In honor of
Mamie D. Eisenhower
This book is presented by

OCEANSIDE REPUBLICAN
WOMEN'S CLUB, FED.

Project sponsored by National Federation of Republican Women
310 First Street, S.E., Washington, D.C. 20003

EISENHOWER

Volume Two
The President

STEPHEN E. AMBROSE

SIMON AND SCHUSTER
NEW YORK

10   9   8   7   6   5   4   3   2   1

Library of Congress Cataloging in Publication Data

Ambrose, Stephen E.
  Eisenhower.

  Maps on lining papers.
  Includes bibliographies and index.
  Contents: v. 1. Soldier, general of the army,
President-elect, 1890–1952—v. 2. The President.
  1. Eisenhower, Dwight D. (Dwight David), 1890–1969.
2. Presidents—United States—Biography. I. Title.
E836.A828   1983   973.921'092'4   83-9892
ISBN 0-671-44069-1 (v. 1)
ISBN 0-671-49901-4 (v. 2)

For Steve and Cee Cee
and Tim and Ronnie—
They all liked Ike

CONTENTS

INTRODUCTION

DWIGHT EISENHOWER is one of only two Republicans (the other was Grant) to serve two full terms as President. Along with the two Roosevelts, he is the only twentieth-century President who, when he left office, still enjoyed wide and deep popularity. And he is the only President in this century who managed to preside over eight years of peace and prosperity.

Clearly, Eisenhower was doing something right. Just as clearly, Eisenhower's famous luck helped him. What follows is an account of how it was done, and of Eisenhower's role in bringing it about.

Eisenhower is at the center of events. Just as in Overlord, when he was the funnel through which everything had to pass, the one man who was responsible for the whole operation, so too as President, he was the one man who could weigh all the factors in any one decision—the political repercussions, the effect on foreign policy, the economic consequences, and the myriad of other considerations involved—before acting.

Eisenhower probably complained more about the Presidency than most of his predecessors and successors, and probably enjoyed it more. Although he exercised freely the soldier's right to grouse, he wanted to be in the position in which he could have a maximum influence on events. He liked making decisions. The primary reason was that he had such complete self-confidence that he was certain he was the best man in the country to make the decisions. So certain, indeed, that the chief reason he agreed to run for re-election in 1956 was that he could not think of any other man who could do his job.

He was sure he made the best decisions. In my own view, sometimes he did, sometimes he didn't. I think he was badly wrong on McCarthy and segregation, brilliantly right in his management of the numerous war scares of his first term, and during the Berlin crisis of 1959, consistently correct in his opposition to putting ever-greater sums into national defense, ambiguous and confused on nuclear-testing policy and disarmament. But my own prejudices and politics are unimportant, and I hope I have succeeded in resisting the temptation of inserting them into the text. What I have tried to do is present the record, to relate what Eisenhower did, and how and why he did it.

This book is based on the inner record of the Eisenhower Administration. The vast majority of the citations are to primary documents, many of them only declassified in the late seventies and early eighties. With the full record available to me, I quickly learned in writing this book that I could not rely on the memoirs, whether written or oral, nor on the contemporary reporting, nor the public papers and pronouncements, nor the monographs written on the basis of those sources. All were helpful, of course, to one degree or another, but the real story, the whole story, could come only from Eisenhower's own diary, memos, orders, and correspondence, from the minutes of the Cabinet, the National Security Council, and the Republican leaders' meetings, from the transcripts of the telephone calls to and from the Oval Office, from the diaries of such people as Ann Whitman, James Hagerty, and Ellis Slater, and most of all from Andrew Goodpaster's memoranda covering nearly every private conference Eisenhower held.

What the documents show, in my opinion, is how completely Eisenhower dominated events. Eisenhower, not Charlie Wilson, made defense policy; Eisenhower, not Foster Dulles, made foreign policy; Eisenhower, not Ezra Benson, made farm policy. Whether the policies were right or wrong, whether they reflected ambivalence and hesitation, or revealed the way in which Eisenhower was a prisoner of the technologists and scientists, or displayed bold and aggressive action, they were Eisenhower's policies. He ran the show.

As to Eisenhower the man, he is as appealing a human being as President as he was as Supreme Commander. Firm, fair, objective, dignified, he was everything most Americans wanted in a President. There were no real scandals in his Administration. In his private life, he prospered. He loved and cherished his wife, had the pleasure and the pride of having his son work for him in a critical post, and enjoyed to the full his grandchildren. His zest for life was strong. He loved to travel and indulged himself whenever he could. He had a loyal group of close friends, all of them millionaires, his "gang" as he called them. With them he could relax, play golf or bridge or go hunting and fishing, all passions with him, and just be himself.

A word about organization. When I finished the research and began writing, I was sorely tempted to do the book by subjects, breaking it down into chapters on Eisenhower and McCarthy, or Eisenhower and civil rights, or Eisenhower and Vietnam, thereby relating Eisenhower's relations with McCarthy, or his approach to civil rights, or his policies in Vietnam from beginning to end. But I eventually decided that such an organization would make the individual subjects easier to understand at the expense of understanding Eisenhower. What I wanted to convey was the magnitude and multitude of problems that come marching up to the President for solution, and the way in which each event relates to and influences others. For example, a decision Eisenhower made about Vietnam would have a major effect on his defense policy; a decision about Korea would be influenced by Senator McCarthy's latest antics, and in turn would affect what McCarthy did the next day.

I decided that the only way to make the relationship between events and actions understandable, and the only way to get some sense of the factors Eisenhower had to take into account in making a single decision, was to tell the story chronologically. This method of organization has one invaluable advantage—chronologically is the way it happened. The disadvantage is that the book jumps from subject to subject, which does not make for smooth or easy reading. I am convinced, however, that it does give a better understanding of what happened, and why.

And, I hope, a better understanding of Eisenhower the man. His ability to shift from one concern to another, to deal with this problem and then turn to that one, to recall what was said to him months or years earlier on any one of hundreds of subjects, demonstrates the impressive agility, quickness, and intelligence of his mind. His use of his vacation time, and his enjoyment of his many close friends, and most of all the joy he got from his relationship with his wife, son, and grandchildren, demonstrate how healthy he was and the good care he took of himself, psychologically as well as physically. Whether as President, friend, elder statesman, or family man, he remained what he had always been, a great and good man.

CHAPTER ONE

President-Elect

November 1952–January 11, 1953

DWIGHT EISENHOWER actively disliked few people. If a man let him down, or offended his sense of dignity, or insulted him, Eisenhower's practice was to try to put the man out of his mind. If he was forced to work on a regular basis with someone he disliked—Montgomery during the war is the supreme example—he managed to control and hide his feelings, so that their work together could be effective. Eisenhower also tried, usually successfully, never to publicly question another man's motives, even when he felt the man's actions to be selfish, unprincipled, partisan, or stupid.

By November of 1952, Eisenhower actively disliked Harry Truman. He thought the President was guilty of extreme partisanship, poor judgment, inept leadership and management, bad taste, and undignified behavior. Worst of all, in Eisenhower's view Truman had diminished the prestige of the office of the President of the United States.

Eisenhower had not always been so negative toward Truman. He had first met the President at Potsdam, in July of 1945, and at the time liked and admired the man. During Eisenhower's tenure as Army Chief of Staff (1946–1948), he and Truman had enjoyed a mutually beneficial working relationship. Although they never became friends (unlike Arthur Eisenhower and Truman, who had been friends since 1905, when they lived in the same Kansas City boardinghouse), they respected each other. In 1948 Truman offered to support Eisenhower for the Presidency, and in 1949 Eisenhower agreed to work for Truman as his chairman of the Joint Chiefs of Staff (JCS). Further, although Eisenhower strongly disagreed with Truman's domestic policies, especially with regard to labor unions and deficit financing, the two men were in full agreement on foreign policy. Eisenhower supported all of Truman's major decisions—the containment policy, the airlift to Berlin, the commitment to Korea, the program to build a hydrogen warhead, the limitation of the war in Korea, and most important of all, the North Atlantic Treaty and the sending of four American divisions to Germany to provide a military base for NATO. With regard to the last point, in fact, Eisenhower had been Truman's principal and enthusiastic agent in making NATO a military reality. In the process Eisenhower had worked closely with Truman's top advisers, including Dean Acheson, Averell Harriman, Robert Lovett, and George Marshall.

The 1952 campaign destroyed the Eisenhower-Truman relationship. Truman resented the Republicans for their promise to clean up the "mess in Washington" and was bitter about Eisenhower's criticisms of American foreign policy, especially the emphasis on liberation of the Communist satellites and the charge that the Democrats were "soft on Communism." The President was furious with Eisenhower for failing to speak up for Marshall in Milwaukee in McCarthy's presence. Truman thought—and said—that Eisenhower's pledge to go to Korea if elected was the worst sort of political hucksterism. In the last days of the campaign, Truman went after Eisenhower personally, reportedly saying that "the General doesn't know any more about politics than a pig knows about Sunday."

Truman had a long, and legitimate, list of complaints, especially the part about Eisenhower's hypocrisy in attacking a foreign policy he had helped to create and execute. And, of course, Truman hated to lose. Now he had to hand over the government to the hated Republicans. He was going to do so with as much grace and good will as he could muster, but he could not resist some final digs. Thus the day after the election, he sent a telegram to Eisenhower inviting him to the White House for a conference on the transition, then added that the presidential plane, the *Independence,* would be available to Eisenhower for his trip to Korea, "if you still want to go."

Eisenhower, tight-lipped and scowling, replied that any military transport would be fine. Then Eisenhower wrote to Lovett, the Secretary of Defense, thanking Lovett for a recent "kind and thoughtful letter" concerning arrangements for the trip. Eisenhower said Lovett's

communication "creates a feeling of confidence that is not characteristic of some that I have been receiving." One of Truman's objections
to the "I shall go to Korea" pledge had been its implication that in
Korea Eisenhower would find some magic formula to end the war,
one that had escaped the Administration and the JCS. Eisenhower
was sensitive to this charge, especially as the chairman of the JCS
was one of his oldest friends and closest associates, Omar Bradley. So
Eisenhower told Lovett, "I am quite sure that you and my old friends
there [in the Pentagon] know that I am not trying to be clever and
I am not pretending that I will find answers that they have over-
looked."[1]

On November 18, Eisenhower flew to Washington for a 2 P.M.
appointment with the President. The meeting was stiff, formal, embarrassing, and unrewarding. Truman had with him Harriman,
Acheson, John Snyder (Secretary of the Treasury), and Lovett. These
were the men most responsible for containment, for NATO, and for
the commitment to Korea. They were the men with whom Eisenhower
had cooperated handsomely in the past, but whom he had vigorously
criticized during the campaign. Everyone was ill at ease. Acheson was
"perplexed" by Eisenhower's attitude. "The good nature and easy
manner tending toward loquacity were gone. He seemed embarrassed
and reluctant to be with us. Sunk back in a chair facing the President . . . he chewed the earpiece of his spectacles and occasionally
asked for a memorandum on a matter that caught his attention."[2]

The meeting lasted but twenty minutes. Truman offered to leave
some portraits in the Oval Office; Eisenhower curtly told him no
thanks. Then Truman gave him the world globe that Eisenhower
had used in World War II, and that Eisenhower had given to Truman
at Potsdam in 1945. Eisenhower accepted the globe, according to Truman, "not very graciously." Finally Truman tried to give Eisenhower
advice on how to organize his staff, but as the President noted in his
diary two days later, "I think all this went into one ear and out the
other."[3] It did indeed. Eisenhower noted stiffly in his memoirs that
the meeting "added little to my knowledge, nor did it affect my planning for the new administration . . ."[4] It was his only meeting with
the President before Inauguration Day, the only effort to provide for
a smooth transition. January 20, 1953, in fact, saw the most hostile
transition of the twentieth century.

The evening of January 21, 1953, Dwight Eisenhower took a
minute to make an entry in his diary. "My first day at the president's

desk," he wrote. "Plenty of worries and difficult problems. But such
has been my portion for a long time—the result is that this just seems
(today) like a continuation of all I've been doing since July 1941—
even before that."[5]

The contrast between Eisenhower's confident attitude and that
of his predecessor after *his* first day on the job could not have been
greater. On April 13, 1945, Harry Truman had told reporters, "Boys,
if you ever pray, pray for me now. . . . When they told me yesterday
what had happened, I felt like the moon, the stars, and all the planets
had fallen on me."[6]

Eisenhower's preparation for the Presidency was, obviously, much
better than Truman's had been. Roosevelt's death had thrown Truman into a whole new world, one completely strange to him. But
Eisenhower was simply continuing a life that he had long since grown
accustomed to leading. He had not had a private life since June 1942,
when he arrived in London. He had had aides at his elbows and
advisers behind him for ten years. He was used to being surrounded
by reporters whenever he was in a public place, to having his photograph taken, to having his every word quoted. Most important of all,
Eisenhower was accustomed to being held in awe, to being the center
of attention, to having the power to make the decisions.

Eisenhower had resigned himself to the loss of many ordinary
human pleasures, but also learned to accept the privileges that went
with his station. Except for an occasional private banquet, he had
not eaten in a restaurant in ten years. His schedule seldom allowed
him sustained leisure for the serious reading of history he so loved
to do. He had learned to take infrequent and short vacations, to expect them to be interrupted, and to take along plenty of work. To
leave his mind and his time free, he had others to do the most basic
of human chores for him. He did not dress himself—John Moaney,
his valet, put on his underwear, socks, shoes, pants, shirt, jacket, and
tie. Eisenhower did not drive a car, never had to worry about a park-
ing place. He did not even know how to use a dial telephone. He had
never been in a laundromat or a supermarket. He did not keep his
own checkbook or manage his own finances. He handled money only
when it was time to settle up on the golf course or at the bridge table,
where he hated to lose and hated even more having to pay up. (Correspondingly, collecting a $20 bet gave him great pleasure. He was
not above using his rank. Opponents had to hole out their one- or
two-foot putts, while Eisenhower would pick up his eight-footer, grin,

and say thanks for the gimme.[7]) His travel arrangements were always made for him. He did not have to worry about where to stand or what toast to make at the many formal occasions he attended; as he told John Foster Dulles, when Dulles corrected him on a point of protocol, he had never bothered to learn such details because "aides have sat on my right all my life."[8]

Eisenhower was also ready for the physical demands of the Presidency. Three weeks before the election of 1952, he had celebrated his sixty-second birthday. Despite his age, Eisenhower was in good health. At 175 pounds, he weighed only a few pounds more than he had when he played football at West Point. He ate and drank in moderation, and in 1949 had quit tobacco cold turkey. He exercised regularly, either on the golf course or in a swimming pool. His face was usually sun-tanned, his complexion ruddy. His erect military bearing provided convincing evidence of his good muscle tone and strong constitution. Although he was of medium height (five feet ten inches), he somehow seemed taller. Wherever he went, he stood out, not only because of his reputation, but also because of his animation. His immense storehouse of energy and warmth was sensed, felt, communicated to everyone around him. His associates drew on that apparently inexhaustible source of energy; his political opponents were confounded by it.

Among most groups, Eisenhower inspired confidence. Those who knew him well, and millions who did not, looked to him instinctively for guidance and leadership. Partly this was a result of his proved record of accomplishment, partly the result of his personality. He seemed so self-assured, so competent, so open to new ideas and suggestions, so reasonable, so objective (his own favorite word to describe himself), that when associates or reporters or supporters described him, there was one word that almost all of them used. It was "trustworthy." His old comrade-in-arms Bernard Law Montgomery put it best when he said of Eisenhower, "He has the power of drawing the hearts of men towards him as a magnet attracts the bits of metal. He merely has to smile at you, and you trust him at once."[9]

But Harry Truman had his doubts about Eisenhower's trustworthiness, and was certain that Eisenhower would not be able to provide the country with competent leadership. As prepared as Eisenhower was for the life-style the Presidency would force on him, he was not, in Truman's view, at all prepared for the real work facing him in the task ahead. Reflecting on the problems the general-become-President would face, in late 1952 Truman mused, "He'll sit here,

and he'll say, 'Do this! Do that!' *And nothing will happen*. Poor Ike—
it won't be a bit like the Army. He'll find it very frustrating."[10]

Truman was not alone. As Eisenhower prepared to enter the
Presidency, friends as well as critics worried about how unprepared
he was for the job. According to this widely held view, Eisenhower
had spent his life in the sheltering monastery of the U.S. Army, and
therefore knew nothing of such practical matters as economics, partisan politics, the intricacies of the relationship between Capitol Hill
and the White House, race relations and labor legislation, or the
myriad of other subjects he would have to deal with. He was, or so it
was charged, the "captive hero," the tool of the millionaires in the
Republican Party who would use him to suit their purposes, while he
would be content to play golf and preside over ceremonial functions.

The truth is so directly the opposite from the portrayal that the
real problem is to attempt to understand how such analysis could
have attained such popularity. One obvious reason was the American
public's traditional dislike of the professional soldier, its unwillingness
to admit that soldiers knew about anything other than making war.
Another factor was Eisenhower's own frequent self-deprecation. "I'm
just a simple soldier," he would say, or "I'm just a farm boy from
Kansas." His penchant for expressing his distaste about politics and
his insistence that he was a political innocent also contributed to the
popular view. But Eisenhower had lived and worked in Washington
throughout most of the Hoover Administration and on into the New
Deal. His principal job had been to lobby in Congress for the U.S.
Army. He had testified at dozens of congressional hearings; he had
spent countless hours meeting privately with congressmen. After
World War II, first as the Army Chief of Staff and then as chairman
of the JCS, and finally as Supreme Allied Commander, Europe
(SACEUR), he had continued to work closely with both the Executive and Congress. Despite the forebodings about the inexperience of
the President-elect, Eisenhower knew Washington and its *modus
operandi* at least as well as any of his predecessors, and far better
than most.

In foreign affairs, he was undoubtedly the best-prepared man ever
elected to the Presidency. He knew personally numerous world leaders, including his main opponent, Joseph Stalin. He had lived in Asia
(the Philippines), Central America (Panama), Europe (Paris in the
twenties and again in 1951; London in 1942 and 1944), Africa (Algeria in 1943), and had made extended trips to the Near East, the
Soviet Union, Japan, and China. He had a close working relationship

with every major politician in Western Europe, including those currently in power, most notably Winston Churchill and Konrad Adenauer, and those out of power, including Clement Attlee and Charles de Gaulle. He had the respect and admiration of nearly all the world's leaders.

He also knew a great deal about teamwork and the need for aides. "No one man can be a Napoleon in modern war," he had declared in 1942, and he believed the principle applied equally to political leadership in 1953. "Now look," he once explained, "this idea that all wisdom is in the President . . . that's baloney. . . . I don't believe this government was set up to be operated by any one acting alone; no one has a monopoly on the truth and on the facts that affect this country." [11]

Eisenhower's sense of the limitations on the individual, however great the man, was well illustrated in a conversation he had with Churchill during the first week of January 1953. Churchill, who had returned in 1951 to 10 Downing Street, flew to the United States to meet the President-elect.

After only a few minutes of conversation, in which Churchill tried to persuade Eisenhower to help Britain solve its problems in Iran, Egypt, and elsewhere, Eisenhower concluded that Churchill was "unquestionably influenced by old prejudices or instinctive reaction." Eisenhower wrote later in his diary that "Winston is trying to relive the days of World War II." Eisenhower said that "in those days he had the enjoyable feeling that he and our president were sitting on some rather Olympian platform with respect to the rest of the world and directing world affairs from that point of vantage." The image of Churchill and Roosevelt sitting on their mountaintops, hurling thunderbolts at various places around the world, amused Eisenhower. He knew better, because he was one of those "in various corners of the world, [who] had to work out the solutions" in fixing and executing a strategy to win the war. Indeed, in Eisenhower's view, Churchill and Roosevelt had frequently been more of a hindrance than a help, and what they were able to accomplish was only possible because of the dedicated staff work of thousands of others. As one of the most important of those "others" in the war, Eisenhower was under no illusions about hurling thunderbolts, even from the White House. He felt that only with the help of thousands of others could anything be accomplished. [12]

A major part of presidential leadership, Eisenhower believed, was selecting the right men for the right jobs and working with them. He wanted competent, proved administrators, men who thought big and acted big. Completely free of any need to boost his own ego, or to prove his own decisiveness or leadership, he wanted to "build up" the men who worked with him.[13] Always impressed by successful businessmen who had made it on their own and knew how to run huge organizations, he sought out the high achievers, men he could turn to for advice and with whom he could share both responsibility and praise.

Personal friendship counted for nothing. In selecting his Cabinet and White House staff, Eisenhower did not pick a single old friend. Some of the most prominent selections were of men he had never met; the others were men he had met only during the course of the campaign. Walter B. ("Beetle") Smith, his wartime chief of staff, who became Under Secretary of State, was the single exception. Nor did politics count for much; few of his Cabinet choices were prominent Republicans; he did not consult with Tom Dewey, Robert Taft, Richard Nixon, or Herbert Hoover in making his choices; and his Secretary of Labor was a Stevenson Democrat.

Those who actively sought the jobs had no chance of getting them. "No one should be appointed to political office if he is a seeker after it," Eisenhower flatly declared in his diary during the pre-inaugural period. Further, "We can afford to have only those people in high political offices who cannot afford to take them." He did not want professional politicians, nor did he want to make appointments that would be political payoffs. "Patronage is almost a wicked word," he scribbled in the diary. "By itself it could well-nigh defeat democracy."[14] He wanted men from outside government: "I feel that anyone who can, without great personal sacrifice, come to Washington to accept an important governmental post is not fit to hold that post."[15] When he was criticized for taking on the chairmen of giant corporations, he wrote in his diary that opposition to such appointments would result in an inability "to get anybody to take jobs in Washington except business failures, college professors [crossed out and replaced by "political hacks"], and New Deal lawyers. All of these would jump at the chance to get a job that a successful businessman has to sacrifice very much to take."[16]

His first selection was for the premier post of Secretary of State. His choice was John Foster Dulles, and he never seriously considered anyone else. The appointment was, indeed, inevitable. Dulles' maternal grandfather had been Benjamin Harrison's Secretary of State; his uncle, Robert Lansing, had held that post under Woodrow Wilson; in 1919 Dulles had been a part of the American delegation to the Versailles Peace Conference; he was a senior partner in Sullivan and Cromwell, the law firm that represented many of America's greatest corporations in their international dealings; he had written the Japanese Peace Treaty; he had been the Republican spokesman on foreign policy for the past decade. "Foster has been in training for this job all his life," Eisenhower explained to Sherman Adams.[17]

Eisenhower had first met Dulles at SHAPE, in April 1952. He had worked with Dulles on the foreign-policy plank in the Republican Party platform. While Eisenhower regretted some of Dulles' more bellicose statements, especially about liberation of the Communist satellites and the concept of "massive retaliation," he appreciated Dulles' commitment to NATO, foreign aid, and internationalism. Further, Eisenhower was impressed by Dulles' comprehensive knowledge of world affairs. Eisenhower once told Emmet Hughes, "There's only one man I know who has seen *more* of the world and talked with more people and *knows* more than he does—and that's *me*."[18]

In addition, Eisenhower actually liked Dulles. In this he was virtually unique. Nearly everyone else found Dulles impossibly pompous, a prig, and unbearably dull (according to a popular saying, "Dull, duller, Dulles"). Dulles loved to give sermons, to moralize, to monopolize conversations. Even British aristocrats could not bear the man. Anthony Eden told Eisenhower, in May 1952, that he hoped Eisenhower would not appoint Dulles the Secretary of State, "because I do not think I would be able to work with him."[19] Churchill thought Dulles a stupid man and could hardly stand the sight of him. He deliberately lisped his name, calling him "Dullith." When Churchill learned that Dulles' younger brother, Allen, would be the head of the CIA, Churchill groaned, then said, "They tell me that there is another Dullith. Is that possible?"[20]

But Eisenhower appreciated Dulles' penchant for hard work, his mastery of detail, and his willingness to serve. Various incidents during the campaign had convinced Eisenhower that Dulles would never attempt to set his own course (Dulles was fully aware of the fate of his uncle; when Robert Lansing had attempted to follow policies Woodrow Wilson had rejected, Wilson fired Lansing), that he would always do as Eisenhower wished. That Dulles would insist on his share and more of the limelight, that he would attempt—with great success—to create the impression that he was solely in charge of foreign policy, pleased rather than distressed Eisenhower, so long as Dulles accepted—as he always did—the reality of Eisenhower's command.[21]

When Eisenhower informed Dulles of his selection, a few days after the election, Dulles thanked him profusely, then said, "With my understanding of the intricate relationships between the peoples of the world and your sensitiveness to the political considerations involved, we will make the most successful team in history."[22]

Eisenhower's second selection was Joseph M. Dodge; he asked Dodge to work with the Bureau of the Budget on the 1954 budget, making it clear to Dodge that he intended to appoint him the director of the bureau upon his inauguration. Eisenhower had known Dodge in Germany, where Dodge had directed the fiscal affairs of the American occupation; Dodge was president of The Detroit Bank. Eisenhower also asked Henry Cabot Lodge, Jr.—who had lost his seat in the Senate to John F. Kennedy—to represent him as liaison with the government before the transition.[23]

Then Eisenhower called Herbert Brownell, Sherman Adams, and Lucius Clay to a meeting at Morningside Heights. He asked Brownell and Clay to form a team to make suggestions to him about his other Cabinet appointments, with Adams serving as their assistant. When Eisenhower left for Augusta and a few days of golf, the Brownell-Clay team went to work. They had a quite remarkable grant of power, which reflected Eisenhower's willingness to delegate authority, his trust in Clay and Brownell, and his own relative unfamiliarity with the potential candidates.

Brownell and Clay first met with Lodge, offering him any position he might want in the Administration, but letting him know that Eisenhower wanted him to serve as either Assistant to the President (really, chief of staff) or ambassador to the United Nations. Lodge chose the latter post, which Eisenhower elevated to Cabinet rank with seniority just below that of the Secretary of State. Eisenhower then asked Adams to be the Assistant to the President, also according that position Cabinet rank. He had thought of Brownell for the post, but decided he wanted Brownell—one of the top lawyers in New York and Dewey's closest associate—to be his Attorney General. Dewey, still the governor of New York, told Brownell he did not wish to be considered for any position in the Administration.[24]

Dewey's running mate in 1948, Earl Warren, was also a serving governor, in California. Eisenhower called him on the telephone to say that he had been considering Warren for Attorney General, but had decided instead to appoint Brownell. Warren replied that Brownell would make a splendid choice. Eisenhower then said, "I want you to know that I intend to offer you the first vacancy on the Supreme Court." It was something Eisenhower had discussed with Brownell, who—like Eisenhower—was much impressed by Warren's bearing, character, and knowledge. Eisenhower told Warren, "That is my personal commitment to you."[25]

Brownell and Clay, meanwhile, had made their selections for the other Cabinet posts. For Secretary of Defense, the man who would head the department that was the world's biggest employer and purchaser, they picked Charles E. Wilson, president of General Motors, the world's largest private corporation. As the reputedly highest-paid executive in American business, Wilson presumably would know how to run the vast Pentagon empire. For Secretary of the Treasury, they selected George M. Humphrey, president of the Mark A. Hanna Company of Cleveland, a far-flung conglomerate. Eisenhower had never met either man, but he accepted them on his advisers' recommendation. He found Wilson to be narrow and simplistic, but he liked Humphrey enormously. Indeed, Humphrey was the only man in the Cabinet—save Dulles—with whom Eisenhower established a warm and close personal relationship. They were almost exactly the same age, had the same horror of deficit financing, and shared a love for hunting and fishing. At their first meeting, Eisenhower grinned at the balding Humphrey, stuck out his hand, and said, "Well, George, I see you part your hair the same way I do." Humphrey put only one condition on his acceptance; he told Eisenhower, "If anyone talks to you about money, you tell him to go see George." Eisenhower promised to do just that. He also told Wilson that he should run the Department of Defense (DOD). "We both can't do it," Eisenhower said, "and I won't do it. I was elected to worry about a lot of other things than the day-to-day operations of a department."[26]

For Secretary of the Interior, Brownell and Clay picked the outgoing governor of Oregon, Douglas McKay. Before entering politics, McKay had been a successful automobile dealer. Sinclair Weeks, another conservative businessman, from Massachusetts, became Secretary of Commerce. After one of their first meetings, Eisenhower wrote of Weeks in his diary, "[He] seems so completely conservative in his views that at times he seems to be illogical. I hope . . . that he will soon become a little bit more aware of the world as it is today."[27] Eisenhower offered Arthur Summerfield, the chairman of the Republican National Committee (RNC), a choice—he could continue in that post or become Postmaster General. Summerfield wanted both jobs, but Eisenhower insisted that it would have to be one or the other. Summerfield chose to become Postmaster General.[28] For the sprawling Department of Agriculture, Eisenhower turned to Milton for advice, based on Milton's many years of service in the department. Milton named Ezra Taft Benson, a member of the Council of Twelve of the Mormon church, agent for farm cooperatives, and a conservative who had supported Taft for the nomination.

Eisenhower told his advisers he wanted one woman in the Cabinet. They selected Mrs. Oveta Culp Hobby, a Texas newspaper publisher and one of the Texas "Democrats for Eisenhower" who had helped make his nomination possible. Eisenhower had known Hobby during the war, when she was the head of the Women's Army Corps. He told her he planned to ask Congress for the consolidation of health, welfare, and education responsibilities into a single department, and that when it was done he would name her as its head. Meanwhile, he wanted her to serve as head of the Federal Security Agency, and she accepted.[29]

One of the most difficult appointments was that of Secretary of Labor. The Republicans anticipated trouble with organized labor, which was demanding wholesale changes in, if not outright repeal of, the Taft-Hartley Act. Eisenhower told Brownell and Clay that he wanted a man from the ranks of labor itself; after a long search and the rejection of various suggestions, they picked Martin Durkin of Chicago, head of the AFL plumbers' union. Durkin was the only Democrat in the Cabinet, and the only Catholic. Taft was flabbergasted to find that organized labor would hold the key post in labor relations in the Cabinet. "This is incomprehensible!" he protested.[30] Shortly thereafter, Eisenhower met with Taft and promised in the future to consult with him on appointments.[31]

So the Cabinet was selected. *The New Republic* commented, "Ike had picked a cabinet of eight millionaires and one plumber."[32] What was more remarkable about it was the absence of any experienced administrators in government (but then having been out of power since 1933, the Republican Party had none to offer), the relative absence of Old Guard faithful, and the lack of coordination with Taft. But without exception, they were all highly successful businessmen, or lawyers, or plumbers, and nearly all self-made men.

Eisenhower had spent his adult lifetime in one of the most tightly organized bureaucracies in the world, the U.S. Army. He liked things that way, and one of his chief criticisms of Roosevelt and Truman was their slipshod organization of the White House staff.[33] They seemed to thrive on near-anarchy, often putting two men from two distinct agencies to work on the same task. Eisenhower wanted none of that. To him, it was "inconceivable . . . that the work of the White House could not be better systemized."[34]

To that end, during the second half of December 1952, he set about picking his principal White House aides, and organizing them along lines taken from both the SHAEF example and that of the British War Cabinet. He already had his chief of staff, Assistant to the President Sherman Adams, and his press secretary, Jim Hagerty, as well as his liaison with Congress, General Jerry Persons. Tom Stephens, a New York lawyer and Dewey man, took charge of appointments; New Jersey lawyer and Stassen man Bernard Shanley would handle legal questions; Dr. Gabriel Hauge would be his economics adviser. C. D. Jackson of Time-Life and Emmet Hughes were the main speech writers.

Eisenhower intended to upgrade the National Security Council (NSC) into a sort of British War Cabinet. Created by the National Defense Act of 1947, the NSC had played only a small role in the Truman Administration. Eisenhower wanted to look to it for advice, recommendations, and planning for all phases of the Cold War. Members included the secretaries of the appropriate departments (State, Defense, Treasury), their deputies, the Vice-President, the JCS, and the director of the CIA. To coordinate the actions of the NSC, Eisenhower created a Planning Board and named as its chairman General Robert Cutler. A director of the Old Colony Trust Company in Boston, Cutler had worked for Secretary of War Stimson during the war. For overall coordination, Eisenhower followed Marshall's example; during the war Marshall had created the post of Secretary, General Staff, to oversee all the administrative details of the War Department. Eisenhower called the new White House position the Office of Staff Secretary, and named General Paul T. Carroll to the post. Carroll had served with Eisenhower both in the Pentagon and at SHAPE headquarters in Paris.

There were other appointments, other committees, far too many to detail here. Indeed, so many that even before the inaugural, critics were charging that Eisenhower was overorganizing the White House, and that he was putting committees in charge of the country. Eisenhower scoffed at such a notion. He had worked with committees all his life, knew how to draw the best from them, and was confident that his leadership would be enhanced and more efficient thanks to the men and women he had chosen to serve on his team.

In New York, the Eisenhowers continued to live at Morningside Heights, home of the president of Columbia University. Mamie's life was a hectic one of buying clothes for the inaugural and preparing to move once again. She had the consolation that this time, for the first time in thirty-five years, she could count on living in the same house for four straight years. Barbara and the three grandchildren were visiting at Morningside Heights for the holidays, which made Christmas Eve and Day especially nice. Eisenhower gave Mamie a gold bracelet with three heart bangles inscribed "David," "Barbara Anne," and "Susan." On Christmas Day, however, even as Eisenhower was carving the turkey, Mamie fell ill. Dr. Howard Snyder, who had lived with the Eisenhowers for years and was their personal physician, gave her sulfa and confined her to bed. There she stayed for the next few days, meanwhile trying to arrange for the shipment of furniture from New York to Washington. A major problem was remembering which item belonged to her, which to Columbia.[35]

In early January, Mamie learned that John was coming home for the inaugural ceremonies. She asked her husband who had ordered John to leave Korea; he asked Omar Bradley, the Army Chief of Staff; Bradley did not know. John's arrival did for Mamie what the sulfa had not accomplished; her health improved and she was out of bed. After their reunion, John went up to Highland Falls for a few days with his family, then brought his wife and children back to Morningside Heights. During the ten days before the inaugural, Mamie and Barbara shopped, while John attended meetings with his father.[36]

Eisenhower was leading a hectic life, but he was accustomed to it. He had long since learned what it was like to live a life in which virtually all of his time was scheduled, with meetings, interviews, appearances, speeches, working lunches, and trips. Nevertheless, he tried to live by regular habits and insofar as possible did so. In the period between his election and the inauguration, except when he was in Korea, he followed the same routine that he had established when Chief of Staff, president of Columbia, and SACEUR, and that he intended to follow as President.

His day began early, around 6 A.M. He got up quietly, so as not to wake Mamie, went to his dressing room, and selected a suit from those Moaney had laid out. Most of his extensive, custom-made wardrobe was given to him by New York clothes manufacturers; he seldom wore a suit more than twice. Over a light breakfast he would read the morning papers. Although it was one of his little conceits to claim that he never read the papers, in fact he pored over them. An extremely fast reader, he could get the essential stories quickly. He usually read the Washington papers, *The New York Times,* and the *Herald Tribune* (by far his favorite). He was also a regular reader of the newsmagazines. Unlike Truman, he never sent angry letters to the editor, but he would send a quiet word of praise about an article or a column to the publisher. When he was unhappy with a column or a report, he told his closest friends about it, but otherwise kept it to himself. He did not object to criticism of his policies or his actions but fiercely resented criticism of his private life. Shortly after the nominating convention, he had vacationed in Colorado. One day he caught and kept considerably more trout than the legal limit. Enterprising reporters discovered the fact; Eisenhower's violation of the fish-and-game laws of Colorado was the headline item in the Denver papers; Eisenhower was furious and demanded to know, "Who's been counting my fish!"[37]

Eisenhower was in his office by 8 A.M. and worked without a break until 1 P.M. Most of his lunches were working affairs. He would then work at his desk until 6 P.M., sometimes later. There was a wide variety to the type and scope of the problems that came to him for decision. He tried to hear all sides before deciding, to expose himself to every point of view, which required a great deal of reading, listening intently to oral presentations, and asking penetrating questions. Hard work, in other words, that required him to use his mind constantly and intensively.

After a day in the office, he would relax with a cocktail. He was strict with himself about the use of alcohol; his usual limit was a single highball before eating. Food, unless he had done the cooking, was of little interest to him. To Mamie's continuing distress, he bolted down whatever was put in front of him. In 1952 he started another practice that Mamie had to resign herself to—eating off a TV tray while watching the evening news. After dinner, if he had no speaking or other engagements, he would study papers, reports, proposals, until about 11 P.M., when he enjoyed an hour of painting before going to bed. His bedside reading consisted of Wild West stories. In them, there were no complications, no complexities. Decisions were clearcut, because they were based on easily answered questions of right and wrong. To read such stories, Eisenhower had to suspend all his critical facilities and enter into a fantasy world. By doing so, he could clear his mind for its necessary rest. The stories were, for Eisenhower, the most effective sleeping pills available.

More complete relaxation came from his hobbies, fishing, painting, golf, and bridge. They all allowed him complete escape, because they required complete concentration. Whether trying to decide which fly to use, or which color to put on a painting, or what iron club to select for his next shot, or how to bid an unusual hand, he was momentarily free of the burdens of his duties and responsibilities. Ellis Slater, who played a great deal of both golf and bridge with Eisenhower, noted that "I don't believe I've ever known a person with such concentration. When doing anything . . . he has an ability to completely lose himself." [38]

Eisenhower enjoyed his hobbies for their own sake, of course, but also because they gave him a mental rejuvenation he could get nowhere else. It was characteristic of Eisenhower that when he needed to escape his daily cares, he wanted to participate actively, not passively, in the escape. Thus literature had no appeal for him, nor did serious music or art. He could not "lose" himself in a book, a concert, or a masterpiece, but he did "lose" himself when he was on a trout stream, painting, playing golf or bridge. For the most part, he played with his regular "gang." These men, of whom the closest to Eisenhower were Bill Robinson, Ellis Slater, Pete Jones, George Allen, and Cliff Roberts, were all successful men of the world with wide-ranging interests and influence. All had complete relationships with Eisenhower. With them, he could indulge his passion for golf or bridge, with small bets and men's jokes as a welcome addition to the game. He could discuss politics or economics or statecraft seriously. Whatever his mood, the gang adjusted to it, because the members were completely devoted to him. With them he could relax and be himself in a way that was possible with no one else.

He was uncomfortable in the presence of women. A frequent speaker at meetings of women's organizations, he always began with a little joke designed to make certain that the assembled ladies were aware of how ill at ease he felt. He had no women as close friends, had never worked with any woman on a regular or equal basis, and had sharply limited ideas on what women were capable of accomplishing. The limits to Eisenhower's thinking about women were revealed when an adviser suggested, in 1954, that he consider supporting an equal-rights amendment to the Constitution. Astonished, Eisenhower snapped back, "Where are they unequal?"[39] His idea of an appropriate activity for women was volunteer work, preferably for a Republican women's organization.

He had always lived in a world of men. The only genuine relationships he had ever formed with women revolved around role images that he felt comfortable with, specifically those of mother, wife, and secretary. No one can look at a photograph of the general with his mother, or of the general and his wife, and doubt that he had a perfect love for Ida and Mamie. But his relationships with them were limited. He never discussed his professional life with either of them, or otherwise shared his concerns.

His relationship with Mamie was happy, uncomplicated, and old-fashioned. Except during World War II, they had always slept together, and planned to do so in the White House. In 1946, at Fort Myer, Mamie had ordered a huge double bed specially built. In 1948 it had been shipped from Washington to New York City. Mamie was going to install it in the White House. Mamie said she liked to reach over in the middle of the night "and pat Ike on his old bald head anytime I want to."[40]

That bed was her command post. She enjoyed staying in it until noon at least, sometimes all day. From it, she answered her correspondence, ran her household staff, and received visitors. Eisenhower enjoyed pampering her, which added to a general impression that she was lazy, spoiled, and more or less empty-headed. In fact, like her husband, she was hardworking. She was also devoted to him. Although she never engaged in Eisenhower's business, she nevertheless provided him with crucial support, in public as well as in private. When her husband became a world figure, she overcame her natural shyness and became a major asset in his career. She entertained his rich and powerful friends and their wives; she presided over numerous large and formal social affairs; she carefully answered every letter written to her; she made certain that every member of the small army of aides, advisers, and secretaries that existed to do Eisenhower's bidding—and their children—were remembered with gifts at birthdays and Christmas. She appeared cheerfully, well groomed and beautifully dressed, at the general's side on public occasions. She did, in short, all that Eisenhower wanted a wife to do, and more. If her share in his life was limited, it was nonetheless satisfying, rewarding, and giving.

There were two women with whom he did share his professional life. In both cases, they occupied a specific, well-defined role, that of secretary. The first was Kay Summersby, the second Ann Whitman. Kay had been at SHAEF during the war; Ann had joined Eisenhower's team "for a few days" just before the 1952 campaign began; she stayed with him for more than eight years. Both women were extremely competent at their jobs, highly intelligent, comfortable to be around. They knew his professional concerns intimately. He could, and often did, comment to them in detail on matters of world importance. He knew they would understand the most cryptic remark; even better, he knew they would be completely on his side, because their devotion to him was unquestioning. He drove them like slaves, dawn to dusk. He made impossible demands on them—have this paper out by so-and-so, he would say—and they met those demands. First Kay, then Ann, gave him an outlet for that big gutsy laugh, or for that terrible temper. With them, he could be as angry or as contemptuous toward another man as he wished, without having to fear that the story of his outburst would be all over town the next day.[41]

On November 29, 1952, Eisenhower flew to Korea. The trip was carried out in great secrecy—while Eisenhower was gone, daily bulletins were issued from Morningside Heights, announcing Cabinet appointments and giving the impression that Eisenhower was busy making his selections. Eisenhower took with him Bradley, Wilson, and Brownell. En route, they were joined at Iwo Jima by Admiral Arthur Radford, commander in chief, Pacific. Radford so impressed Eisenhower during the next few days that Eisenhower decided to name him as Bradley's replacement when Bradley's tour as chairman of the JCS ended in August 1953. The decision on Radford was one of the few positive results of the trip.

Indeed, what was most noteworthy about the Korean inspection was what Eisenhower did *not* do. South Korean President Dr. Syngman Rhee was anxious to convince Eisenhower that a renewed invasion of North Korea could work, that it would unify the country, turn back the Communists, and contribute to stability in Asia. He also wanted Eisenhower to join him on a reviewing stand in Seoul for a large public military review, and give a speech to the National Assembly. But Eisenhower practically ignored Rhee; he met with him only twice, for a total of one hour, and gave Rhee no opportunity to either enhance his prestige by appearing in public with the American President-elect or to present his plans for an all-out offensive.

Mark Clark, commander in chief of the U.N. forces in Korea, also had worked out plans for an offensive designed to drive the

Chinese back across the Yalu River and unify Korea. To Clark's admitted surprise and probable astonishment, Eisenhower never gave him an opportunity to present his plan. Instead, for three days, Eisenhower did what he had done so often during World War II; he visited frontline units and talked with the senior commanders and their men. Despite the bitter cold and snow-covered ground, Eisenhower bundled up in a heavy pile jacket, fur-lined hat, and thermo boots to see for himself. He flew a reconnaissance mission over the front. He studied an artillery duel with his binoculars, chatted with the troops, ate outdoor meals from a mess kit, and came to the conclusion that the situation was intolerable.[42]

That was the real result of the trip. Not that Eisenhower had not already made up his mind that the Korean War had to be ended, as quickly as possible on the best terms he could get, but that this instinctive judgment was reinforced by his study of the terrain. He regarded Rhee's and Clark's plans for an all-out assault as bordering on madness. "In view of the strength of the positions the enemy had developed," he wrote, "it was obvious that any frontal attack would present great difficulties." With the offensive option eliminated, the remaining choices were to negotiate seriously (armistice talks had been under way for nearly two years, but no agreements had been reached because of the POW issue) or to continue the military stalemate, neither accepting a negotiated peace nor seeking victory. The trouble with a negotiated peace was that, aside from having to agree to a forcible repatriation of the Chinese POWs, it would abandon North Korea to Communism, and this by an Administration that had pledged itself to seek liberation for Communist satellites. The trouble with accepting continued stalemate, however, was even worse; as Eisenhower later wrote, "My conclusion as I left Korea was that we could not stand forever on a static front and continue to accept casualties without any visible results. Small attacks on small hills would not end this war."[43]

On December 5, Eisenhower flew east from Seoul. That same day, General Douglas MacArthur spoke at a meeting of the National Association of Manufacturers. He said that he had "a clear and definite solution to the Korean conflict," one that involved no "increased danger of provoking universal conflict." When reporters pressed him to reveal his solution, he replied that he would give it only to the President-elect.[44]

Eisenhower and his party, meanwhile, reached Guam, where they transferred to the cruiser *Helena*. Informed of MacArthur's speech, Eisenhower said he thought he had better arrange a meeting with his old boss. His advisers demurred. They doubted that MacArthur had anything new to say; they remembered his active support for Taft during the convention; his previous advocacy of all-out war in Korea ran directly counter to Eisenhower's thoughts; MacArthur was altogether too controversial a figure. Further, MacArthur was known to have made numerous slighting remarks about Eisenhower, reportedly referring to him as "a mere clerk, nothing more." But Eisenhower had worked for MacArthur for nearly a decade, knew the man intimately, and was certain that he could handle the bombastic general, whom he regarded as a brilliant, if frequently irresponsible, man. And, after all, MacArthur just might have an idea worth pursuing. It would not hurt to talk to him.

In that case, Eisenhower's advisers then said, at least meet with MacArthur privately. But Eisenhower insisted that a public response was necessary. Eisenhower radioed MacArthur, "I . . . assure you I am looking forward to informal meetings in which my associates and I may obtain the full benefit of your thinking and experience." On December 9 a copy was released to the press.[45]

MacArthur replied with an expression of thanks, then added: "This is especially so because, despite my intimate personal and professional concern therewith, this is the first time that the slightest official interest in my counsel has been evidenced since my return,"[46] an astonishing statement from a man who had spoken to a joint session of Congress and testified at great length before congressional committees on the situation in the Far East.

When Truman read this exchange in the papers, he was livid. He issued his own statement, saying that if MacArthur had a plan for ending the war without starting a greater one, he should present it to the proper authorities—that is, the President—at once. At a press conference the next day, he said that he doubted that MacArthur had such a plan, then characterized Eisenhower's trip to Korea as a "piece of demagoguery," a statement that in turn infuriated Eisenhower.[47]

When the *Helena* reached Wake Island, Humphrey, Dulles, McKay, Dodge, Clay, and Hughes joined Eisenhower's group for the journey to Pearl Harbor. For the next three days, Eisenhower held conferences on prospective foreign and domestic policy. The major problem they faced was what Eisenhower called the "great equation." Simply put, it was a question of how much America could afford to

pay for defense. The Truman budget for fiscal 1954 projected revenues that were some $10 billion short of the anticipated $80 billion
in expenditures. At best, the new Administration could only make
marginal cuts in the domestic expenditures, and Eisenhower was hardly
likely to cut foreign aid. That made the Department of Defense—the
biggest spender—the most obvious place to effect savings. All of Eisenhower's advisers agreed with him on that central point; they also
agreed that the budget would have to be balanced before his term of
office was up, and in addition that taxes had to be cut.

Two self-evident conclusions emerged from these contradictory
demands: first, that the Korean War must be brought to an end; and
second, that the nation had to find some way of defending its vital
interests at a lower cost. Dulles argued—and Eisenhower agreed—that
America could not afford to implement the containment policy by
stationing armies at every spot the Communists might probe all around
the world. Instead, the United States should concentrate on deterring
attack by maintaining a retaliatory power capable of striking back at
the source of aggression. That meant nuclear weapons and the means
of delivering them had to be expanded and improved, at the expense
of conventional forces.

In the campaign, Republicans had attacked Truman for his "Asia
last" policy. On board the *Helena,* Wilson and Admiral Radford
argued for a basic change in foreign policy, one that would put Asia
first. Eisenhower demurred. He said that the NATO alliance was the
key to America's defense, that a strong Europe was essential to everything else, including stability in Asia.

Turning to the domestic scene, the group discussed the related
questions of a tax cut, price and wage controls, and the dangers of
inflation. Dodge had convinced Eisenhower that only minimal cuts
could be made in the fiscal 1954 budget, so any immediate tax cuts
were out. But much as he feared inflation, Eisenhower wanted to get
rid of price and wage controls. Humphrey assured him that it could
be done, that increased productivity would minimize or eliminate inflation, and that in any case the system of controls then in effect simply
was not working, that they were in fact having a depressing effect on
the national economy and thus on federal revenues. Eisenhower therefore sent a letter to Weeks, the Secretary of Commerce-designate, telling Weeks that he wanted to discontinue price and wage controls and
asking him to form an *ad hoc* commission to make recommendations
on how soon it could be done.[48]

Thus was the broad outline of the new Administration's policies set. In foreign affairs, it would end the Korean War as soon as possible, then continue the policies of containment, foreign aid, and Europe first. In national security, it would make major cuts in conventional arms while strengthening nuclear-war capabilities. Tax cuts would be deferred until the budget was balanced. Eisenhower would continue the basic New Deal programs, but not expand them, and strive to save money through more efficient management. Controls would end. The role of the federal government in the nation's economy would be reduced. The program fell far short of what the Old Guard wanted or the Republican platform promised—there would be no victory in Korea, no reversal of the results of the Chinese Civil War, no reduction in foreign aid, especially to Europe, no immediate tax cut or balanced budget, no end to the New Deal. Instead, the nation would follow Eisenhower down the middle of the road, rejecting the extremes and concentrating on moderate, efficient management.

When the *Helena* arrived in Hawaii, on December 14, Eisenhower made a brief statement on Korea. "We face an enemy," he said, "whom we cannot hope to impress by words, however eloquent, but only by deeds—executed under circumstances of our own choosing."[49] The clear implication was that unless the Chinese accepted an armistice in Korea, the new Administration would escalate the war. Eisenhower made no direct threat to use atomic weapons, but nevertheless the Chinese were fully aware that the option was available to him.

The threat was exactly what General MacArthur, who had been advocating escalation all along, had in mind. Three days after Eisenhower got back to New York, he and Dulles went to MacArthur's town house to hear the General's ideas. MacArthur handed Eisenhower a memorandum "On Ending the Korean War." The plan was messianic. MacArthur urged Eisenhower to hold a summit meeting with Stalin, excluding all other heads of government. At the meeting, he should insist that "Germany and Korea be permitted to unite under forms of government to be popularly determined upon," that Germany, Austria, Japan, and Korea be then made into neutral states, their neutrality "to be guaranteed by the United States and the Soviet." The U.S. and the Soviet Union should then "incorporate in their respective constitutions a provision outlawing war as an instrument of national policy."

In the event that Stalin refused these demands, Eisenhower should tell him that it was the intention of the United States "to clear North Korea of enemy forces . . . through the atomic bombing of enemy military concentrations in North Korea and the sowing of fields of suitable radioactive materials . . . to close major lines of enemy supply and communication leading south from the Yalu." In addition, Eisenhower should threaten "to neutralize Red China's capability to wage modern war" through an all-out bombing campaign inside China. MacArthur argued that Stalin would have no choice but to accept.[50]

Eisenhower listened patiently. Privately, he was appalled at MacArthur's willingness—and that of so many others—to advocate the use of atomic weapons by the United States against Asian people only seven years after Hiroshima. To Eisenhower's way of thinking, that was the sure way to make all Asians into enemies of the United States.[51] He also doubted that the Chinese could be made to abandon their North Korean allies to an unconditional surrender, no matter how great the threat. He did think that a compromise solution, one demanding less from the Chinese, such as a return to the *status quo antebellum,* might be achieved through the use of the atomic threat.

Eisenhower kept all such thoughts to himself, however, and when MacArthur finished, said only, "General, this is something of a new thing. I'll have to look at the understanding between ourselves and our allies, on the prosecution of this war because if we're going to bomb bases on the other side of the Yalu, if we're going to extend the war we have to make sure we're not offending the whole world."[52]

That response seemed to MacArthur to border on the cowardly. "The trouble with Eisenhower," he later told a circle of close friends, "is that he doesn't have the guts to make a policy decision. He never did have the guts and he never will."[53] But unfortunately for MacArthur, it was Eisenhower, not he, who had been elected to the Presidency and who would therefore be making the policy decisions.

CHAPTER TWO

Inauguration

January 12–January 20, 1953

ON JANUARY 12, 1953, at the Hotel Commodore in New York, Eisenhower presided over the first preinaugural Cabinet meeting in American history. As the waiters were clearing the table, Eisenhower read a draft of his Inaugural Address. He had been working on it for some weeks and was, according to Hughes, who was helping him write it, "humbled, awed, a little troubled" by the thought of giving such an address. For his part, Eisenhower complained in his diary that "my assistant [Hughes] has been no help—he is more enamored with words than with ideas. I don't care much about the words if I can convey the ideas accurately." In his diary, Eisenhower also set down his objectives. He wanted to warn the free world that "the American well can run dry, but I don't want to discourage any." He did not want to give the Soviets "the idea they have us on the run." He wanted to tell the American people that "internationally, we are entering a new phase, but I don't want to be using the inaugural address to castigate and indict the administrations of the past twenty years." Summing up, Eisenhower sighed, "It's a job."[1]

When Eisenhower finished reading his current draft at the Commodore, there was general applause. Frowning, Eisenhower looked up and remarked, "I read it far more for your blue pencils than I did for your applause." He urged them "to tear it to pieces." Wilson, who had led the banter at lunch and who was already recognizable as the most outspoken, self-confident, bluntest, and ill-informed member of the Cabinet, gave his judgment: "I think I am in favor of flying the flag pretty high." "I am, too," Eisenhower replied. "I would get out and shout it out loud, but you have also got to bring basic principles down to our living, because here is this thing going out to probably one of the greatest audiences that has ever heard a speech."

Then Eisenhower turned to one of his most basic principles of leadership—that it was necessary to give everyone involved the feeling that he or she was making a genuine contribution. He wanted to convey the message that the preacher, the teacher, the mother, the workman, "can help to produce something more to allay this starvation and distress in the world." He hoped to find some way to stress the theme of productivity, the idea that if everyone in America would do just a bit more at his or her job, productivity would rise and then America could do more to fight the Communist menace.

The talk then turned to practical arrangements for Inauguration Day. Eisenhower was worried about the people participating in the parade. "Let me tell you something," he said. "I know more about this parade business than most people. You put all those people there all day long, standing in the cold, and finally they march past the reviewing stand when darkness has hit us, . . . and you have made some enemies." He wished they could start the parade earlier in the day, but was resigned to the impossibility of it, since the swearing-in ceremony could not take place until noon. After that, there was a lunch before the parade. Eisenhower promised that he and Mamie would bolt their lunches in fifteen minutes.

After a prolonged discussion of what type of hats to wear—Eisenhower insisted on Homburgs rather than the traditional silk hats—Eisenhower explained his ideas of how the Cabinet should function. He wanted his Cabinet to be a policy body. Every member of the Cabinet should feel free to discuss not only the problems of his or her own department, but of the nation as a whole. Then he gave his standard pitch for teamwork, one that he had given at AFHQ, at SHAEF, in the War Department, at Columbia, and at SHAPE: "I hope that before we have gone very long each one of you will consider the rest of you here your very best friends in the world . . . That is the perfect way."

They returned to a discussion of the Inaugural Address. Humphrey referred back to the productivity theme, saying that he agreed that the common people had to be made to understand that they could do more. Eisenhower said that reliance on the common people was axiomatic: "As a matter of fact, they are the only ones who can generate the power to do it. No matter how clever or brilliant a group like this is, it is dependent on them." Nixon said that was right, that was just it. Throughout the meeting, indeed, Nixon limited his remarks to heartily endorsing whatever Eisenhower said.

Humphrey thought that there was perhaps too much emphasis on foreign aid. Eisenhower responded, "Unless we can put things in the hands of people who are starving to death we can never lick Communism. My whole picture of China is claws reaching at you because you looked like you had five cents." Lodge thought that Eisenhower's reference to Moscow as the center of world revolution ought to be dropped, because so many people around the world "would like to have a revolution." Eisenhower agreed to make the change. "In Mexico today," Eisenhower added, "they still talk about the revolution like the second coming of the Lord. While it hasn't worked too well, nevertheless it is better than what they had." Wilson popped up. "We had a little revolution in our country, a peaceful one," he declared. Astonished, Eisenhower looked at him and asked, "Little?"

Harold Stassen, whom Eisenhower had selected as his Mutual Security Director (i.e., the man in charge of the foreign-aid program), said that the sentence on science "tended to give the scientists a rough time." Eisenhower replied, "I said they gave us as our final gift the power to kill ourselves. That is what they have done, too. Just listen to the stories of the hydrogen bomb. [The first had been exploded the weekend before Eisenhower's election; its destructive power was 150 times greater than the atomic bomb.] And it doesn't do any good to run. Some day we will get those boys up to tell us some of the facts of those things. They are terrifying."

Stassen said he wished there could be a bit more on faith in the speech. "I don't want to deliver a sermon," Eisenhower rejoined. "It is not my place. But I firmly believe that our government . . . is deeply embedded in a religious faith." Indeed, after an adult lifetime of never attending church, Eisenhower had joined the National Presbyterian Church in Washington, and indicated that he intended to attend services there on the morning of the inauguration and regularly on Sundays thereafter. He felt it important for the President to set an example. He did not think the denomination important. Theology was a subject about which he knew nothing and cared nothing; he never discussed his idea of God with anyone; he did talk, sincerely and earnestly, about the need for a spiritual force in American life, but the specific form that the religious content should take did not concern him.

The only serious disagreement at the Commodore meeting came when they discussed foreign trade. Eisenhower said that "I have a very deep conviction that there is no instrument in the hands of diplomacy that is quite as powerful as trade," and indicated that he intended to open extensive trade relations with the Iron Curtain countries. Wilson was unhappy. "I am a little old-fashioned," he said. "I don't like to sell firearms to the Indians." Eisenhower replied that attempts to stop all trade with the Communist states were "absurd." He added, "You can't follow blind prejudice on determining trade routes." Looking directly at Wilson, Eisenhower said, "Remember this: you are trying to set up out of Moscow what you might call a series of centrifugal forces. The last thing you can do is to force all these [satellites] to depend on Moscow for the rest of their lives. How are you going to keep them interested in you? If you trade with them, Charlie, you have got something pulling their interest your way."

Wilson protested again. "I am a pretty good compromiser when I understand the facts," he claimed, "but I think I am going to be on the tough side on this one." "Charlie," Eisenhower replied, "I am talking common sense. I am not saying are you tough or are you soft. I am saying how can we most damage the Kremlin." Wilson, unconvinced, replied, "I think we need to look it over. I am not for going on just to make a little money for somebody."

With that, the meeting ended. Eisenhower had managed to pry some helpful criticism from his Cabinet, and had learned that Wilson was going to be something of a problem. For the rest, he was satisfied with the results.[2] At a second meeting, the following day, the members of the Cabinet discussed eliminating wage and price controls (the Weeks committee had reported that the interests of a dynamic economy demanded the prompt lifting of the controls). Lodge and Stassen said they feared the inflationary impact of such action; Humphrey supported the Weeks committee enthusiastically. Eisenhower listened and remained noncommittal. The group then bemoaned the impossibility of lowering taxes or balancing the budget in the near future.

Turning to appointments, Eisenhower said sternly that he wanted everyone to understand that personal friendship with the President was not to be regarded as qualification for office. To the contrary, he added, anyone who advanced a claim of friendship was to be denied consideration for any post.[3]

During the campaign, Eisenhower had asked the people to rally behind him in a "crusade." He was a man who used words in a precise manner, and a crusade has to be directed against the enemies of Christianity. Neither Eisenhower, nor many of his fellow Republicans, really believed that the Democrats fit that description. But now the Democrats were defeated, and Eisenhower could use the crusade imagery and theme with a clear conscience, for now the enemy was Communist Russia, which certainly was the enemy of Christianity. In the week immediately preceding his inauguration, Eisenhower's mind turned increasingly to crusades against the irreconcilable enemy.

That he had concluded that the Russians were irreconcilable there can be no doubt. On his last evening at Morningside Heights, in his final speech as the president of Columbia, he told an audience of faculty and staff that "this is not just a casual argument against slightly different philosophies. This is a war of light against darkness, freedom against slavery, Godliness against atheism."[4]

On January 18 Eisenhower, his wife, son, daughter-in-law, grandchildren, and aides traveled by train to Washington, where the party settled into the Statler Hotel. There his brothers and closest friends met him for a joyous reunion with the family and gang. Even as they celebrated, however, there was business to be done.

In the afternoon, Bill Robinson took Eisenhower aside to discuss the confirmation of Charles Wilson as Secretary of Defense. Wilson and his wife owned some fifty thousand shares of General Motors stock; in addition, a bonus plan entitled him to more stock and salary over the next four years. As General Motors did a huge business with the DOD, this was an obvious conflict of interest, and thus illegal. On January 15, Wilson had attended confirmation hearings before the Senate Armed Services Committee. Before going into the hearing room, Wilson had told reporters, "I've got a feeling that I'm going to be pretty pleased and surprised at how easily those boys can be handled." But the boys trapped him time and again, until finally Wilson blurted out that he could not conceive of a conflict of interest between his position as stockholder of GM and his responsibilities as Secretary of Defense, because "for years I thought that what was good for our country was good for General Motors and vice versa." That seemed a simple enough proposition, but it avoided the question of law—which absolutely required Wilson to sell his stock, which he was refusing to do because of the capital-gains tax involved—and the "vice versa" allowed reporters to reverse the statement, making Wilson sound like the original Daddy Warbucks.

Now Robinson told Eisenhower that Wilson had to sell or go. For nearly half an hour he cited moral, political, and practical reasons. Eisenhower played devil's advocate, saying that if Wilson were forced to sell "it would be very difficult to get competent businessmen into the government." He added that Wilson had already made enough of a sacrifice in giving up his $600,000 salary at GM to take a post that paid $22,000. It seemed to Robinson "that General Ike really didn't have his heart in it." Milton Eisenhower joined the conversation, which went on for a full two hours. It continued into dinner, "with Mamie urging Ike not to eat so rapidly. He finished his dinner in about ten minutes."[5]

The following morning, Inauguration Day, January 20, 1953, the Eisenhower family, accompanied by 36 relatives and some 140 members of the incoming Administration, attended services at the National Presbyterian Church. When they returned to the Statler, Eisenhower said to Mamie, "You always have a kind of special sense of propriety in such matters. Do you think it would be appropriate for me to include a prayer in my Inauguration Address?" Mamie was enthusiastic about the idea, whereupon Eisenhower took ten minutes to write a prayer.[6]

Then it was time to drive to the White House to pick up Harry and Bess Truman. Since the brief meeting in November, Eisenhower had sent only one communication to the President, a telegram of January 15. Eisenhower said in it that he had read in the papers that Truman intended to take the train to Independence, Missouri, immediately after the swearing-in ceremony, and "it occurs to me that it may be much more convenient for you and your family to make the trip in the *Independence* rather than in the Pullman." If Truman wanted the airplane, Eisenhower said he would "be more than glad to express my desire to the Air Force that they make the plane available to you."[7] Truman did not reply (and on January 20, after the ceremonies, he and Bess took the train home).

When the Eisenhower car arrived at the portico of the White House, the President-elect showed his animosity toward the President by refusing an invitation to come inside for a cup of coffee; instead, Eisenhower waited in the car for Truman to appear. They rode together to the Capitol in a frosty atmosphere. According to Truman, Eisenhower broke the silence by remarking, "I did not attend your Inauguration in 1948 out of consideration for you, because if I had been present I would have drawn attention away from you." Truman snapped back, "Ike I didn't ask you to come—or you'd been here."[8] Eisenhower denied that any such exchange took place. He did recall asking Truman who had ordered John back from Korea for the inauguration. According to Eisenhower, Truman simply replied, "I did." According to Truman, what he said was, "The President of the United States ordered your son to attend your Inauguration. The President thought it was right and proper for your son to witness the swearing-in of his father to the Presidency."[9]

Three days after the ride to the Capitol, Eisenhower sent Truman a letter "to express my appreciation for the very many courtesies you extended to me and mine during the final stages of your Administration . . . I especially want to thank you for your thoughtfulness in ordering my son home from Korea . . . , and even more especially for not allowing either him or me to know that you had done so."[10] That was his last communication with Truman, just as January 20 was the last time they were together, until after Eisenhower himself had left the Presidency.

Eisenhower and Truman walked through the Rotunda to the east front of the Capitol, where a platform had been erected for the ceremonies. The crowd was huge—the largest for an inaugural in American history—and festive. The Republicans were there to celebrate with unabashed joy; as movie actor and future Republican senator George Murphy put it, "It is all just so wonderful, it's like walking into bright sunshine after being in darkness for a long time."[11] And indeed, the sun had broken through the clouds—Eisenhower luck, everyone agreed—to turn it into a pleasant, if chilly, day. Eisenhower wore a dark-blue double-breasted overcoat and had a white scarf around his neck. At 12:32 P.M., Chief Justice Fred Vinson administered the oath of office.

As Eisenhower turned to deliver his Inaugural Address, his grim, determined expression gave way to that famous grin, and he shot his hands over his head in the old V-for-Victory sign. After the cheering stopped, he read the prayer he had composed that morning, asking Almighty God to "make full and complete our dedication to the service of the people in this throng, and their fellow citizens everywhere." Not forgetting the Democrats, he added, "May cooperation be permitted and be the mutual aim of those who, under the concepts of our Constitution, hold to differing political faiths; so that all may work for the good of our beloved country and Thy glory. Amen."

Then he began his Inaugural Address. "The world and we have

passed the midway point of a century of challenge," he said. The challenges that had to be faced now, he insisted, were those of the dangers of war and aggressive Communism. In a speech devoted exclusively to foreign policy, he promised that his Administration would "neither compromise, nor tire, nor ever cease" to seek an honorable worldwide peace. But people had to realize that "forces of good and evil are massed and armed and opposed as rarely before in history." The urgency of seeking peace in such a climate of hostility was all the greater because "science seems ready to confer upon us, as its final gift, the power to erase human life from this planet."

Fortunately, America had allies in the worldwide struggle. Faith united all free men, he said, and in reference to foreign aid and trade, he insisted that there was no safety in economic solitude. America needed markets, and access to raw materials. He made a firm commitment to the United Nations. He managed to work in the productivity theme that had bothered him so, although in a less than satisfactory manner: "Moral stamina means more energy and more productivity, on the farm and in the factory." [12]

Taken all together, the speech was hardly what the Old Guard wanted to hear from the first Republican elected to the Presidency since 1928. There was no denunciation of the New Deal, nor of Yalta, no promise to cut taxes or balance the budget. Instead, Eisenhower had summoned the American people to yet another crusade; in so doing, he sounded far more like Truman announcing the containment policy than he did like Taft or indeed any other Republican. Senator Lyndon B. Johnson, the new Democratic minority leader, called it "a very good statement of Democratic programs of the last twenty years." [13]

But for the moment, it hardly mattered. Taft praised the speech, and the Republicans prepared to celebrate. The parade took forever, just as Eisenhower had known it would: "Not until nearly seven o'clock," he complained, "did the last two elephants go by." [14] Then he and Mamie drove to the White House, and as she took his arm, they walked together into their new home.

That evening, the Eisenhowers attended two inaugural balls (the crowds were so large that one hall could not hold them all). At one of the balls, Eisenhower took Wilson aside and told him he would have to sell his stock in GM. [15] Finally, at 1 A.M., the Eisenhowers—accompanied by John, Barbara, and the grandchildren—drove home and went to bed. In the morning, he would begin to do his duty as President of the United States.

CHAPTER THREE

Getting Started

January 21–March 31, 1953

AFTER EISENHOWER had been in office for slightly more than a month, Robert Donovan of the *Herald Tribune* asked him at a news conference, "How do you like your new job?" Eisenhower replied that he had never said nor thought that "I would like it. It is not a job that I suppose it is intended one should like."[1]

Eisenhower was being a bit coy. Despite his almost blasé remark in his diary at the end of his first day in the Oval Office, he was finding the job to be fascinating, absorbing, challenging, and fulfilling. He once—only once—admitted that he found the clash of wits with the German generals during the war to be "exhilarating." In a different way, so was the Presidency. He was not engaged in a direct contest with Stalin and his generals as he had been with Hitler, Rommel, Rundstedt, and the others; the issues were never as clear-cut between right and wrong, good and evil; nor could he expect instant obedience, even from members of his own team, when he handed down his orders. But there were compensations. The range of problems was much greater; so were the possibilities of using his talents to bring about compromise and to find a *modus vivendi* among warring factions. Most of all, even for the former Supreme Commander it was a heady experience to feel that he was "at the center of the world." The "excitement" of working daily on a wide variety of difficult problems of the greatest importance, he confessed, was "exhilarating."[2]

44

On January 23, Eisenhower presided over his first Cabinet meeting. He began with his standard pitch for teamwork. He said he intended to meet on a weekly basis with the Cabinet, and with the Republican leaders in Congress, so that everyone would know what everyone else was thinking and doing, thereby avoiding "any appearance of disunity." He urged "selflessness rather than empire building" on his department heads, and insisted that they cooperate fully with Congress, using Jerry Persons as their liaison. He told them that "there is no use to try to conceal an error," so they should "advertise your blunders, then forget them." Promising to back them up, he added, "I believe in decentralizing—that's why I took so much care in picking this gang."

Eisenhower said he was concerned about the State of the Union message he would have to deliver to Congress in a little more than a week. It was much too early, he thought, for him to be presenting a program, but the date was fixed and he would have to go through with it. He was concerned "about the lack of detailed substance in the message," and said he did not "want to assemble Congress without having something to give them. I would like more from each member of the Cabinet in specific terms."

Next Eisenhower turned to an issue that much concerned him and his colleagues—getting control of the bureaucracy. Eisenhower had not heard Truman's warning—Poor Ike, Truman had said, "He'll sit here, and he'll say, 'Do this! Do that!' *And nothing will happen.*"— but he did not need to hear it to know it. The Democrats had complete control of the bureaucracy, and had managed to protect, through Civil Service, more than 95 percent of the officeholders. Eisenhower feared they would sabotage his programs. The Republicans, naturally enough, wanted their own people in those jobs and, of course, they had thousands of party faithful who expected rewards for their services.

Intertwined with the problem of getting Democrats out and Republicans in was the question of security. It was an article of faith among the Republicans that the Democrats had allowed thousands of Commies, pinks, queers, and other undesirables into the bureaucracy. To emphasize the Republican devotion to national security, Eisenhower had already announced that all new appointees—including Cabinet members—would have to undergo a security check by the FBI. Brownell now expounded on that theme. He said he did not like loyalty oaths, because they were inefficient and difficult to administer. He suggested that the basic criteria for appointment to office be changed from those of loyalty to those that put the emphasis on the security risk involved. A drunk or a homosexual could be as loyal as Uncle Sam himself, and still be a security risk because he could be blackmailed. Eisenhower seized on that idea and in his formal message announced that henceforth "security," not "loyalty," would be the test for appointments and retention.

Identifying the security risks, and removing them, was the next problem. Eisenhower said he intended to set up review boards in each department. He would encourage the bureaucrats to inform on each other; the review board would then hear the case; it would make a recommendation for retention or firing to the department head, who would have the final authority. Nixon pointed out that if the review-board members were picked from existing employees, all Democrats, they would protect each other. The boards, Nixon said, "should consist of people *new* to the department"—meaning Republicans—or nothing would happen.

Humphrey said he thought it important to get rid of the subversives "as quietly as possible." He urged caution—"don't start with wholesale firings"—and prudence. "Let's make certain our cases are strong—we've got to win the first one." Eisenhower, more aware than Humphrey of how badly the Republicans wanted dramatic action on the subversive front, disagreed. He wanted strong cases, but when undesirables were found and fired, he wanted maximum publicity. Dodge said there were already lists "of persons on whom disloyalty cannot be proved—but they are nevertheless poor security risks." Eisenhower said he wanted to be fair and to protect the rights of the individuals involved, "but I want positive action taken when we are in the right." And in the "hot" departments of Defense and State, "no doubt can be tolerated."

Turning from security to other grounds for cleansing the stables, Eisenhower said he felt that "talkativeness is a good basis for firing a man." He did not want to read any quotes from staff officers in the newspapers; he wanted them to know that leaking information to reporters was "tantamount to resignation." Then he warned the Cabinet that "there is nothing so dangerous as the Washington cocktail party. As a young officer I was horrified by the arbitrary comments of upper-level officials. Those parties are an abomination of the devil."[3]

The next week, Eisenhower read his latest draft of the State of the Union speech to the Cabinet, then asked for reactions. Nixon wished he had laid into the Democrats more; Eisenhower said he did not want to be critical of the past, but forward-looking and positive.

He pointed out that he would need Democratic support to put his program through. Besides, he said, he had hammered the Democrats hard enough on Yalta with his promise to ask Congress at a later date for a resolution "making clear that this government recognizes no kind of commitment contained in secret understandings of the past with foreign governments which permit enslavement." Further, his announcements on his Korean policy all implied severe criticism of Truman's policy. Eisenhower intended to say that he was stepping up military assistance to the Koreans, so that the Republic of Korea (ROK) forces could do more of the fighting, allowing American troops to be pulled back into reserve. More dramatically, he would announce that Truman's order to the U.S. Seventh Fleet to patrol the waters between Formosa and China in order to keep the two sides apart was being rescinded. "I am," he read, "issuing instructions that the Seventh Fleet no longer be employed to shield Communist China." In fact, under secret orders from Truman, the Seventh Fleet had long since encouraged Nationalist raids on a regular basis against the Chinese coast, but nevertheless all agreed that the Old Guard would be delighted at Eisenhower's decision to "unleash" Chiang Kai-shek.

There were other items designed to delight the Old Guard, including Eisenhower's decision to end price controls. This policy, he said, should have a "great effect on Taft," who not only wanted a free economy but who would be delighted by the elimination of the twenty-five thousand federal employees who administered the program. Humphrey expressed his satisfaction with this, and was overjoyed to hear the President say that "the first order of business is the elimination of the annual deficit."

Eisenhower wanted to give the Old Guard as much as he could, because on the most basic issues he was setting policies that ran directly counter to its wishes. Unleashing the Nationalist Chinese, for example, sounded good, but it merely disguised the more fundamental decision *not* to seek an all-out victory in Korea. So too with the balanced-budget pledge—Republicans wanted that, but they also wanted an immediate tax cut. Eisenhower was refusing to give it to them. Eisenhower knew too that the Old Guard would be unhappy with his strong support of foreign-aid programs, especially to the NATO countries, and with his determination to cut back on defense spending (the key line read, "To amass military power without regard to our economic capacity would be to defend ourselves against one kind of disaster by inviting another."). Further, although the Old Guard would be pleased by Eisenhower's firm commitment to find and fire the security risks within the bureaucracy, McCarthy and his friends expected the files of all government agencies to be thrown open to their investigations. Eisenhower could hardly expect them to give him their "understanding and cooperation," as he put it, in leaving such investigations to him and his Cabinet.

On the tariff, too, Eisenhower anticipated trouble with the Old Guard. The last time the Republicans were in power, they had pushed through the highest tariff in American history (the Hawley-Smoot Tariff Act of 1930); since then, the Democrats had cut the tariff in half, primarily through the Reciprocal Trade Agreements Act (RTAA) of 1934, which gave the President the power to raise or lower tariffs by executive agreement. The act was due to expire in six months—and good riddance, most Republicans felt—but Eisenhower had a theoretical commitment to free trade and a practical need to encourage foreign trade, so he intended to announce that he wanted RTAA "studied and extended." Weeks feared that any Republican-dominated commission set up to study RTAA would end up recommending its elimination. Eisenhower disagreed. "Put reasonably intelligent men in possession of all the facts," he said, "and they will come to general agreement in support of extension."

Other items sure to make members of the Old Guard wish they had Taft rather than Eisenhower for a President included his call for "some corrective action" on Taft-Hartley, and his reminder that "we are—one and all—immigrants or sons and daughters of immigrants," which led him to demand new, nondiscriminatory immigration legislation. And although no one in the Cabinet disagreed with Eisenhower's proposal not only to retain but actually to extend Social Security to "millions of citizens who have been left out," the department heads were apprehensive about the effect of this decision on the Republicans in Congress.

Overall, the Cabinet liked Eisenhower's address. The department heads were especially pleased by his concluding paragraph, for it expressed his philosophy clearly: "There is, in our affairs at home, a middle way between untrammeled freedom of the individual and the demands for the welfare of the whole Nation. This way must avoid government by bureaucracy as carefully as it avoids neglect of the helpless."[4]

On February 2, just before going to the joint session to make his speech, Eisenhower noted in his diary that it was much too soon to be announcing specific policies. "But," he realized, "the Republicans have been so long out of power they want, and probably need, a pronouncement from their president . . ."—one that would convince

them that real and drastic changes in policy were under way.[5] He
satisfied them by putting the repudiation of Yalta and the unleashing
of Chiang at the beginning of the speech. These two items got by far
the most attention. Democrats told reporters they had no intention
of repudiating Yalta (and thus FDR); Europeans, led by the French,
feared that the supposedly new Formosa Straits policy would lead to
à wider war. The British were also upset; later that week Dulles had
to reassure them privately that there would be no real change, and
certainly no wider war.[6] "I hope, and pray," Eisenhower had written
in his diary, "that [the speech] does not contain blunders that we will
later regret."[7] After gauging the reaction, he decided that it had not,
and that he had passed this first test successfully.

   Now it was time to turn away from public relations to the serious
problems of statecraft. One of Eisenhower's major goals was the creation of a United States of Europe. During his year and a half as
SACEUR, 1951–52, he had pushed that concept hard, in public and in
private. In his State of the Union message, he called for a "more
closely integrated economic and political system in Europe."[8] He sent
Dulles and Stassen on a tour of the European NATO capitals, with
instructions to pressure the Europeans toward a ratification of the
European Defense Community (EDC), which was designed to create
an all-European army. Eisenhower's idea was that no political unity
could be achieved in Europe without a spur, and that EDC was the
best possible spur. A treaty had been signed creating EDC; the French
were holding up ratification; Eisenhower wanted to force action.
   Before leaving for Europe, Dulles had begun to apply the pressure by announcing, in a television speech, that "if it appeared there
were no chance of getting effective unity . . . then certainly it would
be necessary to give a little rethinking to America's own foreign policy
in relation to Western Europe." The press described this speech as a
"shock treatment," and Eisenhower's many friends in Europe protested privately to him at this implied threat by the Republicans to
return to a policy of isolation.[9]
   Eisenhower wrote a long letter to the SHAPE chief of staff, his
old friend Alfred Gruenther, with instructions to Gruenther to pass
the word at the various NATO capitals. He said he had sent Dulles
and Stassen to Europe to remind the Europeans that American aid
"was bound to be weakened unless they move definitely in the direction of greater unification." Eisenhower said he was "amazed" that
the NATO leaders could believe he intended to desert them.[10]
   Eisenhower's amazement at European nervousness about the di-

rection of his policies was itself surprising. The all-out Republican assault during the campaign on the Truman-Acheson policies and Republican promises for major changes inevitably made Europeans sensitive and worried. The British, who liked to think they had a "special relationship" with the Americans, and especially with Eisenhower, were greatly concerned. They showed their sensitivity when Eisenhower appointed Winthrop Aldrich as his ambassador to the Court of St. James's without first consulting with the Churchill government. In fact, Eisenhower had warned Dulles to inform Anthony Eden, the Foreign Secretary, before making the announcement, but Dulles had failed to do so. In his diary, Eisenhower recorded his reaction: "I am going to advise Anthony . . . to lay the blame for this whole unfortunate occurrence squarely on me. He will have the logical explanation that my lack of formal experience in the political world was the reason for the blunder. Actually, I was the one who cautioned against anything like this happening, but manifestly I can take the blame without hurting anything or anybody; whereas if the secretary of state would have to shoulder it, his position would be badly damaged."[11]

The Europeans, meanwhile, were telling Dulles—and Eisenhower's special representative to NATO, William Draper—that they could not afford to spend any more on defense, and that their idea was that the United States ought to increase its nuclear arsenal in Europe (which currently stood at sixteen bombs of twenty kilotons each).[12] Eisenhower told Draper to remind the Europeans that "if, on the other side of the Iron Curtain, a backward civilization with a second-rate production plant can develop the power to frighten us all out of our wits, then we, with our potential power can, through work, intelligence and courage, build any countering force that may be necessary."[13]

Thus early were patterns established. Eisenhower was determined to force the Europeans to spend more on defense, and to achieve political and military unity. Dulles, highly visible and quotable, flew around the world, apparently acting on his own but in fact operating under instructions from Eisenhower. So tightly did Eisenhower control Dulles that Dulles, each evening that he was on a trip, sent a cable reporting on what had transpired that day and what he intended to say the following day. Dulles carried messages; he did not make policy. And, frequently, Dulles had to be saved from his own mistakes, which Eisenhower was more than willing to do, even at his own expense.

• •

NATO was a matter of great concern to Eisenhower, but the war in Korea was of more immediate importance. On February 11, Eisenhower met with the NSC to consider the situation and the options. Bradley gave a briefing in which he discussed recent reports, and a request, from General Clark. The reports concerned a Chinese buildup in the Kaesong sanctuary, a twenty-eight-square-mile area created through the armistice negotiations and which "was now chock-full of troops and material." Clark believed the Chinese were preparing an offensive; he asked permission to attack Kaesong "as soon as he believes that the Communist attack is imminent." Dulles agreed with Clark; he said the time had come to end the arrangements for immunity at Kaesong, which had been designed to facilitate armistice negotiations, which were now defunct. Eisenhower asked about the possibilities of using atomic weapons on Kaesong, as "it provides a good target for this type of weapon." He did not like that option, but "we can not go on the way we are indefinitely."

Bradley thought it unwise to consider using atomic weapons. Dulles mentioned the moral problem "and the inhibitions on the use of the A-bomb, and Soviet success to date in setting atomic weapons apart from all other weapons as being in a special category." He said in his opinion "we should try to break down this false distinction." Eisenhower knew that the U.N., and especially Britain and France, would object strongly to using atomic weapons; in that case, he added, "we might well ask them to supply the three or more divisions needed to drive the Communists back." But, on reflection, he concluded that there should be no discussion "with our allies of military plans or weapons of attack." As to Clark's request to attack Kaesong, Eisenhower said he "doubted the validity" of any advance information Clark might obtain on Chinese intentions. He said that although "I have never been able to understand why the U.N. command had ever abandoned its rights of hot pursuit of enemy aircraft to the bases" in Manchuria, he nevertheless would not give Clark the authority to attack Kaesong. He also told Dulles not to broach the subject of ending Kaesong's immunity with the NATO allies.[14]

The next day, February 12, at a Cabinet meeting, Korea came up again during a discussion of the timing of the removal of price and wage controls. Dulles had been in Europe when Eisenhower ordered the controls ended; he was back for the February 12 meeting and at it expressed his concern. He said he did not want to recommend reversing Eisenhower's decision, but he did want to warn the President that "the situation has never been so grave as it looks today." He said that the Russians were on the move in Berlin and in the Arab world, and that the Chinese were about to launch an offensive in Korea. Under the circumstances, he thought the President might have to "backtrack" on the removal of controls.

Eisenhower stared at his Secretary of State, then said slowly and deliberately, "We are living on a high plateau of tension and we cannot risk living all our lifetimes under emergency measures." To do so would risk turning the United States into a police state.[15]

Instead, Eisenhower wanted to increase the psychological pressure on the Chinese. He intended to let them know, "discreetly," that unless the armistice negotiations resumed and satisfactory progress was made, the United States would "move decisively without inhibition in our use of weapons . . . We would not be limited by any world-wide gentleman's agreement."[16] Unleashing Chiang was a part of the pressure; so was Eisenhower's announcement that he was increasing military assistance to the ROK; so were his frequent statements that the situation in Korea was "intolerable." But the greatest pressure, by far, was his own reputation. The Chinese were fully aware that in the war against Germany, Eisenhower had used every weapon at his disposal. They knew that he had atomic weapons available in the Far East, that he would not accept a stalemate, and that he was not demanding their unconditional surrender, but only that they agree to an armistice. The substance behind Eisenhower's threats was Eisenhower's reputation, backed by America's atomic arsenal.

On Tuesday, February 17, Eisenhower held his first presidential news conference. He had already announced, through Hagerty, that he intended to meet with the press on a regular basis, weekly if possible, and that he was considering allowing TV cameras into the Executive Office Building for the conferences. Eight years later, he had met with the press on 193 occasions, and starting in 1955 with the cameras present. He thus subjected himself to the questions of the press far more often than any other President in American history. He did so despite the jeers of his critics, who had great fun with his jumbled syntax, his confessions that he "did not know" about this or that issue, and his often inappropriate or impossibly confusing answers.

Eisenhower was proud of his command of the English language, as he had a right to be—he had written MacArthur's speeches in the thirties, and in 1945, at Guildhall, he had delivered a speech (which he wrote by hand) that the London *Times* ranked with Lincoln's

Gettysburg Address and Churchill's "blood, sweat and tears" speech. But showing that he could get his verbs and nouns to agree, that he knew better than to end a sentence with a preposition, or that he could turn a phrase, was not part of his purpose in the news conferences. Rather, he used the reporters, and later the TV cameras, to reach out to the nation. One of his basic principles of leadership was that a man cannot lead without communicating with the people. Through the conferences, he could educate and inform, or confuse if that suited his purpose. The conferences helped him stay in control; through his answers, he could command the headlines and the national discussion of issues. The Tuesday-morning meetings allowed him to set the national agenda for that week. By downplaying an issue, he could get it off the front pages; by highlighting an issue, he could make it the prime item of national interest. He could, in short, decide when there was a crisis, and when there was not. He could also obfuscate an issue when he was not yet sure how he would deal with it.

As he had done during the war, and in the period 1945–1952, he cultivated the press corps, especially the senior members. Reporters who covered his vacations would find themselves invited to a feast of fresh-caught trout, cooked by the man who had caught them, the President himself. Sometimes he played golf with reporters. And although he could not, and did not, expect the kind of loyal cooperation he had gotten from the press during the war, when he considered the reporters to be quasi members of his staff, he never allowed his relationship with them to degenerate into one of antagonism. In his opening remarks at his first news conference, he praised the American press corps, saying that in the eleven years he had been a world figure, "I have found nothing but a desire to dig at the truth . . . and be openhanded and forthright about it." And he was aware of, and thanked the reporters for, the sympathetic treatment he had received: "I feel that no individual has been treated more fairly and squarely over the past many years . . . than I have by the press."

There was an obvious major difference between being Supreme Commander and being President. In the first instance, Eisenhower was executing policies made by Roosevelt, and in his press conferences he could concentrate on *how* he was carrying out his responsibilities. Reporters did not ask him about, much less criticize, his plans and intentions. As President, he was making policy, which meant that his conferences concentrated on *what* he was going to do, and *why*. Further, all reporters were on his side as a general, but as President he faced a press corps of which at least half the working members were Democrats. Despite the differences, it was as true of President Eisenhower as it was of General Eisenhower that he established and maintained an excellent rapport with the press.

In this first presidential news conference, Andrew Tully of Scripps-Howard Newspapers wanted to know if he had "discovered any other secret agreements besides the one signed at Yalta?" No, Eisenhower responded, he had not. What about the repudiation of Yalta? Eisenhower had promised to send an appropriate resolution to Congress on that subject; he now explained, "I am merely talking about those parts of agreements that appeared to help the enslavement of peoples, or, you might say, have been twisted by implication to mean that." In so saying, he made a major concession to the Democrats. The Republican position was that Roosevelt had handed over East Europe to Stalin; the Democrats maintained that Roosevelt had entered into the best possible agreement, one which should have guaranteed freedom to the Poles, but that Stalin had violated his pledged word.

May Craig of the Portland *Press Herald* then asked if he was aware that "many members of Congress feel that the agreements were never binding, anyway, because they were not presented to the Senate" for ratification. Of course he was aware, but he confused the issue: "Well, I think there are, in our practice, certain things that are of course binding when the people are acting as proper representatives of the United States—say, in war, as in establishing staffs and that sort of thing. That extends out into some fields that are almost politico-military in nature."

Unsatisfied, Craig pressed on. "Are you aware that many members of Congress also feel that the President had no right to take us into Korea without consulting Congress, also that he had no right to send troops to Europe?" Eisenhower cut her off: "That all took place long before I came to this office. I have a hard time trying to determine my own path and solve my own problems. I am not going back and try to solve those that someone else had." (Two weeks later, Craig pressed again; Eisenhower then told her, sharply, "I have no interest in going back and raking up the ashes of the dead past.")

Eisenhower also used his news conferences to send messages to Congress. When a reporter wanted to know if he intended to sponsor a bill to retain the excess-profits tax, which was due to expire on June 30, he replied, "I would say this—I can't answer that in exact terms—I shall never agree to the elimination of any tax where reduction in revenue goes along with it." Then, giving the reporters a wave

and a big grin, he left the room, leaving them to figure out what he
had said and what he meant, but with the distinct impression that
everything was under control.[17]

Like most Presidents, Eisenhower had difficulty distinguishing
between attacks on his policies and attacks on himself. When Ken
Crawford of *Newsweek* wrote a critical piece, Eisenhower told an aide,
"I don't understand how he could write a piece like that because I've
always regarded him as a friend of mine." The aide replied, "Well, he
admires you and he *is* a friend of yours. His trouble is that he hates
Republicans." Eisenhower rubbed his chin, grinned, and replied, "He
may have something there."[18]

Indeed, in his first months in office, Eisenhower had far greater
difficulty with his own party than with the Democrats. On February 7,
Eisenhower had noted in his diary, "Republican senators are having
a hard time getting through their heads that they now belong to a
team that includes rather than opposes the White House."[19] He had
in mind the Old Guard, and most especially Senator McCarthy.

A fight between Eisenhower and McCarthy was inevitable. The
senator was not about to give over to the Administration the issue
that had catapulted him to international prominence, Communism in
government. And he was hardly alone. With control of the congressional committees in hand, the Republicans were determined to use
their investigative powers to expose the undesirables who, in their
view, had taken over the federal bureaucracy. By the time Eisenhower
made his diary entry, congressional committees had already launched
eleven different investigations of just the State Department. Nearly
every Republican wanted to participate; of the 221 Republican representatives, 185 had requested assignment to the House Un-American
Activities Committee (HUAC).[20] But, as had been true since February
1950, McCarthy stood preeminent in the anti-Communist crusade.

During the 1952 campaign, Hughes, Shanley, and others on Eisenhower's staff had urged him to denounce McCarthy. He refused to do
so because, he said, he could not repudiate a fellow Republican. Now,
as President, he needed the support of the Republican senators, and
according to popular belief (shared by Eisenhower), McCarthy controlled seven or eight votes in the Senate. These included Herman
Welker, Pat McCarran, and George Malone, who were relatively inconsequential, and Styles Bridges, William Jenner, Everett Dirksen,
and William Knowland, who were of consequence, as they each headed
a Senate committee and thus were the party's leaders in the Senate.

In addition, Taft frequently sided with McCarthy (a friend of Taft's explained, "McCarthyism is a kind of liquor for Taft. He knows it's bad stuff, and he keeps taking the pledge, but every so often he falls off the wagon."[21]).

Eisenhower had said repeatedly that he intended to cooperate with Congress. This fit exactly the Republican mood. All the Republican complaints about FDR and Truman could be summed up in one phrase—usurpation of executive power. In every way possible, the Republicans wanted to cut back on the size and scope of the President's activities, while enhancing the powers of Congress. This was the prime motivation for the demand for a repudiation of Yalta, for the Bricker Amendment, for the two-term amendment, and other attempts to substitute a *de facto* parliamentary system for the United States. As Eisenhower fully agreed with the basic criticism of FDR's and Truman's activism, he was willing to cooperate in this endeavor— to some extent. He drew the line at such fundamental points as the Executive's right to conduct foreign policy or to provide for security in government. It was at precisely these points, however, that the Republicans, and especially McCarthy, were most determined to exercise control.

Their first opportunity came when Eisenhower sent to the Senate his appointees for State Department and foreign posts. With a Republican majority, albeit of only one vote, Eisenhower expected a *pro forma* confirmation. He was therefore astonished and furious when he learned, on January 22, his second full day in office, that McCarthy was holding up his first nominee's confirmation. That nominee was Walter B. Smith, a man whom Eisenhower trusted and admired without stint. Smith had conservative views, to say the least—he once told Eisenhower that he thought Nelson Rockefeller was a Communist— and he had served the Truman Administration as head of the CIA, as well as ambassador to Russia. Eisenhower could not conceive of any possible objection to Smith, but his morning *Times* informed him that McCarthy was taking "an interest" in the case, because Smith had defended John Paton Davies, who was on Smith's staff in Moscow. Smith had characterized Davies as "a very loyal and capable officer." Insofar as Davies was one of McCarthy's favorite targets, high up on the senator's famous list of known Communists in the State Department and a prime example of bumbling State Department China hands, Smith's praise for Davies made Smith, in McCarthy's view, a possible fellow traveler.

To make Smith into a suspect was, in Eisenhower's view, pre-

posterous, degrading, embarrassing. It gave Eisenhower an intimate
sense of the true meaning of McCarthyism. Eisenhower came to loathe
McCarthy, almost as much as he hated Hitler. He was determined to
destroy McCarthy, as he had destroyed Hitler, but his campaign
against the first was much different from his campaign against the
second. The direct assault against Hitler was replaced by an indirect
assault against McCarthy, one so indirect as to be scarcely discernible,
and one which contributed only indirectly—at best—to McCarthy's
downfall. Eisenhower went after Hitler with everything he had; with
McCarthy, he kept all his ammunition in reserve. During the war, he
had insisted on keeping Hitler at the center of everyone's attention;
in his first years as President, he did his best to get people to ignore
Joe McCarthy.

Why the difference? Beyond such obvious factors as nationality
and party affiliation, Eisenhower cited two basic reasons for his nonapproach to McCarthy. The first was personal. "I just won't get into a
pissing contest with that skunk," he said to his friends, many of
whom—including Milton—were encouraging him to do just that.[22]
But Eisenhower never adversely mentioned McCarthy by name. Not
once.[23] He explained his position to Bill Robinson: "No one has been
more insistent and vociferous in urging me to challenge McCarthy
than have the people who built him up, namely, writers, editors, and
publishers." He thought they should have a touch of guilty conscience,
protested that McCarthyism existed "a long time before I came to
Washington," and complained that as McCarthy grew in headline
value, "the headline writers screamed ever more loudly for me to enter
the list against him. As you and I well know—and have often agreed—
such an attempt would have made the Presidency ridiculous."[24]

Aside from the dignity of the Presidency, Eisenhower refused to
speak against McCarthy because he convinced himself that ignoring
McCarthy was the way to defeat McCarthy. He explained his reasoning in his diary: "Senator McCarthy is, of course, so anxious for the
headlines that he is prepared to go to any extremes in order to secure
some mention of his name in the public press." Eisenhower, with
Smith in mind, knew what he was talking about. Thus his conclusion:
"I really believe that nothing will be so effective in combating his
particular kind of troublemaking as to ignore him. This he cannot
stand."[25]

Eisenhower's second reason for attempting to ignore McCarthy,
and indeed to appease him whenever possible, was his need for Mc-
Carthy's support in the Senate. Some of his advisers strongly disagreed.

C. D. Jackson argued that to cooperate with McCarthy would only embolden him further, while costing the President independent and moderate support.[26] But Eisenhower insisted that if anyone should censure McCarthy, it should be the Senate itself, not the President, and that anyway if given enough rope, McCarthy would hang himself. Jackson retorted that appeasing McCarthy was poor arithmetic (referring to the Senate votes) and worse politics. But Nixon and Jerry Persons urged Eisenhower in the direction his feelings were already taking him. They said that an attack on McCarthy would only divide the party and publicize the senator even more. "The best way to reduce his influence to the proper proportion," Nixon said, "is to take him on as part of the team."[27]

That was no part of Eisenhower's view. He never saw McCarthy as a possible member of his team. But McCarthyism, broadly considered, was the most divisive issue of the day. Eisenhower wanted to bring the nation together, through cooperation, not tear it further apart through confrontation. Behind McCarthy stood millions of Americans; they were an important part of the electorate that had put him in office; to attack and alienate McCarthy would be to alienate the senator's millions of supporters, driving them farther away from the middle road in American politics.

Further, Eisenhower was more on McCarthy's side than not on the issue of Communism in government. It was McCarthy's methods he disapproved of, not his goals or his analysis. At a February 25 news conference, Eisenhower said he had no doubt at all that "almost one hundred percent of Americans would like to stamp out all traces of Communism in our country," and added that if there had been a known Communist on his faculty at Columbia, he would have had the man fired, or resign himself.[28]

But he was no McCarthyite. The senator's methods, the way in which his charges and investigations set American against American, leaving innocent victims in the wreckage, were themselves evil. Eisenhower knew this, he felt it in his bones, but he was faced with the fact that McCarthy was an enemy of his enemies, and a friend of a good many of his friends. So while McCarthy had to be destroyed, his followers had to be educated and brought into the mainstream, not alienated. The best way to do that, Eisenhower thought, was to destroy McCarthy by ignoring him, or by letting him destroy himself. He believed this so strongly that he even ignored McCarthy when the senator called into question the good name of his old friend Beetle.

Instead, Eisenhower worked behind the scenes, as he would do countless times in the future, for he was not adverse to hastening the process of McCarthy's withering away.[29] In this instance, he called Taft and told him to put an immediate stop to this nonsense about Beetle. Taft did as told, it worked, and Eisenhower began to have a better impression of Taft.[30] Smith was confirmed, McCarthy got no headlines out of the case, battle had been avoided.

Then came the case of Dr. James B. Conant. Eisenhower had nominated Conant, Harvard's president whom Eisenhower had known for years, as U.S. High Commissioner to Germany. McCarthy told Eisenhower that he would oppose the nomination in the Senate, primarily because Conant had once said there were no Communists on the Harvard faculty—a statement that ran so counter to McCarthy's world view that he could only conclude that the man who made it must be a pink or worse. Eisenhower had Nixon talk to McCarthy— the first of many trips, as Nixon became Eisenhower's ambassador to the senator—and himself called McCarthy on the phone. Eisenhower later told his Cabinet that he had "conclusive evidence" that the Republican senators "are trying to cooperate." His evidence was a letter from McCarthy with regard to Conant; McCarthy wrote that although he was "much opposed" to Conant he would not make a floor fight against his nomination because "he doesn't want to make a row."[31]

Two days later, on February 5, Eisenhower put forward the name of Charles E. "Chip" Bohlen for the post of ambassador to the Soviet Union. McCarthy had had enough. Or rather, he now had something more substantial to fight with than questioning men like Smith and Conant about their supposed Communist tendencies. Bohlen made a much better target, because he was a career Foreign Service officer, by itself suspect, and had been at Yalta. Worse, he refused to reject Yalta. In confirmation hearings he upheld the agreements as the best possible and said he would have no part in repudiating them. McCarthy then obtained FBI reports that carried various damaging rumors about Bohlen's family life. A furor erupted when McCarthy demanded that the FBI reports be made available to the Senate before it confirmed Bohlen. Eisenhower refused to make them available. Instead, he again sent Nixon to talk to McCarthy. Nixon was unable to keep McCarthy from opposing Bohlen on the floor of the Senate, but he did win a minor victory. As Persons later explained, "McCarthy had two speeches ready to use in fighting us. Both were pretty rough, but one was *real* dirty. So he [asked Nixon] which he ought to give. So Dick told him—and he didn't use the real *dirty* one."[32]

The Senate debate over Bohlen lasted from March 23 to 27, and was bitter and heated. Before it began, Eisenhower discussed it with his staff. Shanley recorded in his diary that Eisenhower "said, 'Mc-Carthy has the bug to run for the Presidency in 1956.' He slapped his knee and shouted, 'The only reason I would consider running again would be to run against him.'"[33] In public, however, Eisenhower refused to say the man's name. He did come forthrightly to the defense of the much maligned Bohlen. At a March 25 news conference, he declared, "I have known Mr. Bohlen for some years. I was once, at least, a guest in his home, and with his very charming family. I have played golf with him, I have listened to his philosophy. So far as I can see, he is the best-qualified man for that post that I could find."[34]

Eisenhower also backed Bohlen privately. Dulles was wavering badly on the case, ready to cut and run because, as he told Eisenhower over the telephone, of the rumors of embarrassing incidents in Bohlen's "family life" (a standard euphemism in the early fifties for homosexual tendencies). Eisenhower assured Dulles that he had already checked with an old Foreign Service man who had known Bohlen "intimately for many years and feels confident that Bohlen has a normal family life." Thus reassured, not incidentally being informed sternly by Eisenhower that there would be no cutting and running on Bohlen, Dulles stayed behind the nominee.[35]

McCarthy continued to demand the FBI files on Bohlen. Attorney General Brownell was adamantly opposed, on the grounds of establishing a bad precedent for executive privilege, and because no one was allowed to see raw FBI files. Dulles suggested a compromise— have two senators look at the files and report to the Senate. Eisenhower thought that reasonable. Brownell thought it dangerous. Eisenhower nevertheless ordered it done.[36] After much wrangling, the Senate agreed to have Taft and John Sparkman examine the files. They did so, reported to the Senate that there was nothing in them, and Bohlen was confirmed, 74 to 13, with Republicans dividing 37 to 11 in Bohlen's favor. McCarthy, Bricker, Dirksen, and Hickenlooper were among those voting against Bohlen. When Taft was asked immediately afterward by reporters if there now was an "open break" between the Old Guard and Eisenhower, Taft responded, "No, no, no, no."[37] But Taft also sent a clear message to Eisenhower: "No more Bohlens."

For his part, Eisenhower was pleased with the result. He appreciated Taft's support ("I think it is scarcely too much to say that Senator Taft and I are becoming right good friends," he wrote in his diary), but he was worried about the eleven Republican votes against Bohlen. He thought the eleven "the most stubborn and essentially small-minded examples of the extreme isolationist group in the party." Barry Goldwater's vote against Bohlen, he confessed, surprised him, because he thought Goldwater "a little bit more intelligent than the others."[38]

Irritating and embarrassing as McCarthy's attacks on Smith, Conant, and Bohlen were to Eisenhower, far more ominous was McCarthy's assumption of the chairmanship of the Senate Committee on Government Operations. McCarthy named himself the head of that committee's Permanent Subcommittee on Investigations. Originally, the Administration thought that by getting McCarthy to take those posts, it had outmaneuvered the senator. Jenner replaced McCarran as chairman of the Internal Security Subcommittee, the traditional Communist-hunting unit of the Senate, and Jenner was thought to be a team player. As Robert Griffith remarks, "[Jenner] could be trusted to pummel the Democrats without embarrassing the Republicans."[39] McCarthy would be out of the anti-Communist business, and thus rendered impotent. Taft bragged, "We've got McCarthy where he can't do any harm." But in fact the opposite was true. The subcommittee he headed had a very broad hunting license: to carry out "the investigation of the operation of all government departments at all levels, with a view of determining their economy and efficiency."[40]

Initially, in January, McCarthy promised to behave. He said he would investigate "graft and corruption" in government, and leave the job of finding and firing Communists to Eisenhower. But in mid-February, McCarthy launched an investigation into subversion in the Voice of America, a propaganda agency that had assumed huge proportions (it had a staff of ten thousand, comprising 40 percent of the total personnel of the State Department, and spent some $100 million a year; it transmitted fifty hours of programming daily in as many languages). Republicans were convinced that the Voice was filled with "Communists, left-wingers, New Dealers, radicals and pinkos," and it was thus a target that McCarthy could not leave alone.[41]

McCarthy's investigation consisted primarily of wild and unsubstantiated charges made by disgruntled lower-level employees. These "tips" fed McCarthy's closed-door hearings, and led to enough rumors to force the resignation—brusquely accepted by Dulles—of the chairman of the Voice. McCarthy then turned to material used in Voice broadcasts and included in the libraries of State Department Information Centers in sixty-three countries. McCarthy said that the presence in the broadcasts or in the libraries of the works of such fellow travelers as Arthur Schlesinger, Jr., John Dewey, Robert M. Hutchins, and Edna Ferber proved infiltration of the Voice. Eisenhower and Dulles tried to appease McCarthy—on February 19 the State Department issued a directive that forbade the Voice to quote from the works of "any Communist, fellow travelers, etc." When High Commissioner Conant embarrassed State by cabling from Germany to ask for a clarification of "etc.," State modified the directive to urge "great care" when using Communist sources, and to quote them solely to "expose Communist propaganda or refute Communist lies."[42] In the madness that followed, nervous librarians discarded and even burned books.[43]

When Robert Spivack asked Eisenhower at a February 25 news conference whether "McCarthy's investigation of the Voice of America is helping the fight against Communists," Eisenhower responded with typical vagueness: "Well, I don't know exactly what he is aiming to do, . . . because I just haven't thought about his particular function—what he can do and what would happen if he didn't do it."[44] Ten days later he promised that "if the Senate investigation into the Voice . . . reached a point of inviting international misunderstanding and difficulties, I might intervene."[45] But his much more consistent position was that "it would be extremely dangerous to try to limit the power of Congress to investigate," and he added in response to a question about McCarthy's methods, "I think it would be completely inappropriate for me to comment specifically on individuals in Congress and their methods, because presumably the Congress approves these, or they wouldn't go on."[46] Dulles, meanwhile, made it clear that he would cooperate with McCarthy's investigation, and the general impression was that the Eisenhower Administration had surrendered to McCarthy.

That impression was strengthened by the Greek shipowners' case, which McCarthy broke on March 28, when he announced that he had arranged an "agreement" with the Greek owners of 242 merchant ships to break off all trade with Communist China. McCarthy said he had negotiated the agreements "secretly" because of their "extremely delicate" nature. In fact, the American and Greek governments had just finished an eighteen-month-long negotiation process, finally agreeing to "prohibit the shipment of strategic materials by Greek ships to the Peiping regime." This was a favorite issue of the Old Guard (and some who were not; McCarthy's chief assistant on the Greek deal was Robert F. Kennedy), which had long since been demanding a complete embargo of China. The British, however, had refused to stop trading with China. One Eisenhower aide called McCarthy's claims as "phony" as his procedures were "irregular."[47]

Stassen, the head of the MSA and thus the man in charge of co-ordination of trade agreements, testified on March 30 before Mc-Carthy's subcommittee. Stassen told McCarthy, "You are in effect undermining and are harmful to our objective." Stassen added the elemental point that such agreements could only be made between governments.[48] At an April 2 news conference, James Reston asked Eisenhower for a clarification about McCarthy's "negotiations." Eisen-hower replied with a rhetorical question, "How do you negotiate when there is nothing to commit?" He then gave the reporters a simple civics lesson: Congressional investigators had no power to negotiate and moreover they "cannot possibly have the facts that would make such negotiations really profitable." As to Stassen's use of the word "undermining," Eisenhower said that Stassen probably meant "in-fringement," but added that he was not "the slightest bit unhappy" about what Stassen had said. To further confuse everyone, he added, "I am not going to say there never could be any good come out of such [negotiations]." Indeed, he thought that so long as McCarthy was discussing, suggesting, or advising, "he is probably in his proper function." When Robert Spivack suggested that Eisenhower had to be angry at one or the other man, Stassen or McCarthy, Eisenhower snapped back, "The mere fact that some little incident arises is not going to disturb me. I have been scared by experts, in war and in peace, and I am not frightened about this."[49] After Stassen said, the next day, that he indeed meant to say "infringement" rather than "undermining," and after Dulles, Nixon, and McCarthy got together to negotiate what amounted to their own internal treaty, the issue gradually died away.[50]

Eisenhower's policy of denial—denial that McCarthy had any right to negotiate with foreign governments, denial that he had done so, denial that Stassen had said what he said, denial that there was any difference on basic issues between himself and McCarthy—plus the inner complexities of the case (British goods on Greek-owned ships flying foreign flags destined for Hong Kong to be sold to China), de-fused McCarthy's attack and avoided a crisis. Many of Eisenhower's aides were unhappy with Eisenhower for not standing up to the senator, especially in a case where McCarthy had so clearly exceeded his authority, and prophesied that no amount of appeasement of the junior senator from Wisconsin would ever make him behave.[51]

For all that Eisenhower shuddered at McCarthy's methods, the

President himself, at his first Cabinet meeting, urged aggressive action against Communists in government. He especially urged Dulles to crack down on the State Department. Dulles hardly needed the encouragement, as he had reasons of his own to conduct a purge. Virtually every senior official in the Foreign Service was a Democrat, most of them were guilty of personal devotion to Acheson and had a strong dislike for Dulles. Further, Dulles wanted to avoid the antagonistic relationship that had plagued Acheson in his dealings with Congress. Nothing, Dulles knew, would please the Old Guard more than his firing men whom Acheson had defended from McCarthy and his friends. In addition, Dulles had to prove his own anti-Communist zeal. The skeleton in his own closet, of which he was embarrassingly aware, was his endorsement of Alger Hiss as director of the Carnegie Endowment and his offer of a deposition in Hiss's behalf during Hiss's subsequent trial. So Dulles, acting under Eisenhower's direction, made a purge his first priority.

On January 23, Dulles sent a letter to 16,500 State Department personnel demanding "positive loyalty" to the new Administration. That same day, the first Eisenhower bill to pass the initial legislative stage emerged from the Senate Foreign Relations Committee; it provided for an Under Secretary of State for Administration and Operations, with the specific task of housecleaning in the State Department. Dulles appointed Donald B. Lourie, president of the Quaker Oats Company, to the new post. For his chief security officer, Lourie chose Scott McLeod, a former FBI agent and assistant to Styles Bridges, who was one of McCarthy's closest supporters in the Senate. McLeod, turned loose on the internal State Department files, hired two dozen ex-FBI agents and went to work immediately. Within three weeks, he fired twenty-one employees for alleged homosexuality. Later, he proudly announced that he had removed 306 civilian employees and 178 aliens without a single hearing. He also began feeding information to McCarthy, including the tips about Bohlen's supposed immorality.[52]

Dulles, meanwhile, was actively appeasing McCarthy on other fronts. He dismissed from the service John Carter Vincent, one of the State Department's most respected China experts, despite admitting that there could be "no reasonable doubt" about Vincent's loyalty. Even this did not satisfy McCarthy, who criticized Dulles for allowing Vincent to keep his pension.[53]

Eisenhower played no public role in the purges, but behind the scenes he was pushing Dulles hard. On March 18, he sent Dulles a memo saying that the senior posts in State were all held by people "who believe in the philosophy of the preceding Administration." These men had risen to the top, Eisenhower said, "through a process of selection *based upon their devotion to the socialistic doctrine and bureaucratic controls practiced over the past two decades.*" Eisenhower feared that if "any sizable reductions" in State were made "*before* these top individuals are removed . . . the result will be that down through the organization there will be a studied effort to hang on to those believing in the New Deal philosophy and to eliminate those who show any respect for ideals of self-dependence and self-reliance."[54] Dulles gladly complied with Eisenhower's orders to get rid of the top people first. As a result of this, and of McLeod's activities, and of the Vincent case, morale in the State Department sank. Many spoke of a police-state atmosphere.

Eisenhower was no Hitler, and he did not preside over a police state. But he was deeply concerned with the Communist menace, and he knew the value of military secrets, which made him fearful of spies within the government. As the Rosenberg case showed, he was ready to deal with them without mercy. Julius and Ethel Rosenberg had been convicted of giving atomic secrets to the Soviets and had been sentenced to death. They had appealed, unsuccessfully, to the Supreme Court. By January of 1953, the Rosenbergs only hope was executive clemency. There was an immense international campaign, by no means exclusively Communist, to convince Eisenhower to stay the execution. The grounds were that the Rosenbergs had been framed, that their death sentence was the result of anti-Semitism and runaway McCarthyism. But on February 11, Eisenhower issued a public statement rejecting clemency, because "the nature of the crime for which they have been found guilty and sentenced far exceeds that of the taking of the life of another citizen; it involves the deliberate betrayal of the entire nation and could very well result in the death of many, many thousands of innocent citizens." He insisted that the Rosenbergs had had a fair trial and received "their full measure of justice."[55] Execution was scheduled for mid-June.

What McCarthy and his friends really wanted from Eisenhower and Dulles was much bigger than just firing a few queers and Communists, or the execution of the Rosenbergs. The senator wanted major policy and structural changes. In policy, the Old Guard wanted a flat repudiation of the Yalta agreements, to be followed by action—

the form of which was unspecified—to free the East European satellites. In structure, the Old Guard wanted to amend the Constitution so that neither Eisenhower nor any future President could enter into such agreements. For the nation and the world, these were matters of transcendent importance, beside which the fate of State Department employees paled into insignificance. Eisenhower and Dulles were well aware of this, but so was McCarthy, who would not be bought off or diverted by Dulles' petty purge. The Yalta resolution would give Eisenhower some of his most difficult moments in his first months in office; the Bricker Amendment, named after Senator John Bricker of Ohio, plagued him for the next two years.

As a candidate, Eisenhower had felt free to denounce Yalta. As President, his freedom of action was much more limited. When he turned to serious consideration of the effect of a repudiation of the agreements, he realized that such an action would have negative effects on American foreign policy and would needlessly alienate the Democrats. Further, having assumed power, he did not want to waste his assets by scavenger hunting into the past. Yalta had given the Americans their occupation rights in West Berlin and in Vienna; how could such guarantees be continued if they had been granted by an invalid agreement? The British, among others, warned that if the Americans could repudiate their pledged word, so could the Russians. Eden said bluntly that the U.K. would never participate in a repudiation. And of course the Democrats would resist with all their power any implied or real repudiation of FDR. Any resolution that passed Congress by a slim, partisan majority would have little if any effect. Eisenhower told the Republican leaders that "solidarity is the important thing." He wanted politics to stop at the water's edge.

So, on February 20, when Eisenhower presented to Congress his proposed resolution on Yalta, it did not repudiate the agreements, but instead merely criticized the Soviet Union for violating the "clear intent" of Yalta and thereby "subjugating" whole nations. The United States, Eisenhower's resolution declared, rejected "interpretations" of Yalta that "have been perverted to bring about the subjugation of free peoples." It "hoped" that these peoples would "again enjoy the right of self-determination."[56]

The Old Guard denounced Eisenhower for this betrayal of basic Republican principle. Taft, under pressure from Eisenhower to go along, tried to bridge the gap by proposing a reservation to Eisenhower's resolution: "The adoption of this resolution does not constitute any determination by the Congress as to the validity or invalidity of any of the provisions of the said agreements." The Democrats, meanwhile, led by Lyndon B. Johnson of Texas, hailed Eisenhower's original resolution and opposed any change in it. This put the Old Guard in a dilemma. If it allowed Eisenhower's resolution to pass unamended, it would imply acceptance of Yalta; if it amended the resolution, it would be guilty of partisanship and of splitting with a Republican President. But the Old Guard could not simply drop Yalta. Senator Hickenlooper wanted a clear and strong repudiation, and he had a number of allies on the Senate Foreign Relations Committee, which held hearings on the subject.

Then Stalin, of all people, came to Eisenhower's aid. On March 4, word came from Moscow that the Soviet dictator was near death. Under the circumstances, passing a repudiation resolution would be regarded as particularly callous; further, the imminent change in Soviet leadership made it inopportune to reopen old wounds. Nevertheless, Eisenhower was ready to go ahead with his own resolution. On March 5 he told a news conference that "what I really want to do is to put ourselves on record . . . that we never agreed to the enslavement of peoples that has occurred." When he was asked to comment on suggestions that the Taft amendment represented "a break between you and Senator Taft," Eisenhower replied, "So far as I know, there is not the slightest sign of a rift or break between Senator Taft and me. And if anyone knows of any, I don't." Four days later, Eisenhower met with Taft and other Republican leaders to discuss the issue. Taft admitted that it was probably better "to forget the whole thing." Eisenhower's "powder-puff resolution" was not worth fighting for, while opposing it or amending it would be too costly.[57] Stalin's death, on March 5, allowed everyone to escape the dilemma by shelving permanently any resolution on Yalta.

The death of the man who had single-handedly led the world's second most powerful nation, and America's principal enemy, was an event of momentous importance. The trouble was that no one in the United States knew what to do about it, how to take advantage of it, or what was going to happen next. Eisenhower, relieved to have escaped the need to denounce FDR in public for Yalta, privately told his Cabinet that American unpreparedness was a "striking example of what has *not* been done" by the Democrats while they held power. Since 1946, he said, there had been much talk about what would happen when Stalin died, but the net result of seven years' talk "is zero. There is no plan, there is no agreed-upon position." He added that was why he had brought Robert Cutler down from Boston to give some form, direction, and organization to the work of the NSC. SHAEF had always had contingency plans ready in the event of Hitler's death, and he wanted the NSC to be equally prepared in the future.[58]

The Constitution of the United States, in Article VI, makes treaties the "supreme law of the land." Conservative Republicans, and many others, were unhappy with this provision and wanted an amendment to modify it. There were many motives. Back in 1920 the state of Missouri, for example, had challenged the federal government's right to enter into a treaty with Canada to prevent the extermination of migrating ducks; Missouri took the position that no one could take away the rights of its citizens to shoot ducks within the state. The Supreme Court ruled against Missouri. The issue lay dormant for some decades, but Yalta revived it. So did American entry into the United Nations. Southern leaders feared that the U.N. commitment to human rights would imperil segregation; the American Medical Association feared it would bring about socialized medicine. In addition, there was widespread, and strong, support for limiting the powers of the President to enter into binding agreements with foreign nations.

So strong, in fact, that when Bricker introduced Senate Joint Resolution 1, on January 7, 1953, he had the cosponsorship of sixty-two other senators, including forty-four of the forty-seven other Republicans. The president of the American Bar Association was a supporter; so were the U.S. Chamber of Commerce, the Daughters of the American Revolution, the AMA, the American Legion, the Veterans of Foreign Wars, and many other national organizations. The proposed amendment carried a much-celebrated "which" clause. It declared that "a treaty shall become effective as internal law in the United States only through legislation which would be valid in the absence of a treaty." No one really knew what this meant. Some feared that future treaties would have to be ratified by all forty-eight states. Eisenhower thought that "the logic of the case is all against Senator Bricker," but noted ruefully that "he has gotten almost psychopathic on the subject." Eisenhower realized that a great many lawyers, including his own brother Edgar, were supporting Bricker, but "this fact does not impress me very much. Lawyers are trained to take either side of any case . . . [which] tends to create a practice of submerging conviction in favor of plausible argument."[59]

Eisenhower once characterized the proposed amendment as "an addition to the Constitution that said you could not violate the Constitution. How silly."[60] It was, nevertheless, an issue of fundamental significance. Peter Lyon is surely correct in stating that without Eisenhower's opposition, the Bricker Amendment would have been adopted. With what results, no one knows. Bricker and his supporters gave the impression that the amendment would have prevented any future Yaltas, which was nonsense, as nothing in Yalta had any effect within the United States. More generally, the amendment was designed to take power in foreign relations from the President, although even here it was hardly precise on how that would be accomplished.

"I'm so sick of the Bricker Amendment," Eisenhower told his Cabinet.[61] His preference was to drop it and forget it, but that was hardly possible with an amendment that had two-thirds of the Senate as sponsors, and which had the near-unanimous support of the Republican Party. He therefore tried to talk Bricker into dropping the "which" clause and accepting an amendment that merely said no treaty could violate the Constitution—something Eisenhower regarded as meaningless enough that he could support it. He met with Bricker privately; he met with Bricker and Dulles (who was opposed); he met with Bricker and Brownell (who thought that the whole thing was ridiculous). Bricker could not be moved. Eisenhower thought the senator merely wanted something with his name on it "as a permanent monument." Unable to change Bricker's mind, Eisenhower appealed to Dulles to "write anything which will provide the monument" without detracting from the President's power to enter into treaties and agreements. He informed the Cabinet that he had a copy of the Federalist Papers on his desk, and was reading them "in every spare minute" on the subject of the balance of powers between the President and Congress. The Founding Fathers, Eisenhower said, "had so distinctly in mind the separation of powers." But he could not convince even his own Cabinet. Wilson thought the Bricker Amendment would "strengthen the Constitution"; Weeks also supported Bricker; Nixon urged caution; Humphrey wanted to avoid a "head-on fight" with Bricker.[62]

Eisenhower continued to work on Bricker, to no avail. Dulles wanted the President to join the issue more directly. "I haven't been fuzzy about this," Eisenhower protested. "There was nothing fuzzy in what I told Bricker. I said we'd go just so far and no further." Dulles replied, "I know, sir, but you haven't told anybody else."

Dulles himself was a problem. He sent Eisenhower a copy of a

speech he intended to make on the amendment; in it, Dulles said that
such an amendment might be necessary under different leadership,
but that it was not required so long as Eisenhower was in charge.
Eisenhower told Dulles that if the Secretary really believed that, then
he should withdraw his opposition to Bricker.

Eisenhower tried to make the amendment ridiculous ("Bricker
seems determined to save the United States from Eleanor Roosevelt,"
he told one Cabinet meeting; on another occasion he passed along a
joke he had heard, that the Constitution was being demolished "brick
by brick by Bricker"). Nothing worked. Bricker could not get the
amendment on the Senate floor, because of the parliamentary maneuvering of Eisenhower's supporters, but Eisenhower could not kill it.
Still, through the year 1953 Eisenhower managed to keep the amendment in hearings, avoiding a vote.[63] But the issue droned on.

Eisenhower was not the only man to oppose Bricker, but he was
obviously the most important member of the minority that did so. He
was in a similar position with regard to the defense budget. Eisenhower ordered Wilson to cut back sharply. Except for Humphrey,
only a handful of Republicans supported Eisenhower on these cuts,
although few went public with the opposition. The Democrats felt
no such constraints. After Wilson announced his program of major
reductions, Senator Symington launched an attack—one that the
Democrats would continue and intensify over the next eight years—
charging that Eisenhower's determination to balance the budget
through defense cuts was leaving the United States vulnerable to
Soviet aggression.

When Eisenhower was asked about Symington's charges, at a
March 19 news conference, he used the occasion to attempt to educate the American people. "Ladies and gentlemen," he said, "there is
no amount of military force that can possibly give you real security,
because you wouldn't have that amount unless you felt that there was
almost a similar amount that could threaten you somewhere in the
world."[64]

At a Cabinet meeting the following day, the President was even
blunter. Dulles was opposed to making a balanced budget top priority.
He warned Eisenhower that if the United States cut back on defense
spending, it would have the effect of saying the crisis was over. The
Europeans would then feel that in that case, they too could cut back
on military expenditures. This, he gravely warned, "would take the
heart out of NATO." Eisenhower immediately disagreed. There could

be no security, he told Dulles, without a sound economy, which was dependent upon a balanced budget. Dulles charged that the decision to balance the budget was made in a vacuum. He then tried to pose a dilemma for Eisenhower: What were they going to do about Korea? Continue the stalemate? If so, they would lose congressional support. Try to win? If so, they needed more money for defense. Eisenhower held his position. "There is a limited kind of striving for a victory," he said, "but we simply cannot have these succeeding deficits." Dulles tried another approach. The French were coming to Washington to ask for more help in Vietnam. Dulles thought that "we can clean up Indochina by an eighteen-month all-out effort" of military aid to France. It made good sense to Dulles to spend the money now, in order to effect greater savings later. So too in Korea—victory there now, whatever the cost, would mean savings later.

Eisenhower admitted that there was some truth in what Dulles said, but not enough. He pointed out that just getting sufficient force in Korea to drive the Communists back a few miles, so that the front lines would run across the narrow waist of the peninsula, would cost $3 or $4 billion. "How much better off are we at the waist," he wondered, "and how much do we want to pay to get there?" Dulles said driving forward to the waist would improve Korean morale. Eisenhower replied that was "an imponderable."

Turning to a broader theme, Eisenhower flatly declared that "the defense of this country is *not* a military matter. The military has a very limited sector." If military spending continued at present levels, "then we've got to call for drastic reductions in other things," such as veterans' benefits, Social Security, farm programs. Eisenhower also warned his Cabinet that "any notion that 'the bomb' is a cheap way to solve things is awfully wrong. It ignores . . . the basic realities for our allies. It is cold comfort for any citizen of Western Europe to be assured that—after his country is overrun and he is pushing up daisies—someone still alive will drop a bomb on the Kremlin."[65]

Shortly after taking office, Eisenhower had a telephone conversation with Omar Bradley about the situation in Korea. Hanging up the phone, he turned to Ann Whitman and said, "I've just learned a lesson." Bradley had called him "Mr. President," after a lifetime of calling him "Ike." Eisenhower told Ann that it was a shock to hear it, and made him realize that as long as he was in the White House he would "be separated from all others, including my oldest and best friends. I would be far more alone now than [during the war]."[66]

To overcome those feelings of loneliness, Eisenhower turned first of all to his wife. They almost always ate their evening meal together, in the West Sitting Hall, usually with Mamie's mother, Mrs. Doud, who lived in the White House with them. Later in the evening, when Eisenhower painted, Mamie would sit with him, reading or answering correspondence. They took their vacations together, whether to Augusta in the winter or Colorado in the summer. In the late winter of 1953, following Mamie's first visit to the presidential retreat in Maryland's Catoctin Mountains, named Shangri-La by FDR, Mamie announced that she would not go back to the rustic, rather shabby place unless it was modernized. But there was no money in the White House budget to do so. A member of the staff suggested to Mamie that since the place was operated by the Navy, the Navy might pay for remodeling. Mamie said, "I think I'll just pass a hint along to the Commander-in-Chief." The work was done; Eisenhower renamed the retreat Camp David after his grandson; thereafter, until the Gettysburg farm was remodeled, the President and Mamie spent numerous weekends together in the mountains.[67]

Eisenhower's son, daughter-in-law, and grandchildren also helped him preserve some modicum of a normal family life. John and Barbara stayed in the White House until after the inaugural; Eisenhower liked having them around, and they liked being there. The morning of January 22, Mamie had discovered Barbara sitting in a big four-poster in the Royal Suite, having her breakfast served to her. Mamie had laughed at the sight; Barbara had said that she would "never be nearer heaven than right then."[68] In the months and years that followed, Barbara was often back, with her children, which added immeasurably to Eisenhower's pleasure, and to his sense that the White House was a real home, not an institution.

But neither Mamie nor the family could fully satisfy Eisenhower's need for friendship and companions. Mamie seldom woke before 10 A.M., and did not get out of bed before twelve. "I believe that every woman over fifty should stay in bed until noon," she said, quite seriously.[69] She would study the papers, looking for bargains, whether in food, clothes, or gifts, which she would then order over the telephone. She closely supervised the White House staff and took charge of the social functions, deciding on the menu, flowers, and seating arrangements. "I have only one career, and his name is Ike," she frequently declared, but in fact she was so busy—not to mention his schedule—that they seldom saw each other in daylight. John had his own career to pursue—he returned to Korea and the front lines shortly after the inaugural—and Barbara and the grandchildren lived in New York State. Further, Mamie never played golf, and she refused to play bridge with her husband, for the good reason that he yelled at her every time she misplayed.

Fortunately, he had friends who shared his love of golf and played bridge to his satisfaction. Even better, they were devoted to him. Following his elections, his gang got together and agreed that they would always be available to the President whenever he had a free moment for golf or bridge. They were men of large affairs with crowded schedules of their own, but they felt they had played a major role in convincing their friend to take on the Presidency, and they now felt they owed him whatever they could give him—which was primarily their time and their friendship. Over the next eight years, they were always available. Ann could telephone them in the morning, tell them that the boss wanted to play, and they would immediately get on a plane to Washington. Or, on a few occasions, to England or the Continent.[70]

Eisenhower told Slater he was especially delighted at the gang's willingness to come to Washington at a moment's notice, because most of his favorite partners and opponents in Washington were Democrats. He enjoyed playing with Chief Justice Fred Vinson, Senator Symington, and others he had known for years in the capital, but he feared that if he continued to play with them "some Republicans might not understand."[71] Another criterion his bridge partners had to meet was getting along with Mamie. As one of the gang told an interviewer, "Mamie wants her soldier boy around, and Ike likes to be around her. So when you play bridge, you play at Ike's place. He doesn't go out with the boys at night."[72]

In his memoirs, Eisenhower paid a handsome tribute to his gang. "These were men of discretion," he wrote, "men, who, already successful, made no attempt to profit by our association. It is almost impossible for me to describe how valuable their friendship was to me. Any person enjoys his or her friends; a President needs them, perhaps more intensely at times than anything else."[73]

In the middle of February, Robinson, Roberts, and Slater came down from New York to spend the weekend at the White House. After golf in the afternoon and dinner on Saturday night, the party went to the movie theater in the White House to see *Peter Pan*. The next morning, Eisenhower and his gang marched into Mamie's bedroom about 10:30 A.M. Mamie refused to go to church with them, saying that she planned to stay in bed all day; nevertheless, Robinson noted in his diary, "she hoped we wouldn't completely neglect or forget her." Slater asked Eisenhower how the Presidency was going to work out for him financially. "Hell," Eisenhower replied, "this job is no easy touch. Truman says I'll be lucky if I don't use $25,000 a year of my own money." Mamie added that the government only allowed her $3,000 for redecoration, and complained about "the stingy, small bath towels."[74]

Later in the afternoon, Robinson accompanied Eisenhower to the study in which he did his painting. As Eisenhower worked on a self-portrait Milton had requested, he talked to Robinson about various political problems. "Ike always likes to be in motion of some kind when he is talking and thinking," Robinson noted. "He seldom sits in the same chair for very long during a discussion and abhors sitting behind a desk in any extended conference. During our two- or three-hour talk he was all over the room and he continued to talk animatedly while he worked on the painting."[75]

The previous day, Adlai Stevenson had charged that the "Big Deal" was succeeding the New Deal. Eisenhower told Robinson he thought Stevenson was "very clever" in making the charge, and said he wished he had someone "who could turn the Stevenson kind of satire into a boomerang with cleverly turned phrases and labels." Eisenhower stressed the value of "catch phrases" and pointed to FDR's "nothing to fear but fear itself" line as an example. "Ike pointed out that this was the least important thing that Roosevelt had said in that speech but because of the catchy phrase it was the one thing that people remembered."[76]

Eisenhower consistently used his gang and his friends to try out ideas. On one occasion, he startled Slater by remarking that "I think I'm going to get along well with Taft, and if things work out the way I hope, Taft might be available to us as candidate for the top job in 1956."[77] He had found Taft to be "solid" on domestic affairs and thought he could be educated about foreign affairs. What Eisenhower liked best about being able to think out loud with his companions was that none of them was ever guilty of a leak, or even an indiscretion; as Eisenhower put it in his memoirs, "not one of [my] friends . . . has ever . . . written a sentence or uttered a word that could have been embarrassing to me."[78]

When Robert Donovan asked Eisenhower on February 25 how he liked his job, Eisenhower mentioned "the confinement, and all the rest—those things are what you pay." Wanting always to be in motion, he hated having to spend hours, days, or weeks on end in his office, without a break from the routine, and he got away as often as possible. Dr. Snyder always encouraged him to do so, even if only for half a day. On February 7, Ann noted in her diary that "today the President wanted to play golf, very, very badly. He awoke to a cold and drizzly rain. He peered at the sky frequently during the morning, and finally, after another excursion out to the porch, announced, 'Sometimes I feel so sorry for myself I could cry.'"[79]

Later that month, Eisenhower was delighted when the American Public Golf Association offered to build a putting green on the south lawn. Eisenhower accepted, and had it placed just outside his office window. He practiced his approach shots and putts on his way to and from the office. He was furious with the squirrels, which were almost tame because Truman liked to feed them, and who buried acorns and walnuts in the green. Eisenhower told Moaney, "The next time you see one of those squirrels go near my putting green, take a gun and shoot it!" The Secret Service talked him out of that idea, substituting traps instead; soon most of the squirrels had been transported to Rock Creek Park.[80]

Eisenhower's favorite place to play golf was not on the White House lawn, or at the Burning Tree golf club outside Washington, but at Augusta National. There he and Mamie could entertain their friends, relax, and play cards. On February 27, he made his first trip there for a weekend; the gang flew down from New York in a Chase National Bank plane; everyone had a great time; Eisenhower played golf with the world's most famous golfer, Bobby Jones; he vowed to return often.[81]

By the end of March, Eisenhower was satisfied with what he had accomplished to date. Defense spending was coming down. There was some movement in Korea toward an armistice. He had managed to put off any immediate tax cut. Price controls had been lifted without any major swing in prices up or down. The Cabinet and the NSC were both functioning the way he wanted them to, showing "a spirit of teamwork and of friendship that augurs well for the future."[82] He had managed to avoid a repudiation of Yalta and the passage of the Bricker Amendment. Congress was acting on his requests for reorganization, the most important of which was the creation of a Department of Health, Education, and Welfare.[83] He had set various long-range studies in motion, most of all by Cutler and the NSC staff on the subject of the strategic options in the Cold War. He had put his economics adviser, Dr. Hauge, to work on a study for building "high-speed highways traversing" the country, cautioning Hauge that "the timing of construction should be such as to have some effect in leveling out peaks and valleys in our economic life." [84] Stalin's death gave some hope of a new beginning in Soviet-American relations.

His chief worry was the Old Guard. Not Taft, whom he was beginning to admire, but McCarthy, Hickenlooper, Bricker, Bridges, Goldwater, and the others. The apparent hopelessness of working effectively with such men led Eisenhower to muse about the possibility that "I should set quietly about the formation of a new party." He was considering making a "personal appeal" to every congressman and governor "whose general political philosophy [is] 'the middle way.'" He feared that such a drastic step might "be forced upon us," but hoped that he could avoid it by educating the Old Guard about "teamwork and party responsibility." He thought "this will be much the better way." [85]

CHAPTER FOUR

The Chance for Peace

April 1–June 30, 1953

EISENHOWER, ACCORDING TO C. D. Jackson, suffered from an "exaggerated desire to have everybody happy," which prevented him from making "clean-cut decisions."[1] The case of the generators for the Chief Joseph Dam was one example. It was hardly a major issue, although Eisenhower and his Cabinet spent hours discussing it, but it was illustrative of Eisenhower's willingness to abandon principle when faced with practical problems or political resistance. The case involved procurement of generators for the dam, which was being built by the Corps of Engineers. To Secretary Wilson's consternation, a British firm came in 12 percent below the lowest American bidder, Westinghouse. Wilson refused to make a decision to award the contract to the British (Wilson's habit of bucking his decisions up to Eisenhower was already causing the President much anguish, leading Eisenhower to wonder to his aides how a man who was so hesitant to take control could ever have run General Motors).[2] At a Cabinet meeting in early March, Wilson had outlined his problem. Westinghouse wanted the contract badly, he said, and the Corps of Engineers was arguing that maintenance was easier on American equipment. On the other hand, Wilson knew that Eisenhower was committed to free trade, and that the President wished to strengthen the economies of the NATO allies. And of course there were budgetary considerations—a significant sum of money could be saved by buying British. Wilson concluded his presentation, then said, "Well, Mr. President?"

Eisenhower replied, "Well, just shooting from the hip, I'd say to give the order to the British."[3]

A month later Wilson still had not placed the order. The Cabinet took up the subject again. Dulles reminded Eisenhower that the NSC had made a decision to encourage procurement abroad. Stassen and Lodge warned that the British were watching this one closely, to see if Eisenhower really was committed to free trade. Eisenhower said, "My own mind is made up on what is right in the long term. But if the protectionists can exploit this case, we'd be foolish to do it."

On the other hand, he added, "If we can do it without trouble, let's do it, because I can see no excuse for us to be a high-protectionist country." Brownell reminded him that the bill extending the Reciprocal Trade Agreements Act was before Congress, that most Republicans opposed extension, and that giving the contract to the British would increase anti-RTAA sentiment. But Dulles told the President, "We've got to lead on this one. We can't bend to the 'Buy American' cry." Eisenhower responded that "it is not a matter of courage; I'm just wondering about the effect." "Exactly," Dulles said. "Without our leadership we can't expect Congress to favor RTAA." Eisenhower pointed out that "if we're going to do anything at all about building up foreign economies, we've got to buy foreign someplace along the way." Nixon warned about the political effect; Wilson said Westinghouse would be hurt if it lost the order. "Bunk!" Eisenhower snapped. "If a big American company has to worry over this endangering its positions, I regard that as bunk." Wilson suggested that he ask for rebids. "Let's not pussyfoot," Eisenhower replied. "We have to swim or sink sometime." Nixon repeated what Eisenhower had said about having to buy abroad sometime. The Vice-President agreed that it was "risky," but added, "Let's start educating Congress. We'll still get RTAA." Wilson finally said he would place the order with the British, shrugging that he could take the heat, if only because "I haven't been in much trouble lately."[4]

But by the time of the next meeting, on April 10, Wilson had backslid. He said he wanted to reject the present bids, change the specifications, and ask for new bids. Well, said Eisenhower, "I trust you will not load the specifications in favor of Westinghouse." Dulles, grim-faced, mumbled, "I'll bet ten to one that the foreign stuff is not taken." Don't give up too soon, said Wilson. "You are never going to buy the British materials," Dulles replied.[5]

In May, Wilson did call for new bids. When George Sloan of Chrysler, who was in Vienna for an international meeting of businessmen trying to promote a freer flow of goods, complained to Eisenhower about Wilson's refusal to give the contract to the British, the President assured Sloan that "foreign bidders will receive fair treatment in the judging of bids . . . It is our purpose to help other nations earn their way and in return we will expect them to conduct their affairs so as to maximize world trade."[6] At a Cabinet meeting, Eisenhower told Wilson that "I have a personal interest in hoping the British get it," but added, "My personal beliefs can't decide the issue." He thought "our policy should vary as depending on our employment level at home," and pointed out that Westinghouse was already working at full capacity. But, said Wilson, who could understand, the company still wanted the order, and in the end he gave it to them. Six months later, Wilson did award one small contract to the British.[7]

Emmet Hughes, like C. D. Jackson, was distressed at Eisenhower's refusal to set a course and hold to it. It seemed to Hughes that Eisenhower had no clear convictions, or if he did, that he was always ready to compromise them.[8] The extension of RTAA provided him with another example. Eisenhower had asked for a two-year extension, but Republican leaders in Congress wanted to scrap RTAA and raise tariffs. On May 25, Charles Halleck, majority leader in the House, told the President that Dulles had said in closed hearings on the extension that "we're not going to make anymore reciprocal agreements, so perhaps we don't need to extend the act." Eisenhower shot back, "I promise you that we'll have a new Secretary of State if that is so!"[9] But then he agreed to a compromise. He accepted a one-year extension in return for congressional support for a commission created to study foreign economic policy and make recommendations. Eisenhower appointed Clarence Randall, chairman of Inland Steel, as chairman.

Eisenhower's aides felt that his eagerness to hear all sides before making a decision was a source of weakness, that his sensitivity to every pressure group led him to seek the lowest possible common denominator as the basis for decision. Eisenhower felt that this trait was a source of strength. He wanted to hear every legitimate point of view, to take all possible repercussions into account, before acting. Among other things, this meant he abhorred yes-men. During a Cabinet discussion over ways to cut spending, for example, Lodge suggested reducing grants to the states for highway programs. Eisenhower replied that "my personal opinion is that we should spend more for highways." Lodge mumbled, "I withdraw." Eisenhower wanted none of that. "It's open to discussion," he told Lodge, and reminded him that "I've given way on a number of personal opinions to this gang."[10]

Eisenhower actively sought conflicting views. When he took office, the Canadians were threatening to build the St. Lawrence Seaway on their own if the United States would not join them in the project. Eisenhower wanted to participate, but he knew there was strong opposition, because Milton Eisenhower and George Humphrey were leading spokesmen for the Pennsylvania and Ohio railroad and coal companies that opposed the project. Eisenhower thought the Pennsylvania and Ohio crowd were putting their selfish interests ahead of the obvious long-term good of the United States, but he insisted on hearing their point of view. In late April, he told Milton he realized he was "hearing only the pro side of the argument," so he invited a group of railroad presidents to the White House, and for three hours listened to their side. They claimed that the seaway would cost the United States more than $2 billion; proponents were suggesting that the cost would be less than $500 million. "In such a confused situation," Eisenhower told Milton, "you have to dig pretty deep to find out what the facts really are because each allegation is presented with a very large share of emotionalism and prejudice."[11]

Eisenhower decided to support the seaway, on grounds that he regarded as irrefutable—it was necessary for national defense. Experts convinced him that the country's principal source of high-grade iron ore, the Mesabi Range in Minnesota, was running out, and that the United States needed a sure way, in time of war, to ship high-grade ore from Labrador to the steel mills along the Great Lakes. It also helped that Senator Alexander Wiley, chairman of the Senate Foreign Relations Committee, introduced a new bill that cut American costs for the project from $566 million to less than $100 million, with a provision that the Treasury would be paid back by users' fees. That bill, with strong Administration backing, emerged from the Foreign Relations Committee in June.[12]

Of all Eisenhower's backings and fillings, none distressed such aides as Hughes and Jackson more than his refusal to denounce McCarthy. The senator continued to make his charges, allegations, and threats. That spring, Eisenhower got word that McCarthyites in the FBI were passing on to the senator information branding the 1950 Nobel Peace Prize winner, Dr. Ralph Bunche, a Negro American who was working at the U.N., as a Communist. Eisenhower, visibly upset, told Maxwell Rabb, an aide in charge of relations with minority groups, that he felt "very strongly about this. Bunche is a superior man, a credit to our country. I can't just stand by and permit a man like that to be chopped to pieces because of McCarthy feeling. This report will kill his public career and I am not going to be a party to this." Eisenhower instructed Rabb to go to New York and tell Bunche that the President was ready to support him in public. Bunche told Rabb that he would stand alone. The next month, he did so before HUAC. While the hearings were going on, Eisenhower invited Bunche to dine at the White House—secretly. Bunche survived the inquisition without any help, beyond moral support, from Eisenhower.[13]

McCarthy, in Eisenhower's view, sought headlines, not Communists. A whirlwind tour of Europe that spring by McCarthy's young men, Roy Cohn and G. David Schine, seemed to the President to prove the point. Cohn and Schine were "investigating" Communist penetration of the Voice of America by examining the holdings of America's overseas libraries. Those libraries had already been pretty thoroughly purged by Dulles' orders, but still Cohn and Schine were shocked at what they discovered. They announced that they had found books written by 418 Communists or fellow travelers still being circulated. McCarthy demanded that Dulles trace the book orders and find out who had authorized the purchase of books by such people as Foster Rhea Dulles (the Secretary's cousin, a distinguished historian), John Dewey, and Robert M. Hutchins. Dulles then banned "the works of all Communist authors" and "any publication which continuously publishes Communist propaganda."[14] Some books were burned. Dulles also dismissed some 830 employees of the Voice.

The spectacle was more than many columnists could bear. Richard Rovere, Walter Lippmann, Bruce Catton, and others demanded that Eisenhower speak out. He refused. "I deplore and deprecate the table-pounding, name-calling methods that columnists so much love," he explained to one correspondent. "This is not because of any failure to love a good fight; it merely represents my belief that such methods are normally futile."[15] On May 9, Eisenhower's friend Harry Bullis of General Mills warned him "that the senator has unlimited personal ambitions, unmitigated gall, and unbounded selfishness. In the opinion of many of us who are your loyal friends, it is a fallacy to assume that McCarthy will kill himself. It is our belief that McCarthy should be stopped soon." Still Eisenhower refused. He told Bullis that "this particular individual wants, above all else, publicity. Nothing would probably please him more than to get the publicity that would be generated by public repudiation by the President." That would only "increase his appeal as an after-dinner speaker and so allow him to raise the fees that he charges," which Eisenhower thought was McCarthy's chief motivation. Eisenhower said he realized "it is a sorry mess," and admitted that "at times one feels almost like hanging his head in shame."[16] But shame or no, he would not act.

Even if Eisenhower tried to ignore McCarthy, no one else would. Cohn and Schine were dominating the news, pushing the major issues of statecraft off the front pages, and there was a veritable national uproar over the holdings of America's overseas libraries. In Europe, if possible, the uproar was even greater. Philip Reed of General Electric went to Europe to assess the damage for Eisenhower. Reed reported that "it was surprising how seriously McCarthy and his tactics are taken in Europe" and spoke of the "shattered morale" in America's leading propaganda agency. He advised Eisenhower to "take public issue with McCarthy" in order to correct the European impression of "abject appeasement."[17]

On June 14, at Dartmouth College commencement exercises, Eisenhower did speak out. Talking without notes, he began with a rambling discourse on college life, golf, and patriotism. Then, leaning forward, he admonished the graduates, "Don't join the book burners. Don't think you are going to conceal faults by concealing evidence that they ever existed. Don't be afraid to go in your library and read every book."[18]

The pronouncement caused great excitement among the press, which speculated that Eisenhower was finally, at last, going to go after McCarthy. But it was not to be. The next day, Dulles asked Eisenhower if he wanted recent restrictions on material in the overseas libraries lifted. Eisenhower said no, "it would be undesirable to buy or handle books which were persuasive of Communism."[19] At a news conference on June 17, Merriman Smith asked the President whether the Dartmouth speech was "critical of a school of thought represented by Senator McCarthy." Eisenhower immediately backtracked. "Now, Merriman," he began gently, "you have been around me long enough to know I never talk personalities." He said he was opposed to the "suppression of ideas," but then he backtracked. He said, "If the State Department is burning a book which is an open appeal to everybody in those foreign countries to be a Communist, then I would say that falls outside of the limits I was speaking, and they can do as they please to get rid of them."[20] Did that mean he approved of book burning? Well, no, not exactly.[21]

Eisenhower was equally vague in the privacy of his Cabinet meetings. On June 26 he told Dulles it was all becoming too embarrassing, and he wanted the Secretary to issue yet another statement on book policy (seven had already been sent out). Dulles, harassed himself, charged that Voice employees were burning books "out of fear or hatred for McCarthy," and out of a desire to embarrass the Secretary of State. Eisenhower said that he "could not conceive of fighting the Commies by ducking our heads in the sand," but then, on the other hand, he did not want American libraries distributing Communist propaganda. On still another hand, he said he knew for a fact that the German people "love our libraries," that he was proud to know that a library in Bonn carried a book that "severely criticizes me—on the battle of the Rhine or something," and that "I hate censorship."[22] Dulles finally escaped his predicament by issuing yet another directive, which said that books in overseas libraries should be "about the United States, its people and policies." McCarthy, meanwhile, was off after new targets, and Eisenhower had avoided an open break with the senator.

The execution of the Rosenbergs was intimately associated with the national hysteria that McCarthy fed on. By May, all the Rosenbergs' appeals had been turned down, and their only hope was executive clemency. Eisenhower had made the decision once to allow the execution to go forward, but now—with the date near at hand—he found himself subjected to increased pressure to commute the sentence. By no means was the intense, worldwide pressure confined to liberals, humanitarians, or the Communist press. Allen Dulles proposed that the Rosenbergs be presented with CIA information on the persecution of Jews in the Soviet Union, then given an offer of clemency if they would "appeal to Jews in all countries to get out of the communist movement and seek to destroy it."[23] From Paris, Ambassador C. Douglas Dillon cabled an urgent plea to commute because of the effect of the execution on European public opinion. Dillon thought there were legitimate reasons for doubting the Rosenbergs' guilt, and said that even those who were convinced of their guilt thought that execution was "completely unjustified from moral standpoint and is due only to political climate peculiar to the United States." Citing the disastrous impression Cohn and Schine had just made in Europe, Dillon warned that virtually all Europeans would regard the killing of the Rosenbergs as another example of craven appeasement of McCarthy.[24]

C. D. Jackson, worried as always about the psychological repercussions of a decision, also urged clemency. His motive included wanting to use the Rosenbergs. Jackson asked Brownell to find a Jewish
matron who could "ingratiate herself" with the Rosenbergs, and
through the matron to get them to break and name their superiors
and repudiate Communists.[25] Clyde Miller, a professor at Columbia,
asked the President to commute on the grounds that it would serve to
enhance America's reputation and standing in the world.

Eisenhower would not be moved. He told Miller that Communist
leaders believed "that free governments—and especially the American
government—are notoriously weak and fearful and that consequently
subversive and other kind of activity can be conducted against them
with no real fear of dire punishment." The Rosenbergs, Eisenhower
argued, had "exposed to greater danger of death literally millions of
our citizens." That their crime was a real one, and that its potential
results were as grave as Eisenhower said they were, "are facts that seem
to me to be above contention." Eisenhower pointed to another difficulty; if he commuted the sentence, the Rosenbergs would be eligible
for parole in fifteen years.[26]

Still, the case bothered him. On June 16 he wrote John, in Korea,
about it. He admitted that "it goes against the grain to avoid interfering where a woman is to receive capital punishment." But he felt
there were two good reasons not to go soft. First, "in this instance it is
the woman who is the strong and recalcitrant character; the man is
the weak one. She has obviously been the leader in everything they
did in the spy ring." The second reason was that if he commuted
Ethel's sentence while letting Julius die, "then from here on the Soviets
would simply recruit their spies from among women."[27]

By June 19, with the Rosenbergs scheduled to die that evening,
the White House had an avalanche of mail from around the world,
while demonstrators marched around the White House carrying signs
pleading for clemency. Inside the White House, at a Cabinet meeting,
Eisenhower confessed that he was "impressed by all the honest doubt"
expressed in the letters he had received. He said he could not remember a time in his life when he felt more in need of help from someone
more powerful than he. Brownell, worried that the President might
weaken, said that "the Communists are just out to prove they can
bring enough pressure . . . to enable people to get away with espionage. . . . I've always wanted you to look at evidence that wasn't
usable in court showing the Rosenbergs were the head and center of
an espionage ring here in *direct* contact with the Russians—the *prime*

espionage ring in the country."[28] Eisenhower then issued a statement declining to intervene. In it, he assured the world that the Rosenbergs "have received the benefit of every safeguard which American justice can provide."[29] That evening, just before sunset, the Rosenbergs were electrocuted.

In Eisenhower's view, the complaints by his aides about his refusal to exercise real leadership, as evidenced by his continuing appeasement of McCarthy and his refusal to stand by his guns on the tariff or the generators, were misdirected. They were watching the periphery, while he concentrated on the main battles. These included taxes, the budget, the war in Korea, the level of defense spending, foreign aid, and the general problem of world peace. On all these momentous issues, Eisenhower insisted, he provided firm, direct, and, most of all, effective leadership.[30] He used all the weapons at his command, including private meetings with congressional leaders, his persuasive powers with the Cabinet, patronage, and his ability to mold public opinion through his news conferences and speeches. He left no doubt where he stood on any of the issues he felt were important, and he got his way—despite intense opposition—on every one of them.

Taxes are a problem for every President, of course, but they were especially irksome for Eisenhower because of Republican insistence that they be cut, at once, regardless of the size of the deficit. To that end, seventy-seven-year-old Congressman Daniel Reed of New York, chairman of the House Ways and Means Committee, had introduced a bill (H.R. 1) to advance from January 1, 1954, to July 1, 1953, a scheduled elimination of the 11 percent increase in personal income taxes adopted because of the Korean War. He also announced his intention to let the Korean War excess-profits tax expire as scheduled on June 30, 1953. These two measures would cost the government some $3 billion in revenue. Eisenhower repeated over and over that he would not allow a tax cut until he had a balanced budget; he wanted to postpone the cut in excise taxes and to extend the 11 percent increase in income taxes.

The battle lines were clearly drawn. "I used every possible reason, argument, and device," Eisenhower later recalled, "and every kind of personal and indirect contact to bring Chairman Reed to my way of thinking."[31] Nothing worked. Eisenhower made it plain to other Republican congressmen that if they wanted their share of the patronage, they would have to give him their votes on taxes. That brought a few members around. Eisenhower asked Taft to use his influence, which the senator—reluctantly—did. In July, Eisenhower finally got what he wanted.

Part of his success was due to his promise to bring down federal spending. That was the argument that had moved Taft. The senator was therefore appalled when, at a Legislative Leaders' Meeting on April 30, Eisenhower outlined his budget for the coming fiscal year. Although it made heavy cuts in defense, they were not enough to satisfy Taft; he objected strongly to the continuation of foreign aid at levels only slightly less than those of Truman; he refused to believe that more cuts could not be made and the first Republican budget in twenty years come out balanced.

Red-faced, raising his voice, snapping out his words, Taft declared, "I can't express the deepness of my disappointment at the program the Administration presented today." As Eisenhower recounted in his diary, "[Taft] accused the security council of merely adopting the Truman strategy and, by a process of nicking here and chipping there, built up savings which he classed as 'puny.' He predicted that acceptance by the Congress of any such program would insure the decisive defeat of the Republican party in 1954. He said that not only could he not support the program, but that he would have to go on public record as fighting and opposing it." Eisenhower found himself "astonished at the demagogic nature of his tirade, because not once did he mention the security of the United States . . . He simply wanted expenditures reduced, regardless."[32]

In fact, Taft *had* discussed security, extensively and directly. He said, "With all due respect to the National Security Council, they don't know any more than I do." He said he had no confidence in the people who recommended such high military expenditures, and reminded Eisenhower that Bradley had testified in early 1950 that $13.5 billion was sufficient for defense, and now three years later Bradley was saying that $50 billion was not enough. Taft wanted a "complete reconsideration" of the entire military program. He knew that the NSC relied on the JCS for its opinions, and those JCS people, "they can't change." There had to be a less costly way to defend the country, Taft said, and he wanted "a complete resurvey by the best military people who are not already committed." Why, for example, should the United States be paying for a land army in Germany when no one expected to fight a land war there? Taft admitted that he did not know the answers, but insisted that they "must be studied."

Taft had made a solid presentation on the question of national security. Eisenhower did not hear him. Eisenhower could not hear anyone who was advocating less spending on national defense than he was, partly because the clamor from the other side—demanding more spending on the military—was so much louder; partly, too, because Eisenhower was who he was. He had watched MacArthur beg FDR for more defense spending in the thirties; he had seen the results of FDR's refusal to do so on the battlefield of Kasserine; he would never allow his country to be caught unprepared again. But as a professional soldier, he knew that the Pentagon could meet its responsibilities with far less money than his civilian critics (save for Taft) said it needed. The battles Eisenhower had to fight were with those who wanted more, not less, spending; thus Taft's case was one Eisenhower could not hear.

Or so he said in his diary. At the time, he heard it well enough. But he lost his temper when Taft summed up by threatening to withdraw his support on taxes if Eisenhower did not cut his projected defense spending. Humphrey, fearing an explosion as he watched Eisenhower's face flush red, jumped in with a plea for Taft to be reasonable. He pointed to the difficulties inherent in the situation. He got Taft to arguing over figures. For half an hour, they argued.

Finally Eisenhower broke in. "Let's go back," he said. Looking directly at Taft, he continued. "The essentials of our global strategy are not too difficult to understand." Europe must not fall; we can't take it over; we must make it stronger. "Next, the Middle East. That's half of the oil resources. We can't let it go to Russia." Southeast Asia was another critical point; we had to support the French in Vietnam. Taft's idea about relying exclusively on atomic weapons, based in the United States, brought from Eisenhower a scornful comment: "Reprisal alone gives us no assurance of security." America had to maintain a position of strength, or the Russians "will take these over gradually without fighting." He then gave Taft a detailed explanation of his defense policy. Eisenhower defended the NSC, saying, "It has the competency that any group could have by living with it day by day and constant study. They don't claim any more than that."

Finally, a simple conclusion: "I cannot endanger the security of my country." [33] And the meeting ended. Eisenhower commented in his diary that Taft did not have "considered judgment," because "he attempts to discuss weighty, serious, and even critical matters in such an ill-tempered and violent fashion." And, in a telling judgment on the subject of self-control, Eisenhower said of Taft, "I do not see how he can possibly expect . . . to influence people when he has no more control over his temper [than that]." [34]

• •

Aside from the basic question of war or peace, the most important problem any modern President faces is the size of the defense budget. Everything else—taxes, the size of the deficit, the rate of unemployment, the inflation rate, relations with America's allies and with the Soviet Union—is directly related to how much DOD spends. All of Eisenhower's major goals—peace, lower taxes, a balanced budget, no inflation—were dependent upon his cutting the defense budget.

He knew it and was determined to do it. Indeed, an important factor in his decision to enter politics was his unhappiness with Truman's defense policy. As Taft had noted, spending for the military went up and down between 1945 and 1953 at a dizzying pace. On the eve of the Korean War, Truman had reduced defense to $13.5 billion. Eisenhower had opposed such drastic cuts, and often said that he personally believed there never would have been a Korean War if Truman had not demobilized so rapidly as to force the Army to withdraw its divisions from South Korea in 1948. By 1952, Truman was projecting more than $50 billion for defense, and had committed the United States to building up to maximum strength—to a near total-war footing—by 1954, the so-called "year of maximum danger." (By 1954, according to the Pentagon, the Soviet Union would have a hydrogen bomb and possess the means of delivery.)

Eisenhower told Republican leaders that this target date business was "pure rot." He said, "I have always fought the idea of X units by Y date. I am not going to be stampeded by someone coming along with a damn trick formula of 'so much by this date.'"[35] What he wanted, instead, was a steady buildup, based on what the country could afford. When he announced his program, however, all the services objected strenuously. The Air Force, which had been scheduled to get the largest share of the Truman buildup, was especially upset, and not in the least hesitant in going public with its criticisms. Air Force objections got wide publicity. The Air Force argued that it had to have 141 groups by 1954 or it could not meet its responsibilities.

"I'm damn tired of Air Force sales programs," Eisenhower told the Republican leaders. "In 1946 they argued that if we can have seventy groups, we'll guarantee security for ever and ever and ever." Now they come up with this "trick figure of 141. They sell it. Then you have to abide by it or you're treasonous." Eisenhower said he had told Wilson to put his house in order, to force the generals and admirals to keep their mouths shut. "I will not have anyone in Defense who wants to sell the idea of a larger and larger force in being." The main Air Force spokesman on Capitol Hill, Senator Symington, was charging that Eisenhower's program would leave the United States open to a Russian strategic bombing campaign. Eisenhower thought that too was "pure rot." "We pulverized Germany," he reminded the congressmen, "but their actual rate of production was as big at the end as at the beginning. It's amazing what people can do under pressure. The idea that our economy will be paralyzed is a figment of Stuart Symington's imagination."[36] Eisenhower looked at the problem from the other end—he pointed to the effect on the economy if the United States continued to build toward Truman's target date. What would happen after 1954? Could the country simply shut down the plants that had geared up to produce all those tanks, ships, and planes?

Still the politicians objected to Eisenhower's cuts. Surely the Air Force knew better than anyone else what its needs were. Eisenhower said that was "bunk." He reminded the congressmen that "I've served with those people who know all the answers—they just won't get down and face the dirty facts of life."[37] The politicians were not convinced. How could they, mere civilians, argue with the Pentagon? Eisenhower replied that he knew the Pentagon as well as any man living; he knew how ingrained was the tendency to overstate the case, to ask for more than was really necessary. He dismissed as nonsense the idea that anyone could predict the "year of maximum danger." He insisted that "we're not in a moment of danger, we're in an age of danger."[38]

These remarks were made in private meetings, but Eisenhower was just as emphatic in public. At an April 23 news conference, Richard Harkness of NBC asked him if the "stretch out" in defense spending meant that he was looking to a ten-year buildup. "Well," Eisenhower responded, "I would object to ten years just as much as I object to '54. Anybody who bases his defense on his ability to predict the day and the hour of attack is crazy. If you are going on the defensive, you have got to get a level of preparation you can sustain over the years . . . We have got to devise and develop a defensive program we can carry forward."[39] A week later, when the subject came up again, Eisenhower gave a history lecture. The situation in the 1950s, he said, was not at all like the situation in June of 1944 when "I went across the Channel." At that time, he said, "We picked the day. We knew when we wanted our maximum force. We knew the buildup we wanted. We knew exactly what we were up against." None of that was true in 1953.[40]

Eisenhower had cut Truman's request for new spending by nearly $10 billion, the great bulk of the savings coming from defense. Still

निब

more cuts were necessary to balance the budget. Wilson was unhappy with this prospect; so was Dulles. The Secretary of State warned the President that "we don't know yet what we're going to do in Korea—or in the whole Far East, for that matter." He wanted the whole business of cutting back re-examined.[41] Other Cabinet members thought that more money could be squeezed out of the domestic budget. Humphrey was practically Eisenhower's only supporter—he told his colleagues that the domestic entitlement programs were "untouchable." So far, he warned, the Eisenhower cuts in defense had only "scratched the surface. We have to do a hell of a lot more. . . . And this means *surgery.*"

Wilson was startled. "That means you want at least $10 billion more cut out of defense . . ." he said, unbelieving. Humphrey used images that Wilson could understand in his reply: "Charlie, that's right. You just got to get out the best damn *streamlined model* you ever did in your life. . . . This means *a brand-new model—we can't just patch up the old jalopy.* . . . It's *just* like reorganizing a whole *business.* It's got to be done from top to bottom."[42]

Eisenhower had told Wilson to take control of the Pentagon. When it became obvious that Wilson would not or could not do so, Eisenhower intervened directly. He wrote long letters to old friends in the armed services, explaining his position and asking for their help. If they felt they could not support him, he asked for at least their silence. To Tooey Spaatz, his wartime comrade who was in retirement and writing critical articles about the cuts in Air Force appropriations, Eisenhower wrote a heartfelt plea. The President asked Spaatz to come in and express his views privately, rather than going public with them.[43] Eisenhower told Admiral Radford that when he replaced Bradley as chairman of the JCS in August, he wanted Radford to issue a statement to the effect that with his confirmation as chairman "will come a divorce from exclusive identification with the Navy." He told Radford to stress that his loyalty would be to the Defense Department as a whole, and that he would henceforth serve as "the champion of *all* the services, governed by the single criterion of what is best for the United States."[44]

An integral part of Eisenhower's defense posture was reliance upon allies. That meant specifically that he wanted more funds for MSA, so that he could distribute military hardware to the Koreans, to the NATO allies, and to other friends around the world. Eisenhower believed that it was cheaper for the United States to pay the costs of keeping a British or a German force on the Elbe River, or a

French force in Vietnam, than it was to keep an American force there. Here he ran into the firm opposition of a majority of Republicans in Congress. They were tired of the Marshall Plan, tired of foreign aid, tired of "giving away" America's money. It was in this area, rather than in Pentagon appropriations, that they saw an opportunity to cut spending. Like Taft, they wanted a "Fortress America" program, although unlike Taft they were unwilling to reduce the size of the fortress. To Eisenhower, this was just another instance of congressional stupidity. "Consider British bases," he told the Republican leaders. From Britain, the United States could strike the Soviet Union with B-47 bombers instead of having to use B-52s. He reminded them of the "huge difference" in initial costs, in operation, and in maintenance.[45]

Eisenhower found that trying to talk sense to Congress about defense and MSA appropriations was frustrating. But he seldom lost his temper or his patience, and he kept after it. In the privacy of the Cabinet room, he did not hesitate to complain. By late May of 1953, his Administration was coming close to exceeding the statutory debt limit. Congress would have to raise the limit, but those same congressmen who wanted to spend more on defense while simultaneously cutting taxes were hesitating to do so. Eisenhower asked his Cabinet, "If we exceed that debt limit, who goes to jail?" Humphrey replied, "We've got to go to Congress." "Oh!" Eisenhower exclaimed. "That's worse!"[46]

But go to Congress he did, and he got the debt limit raised, and he managed to get most of what he asked for on MSA, and the Pentagon budget did go down. Together with maintaining the existing level of taxes, these were major triumphs. Eisenhower, more than any other individual, was responsible for winning them.

The most obvious way for Eisenhower to reduce defense spending was to reduce the level of tension in the world. Since 1945 the United States and the Soviet Union had been hurling the most horrendous charges at each other as they built and maintained armed forces designed to fight the battle of Armageddon. Eisenhower's election and Stalin's death provided an opportunity for a fresh start. Stalin's immediate successor, Georgi Malenkov, seized the chance. On March 15, he declared that there was no existing dispute between the two countries that "cannot be decided by peaceful means, on the basis of mutual understanding." The Soviet propaganda machine then went into high gear on a "peace offensive." Eisenhower had to respond. He had a sense of urgency about the need to do so, because he had just read a CIA report on the world reaction to the Soviet moves. "It begins to look to me," he told Dulles, "that if I am to make a speech on this question of peace, I should do it soon."[47] Dulles was opposed—he did not believe a word of what Malenkov was saying—but Eisenhower insisted.

In late March, Eisenhower met with Hughes in the Oval Office. After going over some routine matters, Eisenhower "began talking with the air of a man whose thoughts . . . were fast veering toward a conclusion." The President paced the room, speaking slowly and forcefully. "Look," Eisenhower said, "I am tired . . . of just plain indictments of the Soviet regime. . . . Just *one* thing matters: what have *we* got to offer the world? . . . If we cannot say these things— A, B, C, D, E, F, G, just like that—then we really have nothing to give, except just another speech. For what? Malenkov isn't going to be frightened with speeches. What are we *trying* to achieve?" Hughes recalled the scene vividly—Eisenhower's head "martially high," his "strong mouth tight, the jaw set—and the blue eyes agleam and intent." Eisenhower "wheeled abruptly" toward Hughes and went on: "*Here* is what I would like to say. The jet plane that roars over your head costs three-quarters of a million dollars. That is more money than a man . . . is going to make in his lifetime. What world can afford this sort of thing for long? We are in an armaments race. Where will it lead us? At worst, to atomic warfare. At best, to robbing every people and nation on earth of the fruits of their own toil."

Eisenhower said he wanted to see the resources of the world used to provide bread, butter, clothes, homes, hospitals, schools, "all the good and necessary things for decent living," not more guns. To help bring that about, he wanted to make a speech that would *not* include the standard indictment of the Soviet Union. "The past speaks for itself. I am interested in the future. Both their government and ours now have new men in them. The slate is clean. Now let us begin talking to each other. *And let us say what we've got to say so that every person on earth can understand it.*"

Hughes injected a word of caution. He said he had just talked to Dulles about how the United States would react if the Communists accepted an armistice in Korea. Dulles had said he would be sorry, because "*I don't think we can get much out of a Korean settlement until we have shown—before all Asia—our clear superiority by giving the Chinese one hell of a licking.*" Eisenhower's head snapped around. He stared at Hughes. Then he said, "All right, then. If Mr. Dulles and all his sophisticated advisers really mean that they can *not* talk peace seriously, then I am in the wrong pew. For if it's *war* we should be talking about, I *know* the people to give me advice on that—and they're not in the State Department. Now either we cut out all this fooling around and make a serious bid for peace—or we forget the whole thing."[48]

Eisenhower told Hughes, and C. D. Jackson, to get to work on a speech on peace. He monitored every word of the many drafts, often providing them with imagery and telling phrases. Over the next two weeks, they worked hard at it.

The President's eagerness to seek peace was based not only on his resistance to the cost of the arms race, but also on his horror at the thought of the amount of destructive force available to him. In 1948, when he was Army Chief of Staff, the American atomic arsenal contained two twenty-kiloton bombs. But following the Berlin blockade of that year, Truman had ordered a crash program to build more bombs. They had been built at a rate of nearly one per day, so that by the time Eisenhower became President, the arsenal had grown to sixteen hundred nuclear bombs. Although most of these weapons were relatively small atomic bombs, nevertheless the total destructive power was awesome. Construction was still going forward at the rate of almost one per day—and this under Eisenhower's direct orders—but he felt a terrible unease about it all. His knowledge, not incidentally, was a major reason for his resistance to even greater defense expenditures, and for his scoffing at Symington and others who warned that the Soviets were getting ahead. In 1953 the Soviet Union had *no* nuclear weapons deployed operationally.*

In early April, the Masters golf tournament took place at Augusta. On the Monday after the event, Eisenhower and Mamie, accompanied by Barbara and the grandchildren, flew down to Augusta. They stayed at Bobby Jones's cottage. Eisenhower played a round of golf with the Masters' winner, Ben Hogan, and in the evenings played bridge with

---

* Getting reliable facts and figures on the American nuclear arsenal was the most difficult part of the research for this book. This is the most closely guarded secret of the U.S. government. All Atomic Energy Commission reports to Eisenhower on the arsenal were given verbally. All references to numbers and size are deleted from every document in the NSC, Cabinet, Defense, and other papers in the Eisenhower Library. The figures used here are taken from the Brookings Institution, which does not cite its sources.[49]

his gang. Priscilla Slater was there to provide Mamie with company
and a canasta partner. The gang was building a place for the Eisenhowers on the edge of the golf course; Slater noticed "Ike standing
with David by the hand watching the tractor digging the foundation
for Mamie's cottage." Senator Taft flew down for an afternoon of golf,
but he had to quit because of a pain in his hip. Eisenhower did not
feel well either. He had a persistent stomach upset that forced him to
use a golf cart to get around.[50]

On April 16, 1953, Eisenhower went to the Statler Hotel in Washington to give the American Society of Newspaper Editors the finest
speech of his Presidency. He called it "The Chance for Peace." Insofar as it was a response to the Soviet peace offensive, it was propaganda—eloquently put, but still propaganda. Eisenhower began by
indicting the Soviets for their past actions. Following World War II,
he said, when the United States followed the path of peace, the Soviets
stayed on a war footing, which forced the free nations to rearm. But
despite all Soviet provocations, the free world was still ready to seek
peace. Eisenhower welcomed recent Soviet statements on the need for
peace and said that he would believe they were sincere when the words
were backed with deeds. Specific deeds, including the release of POWs
held since 1945, a Soviet signature on an Austrian treaty, the conclusion of "an honorable armistice" in Korea, Indochina, and Malaya,
agreement to a free and united Germany, and the "full independence
of the East European nations."

In return for such actions by the Russians, Eisenhower said he
was prepared to conclude an arms-limitation agreement and to accept
international control of atomic energy designed to "insure the prohibition of atomic weapons." All this would be supervised by "a practical
system of inspection under the United Nations."

Eisenhower knew that most of his demands for proof were unacceptable to the Russians. Under no circumstances would they pull
out of East Europe; the idea of German reunification gave them night-
mares; they could not be expected to (or even be able to) call off the
guerrilla warriors in Vietnam and Malaya; and their opposition to
on-site inspections within the Soviet Union was implacable, and well
known.

The specific charges, demands, and proposals in "The Chance
for Peace," in other words, were little more than a restatement of
some of the oldest Cold War rhetoric. They were not what made the
speech great. What did make it great was Eisenhower's warning about
the dangers and the cost of continuing the arms race.

"The worst to be feared and the best to be expected can be simply stated," he declared. "The worst is atomic war. The best would be this: a life of perpetual fear and tension; a burden of arms draining the wealth and the labor of all peoples." Then he added up the price: "Every gun that is made, every warship launched, every rocket fired, signifies, in the final sense, a theft from those who hunger and are not fed, those who are cold and are not clothed."

Suddenly Eisenhower began perspiring. As the sweat beaded up on his face, he became so dizzy he feared he would faint. Then he was racked by chills. He reached forward and grabbed the podium with both hands to steady himself. He had had an intestinal attack the previous evening, and that morning Dr. Snyder had given him sedatives, but now the attack was worse than ever. With an effort of will, Eisenhower drew himself together, managed to concentrate on the text, and read on, skipping some passages so as to emphasize the important ones.

"This world in arms is not spending money alone," he continued. "It is spending the sweat of its laborers, the genius of its scientists, the hopes of its children." He picked up his voice, looked out at his audience, and began ticking them off: "The cost of one modern heavy bomber is this: a modern brick school in more than thirty cities. It is two electric power plants, each serving a town of sixty thousand population. It is two fine, fully equipped hospitals." Sweat was pouring from his brow, but he read on: "We pay for a single fighter plane with a half-million bushels of wheat. We pay for a single destroyer with new homes that could have housed more than eight thousand people."

Looking out again, he pronounced his judgment. "This is not a way of life at all, in any true sense. Under the cloud of threatening war, it is humanity hanging from a cross of iron."

Eisenhower's conclusion, pointing to the alternative, was as splendid as his evocation of the costs of the arms race. He said that if the Soviets showed by deeds that they too were ready for peace, the United States would devote "a substantial percentage of the savings achieved by disarmament to a fund for world aid and reconstruction . . . to assist all peoples to know the blessings of productive freedom. The monuments to this new kind of war would be these: roads and schools, hospitals and homes, food and health."[51]

After the speech, Eisenhower took the time and spent the energy to throw out the first ball at the Washington Senators' opening-day ball game (he really was a tough old soldier; his stomach felt as if it was on fire). He then made a short talk in North Carolina. Finally he flew to Augusta. There Dr. Snyder gave him another sedative and put him to bed. The next morning he woke to find that the reception to his speech, in the Western world, was overwhelming. The American press outdid itself in praising him; so did the British and Continental newspapers; messages from American embassies around the world reported the greatest enthusiasm to any statement by an American since George Marshall outlined the European Recovery Program. The Indian ambassador to Egypt said it was a wonderful speech that could not have been made by any other living man. Chip Bohlen, in Moscow, was told by the ambassador from Burma that the speech was in the "best tradition of the Founding Fathers of the United States."[52] The State Department, recognizing a winner, distributed copies all over the world, in dozens of languages.

Actually the head of the State Department had never been happy with the speech. Dulles could see no reason to reach out to the Russians, and had told Eisenhower so. Indeed it was at Dulles' insistence that Eisenhower had asked for so many obviously impossible concessions from the Russians as "proof" of their good intentions. Dulles was especially concerned about the Far East, where he feared the President would be willing to accept a simple battlefield armistice in Korea rather than press on for the unification of the country and the settlement of the other wars going on in Asia. In the context of his speech, Eisenhower had indeed demanded an Asia-wide peace, but the spirit of the address was otherwise—it seemed clear to most observers that Eisenhower would grasp at any conciliatory act by the Soviets as a meaningful gesture. There was much in "The Chance for Peace" that was pure propaganda, but the overall tone of the speech was so reasonable and moderate, Eisenhower's sincerity so apparent, and his willingness to speak the blunt truth about the arms race in such vivid terms, and the reception of the speech so favorable, that the Soviets had to respond.

While Eisenhower waited for them to do so, he recuperated from his stomach troubles in Augusta. The gang was there, and he played ten rubbers of bridge the second night. The following day he played eighteen holes of golf, making sixteen bogeys and two pars, which was relatively good scoring for him. He told Slater he "wouldn't have missed the day for anything." That evening Slater talked to him about getting a herd of purebred Angus heifers for the farm in Gettysburg. Eisenhower liked the idea, so long as it was "worked out on a strictly business basis." They agreed to do it, with the idea that after his retirement in 1957 Eisenhower would take up full-time cattle ranching.[53]

• •

When Eisenhower returned to Washington, Korea was at the center of his attention. The Communists said they were ready to begin again the armistice talks with the U.N. team at Panmunjom. Dulles wanted to reject the offer. At an NSC April 8 meeting, he told Eisenhower that "it was now quite possible to secure a much more satisfactory settlement in Korea than a mere armistice at the thirty-eighth parallel, which would leave a divided Korea." Dulles believed that if a military armistice was not followed by a "political settlement," meaning the unification of Korea, the United States would have to break the armistice.

Eisenhower would have none of that. He told Dulles "it will be impossible to call off the armistice and to go to war again in Korea. The American people will never stand for such a move." Dulles persisted. At least, he said, let us tell the Communists that unless Korea were divided along the waist, rather than at the 38th parallel, "we will call off the armistice." Wilson supported Dulles, and added that he thought it shameful that the South Koreans had not been brought into the negotiations. Eisenhower admitted that the Communists "will void the armistice with impunity whenever they think it convenient," but he had a "strong reaction" against his announcing that the Americans would do so.[54] Besides, he had already told Dulles that he personally would regard the exchange of sick and wounded prisoners as a "test of good faith on the part of the Soviets."[55] On April 20, Operation Little Switch, the first exchange of prisoners, began. Within a week, plenary talks between the Communists and the U.N. negotiating team were resumed.

Dulles was not the only free-world leader who was upset at the sudden prospect of peace. Syngman Rhee was desperate to reunify his country and had objected strenuously to any armistice that would leave Chinese armies in North Korea. If the United States signed such an agreement, Rhee told Eisenhower, then South Korea would ask her allies to get out of the country, except for those who were willing to join in a drive north to the Yalu. Eisenhower, in a carefully drafted reply of April 23, warned Rhee bluntly that "any such action by your government could only result in disaster for your country, obliterating all that has been gained at such sacrifice by our peoples." Eisenhower said that the U.N. had entered Korea in order to drive the North Korean invaders back across the 38th parallel, which had been accomplished. He added that while it was true that the U.S. and the U.N. were committed to the unification of Korea, he claimed that they had never agreed to the use of force to achieve this objective (which was not true; when MacArthur crossed the 38th parallel in September 1950, intending to drive to the Yalu and reunify the country, he did so with the full and formal backing of both the U.S. government and the U.N.).[56]

In Panmunjom, meanwhile, both sides were negotiating seriously, taking new positions on the complex problem of Chinese and North Korean POWs who did not want to return home. The Indian government was proposing a compromise solution that appealed to both sides. But not to Dulles. He flew to Karachi for talks with Prime Minister Jawaharlal Nehru. This trip has since become famous, because during the talks Dulles supposedly told Nehru that the United States might feel compelled "to use atomic weapons if a truce could not be arranged."[57] In fact, no such direct warning was made, nor was it necessary. The full text of Dulles' report to Eisenhower on his conversation with Nehru read: "Nehru brought up Korean armistice, referring particularly to my statement of preceding day, that if no (repeat no) armistice occurred hostilities might become more intense. He said if this happened it difficult to know what end might be. He urged withdrawal our armistice proposals as inconsistent with the Indian resolutions. He made no (repeat no) alternate proposal. He brought up again my reference to intensified operations, but I made no (repeat no) comment and allowed the topic to drop."[58]

Dulles did not need to make any direct threats, much less depend on Nehru to pass them along to the Chinese. The Communists already knew that Eisenhower had a nuclear option; they knew that his patience was limited; they knew that he was under pressure to widen the war; they knew that the Americans had atomic warheads in Okinawa.[59] On June 4, the Chinese presented a POW proposal that was in substantial accord with the latest U.N. offer. Peace was in sight.

Rhee was furious. He had already told Eisenhower that a simple military armistice would mean "a death sentence for Korea without protest." He proposed, instead, a simultaneous withdrawal of both the Chinese and U.N. forces in Korea, a mutual-defense pact between South Korea and the United States, and an increase in military aid. If this program was unacceptable, he begged Eisenhower to allow the Koreans to continue the fighting, for this "is the universal preference of the Korean people to any divisive armistice or peace."[60] In a long and sympathetic reply, Eisenhower told Rhee that "the moment has now come" for peace. "The enemy has proposed an armistice which involves a clear abandonment of the fruits of aggression." As the cease-fire line would follow the front lines, which were slightly north of the 38th parallel, Rhee would emerge from the conflict with his territory intact, "indeed somewhat enlarged." Eisenhower pledged that the United States "will not renounce its efforts by all peaceful means to effect the unification of Korea," agreed to a mutual-defense pact, and promised substantial reconstruction aid for South Korea. He concluded, "Even the thought of a separation at this critical hour would be a tragedy. We must remain united." [61]

The Old Guard, like Rhee and Dulles, was upset. With its close identification with the China lobby and its persistent emphasis on Asia first, the Old Guard wanted victory, not armistice. Members were heard to mutter that if Truman had signed the conditions Eisenhower was willing to accept, they would have moved to impeach him. One of the Old Guard's chief concerns was Chiang Kai-shek. Europeans were saying that once an armistice had been achieved, the problem of the Chinese seat on the U.N. Security Council could be settled by replacing the Nationalist with the Communist Chinese. To prevent this, on May 28 the Senate Appropriations Committee reported out a bill with a rider barring any American financial contribution to the U.N. if the Red Chinese were seated.

Foreign policy was an area in which Eisenhower would not appease the Old Guard. However muddled his leadership on McCarthyism or generators, he was clear and forceful and effective as a leader on foreign affairs. Although Styles Bridges, chairman of the committee, told the President that all Republican senators supported the rider, and no Democrat would dare to oppose it, Eisenhower was determined to stop it.

Eisenhower's own thoughts about what to do concerning China ran in the opposite direction of those of the Old Guard. He thought that with the end of the hostilities, the United States ought to reexamine its China policy. Keeping China out of the U.N., and refusing to recognize the existence of the Communist government, made no sense to him. But the art of leadership includes the art of the possible, and Eisenhower believed that the American public was not ready to think about a new relationship with China. He would not, however, allow the Old Guard to achieve one of its major objectives, the destruction of the U.N., especially not over the question of who sat in China's seat on the Security Council. [62]

Eisenhower wrote Nixon a three-page letter strongly opposing the rider and asking Nixon to present his views to the Senate. [63] Not satisfied with that approach, he then called a special meeting of the Republican leaders in Congress. "I am distressed," he told them, "that this rider might become law. I oppose it because I believe that the United States cannot properly serve notice on the United Nations in such a manner, and more fundamentally, that the United States cannot live alone." The U.N., he said, was "essential because global war is now unthinkable." He warned that "it is not wise to tie our own hands irrevocably about affairs in advance." He reminded the congressmen that back in 1945, "Germany was our deadly enemy; who could then have foreseen that in only a few years it would become a friendly associate?" Perhaps China too might someday become America's ally. Slowly, painfully, the Republican leaders backed down. Finally Knowland suggested a resolution that would have no legal effect and cut off no funds, but which would express congressional disapproval of seating Red China. That was meaningless enough to be acceptable to Eisenhower, who thereby managed, as he put it, "to preserve the executive branch from congressional encroachment." [64]

Korea was not the only place in Asia where Communists were fighting the forces of the free world. In the Philippines, the Huks were challenging the government. In Malaya, the British were fighting insurgents. And in Vietnam, the French were engaged in a costly struggle with the Vietminh. It was an axiom of American political thinking at this time that all these insurrections were part of a master conspiracy directed by the Kremlin, and that the Kremlin could, if it wished, call them all off. Dulles was a leading spokesman for this view. Eisenhower did not disagree with it, but he did not accept Dulles' contention that all these wars had to end before there could be a meaningful peace in Korea. The President thought that the way to achieve peace in Vietnam was not to link it to Korea but to strengthen the French forces there while simultaneously offering a full and genuine independence to the people of Indochina.

The French were using the war in Vietnam to blackmail the United States. Paris argued that the cost of the war precluded any increases in the French contribution to NATO, and they made French ratification of EDC contingent upon receiving additional military aid. Eisenhower was willing to provide such aid—indeed he had already asked Congress for an additional $385 million for that purpose—but he was convinced that increased military pressure alone would not solve the problem. So, while he was agreeing to surreptitiously furnish the French with "sanitized" American aircraft for use in Vietnam,[65] he was also instructing Ambassador Dillon to tell the French that there were two things they had to do. First, find "a forceful and inspirational leader" to take charge of military operations. Second, make a "clear and unequivocal announcement . . . that France seeks self-rule for Indochina and that practical political freedom will be an accomplished fact as soon as victory against the Communists is won." Such a declaration, he said, "would place this tragic conflict in an appealing perspective" and end the accusation that the French were fighting nothing more than a colonial war.[66]

The French, however, had no intention of giving up Vietnam. They knew that, despite what the Americans thought, their enemies were in the interior of Vietnam, not in Peking or Moscow, and they were not fighting the war in order to leave Vietnam after they had won it. When Eisenhower was SACEUR, he had pleaded with the French to make such a "clear and unequivocal" statement about their intention to grant full independence to Vietnam, Laos, and Cambodia; they had not responded then; they would not respond now. The war went on.

On June 8, the Communists at Panmunjom agreed to the voluntary repatriation of POWs, with the provision that the processing of the prisoners would be observed by representatives of both sides. All that now remained was to establish a cease-fire line. That, and bringing Rhee around.

Rhee was in a strong position. Two-thirds of the battle line was manned by his troops. He could upset any armistice agreement by marching north. Further, his soldiers were the guards at the POW compounds. He had the sympathy of many Americans. And he had the apparent complete support of his own people. When the announcement of the POW agreement was made in Seoul, some 100,000 South Koreans took to the streets in a massive demonstration demanding a march to the north. The South Korean assembly rejected the proposed truce by a vote of 129 to 0.[67]

On June 19, Eisenhower was holding a regular Cabinet meeting. Dodge was reporting on the budget. An aide came in with a message. Eisenhower read it, then went into a huddle with Dulles and Cutler. Rhee had released some twenty-five thousand POWs, Chinese and Korean, and they had quickly scattered over the countryside. This was a direct violation of the armistice agreements, and inevitably made the Chinese ask "whether the United States was able to live up to any agreement to which the South Koreans might be a party."[68] Eisenhower turned to his Cabinet, reported on what he had just learned, and commented that "we are coming to the point where it is completely impossible." He said he could not understand the "mental processes of the Oriental. One thing I learned in five years out there is that we don't know to what they will react." Rhee, in Eisenhower's view, was committing his people to national suicide. Dulles thought Rhee had a legitimate point of view and suggested, "Let's merely hold the line; try to carry on what we've done the last two years," that is, continue the war. Eisenhower objected: "This would be a complete surrender to his blackmail." Wilson said that was the other side of the "Oriental mind—he doesn't consider it blackmail. After all, we dumped him out of the truce talks."

Eisenhower said he would be tempted to follow a policy of nonresponse to Rhee's threats "if there were some hope—like a palace revolt" against Rhee. But "what hope have we got?" And he warned that "if Rhee succeeds now, his prestige in Korea goes up," and he would be even more difficult to deal with. The Cabinet then discussed the possibilities of getting rid of Rhee. Eisenhower wanted to know about the attitude of the ROK chief of staff. Would he support a palace coup, or was he loyal to Rhee? Cutler thought the ROK generals would come to their senses and overthrow Rhee. Humphrey said the Americans should get an advance commitment from them. Wilson warned that "we can't count on what they say."

"We've got to figure out our next step," Eisenhower declared. "We can't sit in a state of suspended animation." Then he turned to Dulles and asked, "What about Allen [Dulles]?" Lodge jumped in to say that he had ridden on an airplane with General MacArthur that day, and informed the Cabinet that "MacArthur thinks Rhee will be killed within two weeks." "What's his basis for saying that?" Eisenhower asked. Lodge replied that MacArthur had told him that "after the emotion dies down, the more reflective elements [in the ROK] will act." In that case, said Wilson, "let events take their course." Eisenhower worried about the American troops in Korea, one of whom was his only son. Could they be supplied and maintained independently of the ROK? It appeared that they could be. Humphrey said that the "only thing for us to do is what we can to keep face." Eisenhower burst into laughter—"Imagine," he said, "Westerners saving face!"

Dulles had the last word. He gravely informed Eisenhower that "this situation is inherent in the type of foreign policy we're trying to pursue." Failure to fight the Communists everywhere, failure to drive them back behind the Yalu, failure to support Chiang in an offensive on the mainland, failure to go for an all-out victory in Vietnam, all coupled with Eisenhower's glittering promises in "The Chance for Peace," made it impossible for the United States to pursue a clear and direct policy of resistance to Communism. The implication of Dulles' remarks was clear—break off the truce talks and go for victory.[69]

Eisenhower would not consider that. Nor did he send out any orders to have Rhee assassinated. Instead, he sent Walter Robertson, an Assistant Secretary of State, to Seoul to try to talk reason to Rhee. Eisenhower also sent a stern warning to Rhee. Reminding the South Korean President that the Koreans had agreed to give the U.N. Command "authority over all land, sea, and air forces of the ROK during the period of the present state of hostilities," Eisenhower said that the release of the prisoners "constitutes a clear violation of this assurance and creates an impossible situation." Eisenhower told Rhee that "unless you are prepared immediately and unequivocally to accept the authority of the U.N. Command to conduct the present hostilities and to bring them to a close, it will be necessary to effect another arrangement."[70] Robertson, acting under Eisenhower's direction, told Rhee what those "other arrangements" would be—a withdrawal of American troops, no more military support for the ROK, no reconstruction funds for South Korea, no mutual-defense pact.

Eisenhower's June 19 Cabinet meeting illustrated well the diversity and scope of his problems. On that date, he discussed the Rosenberg case, a tax bill (with Congressman Reed still insisting on cutting taxes, Eisenhower referred at one point to "Dr. Syngman Reed"), an upcoming New Jersey election, reorganization plans, patronage, problems with Secretary Benson's farm policy, DOD appropriations, the leaks and squabbles among the JCS, whether or not to ask for a wire-tapping bill, McCarthy, the State Department's book-burning policy, and a half dozen other problems.

Small wonder that Eisenhower opened the next meeting, on June 26, by saying that he had just had a "week of trouble." But in spite of all the frustration, he told the Cabinet that "long faces do not win battles." He wanted his colleagues to remain optimistic and to keep their "faith in God and in themselves." He said this was a "very real matter with me though it may seem obvious to others."[71] After the meeting, the Eisenhowers, joined by their daughter-in-law and grandchildren, went up to the remodeled Camp David for the weekend, where—Eisenhower later informed the press—they spent their time "very quietly, doing nothing."[72]

CHAPTER FIVE

Peace in Korea, Coup in Iran

July 1–September 30, 1953

AT EISENHOWER'S July 1 news conference, Merriman Smith asked the first question. He wanted to know if the President was "hopeful or optimistic about the prospects of an armistice." Eisenhower said he was. He admitted that "we are having an acute example of the difficulties that arise among allies . . . It is the history of coalitions; we shouldn't be too discouraged about it." Without mentioning Rhee's name, Eisenhower pointed out that "people in emotional states are very apt to even overstate their cases, and it becomes extraordinarily difficult to get a reasonble solution." But by no means was he ready to throw up his hands: "I still, in my own mind and in my very deepest convictions, believe that a satisfactory solution is coming out of it."[1]

In Seoul, meanwhile, Walter Robertson and General Clark were conferring daily with Rhee, threatening him with an American pull-out if he did not cooperate in the armistice, promising him virtually unlimited American aid if he did. Rhee resisted the pressure, helped by reports from the States that seemed to indicate a near revolt by Republican senators against their own Administration. Ralph Flanders had said that Robertson and Clark were putting "us in the position of threatening the Korean government with an attack from the rear while the ROKs were attacking the Communists at the front." Bridges and McCarthy believed that "freedom-loving people" should applaud Rhee's defiance of the armistice. An Old Guard representative introduced a resolution in the House commending Rhee for releasing the prisoners. And on July 5, the acting majority leader, Senator Knowland (Taft was in the hospital for treatment of a cancer in his hip), blamed Eisenhower for a "breach" with Rhee and announced his support for Korean unification before any armistice agreement was signed.[2]

Despite the clamor, Eisenhower insisted that Robertson and Clark be firm with the old man. They were, and ultimately persuaded Rhee that it was futile for South Korea to try to go it alone. On July 8, Rhee finally issued a public statement promising to cooperate.

On July 12, with peace imminent, the Communists launched a massive assault, several corps strong, against an ROK division and its supporting American field artillery battalion. The attack evidently had a twofold purpose—to get better defensive positions before the final cease-fire line was established, and to demonstrate to Rhee how vulnerable his ROK units were. Clark rushed the U.S. 3d Infantry Division (Eisenhower's old outfit, which had been pulled out of the line the night before) into the breach. One of the regimental officers in the 3d Division was John Eisenhower. When the Americans appeared on the line, the Chinese called off their attack at that spot, resuming it the next day farther to the east, against only ROK targets.

Eisenhower wrote a furious memorandum to Wilson. He reminded the Secretary of Defense that he had suggested, some weeks earlier, strengthening American forces in Korea. At that time the JCS had rejected his suggestion, on the grounds that unless the U.N. intended to undertake an offensive, more troops were not needed. "Moreover," Eisenhower complained, "there was no great value attached by anyone to my further suggestion that the arrival in that region of reinforcements might have a good effect upon the hostile negotiators at Panmunjom." Now several ROK divisions, and an American artillery battalion, had been overrun, which "would seem to indicate that some of the confidence in our defensive strength was misplaced." He instructed Wilson to undertake a "complete review" of the situation, and insisted that "we must take no gamble with the integrity of our defensive position." He wanted two additional divisions sent to Korea immediately.[3]

On July 23, at an NSC meeting, Eisenhower pointed out that the truce that was about to go into effect would mean that no more troops could be brought in on either side. He therefore ordered two American divisions already in Japan, plus one still in the States, sent to Korea. He also ordered that there be "no publicity."[4]

The next day, Dulles called Eisenhower on the telephone to inform the President that Rhee had just sent a message demanding iron-clad guarantees of post-truce American aid. Dulles said that it appeared to him "as if Rhee at the last minute was trying to run out on his commitment to us." Eisenhower said he was "astonished" at this development and instructed the Secretary to tell Rhee that "this is what we can do and beyond that we cannot go." [5] Dulles sent the word to Rhee, and when the truce was finally signed, two days later, Rhee made no public protest.

At 9:30 P.M. on July 26, Eisenhower received word of the signing. A half hour later, he made a radio and television address to the American people. The shooting was over, he said, a fact that he greeted with "prayers of thanksgiving." Still, he felt it necessary to remind the American people that "we have won an armistice on a single battle-ground—not peace in the world. We may not now relax our guard nor cease our quest." He concluded his low-key remarks with a quotation from Lincoln ("With malice toward none; with charity for all."). There were no victory celebrations, no cheering crowds in Times Square, no sense of triumph. Instead Republicans like Jenner, Dewey Short, McCarthy, and House Speaker Joe Martin complained because the Administration had not sought victory, while Lyndon Johnson warned that the armistice "merely releases aggressive armies to attack elsewhere." [6]

The armistice was, despite its reception, one of Eisenhower's greatest achievements. He took great pride in it. He had promised to go to Korea; he had implied that he would bring the war to a close; he had made the trip; despite intense opposition from his own party, from his Secretary of State, and from Syngman Rhee, he had ended the war six months after taking office. Just as de Gaulle almost nine years later was the only Frenchman whose prestige was great enough to allow him to end the war in Algeria without himself being over-thrown, so too was Eisenhower the only American who could have found and made stick what Eisenhower called "an acceptable solution to a problem that almost defied . . . solution." [7] His solution was acceptable only because he had put his own immense prestige behind it; he knew that if Truman had agreed to such a settlement, Republican fury might have led to an impeachment attempt and certainly would have had a divisive effect on the country.

What stands out is Eisenhower the leader. The Supreme Allied Commander of 1945, the victor who would accept nothing less than unconditional surrender, had become the peacemaker of 1953, a man who would accept a compromise settlement that left him far short of victory, much less unconditional surrender. There were fundamental differences in the two situations, obviously, but this should not obscure the truth. The truth was that Eisenhower realized that unlimited war in the nuclear age was unimaginable, and limited war unwinnable. This was the most basic of his strategic insights.

The alternative between unimaginable and unwinnable was continued stalemate. That was the policy urged on him by nearly all his advisers, Republican colleagues, and most Democrats. At this thought, Eisenhower the man rebelled. The U.S. Army had suffered nearly one thousand casualties a week in Korea during the time since Rhee released the prisoners, on the eve of a successful completion of the truce. The thought of those five thousand dead and wounded boys made Eisenhower sick. The man who had ordered the Allied troops back onto the Continent and into the hell of the Bulge could not bear the thought of American boys dying for a stalemate. He wanted the killing ended, and he ended it.

Eisenhower liked to make up lists in his diary, lists of men who had pleased him or disappointed him, of events, of accomplishments. From the end of July 1953 onward, whenever he listed the achievements he was proudest of, he always began with peace in Korea.[8]

Immediately upon the conclusion of the armistice, Eisenhower moved to make good on his promises to Rhee. On July 27 he sent a special message to Congress, asking for authorization to spend $200 million for reconstruction in Korea, the money to come from savings in the Defense Department "that result from the cessation of hostilities." One week later, Congress responded positively.[9]

Eisenhower had a much more ambitious plan in mind, one that went far beyond a mere $200 million. On July 31, he sent a memorandum to Dulles, Wilson, and Stassen on "Assistance to Korea." Eisenhower said that "it strikes me that never before have the armed forces of the United States had a better opportunity to contribute more effectively than they now have in Korea toward helping win the Cold War." He felt that if the U.S. Eighth Army in Korea, then commanded by General Maxwell Taylor, could develop a "proper understanding" of the opportunity, and "if we can produce the enthusiasm that leadership should be able to develop," then the Eighth Army could go to work rebuilding South Korea. It would be "something almost unique in history. It is the opportunity of an army in a foreign land to contribute directly and effectively to the repairing of the damages of war; to rebuild and revive a nation, to give to itself the satisfaction of constructive and challenging work, dedicated to the preservation and enhancement rather than to the destruction of human values."

Eisenhower was quite specific about his vision. He wanted Taylor to use his men to restore productive facilities such as roads, railways, lines of communications, and in addition to rebuild schools, restore hospitals, train teachers and medical staffs, and engage in "countless other activities that would bring into play all of the talents present in this great Army." Eisenhower thought that if Taylor and the Eighth Army put their hearts into it, "an amazing transformation could come about, within the space of months, almost weeks. The effect of this upon the world would, in my opinion, be electrical." It would demonstrate that America was "engaged in helping humans, not merely in asserting and supporting any particular government system." It would cement the bonds of friendship between the Korean and American people. It would overcome the boredom "that always attacks an occupying army." Most of all, it would "improve the health and living standards of the Korean people, and assure that that region will remain a real bulwark of freedom."[10]

But however grand the opportunity seemed to Eisenhower, it held no interest for Dulles, Wilson, or Taylor. They simply ignored it. Eisenhower, with other things on his mind, failed to follow up until the end of September, when he asked an aide what was being done. The answer was, nothing. Taylor was preoccupied with building a defensive line in the rear of the neutral zone; Dulles was worrying about Vietnam, Iran, and other crises around the world, and had put Korea out of his mind; Wilson was trying to cut costs, not find new ways to spend DOD money.

On September 30, Eisenhower wrote Wilson another memo. Rather than accuse Wilson directly of ignoring his orders, he began: "Because it appears that a memorandum I wrote last July to express some thoughts of mine was probably lost, I am attaching hereto a copy." He said he realized that Taylor was concerned with building his defensive line, but "this work should be well along by now," so there should "certainly be available technical personnel whose enthusiastic cooperation can make every appropriated dollar do the work of ten." Eisenhower offered to talk to Wilson "at any time about this problem."[11] Again, nothing happened. Wilson was not interested, Taylor was not interested, and Eisenhower—despite his splendid vision—was not interested enough to follow through. Korea was in the past.

•   •

Back in January 1953, Eisenhower had received a three-page cable from the Iranian Prime Minister, Mohammed Mossadegh. "Old Mossy," as he was called by contemptuous Westerners, headed a government that had nationalized the oil fields and refineries of the Anglo-Persian Oil Company. The British had responded by shutting down the world's largest refinery, at Abadan, and by charging that any oil sold by Iran was in fact stolen goods. The British threatened to take any purchasers to court; the result was a *de facto* blockade on the sale of Iranian oil. In October 1952, Mossadegh broke diplomatic relations with the British. That act increased his popularity, but not his revenues—Iran was broke. In his cable to Eisenhower, Mossadegh set forth the Iranian position, summing up his theme in one sentence: "For almost two years the Iranian people have suffered acute distress and much misery merely because a company inspired by covetousness and a desire for profit supported by the British government had been endeavoring to prevent them from obtaining their natural and elementary rights." In a hand-drafted reply, Eisenhower said that his own position was impartial, that he had no prejudices in the case, and that he hoped future relations between Iran and the United States would be good.[12]

Everything Eisenhower was hearing about Iran, however, was anti-Mossadegh. Because Mossadegh had accepted the support of the Iranian Communist Party, the Tudeh, Americans leaped to the conclusion that he was himself a Communist. The American ambassador to Iran told Eisenhower that Mossadegh's supporters in Teheran were "the street rabble, the extreme left . . . extreme Iranian nationalists, some, but not all, of the more fanatical religious leaders, intellectual leftists, including many who had been educated abroad and did not realize that Iran was not ready for democracy."[13] Eisenhower's own friends in the oil business, including Sid Richardson, a Texas oil magnate, and Pete Jones of Cities Service (a charter member of Eisenhower's gang), told the President that nationalization was "disruptive" and not in the best interests of Iran, Britain, or the United States. Dulles feared that the chaos in Iran, coupled with the Tudeh's growing influence under Mossadegh, would give the Soviets an opportunity to take over the country.

In the spring of 1953, Foreign Secretary Eden had come to Washington for talks. There had been much to discuss—the war in Korea, British trade with China, Vietnam, NATO, ferment in Egypt, and of course Iran. In his meeting with Eisenhower, Eden noted later, the President "was extremely worried about the position in Iran." By this

time, Mossadegh was engaged in a test of will with the young Shah of
Iran, who was pro-British and who opposed nationalization. Eden told
Churchill that Eisenhower "seemed obsessed by the fear of a Communist Iran." Eden was in a delicate position; he wanted Anglo-Persian's
monopoly restored, but he did not want it done by the Americans, because if they intervened successfully, their oil companies would demand a share in Iranian oil. "The difficulty of this situation," Eden
reported to Churchill, "remains that the Americans are perpetually
eager to do something. The President repeated this several times." Further, the Americans had "a desire to reach a quick solution at almost
any cost," coupled with "an apparent disinclination to take second
place even in an area where primary responsibility was not theirs."[14]

Unfortunately for the British, they did not have the resources to
drive Mossadegh from power by themselves. Anglo-Persian and the
British government had therefore called on the CIA for help. British
Secret Service agents had talked to Kermit ("Kim") Roosevelt, TR's
grandson and FDR's cousin, a former OSS man now working for the
CIA, about the possibilities of cooperative action toward a coup en-
gineered by the CIA, supported by the British communications net-
work in Cyprus. Roosevelt told the British that the chances of convincing the Eisenhower Administration to act were good.[15]

He thought so because of the emphasis the new President was putting on both the underdeveloped world and on the CIA. Eisenhower
and Foster Dulles spent many a cocktail hour together, holding wide-
ranging discussions. More often than not, their talk came around to
the underdeveloped world and the need to keep the poorer nations
from going Communist. With NATO in place, with EDC about to be
ratified, with a firm defensive line established in Europe, with an
armistice in Korea, the battleground for the Cold War had shifted to
the so-called Third World. Latin America, India, Egypt, Iran, Vietnam—these were the places where the free world was being challenged,
or so Eisenhower and Dulles believed.

In meeting the challenge, Eisenhower intended to use the CIA in
a much more active role than Truman had given it. Under Truman,
the Agency had concentrated on its first responsibility, gathering and
evaluating intelligence from around the world. It had occasionally intervened in the affairs of other nations, but only by providing campaign funds for political parties favorable to the West, such as the
Christian Democrats in Italy in the 1948 election. Eisenhower believed
the Agency could be used more effectively, indeed could become one
of America's chief weapons in the Cold War. Partly this was based on

his experiences in World War II; he had been impressed by and grateful for the contribution to victory made by the British Secret Service,
the French Resistance, and the OSS. More important was Eisenhower's
fundamental belief that nuclear war was unimaginable, limited conventional war unwinnable, and stalemate unacceptable. That left the
CIA's covert action capability. Under Eisenhower's leadership and
Allen Dulles' direction, the size and scope of the CIA's activities increased dramatically during the 1950s. The beginning came in Iran in
1953.

In May of that year, Mossadegh again wrote Eisenhower, asking
the President to remove the British obstacles to the sale of Iranian oil
and to provide Iran with American economic assistance. Eisenhower
refused. After waiting more than a month to reply, Eisenhower told
Mossadegh, "I fully understand that the government of Iran must determine for itself which foreign and domestic policies are likely to be
more advantageous to Iran . . . I am not trying to advise the Iranian
government on its best interests. I am merely trying to explain why,
in the circumstances, the government of the United States is not pres-
ently in a position to extend more aid to Iran or to purchase Iranian
oil." [16]

That cable was sent on June 30. By that time, a high-level meeting in the Secretary of State's office had already produced the decision
to mount a coup against Mossadegh, directed by Kim Roosevelt, with
the aim of restoring the Shah to power. Beetle Smith, Robert Murphy,
the Dulles brothers, and Charlie Wilson were there. The plot involved
using CIA money—the total amount spent is in dispute, but some
millions of dollars were involved—to bribe Iranian army officials and
to hire a mob in Teheran in order to turn out Mossadegh and bring
back the Shah. It was code named Ajax. Secretary of State Dulles was
delighted by the plan. "So this is how we get rid of that madman
Mossadegh!" he exclaimed. [17]

Before going into operation, Ajax had to have the approval of
the President. Eisenhower participated in none of the meetings that
set up Ajax; he received only oral reports on the plan; and he did not
discuss it with his Cabinet or the NSC. Establishing a pattern he
would hold to throughout his Presidency, he kept his distance and left
no documents behind that could implicate the President in any projected coup. But in the privacy of the Oval Office, over cocktails, he
was kept informed by Foster Dulles, and he maintained a tight control
over the activities of the CIA. [18]

In July, Mossadegh dissolved the parliament and began ruling by decree. He called for a plebiscite. Meanwhile, the Tudeh Party was staging riots in Teheran. Mossadegh, Eisenhower believed, "was moving closer and closer to the Communists." In early August, the Shah fled his riot-torn capital. On August 5, Mossadegh won 99.4 percent of the vote in his plebiscite. And on August 8 the Soviet Union—which Eisenhower had been told had already provided Mossadegh with $20 million to keep his government afloat—announced that it had initiated negotiations with Iran for financial aid. Different observers drew contradictory conclusions from these events, but Eisenhower's was clear. "Iran's downhill course toward Communist-supported dictatorship was picking up momentum." Eisenhower told Allen Dulles to tell Kim Roosevelt to put Ajax into operation.[19]

Eisenhower wanted to wage the Cold War not only on the diplomatic and covert fronts, but also for world public opinion. Jackson was full of psychological-warfare ideas, many of which Eisenhower approved of and implemented. One such was to offer Communist pilots a $100,000 reward if they would deliver a MIG jet airplane to American authorities. The idea was not so much to study the MIG—enough had been shot down in Korea to do that—as to exploit the propaganda angle of a defection.

In September, a North Korean pilot did fly his MIG across the 38th parallel and land on an American airstrip. Although Eisenhower had approved the offer, he now found himself embarrassed by it. Even for the Americans, $100,000 was a fair sum of money, especially for a plane that, as Eisenhower said, "is no longer of any great interest to us." Eisenhower felt that the CIA had a moral obligation to pay the money, but thereafter he wanted the offer withdrawn. He was also ready to tell the Communists that they could have the plane back. Allen Dulles objected to all of this, on the grounds that great propaganda victories were possible, and it might even be that hundreds of pilots would defect. Eisenhower told Dulles that if that happened, "I will eat crow." He explained that Communist "methods of punishing people through torturing families are too well known and too effective to give rise to any great hope that we are going to wreck the Communist Air Force in this fashion."[20] Beetle Smith then worked out a compromise; the pilot "rejected" the bribe "on the basis that his action was because of his own convictions and not for money." Instead, Smith arranged for the pilot to be taken over as a ward by the National Committee for Free Asia (which was funded by the CIA) and provided with a technical education and financial support equal to the reward. Smith concluded a memorandum to Eisenhower, "C. D. and I feel that there is real propaganda value in this." Eisenhower scribbled at the bottom of the memo, "Now we're clicking. D. E."[21]

CIA control of funds that did not have to be accounted for gave Eisenhower flexibility in expenditures. The National Committee for a Free Europe, for example, an organization guided by C. D. Jackson that was dedicated to liberation and ran Radio Free Europe, received 90 percent of its operating budget from the CIA. Jackson was a bit embarrassed by this fact, while Eisenhower was anxious to save the government's money. They agreed to hold a private dinner at the White House for "business and national organization big shots." Jackson managed to raise $10 million from the dinner, so the government saved that amount, and Radio Free Europe became, according to Jackson, "credible."[22]

That dinner was not publicized, but on most occasions when Eisenhower hosted his stag dinners, Hagerty gave a notice and a guest list to the press, which had been clamoring for more information about the dinners. Publication excited widespread comment. Republicans were delighted that the President had sense enough to gather around him the biggest businessmen in America; Democrats were outraged that the President sat down only with millionaires. That was not exactly true—Eisenhower liked to mix his company, with private businessmen sitting beside high government officials. At a September 23 stag dinner, for example, C. D. Jackson sat next to Henry Ford II; Charlie Wilson sat next to the head of Goodyear; Beetle Smith sat beside Richard Mellon; Allen Dulles was across from John J. McCloy of the Chase National Bank; and as a special treat for Eisenhower, his son was there, home from Korea, sitting at the end of the table.[23] The dinners had a set pattern; formal dress, cocktails, dinner, retirement to the Red Room, where they all sat in a circle and discussed philosophical points or current issues.

Democratic fears that Eisenhower was allowing himself to be unduly influenced by his rich friends were misplaced. Although it was true that the President listened more than he talked, and although he occasionally did pick up an idea or two, his actual purpose was to impose his views and ideas on his guests. At a dinner in July, for example, the subject for discussion was a return to the gold standard. Eisenhower entered into it with preconceived notions; he had told George Whitney recently that as far as he could tell, the gold bugs "are merely another type of isolationist (I think some of

them own some gold stocks.).″[24] Still he listened patiently as the
guests made their case for gold. He was not convinced. When he
pressed them on their ideas, he discovered that "they had no clear
idea as to the method by which this should be done; indeed, they
had no real idea of what they were talking about." Eisenhower concluded a diary entry on the dinner, "As usual, everybody went away
carrying with him the opinion with which he came."[25]

Eisenhower knew better. He did change many minds in the course
of eight years of stag dinners. He used the occasions for a sales pitch
for his favorite programs, most especially MSA and NATO. He always spoke last, summing up the evening's conversation in a few sentences and then pronouncing his judgment and asking his guests to
help him put over his program. Since the guests were among the most
powerful and influential men in American life, the dinners gave
Eisenhower an opportunity to exercise leadership the way he liked
to do it, through reason and persuasion of other American leaders.
He was so earnest about MSA, so convincing about NATO, and so
open and honest in his appeals for help, that virtually every guest
went away a missionary determined to "go out and help Ike on this
one." Eisenhower's virtuosity, and his intelligence, impressed even
such a high-powered intellectual as George Kennan. After attending
one stag dinner, Kennan remarked, "In summarizing the group's conclusions, President Eisenhower showed his intellectual ascendancy over
every man in the room."[26]

On July 2, Eisenhower wrote in his diary, "Daily I am impressed
by the shortsightedness bordering upon tragic stupidity of many who
fancy themselves to be the greatest believers in and supporters of
capitalism."[27] He had in mind such organizations as the American
Medical Association, with its knee-jerk opposition to any role for the
government in the nation's health care, or the general clamor he heard
from the heads of large corporations about the need to cut taxes.
Lobbyists were a special bête noire; in the summer of 1953, the lobby
that irritated him most was the one that spoke for the motion-picture
industry. The movie people had persuaded Congress to eliminate the
tax on admission tickets. Eisenhower was opposed to special favors
for anyone, and he hated to lose revenue, so he was opposed to the
movie-tax elimination on general principles. He also had specific objections.

The movie industry was in trouble, he said, not only because of
the competition of television, but because "the cost of motion pic-

tures has gone into extravagant and almost senseless competition" for "stars" whose only qualifications were good looks. Eisenhower felt he knew what he was talking about, because "I have personally met a number of these stars; those with whom it is a pleasure to talk informally constitute a very small portion of the whole. I think one out of ten would be an exaggeration." Further, "the movies ran the old-fashioned vaudeville practically off the stage; they enjoyed for many years practically a monopoly in popular indoor entertainment." With their monopoly, they "grew careless indeed in the kind of pictures that they produced." Then came television, and now Hollywood was begging for tax relief. Eisenhower thought the movie people ought to pay for their own sins, and he vetoed the tax-relief bill.[28]

Eisenhower's tightfistedness about movie tickets and defense expenditures did not reach clear across the board. In some areas he was not only willing to continue, but actually wished to increase, public spending. Social Security was one. On August 1, he sent to Congress his program for expansion of the system. He called for extension of coverage to some 10.5 million people, plus increased benefits.[29] At a Cabinet meeting in early July, when the discussion turned to the budget, Secretary Hobby said that HEW could make significant cuts. Eisenhower was enthusiastic about the prospect until he heard her say that federal grants for education was an area in which she expected to make savings. Eisenhower protested that he "hadn't heard of this before. I am amazed at the thought of an education cut!!! This is the most important thing in our society." He told Hobby that "every liberal—including me—will disapprove." Hobby protested that the cuts were popular with Congress. "Then we can play some politics," Eisenhower responded. "If Congress can increase its expense accounts, we shouldn't cut vital education programs."[30]

Eisenhower frequently characterized himself as "liberal on human issues, conservative on economic ones." His liberalism, however, was usually closely connected with national security. He wanted better educational opportunities for Americans, for example, not so much for their own sake as for. creating the scientists and technologists who could keep America ahead in the arms race. That was equally true of immigration legislation, where he took a "liberal" stance that had its real origins in the needs of the Cold War. In 1952 Congress had passed, over Truman's veto, the McCarran-Walter immigration bill, a restrictive measure that tied quotas to national origins based on the U.S. population of 1924. The practical effect was to exclude hundreds of thousands of potential refugees from Eastern Europe, one of the major Cold War battlegrounds. Eisenhower wanted to let these people in, both to reap the propaganda advantage and to obtain the benefit of their skills and labor. He therefore proposed supplementary legislation to provide for the admission of about 250,000 escapees from Communism. Old Guard senators were firmly opposed to this "surplus-population bill" and turned Eisenhower's Cold War motivation on its head by charging that such wholesale admissions would make it possible for Communist agents to infiltrate the country. Eisenhower met privately with McCarran, but as he told a Republican leaders' meeting, "I made about as much impression on him as beating on a steel lid with a sponge." Still, he insisted that this was "must" legislation and he forced the Republican leaders to support it. On August 7, he signed the bill into law.[31]

When there was no direct Cold War connection on a domestic issue, Eisenhower's liberalism faded. TVA provided one example. Liberals wanted to extend the system itself, and expand the principle by building federal dams and generators on other rivers. Conservatives wanted to sell it. So did Eisenhower, but he realized it was politically impossible, so he concentrated on stopping any expansion of TVA while encouraging private power company growth. He explained to the Cabinet, "TVA taxes Massachusetts to provide cheap power in the TVA area to lure Massachusetts industry away."[32]

In these areas and others, such as his effort to put the Post Office on a self-sustaining basis, Eisenhower sought the middle of the road. He explained to Swede Hazlett that he tried to prepare himself for every decision through intensive study, but because "of the infinite variety of problems presented, and the rapidity with which they are placed in front of me," he often could not do the research he wanted to do. Further, the people who came into his office to discuss specific issues "always have an axe to grind," so that the advice he received was "distorted and selfish." His own solution was to "apply common sense—to reach for an average solution."[33]

But when basic decisions affecting the economy were involved, his average solutions usually came down on the side of business. His stance on revision of Taft-Hartley was a prime example. During the campaign, he had promised to amend Taft-Hartley so that it could not be used for union busting. And he added that any changes he recommended would incorporate the views of organized labor. His appointment of Martin Durkin as Secretary of Labor flowed directly out of that pledge. Durkin set up a committee to study revision, with representatives from management, labor, and Weeks's Department of Commerce. Durkin wanted to abolish the right-to-work provision of Taft-Hartley, to minimize the jurisdiction of state courts in labor disputes, and to permit secondary boycotts. Weeks opposed any basic changes. On June 18, while the group was meeting in Sherman Adams' office, Eisenhower walked in. He said he was interested in the subject and wanted to listen to the discussion. But when Durkin stated his position on right-to-work, Eisenhower interrupted to say that it was imperative that the states retain their rights in that field. He told Durkin that the Secretary of Labor should be representing the government and not the AFL.[34]

With Durkin blocked by Weeks, two of Eisenhower's aides, Bernard Shanley and Gerald Morgan (one of the principal drafters of Taft-Hartley), drew up a memorandum containing nineteen revisions to be recommended to Congress; among them was a repeal of right-to-work. They told Durkin that the President had agreed to send the message to Congress on July 31. But that day, Senator Taft died. Shanley and Morgan then told Durkin that amending Taft's bill on the very day of his death would be tactless. They did promise that the message would go to Congress shortly. Someone then leaked the proposals to *The Wall Street Journal,* which published them on August 3 under a headline that charged Eisenhower with favoring the unions. That article brought forth a flood of outraged complaints from big business. Nixon told Eisenhower that repealing right-to-work would alienate both business and southern support. Eisenhower therefore held back the message on revisions.

On August 19, Durkin had lunch with Eisenhower. According to Durkin, Eisenhower promised support for the nineteen amendments; according to Eisenhower, he urged Durkin to take a broader view of his responsibilities and stop being a special pleader for labor (the President, his critics were quick to note, never told Weeks to stop being a special pleader for business). On September 10, Eisenhower informed Durkin that he had withdrawn his support for the amendments. Durkin then resigned, charging that he had been double-crossed.[35]

Accusing Eisenhower of being a liar was guaranteed to set Eisenhower off into a furious rage. He had spent his life making his word his bond. Both his prestige and power flowed directly from his reputation, and he guarded it jealousy. In this case, he immediately sent a long memorandum to Shanley, asking Shanley if he could remember what had been said. Shanley assured him that he had made no promises to Durkin.[36] At a news conference later that week, Eisenhower was asked for his version of the Durkin resignation. "To my knowledge," Eisenhower replied, "I have never broken an agreement, it was something that I did not understand was made. Now, I have never broken one that I know of. And if there is anyone here who has contrary evidence, he can have the floor and make his speech."[37] Eisenhower, who could use his temper constructively, had adroitly shifted the issue over to his integrity—an area where he could not lose—and away from right-to-work. And with that news conference outburst, the Eisenhower commitment to revise Taft-Hartley faded away. James P. Mitchell, a vice-president of Bloomingdale's in charge of labor relations for the department store, was Durkin's successor. He made some feeble efforts to recommend amendments, but nothing was done, and the original Taft-Hartley, including right-to-work, stayed on the books.

Taft's death was a blow. The senator had surprised and pleased Eisenhower by his cooperative attitude. Despite Taft's outburst when first informed of the Administration's budget plans, he had persuaded many of the Old Guard congressmen to go along with Eisenhower's proposals on such basic matters as taxes and expenditures. Responding to Eisenhower's heartfelt pleas, he had managed to save much of the MSA appropriation. With Taft's help, Eisenhower could deal with the Old Guard; without it, he anticipated great difficulties. Eisenhower released a statement saying that America had "lost a truly great citizen and I have lost a wise counsellor and a valued friend."[38] Along with Mamie, Eisenhower paid a call on Taft's widow in Georgetown. Holding Martha Taft's hand in both of his, Eisenhower said, "I don't know what I'll do without him; I don't know what I'll do without him."[39]

Eisenhower meant what he said, if only because Taft's successor as majority leader in the Senate was William Knowland. Eisenhower's contempt for the California senator was complete. "In his case," Eisenhower wrote of Knowland in his diary, "there seems to be no final answer to the question 'How stupid can you get?' "[40]

One of Knowland's problems was his opposition to MSA funding. He wanted MSA done away with. Truman had called for $7.6 billion for 1954; Eisenhower reduced the figure to $6 billion and then, after Knowland and others complained, to $5.5 billion. He assured Congress that "by far the largest single element will be the direct provision of military end items" to NATO, but his concessions and explanations were not enough to satisfy the Old Guard.

Eisenhower waged an all-out struggle on behalf of MSA. It was a constant theme at his stag dinners; in addition, he had breakfasts, luncheons, and evening sessions with both Democrats and Republicans, appealing to their patriotism and sense of duty. He told congressional leaders that "the most expensive way to insure security is to pile up our money in a defense," and that "we're not doing this for altruism. We're talking about the security of our country—nothing less." He swore he would "plead, cajole, and push" until he got the funds. Knowland told him he was unhappy because there had been no basic change in foreign policy; he wondered what was the point of electing a Republican President if he continued Truman's same old line. Eisenhower's response was to complain that "people rant and rave that we haven't revolutionized foreign policy. We can't ever revolutionize. The facts of the world situation don't change that much." But despite his vow to "fight to the bitter end" on MSA, the Republicans cut his request by 22.3 percent, leaving him with only slightly more than half of what Truman had projected. Still, Eisenhower felt, it could have been worse, and certainly would have been save for his personal involvement.[41]

One reason Eisenhower wanted more MSA funds was to get on with the rearming of Germany. He not only wanted Germany rearmed, but he wanted the country unified and brought into NATO and EDC as a full partner. Field Marshal Montgomery, commanding the NATO ground forces, warned him not to push his projects too fast, because he could not have everything he wanted. His program was unrealistic, Montgomery said, because neither the Russians nor the French would ever allow Germany to both unify and rearm. If Eisenhower continued to insist, Montgomery feared the result would be to heighten tensions in Europe, and possibly to kill EDC, and certainly to put back the cause of German unity.

Eisenhower disagreed. He told Montgomery that "a steady social, political, military, and economic advance in West Germany" would act like a magnet to the East Germans. "It might even become impossible for the Communists to hold the place by force." He admitted that German unity within the NATO alliance might be "provocative of a general war," but said that would happen only after Germany had united, rearmed, and joined EDC. Those developments would have "a sobering effect on any Russian plan for risking a global war."

Summing up, Eisenhower asserted that "I do not believe there is anything incompatible between German unification and German participation in the EDC." Why? Because Eisenhower was convinced that
EDC, "like NATO and the U.N., is a peaceful concept."[42]

Convincing the Russians, not Montgomery, was the trick. Chancellor Adenauer, like almost everyone else, doubted that it could be
done. Although Adenauer continued to give *pro forma* support to the
idea of unification, he had reconciled himself to the fact that the division of Germany was one of the most basic and permanent results
of the war. Not Eisenhower. He continued to dream about German
unification and a major German contribution to EDC, and beyond
that to the liberation of all the East European satellites. How to
achieve such goals was a problem, but he was convinced that backing
off on a peace treaty, all-German elections, and full German participation in NATO was not the way to begin.[43]

The creation of an all-European army through EDC, to be followed by the creation of a United States of Europe, had been one of
Eisenhower's major goals as SACEUR, and he continued to make it
the centerpiece of his European policy as President. Through Dulles,
and through his private correspondence with European leaders, he
pushed the project. In September, he told French Premier Joseph
Laniel that it was "urgent" that the French, in their relations with
West Germany, "be guided by a new spirit of friendship and trust."
He said he was aware of the difficulties for the French involved in ratifying EDC, as "we are not blind to history." But still he urged Laniel
to "not miss this historic opportunity for a Franco-German rap-
prochement."[44]

Eisenhower's high hopes for EDC involved not only what he felt
it could accomplish for Western Europe, but also the promise it held
for the United States. A closely knit Western European community,
held together by economic and military ties, protected through NATO
by the American nuclear umbrella and through EDC by numerous
all-European ground divisions, would not only be a source of security
for the world but would end the need for MSA funds and allow Eisenhower to cut even further the American military budget. EDC, in
short, would simultaneously provide greater security for the West, a
smaller defense establishment for the United States, and lower taxes.
Anticipating its ratification, Eisenhower told Wilson to have the
newly appointed Chiefs of Staff, headed by Admiral Radford, undertake a basic study of America's strategic concepts, the roles and missions of the services, the nuclear option, and MSA, all with a view to

reducing conventional forces and military aid.[45] The re-examination, and EDC ratification, received a new emphasis on August 12, when the Soviets successfully tested their own hydrogen bomb.

In mid-July, just as Kim Roosevelt was implementing Operation Ajax in Iran, Senator McCarthy threatened to disrupt the CIA by launching a full-scale investigation of it. His immediate motive was Allen Dulles' appointment of William Bundy to the post of liaison officer between the NSC, the AEC, and the CIA. McCarthy challenged Bundy's fitness on the grounds that he was Dean Acheson's son-in-law and had contributed $400 to the Alger Hiss defense fund. McCarthy issued a subpoena to Bundy to appear before his committee, but Allen Dulles flatly refused to allow âny CIA employee to appear before any congressional committee. Unlike his brother, he would not be cowed by McCarthy. The senator then declared that the CIA was neither "sacrosanct" nor immune from investigation.[46]

Both Eisenhower and Allen Dulles asked Nixon for his help. Nixon went to McCarthy. "Joe," Nixon explained to McCarthy, "you have to understand how those people up in Cambridge think. Bundy graduated from the Harvard Law School, and Hiss was one of its most famous graduates." McCarthy, for one of the few times in his career, backed down. Eisenhower breathed a sigh of relief.[47]

McCarthy's retreat on the CIA seemed to provide proof of the effectiveness of Eisenhower's policy of ignoring the senator. Bill Robinson, for one, said so, and he told Eisenhower, "a gratuitous castigation of McCarthy by you would be inappropriate as well as unwise," while Allen Dulles was "satisfied" with the result.[48] Swede Hazlett was "delighted," not only because the CIA was protected, but because the incident seemed to him to "indicate that at last you are ready to crack down on McCarthy."

Eisenhower hastened to correct Swede's misperception. "I disagree completely with the 'crack down' theory," he wrote Swede. He would continue to fight McCarthy with "indirect methods," which he felt would produce "results that may not be headlined, but they will be permanent . . . To give way in anger or irritation to an outburst intended to excoriate some individual could do far more to destroy the attacker than it would do to damage the attacked." Linking McCarthy to Huey Long, Eisenhower said that "the average honorable individual cannot understand to what lengths certain politicians would go for publicity," and he assured his friend that he had no intention of adding to McCarthy's notoriety.[49]

That was Eisenhower's position, and he stuck to it, despite pressure from his aides as well as his friends to speak out. Shanley noted sadly in his diary, "We have really abdicated to McCarthy which is the entire source of his strength."[50]

By the end of the summer, Eisenhower badly needed a vacation. He had been stuck in Washington for nearly two straight months. He had been hoping to find a weekend place close to the capital, something more homey than Camp David, and in late July had almost bought a country place in Virginia. He intended to sell the Gettysburg farm to pay for it. Then he discovered that although Mamie too was impatient for the rebuilding at Gettysburg to take place, "her heart is really set on it. When I talked about getting rid of Gettysburg, she looked as if she were about to lose her last friend." So he decided to do without a weekend home until the work at Gettysburg was finished.[51]

Instead of going to Virginia, Eisenhower and Mamie spent the last four weeks of summer in Denver. On the eve of going, Eisenhower told Sid Richardson that "I am going to forget all of this political yammering—I hope to go up in the hills, catch a fish and cook a pancake; and, when I get on the golf course, try to stay under 120."[52]

But although he was able to play some golf, catch some trout, and otherwise enjoy the marvelous air, weather, and scenery of the Rockies in late summer, he found he could not escape the work or the pressure. The press was still with him, covering his every move, asking questions. Sherman Adams was there, with his reminders, memos, and queries. Hagerty was along, and so were most of the aides. After sending a three-page, single-spaced memo to Charlie Wilson about a new type of radar, Eisenhower wrote, "This is supposed to be a vacation— actually the problem presented in this letter is only a small item compared to the constant pounding I am getting from all sides."[53]

Despite the irritating interruptions, and despite the temptations of the mountains, Eisenhower used his vacation to do some serious thinking about a fundamental problem. The problem was post-Korea foreign policy. Eisenhower's way of working on it was to bring along to Denver a long memorandum from Dulles. He also had Dulles come to Denver for a day of talk. At the end of his vacation, Eisenhower sent a memorandum of his own to Dulles. He began by rejecting Dulles' suggestions, which had been that the United States increase its nuclear-weapon production and withdraw its troops from Asia and Europe. Eisenhower then outlined what he thought the basic needs were in the post-Korea foreign policy. First, educate the people. Other-

wise, "we will drift aimlessly, probably to our own eventual destruction." The people had to be told the truth. As things stood, "The individual feels helpless to do anything about the foreign threat that
hangs over his head and so he turns his attention to matters of immediate interest," namely taxes.

Educate the people about what? "Among other things, we should
describe the capabilities now and in the near future of the H-bomb,
supplemented by the A-bomb." That was an idea that had been running through Eisenhower's head ever since he read the report on the
effect of the first hydrogen device. He had frequently mused to his
aides, "We've just got to let the American people know how terrible
this thing is."[54] AEC and JCS objections had so far deflected his desire, but he resolved to put new effort into making the horrors of
nuclear war the subject of a major speech in the fall.

After explaining, in some graphic detail, the results of a hydrogen
explosion, Eisenhower said, "We should patiently point out that any
group of people, such as the men in the Kremlin, who are aware of
the great destructiveness of these weapons—and who still decline to
make any honest effort toward international control by collective
action—must be fairly assumed to be contemplating their aggressive
use." Then the citizen would realize that "we have to be constantly
ready, on an instantaneous basis, to inflict greater loss upon the enemy
than he could reasonably hope to inflict upon us."

That was exactly Dulles' point—he recommended a defense policy based on a massive overkill capacity. Eisenhower agreed that such
a capacity "would be a deterrent," but he warned that "if the contest
to maintain this relative position should have to continue indefinitely,
the cost would either drive us to war—or into some form of dictatorial
government. In such circumstances, we would be forced to consider
whether or not our duty to future generations did not require us to
initiate war at the most propitious moment that we could designate."
First strike, in other words. Preemptive war. Back in the late thirties,
Eisenhower had wondered how long a democracy would be willing to
pay the cost of maintaining its defensive strength before it lashed out
at the source of the threat and removed it. Now he wondered the same
thing about the Russian nuclear threat.

Eisenhower was not advocating a first strike. He was not the man
to launch a second Pearl Harbor. But he believed that a prolonged
nuclear arms race would bankrupt the world, then destroy it. Anything was better than that, he was telling Dulles. Therefore the tone
of the new, post-Korea foreign policy was to be one of an all-out effort

to find a way to disarmament. And he was convinced that the way to prepare the people for such a move was to inform them of the horrors of nuclear war. Eisenhower thought that "a carefully thought out program of speeches, national and international conferences, articles, and legislation, would be in order."

As a part of the preparation campaign, Eisenhower told Dulles to tone down a speech he was to make shortly before the U.N. Eisenhower was gentle with his Secretary. He said he had the "impression" that the speech "is intended as a new indictment of the Bolshevik Party . . . Now I have no quarrel with indicting and condemning them," but he wanted Dulles to "be positive and clear, without giving the impression we are merely concerned with showing that we have been very nice people, while the others have been very wicked indeed."[55]

Dulles replied, "I see on rereading that my language can be much improved and I shall do this along the lines of your suggestion, which certainly has validity."[56]

Another Cabinet visitor to Denver was the Attorney General. He was welcome. Eisenhower had developed an unbounded admiration for Brownell. Eisenhower thought Brownell was a man of consummate honesty, incapable of an unethical practice, a lawyer of the first rank, and an outstanding leader. After outlining these qualities of Brownell's in his diary, Eisenhower summed up, "I am devoted to him and am perfectly confident that he would make an outstanding president of the United States."[57]

Eisenhower was not so happy with Brownell's mission in Denver as he was with the man himself. Brownell had come to discuss the school segregation cases that were coming up before the Supreme Court. He told Eisenhower that the Court had requested the Attorney General to file a brief and an opinion in the cases. Requests for such *amicus curiae* briefs from the Court, Brownell assured Eisenhower, were not unique, although by no means was it an established practice.[58] Eisenhower was not bothered by the Court's request for a statement of fact on the Fourteenth Amendment as it related to segregation in the schools, but he did object to the Court's further request that the Justice Department also submit its opinion on the subject. This, to Eisenhower, represented an abdication of responsibility. One reason he felt that way was his attitude toward separation of powers. "As I understand it," he told Brownell, "the courts were established by the Constitution to interpret the laws; the responsibility of the

Executive Department is to execute them." He suspected the Court was trying to duck out of or avoid the most controversial social problem in America, that "in this instance the Supreme Court has been guided by some motive that is not strictly functional." After talking to Brownell, Eisenhower dictated to Ann Whitman a "memorandum for the record" on their conversation; in it he concluded, "The Court cannot possibly . . . delegate its responsibility and it would be futile for the Attorney General to attempt to sit as a court and reach a conclusion as to the true meaning of the Fourteenth Amendment." He wanted Brownell to limit himself to a presentation of "fact and historical record," and to avoid giving his own opinion.[59]

Brownell very much wanted to give his own opinion, which was that segregation by race in public schools was unconstitutional. There was the rub. Eisenhower did not necessarily disagree with Brownell— the President tried to remain neutral on the constitutionality of segregation—but Eisenhower was fearful of the effect of a ruling outlawing segregation. Partly this reflected his own background and attitudes. Eisenhower was six years old when *Plessy* v. *Ferguson* established the doctrine of "separate but equal"; he had lived all his life with it. There were no Negroes in his home town, none at West Point. Eisenhower had spent virtually all his prewar career at army posts in the South (or in the Canal Zone or the Philippines, where racism was, if possible, even more blatant). During the war, he had commanded a Jim Crow Army. In December 1944, he had responded to the manpower crisis by offering to integrate Negro port workers and truck drivers into white units, if the Negroes would volunteer for combat duty. Thousands did, and fought well, but when the crisis was over, Eisenhower quietly returned the volunteers to their all-Negro noncombat units. Eisenhower had left the Army before Truman, in 1948, ordered the armed forces desegregated. Eisenhower had many southern friends and he shared most of their prejudices against Negroes. When he went down to Augusta, he listened to the plantation owners tell their jokes about the "darkies"; when he returned to Washington, in the privacy of his family, he would repeat some of those jokes.[60]

During the campaign, Eisenhower had denied that race relations were an issue, a startling statement in view of the Democratic Party split in 1948 over the Fair Employment Practices Commission (FEPC). Indeed, Eisenhower had bid for southern votes by his own refusal to endorse FEPC. But one of his core beliefs about the office he now held was that he was the President of all the people. That included Negro Americans. He had therefore announced, in his State of the Union

message, that he would use his full authority to end segregation in the
District of Columbia and in the armed forces.[61] Two months later,
when Alice Dunningham of the Associated Negro Press asked him
about the apparent contradiction between his announced policy and
the continued segregation of military posts in the South, Eisenhower
replied, "I have said it again and again; wherever federal funds are
expended for anything, I do not see how any American can justify—
legally, or logically, or morally—a discrimination in the expenditure
of those funds as among our citizens. If there is any benefit to be derived from them, I think it means all share, regardless of such inconsequential factors as race and religion."[62]

Eisenhower did move vigorously to eliminate discrimination in
those areas where his authority was clearly established. He assigned an
aide, Max Rabb, to oversee the task. Rabb consulted with Secretary of
the Navy Robert Anderson, a Texas oilman; with Rabb's encouragement, Anderson desegregated the naval installations in Norfolk and
Charleston. Anderson did it quietly, without fanfare, and effectively;
he thereby earned Eisenhower's "intense admiration" and undying
gratitude.[63] Rabb and Eisenhower also worked on the other services;
by the end of 1953 Eisenhower could boast that segregation in the
Navy and the Air Force "was a thing of the past," and the Army was
on the verge of eliminating its last all-Negro unit. Eisenhower also
ordered all public facilities in Washington desegregated, while Brownell argued before the Supreme Court that discrimination by restaurant owners in the capital was unconstitutional (the Court, on June 8,
agreed).

These were real accomplishments, but they had little or no effect
on the great bulk of Negro Americans. *Plessy* remained the law of the
land. In the South, in the border states, even in abolitionist Kansas,
schools remained segregated. The NAACP had been working for years
within the court system to break down *Plessy;* by 1953 it had won a
number of significant victories in special cases (admission to law or
medical schools) and had cases moving toward the Supreme Court that
challenged the basic constitutionality of segregation in the public
schools.

Southern politicians were alarmed. On July 20 South Carolina
Governor Jimmy Byrnes, once Truman's Secretary of State, came to
the Oval Office to talk to the President. Byrnes said he was "very fearful" of the consequences of integration in the South. He mentioned
the possibility of riots, and said in his opinion a number of southern
states "would immediately cease support for public schools." Byrnes

assured Eisenhower that "the South no longer finds any great problem in dealing with adult Negroes," but said we "are frightened at putting the children together . . ." He also warned Eisenhower that if the President supported a desegregation decision, "that would forever defeat any possibility of developing a real Republican Party in the South."

Eisenhower assured Byrnes that he realized "that improvement in race relations is one of those things that will be healthy and sound only if it starts locally." Prejudice would not "succumb to compulsion." Any federal law that set up a conflict "of the police powers of the states and of the nation would set back the cause of progress in race relations for a long, long time."[64]

While in Denver, Eisenhower wrote further to Byrnes on the subject, which he said "has scarcely been absent from my mind" since their talk. He thought it was up to leaders to lead. "We who hold office not only must discharge the duties placed upon us by the Constitution and by conscience," he told Byrnes, "but also must, by constructive advances, prove to be mistaken those who insist that true reforms can come only through overriding federal law and federal police methods." He appealed to Byrnes to use his influence, not only in South Carolina but among the other southern governors, to achieve some real progress in race relations. That seemed to Eisenhower to be the only alternative to a federally enforced end to segregation.[65]

Eisenhower sent a copy of his letter to Nixon, asking the Vice-President to make a public statement along the lines he had suggested to Byrnes. But Eisenhower also told Nixon that he remained opposed to FEPC, on the grounds that it would be ineffective, would create antagonisms, and would set back the cause of progress by many years. Returning to his theme of voluntary cooperation, he told Nixon that every elected official in the United States should "promote justice and equality through leadership and persuasion; no man is discharging his full duty if he does nothing in the presence of injustice."[66]

Thus the sum total of Eisenhower's program for the 16 million Negro Americans who were outside the federal establishment was to appeal to the southern governors for some sign of progress. Since every one of those governors had been elected by a virtually all-white electorate, and since every one of them was thoroughly committed to segregation as a way of life, as were the vast majority of their white constituents, the President could not have anticipated rapid or dramatic progress.

•   •

On the morning of September 8—Eisenhower was still in Denver—
the President was informed that Chief Justice Fred Vinson had died
of a heart attack. Eisenhower flew back to Washington for the funeral.
He mourned the passing of his old bridge-playing friend, but inevitably his mind turned to the appointment of a successor. Eisenhower
had already promised Earl Warren that he would have the first vacancy on the Court, but when Eisenhower made that promise he did
not expect that the vacancy would be that of the Chief Justice himself.
Eisenhower therefore felt free to canvass other possibilities, and did
so—including considering John W. Davis of West Virginia, the 1924
Democratic nominee for the Presidency and a lawyer who was arguing
the South's side in the segregation cases. Eisenhower also thought of
John Foster Dulles, and indeed asked Dulles if he would take the appointment. Dulles said no, he preferred to stay with the State Department.[67]

It was not that Eisenhower wanted to renege on Warren. Eisenhower had talked to Warren about his basic philosophy and was much
impressed by the California governor. Brownell later recalled that
Eisenhower "saw Warren as a big man; and his respect turned into a
real crush." To his brother Edgar, Eisenhower wrote that "from the
very beginning of my acquaintanceship with Warren, I had him in
mind for an appointment to the high court."[68]

But Eisenhower wanted to think long and hard before making
what probably would be the most important appointment of his Presidency. "I'm not going to make any mistakes in a hurry," he told one
consultant. To the dean of the Columbia Law School, who had suggested some names, Eisenhower explained his approach. "My principal concern is to do my part in helping restore the Court to the position of prestige that it used to hold, and which in my opinion was
badly damaged during the New and Fair Deal days." He said he was
seeking "a man of broad experience, professional competence, and
with an unimpeachable record and reputation for integrity."[69]

Warren had all those qualifications, and others. Eisenhower could
not be accused of paying off a political debt, because Warren had
stayed in the race against him until the end at the convention. Warren
was from the West Coast, but he was identified with Dewey and that
wing of the Republican Party that Eisenhower wished to see prosper
at the expense of the Old Guard. Warren was middle-of-the-road, so
much so that Eisenhower's reactionary brother Edgar denounced him
as a left-winger, while Milton reported that he and his friends considered Warren to be dangerously to the right. Eisenhower responded

to Milton: "Warren has been very definitely a liberal-conservative; he represents the kind of political, economic, and social thinking that I believe we need on the Supreme Court." [70]

In late September, Eisenhower announced a recess appointment of Warren as Chief Justice (Congress was not in session). Eisenhower made the appointment for all the reasons cited above, but the one that stands out is simplicity itself. Eisenhower personally knew many great lawyers, great judges, great men. He was a shrewd judge of character and talent. He wanted this appointment to be his best. He was convinced that Warren was the best man in the country for the post of Chief Justice.

During his Presidency, Eisenhower never doubted that he had been right. When Congress gathered again in January 1954, Eisenhower sent Warren's formal nomination to the Senate. There Senator Langer, helped by some Old Guard senators, held up confirmation. Eisenhower scribbled in his diary, "[If the] Republicans as a body should try to repudiate him [Warren], I shall leave the Republican Party and try to organize an intelligent group of independents, however small." [71] Despite his many difficulties with Warren over the next seven years, he remained convinced that he had made the right choice.

While Eisenhower was in Denver, he also got the news of the CIA's successful coup in Iran. On August 22, the Shah returned to his country; Mossadegh had been arrested by the Iranian Army, acting in concert with Kim Roosevelt. Eisenhower was careful not to meet publicly with Roosevelt when he returned to the States, or have any other connection with Operation Ajax, but he did read Roosevelt's report while in Colorado. In his memoirs, Eisenhower quoted a bit of that report, but stated flatly that the report was prepared by "an American in Iran, unidentified to me." [72] On September 23, in fact, Eisenhower had personally awarded, in a closed-door ceremony, the National Security Medal to Roosevelt. And, in his diary, he wrote, "The things we did were 'covert,'" and he admitted that the United States would have been embarrassed if the CIA's role in the coup became known. Of Roosevelt himself, Eisenhower wrote that he "worked intelligently, courageously and tirelessly. I listened to his detailed report and it seemed more like a dime novel than an historical fact." [73]

It was real enough. The Shah was back, and he entered into a new oil deal with the West. The British, despite their help on Ajax, lost their monopoly, retaining only 40 percent of Iran's oil. The French got 6 percent, the Dutch got 14 percent, and the Americans

(Gulf, Standard of New Jersey, Texaco, and Socony-Mobil) got 40 percent. Delighted with this outcome, Eisenhower in late September announced an immediate allocation of $45 million in emergency economic aid to Iran, with another $40 million to follow. On October 8, he wrote in his diary, "Now if the British will be conciliatory . . . if the Shah . . . will be only a little bit flexible, and the United States will stand by to help both financially and with wise counsel, we may really give a serious defeat to Russian intentions and plans in that area."[74]

Eisenhower had ordered the Mossadegh government overthrown, and it had been done. It seemed to him that the results more than justified the methods. That was an additional side of the man who had insisted on making peace in Korea and trying new approaches to Russia on disarmament. Where he thought it prudent and possible, he was ready to fight the Communists with every weapon at his disposal—just as he had fought the Nazis. There was no squeamishness, no doubts. Do it, he told the CIA, and don't bother me with any details.

CHAPTER SIX

Atoms for Peace

October 1–December 31, 1953

ON OCTOBER 8, Eisenhower opened a news conference with a prepared statement. The subject was the recent Soviet test of a hydrogen bomb. The President said the test had not come as a surprise, and added that the Soviets "now possess a stockpile of atomic weapons . . . and the capability of atomic attack on us, and such capability will increase with the passage of time." Turning to the American situation, he said, "We do not intend to disclose the details of our strength in atomic weapons of any sort, but it is large and increasing steadily." He assured the press that the armed forces had sufficient nuclear arsenals to carry out the specific tasks assigned to them. And he warned that "this titanic force must be reduced to the fruitful service of mankind."[1]

Millions agreed with Eisenhower's final sentence. More important, leading American scientists agreed, and indeed had already been calling for disarmament followed by research on peaceful uses of atomic power. Most important, the former scientific head of the Manhattan Project, J. Robert Oppenheimer, agreed. In July of 1953 Oppenheimer had published, in *Foreign Affairs,* an article titled "Atomic Weapons and American Policy." In the article, Oppenheimer warned that an atomic arms race between the superpowers could only have disastrous results, and in any case it made no sense, because when America built its "twenty-thousandth bomb it . . . will not offset their two-thousandth." In a vivid image, Oppenheimer compared the

United States and the Soviet Union to "two scorpions in a bottle, each capable of killing the other, but only at the risk of his own life." He insisted that the American people had to be told the truth about the size and power of their atomic arsenal, and called for "candor on the part of the representatives of the people of their country."[2]

Oppenheimer's article sharpened, but did not begin, the debate in the Eisenhower Administration over atomic policy. As this was un-questionably the most momentous problem Eisenhower faced, he treated it with the utmost seriousness. He had made Oppenheimer the head of an advisory group to report to the President on what to do about the arms race; in addition, Oppenheimer had been chair-man of the General Advisory Committee of the AEC. Eisenhower read and was impressed by Oppenheimer's views; he agreed with the physi-cist that an atomic arms race was madness; he also believed that if the American people were told, in graphic detail, of the destructive power of the H-bomb that they would support him in any genuine disarma-ment proposal. The President therefore put C. D. Jackson to work on a speech designed to meet Oppenheimer's call for candor. Jackson called the preparation of the speech "Operation Candor," and worked on it through the spring and summer of 1953. He was an enthusiastic supporter of Oppenheimer's basic idea.

Other top advisers were firmly opposed. Dulles had no faith what-soever in any disarmament proposal. He believed in dealing with the Russians only from a position of overwhelming strength, and insisted that the various Soviet proposals so far received for disarmament were merely propaganda devices, designed to weaken NATO and to dis-courage the French from ratifying EDC. Admiral Lewis Strauss, chair-man of the AEC, agreed with Dulles.

Strauss was a self-made millionaire (on Wall Street) and had been James Forrestal's assistant during the war (thus his rank of admiral). Truman had first put him on the AEC in 1946; three years later Strauss had engaged in a bitter dispute with the then AEC chairman, David Lilienthal, and with Oppenheimer, over the hydrogen bomb. They did not want to build one, while Strauss—and Truman—did. In July 1953, Eisenhower appointed Strauss the chairman of the AEC (although he hardly knew the man). After Strauss's swearing-in cere-mony, Eisenhower took him aside and told him, "My chief concern and your first assignment is to find some new approach to the dis-arming of atomic energy." Strauss ignored the President's directive. His concern was to stay well ahead of the Russians, and he had no interest in promoting disarmament, especially by so dangerous a method as Operation Candor. Strauss wrote in his memoirs that Candor "would not have advantaged the American public but certainly would have relieved the Soviets of trouble in their espionage activities."[3]

Eisenhower was between Oppenheimer and Strauss in his thinking, "encouraging both without offending either." The President said that Jackson's various drafts (which insiders were calling the "Bang! Bang! papers"), with their descriptions of atomic horrors leaving "everybody dead on both sides with no hope anywhere," were too frightening to serve any useful purpose. "We don't want to scare the country to death," Eisenhower told Jackson, because he was afraid it would set off a congressional demand for outlandish and largely ineffective defense spending. On the other hand, ever since he had read his first report on the initial H-bomb test, he had had an impulse to inform the public about the awesome destructive power thereby unleashed. But each time he read another of Jackson's drafts, the fear of an overreaction by Congress to a "Bang! Bang!" presentation overcame his instinct to tell the truth, and he kept instructing Jackson to tone it down. "Can't we find some hope?" he asked Jackson.[4]

Hope was difficult to locate. Not even the President could find much of it, and he was beginning to despair of ever delivering a Candor speech. He asked Strauss if he could possibly balance the "Bang! Bang!" aspect of the speech with "some kind of equally significant hopeful alternative."[5] Strauss thought not. In September, in Denver, Eisenhower talked to Dulles about it, complaining that "everything was still very vague." Eisenhower wanted to "bring things to a head," to make a "fair offer" to the Russians and then, if it was rejected, face the fact that "we had no alternative but to look upon the Soviet Union as a potential aggressor and make our own plans accordingly."[6]

Later that month, back in Washington, Eisenhower conferred again with Jackson, telling him that any speech on atomic power had to "contain a tremendous lift for the world—for the hopes of men everywhere." Having been rebuffed so many times in his attempts at candor, Jackson was enthusiastic about the prospect of turning from the negative to the positive. He told Eisenhower that the speech "can not only be the most important pronouncement ever made by any President of the United States, it could also save mankind."

At Eisenhower's insistence, Jackson then began hosting a series of breakfast meetings (and in the process changed the code name from Candor to "Operation Wheaties") with Strauss, Beetle Smith, Radford, and Dulles. Together, they came up with a "package." They insisted that any proposal Eisenhower made—the nature was unspecified—must meet three requirements. First, it had to be "new and fresh, and acceptable to the Russians if they possess a shred of reasonableness or desire." Second, it must not lessen the American defensive posture. Third, it must be of such a nature that if the Russians did reject it, or drag their feet, then it would be "clear to the people of the world that we must all prepare for the worst, and that the moral blame for the armaments race, and possibly war, is clearly on the Russians."[7]

Eisenhower mulled it over. The advice he was getting was contradictory and not very helpful. He realized that he would have to come up with an idea of his own for a disarmament proposal, one that would not endanger security, that the Russians would not be likely to dismiss out of hand, and that would contain some genuine hope. Finally he hit on it. The United States and the Soviet Union could, he thought, make donations of isotopes from their nuclear stockpiles to a common fund for peaceful purposes, such as developing nuclear generators. In one stroke, the proposal would solve many problems. It would replace despair over atomic energy with hope; it did not require on-site inspection, always a stumbling block in any disarmament proposal; its propaganda advantages were obvious and overwhelming. Further, it would reassure the American people "that they had not poured their substance into this whole development with the sole purpose of its being used for destruction." Best of all, as Eisenhower wrote in his diary, if the Russians cooperated, "The United States could unquestionably afford to reduce its atomic stockpile by two or three times the amounts that the Russians might contribute . . . and still improve our relative position in the cold war and even in the event of the outbreak of war." Finally, "Underlying all of this, of course, is the clear conviction that as of now the world is racing toward catastrophe."[8]

Eisenhower called in Bobby Cutler of the NSC to discuss the idea with him. After leaving the White House, Cutler wrote Strauss: "The President suggested that you might consider the following proposal which he did not think anyone had yet thought of. . . . Suppose the United States and the Soviets were to turn over to the United Nations for peaceful uses X kilograms of fissionable matter." The Wheaties talks finally had something to plan. Through October and November, Strauss and Jackson worked on the details of the speech.[9]

•   •

Wheaties had just about abandoned the original Candor motivation for the speech, especially any mention of the numbers of bombs in the American arsenal. That bothered Eisenhower, both in the general sense that he had a theoretical commitment to the principle of an informed public, and in the specific sense that he thought the public had to be made aware of the realities of the atomic age. At a stag dinner on November 6, Eisenhower began the after-dinner discussion by expressing "his worry over people's seeming reluctance to recognize the threat of the hydrogen bomb." Dr. Vannevar Bush, head of the wartime science program, "immediately took up the case for scaring the people into a big tax program to build bomb defenses." That was exactly the reaction Eisenhower had feared, and the reason for his opposition to Candor. "Is this all we can do for our children?" he asked. Bill Robinson, who was present, recorded in his diary that "Ike became greatly spirited and said that our great advantage was spiritual strength—this was our greatest offensive and defensive weapon." [10]

Spiritual strength presumably included truth telling, but Eisenhower had not needed to hear Bush's reaction to realize the dangers in telling too much of the truth. That applied to the activities of the CIA as well as to the horrors of nuclear war. Senator Mike Mansfield had introduced a resolution for a Joint Congressional Oversight Committee for the American Clandestine Service. Eisenhower was unalterably opposed to any oversight committee for the CIA. Stuyvesant Wainwright II, a freshman congressman from Long Island, had supported Mansfield. That fall, Eisenhower had Wainwright come to the White House for breakfast. Wainwright recalled that "he told me that this kind of a bill would be passed over his dead body." The President said he was appalled at the thought of letting out the secrets of the CIA. And he was shocked by Wainwright's support for Mansfield, because Wainwright had been on his staff at SHAEF, had been in on the Ultra secret, and should have known better. It was Wainwright's turn to be shocked; he was a very junior member of the SHAEF staff and could recall seeing Eisenhower only four or five times during the war. That Eisenhower remembered him was remarkable. "He had a politician's kind of memory," Wainwright later said.[11] He also had a politician's adroitness; through such private conversations with key congressmen, Eisenhower was able to stave off Mansfield's bill and allow the CIA to continue to operate without interference or publicity.

•   •

With regard to the struggle against the Communist enemy within, Eisenhower definitely did want publicity about his efforts. At Cabinet meetings in late September and early October, the President led a discussion about getting maximum value out of the results of his executive order changing the basis for employment by the government from loyalty to security. How many Communists had been found, he wanted to know, and how many dismissed? Nixon, Brownell, and Summerfield all wanted to make a public announcement that would demonstrate the progress made by the Republicans in finding and eliminating the undesirables. Eisenhower was for it, but he did not want any names released, only numbers, for fear of prejudicing the prospects of dismissed employees.

Eisenhower had another worry. Publicizing numbers was risky. How many employees had been dismissed because of their politics? How many because they were simply excess? The Eisenhower Administration was cutting federal personnel across the board; thousands had been dismissed; surely not all of them were Communists. When Jackson told Eisenhower at an October 2 Cabinet meeting that some twenty-five hundred employees had been dismissed by Commerce alone, Eisenhower interrupted to say, "If we have twenty-five hundred security risks in one office, I'm going to quit!" Jackson then admitted that they were not "all" security risks.[12] Eisenhower also worried about the problem of who was accusing whom within the bureaucracy. He told Brownell to take a long look at any accusation coming from an ex-Communist. The Communists, he explained, "are such liars and cheats that even when they apparently recant and later testify against someone else for his Communist convictions, my first reaction is to believe that the accused person must be a patriot or he wouldn't have incurred the enmity of such people." Eisenhower told Brownell to "search out some positive way to put ourselves on the side of individual right and liberty as well as on the side of fighting Communism to the death."[13]

Brownell finally came up with a figure on the number of security risks fired by the Administration, and on October 23 Hagerty announced on behalf of the President that 1,456 persons had been driven from the federal payroll. A numbers game ensued. Were they all spies? reporters asked Hagerty. No, Hagerty replied, he had not said that. Were they all Communists? No, not exactly, but they were all security risks. At this point McCarthy jumped into the game; it all proved, he declared, that the Truman Administration had been "crawling with Communists."[14]

Fear of McCarthy then prompted the President and the Attorney General to ignore the basic principles Eisenhower had set forth, such as ignoring accusations made by ex-Communists and giving every man a fair hearing. In an effort to prove that McCarthy and his friends could trust Eisenhower to carry out the hunt for Communists, Brownell decided—with Eisenhower's approval—to go after Truman himself by reviving the case of Harry Dexter White. Back in 1946, ex-Communists Whittaker Chambers and Elizabeth Bentley had accused White, an official in the Treasury Department, of being a Russian spy. White denied it and a federal grand jury refused to indict him. The FBI, however, had sent further evidence about White to Truman. Truman read the FBI report and decided it contained only the evidence offered by "a crook and a louse" (Chambers and Bentley). The only thing new was a charge that White had shown "friendliness to Russia" during the war. Truman dismissed the charges from his mind, and indeed promoted White (who died of a heart attack in 1948).[15]

Brownell looked through the record (evidently prodded by J. Edgar Hoover) and decided that Truman was wrong. Brownell felt that the record showed White to be clearly guilty, and he could not understand how Truman could have promoted the man after reading the record. Brownell met with Eisenhower. He told the President the case was too important to cover up, that he felt a personal obligation to make it public, and that "disclosure was justified political criticism and that it would take away some of the glamour of the McCarthy stage play." Eisenhower told him to go ahead.[16]

On November 6, Brownell told the Executives Club in Chicago that on the eve of White's promotion, the FBI had sent a report to the White House that proved White was a Soviet spy. He said that the White case was "illustrative of why the present Administration is faced with the problem of disloyalty in government," and charged that it was "typical of the blindness which infected the former Administration on this matter."[17] Chairman Velde then served a subpoena on Truman, calling on him to appear before HUAC. Truman denied that he had ever seen a report on White and, citing the constitutional separation of powers, loftily refused to appear before HUAC.

Eisenhower strongly supported Truman on the matter of the subpoena. He called Brownell the next morning and told him he deplored what Velde was doing and wanted it stopped. He also told Brownell that Dulles had done some searching and could prove that Truman had indeed read the report; nevertheless he informed Brownell that he intended to emphasize that no one had said Truman had personally seen the file, only that it had been sent to the White House "for delivery to the President." If Truman said he had not seen it, Eisenhower was not going to contradict him. He did tell Hagerty to correct Truman's statement that "as soon as we found out White was disloyal we fired him." Hagerty reminded the press that in fact Truman had promoted White *after* the FBI report was delivered to the White House.[18]

Then it was Eisenhower's turn to face the press. The media was obsessed with the subject, because of its sensational nature. In effect, Eisenhower had accused Truman, through Brownell, of not only harboring but actually promoting a known Communist spy. The reporters put Eisenhower through one of the most difficult news conferences of his eight years in office. It lasted but nineteen minutes, and every question dealt with White. All were hostile. Later that day, Eisenhower told his Cabinet he was "amazed at the press unanimity in leaping to the defense of Truman and White. They were prosecutors, I was defendant."[19] He was asked if he thought Truman "knowingly appointed a Communist spy to high office." "No, it is inconceivable," Eisenhower replied. Well, then, Ray Brandt asked, "Do you think the Administration's action in virtually putting a label of traitor on a former President is likely to damage our foreign relations?" "I reject the premise," Eisenhower replied, "I would not answer such a question." Anthony Leviero of *The New York Times* told the President, "I think this case is at best a pretty squalid one." White had had his day in court and had been found innocent, Leviero said. Under those circumstances, "Is it proper for the Attorney General to characterize that accused man, who is now dead, as a spy and, in effect, accuse a former President of harboring that man?" Eisenhower said to put that question to Brownell. Leviero responded that Brownell refused to see the press. Other reporters wanted to know when the new evidence would be released, and what it consisted of. Eisenhower's patience broke. "Ladies and gentlemen," he broke in, "I am going to answer my last question right now on this subject. I told you exactly, Mr. Brownell came in and reported to me. He said the evidence was so clear that he considered it his duty to lay it out. 'I am not going to be a party to concealing this' is the way he explained it to me. I said, 'You have to follow your own conscience as to your duty.' Now that is exactly what I know about it."[20]

That afternoon, in a Cabinet meeting, Eisenhower asked Brownell how convincing was the evidence in the report; the President added that what he had seen had not convinced him, and pointed out that "friendliness toward Russia" during and immediately after the war was hardly proof. Indeed, he himself had been friendly toward Russia at that time. Brownell said he had four sources, not just Chambers and Bentley, "and papers in White's handwriting." Brownell added, "We got much more against White than against Hiss." Eisenhower reminded him that "they never proved more than perjury against Hiss." Eisenhower then tried to reassure himself that the case was important enough to warrant all the attention; he said the fact that the Democrats were "scared" proved it.[21]

Then it was Truman's turn to contradict himself and get caught in his own maze of half-truths and outright falsehoods. On national television, Truman said that the Eisenhower Administration had "fully embraced, for political advantage, McCarthyism," which he called "this evil at every level of our national life." Turning to the White case, Truman now admitted that he had indeed read the report, but he did not say that he had decided to disregard it. Instead he claimed that he had entered into a plot with J. Edgar Hoover. They would keep White on the job because firing him would tip off others under surveillance who were a part of White's spy team. (Hoover immediately denied such a deal ever existed.) Then Truman completely contradicted himself by arguing for White's innocence, citing as proof the failure of the federal grand jury to indict White. In a diary entry, Truman left no doubt that he believed White to be innocent; in his scathing view, "convicting a dead man of treason on a communist F.B.I. report is in line with present administration policy."[22]

At the height of the furor, the Eisenhowers were able to escape Washington and spend Thanksgiving in Augusta. John, Barbara, and the grandchildren were there, along with Eisenhower's gang. Mamie's cottage was ready, it was delightful, and she loved it. Priscilla Slater wrote in her diary that Mamie "spends the mornings in bed but sees everyone passing through the open venetian blinds. Sociable, gregarious and warmhearted, she seldom lets anyone pass without calling him in . . ." Eisenhower, meanwhile, was busy cooking breakfast for his grandchildren, or was otherwise "active every minute, trying to crowd in as many games of golf, hours of fishing, fun with the children, and bridge with his friends as he can . . ." Cliff Roberts complained that he was exhausted after eighteen holes of golf and wanted to stretch out to rest, when Moaney appeared to announce, "The Boss is ready to play bridge!"

That evening the women played bolivia while the men played

bridge. Mrs. Slater took some mental notes on Mamie, later recording them in her diary. Mamie, she wrote, "has great concentration powers, a good memory, and is sharp and alert. She is feminine, really luscious looking, dainty and loveable, appealing in an almost childlike way. [She is] a very efficient wife, mother and hostess, who has her fingers on every detail of her part of the tremendous role of being the First Lady. She is tactful, but no individual would impose upon her more than once. She has a forceful personality, but her warmth and affectionate regard for her friends more than makes up for her decisiveness."

The following day, when Bill Robinson saw young David Eisenhower playing with his grandfather, he suggested that David looked like presidential timber. "Ike said feelingly, 'Oh, no! Be kind to him.'"[23]

When Eisenhower returned to Washington, he discovered that the price he and Brownell had to pay for digging up Harry Dexter White was going higher. Eisenhower had told the reporters that Brownell would supply evidence of White's guilt, but Brownell objected to releasing FBI files, because he feared the consequences of setting such a precedent. Eisenhower told Brownell, over the telephone, to say, "We long ago decided that the records of the Departments would be opened up more widely to the public, and I used this case to illustrate the kind of laxity, of what appeared to us to be indefensible."[24]

Fortunately for Brownell, interest in the White case disappeared, to be replaced at center stage by Joe McCarthy. The senator from Wisconsin demanded and got equal time from the national TV networks to reply to Truman's presentation. McCarthy used some of his time to denounce Truman, but he also declared that "the raw, harsh, unpleasant fact is that Communism is an issue and will be an issue in 1954." This directly contradicted Eisenhower, who had said in his news conference that "he hoped the Communist-in-government question would not be an issue in the 1954 congressional campaign." Eisenhower's aides thought McCarthy's contradicting Eisenhower so directly was a part of a bid by McCarthy to take control of the Republican Party. Hagerty said McCarthy's motive was to make himself the issue in 1954, and then the candidate in 1956. He called McCarthy's speech "sheer fascism." Jackson was furious. He told James Reston that McCarthy's speech was "a declaration of war against the President."[25] But still the President refused to denounce McCarthy.

Jackson was almost distraught. "All the vague feelings of un-happiness I have had regarding 'lack of leadership' over the past many months, which I have always put down, really bounced up this week, and I am very frightened." He warned the staff that "this Three Little Monkeys act was not working." On December 1, at a press-conference briefing, Jackson wrote out a statement on McCarthy for the President to read to the reporters. Eisenhower read the draft, Jackson recorded in his diary, "with visible irritation, and made some mumbling comments." Jack Martin, a former assistant to Taft who had recently joined the White House staff, "pitched in with great courage and said that a vacuum existed in this country, and it was a political vacuum, and unless the President filled it somebody else would fill it." Jackson wrote that Eisenhower "twisted and squirmed." Jackson told the President that "the people were waiting for a sign, and a simple sign—and now was the time." Eisenhower read the text again, "slammed it back at me and said he would not refer to Mc-Carthy personally—'I will not get in the gutter with that guy.'"[26]

What Eisenhower was willing to do was read to the news con-ference a paragraph repeating that Communism in government would not be an issue in 1954. "Long before then," Eisenhower said, "this Administration will have made such progress in rooting them out that this can no longer be considered a serious menace." He then asserted that "about fifteen hundred persons who were security risks have al-ready been removed."[27]

And with that, he hoped, he had put McCarthy behind him, at least for now. But as he often said, McCarthyism was around long before McCarthy, and he predicted that it would outlast the senator. At the height of the furor over McCarthy's bid to define the issues of 1954, Eisenhower got a telephone call from Wilson, who said that he had yet another report. This one was on Oppenheimer. It consisted of a letter from William Borden, the former director of the Joint Congressional Committee on Atomic Energy, to the Secretary of De-fense. Borden charged that it was "more likely than not that J. Robert Oppenheimer is a Communist spy." Borden had no new evidence to substantiate this charge, which had been around a long time, had been investigated, was widely known, and was widely disbelieved. What disturbed Wilson—and Eisenhower—was not so much what Borden was saying, but that McCarthy had become aware of the charges. It was imperative that the Administration act before Mc-Carthy made the Oppenheimer charges *his* case.

The following morning, December 3, Eisenhower convened Strauss, Brownell, Wilson, Cutler, and Allen Dulles in the Oval Office. Eisenhower demanded to know how on earth Strauss could have cleared Oppenheimer for the AEC back in 1947, and why there had been no investigation of him since the Republicans took office. Strauss muttered that they could not have built the atomic bomb without Oppenheimer. Eisenhower then said that while he "wished to make it plain that he was not in any way prejudging the matter," he wanted a "blank wall" placed between Oppenheimer and any further access to top-secret information until such time as a hearing had been completed. He told Brownell to get the entire FBI file on Oppenheimer and study it. He said he had himself examined the Borden charges and thought they provided "no evidence that implies disloyalty on the part of Dr. Oppenheimer." However, Eisenhower added, "this does not mean that he might not be a security risk." Eisenhower said he realized that if Oppenheimer had been feeding information to the Soviets, then cutting him off at this point "would not be a case of merely locking the stable door after the horse is gone; it would be more like trying to find a door for a burned-down stable."[28] He appointed a three-man committee to investigate the charges; Oppenheimer meanwhile was put into a state of suspension; McCarthy was blocked from exploiting the case.

Simultaneously with the White incident, McCarthy's challenge, and the Oppenheimer case, Eisenhower had to deal with the segregation cases coming up before the Supreme Court. Unhappy with the idea of the Attorney General expressing his opinion on the unconstitutionality of segregation in the schools, Eisenhower nevertheless accepted Brownell's advice that it had to be done. Indeed, he helped Brownell write his opinion. Still he worried. As always when he got back from Augusta, Eisenhower was full of sympathy for the white southerners' point of view. He asked Brownell what would happen if the southern states abandoned public education, as Byrnes and others were threatening to do. Brownell said he would try to convince Byrnes that the Court would give the South "a period of years" to adjust, so "he wouldn't have to declare war so to speak." Eisenhower repeated his fear that the Court would make education a function of the federal government. Brownell assured him that the South "will work it out in ten to twelve years."[29]

Byrnes came up to Washington for further talks with the President, who later, on December 1, wrote the South Carolina governor.

Eisenhower said he recognized the "very serious problems" the South had to face. He warned Byrnes that the last-minute southern attempt to put some money into Negro schools, so that there could be some appearance of the "equal" to go with the "separate" in *Plessy,* was going to involve "extraordinary expenditures." And he wondered just who would decide "when facilities were exactly equal." Then, knowing full well that Brownell was that day expressing to the Court his opinion that segregation was unconstitutional, Eisenhower nevertheless told Byrnes that in rendering any opinion Brownell would be acting according to "his own conviction and understanding." The President assured Byrnes that he himself was disassociated from the case.[30]

On December 2, Brownell told Eisenhower that Justice Warren "told me last night that my brief on the segregation cases was outstanding."[31] Eisenhower made it clear that he wanted no part for himself in the compliment. He had begun the process of refusing to associate himself and his prestige in any way with *Brown* v. *Topeka.*

The level of post-Korea defense spending continued to be a problem. In October, to Eisenhower's great irritation, Wilson leaked to the press the Administration's plans to sharply reduce personnel. The Europeans, fearing reduction in American combat strength in NATO, immediately protested to Gruenther (who had risen to the position of SACEUR), who passed along their alarm to Eisenhower. In response, Eisenhower began by complaining about Wilson, saying that "some people have more trouble in controlling their tongues than they do their wives." But he also told Gruenther to remind his European friends that the stationing of American troops in Europe was always intended to be on a "temporary or emergency" basis. When Eisenhower was SACEUR, he had frequently expressed the hope that American boys could go home in three or four years. Now he reminded Gruenther that the United States could neither build nor afford to maintain "a sort of Roman Wall to protect the world." He also worried about the troops themselves; how long, he wondered, before European gratitude for their presence would turn to hostility toward foreign troops on their soil.[32]

When Gruenther passed along some more European criticism, Eisenhower began to lose his temper. "I get weary of the European habit of taking our money," the President wrote, "resenting any slight hint as to what *they* should do, and then assuming, in addition, full right to criticize us as bitterly as they may desire. In fact, it sometimes appears that their indulgence in this kind of criticism varies in direct ratio to the amount of help we give them." In fact, the whole thing made him mad as hell, and "makes me wonder whether the Europeans are as grown up and mature as they try to make it appear."[33]

Eisenhower decided to go ahead with his cuts, despite the Europeans. At a November 11 meeting with Dulles, Humphrey, and Wilson, he agreed with Dulles' recommendation that the United States should begin to withdraw ground troops from Korea. Such an act would both save money and "show confidence in our air and naval strength." Further, Eisenhower ordered reductions in service and support units in Europe; he wanted them "skeletonized." He also wanted manpower reductions in the Navy. To balance these cuts, he ordered a continuation of nuclear weapons' production at the rate of one per day.[34] He noted in his diary, "The dependence that we are placing on new weapons [will] justify completely some reduction in conventional forces."[35]

The JCS was unhappy (even the Air Force was scheduled to take some cuts in personnel). Eisenhower, in a long memorandum to Budget Director Dodge, met their objections. "We are no longer fighting in Korea," the President declared, "and the defense establishment should show its appreciation of this fact and help us achieve some substantial savings—and without wailing about the missions they have to accomplish." As an old-timer at the Pentagon, the President said he was sure that "if they put their hearts into it, they can make substantial savings with little damage to the long-term efficiency of the establishment." Then Eisenhower warned Dodge not to expect any dramatic changes for fiscal '55 in procurement costs, which were pretty well fixed. That made personnel savings even more essential; Eisenhower said he was going to tell Wilson to "place everything except a few units on an austerity basis."[36]

At a mid-December meeting with the Republican congressional leaders, Eisenhower explained his strategy. "The things we really need are the things that the other fellow looks at and respects," he declared. The Russians did not respect the handful of American divisions in Europe, but they did respect the bomb. Eisenhower said the United States "must take risks in certain areas," and "must make a long-term effort," so that "we do not get to the point where we must attack or demobilize." Asia-firsters among the Old Guard congressmen protested against the planned reductions in ground strength in Korea. Eisenhower told them that he did not believe "Korea will be stabilized greatly by the continued presence of ground troops. We must put more dependence on air." He said that if the Communists broke the armistice, "we go all out" in nuclear retaliation.[37] At the end of December, while Wilson was reducing the 3.5-million-man armed forces to under 3 million, Eisenhower announced the withdrawal of two American combat divisions from Korea.[38] He was putting his own stamp on defense policy; that stamp was a stronger emphasis on nuclear retaliatory power.

But, as always, Eisenhower also expected help from his allies. By December, the time had come to meet with his two principal allies, Churchill and Premier Laniel of France. Indeed, Eisenhower had been scheduled to meet with them in June, but then Churchill became ill; by the time he had recovered, the French were in the midst of another change-of-government crisis, and the meeting had twice been postponed. The Russians had added to the pressure for consultation by calling for four-power talks at the Foreign Ministers' level. The British and the French wanted to hold such a meeting. Dulles did not. On December 2, two days before the Western Allies met in Bermuda, Ann Whitman made notes on Dulles' advice to the President on four-power talks. "He says the Russians are going to stress that you can never have peace until Red China is brought into the council of great nations; that they will attack the United States for having bases on other countries' territory as being a war threat; will attack NATO as being warmongering." Dulles doubted that "anything constructive" could come out of such a meeting; he thought the real question was "how do you get it over with with as little damage as possible." Eisenhower disagreed. He was ready to try, if only "to convince public opinion of our good faith."[39]

The following day, December 3, Eisenhower met with the NSC and obtained from it a statement of policy on the exchange of atomic information with allied countries. Eisenhower had long disapproved of the McMahon Act of 1946, which forbade the sharing of atomic information with foreign nations. Britain had played a major role in the Manhattan Project, had since the war developed its own atomic bomb, and remained America's staunchest ally. The British could go much faster and farther with their atomic arsenal if the Americans would provide them with the results of their research. Eisenhower wanted to do it. He also wanted more Anglo-American sharing of atomic weapons, means of delivery, and strategy. The kind of mutual cooperation he had created at SHAEF was his goal. He therefore had the NSC agree that after appropriate revision of the McMahon Act, "the

United States should increase its disclosure to selected allied governments of information in the atomic energy field." The "objectives of
greater disclosure" included point 2.b: "Inspire them to act with the
United States in crises and thus give the United States greater freedom
of action to use atomic weapons as required." Other points were to
gain access to uranium ore and to benefit from the results of British
research.

This statement of policy, called NSC 151/1, then spelled out in
some detail the extent of sharing Eisenhower was willing to do. He
wanted to inform the NATO allies "of the existence of a family of
weapons ranging from relatively small yields to the very large," and
to inform them in a general way about the total American nuclear
force "available for tactical support of NATO forces in the event of
war." He wanted them informed about the targets. What he would
not do was to give them information "concerning the manufacture
and design of atomic weapons," or any figures on the total U.S. arsenal, "existing or past."[40]

With NSC 151/1 adopted, Eisenhower was ready for Bermuda.
He wanted to talk to Churchill and Laniel about his Wheaties speech,
scheduled for the U.N. General Assembly later that week, about
atomic sharing, and about EDC. Churchill wanted to talk about British problems in Egypt and Jordan. Laniel wanted to talk about Vietnam. Eisenhower thought both European leaders were just hopeless
on these colonial questions. In the President's view, they were simply
blind to the strength of nationalism as a force, and he feared that
their refusal to meet demands for self-government would lead to the
loss of the Third World to Communism. So he did not want to talk
about colonial problems. He insisted, instead, that they go into the
talks without an agenda, and that the talks be informal throughout.

Eisenhower did not look forward to a high-level meeting with
Churchill. The Prime Minister was deaf, he could hardly keep awake
in the afternoon, he refused to face reality, either about his age or
about Britain's position in the world. ("In many ways," Eisenhower
told his Cabinet, "he's just a little Peter Pan."[41]) Eden was growing
old waiting for Churchill to face facts and retire, and he was beginning to show his irritation. But if Eisenhower could get Churchill's
prestige behind his idea for an international atomic energy pool, putting up with the old man for a few days would be worth it.

Churchill surprised Eisenhower. As the meeting was on British
soil, he was the host, and a most gracious one—the British put on a
grand show of pomp and pageantry. In the restricted sessions (heads

of government and Foreign Ministers only), Churchill stayed alert, made his contribution, and gave his support. He listened carefully as Eisenhower explained his idea. Eisenhower wanted to bring the British in on it; he suggested that "we might put in a thousand kilos, the U.S.S.R. two hundred, and the U.K. forty." The material could then be made available "to the scientists of the world to use for practical purposes." Eisenhower fairly glowed as he explained his high hopes: "We know that atomic energy could be used to generate power, to run tractors—in fact, we have a ship ready to run—its engine was built. This was very expensive, but scientists might find a way to make it cheaper. It had great capabilities in the medical field, in the field of agriculture, and tremendous possibilities if used peacefully instead of for destruction."

Eisenhower saw other advantages to his idea. It would "make other nations feel they had a stake in all this. Men needed power everywhere. If we could give hope, it would give these nations a stronger feeling of participation in the struggle of East and West, and such a feeling of participation would be on our side, and hope might be engendered from a fairly insignificant start." Eisenhower then gave the latest draft of his Wheaties speech to Churchill and Laniel, asking them to consider it very secret, because "he had not yet even made a definite decision as to whether the talk would be given." Churchill responded to the flattery. He read the draft, then said he found the whole concept to be splendid and pitched in enthusiastically. He made a number of editorial changes, and recommended deleting two passages that were unnecessarily provocative.[42]

Eisenhower, Dulles, and Jackson then got on the airplane for the flight to New York and the General Assembly appearance. Eisenhower incorporated Churchill's suggestions; Ann Whitman frantically typed the last version; as the plane circled New York to give them enough time to finish the job, Dulles and Jackson ran the mimeograph machine to make advance copies for the press.

At 2 P.M. on December 8, Eisenhower gave his "Atoms for Peace" speech to the General Assembly. After opening words of praise for the U.N., Eisenhower launched into the Candor part of his speech. It was much reduced from his original intention. He informed the world that the United States had conducted forty-two test explosions since 1945, that America's atomic bombs were now twenty-five times more powerful than the original bombs used against Japan, "while hydrogen weapons are in the ranges of millions of tons of TNT equivalent."

Oppenheimer's and Jackson's thought that the President ought to reveal the size of the American arsenal gave way to this paragraph: "Today, the United States stockpile of atomic weapons, which, of course, increases daily, exceeds by many times the explosive equivalent of the total of all bombs and all shells that came from every plane and every gun in every theater of war in all of the years of World War II." Eisenhower gave one additional illustration: "A single air group can now deliver to any reachable target a destructive cargo exceeding in power all the bombs that fell on Britain in all of World War II." Atomic weapons, he added, had now achieved "virtually conventional status within our armed services."

But the Russians also had the bomb, and were building more. An atomic arms race was under way. To continue it, Eisenhower said, "would be to confirm the hopeless finality of a belief that two atomic colossi are doomed malevolently to eye each other indefinitely across a trembling world." Anything would be better. Eisenhower asserted that he was prepared to meet with the Soviets (and he announced that the four-power talks the Russians had requested would begin promptly) to discuss such problems as an Austrian treaty, Korea, and Germany, as well as disarmament.

In such talks, Eisenhower said, the United States "would seek more than the mere reduction or elimination of atomic materials for military purposes." It was not enough "to take this weapon out of the hands of the soldiers. It must be put into the hands of those who will know how . . . to adapt it to the arts of peace." Then, "this greatest of destructive forces can be developed into a great boon, for the benefit of all mankind."

Eisenhower thereupon made his specific proposal. The U.S., the U.K., and the U.S.S.R. should make joint contributions from their stockpiles of fissionable materials to an International Atomic Energy Agency. That agency would be set up under the aegis of the U.N. He recognized that initial contributions would be small, but "the proposal has the great virtue that it can be undertaken without the irritations and mutual suspicions incident to any attempt to set up a completely acceptable system of worldwide inspection and control."

The proposed agency would draw on the talents of scientists from all over the world, who would study ways to use atomic energy for peaceful activities. "A special purpose would be to provide abundant electrical energy in the power-starved areas of the world. Thus the contributing powers would be dedicating some of their strength to serve the needs rather than the fears of mankind." He outlined other advantages inherent in his proposal: a reduction in the world's atomic stockpile dedicated to destruction; proof that the superpowers were "interested in human aspirations first"; and the opening of "a new channel of peaceful discussion." He closed with a pledge: The United States was ready "to devote its entire heart and mind to find the way by which the miraculous inventiveness of man shall not be dedicated to his death, but consecrated to his life."[43]

Eisenhower had not been interrupted once by applause, and when he finished there was dead silence. Then the thirty-five hundred delegates began to cheer—even the Russians joined in—in an outburst of enthusiasm unprecedented in U.N. history. Outside the Communist countries, world reaction was overwhelmingly positive and even extravagant. Eisenhower appeared to have cut the Gordian knot. He had replaced fear with hope.

But the Russians stalled. They gave no immediate response, nor did they respond during the next year, or the next. Not until 1957 was an International Atomic Energy Agency created. By that time, the arms race had moved on to new levels and such an agency was irrelevant to current problems.

A great opportunity had been lost. Eisenhower's proposal of atoms for peace was the most generous and the most serious offer on controlling the arms race ever made by an American President. All previous offers, and all that followed, contained clauses about on-site inspection that the Americans knew in advance were unacceptable to the Russians. But it was the strength of Eisenhower's proposal, the measure of his genius, and the proof of his readiness to try something new to get out of the arms race that atoms for peace seemed to have a real chance of acceptance. It was not loaded against the Russians. Eisenhower believed that, to the contrary, the proposal *had* to be tempting to them. He hoped they would accept it and he thought that they would.

They did not. The Communists allowed their suspicions to override their judgment. They felt, evidently, that a reduction of their stockpile of fissionable matter would only widen the American lead. They were right, of course, and indeed Eisenhower had made that point in his diary and in selling the idea to Churchill. But Eisenhower had proposed contributions at a level of five American units to one Russian, and that was only a starting figure, open to negotiation. Still the Russians were not interested. They let the numbers frighten them. The United States might get two or three thousand bombs ahead of them.

Thus did the logic of the nuclear arms race take over. It was a logic unique to itself, with no connection to experience or reality. Everyone agreed that the sole purpose of making atomic weapons was to deter the enemy from aggression. All agreed that to deter you need only be in a position to threaten to destroy one major city. (Eisenhower once told this author, "There is nothing in the world that the Communists want badly enough to risk losing the Kremlin.") Why then build arsenals of thousands of bombs, when a few hundred would be more than enough to make the threat meaningful? At this point the numbers game took over. Strategists and leaders on both sides were terrified at the thought of the other side getting too far ahead. Eisenhower and the Americans wanted—demanded—a clear American superiority. How they would use that lead—except to insure deterrence, which could be assured with one hundred bombs anyway—they did not know. For their part, the Russians could not accept such a huge American advantage. They were determined to close the gap, if not catch up. Like the Americans, they did not know what they were going to do with all those bombs. They only knew they wanted them.

So they spurned Eisenhower's proposed atoms-for-peace plan. It was a true tragedy. With only a bit of exaggeration, it can be said that Eisenhower's proposal was the best chance mankind has had in the nuclear age to slow and redirect the arms race. Had the Russians put their own enthusiasm into it, it is possible to project an idyllic scenario: a generation of money, energy, and scientific skill going into peaceful uses for the atom, with both sides content to maintain but not add to their existing arsenals. To Eisenhower, the worst possible outcome, as he looked ahead in 1953, would have been a continuation of the numbers game, only by the 1980s at a level of tens of thousands of bombs, and with peaceful uses of atomic power generally unexploited, or—when in place—highly controversial and expensive. But that is exactly how it turned out.

Part of the blame is Eisenhower's. He played the numbers game in nuclear weapons vigorously, although not so vigorously as all the JCS, nearly all Democrats, and most Republicans wanted him to. Atoms for peace was his one great bid to get out of what he knew was a losing game. He had pride of authorship in the original idea, which added to his depression when the Russians stalled on the proposal. He thought his idea was worth a try, and the lack of Russian response made him harden his attitude toward the Soviet Union. He had been rebuffed on the major goal of his Presidency. His attempt to explore a new approach to arms control was never even tried. That was the sad result of atoms for peace.

In December 1953, Eisenhower had little time to gauge reaction to his speech, because he had to descend from the rarefied atmosphere of a peace talk before the U.N. to the level of hard-core American domestic politics. Congress would soon be back in session; he needed to finish work on his first budget (fiscal 1955) and prepare his legislative program. In November, he had outlined a part of that program for Dodge, for Dodge's use in making up the budget. Eisenhower said he wanted "to put ourselves clearly on record as being forward-looking and concerned with the welfare of all our people." He said Dodge should budget for slum clearance and public housing, for dams on the western rivers, for the extension of Social Security, and for public housing. Eisenhower was even ready to accept "a few *small* public-works projects."[44]

The Old Guard senators wanted none of this program, nor of Eisenhower's request for MSA funds or other projects. They did want the Bricker Amendment. Beyond the Old Guard, Eisenhower was having trouble with Republicans generally, who were furious with Sherman Adams for not handing out enough jobs fast enough for their deserving constituents. Eisenhower could not get them interested in anything beyond Bricker and patronage, and certainly not in his middle-of-the-road program. The Republicans, Eisenhower complained to Emmet Hughes, "did not look upon the results of the election as the threshold of opportunity; rather it was the end of a long and searing drought, and they were at last reveling again in luxurious patronage."[45]

Eisenhower professed to hate the very word "patronage," but he was ready to use it to pursue greater goals. The difficulty was that the Democrats had managed to protect nearly everyone in government through Civil Service. At a mid-December Cabinet meeting, Eisenhower told Phil Young, a Columbia dean who had taken over as head of the Civil Service, that one way to get rid of a Democrat was to "transfer him around until he's sick of it." Eisenhower said that when he was Chief of Staff, "we had a general who didn't want to retire. After we got through with him, he was ready!!!" He also told Young that it was "better to abolish a job than keep an opponent in it."[46]

The next week, Eisenhower told the Cabinet that he was sick and tired of Republicans who opposed his programs coming to him to demand patronage. "From here on," he declared, he was going to say to such men, "either you're for the Administration program or not. If not, expect no more help from us, no patronage, no nothing." The Cabinet applauded this tough stance. Eisenhower immediately retreated. "Now I don't want to put it up as an ultimatum," he said.[47]

The week before Christmas, Eisenhower held a three-day meeting with Republican congressional leaders. He wanted to talk about his program for the upcoming session; they wanted to talk about Bricker and patronage. Again and again the Republican leaders told Eisenhower that "if we could get the Bricker Amendment through quickly it would be the most helpful thing." The President would mumble that he hoped they could get an agreed-upon (that is, meaningless) wording, so that he could support it. Congressman William Miller of New York then charged that the "Interior Department is still being sabotaged by rabid New Dealers." He thought Eisenhower should "fire Phil Young." Eisenhower snapped back, "I told you, Mr. Miller, I love to have your advice but when it comes to picking my assistants, I pick them." Miller rejoined, "And I told you my advice was I would fire Young."

After three days of such pounding, Eisenhower frankly confessed to the group, "My greatest troubles come up within the Republican Party." He spit out the word "patronage." He said, "I'll be damned if I know how the Republicans ever held a party together all these years." He said he "used to go on the theory that the Republicans had quite a bit of brains." After the ordeal was over, he scribbled in his diary, "Impressions of three-day conference. Amount of caution, approaching fright, that seems to govern the actions of most politicians."[48]

It was a gloomy onset of winter for Eisenhower. He had had the distasteful business of Oppenheimer to deal with, and the challenge from McCarthy, and the misguided effort to revive the White case. The Russians were stalling on atoms for peace. And the Republicans were impossible. So impossible that he told Bill Robinson, as Robinson recorded it in his diary, "that if the die-hard Republicans fight his program too hard, he may have to organize a third party. Later he smiled ruefully, saying that could, of course, be an impractical alternative but he wasn't ready to abandon the idea."[49]

To Milton, Eisenhower expressed his personal feelings. Referring to the 1956 presidential election, he said "if ever for a second time I should show any signs of yielding to persuasion to run, please call in the psychiatrist—or even better the sheriff."[50] That was before the meeting with the Republican leaders; after it ended, Eisenhower told

Swede Hazlett, "I shall never again be a candidate for anything. This determination is a fixed decision." He told Swede his first choice for his successor was Milton, but he did not want to have any part in establishing a dynasty, and in any case Milton was not "physically strong enough to take the beating." Eisenhower therefore was going to build up some of the younger men on his team. He said he could support Lodge, Nixon, Brownell, Stassen, or a number of others, and he wanted to put all of them in the spotlight so that the Republicans wolud have a well-trained, well-known candidate for 1956.[51]

After Christmas at Augusta, Eisenhower returned to the White House, where on New Year's Eve he replied to a suggestion from C. D. Jackson. Jackson had advised him to follow up on atoms for peace with proposals for complete atomic disarmament. That was far beyond anything Eisenhower was willing to do. He said that before making any such proposal, "I should like to discuss just what would be the effect on us and our position if atomic weapons could be wholly eliminated from the world's armaments." What, in other words, would then stop the Red Army from marching across the Elbe? Eisenhower also told Jackson, "The mere argument that because we are ahead of the Russians in atomic weapons that this one phase of our armament activity should be pushed to the limit, must be taken into account."[52]

That was the dilemma that left Eisenhower alternately encouraged and discouraged that New Year's Eve. He had brought about peace in Korea—but only through the implied threat to use atomic weapons. He anticipated major reductions in the defense budget—but only by putting increasing reliance on an ever-expanding nuclear arsenal. The prospective balanced budget would mean prosperity, stability, and lower taxes—at the cost of a nuclear arms race. There was the dilemma. A nuclear arms race was the cheapest way to counter the Russian military threat, but it was simultaneously the most dangerous. The arsenal could not be used, it could only grow and grow. With no response from the Russians on atoms for peace, and seeing no incentive for America in atomic disarmament, Eisenhower knew he was stuck. "Those horrible things," as he called them, would dominate his Presidency. His attempt to persuade the Russians to turn the direction of atomic research and stockpiling from destructive to constructive purposes, so brilliantly and sincerely expressed in "Atoms for Peace," had failed. It was most discouraging.

CHAPTER SEVEN

Bricker, McCarthy, Bravo, Vietnam

January 1–May 7, 1954

AT THE BEGINNING of the new year, C. D. Jackson, who was about to leave the Administration to return to Time-Life (Emmet Hughes had already done so), wrote that he thought Eisenhower had grown immensely in the past year as a professional politician, but added that "he is still mystified in a sincere and uncomplicated way at the maneuvers of politicians."[1] The politicians who mystified Eisenhower most were those senators, a majority of the whole, who supported the Bricker Amendment. Through the winter of 1953–1954, the amendment dominated the political news. It went through a complex and incomprehensible series of changes, as various senators struggled to find a precise wording that would satisfy both the President and Bricker. But the substance remained. Bricker insisted that executive agreements, such as Yalta, would be regulated by Congress, and that treaties "shall become effective as internal law in the United States only through legislation which would be valid in the absence of a treaty." Eisenhower told the Republican leaders on January 11 that no one knew enough about what the amendment meant to talk about it with any authority, and "probably less than one percent are familiar with the basic issues involved."[2]

Eisenhower's position was clear; he opposed any amendment that would reduce the President's power to conduct foreign policy. On January 14, Eisenhower told Hagerty he was going to start "calling names—say this was stupid, a blind violation of the Constitution by

154

stupid, blind isolationists."[3] When Edgar Eisenhower wrote a letter strongly supporting the amendment, Eisenhower replied that he would not normally answer a letter so filled with "hackneyed criticisms and accusations palpably based on misinformation and deliberate distortion." But he said he was replying to Edgar because he was so disturbed to find that Edgar believed "that I am a poor, helpless, ignorant, uninformed individual, thrust to dizzy heights of responsibility, who has been captured by a band of conniving 'internationalists.' "[4] Similar letters, although less strong and angry, went to his rich friends who supported Bricker.

At his meetings with Republican leaders, Eisenhower emphasized his "utter opposition" to the amendment. He also tried to educate the Republicans. The amendment, he declared, could never have stopped Yalta, because at Yalta the President had been acting as Commander in Chief during time of war. He said he wished FDR had not been so "indiscreet and crazy,"[5] and claimed that he had told Roosevelt that he did not have the right to make decisions that properly belonged in the peace treaty, but still he insisted that the Bricker Amendment could not have stopped the process. Gene Millikin of Colorado said the amendment was a step in the right direction, nevertheless, and insisted that "no one ever got to heaven in one jump." Eisenhower snapped back, "There's a lot of stairs." Nixon wanted to find a substitute amendment that would be acceptable to Eisenhower, and advised the President, "As in any battle, you need a second line of retreat." Eisenhower replied, "No, Dick, you need two to go ahead, only one to retreat."[6]

In February, there was a series of votes on various forms of the amendment. Eisenhower agonized through every one of them (one substitute motion came within a single vote of adoption by two-thirds of the Senate). Eisenhower used all his persuasive powers—in stag dinners, at meetings, in private, in correspondence, even on the golf course—to kill the amendment. He hated wasting his time on Bricker; early in February, he told Hagerty, "If it's true that when you die the things that bothered you most are engraved on your skull, I am sure I'll have there the mud and dirt of France during the invasion and the name of Senator Bricker." He also complained, "If our Republican leaders had any guts this would all have been over."[7]

Simultaneously with the fight over Bricker, Eisenhower had to struggle with the Republican leaders over the tariff. In January, Eisenhower asked for a three-year extension of RTAA, based on a report from the Randall Commission on the necessity of promoting free trade around the world. Predictable complaints from high-tariff advocates, such as Edgar, brought from Eisenhower some straightforward presentations of fact. American capital and trade had to go into the underdeveloped world, Eisenhower said, because "only in this way can they absorb our industrial and agricultural surpluses; only in this way can we get the vital raw materials we must have."[8] Intermixed with RTAA were various Old Guard proposals to stop all trade with Communist states, to blockade China, and to prevent the NATO allies from trading with Russia. Eisenhower told the Republican leaders, "The unpleasant truth we have to face is that we're going to have to fight Russia either in a trade war or in a hot war. We've got to win a lot of people to our side. Our allies say, 'All right, you want to limit trade with us; you won't let us trade with Russia; what do you want us to do—starve?' "

Dan Reed warned about the dangers of letting cheap Japanese goods into the United States. The congressman said he had a doll in his office, "all dressed up, hair, clothes, the works. It's from Japan, and the price is three cents." Eisenhower cut him off: "Never mind the dolls." He urged Reed to think about real problems, such as nuclear testing and containment. Millikin interrupted to say it reminded him of a man who had been told of all the terrible things that were about to happen. The man said, "Well, I guess we might just as well paint our asses white and run with the antelopes." Eisenhower strongly disapproved of such language in a formal meeting (he always apologized when a "damn" or a "hell" slipped out when he was talking). Turning red, the President said tartly, "That's quite a story. Unless we act, we better start running now." Later, Eisenhower said of Millikin, "He's the most fearful man I ever met—he fears everything." On this occasion, he told the Republicans, "We cannot live alone, and we've got to find some way for our allies to earn a living, because we do not want to carry them on our backs."[9]

The Old Guard was not convinced. Eisenhower threatened, telling his Cabinet he would not support for re-election any Republican who would not support him on RTAA. "If the man changes," Eisenhower added, "look upon him as a prodigal son and kill the fatted calf for him, but if not, I have need for my own beef." And he told Hagerty that he was about to give up on working with Republicans. But in the end he compromised, accepting a one-year extension of RTAA, instead of the three he had demanded.[10]

• •

Eisenhower was not always at odds with the Republican leaders. Most of his domestic program was acceptable to the party, and even the Old Guard was enthusiastic about parts of it. In his State of the Union message of 1954, Eisenhower repeated his call for legislation on a number of issues that he had first proposed in 1953. One dealt with controlling the Communists. Some liberals, such as Hubert Humphrey, were trying to outlaw the Communist Party. Conservatives, such as J. Edgar Hoover, who had no need to establish their anti-Communist credentials, warned that outlawing the party would only make surveillance more difficult, while Eisenhower was worried about the constitutionality of a bill making membership in a political party a crime. Instead he asked for, and eventually got, the Communist Control Act of 1954, which stripped anyone who advocated the violent overthrow of the government of his or her citizenship. The bill also included "immunity-bath" legislation, which allowed the Attorney General to grant immunity from prosecution to witnesses testifying before a grand jury or a congressional committee.[11]

That bill pleased the Old Guard. So did Eisenhower's decisive endorsement of private development of nuclear power. Democrats had wanted to retain a federal monopoly on nuclear power, through the AEC, while most Republicans wanted to encourage commercial production of electricity. Eisenhower asked for, and got, legislation that permitted the private manufacture, ownership, and operation of atomic reactors under licensing systems administered by the AEC, and that directed the AEC to provide private manufacturers, at cost, with materials and services. With such inducements, the utilities were quick to respond; on Labor Day 1954, at Shippingport, Pennsylvania, groundbreaking ceremonies marked the beginning of the first civilian atomic power plant in America.[12]

Health care was another area that pitted private against public development. Some Democrats, most notably Harry Truman, were advocating a form of national health insurance; Republicans, with the solid support of the AMA, denounced any such plan as socialism. Eisenhower asked for—but did not get—a program instituting a limited federal reinsurance program that would provide financial support for the private health-insurance industry. To the AMA and its friends in the Old Guard, Eisenhower's proposal was no more than the entering wedge of socialized medicine.[13] Eisenhower suffered other defeats; his call for Hawaiian statehood failed, in part because the southern Democrats were afraid of Hawaii's mixed population. The Democrats wanted Alaska brought in simultaneously, but Eisenhower opposed statehood for Alaska on the grounds that the population was insufficient to provide a state government. He also failed on his proposal for the vote for eighteen-year-olds, and on his call for some minor revisions in Taft-Hartley.[14]

But Eisenhower won more than he lost. His Housing Act was one example. Democrats, responding to the nation's urgent need for more housing, brought on by the postwar baby boom, proposed a major role for the government in building housing projects; Republicans wanted to leave the problem to the construction industry. Eisenhower came down in the middle, calling for the construction by the government of 140,000 homes over a four-year period (which was far below the figures the Democrats had in mind, and even Senator Taft had advocated a larger federal role). Eisenhower put a four-year limit on the program with the idea that after that time he could replace government-financed projects with a program to insure long-term loans to mortgage holders.[15]

Eisenhower's most significant legislative victory was Social Security. He had tried to expand the system in 1953, failed to get action, and repeated his request in 1954. With an election coming in November, Republicans were more amenable to improving rather than destroying the system, and Eisenhower got a bill that increased benefits and put ten million people not previously covered into Social Security.[16] He also got the funds for American participation in the St. Lawrence Seaway and put through a tax-revision bill that did not lower rates but did increase deductions, thereby providing a tax cut of $7.4 billion for 1954.[17] Thanks to reductions in defense expenditures, he was bringing the budget into balance despite the tax cut.

In the spring of 1954, the country went into a mild, post-Korea recession. Eisenhower was determined that the Republican Party shed the label of "party of depression," and repeatedly warned his Cabinet and the Republican leaders that they could not afford to "get tagged like Mr. Hoover did, unjustly, of not doing anything to help in economic bad times." Eisenhower spent an enormous amount of his time studying the state of the economy with his chief economics adviser, Dr. Arthur Burns, and with his associates. He was ready to move decisively in the event unemployment got much above 5 percent (it had been 2.9 percent in 1953, and peaked at 5.5 percent in 1954). As unemployment pushed toward 6 percent, Eisenhower warned the Cabinet, "Now is the time to liberalize everything we can, because the fear in America is not the fear of inflation; it is the fear of deflation, of going down, not up."[18] In a long memorandum to Burns of February 2, he pointed out that he was committed to "keeping in a high state of readiness all applicable plans for combating, or rather preventing, depression or serious deflation." Specifically, he wanted the government ready to speed up spending in such areas as soil conservation, dam construction, roads, public buildings, defense procurement, and shipbuilding.[19] In early May, he got from Congress a bill that authorized some $2 billion for road construction, the largest sum ever invested to date by the federal government in the nation's highways. If necessary, he was prepared to do more. On April 2, he told the Cabinet to "be ready to act *every day.*" He wanted the departments, especially such big spenders as Defense and Agriculture, to hurry up with their purchases, and he made it clear that he wanted it done well before the fall elections. He added that if the economy continued to decline, he would not hesitate to cut taxes.[20]

Fortunately for Eisenhower and the Republicans, the recession was short-lived. Whether the early recovery (by 1955, the GNP was up sharply, while unemployment was down to 4.4 percent) was due to the Administration's policies, or to simple good luck based on the inherent strength of the economy, was unclear. In any event the Republicans had avoided a depression, and thereby laid to rest at least some of the fear, so widely held from 1929 onward, that a Republican Administration meant widespread unemployment and an uncaring government. In the economic field, Eisenhower was approaching or realizing his major goals—a balanced budget, no inflation, tax reduction, a growing GNP, and a low rate of unemployment.

He was not so fortunate in his farm policy. In this area, his major goal was to get the government out of agriculture, and his main agent was Ezra Taft Benson. Together, Eisenhower and Benson agreed that the Democratic policies of the past twenty years were a disaster. The Democrats had instituted a compulsory fixed price support of 90 percent of parity on basic crops. Nevertheless, commodity prices had fallen steadily in relation to the rest of the economy. Meanwhile, the government had, by 1954, enough wheat and cotton and other crops in storage bins to supply all the needs of the market for a full year. This immense surplus was a problem of immense proportions; it was expensive to keep the crops in storage; the surplus had a depressing effect on prices; storage capacity was about gone. The government had been selling off the surplus slowly and ineffectively; Eisenhower wanted to get rid of it by giving it away through such programs as a free school lunch, disaster relief, and emergency assistance to foreign countries. For the future, he wanted to reduce price supports immediately by instituting a flexible system that would range from 75 percent to 90 percent, with the aim of implementing a long-term solution to the problem of overproduction by allowing a free market in farm products. Thus his ultimate goal was to end both parity and the government controls that went with it.[21]

Farm policy was an area in which he had deep and unchangeable convictions. Nowhere did his turn-of-the-century upbringing in Abilene show more clearly. As he often told his Cabinet, farmers in central Kansas had done without federal programs, and indeed had rejected the candidacy of William Jennings Bryan in 1896 despite hard times and Bryan's major plank of helping farmers through monetary relief (the free coinage of silver). Eisenhower himself, as a six-year-old, had carried a torch in a McKinley parade. (When Truman accused Eisenhower of "creeping McKinleyism," it gave the President a good laugh.[22]) But however strongly Eisenhower felt about the need to get the government off the farmers' backs, he was never able to do so. Benson waged titanic struggles with the dairy producers, the corn growers, and other groups over flexible price supports, but he scored only minor victories. The basic structure remained in place.

Farm policy was the only area in which Eisenhower called for a repudiation of the basic New Deal economic structure. In most instances, such as TVA, he was willing to continue, although not expand, the New Deal reforms; in some cases, most notably Social Security, he was willing to both continue and expand. Overall, save for agriculture and the level of defense spending, he continued the policies of the Truman Administration. That gave him the support of many Democrats, enough to make up for the loss of some of the Old Guard on his proposals, and allowed him to boast that his Administration had gotten most of what it requested from Congress. True enough, his critics responded, but that was only because what he had requested was so bland.[23]

Whatever else Joe McCarthy was, he certainly was not bland. The President's attempt to undercut McCarthy by ignoring him had failed, utterly. To Eisenhower's dismay, McCarthy continued to dominate the headlines and the White House news conferences. Eisenhower was genuinely perplexed by this situation; insofar as he felt he could explain it, he laid the blame on the news media. He told Bill Robinson, "We have here a figure who owes his entire prominence and influence in today's life to the publicity media of the nation," and he complained that "now these same media are looking around for someone to knock off the creature of their own making."[24] In his diary, he wrote, "The members of this group [the press] are far from being as important as they themselves consider," but immediately contradicted himself by noting that in Washington, every politician courted the press shamelessly. His real objection was that the reporters "have little sense of humor and, because of this, they deal in negative criticism rather than in any attempt toward constructive helpfulness." In other words, he wanted the press to be a part of his team, working together for the good of the country, just as the press in North Africa and Europe had been on his side.[25]

On a more realistic level, Eisenhower wanted the press to provide, at a minimum, accurate reporting. At the end of January, Ellis Slater came down to spend a weekend in the White House. On Sunday morning, the two men read the papers while eating breakfast. Slater recorded that Eisenhower "remarked that after twelve years in public life, during which he had been in a position to know the real stories back of the news, he had about come to believe it was virtually impossible for a news reporter to get any story exactly right."[26]

A prime example was Secretary of the Army Robert T. Stevens' "surrender" to McCarthy. The incident had its origins in McCarthy's various investigations of Communist infiltration into the Army, which had led him to discover that a dentist, Dr. Irving Peress, who had been drafted, was a "Fifth Amendment Communist." But although Peress had refused to sign a loyalty oath, or to answer McCarthy's questions in a hearing, he had been promoted (the promotion was required by the doctors' draft law) and then given an honorable discharge. McCarthy, furious, called the Camp Kilmer commanding officer, General Ralph Zwicker, to testify. Through most of February, McCarthy's sole question of Zwicker—"Who promoted Peress?"—dominated the national news. Zwicker said he knew nothing about it. McCarthy browbeat Zwicker in the most abusive fashion, telling the general that he did not have "the brains of a five-year-old child" and that he was "not fit to wear" his uniform. Stevens then ordered Zwicker not to testify further. McCarthy thereupon ordered Stevens himself to appear before his committee. On February 24, Stevens had lunch with McCarthy in Everett Dirksen's Senate office. Karl Mundt was also there. They struck a deal—McCarthy promised to stop abusing his witnesses in return for Stevens' promise to permit further testimony by Zwicker and to release "the names of everyone involved in the promotion and honorable discharge of Peress."[27]

The luncheon was supposed to be a secret (it was a mark of

Stevens' political innocence that he could believe a lunch with McCarthy and the members of his committee, in the Senate office building, with Nixon's office across the hall, could be kept secret). When Stevens emerged, McCarthy beside him, the reporters and photographers were waiting. McCarthy announced that Stevens had capitulated. The Secretary and his subordinates would come back to the hearings. He neglected to add that he in turn had promised to act responsibly, and Stevens did not think to point this out to the press.

As the newspapers then broke the story, Eisenhower and his Administration had surrendered. *The New York Times* headlined its story, "Stevens Bows to McCarthy at Administration Behest. Will Yield Data on Peress." [28] Eisenhower, returning from a speaking trip to California, was "very mad and getting fed up." Hagerty noted in his diary, "It's his Army and he doesn't like McCarthy's tactics at all." Eisenhower swore, "This guy McCarthy is going to get into trouble over this. I'm not going to take this one lying down . . . He's ambitious. He wants to be President. He's the last guy in the whole world who'll ever get there, if I have anything to say." [29]

Over the telephone, that afternoon, Eisenhower told Lucius Clay that Stevens, a wealthy textile manufacturer from South Carolina, was so chagrined by his blunder that he had offered to resign. Eisenhower said Stevens was "in a state of shock and near hysteria." Eisenhower refused to hear of a resignation, and he told Stevens to admit that the Army had made an administrative error, then talk about "loyalty, honesty, integrity." Clay then warned Eisenhower that "I'm willing to bet he [McCarthy] has information on honorable discharges while you were Chief of Staff." Eisenhower bristled: "Never in my life has any Communist been brought to my attention. He never could be able to prove there was anything where I authorized a man's discharge." Clay cursed Dirksen for double-crossing the Administration, but Eisenhower said Dirksen was "not so bad," that he was "just frightened." Ninety-five percent of McCarthyism, Eisenhower said, was "just fear." [30]

Behind the scenes, Eisenhower was meeting with Dirksen and Mundt, extracting from them promises to make Joe behave. But his more significant act was a telephone call he placed to Brownell. His subject was the power of a committee of Congress to subpoena. "I suppose the President can refuse to comply," Eisenhower said, "but when it comes down to people down the line appointed to office, I don't know what the answer is. I would like to have a brief memo on precedent, etc.—just what I can do in this regard." [31] Eisenhower thereupon prepared the foundation for what would be his sole significant action against McCarthy, denial of access to executive personnel and records.

On March 3, Eisenhower had a prepared statement for his news conference. He said that the Army had made "serious errors" in the Peress case, that it was correcting its procedures, and that he had complete confidence in Stevens. He then read some homilies about McCarthyism ("In opposing Communism, we are defeating ourselves if we use methods that do not conform to the American sense of justice"), about the Army (it was "completely loyal and dedicated"), and about Congress (which had a responsibility "to see to it that its procedures are proper and fair"). After asserting his own "vigilance against any kind of internal subversion," Eisenhower ended curtly: "And that is my last word on any subject even closely related to that particular matter."[32]

McCarthy answered within the hour. He declared defiantly that "if a stupid, arrogant, or witless man in a position of power appears before our committee and is found aiding the Communist Party, he will be exposed. The fact that he might be a general places him in no special class as far as I am concerned." Then, in a classic McCarthyism, delivered by the master himself, McCarthy said, "Apparently the President and I now agree on the necessity of getting rid of Communists." To make sure his followers got the point, he publicly deleted the "now" a half hour later.[33]

Still Eisenhower held back from any direct attack against McCarthy. He continued to urge the Republican senatorial leaders, especially Knowland, Dirksen, and Mundt, to keep the Army-McCarthy hearings (which were about to begin) orderly and fair. He told his Cabinet, in a formal memorandum, that "each superior, including me, must remember the obligations he has to his own subordinates. These comprise . . . the protection of those subordinates, through all legal and proper means available, against attacks of a character under which they otherwise might be helpless."[34] Beyond that, he would not go. His belief was that McCarthyism was based on fear, and that the fear would subside, and McCarthy would lose his power and influence as the nation concentrated its interest on matters of substance. In a series of letters and diary entries, many in response to strong letters from men he respected urging him to denounce the senator from Wisconsin, Eisenhower cursed the amount of time the nonissue took. "Doctrine, ideas, and ideals have a tough time competing for headlines with demagogues." To Bill Robinson, he complained that "we have sideshows and freaks where we ought to be in the main tent with our attention on the chariot race." He also bemoaned "the tremendous importance that America places on personalities, and particularly upon clashes between personalities."[35]

Much of Eisenhower's incoming mail was telling him that McCarthy "has it within his power to destroy our system of government." He scoffed at the notion: "When the proposition is stated as baldly as this, then it becomes instantly ridiculous." He also scoffed at Adlai Stevenson's charge "that the Republican Party was one-half Eisenhower and one-half McCarthy." When asked at a news conference to comment, Eisenhower replied, "At the risk of appearing egotistical, I say nonsense."[36]

Thus Eisenhower decided, again, that McCarthy was not so great a threat to the nation or to the party as so many feared. But the forces McCarthy represented, and the methods he used, were another matter. "There is a certain reactionary fringe of the Republican Party that hates and despises everything for which I stand," he told Robinson. He thought that if the Republican leaders had done their job, McCarthy would have long since been relegated to his proper sphere. Knowland, especially, had let him down; Eisenhower wrote of the majority leader in the Senate, "It is a pity that his wisdom, his judgment, his tact, and his sense of humor lag so far behind his ambition."[37] As to McCarthy's methods, Eisenhower said, "I despise them." Nevertheless, he thought that his many close friends who were urging him to publicly label McCarthy with derogatory titles were badly mistaken. It would make "the Presidency ridiculous and in the long run make the citizens of our country very unhappy indeed." Instead of speaking out, he would stick to his lifelong principle, so often stated so vehemently: "To avoid public mention of any name unless it can be done with favorable intent and connotation; reserve all criticism for the private conference; speak only good in public." Eisenhower insisted that such a stance "is not namby-pamby. It certainly is not Pollyanna-ish. It is just sheer common sense. A leader's job is to get others to go along with him in the promotion of something. To do this he needs their good will."[38]

Sound principle, but there were other principles Eisenhower also held, one of which was loyalty. He was, after all, not only the Commander in Chief but also the former Chief of Staff of an Army that McCarthy was viciously attacking. He was also the Supreme Commander of 1944; under his orders, General Zwicker, a West Pointer, had gone ashore on D-Day as chief of staff for the 2d Division, been wounded, and won a decoration. Since the war, Zwicker had had a distinguished career. Now Eisenhower was standing aside while

McCarthy told Zwicker that he was not fit to wear the uniform. One might have thought that such assaults on such targets would have brought Eisenhower charging into the action. He himself had said (of the Republican senatorial leaders), "They do not seem to realize when there arrives that moment at which soft speaking should be abandoned and a fight to the end undertaken. Any man who hopes to exercise leadership must be ready to meet this requirement face to face when it arises; unless he is ready to fight when necessary, people will finally begin to ignore him." [39] But despite McCarthy's extreme provocations, Eisenhower was not ready to abandon soft speaking.

The next storm broke when McCarthy announced that he would hold his seat as a voting member of the committee, despite the fact that he was on trial as much as the Army was (the Army charged that Roy Cohn, counsel to McCarthy's subcommittee, had used his position to exert pressure for special favors for G. David Schine, Cohn's former associate, who had been drafted). At a news-conference briefing, Eisenhower's aides were split on how to respond. Jerry Persons, always the most conservative of the advisers, wanted the President to say that McCarthy's vote was a matter for the Senate to decide. Hagerty, Cutler, and others said that the President was the moral leader of the nation and that if he did not speak out he would "get murdered on this one." Eisenhower stopped their arguing by announcing, "Look, I know exactly what I am going to say. I'm going to say he [McCarthy] can't sit as a judge. I've made up my mind you can't do business with Joe and to hell with any attempt to compromise." [40]

At his news conference, he was not quite so tough. "I am perfectly ready to put myself on record flatly," he said, "that in America, if a man is a party to a dispute, directly or indirectly, he does not sit in judgment on his own case, and I don't believe that any leadership can escape responsibility for carrying on that tradition." [41] No one could disagree with that statement, and so McCarthy was considered "spanked," and he abandoned his demand to have a vote, although he did retain his right to cross-examine witnesses. And, of course, the right to subpoena.

It was this last point that had Eisenhower worried. He did not want McCarthy running rampage, demanding that personnel from the Executive Branch appear before him, and that they produce records. McCarthyism was the result of fear, the President had insisted, but he was reluctant to admit that he was also afraid. He feared that McCarthy would get into the records or haul government officials before him. On March 29, he again asked Brownell to prepare a state-

ment that he could use in the event that he had to order his subordinates to not appear before McCarthy.[42]

What Eisenhower feared specifically was the Oppenheimer case.
Eisenhower's withholding of Oppenheimer's top-secret clearance, pending investigation, had been done secretly, but inevitably word was
getting out. What bothered Eisenhower most was that McCarthy had
just charged that the H-bomb development had been held up for
eighteen months "because of Reds in the government." Joe's statement
was getting uncomfortably close to Oppenheimer. "We have to move
fast," Hagerty noted, "before McCarthy breaks the Oppenheimer investigation and it then becomes our scandal."[43] Hagerty worried about
the public-relations aspects: "It's just a question of time before someone cracks it wide open and everything hits the fan—if this breaks it
will be the biggest news we've had down here yet—real hot."[44] Eisenhower worried about something much bigger than public relations;
his concern was the morale of the nation's scientists and the state of
the nation's defenses.

The seriousness Eisenhower assigned to keeping McCarthy out of
the Oppenheimer case was best illustrated by the fact that the President spent most of three full days, April 9 through 11, on the Oppenheimer matter. Strauss gave the President information that made it
clear Oppenheimer had indeed tried to delay the H-bomb project.
Eisenhower was not particularly concerned about the politics of Oppenheimer's wife, or those of his brother and sister-in-law, or even
about Oppenheimer's having lied, under oath, about his associations.
Eisenhower respected the man for his accomplishments, thought that
such a unique genius should be given maximum leeway for idiosyn-
crasies, even in politics, and had been impressed by the moral arguments Oppenheimer had made against the H-bomb. What Eisenhower
found inexcusable was that once Truman had made the decision to go
ahead with the H-bomb, Oppenheimer did not get on the team.
Worse, he tried to slow down the project. Eisenhower wanted him removed from all contact with the AEC, because he did not want to give
Oppenheimer the opportunity to spread moral doubts in the minds of
the scientists. Oppenheimer's removal from the AEC had to be done
carefully, however, because of his unique stature and prestige among
his fellow scientists, men on whom the fate of the nuclear arms race
rested. Eisenhower also did not want to let McCarthy give the country
the impression that all scientists were disloyal. "We've got to handle
this so that all our scientists are not made out to be Reds," Eisenhower
told Hagerty. "That goddamn McCarthy is just likely to try such a
thing."[45]

Adding to the difficulties, as Hagerty noted, was that "McCarthy knows about case and it was Nixon who talked him out of using it earlier because of security reasons." And Hagerty realized, as did Eisenhower, that McCarthy, "with back to wall, could easily try to get out from under by splashing Oppenheimer."[46]

So Eisenhower decided to back off, or rather to stay backed off, from McCarthy. He would not push the senator, but allow events to run their course, including ignoring McCarthy's gross insults to Zwicker, hoping that McCarthy would not get so far back against the wall that he opened an Oppenheimer investigation. When Eisenhower was asked at a news conference about McCarthy's charge of an eighteen-month delay in the H-bomb, he denied any knowledge of it at all. "I never heard of any delay on my part, never heard of it."[47] Even in his memoirs, written after the accusation had been made that Oppenheimer had been removed from the AEC because of his opposition to the H-bomb, Eisenhower said, "Certainly I . . . gave no weight to this fact."[48] But in private, at the time, he told a different story. James Conant, from Bonn, wrote a strong defense of Oppenheimer. Conant said he knew all about the charges and they were false. Eisenhower replied that he was responding to the new charges, that is that Oppenheimer "attempted to induce personnel to abstain from working on the project and used such other influence as he thought would adversely affect the proposition." On reflection, Eisenhower did not send the letter to Conant, but he did send a copy to Strauss.[49]

In his memoirs, Eisenhower said his main concern about the Army-McCarthy hearings was that they be done "with minimum publicity and maximum dispatch." He certainly failed in that goal. But his real aim was to keep McCarthy away from Oppenheimer, and to avoid a debate among scientists about the morality of working for the government on the H-bomb. In this goal he succeeded brilliantly.

The hearings began on April 22 and dragged on for two months. They were on national TV and attracted a huge and fascinated audience. McCarthy got maximum publicity with minimum dispatch—indeed too much publicity. The senator had put himself into an impossible position, because it had come down to the Army versus McCarthy, the Senate versus McCarthy, and, offstage, Eisenhower versus McCarthy. Despite his histrionics, McCarthy could not win against such odds. He could only expose himself before the biggest audience of his career. Eisenhower watched the spectacle on TV (although he denied it), as fascinated and appalled as everyone else. "The McCarthy-Army argument, and its reporting, are close to disgusting," he told Hazlett. "It saddens me that I must feel ashamed for the United States

Senate."[50] As the spring wore on, he was content to watch McCarthy hang himself, and quite pleased that the subject of the H-bomb never came up in the hearings.

The H-bomb was very much at the center of the President's attention. On March 1, the AEC had detonated a multimegaton nuclear device on Bikini island. Code named Bravo, the blast was the first in a series called Castle. Eisenhower had given his approval to Castle after being told by Strauss that it was probable that the Russians were ahead of the Americans in H-bomb technology. The device the AEC had set off in November 1952 had not been small enough to carry in an airplane, while the Russians seemed to have accomplished that goal in their test. American scientists needed to increase their efforts, which was one reason Eisenhower was so concerned about the Oppenheimer case breaking just as the United States prepared to start Castle. Eisenhower wanted to keep the tests themselves secret too, but it proved impossible to hide them. Among other problems, a Japanese fishing boat had been showered with radiation, the crew fell ill, and the Japanese government and people raised a roar of protest. On March 24, at a news conference, Eisenhower decided he had to respond to persistent questions about radiation, even though he had promised Hagerty he would tell reporters to wait for Strauss's return from the Pacific testing grounds. Eisenhower told the press, "It is quite clear that this time something must have happened that we have never experienced before, and must have surprised and astonished the scientists. Very properly, the United States has to take precautions that never occurred to them before."[51]

The President's admission allowed the reporters to speculate that the H-bomb testing had gotten out of hand, that the blast was uncontrollable. Then on March 30 the AEC, no longer attempting to hide the basic testing, announced that a second H-bomb had been tested that morning. That led to more concerned headlines. Meanwhile, Strauss had returned to Washington, and on March 31 Eisenhower took him to his news conference. Eisenhower had told Strauss to read a prepared statement "setting at ease fears that bombs had gotten out of control," then answer questions about Bravo, and finally try to relieve people's worries.

Strauss told the press that Bravo was never out of control, that the main problem had been a shift in wind that blew the radioactive material over the Japanese fishing boat, that there was no truth to stories about contaminated tuna fish or about radioactive currents moving on

Japan, and that overall the fallout danger was being greatly exaggerated. The radioactivity would disappear quickly, but the military gains for the United States would be enduring. He said the nation should "rejoice" that the tests had been so successful and that "enormous potential has been added to our military posture by what we have learned."

That piqued the reporters' curiosity, and one of them asked how big an H-bomb might be made. Strauss replied, "It can be made to be as large as you wish, as large as the military requirement demands, that is to say, an H-bomb can be made as—large enough to take out a city." Cries of "What?" went up around the room. "How big a city?" "Any city," Strauss replied. "Any city, New York?" "The metropolitan area, yes."[52]

On the way back to the Oval Office, Eisenhower told Strauss, "Lewis, I wouldn't have answered that one that way." Instead, the President said, Strauss should have told the reporters to "wait for the movie." He was referring to a movie the AEC had made on Bravo. Eisenhower said he wanted the truth told—"Hell, I'd let everyone see the movie," he told Hagerty. "That's the purpose of it, to let everyone in." But then he let Strauss change his mind and decided not to release the movie, for fear of frightening people even further.[53]

On April 7, the AEC announced that the third shot in the Castle series had taken place. That same day, Merriman Smith asked Eisenhower at his news conference whether the United States was "going to continue to make bigger and bigger H-bombs." Eisenhower was direct in his answer. "No," he said, "we have no intention of going into a program of seeing how big these can be made. We know of no military requirement that could lead us into the production of a bigger bomb than has already been produced. I don't know what bigger ones would do."[54] And indeed, as Robert Divine points out, Bravo was "the biggest bomb the United States ever detonated."[55] Further, despite the assurances of the AEC and other leading scientists, Eisenhower was worried about fallout, especially as reports from Japan on the condition of the fishing boat's crew became more alarming (one man had died already). And he was quite honest in saying that he could see no point to making any bigger weapons, which led him to wonder why it was necessary to continue testing.

He brought up the subject with Dulles even as Castle was going on. He told the Secretary of State (an enthusiastic supporter of testing) on April 19 that he wanted Castle completed "as rapidly as possible."

After that, he thought the United States "should advocate a moratorium." He said he was "willing to have a moratorium on all further experimentation whether with H-bombs or A-bombs."[56] Dulles was opposed to a moratorium, citing the verification problem. Meanwhile Castle went on, reaching its end on May 5 with a blast of almost seven megatons and on May 14 of two megatons. Divine speculates that the purpose of the series was to test various explosive configurations for the Atlas intercontinental ballistic missile, which had gotten started in February on a crash basis in response to Eisenhower's order.[57]

The Oppenheimer case, meanwhile, became public knowledge when the committee Eisenhower had charged with investigating Oppenheimer reported, by two votes to one, that while Oppenheimer was not disloyal, he had "fundamental defects of character" and therefore recommended that his security clearance be taken away. (By a vote of 4 to 1, with Strauss leading the way, the AEC later upheld that decision.) The announcement of the committee recommendation met Hagerty's objective of beating McCarthy to the headlines on Oppenheimer, but it also set off the split that Eisenhower had feared in the American scientific community. The ensuing uproar also met Eisenhower's objective of keeping the development of the H-bomb out of the debate. The ugly charge of anti-Semitism was hurled about, and Oppenheimer's supporters said that Eisenhower had done it only to appease McCarthy.[58] Eisenhower was careful to point out that he was not punishing Oppenheimer in any way, nor finding him guilty of anything, merely separating him from the AEC. He was not even adverse to having Oppenheimer work for the government, if the project was safe enough. "Why do we not get Dr. Oppenheimer interested in desalting sea water?" Eisenhower wrote to Strauss.[59] And in a press conference, he was ready to praise Oppenheimer, albeit in a rather muddled way: "I have known Dr. Oppenheimer and, like others, I have certainly admired and respected his very great professional and technical attainments; and this is something that is the kind of thing that must be gone through with what I believe is best not talked about too much until we know whatever answers there may be."[60] And with that, and with the end of the Castle series, and with the Army-McCarthy hearings reaching their height, the public interest in Bravo and its implications faded.

Throughout the period of Castle and the announcement about lifting Oppenheimer's security clearance, Eisenhower complained about the way in which the Army-McCarthy hearings were detracting public attention from the real issues. But he was the chief beneficiary. He wanted Bravo and Oppenheimer kept as quiet as possible, and McCarthy diverted enough attention so that few noticed, in the spring of 1954, that Eisenhower had launched the United States into an H-bomb race with the Soviets, including a race to build intercontinental missiles. Eisenhower had made momentous decisions about this most critical of issues, and had done so with a minimum of public debate. He had even managed to keep Oppenheimer's dismissal from raising the question of the morality of building the H-bomb.

Eisenhower, depressed by the failure of the Russians to respond to Atoms for Peace, was fully committed to the H-bomb. It had become the centerpiece of his strategy, and of his defense policy. It had allowed him to cut spending while increasing America's nuclear lead. It made possible the "New Look," as Wilson's Pentagon public-relations people called it—fewer conventional forces, more atomic firepower, less cost. In the privacy of his Cabinet meetings, Eisenhower liked to stress what was "new" in the New Look; at his news conferences, he stressed continuity rather than change. When Ed Folliard of the Washington *Post* asked him about the subject, he replied, " 'New Look.' What do we mean? We mean this: We are not fighting with muzzle-loaders in any of the services." The kind of force he took across the Channel in 1944, Eisenhower said, "cannot possibly have any usefulness today whatsoever," because two small atomic bombs would have been enough to wipe out the beachhead. He said he had heard people calling for a bigger Army. "Now, our most valued, our most costly asset is our young men," he asserted. "Let's don't use them any more than we have to." He was maintaining a one-million-man Army, the largest peacetime Army in American history, and regarded calls for an even larger force as irresponsible. He thought the reasons for such demands were that "there is too much hysteria." Americans were afraid of the "men in the Kremlin," afraid of "unwise investigators," afraid of subversion, afraid of depression, afraid of radiation. The New Look was designed to meet one of those fears, that of a sudden massive Pearl Harbor-type attack on the United States. "To call it revolutionary or to act like it is something that just suddenly dropped down on us like a cloud out of the heaven is just not true, just not true." [61]

The basic structure of the New Look was an expanded strategic air force and a much-reduced conventional force on land and at sea. It depended upon a huge American lead in nuclear weapons. Critics,

led by Army Chief of Staff Matthew Ridgway, charged that it was un-
balanced and thereby forced America into an "all or nothing" posture.
Ridgway was right, of course, as Dulles made clear in a mid-January
speech, when he announced that Eisenhower and the NSC had made
a "basic decision" that in the future the United States would confront
any possible aggression by "a great capacity to retaliate instantly by
means and places of our own choosing." Eisenhower, asked to comment, said that Dulles "was merely stating what, to my mind, is a
fundamental truth and really doesn't take much decision; it is just a
fundamental truth." [62]

But that only deepened and did not elucidate the mystery. If
American policy was to retaliate instantly and massively against Soviet
aggression, what happened to the congressional power to declare war?
In March, Dulles explained: "If the Russians attacked one of America's allies, there was no need for the President to go to Congress for
a declaration of war." Congress was unhappy with that response; so
were the reporters. Through the spring, they pressed Eisenhower for
clarification. He explained that "there is a difference between an act
of war and declaring war." If he was faced with a Soviet assault against
the United States, "a gigantic Pearl Harbor," he would act instan-
taneously, but he would also assemble Congress as fast as possible,
because "after all, you can't carry on a war without Congress." As to
the precise legal and constitutional question, Eisenhower admitted, "I
could be mistaken, and I would not argue it." In a sentence that said
volumes about the Eisenhower-Dulles relationship, the President
added, "I would like to discuss it with Foster Dulles, but having
talked to him, I am sure that we are absolutely in agreement as to
what we mean about it."

The point was that the reporters wanted to know what he meant
by "it." Did it mean that if there was a war in Korea or the Americans decided to support the French in Vietnam, that nuclear weapons
would be delivered against Moscow or Peiping? "No war ever shows
the characteristics that were expected," Eisenhower replied. "It is always different." Avoiding the question of how massive retaliation
could work in a small war far outside Russian or Chinese borders,
Eisenhower returned to the Pearl Harbor theme, again warning that
in the age of nuclear weapons a surprise attack could be horrendous.
Under those circumstances, if the President did not act immediately,
he "should be worse than impeached, he should be hanged." The reporters persisted. Richard Wilson said that Dulles' speeches had indicated that if the United States were to take part in a local conflict, it

would be done "with a direct attack upon the major aggressor at some point most desirable for us."

"Well, now," Eisenhower replied, "I will tell you. Foster Dulles, by no stretch of the imagination, ever meant to be so specific and exact in stating what we would do under different circumstances. He was showing the value to America to have a capability of doing certain things, what he believed that would be in the way of deterring an aggressor and preventing this dread possibility of war occurring."[63]

The war raging in Vietnam made the subject of massive retaliation more than academic. The French were holding their own, but barely. Paris was weary of war. The cost, in lives and money, had become unendurable. For the Americans, too, the situation was intolerable. A continued stalemate would drain French resources to such an extent that France would never be able to meet its NATO obligations, always a prime consideration with Eisenhower. Further, the French were demanding more American money, and even American planes and troops, and they were simultaneously using EDC, which Eisenhower very much wanted, to blackmail the United States. Without support in Indochina, the French were saying, they could not ratify EDC.

A French defeat in Vietnam would be worse than continued stalemate. There was first of all the global strategic balance to consider. As far back as December 1952, Dulles had told Eisenhower that "Korea is important, but the really important spot is Indochina, because we could lose Korea and probably insulate ourselves against the consequences of that loss; but if Indochina goes, and South Asia goes, it is extremely hard to insulate ourselves against the consequences of that."[64] There was in addition the political position of the Republican Party to be considered. A major theme of Eisenhower's campaign had been a rejection of containment and an adoption of a policy of liberation. Now the Republicans had been in power for more than a year. They had failed to liberate any Communist slave anywhere. Indeed in Korea they had accepted an armistice that left North Korea in Communist hands. Eisenhower was keenly aware that by far his most popular act had been to achieve peace in Korea, but he was just as aware that Republican orators had been demanding to know, ever since 1949, "Who lost China?" Could he afford to allow Democrats to ask, "Who lost Vietnam?" He told his Cabinet he could not.[65]

The obvious way out of the quandary was a French victory, but the problem was how to achieve it without introducing American planes and troops. Under no circumstances was Eisenhower going to send American troops back onto the Asian mainland less than a year after signing an armistice in Korea. Even had he wanted to do that, the New Look precluded such an effort—the troops simply were not available.

The only hope was through a judicious use of American resources to support allied forces, and not only the French. Eisenhower put Beetle Smith at the head of a committee to advise him. Smith recommended using Nationalist Chinese troops, adding that he had made a similar recommendation to Acheson in 1950 with regard to Korea. Smith admitted to Eisenhower that he and Acheson "had some very sharp words about this but I think I was right." Eisenhower thought he was wrong. Putting Chiang Kai-shek's troops into Vietnam would be a sure way to bring on a massive Red Chinese intervention. Besides, he told Smith, "We do not have an overall plan which provides for alternate lines of action in the event things go bad in Indochina regardless of our assistance."[66]

What Eisenhower had in mind was a joint British-U.S. intervention, not with troops but with air support and military hardware. That would be in accord with his basic principle of collective security, it would relieve the Americans of the charge of colonialism, and it would save the French position. Convincing himself, however, was much easier than convincing the British, who wanted no part of an involvement in another war in Asia. Eisenhower wrote directly to Churchill, appealing to his sense of history. Eisenhower said that "I've been thinking a bit of the future. I am sure that when history looks back upon us of today it will not long remember any one of this era who was merely a distinguished war leader whether on the battlefield or in the council chamber." Rather, history would remember those who established ties among the free nations that would allow them to "throw back the Russian threat and allow civilization to continue its progress." In conclusion, Eisenhower declared, "Destiny has given priceless opportunity to some of this epoch. You are one of them. Perhaps I am also one of the company on whom this great responsibility has fallen."[67]

Churchill was unimpressed by Eisenhower's dramatic presentation. Shortly after receiving it, Churchill met with Dulles. The Secretary of State reported to Eisenhower, "The Prime Minister followed his usual line. He said that only the English-speaking peoples counted; that together they could rule the world."[68] Eisenhower deplored such thinking as hopelessly out of date, but he continued to work on Churchill.

Meanwhile, Eisenhower increased direct American military assistance to the French. How much of the war the Americans were paying for at this time is impossible to say because the figures were hidden in so many different ways, but the general estimate is around 75 percent. The French wanted more; specifically and immediately they wanted some B-26 bombers and the technicians to go with them. Eisenhower was terribly exasperated by the French—he blamed their refusal to grant full and free independence to the nations of Indochina for the continuation of the war—but the latest reports he was getting were quite positive about French chances. Eisenhower had not wanted to put American money and prestige into a losing cause, but his special study mission to Indochina, headed by General John O'Daniel, had just reported to him that the Dien Bien Phu fortress could "withstand any kind of attack the Vietminh are capable of launching." [69] The French were on the offensive, or so they said, although Eisenhower found it difficult to see how putting their most famous units into a fortress that was surrounded by high ground that was held by the enemy constituted taking the offensive. But he needed the French vote for EDC; he wanted to keep the French fighting in Vietnam; he could not bear the thought of losing the place through neglect; perhaps this time, with the bombers, the French would stiffen their backs and really go after the enemy. Eisenhower decided to give them something less than half of what they asked for. The French had wanted twenty-five bombers and four hundred Air Force personnel to service them; Eisenhower gave them ten bombers and two hundred people.

On February 8, at a meeting of Republican leaders, Senator Leverett Saltonstall anxiously raised the question about American servicemen going to Indochina. Was yet another President, this one a Republican, going to take the country into yet another war by the back door? That was Saltonstall's implied question, and Eisenhower took it seriously. He carefully explained his reason for giving U.S. Air Force weapons to the French to be used against the Vietminh, and assured Saltonstall that none of the personnel would be in a combat zone. Eisenhower admitted that he was "frightened about getting ground forces tied up in Indochina," and promised that he would pull all two hundred men out of the area on June 15. "Don't think I like to send them there," he added, "but we can't get anywhere in Asia by just sitting here in Washington and doing nothing—my God, we must not lose Asia—we've got to look the thing right in the face." Then he allowed himself Beetle Smith's little fantasy: "I'd like to see Chiang's troops used in Indochina"—and immediately caught himself up—"but the political risk of Chinese Red moves would then be too great."[70]

Still, for all Eisenhower's emphasis on reduced numbers and a definite date for withdrawal, he had sent the first American military personnel to Vietnam. Of course, as Eisenhower insisted, it was hardly an irrevocable step. But still, it had been taken. He was worried about what it might lead to. Earlier, in January, he had told the NSC (in the words of the stenographer), "For himself, said the President with great force, he simply could not imagine the United States putting ground forces anywhere in Southeast Asia, except possibly in Malaya, which we have to defend as a bulwark to our offshore island chain. But to do this anywhere else, said the President with vehemence, how bitterly opposed I am to such a course of action. This war in Indochina would absorb our troops by divisions!"[71]

Long before the Gulf of Tonkin Resolution of 1964, Eisenhower was even more emphatic and prophetic about an American ground involvement in Vietnam. When writing his presidential memoirs, in 1963, he declared, "The jungles of Indochina . . . would have swallowed up division after division of United States troops, who, unaccustomed to this kind of warfare, would have sustained heavy casualties . . . Furthermore, the presence of ever more numbers of white men in uniform probably would have aggravated rather than assuaged Asiatic resentments." (When he published the memoirs, nearly a year later, he deleted that passage, because by then the country was getting involved in Vietnam and he did not want to be critical of the President.[72]) Nevertheless, throughout the long period in 1954 of the French agony at Dien Bien Phu a grim specter dominated his thinking.

In mid-March, the upbeat reports from Vietnam suddenly reversed. Allen Dulles said the French now felt they had only a 50-50 chance at Dien Bien Phu. Furthermore, French Premier René Pleven told ambassador to France Douglas Dillon that "there was no longer the prospect of a satisfactory military solution." Eisenhower was distraught on learning of Pleven's defeatist attitude. "Why don't they withdraw request for military aid?" he wrote Smith. "Might be well to ask."[73]

Eisenhower soon had a chance to ask himself. On March 23 French Army Chief of Staff Paul Ely came to Washington to discuss increasing the flow of American material. Eisenhower and Dulles had a series of meetings with Ely. He wanted additional American aircraft, while Eisenhower pressed him on the status of granting independence. Finally, Eisenhower agreed to furnish the French with some C-119

Flying Boxcars that could drop napalm, "which would burn out a considerable area and help to reveal enemy artillery positions." But Eisenhower would not commit the United States to any military policy of direct intervention until he "got a lot of answers" from Paris on outstanding issues, primarily EDC and Indochinese independence.

Then Eisenhower set about building the support he would need to withstand the strident demands for intervention that he knew would come when Dien Bien Phu fell. He did so by putting conditions on American involvement. They were deliberately created to be impossible of fulfillment, and there were a number of them. First, a full and clear grant of independence by the French. Second, British participation in any venture. Third, at least some of the nations of Southeast Asia had to be involved. Fourth, Congress had to give full and clear prior approval. Fifth, he would want the French to turn the war over to the Americans, but keep their troops in combat. Sixth, the French had to prove that they were not just asking the Americans to cover a fighting withdrawal.

Eisenhower's conditions, impossible as they were, seemed to him to be based on principles that could not be broken. As Dulles told Ely point-blank, the United States could "not afford to send its flag and its own military establishment and thus to engage the prestige of the United States," unless it expected to win.[74] Eisenhower expressed for himself another basic principle, when in an unpublished portion of his memoirs he wrote that "the strongest reason of all for the United States [to stay out] is the fact that among all the powerful nations of the world the United States is the only one with a tradition of anti-colonialism. . . . The standing of the United States as the most powerful of the anti-colonial powers is an asset of incalculable value to the Free World. . . . The moral position of the United States was more to be guarded than the Tonkin Delta, indeed than all of Indochina."[75]

So Eisenhower refused to go very far in meeting Ely's demands. The French general went to Radford, who was much more forthcoming. Together they approved joint U.S.-French plans, made in Saigon, for Operation Vulture, an air strike against the Vietminh around Dien Bien Phu. Ely's hope, and Radford's, was that as the end drew near at Dien Bien Phu, Eisenhower could not resist the pressure to intervene. Indeed, some of Eisenhower's aides thought that the French were deliberately losing at Dien Bien Phu in order to force an American intervention.[76] Radford had reason to suppose the President might approve a strike too; just the day before he met with Ely, Eisenhower had told him that he would not "wholly exclude the possibility of a

single strike, if it were almost certain this could prove decisive results."
But as always, Eisenhower had put on a condition that was impossible
to fulfill.[77]

Eisenhower's most impossible conditions were the ones that required allied participation and congressional support. On March 29,
Dulles in a speech put forward an idea that he had been given by
Eisenhower, that the United States take the lead in forming a "United
Action" in Vietnam. Britain, France, Australia, New Zealand, Thailand, the Philippines, and the Associated States of Indochina would
all intervene together. It was an absurd idea, except that it accomplished two objectives for Eisenhower—it allowed a national debate to
take place on the wisdom of intervention (which debate, Eisenhower
was sure, would convince most people that it was a mistake), and it began building the American fallback position. Eisenhower had reconciled himself to the loss of some of Vietnam, but not all, and certainly
not all of Southeast Asia. Already he was committed, in other words,
to a division of Vietnam, with the United States then coming in to
support the non-Communist south. But he never said so in public,
where he continued to insist that a negotiated settlement was out of
the question. He still had some faint hopes that the French might pull
themselves together, and that the British might at least put in a little
material help.

For the record, and to protect himself against right-wing assaults,
Eisenhower then tried to get both prior congressional approval and
British participation. On April 2, with the situation at Dien Bien Phu
growing worse every day, Eisenhower had Dulles and Radford meet
with the leaders of both parties in Congress. Dulles said Eisenhower
wanted a resolution from Congress that would give him the discretion-
ary authority to use American air and sea power to prevent the "extension and expansion" of Communist aggression in Southeast Asia.
The authority would expire on June 30, 1955, and would in no way
"derogate from the authority of Congress to declare war."[78] The congressmen, as Eisenhower expected would be the case, were aghast.
They cried out "No more Koreas." The only way Eisenhower could
get a resolution, they said (thus protecting themselves as carefully as
Eisenhower was protecting himself), was if the British and other allies
joined in, and if the French promised independence. Dulles decided
not to submit the resolution to Congress.[79]

On April 4, Eisenhower sent a telegram to Churchill. He expressed hope about Dien Bien Phu, but warned that "I fear that the
French cannot alone see the thing through." Worse, defeat would

mean "that the future of France as a great power would be fatally affected." He urged Churchill to join United Action, and between the lines implied to the Prime Minister that he had in mind putting the plan into effect after Vietnam was partitioned.

Then, Eisenhower drew the most telling historical parallel he could think of in appealing to Churchill: "We failed to halt Hirohito, Mussolini, and Hitler by not acting in unity and in time. That marked the beginning of many years of stark tragedy and desperate peril. May it not be that our nations have learned something from that lesson?"[80] But for all the rhetoric, what Eisenhower was really doing was building a negotiating position for a conference in Geneva, scheduled for late April. The meeting had been called earlier to deal with Korea, but the Russians had insisted on putting Indochina on the agenda. Dulles was unhappy because he suspected, rightly, that the French wanted to use Geneva to negotiate themselves out of Vietnam. But he had failed to keep Indochina off the agenda, and partition was in the air, not least because of Dulles' United Action proposal. The Americans knew they had to prepare for the probability of a French withdrawal.

On the morning of April 5, Dulles called Eisenhower to inform him that the French had told Ambassador Dillon that their impression was that Operation Vulture had been agreed to, and hinted that they expected two or three atomic bombs to be used against the Vietminh. Eisenhower told Dulles to tell the French, through Dillon, that they must have misunderstood Radford. Eisenhower said that "such a move is impossible," that without congressional support an air strike would be "completely unconstitutional and indefensible." He told Dulles to "take a look to see if anything else can be done," then again warned, "We cannot engage in active war."[81]

So Eisenhower had rejected intervention. But he had not decided to leave Southeast Asia to its own devices. He very definitely wanted to form a regional grouping for United Action that could draw a line and thus institute a policy of containment. As Truman had done in Europe in the late forties, Eisenhower would seal off the Communists in Southeast Asia. To achieve that goal, he first of all had to convince Congress, the American people, and the potential allies that Indochina was worth the effort. After all, if the Americans were not ready to fight beside the French, why should they, or anyone else, be prepared to fight for whatever was left of a non-Communist Indochina?

At his April 7 news conference, Eisenhower made his most important—and his most famous—declaration on Indochina. Robert Rich-

ards of Copley Press asked him to comment on the strategic importance of Indochina to the free world. Eisenhower replied that first of
all, "You have the specific value of a locality in its production of materials that the world needs." Second, "You have the possibility that
many human beings pass under a dictatorship that is inimical to the
free world." Finally, "You have the broader considerations that might
follow what you would call the 'falling domino' principle. You have a
row of dominoes set up, you knock over the first one, and what will
happen to the last one is the certainty that it will go over very quickly.
So you could have a beginning of a disintegration that would have the
most profound influences." He thought that the "sequence of events,"
if the United States abandoned Southeast Asia altogether, would be
the loss of all of Indochina, then Burma, then Thailand, then Malaya,
then Indonesia. "Now you begin to talk about areas that not only mul-
tiply the disadvantages that you would suffer through loss of materials,
sources of materials, but now you are talking really about millions and
millions and millions of people." Even worse, the loss of Southeast
Asia would be followed by the probable loss of Japan, Formosa, and
the Philippines, which would then threaten Australia and New
Zealand.[82]

The President had painted a cataclysmic picture. If he was right
about the probable consequences of the loss of Indochina, the need for
United Action became clear and overwhelming. It was at this point,
based on Eisenhower's reasoning, that the United States made its commitment to Vietnam. Not to the whole of Vietnam, but to whatever
was left of non-Communist Vietnam after the Geneva Conference finished partitioning the place. He was taking a halfway position, between those who were demanding an all-out effort to save the French
at Dien Bien Phu and those who wanted America to get out and stay
out of Southeast Asia.

As the situation at Dien Bien Phu deteriorated, demands for intervention from right-wing American politicians, military leaders, and
from the French, increased. On April 16, the Vice-President spoke to
the American Society of Newspaper Editors. Nixon was asked whether
he thought the United States should send troops into Indochina if the
French decided to withdraw. Nixon replied that if sending American
boys was the only way to avoid further Communist expansion in Asia,
"I believe that the Executive Branch of the government has to take
the politically unpopular position of facing up to it and doing it, and
I personally would support such a decision."[83] Since Nixon mentioned
neither Congress nor allied participation, his statement seemed to

represent a major shift in policy. Eisenhower was in Augusta for the weekend, so Hagerty had to face the reporters. He asked Nixon if there had indeed been a policy shift, but Nixon "played dumb" and said he was only answering hypothetical questions. Hagerty commented, "Think it was foolish for Dick to answer as he did but will make the best of it."[84]

At a meeting of the Republican leaders the next week, Charlie Halleck told Nixon that his statement "had really hurt" and that he hoped there would be no more talk of that kind. Eisenhower defended Nixon, saying that it was a good thing to keep the Communists guessing about American intentions.[85]

By April 23, the situation at Dien Bien Phu had become desperate. Dulles, who was in Europe trying to get United Action under way, sent a series of alarming cables to Eisenhower. "France is almost visibly collapsing under our eyes," the Secretary declared. He deplored the worldwide publicity being given to Dien Bien Phu, because "it seems to me that Dien Bien Phu has become a symbol out of all proportion to its military importance." Dulles insisted that there was "no military or logical reason why loss of Dien Bien Phu should lead to collapse of French will, in relation both to Indochina and EDC."[86] In another cable, Dulles said the French insisted there were only two alternatives; Operation Vulture or a request for a cease-fire. (There was great confusion about Vulture; Radford, Ely, and Nixon all believed it involved three atomic bombs, while Dulles thought it would be a "massive B-29 bombing" by U.S. planes using conventional bombs.[87])

Eisenhower phoned Beetle Smith. They agreed that there should be no intervention, no air strike, without allies. Eisenhower then cabled Dulles, saying that he could fully understand Dulles' frustration, but urging the Secretary to keep trying.[88] Dulles replied that it was not at all certain in any case that an air strike would save Dien Bien Phu at this late date. "It is my opinion," the Secretary continued, "that armed intervention by executive action is not warranted. The security of the United States is not directly threatened."[89]

On April 26, the opening day of the Geneva Conference, Eisenhower met with the Republican leaders. He told them that "the French are weary as hell," that Dien Bien Phu would fall within the week, although "the French go up and down every day—they are very voluble. They think they are a great power one day and they feel sorry for themselves the next day." When the congressmen asked the President why the British were so reluctant to get involved, he said that the Churchill government was "worried about Hong Kong and hope it will be left alone. They are fearful that if they move in Indochina the Chinese Reds will move against Hong Kong and could take it easily." Eisenhower said he tried to convince the British that "if we all went in together into Indochina at the same time, that would be fine but if they don't go in with us, they can't expect us to help them defend Hong Kong. We must have collective security or we'll fall." He then assured the leaders that "I don't see any reason for American ground troops to be committed in Indochina, don't think we need it," because "there are plenty of people in Asia, and we can train them to fight. It may be necessary for us eventually to use some of our planes or aircraft carriers off the coast and some of our fighting craft we have in that area for support."

Milliken said that if the British and French "deserted, we would have to go back to fortress America." Eisenhower turned on him angrily and ended the discussion by saying, "Listen, Gene, if we ever come back to fortress America, then the word 'fortress' would be entirely wrong in this day and age. Dien Bien Phu is a perfect example of a fortress. If we ever came back to the fortress idea for America, we would have one simple, dreadful alternative—we would have to explode an attack with everything we have. What a terrible decision that would be to make."

After the meeting, Eisenhower walked to the Oval Office with Hagerty. The President told his press secretary to prime a reporter to ask him at the next news conference about the Geneva Conference. Eisenhower would then try to emphasize "that all is not lost if Dien Bien Phu falls, which probably it will within a week."[90]

Eisenhower then wrote a long, thoughtful letter to Gruenther, whom he depended upon as his most reliable link to the French leadership. After repeating once again that unilateral American intervention was out of the question ("it would lay us open to the charge of imperialism and colonialism or—at the very least—of objectionable paternalism"), Eisenhower complained that "ever since 1945 France has been unable to decide whether she most fears Russia or Germany. As a consequence, her policies in Europe have been nothing but confusion; starts and stops; advances and retreats!" Eisenhower said of Dien Bien Phu, "This spectacle has been saddening indeed. It seems incredible that a nation which had only the help of a tiny British Army when it turned back the German flood in 1914 and withstood the gigantic 1916 attacks at Verdun could now be reduced to the point that she cannot produce a few hundred technicians to keep planes flying properly in Indochina." Eisenhower thought the French problem was one of leadership and spirit. "The only hope is to produce a new and inspirational leader—and I do *not* mean one that is 6 feet 5 and who considers himself to be, by some miraculous biological and transmigrative process, the offspring of Clemenceau and Jeanne d'Arc."

Then Eisenhower turned serious, ticking off points he wanted Gruenther to make to the French. The loss of Dien Bien Phu did not mean the loss of the war. The French should join United Action to stop "Communist advances in Southeast Asia": not to hurl back, but to stop such expansion; i.e., after partition. Eisenhower wanted the French Army to remain in Vietnam and promised that "additional ground forces should come from Asiatic and European troops already in the region" (that is, there would be no American troops but America would pay the bills). The French should grant independence. The ultimate goal, Eisenhower told the SACEUR to pass on to the French, was to create a "concert of nations" in Southeast Asia on the NATO model.[91]

This was Eisenhower's first direct mention of the idea of a Southeast Asia Treaty Organization (SEATO), and it was significant that he made it to the SACEUR. He thought first of NATO. His own vehement anti-Communism certainly played the major role in his Vietnam policy, tempered of course by his realism, but his anxieties about the French were also important considerations. He felt the French had to be dealt with like children, but he rejected the de Gaulle alternative. He had to support Pleven, now reportedly his only hope for getting EDC ratified by the French. And if EDC failed, German rearmament would be even more difficult to achieve. And without German rearmament, NATO would continue to be a hollow shell. In some part, then, SEATO came about because of the needs of NATO.

On the morning of April 29, at a news conference, Eisenhower referred obliquely to partition in response to a question from Joseph Harsch about Eisenhower's recent use of the phrase *"modus vivendi"* in Indochina. Eisenhower said he was "steering a course between two extremes, one of which, I would say, would be unattainable, and the other unacceptable." It would not be acceptable, he explained, "to see the whole anti-Communistic defense of that area crumble and disappear." But because the Vietminh were winning, there could be no hope of getting a "satisfactory answer" from them. "The most you can work out is a practical way of getting along." Eisenhower then mentioned divided Germany and Berlin as an example of "getting along one with the other, no more. Now, I think that for the moment, if you could get that, that would be the most you could ask."[92]

Immediately after the news conference, Eisenhower went to a three-hour NSC meeting, most of it devoted to Vietnam. According to notes Nixon kept, "Stassen said that he thought that decision should be to send ground troops if necessary to save Indochina, and to do it on a unilateral basis if that was the only way it could be done. The President himself said that he could not visualize a ground troop operation in Indochina that would be supported by the people of the United States and which would not in the long run put our defense too far out of balance. He also raised the point that we simply could not go in unilaterally because that was in violation of our whole principle of collective defense against communism in all places in the world."[93]

Eisenhower told Stassen that there would be the most serious repercussions among the NATO allies, especially Britain, if the United States went in on its own. He then turned the discussion to a postpartition "Pacific coalition." Eisenhower said that future American efforts would be toward organizing a regional coalition, obtaining British support for it, and pressing France to grant independence. Eisenhower would not seek congressional approval for American participation in a collective intervention until a coalition could be put together.[94]

The following morning, Bobby Cutler brought him a draft of an NSC paper that was exploring the possibilities of using atomic bombs in Vietnam. Eisenhower told Cutler, "I certainly do not think that the atom bomb can be used by the United States unilaterally." Eisenhower turned on Cutler. "You boys must be crazy. We can't use those awful things against Asians for the second time in less than ten years. My God."[95]

On May 7, Dien Bien Phu surrendered. Eisenhower tried to keep up the pretense that the French had lost only a battle, not the war. He told the NSC of his "firm belief that two, and only two, developments would really save the situation in French Indochina." First, Paris had to grant independence; second, the French needed to appoint a better general to take charge of the campaign. The French could still win, but time was running out. Cutler then joined Nixon and Stassen in again urging a unilateral American intervention. Eisenhower ignored them.[96]

So Eisenhower's policy was set: to accept partition, although only after obstructing and delaying the process as long as possible, and then to create SEATO. He had managed to avoid involvement in the war, but he was determined to make as firm a commitment to the non-Communist remainder of Southeast Asia as America had made to the NATO countries.

Of all Eisenhower's reasons for staying out of Vietnam, the one that meant most to him was the potential effect of intervention on the American people. The Korean War had been divisive enough; Eisenhower shuddered to think of the consequences of getting into a war to fight for a French colony less than a year after the armistice in Korea. That was the reason for his stress on prior congressional approval; if he could get it, he would be leading a united nation. But he doubted that he could get it, precisely because the nation was badly divided.

Eisenhower's decision to stay out of Vietnam did not have the dramatic quality to it that his 1944 D-Day decision had, because it was made over a longer period of time. Nevertheless, it was as decisive, in its way, because in both cases what happened next depended solely upon his word. At any time in the last weeks of Dien Bien Phu he could have ordered an air strike, either atomic or conventional. Many of his senior advisers wanted him to do just that, including his chairman of the JCS, his Vice-President, his head of the NSC planning staff, his MSA adviser, and (sometimes) his Secretary of State. Eisenhower said no, decisively. He had looked at the military options, with his professional eye, and pronounced them unsatisfactory. On June 5, 1944, they had been satisfactory, and he said go; in April 1954, they were unsatisfactory, and he said don't go.

From that moment on, Eisenhower supporters could claim, "He got us out of Korea and he kept us out of Vietnam."

CHAPTER EIGHT

McCarthy, Guatemala, SEATO

May 8–September 8, 1954

IN HIS MEMOIRS, Eisenhower complained that the day Dien Bien Phu fell, the banner headlines covered not that event but rather McCarthy's demand for a test of Eisenhower's right to use executive privilege to bar secret data to congressional investigators. Ten years later, Eisenhower said, it was plain to see that the action in Vietnam was far more important than McCarthy, who "ceased to command public attention shortly after that day in history."[1] What Eisenhower could not know was that almost exactly *twenty* years later the precedent of executive privilege he created in his response to McCarthy's demand would play the central role in Nixon's response to Watergate. In May 1974 it would not have been quite so self-evident that the headline writers had put the wrong story on top back in 1954.

Eisenhower took McCarthy's demand far more seriously than he implied in his memoirs. In March, he had asked the Attorney General if the President could order federal personnel to not appear before McCarthy on the grounds that they were being abused. The reply was that there was no such precedent.[2] On May 3 and 5, Eisenhower asked for further briefs on his power to withhold confidential information from Congress.

What bothered Eisenhower was how far down he could extend the blank wall. On May 11, Wilson called him to report that the McCarthy committee had demanded the names of all Army personnel who had any connection with the Peress case. Wilson said that Ridgway "violently objected" to this, and asked Eisenhower what to do. Eisenhower said that in this case the Army had better give in to avoid the appearance of a "cover-up."[3] Two days later, McCarthy was threatening to subpoena White House personnel. Eisenhower began to feel the pressure. In a conference with Adams and Hagerty, Eisenhower said it might be necessary to send one man from the White House, probably Adams, before the committee. He should give his name, and title, and then refuse to answer all questions under presidential order.[4]

The following day, May 14, Eisenhower told Hagerty that he was not even going to send Adams. "Congress has absolutely no right to ask them to testify in any way, shape, or form about the advice that they were giving to me at any time on any subject." Eisenhower was angrier than he had ever been with McCarthy, because McCarthy had now pushed him to the point where he had to act. His response to McCarthy's demands had become the central issue. With Adams, Lodge, and the others before his committee, McCarthy could have a field day. It made Eisenhower shudder to think of what McCarthy might bring up. Worst of all would be Oppenheimer.

What was at stake, as Eisenhower saw it, was the modern Presidency. Previous Presidents had been exceedingly reluctant to withhold information or witnesses from Congress, and Brownell was never able to find any convincing precedent for a doctrine of executive privilege. What Eisenhower felt so keenly was the *need* for such a doctrine for a President in the nuclear age. The reason there were no precedents was precisely because the situation was unprecedented. There were so many things Eisenhower felt he had to keep secret, like Oppenheimer, the H-bomb tests, the CIA's covert activities, and a host of others, that he was willing to vastly expand the powers of the Presidency to do it. He told Hagerty, "If they want to make a test of this principle, I'll fight them tooth and nail and up and down the country. It is a matter of principle with me and I will never permit it."[5]

On May 17, at a leaders' meeting, Eisenhower said that "any man who testifies as to the advice he gave me won't be working for me that night. I will not allow people around me to be subpoenaed and you might just as well know it now." Knowland protested that it would be a terrible thing if Eisenhower challenged Congress' right to subpoena. Eisenhower repeated that "my people are not going to be subpoenaed."[6]

That afternoon, Eisenhower released a letter to Wilson, directing Wilson to withhold information from the committee. The President put his case in sweeping terms: "It is essential to efficient and effective

administration that employees of the Executive Branch be in a position to be completely candid in advising with each other on official
matters." Therefore "it is not in the public interest that *any* of their
conversations or communications, or *any* documents or reproductions,
concerning such advice be disclosed."[7] This was, Arthur Schlesinger,
Jr., writes, "the most absolute assertion of presidential right to withhold information from Congress ever uttered to that day in American
history."[8] Earlier Presidents had held that their conversations in Cabinet meetings were privileged and confidential, but none had ever
dared extend this privilege to *everybody* in the Executive Branch.
Congress was upset, Republicans and Democrats alike. The Army-
McCarthy committee members told reporters that they could not possibly carry on unless Eisenhower relaxed the order. He was asked at a
press conference two days later whether he intended to do so. "I have
no intention whatsoever of relaxing or rescinding the order," he declared. He said he hoped the hearings would end soon, "so these ex-
traneous matters and these things that roam all up and down the al-
leys of government, of every kind of thought and idea, are kept out of
them. Now I hope that disposes of my order."[9]

McCarthy was livid. His real source of power was the power to
subpoena, and he knew at once that his whole career was at stake. He
therefore made a public appeal to federal employees to disregard
Eisenhower's orders and report directly to him on "graft, corruption,
Communism, and treason." Eisenhower took up the challenge. When
Hagerty discussed McCarthy's appeal with Eisenhower, the red-faced
President damned "the complete arrogance of McCarthy." Pacing
around the room, speaking in rapid-fire order, Eisenhower said, "This
amounts to nothing but a wholesale subversion of public service . . .
McCarthy is deliberately trying to subvert the people we have in gov-
ernment. I think this is the most disloyal act we have ever had by anyone in the government of the United States."

Eisenhower told Hagerty to make sure the subject came up at his
next press conference, so that he would have the opportunity to tell
the reporters "that in my opinion this is the most arrogant invitation
to subversion and disloyalty that I have ever heard of. I won't stand
for it for one minute."[10] But between the time of that discussion and
the press conference, Eisenhower spent another afternoon on the Oppenheimer case. He was beginning to think that the case was even
worse than he had feared, that Oppenheimer really was a Communist,
and really had significantly held back H-bomb development.[11] But
whatever the facts, Eisenhower remained determined to avoid a public

debate on Oppenheimer, with its probable demoralizing effect on the atomic scientists. So he did not want to push McCarthy too far against the wall. He did not deliver the rough treatment that he had promised to give McCarthy at the press conference; instead he refused to answer any questions on the subject. He simply held to his order on executive privilege.[12]

Next McCarthy threatened once again to investigate the CIA. Eisenhower was delighted. He explained to his aides, "My boys, I am convinced of one thing. The more we can get McCarthy threatening to investigate our Intelligence, the more public support we are going to get. If there is any way I could trick him into renewing his threat, I would be very happy to do so and then let him have it."[13] In practice, however, he moved to outflank McCarthy by setting up his own committee "to conduct a study of the covert activities of the CIA," and appointed General James H. Doolittle to head it.[14]

The Army-McCarthy hearings, meanwhile, droned on to their doleful conclusion. On June 18, the day after they ended, Eisenhower called Army counsel Joseph Welch to the Oval Office, where he congratulated Welch on his prosecution of the Army's case. Welch said that the only good thing to come out of the hearings was that they had given the nation an opportunity to see McCarthy in action. Eisenhower agreed.[15]

And that indeed was the effective end of McCarthy. He still retained considerable strength in the polls, he still had his committee chairmanship, but he no longer had the power to frighten. The Army-McCarthy hearings had degenerated to ridiculous points of trivia, primarily because Eisenhower denied to the committee access to people and records that could have provided McCarthy with sensational disclosures. But with nothing substantial to go after, McCarthy was reduced to ranting and raving (and increasingly heavy drinking), which cost him his credibility. It was not the things Eisenhower did behind the scenes but rather his most public act, the assertion of the right of executive privilege, that was his major contribution to McCarthy's downfall. At the time, few noticed and fewer commented on Eisenhower's boldness in establishing executive privilege, which quickly came to be regarded as traditional.

In the spring of 1954, the Supreme Court was scheduled to make its pronouncement in the school segregation cases. Brownell told Eisenhower that he thought the Court wanted to delay making a ruling as long as possible. Eisenhower laughingly replied that he hoped they would defer it until the next Administration took over. More seriously, the President said, "I don't know where I stand, but I think I stand that the best interests of the United States demand an answer in keeping with past decisions."[16] He invited Warren to the White House for a stag dinner, along with Brownell, John W. Davis, who was counsel for the segregationists, and a number of other lawyers. Eisenhower had Davis sit near Warren, who in turn was on the President's right hand. During dinner, Eisenhower—according to Warren— "went to considerable lengths to tell me what a great man Mr. Davis was." And as the guests were filing out of the dining room, Eisenhower took Warren by the arm and said of the southerners, "These are not bad people. All they are concerned about is to see that their sweet little girls are not required to sit in school alongside some big overgrown Negroes."[17]

If Eisenhower intended to influence Warren, he failed. On May 17, the Court handed down its decision in the case of *Brown* v. *Topeka*. It declared segregation by race in public schools to be unconstitutional. Eisenhower was "considerably concerned," Hagerty recorded in his diary the next day. The President thought that the southerners might "virtually cancel out their public education system," putting in its place all-white "private" schools to which state money would be diverted. "The President expressed the fear that such a plan if it were followed through would not only handicap Negro children but would work to the detriment of the so-called 'poor whites' in the South."[18]

In his memoirs, Warren wrote that he always believed that Eisenhower "resented our decision in *Brown*." He added that with that decision, "[there] went our cordial relations."[19] Much later, in the sixties, Eisenhower frequently remarked that his biggest mistake was "the appointment of that dumb son of a bitch Earl Warren."[20] But Eisenhower did not have those feelings at the time; he came to them as a result of his disapproval of the Warren Court's decisions in criminal and Communist cases in the early sixties (as Warren himself notes in another section of his memoirs).[21] Although Eisenhower personally wished that the Court had upheld *Plessy* v. *Ferguson*, and said so on a number of occasions (but only in private), he was impressed by the 9 to 0 vote and he certainly was going to meet his responsibilities and enforce the law. But he would not comment on it in public. At a May 19 press conference, he was asked if he had any advice to give to the South as to how to react. "Not in the slightest," Eisenhower replied. "The Supreme Court has spoken and I am sworn to uphold the constitutional processes in this country; and I will obey."[22]

Shortly thereafter, Eisenhower wrote Hazlett, "The segregation issue will, I think, become acute or tend to die out according to the character of the procedure orders that the Court will probably issue this winter. My own guess is that they will be very moderate and accord a maximum of initiative to local courts."[23] He was right about that. He admired Warren for his moderation in the pursuit of desegregation, and continued to support Warren strongly in his correspondence and conversation. In December 1955, when Hagerty asked about the possibilities of getting the Republican nomination for the Presidency for Warren, Eisenhower snapped back, "Not a chance, and I'll tell you why. I know that the Chief Justice is very happy right where he is. He wants to go down in history as a great Chief Justice, and he certainly is becoming one. He is dedicated to the Court and is getting the Court back on its feet and back in respectable standing again."[24]

"Both Eisenhower and Warren," Herbert Brownell once said, "were very reserved men. If you'd try to put your arm around either of them, he'd remember it for sixty days."[25] And William Ewald, an Eisenhower speech writer, puts it perfectly when he says of Eisenhower and Warren, "For more than seven years they sat, each on his eminence, at opposite ends of Pennsylvania Avenue, by far the two most towering figures in Washington, each playing out a noble role, in tragic inevitable estrangement."[26]

What hurt was not Eisenhower's private disapproval of *Brown*, but his refusal to give it a public endorsement. As with McCarthy, Eisenhower insisted time and again that he had neither need nor right to comment. Even as violence flared across the South, as the implementation of desegregation began, Eisenhower refused to ever say that he thought segregation was morally wrong. That allowed the bitter-end segregationists to claim that Eisenhower was secretly on their side, which they said justified their tactics.[27] Warren, and many others, thought that one word from Eisenhower would have made possible a smoother, easier, and quicker transition period. But Eisenhower never said the word. He insisted that it was not his role to comment on Court decisions, just as firmly as he insisted that the Court's ruling had a "binding effect" on everyone. He told Hazlett, "I hold to the basic purpose. There must be respect for the Constitution—which means the Supreme Court's interpretation of the Constitution—or we shall have chaos. This I believe with all of my heart—and shall always act accordingly."[28] That was a long way from President Andrew Jackson's famous dictum, "John Marshall has made his decision; now let him enforce it." But it was also a long way from saying that *Brown* was morally right. He missed a historic opportunity to provide moral leadership. In fact, until Little Rock in 1957 he provided almost no leadership at all on the most fundamental social problem of his time.

One place where he did supply leadership was in the worldwide struggle against the Communists, especially in Central America, although here too he was careful to operate in private, and secretly. Reports from two men he trusted above all others—his brother Milton and Beetle Smith—had convinced him that Guatemala was fast falling to the Communists. Milton had made a fact-finding trip to Latin America for his brother in 1953; when he returned, Milton said that Guatemala had "succumbed to Communist infiltration." Smith, six months later, told Eisenhower that "the Guatemalan government has abundantly proved its Communist sympathies."[29] Many other observers, however, including some in the State Department, said that the "proof" was lacking, that Jacobo Arbenz was a democratically elected President who was trying to carry out a relatively mild land-reform program. According to this view, the critics of Arbenz were using his toleration of the Communist Party as a red flag; their real objection was to Arbenz' nationalization of some of United Fruit's vast idle acreage in Guatemala. And it certainly was true that United Fruit had some highly placed friends in the Administration; among others of Eisenhower's closest advisers, the two Dulles brothers, Bobby Cutler, Henry Cabot Lodge, and Sinclair Weeks—and even Ann Whitman— had a financial stake in United Fruit, and thus a direct interest in overthrowing Arbenz.[30]

Eisenhower, too, wanted Arbenz removed, not so much to protect United Fruit but because he genuinely believed that Arbenz either was himself a Communist or had been taken over by them. Sometime in late 1953 or early 1954 (it is impossible to pinpoint the project's inception), Eisenhower told the CIA to go ahead with Operation Pbsuccess, a covert action designed to drive Arbenz from office and replace him with someone more acceptable to the Americans. Planning took place with utmost stealth, as Richard Immerman writes in his authoritative account of the incident. Only Eisenhower, the Dulles brothers, Cutler, and a handful of others knew that an operation was even being considered. The CIA marked its communications to the President and the Secretary of State "top secret Ita," a superclassification that restricted circulation of the document to the recipient. Later, the Agency burned most of the papers generated by Pbsuccess. All agents brought in on the operation were sworn to secrecy. Eisenhower usually dis-

cussed the project with the Dulles brothers at a Sunday brunch that
Eleanor Dulles hosted for her two brothers each week.[31]

The model for Pbsuccess was Ajax, the CIA coup the previous
year in Iran. It involved turning the Army against Arbenz, frightening
him into leaving the country, then staging a coup. Eisenhower's guide-
lines to the CIA were that there was to be no direct United States intervention. The planners could not use military force; they would
have to use deception, much as they had against Mossadegh. Dulles believed that the Agency could convince Arbenz that Colonel Carlos Castillo Armas, the CIA's chosen successor, was at the head of a major in-
surrectionary force, and that if necessary the United States was ready
to back him up with arms. But as Immerman insists, "The Eisenhower
administration never intended to commit United States troops or substantial equipment to the effort."[32]

In April, the CIA prepared Pbsuccess for action. On May 15, a
Swedish merchant vessel, the *Alfhem,* docked in Guatemala. It contained a load of small artillery pieces and small arms from Czechoslovakia. Foster Dulles announced the arrival in a press conference and
denounced this blatant violation of the Monroe Doctrine. Washington
was in an uproar. Senator Wiley, chairman of the Foreign Relations
Committee, called the shipment "part of the master plan of world
Communism." Eisenhower asserted that this "quantity [of arms] far
exceeded any legitimate, normal requirements for the Guatemalan
armed forces."[33] He was right, but the arms were not intended for the
armed forces. Arbenz distrusted his own military, with good reason, as
the CIA had been busy subverting the colonels and generals with
money and arguments about Arbenz' supposed Communist tendencies.
Arbenz therefore intended to distribute the arms to his supporters in
order to create a people's militia, free of any control by the Army.

Eisenhower moved immediately. He ordered an airlift of fifty tons
of rifles, pistols, machine guns, and ammunition to Guatemala's neighbors, Nicaragua and Honduras, both ruled by fanatic anti-Communist
dictators. Eisenhower also declared a naval blockade of Guatemala,
called for a meeting of the OAS, and ordered the CIA to put the first
phase of Pbsuccess into operation.[34]

Pbsuccess consisted of a handful of Guatemalans, hired by the
CIA, and their leader, Castillo Armas, who had been personally selected by agent Howard Hunt. Richard Bissell was in charge. Its principal asset was a radio station in Honduras, which beamed propaganda
into Guatemala City, along with "flashes" from the "front," where
supposedly major battles were taking place between Castillo Armas'

"invading force" and the Army. Actually, as Bissell himself later explained, Castillo Armas' force was at best a "ragtag" group that had yet to set foot on Guatemalan soil. But the excitement the radio broadcasts created in Guatemala, added to the intense diplomatic and propaganda pressure the United States government was putting on, led Arbenz to order martial law, and to ask the Russians for more arms.[35]

The Soviets responded by arranging to ship ammunition to Guatemala. On June 14, however, American Army officers in Hamburg seized the freighter. The officer in charge admitted that the shipment was perfectly legal and all papers were in order; therefore he had "detained but not confiscated" the ship. The British were furious, both at the seizure and at Dulles' proposal that ships bound for Guatemala voluntarily submit to a search by U.S. Navy vessels. Eden responded, "There is no general power of search on the high seas in peacetime."[36] Robert Murphy and other State Department officials then told Eisenhower that it was "a bad mistake" to violate "the high principle of freedom of the seas."[37]

But instead of calling off the blockade, Eisenhower intensified it. Simultaneously, he told Allen Dulles to put the final stage of Pbsuccess into action. On June 16, at a news conference, Eisenhower limited himself to a few noncommittal remarks about Guatemala, concluding, "I couldn't go beyond that in talking about the situation."[38] Two days later, Allen Dulles reported that "there would be an anti-Communist uprising in Guatemala very shortly," which meant Pbsuccess was in full gear. "Officially we don't know anything about it," Hagerty wrote in his diary.[39] The next day, June 19, *The New York Times'* headline proclaimed, "Revolt Launched in Guatemala: Land-Air-Sea Invasion Reported: Risings Under Way in Key Cities." That was putting it rather grandiloquently. In fact, Castillo Armas' "army" of 150 men had crossed the Honduran border, advanced six miles into Guatemala, settled down in the Church of the Black Christ—and waited for the Arbenz regime to collapse.

But nothing happened. The people did not rally to Castillo Armas' cause, the Guatemalan Army continued to sit in its barracks, refusing to get involved, and the Castillo Armas "army" stayed in its church. Late in the afternoon of June 22, Eisenhower held a meeting in the Oval Office with the Dulles brothers and Henry Holland, Assistant Secretary of State for Latin America. Allen Dulles reported that without some bombing raids against Guatemala City, the "rebellion" might soon die of boredom. The Guatemalan Army would not drive Castillo Armas out of the country, but neither would it turn on Arbenz. Dulles further reported that Anastasio Somoza, the Nicaraguan dictator, had offered to give Castillo Armas two P-51 fighter-bombers if the United States would agree to replace them. Dulles said this was the critical moment for Pbsuccess. Holland interrupted to say that the United States should keep hands off because the Latin-American republics would, "if our action became known, interpret our shipment of planes as intervention in Guatemala's internal affairs." But Allen Dulles insisted that supplying the two P-51s "was the only hope for Castillo Armas, who was obviously the only hope of restoring freedom to Guatemala."

Eisenhower asked Dulles, "What do you think Castillo's chances would be without the aircraft?" Dulles replied, "About zero." "Suppose we supply the aircraft. What would the chances be then?" Dulles thought "about twenty percent." As Eisenhower later put it, he "knew from experience the important psychological impact of even a small amount of air support, . . . our proper course of action—indeed my duty—was clear to me." He told Dulles to give Somoza the P-51s.[40]

So Castillo Armas got his planes. Meanwhile (something Eisenhower did not reveal in his memoirs), American bombers, flown by CIA pilots, were already based at Managua's international airport, and they joined in the air offensive. Arbenz asked the Security Council of the U.N. to put the Guatemalan situation on its agenda. He asked for U.N. observers, something the United States was determined to prevent, because observers would certainly identify the planes as American. But despite American opposition, France and Britain announced that they were supporting Arbenz in the U.N. Their action outraged the President. He told his aides, "We have been too damned nice" to the NATO allies. He singled out the British, who, he declared, "expect us to give them a free ride and side with them and yet they won't even support us on Guatemala." Eisenhower said he would teach them a lesson and show them that "they have no right to stick their noses into matters which concern this hemisphere entirely."[41] He then instructed Lodge to use the veto to keep Guatemala off the agenda, if necessary; America had never previously used the veto.

Lodge met with the British and French representatives. He told them he was prepared to veto, then added that Eisenhower had instructed him to say "if Great Britain and France felt that they must take an independent line backing the present government in Guatemala, we would feel free to take an equally independent line con-

cerning such matters as Egypt and North Africa." Britain and France
then abstained on the vote, the United States did not have to use the
veto, and Guatemala did not get on the agenda.[42]

The bombing raids continued, Arbenz lost his nerve, resigned,
and was replaced by a military dictatorship. The closest observers of
this incident believe that it was not the bombing raids that broke
Arbenz' will so much as it was his knowledge that Eisenhower was
putting his planes into the operation.[43] Arbenz had to assume that
Eisenhower, once committed, would escalate the American military
effort however far he had to go until he had achieved his objective.
Arbenz was almost certainly right in his anticipation of Eisenhower's
probable actions in the event that he, Arbenz, tried to stay in office.
Sometime later, Eisenhower told Andrew Goodpaster that "he had
gone quite deeply into the Guatemalan situation" and the decision
to act had been made. At this "critical period," Goodpaster recalled
Eisenhower saying, "some of those, of his principal associates began
to get nervous about it, after we had committed ourselves. And his
answer to them, which stayed very clear in his mind, was that the
time to have those thoughts was before we started down this course,
that if you at any time take the route of violence or support of violence . . . then you commit yourself to carry it through, and it's too
late to have second thoughts, not having faced up to the possible
consequences, when you're midway in an operation."[44]

Eisenhower was highly pleased by the outcome. At a June 30 news
conference, he announced that he had heard that the "Communists
and their great supporters were leaving Guatemala. If I would try to
conceal the fact that this gives me great satisfaction, I would just be
deceitful. Of course it has given me great satisfaction."[45] On January
19, 1955, when Eisenhower gave his first televised news conference, he
listed the elimination of the Arbenz regime as one of his proudest
accomplishments. In his memoirs, it was the only CIA covert operation that he mentioned, and he did so in some detail and with great
pride.[46]

But he gave his account a lighthearted touch by making it appear
that the only risk the United States took was to send two planes to
Somoza. In fact there were more planes involved, but what really
matters was how much more than planes Eisenhower had put at stake.
First, the prestige of the United States in a military action which he
would not hesitate to escalate if necessary. As he so firmly told Goodpaster, once you start this sort of thing you don't back down. Second,
at a time when the Geneva Conference was at a critical point and

Eisenhower badly needed British and French support for SEATO and EDC, he threatened to break with them—over tiny Guatemala. Third, he declared a naval blockade and enforced it. Fourth, he had authorized the first American use of the veto in the U.N., which would have given away one of America's prize propaganda assets, that only the Russians used the veto.

Clearly, the President took grave risks over Guatemala. He also opened himself to the criticism that American policy toward Central America was dictated by United Fruit (the company, incidentally, got its land back from Castillo Armas). But he did not overthrow the elected government of Guatemala, or risk SEATO and EDC, or declare a blockade, in order to protect the holdings of the United Fruit stockholders. What he feared was not the loss of American profits in Guatemala, but rather the loss of all Central America. Milton had reported to him that the area was a breeding ground for Communism, because of the awful extremes between rich and poor, and that long term the United States had to work to correct the disparity. But short term, Milton had warned, the United States could never afford to allow Communism to establish a foothold in Central America. If the Russians ever got a base there, they could export subversion, arms, a whole guerrilla uprising to the surrounding countryside. In Eisenhower's nightmare, the dominoes would fall in both directions, to the south of Guatemala toward Panama, endangering the Canal Zone, and to the north, bringing Communism to the Rio Grande. "My God," Eisenhower told his Cabinet, "just think what it would mean to us if Mexico went Communist!" He shook his head at the thought of that long, unguarded border, and all those Mexican Communists to the south of it.[47] To prevent the dominoes from falling, he was prepared to, and did, take great risks over tiny Guatemala.

At the height of the uproar over Guatemala, Churchill and Eden arrived for talks. It was June 25, the day the Security Council was to vote on Guatemala. Eisenhower "talked cold turkey" to the British, who then reluctantly and unhappily agreed to abstain and to recommend to the French that they do likewise. Churchill later complained to Eisenhower that "Dulles has said a couple of things to Eden that need not have been said."[48] For the rest of Churchill's visit his time was taken up with an address to Congress, stag dinners, formal and informal receptions, and other social events. Eisenhower found it difficult to talk to Churchill about matters of substance. The PM had had two strokes since he last saw Eisenhower at Bermuda, was in his dotage, quite feeble, could not hear, kept repeating points or asking the same question, and seemed almost to embarrass Eden and the rest of the British delegation. (One Britisher told Hagerty that the leadership no longer gave Churchill confidential information because he was likely to spill it in his next appearance before Commons.[49]) As Churchill was deaf, it was easy to keep information from him. Hagerty noted that during consultations, Churchill "constantly broke in with questions that had to be explained to him by either the President or Eden in a shouting tone of voice."[50]

It was all a great strain on Eisenhower—too many parties, too much shouting, too many people who wanted to meet Churchill and could not be denied (Ann Whitman and the aides were all agog at having the great man in the White House; everyone in the Cabinet wanted at least a few minutes alone with Churchill). Fortunately for Eisenhower, when Churchill left, the President was able to get away to Camp David for a long Fourth of July weekend.

All the gang came to Camp David. Mamie kept the women busy playing bolivia and talking; Eisenhower exhausted the men by insisting on as much bridge and golf as possible. The men and women got together only at their meals. Everyone brought gifts for the Eisenhowers; Pete Jones gave Mamie a solid-gold bracelet and Eisenhower a gold vest-pocket watch. Priscilla Slater questioned Pete's good taste, saying that the gifts seemed a bit lavish. On Sunday they all drove to Gettysburg, where the women inspected the interior decoration while the men checked the construction and talked about getting Eisenhower a good herd of Angus cattle. By Tuesday the various members of the gang were ready to return to their homes and work, but Eisenhower announced that he had been able to readjust his schedule and could stay an extra day. He asked the gang to stay with him. Over that afternoon's bridge game, Eisenhower said he could "not begin to tell us how happy he was." It was the best week of his life, Eisenhower declared, free from Washington, having fun with his pals, seeing the progress at Gettysburg and how happy it made Mamie.[51]

Shortly after returning to Washington, Eisenhower sent a private letter to Foster Dulles. The President said that his wine bill was getting completely out of hand because of all the entertaining he had to do, and that he had especially enjoyed some French white wine Dulles had given to him. He asked Dulles if the ambassador to France might not be able to arrange for importing a few dozen cases of that wine "without the need for paying duty." Eisenhower admitted that he would be "horribly embarrassed" if this deal became public knowledge, but the savings on customs duties would be so great that he wanted it done if it could be done "quietly."[52]

Back in Washington, the business at hand was getting Eisenhower's program through Congress and preparing for the fall congressional elections. Eisenhower was convinced that his middle-of-the-road program was best for the country, and best for the Republican Party. He thought that if the party supported him, Republican congressmen would be assured of re-election. Many Republicans and their supporters strongly disagreed and continued to oppose the President on specific issues. His proposal of a Health Reinsurance Bill for private health-insurance companies was one example. The AMA was dead set against it, and the Old Guard supported the AMA, on the grounds that this was the entering wedge of socialized medicine. When Knowland made that argument to Eisenhower at a leaders' meeting, Eisenhower cut him off. "Listen, Bill," the President said, "what do you think we're going to tell the people of the United States? . . . As far as I'm concerned, the American Medical Association is just plain stupid. This plan of ours would have shown the people how we could improve their health and stay out of socialized medicine." To Charlie Halleck, he said, "I don't believe the people are going to stand for being deprived of the opportunity to get medical insurance. If they don't get a bill like this, they will go for socialized medicine sooner or later and the Medical Association will have no one to blame but itself." He complained that there was no way to do business with the hierarchy of the AMA, "a little group of reactionary men dead set against any change."[53] But he did not get the bill passed.

The reactionaries were giving him trouble on many fronts. He told one friend that Washington was full of people—important people—"who want to eliminate everything that the federal government has ever done that represents social advance. For example, all of the regulatory commissions are anathema to these people. They want to abolish them completely. They believe that there should be no trade union laws and the government should do nothing even to encourage pension plans." To one such reactionary who had made a specific proposal, Eisenhower rejoined, "I must say that if you think you are going to get rid of the graduated income tax, you are certainly planning to live far longer than I am." His own stance, he explained, was that "excluding the field of moral values, anything that affects or is proposed for masses of humans is wrong if the position it seeks is at either end of possible argument."[54]

Eisenhower wanted his entire program put through. He told his Cabinet, "I want to remind you of what Nelson said just before Trafalgar. He told his officers that 'as long as we have any enemy ship afloat the victory is not won.' That's the way I feel about this whole business."[55] When the Republican leaders in Congress told him that they could not stop a bill giving pay raises and the right to form a union to postal employees, Eisenhower lost his temper. This was a "raid on the Treasury," he thundered, at a time when the Administration was within sight of balancing the budget. "What the hell is going on?" he demanded to know. He swore he would veto such a bill, and told the leaders that they were "opening up a Pandora's box." Allowing federal employees to unionize would be "a terrible mistake. Suppose you had an organized Army reporting and responsible to union bosses—wouldn't that be something! I am not going to be slick on this one. I am not going to run around the cabbage patch."[56]

Despite his outburst, the Republicans would not support him on the issue. There were too many votes to be won, and too few to be lost, on a postal pay raise. The representatives were all facing re-election, as were one-third of the senators. Eisenhower could afford to take the high ground; they had to get the votes. The situation led Eisenhower to propose a constitutional amendment to his Cabinet, one that would make the terms of the representatives four years instead of two. If that were done, they would have to run when the President did, and would be much more amenable to party control and to acting for the good of the country rather than for their own re-election. As things stood, Eisenhower said, congressmen were "always running." He said he just tossed out the idea for consideration, "but I've been thinking about it for months."[57] His idea, however, was as much of a will-of-the-wisp as was his continuing notion to form a third party that would stand between the extreme Democrats and the extreme Republicans, and nothing ever came of it.

As Congress prepared to end its business and face the voters, any number of vote-catching bills were introduced and rushed through the legislative process. One of them was to stop TV and radio advertisements for liquor and cigarettes. Eisenhower was opposed: "What are we going to turn out to be—a police state?" Another proposed to insert the words "under God" in the Pledge of Allegiance. Eisenhower was "very much in favor of it. Why not get up a speech and say that the only one who would be opposed to this would be a Communist?"[58]

The economy was improving, but not rapidly, and the Democrats were talking depression. Eisenhower deplored the way they played politics with the economy. "The Democrats are really riding for a hell of a fall if they turn out to be wrong prophets of a depression," he told the Republican leaders. "How a man can preach depression for the sake of a few votes—well, I'll be a son of a sea cook if I don't think a man who does that is—well [expletive deleted]." [59] The President urged his Cabinet members to spend as much of their appropriation as soon as possible, in order to help recovery; he sent a note to Sherman Adams: "Where do we stand on our 'dramatic' plan to get 50 billion dollars' worth of self-liquidating highways under construction?" [60]

One place the President was not willing to spend money was on TVA. The Democrats wanted to expand it; Eisenhower would have liked to sell it to private industry. He never dared to go that far, but he was constantly complaining about TVA to his Cabinet. "Every river valley in America is open to development" was his position. Therefore, "Why favor Tennessee?" He thought that if the government was going to get into the business of producing electricity, it should do so "everywhere." [61] In the West, where the Truman Administration had started or proposed a number of TVA-like power projects, the Eisenhower Administration took most of the sites out of federal hands, including the biggest, Hells Canyon on the Snake River, and sold them to private companies. When Tennessee politicians asked to expand TVA so it could provide for the growing needs of both the AEC and the city of Memphis, Eisenhower flatly refused. Instead, he authorized a contract with Edgar Dixon and Eugene Yates, who had formed a company to build steam plants to provide additional electricity for both the AEC and Memphis. Eisenhower was pleased at his success in preventing the "encroachment of socialistic tendencies" on the utility industry. He could see no reason why the "nation's taxpayers should be forever committed to providing cheap power for the people in the TVA region." [62]

On TVA, most Republicans were with him. On the tariff, most were opposed. The congressmen were concerned with jobs and profits; Eisenhower was concerned about world strategy and economics. Various bills to halt Japanese imports, for example, seemed to him to be shortsighted at best. Without a healthy trade relationship with the United States, he told one trade group that had come to him to protest against Japanese imports, Japan "with its vast population and resources might be lost to the Communists." [63] Long term, he wanted to get the Japanese to sell their goods on the Asian mainland, which was one reason he put such stress on holding on in Indochina. He told the Cabinet, "If China finds that it can buy cheap straw hats, cheap cotton shirts, sneakers, bicycles, and all the rest of that sort of stuff from Japan, it would seem to me that would set up the need within China for dependence upon Japan." In return, Japan could get raw materials from China. "We will have to exercise great care and we will have to watch Japan very closely," he concluded.[64]

The Old Guard wanted to stop all trade with Communist countries. Even Eisenhower's majority leader in the Senate, Knowland, wanted such a blockade. "Knowland has no foreign policy," Eisenhower complained to Gruenther, "except to develop high blood pressure whenever he mentions the words 'Red China.'"[65] Once again, the Old Guard seemed to Eisenhower to be impossibly stupid. He said that trade with the satellite nations "would in the end weaken the Russian hold on them . . . Trade is the strongest weapon of the diplomat and it should be used more." In Eisenhower's view, "Anyone who says that to trade with a Red country is in effect advocating a traitorous act just doesn't know what he's talking about."[66]

As the summer wore on, and the campaign began, the Republicans escalated their political rhetoric, led by the McCarthyites in the Senate, who were hitting hard on the "twenty years of treason" theme. Nixon, out campaigning, was beginning to sound like them. Eisenhower called Nixon into his office to tell him to back off. The President said he needed Democratic votes to get his program passed and Nixon was not helping by calling the Democrats traitors. Nixon explained that he had meant to attack only Acheson and Truman, not the entire party. Eisenhower replied that any talk about treason by the Democrats was "indefensible," and he ordered Nixon to stop it.[67] Nixon stopped—at least for a while.

In early August, McCarthy said that Marshall "would sell out his grandmother for personal advantage." Eisenhower was asked at a news conference what he thought about the charge. Eisenhower launched into a full and spirited defense of Marshall ("a brilliant record") but was careful to note that he "knew nothing" about Marshall's performance in China after the war.[68] Privately, however, he blamed Marshall for the loss of China. As he explained to Nixon, "The reason we lost China . . . was because [Marshall] had insisted upon Chiang Kai-shek taking Communists into his government, against Chiang's judgment."[69]

The reason we know about this, and other private conversations with Nixon and other visitors to the Oval Office, is that the President had wired the office in order to tape-record his conversations. He had a switch under his desk that turned the machine on; Ann Whitman complained that he often forgot to use it, and when he did activate the machine the talk was usually garbled. Still, innumerable records were made. Eisenhower recommended to his Cabinet that the members tape-record all their telephone calls, or at least have them monitored (as were all the President's calls). Laughing, Eisenhower explained, "You know, boys, it's a good thing when you're talking to someone you don't trust to get a record made of it. There are some guys I just don't trust in Washington, and I want to have myself protected so that they can't later report that I said something else."[70] Eisenhower nearly always remembered to turn on the machine when he was talking to Nixon.

With elections in the air, Eisenhower's mind turned to his own political situation. He had been insisting for a year and a half that he would not be a candidate for re-election. On July 27, however, he told Hagerty that "I will run for another term," but warned that "I am telling everyone that they better not speculate on this and let me make the decision. After all, it is my life and it will have to be my decision." He then confessed that for the first time he was beginning to feel the tension of his office. The Geneva Conference had just concluded, on a sour note for the United States, and he was impatient with Congress. He hated "the multiplicity of petty problems that many people bring to me. The selfishness of the members of Congress is incredible . . . They are just about driving me nuts."[71]

Eisenhower did not tell Hagerty that he was also disappointed in his aides, but he was. He missed Emmet Hughes and C. D. Jackson, especially Jackson. On August 4, he wrote Bill Robinson a five-page, single-spaced letter, saying that he needed help. He wished he could find someone—"A man of stature, of good judgment, of complete objectivity"—who could give him advice. "I need a person to evaluate the importance of the decisions I must make," Eisenhower said, "to take over at least some of them . . . make the necessary study, and come up with what seems to be the best possible solution." He hinted that he thought Robinson could handle the assignment, but Robinson was about to take over as president of Coca-Cola and, anyway, wanted to keep his relationship with Eisenhower on an informal basis.[72]

Next to Robinson, Eisenhower wanted Jackson back. But Jackson was making too much money at Time-Life to abandon his post

for the pay of a White House aide. On August 11, he did come down
from New York for a conference with the President and his aides, at
Eisenhower's direct request, to provide a critique of the Administration to date. Jackson said that the first thing that was wrong was the
absence of follow-through. Atoms for peace, for example, had been
launched with great fanfare—and then nothing happened. Eisenhower
interrupted to say that it had taken six full months to get a definite
no out of the Soviets on that one, and that now he was prepared to go
ahead with atoms for peace without the Russians. Jackson then complained about Eisenhower's McCarthy policy, saying that the President
was still allowing the senator to run rampant. Eisenhower's reaction
to McCarthy, Jackson said, was "utterly incomprehensible to really
serious people." He warned that the impression was getting about that
Eisenhower did not like his job. The government was not doing anything dramatic, at home or abroad. There was a sense of stagnation.
Jackson wanted action.

    To that end, Jackson proposed a "world economic plan" and had
brought along a draft on the subject. He thought it necessary, dramatic, and good for both Eisenhower and the Republican Party.
Eisenhower disagreed. He thought "we ought first of all to be content
with little steps, even if we use the occasional dramatic appeal." Eisenhower felt that there had been altogether too much talk about America's role as a world leader, especially by Truman. The President
thought a "world economic plan" much too ambitious, and confessed
that "trying to sell it to Congress scares me." The meeting concluded
on that unsatisfactory note. Jackson agreed to fly down one day a
week to "help out," but that was the only positive achievement of
Eisenhower's attempt to get better advice.[73]

    The most serious problem Eisenhower had to face in the summer
of 1954, and the one of the largest long-term significance, was Vietnam. The Geneva Conference was under way, with Beetle Smith there
as the American representative. With Dien Bien Phu gone, the Communists at Geneva were stalling on the talks while the Vietminh re-
grouped after their victory and prepared to attack the French throughout the delta region of Vietnam. Which upset Eisenhower most—
French defeatism or British refusal to cooperate—would be impossible
to say. Australia and New Zealand had told Dulles they were willing
to join a regional alliance; Eisenhower said that they were "more
realistic and possibly more courageous than those who are apparently
willing to accept any arrangement that allows them . . . to save a bit

of face and possibly a couple of miserable trading posts in the Far East."[74] On May 5, Eisenhower told a news conference that "we will never give up," and again gave a strong pitch for SEATO. That afternoon, Smith sent word that the British were proposing a five-power grouping (the U.K., U.S., France, New Zealand, and Australia) that would have its headquarters in Singapore. That was a bit of an improvement in the British position, but not much—Eisenhower wanted Asian nations included in the alliance—and he instructed Dulles to tell Eden that the United States would "not agree to a 'white man's party' to determine the problems of Southeast Asia."[75] The President also told Dulles to work on Churchill's "sense of history" by implying that the British in their desperate search for a negotiated settlement in Indochina "were really promoting a second Munich."[76]

Meanwhile a major war scare ensued. The French convinced themselves that the Chinese were on the verge of intervening with jet aircraft to aid the Vietminh in their final drive to Hanoi. If that happened, the French wanted a guarantee of a massive and immediate American intervention. The JCS, the NSC, the State Department, and the White House all began to study the options intensively. The JCS, led by Radford, who had already made a series of unauthorized promises of support to the French, were ready to go—not to Indochina, but to China itself. Bobby Cutler reported to the President that the NSC also believed that "there was little use discussing any 'defense' of Southeast Asia; that U.S. power should be directed against the source of the peril, which was, at least in the first instance, China, and that in this connection atomic weapons should be used."[77] (Shortly thereafter, Eisenhower told Dulles that he felt "the NSC work was too hurried, and did not deal sufficiently with the long-range problems."[78])

Dulles was also breathing fire. He thought Chinese intervention in Vietnam would be the "equivalent of a declaration of war against the United States." The Secretary of State advised the President to get a resolution through Congress at once, authorizing him to respond to a possible Chinese intervention as he saw fit. Eisenhower told Dulles (as recorded in notes taken by Cutler), "If he was to go to the Congress for authority he would not ask any halfway measures. If the situation warranted it, there should be declared a state of war with China; and possibly there should be a strike at Russia." That took Dulles' breath away. The President's next point eliminated the idea of a unilateral intervention by the United States. Eisenhower said, "He would never have the United States go into Indochina alone." Returning to his first point, Eisenhower said: "If the U.S. took action against Communist China, the President said there should be no halfway measures or frittering around. The Navy and Air Force should go in with full power, using new weapons, and strike at air bases and ports in mainland China." [79]

Then Eisenhower called in the JCS. He told the Chiefs that an atomic assault against China would inevitably bring Russia into the war; therefore if the United States were to launch a preventive attack, it had to be against both Russia and China simultaneously. Looking directly at Radford, Eisenhower said suppose it would be possible to destroy Russia. "I want you to carry this question home with you: Gain such a victory, and what do you do with it? Here would be a great area from the Elbe to Vladivostok . . . torn up and destroyed, without government, without its communications, just an area of starvation and disaster. I ask you what would the civilized world do about it? I repeat there is no victory except through our imaginations." [80]

With all the loose talk going on in Washington about atomic strikes, reporters inevitably heard about the JCS and NSC recommendations. At a news conference, Eisenhower was asked to comment on preventive war. He replied, "I don't believe there is such a thing; and, frankly, I wouldn't even listen to anyone seriously that came in and talked about such a thing." Was his answer based on military or moral considerations? "It seems to me that when, by definition, a term is just ridiculous in itself, there is no use in going any further," Eisenhower replied. [81]

Syngman Rhee flew to Washington to tell Eisenhower that the moment had come to strike hard at the Communists. "Let me tell you that if war comes," Eisenhower replied to Rhee, "it will be horrible. Atomic war will destroy civilization. War today is unthinkable with the weapons which we have at our command. If the Kremlin and Washington ever lock up in a war, the results are too horrible to contemplate. I can't even imagine them." [82]

Fortunately, the war scare in Indochina went away as quickly as it came on. The Chinese Air Force did not intervene in the delta. It did not have to, as the Vietminh were driving forward on their own, and the Laniel government in Paris was tottering. Gruenther reported to Eisenhower that the French were threatening "a wave of anti-American outbursts in France with great bitterness because the Allies let us down." Eisenhower replied with a long, angry letter, reciting in some detail all that he had done for the French, and expressing his own bitterness that the United States should be blamed for French failures. Most galling was the continued French refusal, "even now," to grant independence to the Associated States.[83]

Four days later, on June 12, the Laniel government fell by a narrow margin, 306–293. On June 18 Pierre Mendès-France took office as Premier on the strength of a pledge that he would secure a peace in Indochina by July 20. Privately, he told Smith—who had flown from Geneva to Paris—that he might be meeting with Chou En-lai. Smith strongly advised him not to. (Smith, who was living a hectic life, was suffering terribly from his ulcers. Eisenhower sent him a handwritten note of thanks for his efforts, concluding, "I am lost in admiration of your patience, ability, and skill."[84] Three months later Smith had to resign.) Smith suspected a French sell-out. Neither he, Dulles, nor Eisenhower wanted to be a part of the surrender arrangements at Geneva. Smith therefore returned to the United States, and the American delegation at Geneva was reduced to an "observer" status.

Meanwhile, Churchill and Eden came to Washington; one of the things they discussed with Eisenhower was the French and EDC. Laniel had been a strong supporter of EDC, but Mendès-France was shaky. The final vote on ratification was imminent. Without EDC, there was no program for German rearmament. Before meeting with the British, Eisenhower told Dulles, "Churchill is not supporting EDC but he won't say so, so both you and I, Foster, had got to be very cagey on this. We are not interested in anything but EDC and we have got to be tough about it."[85] To get British cooperation on EDC, Eisenhower had something to offer Churchill. The British had been building bombers designed to carry atomic weapons, but they had more bombers than they did weapons. Eisenhower told Churchill, "If we ever get into trouble when we need these bombs it is our duty to provide them as quickly as possible to the British Air Force." Eisenhower privately told Dulles his reason: "I don't want to see American crews and American crews alone take the punishment they will have to take to deliver those bombs."[86] To influence both the French and the British on the EDC vote, Eisenhower had Knowland steer through the Senate a resolution, adopted unanimously, authorizing the President to take any steps necessary to "restore sovereignty to Germany and to enable her to contribute to the maintenance of peace and security." In other words, if France and Britain did not get behind EDC, the Americans would help the Germans rearm themselves, outside an all-European army, but inside NATO as a full partner.[87]

After discussing EDC, Eisenhower and Churchill turned to Indochina. They agreed on what their minimum objectives were: independence for Laos and Cambodia, with a Vietminh agreement to withdraw from those countries; partition of Vietnam at the 17th parallel, with the Vietminh taking over in the north.[88] As the Vietminh were demanding the whole of Indochina, and as they anticipated taking it by force in the near future, to ask them to settle for only northern Vietnam was to ask for major concessions from the victorious party. Nevertheless, accepting partition represented a major concession by the Americans, who in public were still insisting that the French should fight on. Eisenhower knew he would have the Old Guard to contend with, as well as his own military, whose inclination remained that it was better to launch an atomic attack on China than to accept the loss of northern Vietnam to the Communists. At a press conference on June 30, James Reston asked the President if he was willing to accept a partition that enslaved millions of people. Eisenhower replied, "I won't be a party to a treaty that makes anybody a slave; but to make such a statement doesn't mean you are not going to study every single region, every single incident that comes up, and decide what to do at the moment."[89]

While Eisenhower was meeting with Churchill, Mendès-France was meeting with Chou En-lai. Those two agreed to a temporary partition of Vietnam, to be instituted with a cease-fire and ended with nationwide elections within two years. They also agreed to independence for Laos and Cambodia, with all foreign troops withdrawn. Chou told Mendès-France that he would see to it that the Vietminh cooperated. It was Mendès-France's task to ensure American cooperation.

The French Premier then sent an urgent request to Eisenhower—that he send either Dulles or Smith back to Geneva to head the American delegation. The presence of either man would convince Chou that the Americans were willing to accept the decisions of the conference. Eden urged the same thing. Dulles firmly opposed going. He announced this decision at a Cabinet meeting on July 9. Eisenhower immediately interrupted him. "I was strong that way the other day," Eisenhower admitted, but he had changed his mind. He wanted Smith sent back. He explained his thinking: "If we are not on record to oppose the settlement when it happens, it will plague us through the fall and give the Democrats a chance to say that we sat idly by and let Indochina be sold down the river to the Communists without raising a finger or turning a hair."[90]

Smith returned to Geneva, although as an observer and not as a participant. On July 21, the Geneva agreements were signed. They established a cease-fire, partitioned Vietnam, called for nationwide elections within two years, forbade the introduction of new military equipment from foreign nations into either part of Vietnam, provided for free movement of people between the two parts of Vietnam, and established a three-nation supervisory commission (Poland, India, and Canada). This was an outcome to which Eisenhower had long since resigned himself. It was acceptable to him because it sealed off the Communist breakthrough and because SEATO was now well on track to establish a new defensive line in Southeast Asia. Ho Chi Minh was the big loser. Nevertheless, Eisenhower and the Republicans were embarrassed by the loss of northern Vietnam to the Communists, so Eisenhower had Smith issue a declaration that said the United States took note of the agreements, would not use force to upset them, but would not sign them. When Eisenhower informed a news conference on July 21 of the refusal to sign, he emphasized that "the United States has not itself been a party to or bound by the decisions taken." He added that he was immediately dispatching ambassadors to Laos and Cambodia, and that he was "actively pursuing discussions . . . with a view to the rapid organization of a collective defense in Southeast Asia."[91]

Old Guard senators, led by Knowland, were denouncing the agreements as appeasement. Eisenhower was asked to comment. He said the agreements certainly were not satisfactory to the United States, "but I don't know, when I am put up against it at this moment, to find an alternative, to say what we would or could do."[92]

What Eisenhower had done was face the realities. The French were not going to continue to fight; if the war went on, Ho Chi Minh would win everything in Indochina. At the critical juncture, the United States had neither the air nor troop strength to prevent a Vietminh victory, short of a unilateral atomic strike. But although there was extreme pressure to do just that, from a majority of Eisenhower's military and civilian advisers, he set political and military obstacles that he knew could not be overcome. Of these, the most important were British cooperation, congressional approval, and a JCS facing of the fact that an atomic strike had to be directed against Russia as well as China, and could hardly be limited to Vietnam. As he had done in the crisis of late April over Dien Bien Phu, Eisenhower in July 1954 again kept America out of Vietnam.

Then he put America into Vietnam. Dulles spent most of August flying around the world, signing up allies for SEATO. By September 8, the process was completed. France, Britain, Australia, New Zealand,

Thailand, the Philippines, Pakistan, and the United States together pledged themselves to defend Southeast Asia. The treaty extended the protection of SEATO to Laos, Cambodia, and South Vietnam. Less than one month later, Eisenhower pledged full American support to the Prime Minister of South Vietnam, Ngo Dinh Diem, whom the CIA said was "the only figure on the political scene behind whom genuine nationalist support can be mobilized."[93] Eisenhower wrote Diem in late September that he was sending American officials to Saigon to confer with Diem to see "how an intelligent program of American aid given directly to your government can serve to assist Vietnam in its present hour of trial, provided that your government is prepared to give assurances as to the standards of performance it would be able to maintain in the event such aid were supplied." The purpose of the offer, Eisenhower said, was to assist Diem "in developing and maintaining a strong, viable state, capable of resisting attempted subversion or aggression through military means." There was a condition to the aid: "The government of the United States expects that this aid will be met by performance on the part of the government of Vietnam in undertaking needed reforms."[94]

Eisenhower's letter, along with the extension of SEATO protection to South Vietnam, violated the Geneva agreements in two ways. First, the agreements had stated explicitly that neither part of Vietnam could join an alliance. Second, it escalated South Vietnam's position from that of one part of a divided country into a sovereign state. In practice, this meant that the United States was going to support Diem in his refusal to hold the promised nationwide elections. Eisenhower had good reason for rejecting elections—the CIA told him that if they were held, Ho Chi Minh would certainly win, perhaps by as much as 80 percent of the vote.[95] To prevent that from happening, the President was willing to—and did—pledge the United States to the support of an independent South Vietnam.

The debacle in Indochina badly strained the NATO alliance. As Gruenther had warned, many Frenchmen put the blame on the United States. They had an opportunity to vent their anger on August 30, when the French Assembly voted on EDC. Dulles had been active in Paris, putting every kind of pressure he could on the French. Eisenhower, at a news conference, added to the pressure by announcing that if the French failed to ratify EDC, the United States would move along to "secure a better relationship with Germany." He wanted the French to know that one way or another there was going to be a German rearmament.[96] Nevertheless, the Assembly voted to reject EDC, 319 to 264, with 43 abstentions.

Eisenhower had suffered a major setback. Since December 1950, he had labored to create EDC and the all-European army that would go with it, not only in order to get German rearmament under way, but also to provide a spur for a United States of Europe. He was disappointed and perplexed. He asked Hagerty, "Are the French deliberately saying they are going to tie up with Russia?" He recalled a meeting he had with the French Cabinet when he was SACEUR, when he had lost his patience and said to the members, "I obviously have a hell of a lot more fear of what happens to France than you do." Eisenhower said that some of the Frenchmen present "broke down and cried," but now look, they were rejecting their own proposal, EDC.

As in Vietnam, Eisenhower had his backup position ready. Immediately upon hearing the result of the vote, he told Smith—who was Acting Secretary of State while Dulles was in Paris—to arrange a meeting of the NATO countries, "with a view of including Germany as an equal partner therein."[97] Thus the chief result of the French vote was to restore German sovereignty, bring Germany into NATO, and create an independent German Army.

Taken together, the loss of North Vietnam and of EDC were serious defeats for Eisenhower. But he had lost only a couple of battles, not the war against Communism. As he so often reminded his Cabinet, "Long faces don't win wars." He insisted on remaining optimistic as much as he insisted on being realistic.

CHAPTER NINE

Quemoy and Matsu, Off-Year Elections

September 3–December 31, 1954

IN LATE AUGUST 1954, Eisenhower went to Denver for the start of his vacation. On September 3, he got word from Washington that there was yet another Far East crisis, this one about halfway between Korea and Vietnam. The Chinese had begun shelling two tiny island groups, Quemoy and Matsu.

Some of the islands were less than two miles off the Chinese coast. Unlike Formosa and the nearby Pescadores, which had been held by the Japanese for some fifty years, Quemoy and Matsu had always been a part of China. When Chiang fled to Formosa in 1949, he retained his hold on the islands, garrisoned them heavily, and used them to observe the mainland, to stage raids against the mainland, and to disrupt Chinese coastal shipping. Eventually, Chiang hoped to use them as stepping-stones for his invasion of the mainland. The U.S. Seventh Fleet had orders, originated by Truman and continued by Eisenhower, to prevent a Chinese assault against Formosa. Whether Quemoy and Matsu were included in the defensive area was unclear. There were technical and political problems; the U.S. Navy could not get its ships between the islands and the mainland for lack of depth of water, and intervention threatened to put the United States squarely into the Chinese civil war at a time when none of America's allies, except Chiang, was willing to risk World War III over two tiny offshore island groups. Nevertheless Chiang insisted that the fall of Quemoy and Matsu would only be a preliminary to the invasion of

Formosa itself, and Eisenhower was told that Nationalist Chinese morale would fall precipitously if no attempt was made to defend them. The JCS informed Eisenhower that although the islands were not militarily necessary to the defense of Formosa, Chiang could not hold them without American assistance.[1]

On September 12, Dulles and the JCS flew to Denver for a conference on what Dulles called "this horrible business." The Chinese were shelling the islands on a regular basis but had not yet invaded. Radford, backed by the Air Force and Navy Chiefs, recommended not only putting American forces on the islands, but also that the United States join Chiang in carrying out bombing raids against the mainland. This was the third time in less than six months that Radford had recommended aggressive action, to include atomic weapons, against China. Eisenhower again rejected the advice. As before, the President said that "if we attack China, we're not going to impose limits on our military actions, as in Korea." And, the President added, "If we get into a general war, the logical enemy will be Russia, not China, and we'll have to strike there."[2]

By late October, the Chinese appeared to be ready to launch their invasion. Despite Eisenhower's dressing down in September, Radford and the JCS still assumed that when China attacked, the United States would strike hard at the Chinese mainland. Eisenhower told them to make no such assumption. He said he was distressed at their lack of understanding of the constitutional responsibilities of the President. The United States had no treaty with Chiang Kai-shek; the President could not plunge America into a war with China (and possibly Russia) without congressional approval, and especially not over the fate of such insignificant places as Quemoy and Matsu. He told the JCS that if the Chinese attacked Formosa, the Seventh Fleet should act defensively; simultaneously, he would call an immediate session of Congress. There would be no retaliation against the Chinese mainland, no invoking the doctrine of massive retaliation, "pending congressional consideration of the matter."[3]

Through November, the threat intensified as the Chinese bombed other small islands held by Chiang's forces and continued their buildup opposite Quemoy and Matsu. Then on November 23, the Chinese announced the verdict of a trial of thirteen American fliers who had been shot down over China during the Korean War. They received prison terms ranging from four years to life for espionage. Insofar as all but two of the fliers had been in uniform, and insofar as the Korean armistice agreements specified that all POWs would be returned, there was a predictable roar of protest in the United States. Senator Knowland spoke for millions of Americans when he demanded a total blockade of the Chinese coast.

The President refused to even consider it. He told a press conference, "The hard way is to have the courage to be patient." He pointed out, "It is possible that a blockade is conceivable without war; I have never read of it historically." (Although he had just done it, successfully, in Guatemala.) He was, therefore, going to turn the problem of the airmen over to the U.N. After all, the prisoners had been fighting under a U.N. flag when captured, so "how the U.N. can possibly disabuse itself of a feeling of responsibility in this matter and retain its self-respect, I wouldn't know." With regard to the cries by Knowland, McCarthy, and others about the "honor of America," Eisenhower declared sternly, "So far as the honor of the United States is concerned, I merely hope that I shall not live long enough to find myself accused of being insensible to the honor of the United States and the safety of her men and soldiers."[4]

But Eisenhower had to respond somehow. Early in December, he signed a mutual-defense treaty with the Nationalist Chinese. It declared that an armed attack on either party would be regarded as an act of war against the other. Chiang agreed not to attack the mainland unilaterally. Eisenhower insisted on restricting the treaty to Formosa and the Pescadores, deliberately leaving out Quemoy and Matsu. On December 20, Chiang's Foreign Minister, Dr. George Yeh, came to Washington for a conference with Eisenhower and Dulles. Yeh said it "would be a good psychological warfare move" for the United States to announce that it would provide logistic support for Chinese forces on Quemoy and Matsu. But Eisenhower said he felt that "any actions against the islands could best be handled, case by case, each on its merits." Eisenhower also told Yeh that it was a mistake to keep putting more and more men on "these small and exposed islands." And he dashed any hopes Yeh may have had about the imposition of a blockade of the mainland.[5]

Farther south along the Asian coast, there were other problems. Allen Dulles had slipped a CIA team, headed by Colonel Edward Lansdale, into Vietnam, with the objective of disrupting the Vietminh take-over in Hanoi through various acts of sabotage. None were very effective.[6] Diem, meanwhile, was having difficulty in establishing himself in command in South Vietnam. On October 30 Eisenhower conferred with Foster Dulles on Vietnam. The Secretary of State had no objection to the CIA's covert actions in North Vietnam, but he did want a "high-ranking" American official in Saigon, preferably an Army officer, who could help Diem build an army and a government. Eisenhower liked the idea and said that General J. Lawton Collins was the perfect man to implement it.[7]

Eisenhower decided to make Collins the ambassador to "Free Vietnam" (neither of the terms "Republic of Vietnam" nor "South Vietnam" was yet being used), thereby making public what had already been done in secret, the elevation of the southern half of Vietnam to the status of a sovereign state. Eisenhower gave Collins control over "all the agencies and resources" of the United States in Vietnam, and said the basic American policy was "to maintain and support a friendly and independent non-Communist government in Vietnam and to assist it in diminishing and ultimately eradicating Communist subversion and influence." Collins' principal task was to help Diem wage a military campaign against the Vietminh and to build an army.[8]

These were serious steps with potentially quite large consequences. Eisenhower knew that when Diem's refusal to hold elections became known, Diem was going to face an insurrection. The President also knew he was putting the United States into the middle of a probable civil war in Southeast Asia. Eisenhower had provided the tools for the French to wage the war in the area; now that the French had quit, he shifted the aid to Diem and his adherents. The President, and Collins, had a model in mind. Before Collins' departure for Saigon, they met (November 3) in the Oval Office. There they agreed that Collins should follow the pattern that had been so successful in Greece and Korea, building an indigenous army that could defend the country by itself, with American arms. Eisenhower had often complained that the French wanted American equipment but not American advice; Diem, he hoped, would be more cooperative, as the leaders in Greece and South Korea had been. To that end, the President agreed to "build up" the American military mission in Saigon, shift a $400 million aid package intended for the French to the South Vietnamese, and put the whole program under the command of a career soldier.[9]

French rejection of EDC, so closely connected with their defeat in Vietnam, had to be dealt with. In September, Eisenhower sent Dulles to Paris to begin preparations for a NATO meeting, at which the United States would propose a restoration of West German sovereignty, the inclusion of Germany in NATO, and the creation of a German army. German rearmament, to Eisenhower, was the linchpin of his strategic design. A German army was crucial to his vision of what NATO could become, and NATO was, as always, his first concern. Other things being equal, he made his foreign-policy decisions on the basis of the question, Will this help or hurt NATO? When Knowland demanded a blockade of China, for example, Eisenhower's first thought was of the havoc the demand would raise with the attempt to promote German rearmament. The French were always questionable, especially when Germany was the issue; Eisenhower had to have the French vote to bring Germany into NATO. Knowland was threatening to upset everything by making the French think that the Americans were irresponsible and bent on war. Damning Knowland, Eisenhower said the senator was playing into the hands of the Communists, who wanted to divide the NATO countries in order to stop German rearmament.[10]

Through September, Dulles met with the NATO representatives. On October 3, he brought home an agreement. By promising the French that there would be a twelve-division limit on the German army, that Germany would promise never to make atomic weapons, and that the ultimate command and control would belong to the SACEUR (presumably always an American), and by threatening that the United States would go it alone with Germany if France failed to sign the agreement, Dulles had managed to achieve nearly all Eisenhower's goals. Eisenhower was absolutely delighted—what he got was even better than EDC. Dulles told him that Adenauer had emerged as the "real statesman" of Europe; Eisenhower agreed and said, "Of course he is one of the great men of our time."[11]

The real credit belonged to Eisenhower, who had thought up the formula, but he was eager to give Dulles the credit. In a statement announcing the agreement, Eisenhower said Dulles had "accomplished one of the greatest diplomatic achievements of our time."[12] To Swede Hazlett, meanwhile, Eisenhower explained privately that "Dulles has never made a serious pronouncement, agreement, or proposal without complete and exhaustive consultation with me in advance and, of course, my approval."[13]

Now Eisenhower had to wait, once again, for ratification by the French National Assembly. Various test votes in the Assembly were close, and generally discouraging. Eisenhower tried to lessen French fears by following a conciliatory line in Asia, by emphasizing that bringing Germany into NATO was the way to control her, and by de-emphasizing the American military presence in Europe. When the U.S. Army put out a publicity release on its sending Honest John atomic missiles to Europe, Eisenhower was furious. French students were already out on the streets, protesting that they did not want to be cannon fodder for a U.S.-U.S.S.R. war. Eisenhower told Goodpaster to find out who was responsible, and said he wanted such shipments kept a secret.[14]

(Goodpaster had come to the White House on October 10, 1954, with the title of Staff Secretary to the President. A West Point graduate with a Ph.D. in international relations from Princeton, Goodpaster had worked for Eisenhower at SHAPE. Eisenhower had unbounded admiration for Goodpaster, and when his first Staff Secretary, General Paul Carroll, died of a heart attack, Eisenhower told Gruenther he would have to give up Goodpaster, because the President needed him. Goodpaster stayed with Eisenhower to the end of the second term. He became, without question, Eisenhower's closest adviser and confidant. Eisenhower had no secrets from Goodpaster, something that could be said of no other man, not even the Dulles brothers. Goodpaster was at the President's side, literally, during all his working hours. To the biographer's delight and profit, he kept notes on the meetings in the Oval Office; to Eisenhower's delight and profit, he was always ready to offer advice or information. Goodpaster became to Eisenhower the President what Beetle Smith had been to Eisenhower the Supreme Commander, and like Smith, Goodpaster never let his boss down.)

In December, Dulles flew back to Paris to put more pressure on the Assembly. When he returned, his only piece of cheerful news was that he had managed to "smuggle back a few cases of wine" as Eisenhower had asked him to do. Otherwise, the prospects for ratification looked slim. Two days before Christmas, a test vote went 280 to 259 against German rearmament. "Damn those French!" Eisenhower exploded. "It's their old game of diplomatic doodling to see how much they can get out for themselves and never mind the rest of the world."[15] But to Eisenhower's intense relief, two days before the New Year the Assembly voted 287 to 260 for the agreements.

On April 1, 1955, the U.S. Senate ratified the protocols. Thus did Eisenhower, the man who had commanded the conquest and occupation of West Germany, come to set it free. In the process, Eisenhower joined West Germany solidly to the United States and NATO.

The major concern of most politicians in America in the second half of 1954 was not Germany, nor Vietnam, nor China, but getting reelected. Eisenhower was also concerned about the elections, if only because of the thin margins the Republicans held in both houses of Congress. He wanted his party to retain control of Congress, and despite his constant reiteration of his nonpartisanship, he exhorted his Cabinet members to do all they could to elect Republicans. In September, from the summer White House, he sent orders to Washington to "step up expenditures to stimulate industrial activity." He ordered the Defense Department "to do the major portion of its buying now and not wait for the last half of the fiscal year. Do not hesitate to use any legal authority I have to get this going." [16]

Hurry-up spending was not enough to satisfy the party leaders, who wanted the President to wage an active campaign. On October 7, after Eisenhower had been in Denver for six weeks, he heard from Tom Dewey, who told him that while he was on vacation "the Republican Party is going down the drain!" [17] In a long and defensive reply, Eisenhower explained why he was not out on the campaign trail. First, he told Dewey, he did not think it proper. "I know that there was nothing that Mr. Truman did that so shocked my sense of the fitting and the appropriate as did his barnstorming activities while he was actually the President." Second, the history of the thing was all against him. Wilson and FDR had tried to influence off-year elections, only to suffer big losses. Third, Eisenhower had his own health to think about. He said he was sixty-four years old, and "the Presidency is a job that would tax the intellectual and physical energies of a far younger man." He said he needed time for "reflection and recuperation." If he did not take the time, he would not be doing his duty to himself, his party, and the country.[18] At his news conferences, Eisenhower took the same line—he was not going to participate actively in the congressional elections.

But then the polls began to show a dangerous shift to the Democrats, and Gabe Hauge warned Eisenhower that if the Republicans lost control of Congress, "the extreme right wing will try to recapture the leadership of the party." That argument was convincing. The President thought the threat a serious one, and deplored it, because "if the right wing really recaptures the Republican Party, there simply isn't going to be any Republican influence in this country within a matter of a few brief years. A new party will be inevitable." [19] Eisenhower therefore entered the campaign to prevent an Old Guard take-over. In the second half of October, he traveled more than ten thousand miles and made nearly forty speeches. He concentrated on the eastern half of the country, and stayed in states where moderate Republicans needed help. He sent Nixon to campaign in the Midwest and West,

Old Guard strongholds. Eisenhower took the high road, emphasizing Republican accomplishments—peace in Korea, less federal spending, an almost balanced budget, and so on. Nixon hammered at the Democrats; Stevenson accused him of indulging in "McCarthyism in a white collar." Eisenhower was nevertheless appreciative of Nixon's efforts; late in October he sent the Vice-President a warm note expressing his gratitude and admiration for all Nixon had done.[20]

Despite Eisenhower's efforts, the Republicans lost seventeen seats in the House and two in the Senate, which gave the Democrats control of both chambers of Congress. Most observers felt that only Eisenhower's last-minute intervention had prevented an even bigger Democratic victory, and Eisenhower pointed out that Republican losses in the off-year election were much less than was customary for the party in power. Nevertheless, it was a bad defeat, and one that helped create a crisis in the Republican Party.

Eisenhower blamed the right wing of the Republican Party for the losses; the Old Guard blamed the President, because he had failed to implement genuinely conservative policies. Edgar Eisenhower agreed with the Old Guard; he wrote Dwight that his policies were no better than Truman's, and just as unconstitutional. In his reply, the President let out some of his anger at and scorn for the right wing: "Should any political party attempt to abolish Social Security, unemployment insurance, and eliminate labor laws and farm programs, you would not hear of that party again in our political history." He said he realized there was a "splinter group that believes you can do these things," but insisted that "their number is negligible and they are stupid."[21] He was, in fact, becoming contemptuous of most politicians, not just the Old Guard. When Merriman Smith asked him, in a private interview, if he thought of himself as a politician, Eisenhower replied that no, he did not, because he had not made politics his career. "But I can say this," he quickly added, "and I think without egotism, in many, many ways I will make smarter political decisions than a lot of guys who are pros."[22]

Senator McCarthy was one such pro. He was back in the headlines, and out in the front of the right-wing movement to take control of the Republican Party from Eisenhower. The latest McCarthy uproar had its origins on July 30, when Senator Ralph Flanders of Vermont introduced a motion to censure McCarthy for behavior unbecoming to the Senate. A select bipartisan committee, chaired by Senator Arthur Watkins, Republican of Utah, considered the motion and recommended censuring McCarthy. On December 2, the roll-call vote revealed that the Senate, for the third time in its history, had censured one of its own, by a vote of 67 to 22. Eisenhower was pleased with the result. On December 4, he called Watkins to the White House to congratulate him. "I wanted to see you," was Eisenhower's opening remark: "You handled a tough job like a champion."[23]

But there was also a major disappointment in the vote. The Republicans had split exactly down the middle, 22 to 22. Even worse, the only Republican leader who supported censure was Leverett Saltonstall; all the others—Dirksen, Bridges, Millikin, and Knowland—voted for McCarthy. Eisenhower tried to be optimistic; he told Cliff Roberts that "I don't believe that so-called 'rightest' thinking in the Republican Party is as prevalent as this Senate ratio might indicate." But he also hinted that he would welcome a split. If McCarthy and his supporters walked out, Eisenhower said he would try to attract Democrats and independents to a new, moderate Republican Party. Such a party, holding the middle, "would go so rapidly that within a few years it would dominate American politics."[24]

On December 7, McCarthy attacked again. He said he was "breaking" with the President, because Eisenhower had congratulated Watkins and Flanders for the censure vote while holding up the work of the investigation of Communism, and at the same time urging patience and niceties toward the Chinese who were torturing American prisoners. McCarthy accused Eisenhower of "weakness and supineness" in ferreting out Communists, and said he wanted to "apologize" to the American people for supporting Eisenhower in 1952.

Eisenhower told Hagerty that he was "glad the break has come." Becoming agitated, he bit the earpiece of his glasses, shoved them into his jacket, sprang out of his chair, and began pacing. He said he was sick and tired of the Old Guard. "If there is one thing that I am going to try to do during the next two years," he went on—but Hagerty interrupted him. "Don't you mean the next six years, Mr. President?" Eisenhower laughed and said right now he was speaking only of the next two years. "I have just one purpose, outside of the job of keeping this world at peace, and that is to build up a strong progressive Republican Party in this country." Warming to his subject, he thundered, "If the right wing wants a fight, they're going to get it. If they want to leave the Republican Party and form a third party, that's their business, but before I end up, either this Republican Party will reflect progressivism or I won't be with them anymore.

"And let me tell you one other thing. If they think they can nominate a right-wing Old Guard Republican for the Presidency, they've got another thought coming. I'll go up and down this country, campaigning against them. I'll fight them right down the line."[25]

Stopping the right wing meant stopping the leaders of the Republican Party. To do that, Eisenhower needed to build up alternative leaders. Further, if he wanted to retire after 1956—always a tempting thought—he also needed to build up someone who could take his place. In the weeks after the election, as the right-wing revolt spread (pro-McCarthy clubs were springing up around the country, and McCarthy was charging that twenty years of treason had become twenty-one years of treason), Eisenhower in his correspondence and conversations with his friends and political associates tried to promote various candidates. His own favorites were Robert Anderson (currently Deputy Secretary of Defense) and Herbert Hoover, Jr., who had just replaced Smith as Under Secretary of State and who had, Eisenhower declared, "all the brains of his dad, and all the charm of his mother." Nixon, Brownell, Halleck, and William Rogers were others whom Eisenhower thought could make good party leaders.[26]

But the truth was that none of those men, no matter how highly Eisenhower thought of them, was capable of saving the Republican Party from itself. Only Eisenhower could do that. Immediately after the elections, the chief concern of Clay, Bill Robinson, Lodge, and the others who had induced Eisenhower to run in 1952 was to once again use Eisenhower to prevent a right-wing take-over. On November 18, after conferring with his associates in New York, Clay flew to Washington to talk to Eisenhower. He came on his subject by a roundabout way. He told Eisenhower there was a feeling among his friends that Dr. Snyder, being seventy-three years old, was really not capable of providing the medical care and advice that the President ought to have. When Eisenhower asked the reason for the sudden concern, Clay said he was interested in Eisenhower's health not just for the moment or for the next two years, but for the next six years. Eisenhower would have to stay in command, Clay argued, if there was to be any hope of modernizing and reforming the Republican Party. Eisenhower agreed that there was a job to be done; he branded the right wing as "the most ignorant people now living in the United States." But he did not agree that he was the only man who could stop the Old Guard. When Clay said he wanted to use the name "Eisenhower Republicans," the President protested strongly. He said if the effort to reform the party was focused on one man, "then it would follow that in the event of my disability or death, the whole effort would collapse." Such an outcome would be "absurd," because "the idea is far bigger than any one individual."

Clay was not listening. He told Eisenhower, "I am ready to work for you at whatever sacrifice to myself because I believe in you. I am not ready to work for anybody else that you can name." Eisenhower gave Clay all the arguments against his running again—his age; the need for younger men in high position in the party; the complexity of the job; the fact that he would be, because of the Twenty-second Amendment, a lame-duck President from the moment he was re-elected. Clay was unimpressed. He referred to Eisenhower's "duty." That was the key word. (As Eisenhower recorded in his diary entry on this conversation: "All that an individual has to say to me is 'the good of the country' . . . and I probably yield far too easily.") The conversation ended with Eisenhower avoiding any promises, but leaving Clay free to work for reforming the party and re-electing Eisenhower.[27]

One part of reforming the Republican Party was bringing the southern strength into it. Eisenhower frequently expressed his great admiration for the southern Democrats, whom he found far more intelligent and responsible than the Old Guard. One such southern Democrat, Robert Anderson of Texas, was consistently Eisenhower's personal choice as his successor. Eisenhower thumped for Anderson whenever he could. He told Hazlett that Anderson "is just about the ablest man that I know. He would make a splendid President."

That observation, plus the fact that Churchill had just had his eightieth birthday, set Eisenhower to write a disquisition to Hazlett on the subject of greatness. Eisenhower thought greatness depended on either achieving preeminence "in some broad field of human thought or endeavor" or on assuming "some position of great responsibility," and then so discharging his duties "as to have left a marked and favorable imprint upon the future." He said Plato was an example of the first type, George Washington of the second. Eisenhower insisted that one had to distinguish between a great man and a great specialist; for example, "Martin Luther was a great man; Napoleon was a great general." The qualities a great man should have were "vision, integrity, courage, understanding, the power of articulation, . . . and profundity of character." Under those definitions, Eisenhower said that Churchill "came nearest to fulfilling the requirements of greatness in any individual that I have met in my lifetime. I have known finer and greater characters, wiser philosophers, more understanding personalities"—but no greater man. From among the Americans he knew personally, Eisen-

SEPTEMBER 3–DECEMBER 31, 1954   223

hower said that "George Marshall possessed more of the qualities of greatness than has any other." Henry Stimson was a close second. Of the pre-twentieth-century Americans, Eisenhower said he admired most Washington, Lincoln, and Lee. Among congressmen, "I think John Quincy Adams would head my list."

When he finished the letter, Eisenhower read it over and was surprised at how few men he thought of as "great." He put in a postscript for Hazlett, lest Hazlett think he was too pessimistic: "Long ago I learned to look for caliber or relative size in individuals rather than for perfection." By that standard, he said, he was satisfied with his Cabinet.[28]

In fact, Eisenhower was not so happy with his Secretary of Defense. For one thing, Wilson had shot off his mouth during the campaign about unemployed auto workers in Detroit. "I've always liked bird dogs better than kennel-fed dogs myself," Wilson announced. "You know, one who'll get out and hunt for food rather than sit on his fanny and yell." It was an absurd comparison—bird dogs live in kennels and they do not hunt, kill, and eat the quail, but only point them out to the hunter—and the unnecessary insult of equating the unemployed with lazy dogs set off a storm that cost the Republicans votes. But the real reason for Eisenhower's unhappiness with Wilson was the Secretary's inability to control the Chiefs. In preparing his budget for the next fiscal year, Eisenhower had again made substantial cuts in the Army and Navy. The Army would drop from 1.4 million to 1 million, with a budget reduction from $12.9 billion to $8.8 billion; the Navy from 920,000 to 870,000, and from $11.2 to $9.7 billion. The Air Force got a slight increase, from $15.6 to $16.4 billion. All the Chiefs were unwilling to accept these figures. Ridgway was the most outspoken—he said he could not be responsible for the security of American troops in Europe, Korea, and elsewhere with so small an army—but the Navy and Air Force Chiefs also went before Congress to denounce the Eisenhower budget and demand more money.

In December, Eisenhower summoned Wilson and the Chiefs to the Oval Office. Goodpaster took notes. Eisenhower gave a brief outline of his military budget, acknowledged that each service could find shortcomings in it, insisted that he had to look at the whole picture, including the state of the economy, and then ordered them to get on the team. "The President stated this [budget] was his own judgment on the matter. As Commander in Chief he is entitled to the loyal support of his subordinates of the official position he has adopted, and he

224 EISENHOWER

expects to have that support." If the Chiefs wanted to complain, they should come to him privately, "but once the decision is made all must follow."[29]

With the Democrats back in control of the Congress, Eisenhower's worries about the economy increased. He feared they would want to spend and spend, tax and tax, citing the glittering goal of full employment as their objective. Two days after the election, Eisenhower complained to his Cabinet that "eight to twelve years are needed to wean people back away from the idea of war prosperity," when everyone had a job. Humphrey pointed out that "we can't have full employment without war." Inflation and national bankruptcy, not unemployment (currently at 4.5 percent), were Eisenhower's chief concern. "We cannot defend the nation in a way which will exhaust our economy," he told the Cabinet. That meant, he added, "that instead of conventional forces, we must be prepared to use atomic weapons in all forms." Russia, he said, "is not seeking a general war," which meant there was no reason to panic. On the specific issue of manpower for the armed services, Eisenhower said, "I have directed a cutting back this year— and more next year—so as to allow us to concentrate on those things which can deter the Russians. This is a judgment of my own, made after long, long study."[30]

A public split between the President and the JCS on defense spending was, of course, a big story for the reporters, who pestered Eisenhower with questions about the "New Look" at his news conferences. Eisenhower would carefully and patiently explain his position on deterrence. What about little wars? the press asked. Ridgway had said that with his tiny army, he could not fight one. Eisenhower did not disagree; he did say that "I just don't believe you can buy one hundred percent security in every little corner of the world where someone else wants to start trouble. I think you have to go ahead, taking certain calculated risks." To be ready to fight all the potential little wars, Eisenhower added, "You would have to have troops stationed in every place in the world where trouble might arise, in advance."[31]

Eisenhower did, however, want nuclear weapons dispersed to potential trouble spots. On December 1, he met with Wilson and Strauss to make arrangements for "increased overseas deployment" of American bombs. There were some problems with the proposal, as Wilson pointed out, including the "possible impact upon the American public, our allies, and the Soviet Union, should the information as to their transfer become generally suspected or known." A particular source of trouble, Wilson added, was the possibility that transferring the bombs from the United States to Europe, the Middle East, and the Far East "might be construed by our allies as an act of mobilization and by the Soviets as an indication or threat of impending attack." But the advantages outweighed the disadvantages. With the bombs in place on the periphery of the Soviet Union, the United States could launch a retaliatory attack almost instantly. In addition to enhancing readiness, overseas deployment and dispersal would greatly decrease the vulnerability of America's atomic stockpile to enemy attack. Eisenhower told Wilson and Strauss to go ahead with a program that would put 36 percent of the hydrogen bombs overseas, and 42 percent of the atomic bombs. He also instructed Strauss to have the AEC turn control of the bombs over to the DOD.[32]

Thus did Eisenhower set the nation's post-Korea, post-Dien Bien Phu defense policy. The New Look put the emphasis on massive retaliation, on more bang for a buck, on cutting costs everywhere except for the Strategic Air Force and its ability to wage atomic war. The New Look meant big savings, and much grumbling. At times it seemed that except for Humphrey, Eisenhower was the only man in Washington who supported it. From 1955 onward, the Democrats would concentrate their criticisms of Eisenhower on his defense policy, charging that the President—and Humphrey—were allowing their Neanderthal fiscal views to endanger the security of the nation. Despite Eisenhower's direct order, the JCS continued to supply his critics with countless facts and figures to prove that more money had to be spent on conventional forces.

So strongly, and so often, did the Chiefs—all of them—object to the New Look that Eisenhower was nearly driven to distraction. "Let us not forget that the armed services are to defend a 'way of life,' not merely land, property, or lives," Eisenhower wrote Swede Hazlett. "So what I need to make the Chiefs realize is that they are men of sufficient stature, training, and intelligence to think of this balance—the balance between minimum requirements in the costly implements of war and the health of our economy." A major problem was that although each Chief agreed that the sums allocated to the other services were entirely adequate, the amounts provided for his own service were entirely inadequate. Eisenhower told Hazlett that he could run a blue pencil through the Pentagon requests for more money because he knew the Pentagon game so well, "but some day there is going to be a man sitting in my present chair who has not been raised in the military services and who will have little understanding of where slashes in their estimates can be made with little or no damage." Eisenhower then expressed his great fear: "If that should happen while we still have the state of tension that now exists in the world, I shudder to think of what could happen in this country."[33]

The more general complaint about Eisenhower's New Look was linked to widespread dissatisfaction with the way he was waging the Cold War. Critics—including not only the opposition party but also the Old Guard, the JCS, the NSC, and often the Secretary of State—wanted a more vigorous prosecution of the conflict, as evidenced by the number of times in 1954 they urged the President to launch an atomic strike against China. But Eisenhower would have no part of nuclear war, unless the Russians actually marched across the Elbe River, and he wanted no more Koreas. He was, however, more than willing to wage an aggressive covert offensive, implemented by the CIA, against the Communists.

Immediately after Knowland issued his call for a blockade against China, Eisenhower called the senator into his office for a bit of straight talking. The President said that "in the conduct of foreign affairs, we do so many things that we can't explain." He had turned on his recorder; Ann Whitman made a transcript of the conversation. Eisenhower told Knowland, "There is a very great aggressiveness on our side that you have not known about and I guess that is on the theory of why put burdens on people that they don't need to know about." He said that he himself "knew so many things that I am almost afraid to speak to my wife." Without providing details, Eisenhower assured Knowland that the Cold War *was* being waged aggressively, that the CIA was busy around the world, "very active, and there are a great many risky decisions on my part constantly . . . but I do try to spare other people some of the things I do." But as for a blockade, or breaking diplomatic relations with the Russians (which Knowland had also demanded be done), "that is a step toward war; if you do that, then the next question is, are you ready to attack? Well, I am not ready to attack."[34]

Not openly, anyway, but under Eisenhower's direction, as he told Knowland, the CIA was carrying on assorted covert operations around the world. Because it was his chief instrument for waging the Cold War, and because it was so controversial, Eisenhower kept a close watch on the CIA. In late October, he spent an afternoon with General Doolittle and the other members of the committee he had created to investigate the Agency. Doolittle's report on the spymaster was mixed. He thought Allen Dulles had as his principal strength "his unique knowledge of his subject; he has his whole heart in it." His weakness was in organization and the relatively poor quality of men he had around him. Further, Doolittle felt that the relationship between the Secretary of State and the head of the CIA was "unfortunate." Eisenhower interrupted Doolittle to say he thought the relationship was "beneficial." Doolittle said that Allen Dulles was "too emotional" for his job, and that he thought Dulles' "emotionalism was far worse than it appeared on the surface." Eisenhower again interrupted, saying, "I have never seen him show the slightest disturbance." Continuing to defend Dulles, Eisenhower pointed out that "here is one of the most peculiar types of operation any government can have, and it probably takes a strange kind of genius to run it."[35]

At the end of the meeting, Doolittle handed Eisenhower the committee's report. Its conclusion was chilling: "It is now clear that we are facing an implacable enemy whose avowed objective is world domination . . . There are no rules in such a game. Hitherto acceptable norms of human conduct do not apply. . . . We must . . . learn to subvert, sabotage, and destroy our enemies by more clever, more sophisticated, and more effective methods than those used against us."[36] That was a concise summary of Eisenhower's own views, and described accurately the methods he had already used in Iran, Guatemala, and North Vietnam.

The CIA's other main function was the less glamorous one of collecting and interpreting intelligence. Like everyone else of his generation, Eisenhower had been deeply scared by the intelligence failure at Pearl Harbor; by the fifties, the advantage of surprise to an attacker who had atomic weapons was incalculably greater than it had been in the early forties. Eisenhower wanted information from within the Soviet Union; he especially wanted an early warning on any mobilization of planes or troops. But the CIA had been unable to set up any spy networks inside Russia. Early in 1954, Eisenhower set up a Surprise Attack Panel to advise him on what to do. The chairman was Dr. James R. Killian, president of MIT. A key member was Edwin H. Land, inventor of the Polaroid camera and winner of a Nobel Prize (1952). Land reported that new cameras were available that made high-level precision photography possible. The trick was to get the cameras over Russia. The Air Force had made several attempts, using redesigned bombers and unmanned balloons, but the results were disappointing. Meanwhile, Clarence ("Kelly") Johnson, the top designer at Lockheed, had proposed a high-altitude single-engine reconnaissance aircraft that was really more a kite with an enormous wingspan, a single jet engine, and an ability to fly long distances above seventy thousand feet. Lockheed called the plane the U-2. Allen Dulles liked it; Killian liked it; Land liked it. On November 24, they went to see Eisenhower to ask authorization to build thirty U-2s at a cost of $35 million. The CIA and the Defense Department would split the bill. Foster Dulles, who was also present, indicated "that difficulties might arise out of these flights, but we can live through them." Allen Dulles put Richard Bissell, who had directed Pbsuccess, in charge. At the conclusion of the meeting, Goodpaster noted, "The President directed those present to go ahead and get the equipment, but before initiating operations to come in for one last look at the plans."[37]

Immediately after the U-2 meeting, Eisenhower, his family, and his gang went to Augusta for Thanksgiving. Accompanying them was Field Marshal Montgomery, who had—Eisenhower complained—"invited himself."[38] At Thanksgiving dinner, the two old soldiers regaled the party with war stories. They got to talking about Gettysburg. Eisenhower gave a lecture on his favorite battle. When he got to Pickett's charge, he said that Lee's reply to Pickett's suggestion that he attack the enemy—"Do it if you can"—was a most unusual one. As a commanding general himself, Eisenhower said, he would never give a subordinate so much leeway. Montgomery said he had good reason to know that was true. Later, Monty got started on all the things he did not know about America. He said he had never heard of Princeton, only Harvard and Yale. On the liner crossing the Atlantic, he recounted, he was introduced at the captain's table to a man named Spencer Tracy. Monty had to ask Mr. Tracy what business he was in. After dinner, the men settled down to play bridge, all except Monty, who did not play cards and therefore had Mamie teach him to play Scrabble.[39]

The following morning, Montgomery asked Eisenhower about what it was like to be the President. "No man on earth knows what this job is all about," Eisenhower replied. "It's pound, pound, pound. Not only is your intellectual capacity taxed to the utmost, but your physical stamina."[40]

The Eisenhowers returned to Augusta for Christmas and New Year's. On this occasion there was an unusual tension in the air because Eisenhower had to wait out the French vote on German rearmament. He worried that he would have to return to Washington if the vote went badly. There was, therefore, great relief all around when on December 30 word arrived that the French Assembly had ratified the agreement.[41]

• •

Thus did Eisenhower's second year in office end on a happy and successful note. French acceptance of his program for Germany had led to a stronger NATO, one of Eisenhower's proudest achievements. There were many other victories to toast that New Year's Eve. Mc-Carthy had been censured. SEATO was functioning. Guatemala was secured. The budget was almost in balance. Defense spending was sharply down. Eisenhower's popularity, according to the polls, was re-markably high—he had a 60 percent or higher approval rating. There had been setbacks, of course. The ones Eisenhower felt most strongly were the loss of North Vietnam, the failure to bring the Old Guard into the mainstream of moderate politics, and the election losses that turned control of the Congress over to the Democrats. There were also ongoing issues, fraught with danger, such as Quemoy and Matsu, the stability of South Vietnam, and of course all the domestic problems. But as Eisenhower looked back on 1953 and 1954, the deep sense of personal satisfaction he felt about his record was based upon, far and above all other considerations, his success in making and keeping peace.

Eisenhower had told Hagerty that his "one purpose" was "the job of keeping this world at peace." At times it appeared that he was the only man who could do it. In mid-1953, most of his military, foreign policy, and domestic political advisers were opposed to accepting an armistice in place in Korea. But Eisenhower insisted on peace. Five times in 1954, virtually the entire NSC, JCS, and State Department recommended that he intervene in Asia, even using atomic bombs against China. First, in April, as the Dien Bien Phu situation grew critical. Second, in May, on the eve of the fall of Dien Bien Phu. Third, in late June, when the French said the Chinese Air Force was about to enter the Indochina conflict. Fourth, in September, when the Chinese began shelling Quemoy and Matsu. Fifth, in November, when the Chinese announced the prison terms for the American fliers.

Five times in one year the experts advised the President to launch an atomic strike against China. Five times he said no. He did so most dramatically in a news conference in late November, when he was asked about the possibilities of a preventive strike against the Chinese, in order to secure the release of the prisoners. Eisenhower took ten minutes to reply, in off-the-cuff remarks that were delivered with visi-ble emotion. After giving a lengthy analysis of the prisoner problem, in which he tried to calm everyone down a bit, Eisenhower leaned for-ward and said he wanted "to talk a little bit personally." He admitted that "a President experiences exactly the same resentments, the same anger, the same kind of sense of frustration almost, when things like this occur to other Americans, and his impulse is to lash out." He said he knew that would be the "easy course" as well. The nation would be "united automatically." It would close ranks behind the leader. The job would become a simple one—win the war. "There is a real fervor developed throughout the nation that you can feel everywhere you go. There is practically an exhilaration about the affair." Eisenhower confessed that he was not immune to those feelings: "In the intellectual and spiritual contest of matching wits and getting along to see if you can win, there comes about something . . . an atmosphere is created . . . an attitude is created to which I am not totally unfamiliar."

Five times in one year the experts had advised him to enjoy that experience once again. But Eisenhower had other memories too. He reminded the reporters of his own favorite line from Robert E. Lee: "It is well that war is so terrible; if it were not so, we would grow too fond of it." He said he had personally experienced "the job of writing letters of condolence by the hundreds, by the thousands, to bereaved mothers and wives. That is a very sobering experience." So he pleaded with the reporters, and through them to the people, to think things through before rushing off to act. Try to imagine the results, he said. "Don't go to war in response to emotions of anger and resentment; do it prayerfully."[42]

Five times in 1954 Eisenhower prayed over the question of war or peace. Each time, he made the decision to stay at peace.

Colorado, August 1953. There was peace in Korea, a booming economy, and Congress was in recess. A happy President enjoys one of his favorite pastimes.

Left, President Eisenhower delivers his inaugural address, January 20, 1953. The sun shone, typical Eisenhower luck.

Above, press conference, April 30, 1953. Ike carefully cultivated his relations with the reporters, with whom he was obviously relaxed. He held more press conferences than any President before or since.

Below, Quantico, Virginia, July 24, 1953. How could one help but like him?

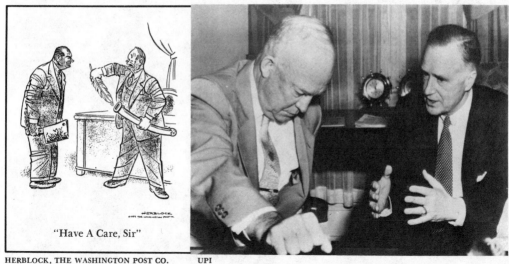

"Have A Care, Sir"

HERBLOCK, THE WASHINGTON POST CO.   UPI

Above right, Eisenhower receives a first-hand report from Walter Robinson, his personal envoy to Korea, who had returned that day, July 15, 1953, from meetings wtih Syngman Rhee, who was being difficult.

Above left, Herblock comments on Eisenhower's approach to McCarthy.

Below, a fateful handshake. Eisenhower and McCarthy, Milwaukee, October 1952, on the occasion of Eisenhower's removal of a paragraph praising George Marshall, in deference to McCarthy. Some of Ike's worst problems as President flowed from this handshake.

EISENHOWER LIBRARY

ASSOCIATED PRESS

Left above, Eisenhower, Jim Hagerty, and Murry Snyder returning to the White House from a press conference at the EOB, March 3, 1954. One can just hear Ike telling Hagerty and Snyder, "Well, boys, we really fooled 'em this time, didn't we?"

Far left, Nixon, Eisenhower, and Earl Warren, February 4, 1954. Ike appointed Warren Chief Justice of the Supreme Court for the simplest of reasons: he knew it was his most important appointment, and he wanted it to be the best. He thought Warren was the best; later, he had his doubts.

Left below, Eisenhower and Douglas MacArthur, March 18, 1954. MacArthur's advice tended to be "Nuke 'em." Ike was dubious.

Above, Eisenhower and John Foster Dulles listen to Chip Bohlen at the conference table in Geneva's Palais des Nations, July 18, 1955. Two days later Eisenhower made his Open Skies proposal.

Below left, Eisenhower and Dulles, October 25, 1954. Typically, they are at the airport, aides are scurrying behind them, the plane is about to take off, and Dulles is waiting for Ike's approval of his next speech before departing for who knew where.

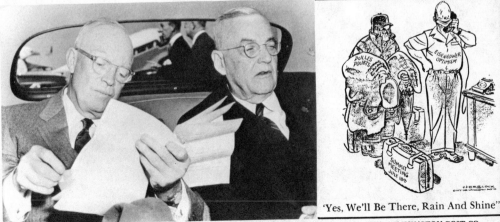

"Yes, We'll Be There, Rain And Shine"

NATIONAL PARK SERVICE

HERBLOCK, THE WASHINGTON POST CO.

Scrabble at Camp David,
July 1954.

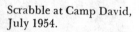

August 1, 1954,
Camp David.
Eisenhower is painting
a portrait of Barbara
and her children,
David, Anne and Susan.

The Eisenhowers
at Gettysburg,
September 1956.

Above, father and son on their way to the Yankee-Dodger opening game of the 1956 World Series. In his father's second term, John became an invaluable member of the White House staff, serving as Goodpaster's assistant. After 1961, he spent two years working for his father on the White House memoirs.

Below, Eisenhower and Field Marshal Montgomery at Gettysburg, with Jim Hagerty. Monty's judgment, loudly expressed, was that both Meade and Lee should have been sacked.

"You Came Here Your Very Self!"

REPUBLICAN
NATIONAL
CONVENTION
1956

HERBLOCK
©1956 THE WASHINGTON POST CO.

Above, Lewis Strauss, just back from Geneva test ban talks, confers with Eisenhower at Lowry Air Force Base, Denver, August 22, 1955. Strauss could always find good reasons to oppose any limitation on testing.

Left, Herblock captures a bit of the ambiguity in the Eisenhower-Republican Party relationship.

Below, Andrew Goodpaster, Roland Hughes, Eisenhower, Gerald Morgan, and Gabriel Hauge, at a budget meeting, January 3, 1956, in Newport, Rhode Island. Ike had a habit of chewing on the earpiece of his glasses when he was in deep thought.

"What Do You Suppose He Means This Time?"

IKE 57

PASS · STOP · TURN · REVERSE

YES · AND NO · DON'T KNOW · ON THE OTHER HAND

SCHOOLS · CIVIL RIGHTS · BUDGET

HERBLOCK

HERBLOCK, THE WASHINGTON POST CO.

Above right, Eisenhower and Nixon on one of the few occasions they played golf together. Ike often complained that "Dick hasn't matured," but he kept him on the ticket in 1956 and supported him wholeheartedly in 1960. Whatever his reservations about Nixon, Eisenhower wanted the best for his country, and he thought Nixon far superior to his competition.

Below, in a famous photo, the President's grandchildren and the Vice-President's children meet for the first time, on Inauguration Day, 1957. Ann and David Eisenhower, Tricia and Julie Nixon.

FOUR CARTOONS:
HERBLOCK, THE WASHINGTON POST CO.

"And All This Time I Was Hoping You'd Speak Up"

Above left, Jim Hagerty advises Eisenhower on camera angles prior to a Presidential talk on the budget. Ike was the first President to take full advantage of television and, as can be seen, prepared carefully for his appearances. May 14, 1957.

Below left, Another fateful handshake, this time with Arkansas Governor Orval Faubus, Newport, R.I., September 14, 1957. Herbert Brownell, in the background, warned Ike that Faubus could not be trusted, but Faubus had just promised he would remove the Arkansas National Guard troops around Little Rock Central High. When he got home, the governor double-crossed the President, forcing Ike to act decisively.

"Tsk Tsk—Somebody Should Do Something About That"

"Well, Men, What'll We Refrain From Doing Now?"

Above left, a meeting of legislative leaders, March 6, 1959. Left to right: Charles Halleck, Allen Dulles, Everett Dirksen, Christian Herter, Sam Rayburn, Neil McElroy, Eisenhower, Lyndon Johnson, Nixon. Eisenhower carefully courted the Congressional leaders.

Below right, Eisenhower presents the Distinguished Service Medal to Admiral Arthur Radford, August 8, 1957. As Chairman of the JCS, Radford often offered recommendations that went beyond anything Eisenhower was willing to do. Still, they worked effectively together.

Above, Sir Winston Churchill rides with the President on his last visit to the United States. May 4, 1959.
Below, Another comrade-in-arms from World War II, Charles de Gaulle, visits the President in the Oval Office, April 22, 1960.

FOUR PHOTOS: NATIONAL PARK SERVICE

Above, Eisenhower and Khrushchev, September 1959, during Khrushchev's visit to the United States. They never liked or trusted each other, but they came close to calling a halt to the arms race. It came to naught at the Paris Summit in May 1960.

Below, Eisenhower and Kennedy on their way to Kennedy's inauguration. The oldest President to that date had to hand over to the youngest man elected to the office, and he hated doing it. His opinion of Kennedy did not go up in the years that followed.

Above, Walter Cronkite interviews Eisenhower for the CBS program, "D-Day Plus Twenty Years." They are sitting in Southwick House, Ike's invasion headquarters, in front of the operation map at SHAEF, set for June 6, 1944.

Below, Eisenhower meeting with Johnson and his advisers in the Cabinet Room of the White House, February 16, 1965. At this critical meeting, Ike was hawkish on Vietnam. From left to right: Robert McNamara, McGeorge Bundy, Johnson, Eisenhower, General Earl Wheeler, and Andrew Goodpaster.

Above, Eisenhower leaves the White House, August 30, 1965, again urging Johnson to go for victory in Vietnam.
Below right, Eisenhower and Andrew Goodpaster. In the White House, Goodpaster was the indispensable man, the one the President leaned on and relied on more than any other. During Ike's retirement, Goodpaster was his liaison with Johnson on the Vietnam War.

Dwight David Eisenhower, 34th President of the United States. October 22, 1953.

CHAPTER TEN

The Formosa Doctrine

January 1–June 20, 1955

ON NEW YEAR'S DAY, 1955, Chiang Kai-shek predicted "war at any time" over Quemoy and Matsu. On the other side of the Formosa Straits, Chou En-lai said that a Chinese invasion of Formosa was "imminent."[1] Thus did the two Chinese rivals intensify the Formosa Straits crisis, which soon became one of the most serious of Eisenhower's eight years in office. Indeed the United States in early 1955 came closer to using atomic weapons than at any other time in the Eisenhower Administration.

On January 10, the ChiCom Air Force raided the Tachen Islands, two hundred miles from Formosa but held by ChiNat troops. (For the sake of simplicity, this account will use the terminology of the Eisenhower Administration in distinguishing the two sides—ChiComs for Chinese Communists, ChiNats for Chinese Nationalists.) A week later, ChiCom troops captured Ichiang, an island seven miles north of the Tachens. On the mainland, meanwhile, the ChiComs were improving their jet airfields opposite Formosa. Eisenhower decided that "the time had come to draw the line."[2] This decision immediately raised the problem of *where* to draw the line, a problem that was never fully resolved and that deepened the crisis. Certainly the Americans were going to fight to defend Formosa—Eisenhower had made treaty arrangements in December of 1954 that required the United States to do so—and the Pescadores were included in the area to be defended. But what of Quemoy and Matsu? They were so close to the Chinese main-

231

land, so unquestionably a part of China, so far from Formosa (and in any case so small that they could not be used as a platform for the invasion of Formosa) that almost no one, except Chiang, thought they were worth defending. The Tachens added to the problem: Were they also vital to the defense of Formosa?

Eisenhower decided to let the Tachens go, while deliberately remaining vague about Quemoy and Matsu. He managed to maintain the vagueness throughout a series of war scares during the crisis. It was the cornerstone of his policy, and he held to it despite the manifold problems it created for him with his European allies, his own military and JCS, Chiang, Congress, and the American public.

On January 19, Eisenhower met with Dulles to discuss a resolution Eisenhower wanted Congress to pass, giving him authority to commit American armed forces to the defense of Formosa and the Pescadores. Dulles agreed there was a need for such a resolution, and with Eisenhower's decision to use the Seventh Fleet to assist in the evacuation of the Tachens. But Dulles wanted to include Quemoy and Matsu in the resolution, which Eisenhower would not permit. Instead, Eisenhower said the wording he wanted would allow the President to react in defense of Formosa and the Pescadores and "such other territories as may be determined."[3]

The resolution Eisenhower wanted was something new in American history. Never before had Congress given the President a blank check to act as he saw fit in a foreign crisis. Fully aware of the unprecedented nature of his request, Eisenhower talked with all the congressional leaders before submitting it. Eisenhower wanted Congress's backing. He was not going to expose himself to the kind of criticism that Taft and other Republicans had made against Truman for entering the Korean War without consulting Congress. He explained his thinking and his wishes to Joe Martin, the minority leader, and Sam Rayburn, the speaker of the House; they assured him that the House would "approve his action and without any criticism whatsoever."[4]

On January 21, Eisenhower met in the Oval Office with the JCS, Dulles, and Wilson. He outlined the resolution he proposed to ask Congress to pass. He gave four reasons for the resolution: (1) its logical purpose; (2) "to tell the ChiComs of our intentions"; (3) "to dispel doubts as to whether we were acting on constitutional grounds"; and (4) to bolster the morale of the ChiNats. Admiral Robert Carney, the Chief of Naval Operations, then protested that the resolution was merely a cover for what was in fact a retreat. Carney did not want to abandon the Tachens. Citing the difficulties inherent in trying to evacuate the forty thousand ChiNats on the Tachens, Carney said it would be easier and wiser to defend them. That would involve using the Seventh Fleet, as the ChiNats were incapable of defending the Tachens alone. Eisenhower told Carney that there was no relationship between the Tachens and Formosa, that he was not going to change his mind, and that Carney should get to work on evacuation plans.[5]

The following day, Eisenhower talked to Hagerty about the public-relations aspects of the resolution. He said this was a "big step" and he wanted it done right. That morning, Eisenhower said, he had ordered three aircraft carriers from Pearl Harbor to join the Seventh Fleet, and told other forces in the Pacific to prepare to go to Formosa if necessary. Eisenhower declared, according to Hagerty's diary entry, that he "had made up his mind to not let the ChiComs get away with murder in the China Sea." Nor would he "sit idly by and permit the Reds to build up any large forces on the mainland for an invasion of either Formosa or the Pescadores." Eisenhower said he would "not draw any definite line as such," and explained to Hagerty: "We are deliberately not going to draw a specific line because we do not believe in giving blueprints to the Communists on just what we will or will not do."[6]

On January 24, Eisenhower sent his message to Congress, asking for a resolution that would "clearly and publicly establish the authority of the President as Commander in Chief to employ the armed forces of this nation promptly and effectively for the purposes indicated if in his judgment it became necessary." The "purposes indicated" included not only the defense of Formosa and the Pescadores, as required by treaty, but also the defense of "closely related localities," which meant—or did it?—Quemoy and Matsu. The President did not, would not, say.[7]

After dispatching the message, Eisenhower worked to build support for it. He wrote Henry Luce, outlining his thinking and asking for a Time-Life endorsement.[8] He talked to Senator Saltonstall, who wanted to know if the resolution "amounted in effect to an advance declaration of war" and asked whether Chiang had a "clear title" to Formosa, which the ChiComs claimed was a part of China. Defending Formosa might put the United States smack in the middle of the Chinese civil war, and defending Quemoy and Matsu certainly would have that effect. Resisting Communist expansion was one thing; involvement in a civil war something else again.

"You know, Senator," Eisenhower answered, "sometimes we are captains of history." Formosa was "part of a great island barrier we have erected in the Pacific against Communist advance. We are not going to let it be broken." Therefore, "I don't think we should worry about any cloudiness to any title . . . We just can't permit the Chi-Nats to sit in Formosa and wait until they are attacked . . . If we see the ChiComs building up their forces for an invasion of Formosa we are going to have to go in and break it up." As to whether he already had the power to act, even without the resolution, Eisenhower said that no one had ever clearly defined the President's constitutional powers in such a situation, and explained that his real reason for the message was "to serve notice on the Communists that they're not going to be able to get away with it."[9]

The House responded as Martin and Rayburn said it would; within the hour of receiving the message, it gave the President unlimited authority to act as he saw fit, by a vote of 410 to 3. The Senate, however, was another matter. It insisted on holding hearings. Initially, these went badly for the Administration, because General Ridgway went to the Hill to testify and took the opportunity to once again denounce Eisenhower's New Look. Ridgway said that because of the New Look, the Army was just too small to defend Formosa. Eisenhower was so angry that he told Dulles over the telephone that the time had come to fire Ridgway. Dulles cautioned him against precipitate action, and Eisenhower agreed to talk to Ridgway privately.[10] Partly because of Ridgway's testimony, mainly because of fears of involvement in the Chinese civil war, Senator Herbert Lehman of New York introduced an amendment to the resolution, drawing the line back of Quemoy and Matsu and confining the use of American forces to the defense of Formosa and the Pescadores. Eisenhower, Dulles, and the Administration went all out to defeat the amendment.

Publicly, Eisenhower had Hagerty release a statement in the President's name that assured the Senate that American forces would be used "purely for defensive purposes" on the basis of a presidential decision "which he would take and the responsibility for which he has not delegated." Eisenhower also said that he would not commit American troops to the defense of Quemoy and Matsu unless he was convinced that an attack against the islands was merely a prelude to an assault against Formosa itself. He had not "made that decision" and would not make it until he knew "the circumstances surrounding any given attack."[11]

After three days of debate the Lehman Amendment was rejected, 74 to 13. On January 28, by a vote of 83 to 3, the Senate passed the resolution. For the first time in American history, the Congress had authorized the President in advance to engage in a war at a time and under circumstances of his own choosing.

The Formosa Doctrine, as Eisenhower called it, confused more than it clarified—exactly as he intended. Chou called it a "war message" and reiterated the ChiComs' intent to liberate Formosa. Chiang was not so sure. The ChiNat leader wanted some assurances about Quemoy and Matsu from the President before he would agree to abandon the Tachens. Eisenhower was unwilling to give any such guarantee. On January 31, he called Radford to his office, to give Radford his orders. The President said that he would defend Quemoy and Matsu "if an attack [on them] were to occur which the U.S. judged to constitute a threat to Formosa," but he did not want Chiang or anyone else informed of that position, as he insisted on reserving the final decision to himself.[12] The President also told Radford that if Chiang asked for help in evacuating the Tachens, the Seventh Fleet should provide assistance. Eisenhower would not, however, authorize any attacks against the Chinese mainland. If the ChiComs "undertook a consistent and persistent air attack against the [evacuation] operation," the Seventh Fleet could attack ChiCom airfields on the mainland, but only after clearing it with the President.[13] The evacuation began on February 4 and was completed within a week; the ChiComs did not attack.

That left Quemoy and Matsu. Eisenhower's ambiguous resolution led the whole world to wonder if he would fight to defend them or not. Aside from Chiang and Eisenhower, it seemed that almost no one else was ready to do so. The Europeans were especially alarmed. Churchill best expressed their fears. He told Eisenhower that while of course the United States could not allow the ChiComs to overrun Formosa, he could not see the point of holding on to Quemoy and Matsu. Churchill said that in the event of a ChiCom invasion, the Seventh Fleet could easily "drown any Chinese would-be invaders of Formosa."[14]

To reassure the Europeans, Eisenhower used his favorite emissary, the SACEUR, General Gruenther. In a long letter to Gruenther (with an almost identical letter to Churchill), Eisenhower explained his position. He said he realized that Europeans "consider America reckless, impulsive and immature," but pointed out that at home he had to deal with "the truculent and the timid, the jingoists and the pacifists." The pressures, in other words, were coming on him from all sides, ranging from advice to immediately launch a full-scale atomic strike against the ChiComs through the spectrum to advice to withdraw from Formosa itself. If he were to announce an intention to defend Quemoy and Matsu, it would mean that the United States would have to assure the defense of islands "that are almost within wading distance of the mainland." That would be costly and "we could get badly tied down."

Why not just pull out? Because, the President explained, the morale of the ChiNats was at stake. Already there were disturbing rumors that ChiNat forces were breaking under Chou's pressure, and the CIA reported the possibility that whole units of Chiang's army were ready to jump to the Communist side. So while Eisenhower was more than ready to agree that Quemoy and Matsu had no relation to the defense of Formosa as such, he argued that they were central to the problem of ChiNat morale. Eisenhower told Gruenther what he had repeatedly told the JCS, that ChiNat morale was the key to everything, because if Chiang's army would not fight to defend Formosa, nothing could be done. And ChiNat morale depended on holding on to Quemoy and Matsu. Why? Because the ChiNats considered the islands as "stepping-stones" to their eventual invasion of the mainland. Abandoning the islands would be, to the ChiNats, equivalent to abandoning all hopes of ever retaking China itself. With that hope gone, Chiang's units might desert wholesale.

The Europeans were worried about what Russia might do if United States armed forces were involved in a war in the China Sea. Eisenhower assured Gruenther that "I do not believe that Russia wants war at this time," that the U.S.S.R. would not involve itself in a fight for Formosa nor would it use the opportunity to march across the Elbe River. The Russians would, Eisenhower said, provide the ChiComs with supplies, "but I am convinced that Russia does not want, at this moment, to experiment with means of defense against the bombing that we *could* conduct against her mainland." [15]

In his letter to Churchill, Eisenhower emphasized the importance of the ChiNat Army. He reminded the Prime Minister that "only a few months back we had both Chiang and a strong, well-equipped French Army to support the free world's position in Southeast Asia. The French are gone—making it clearer than ever that we cannot afford the loss of Chiang unless all of us are to get completely out of that corner of the globe. This is unthinkable to us—I feel it must be to you." [16]

Dominoes again—Eisenhower was saying that the loss of Quemoy and Matsu would lead to the loss of the entire Western position in Asia. Churchill was not convinced. He said that all the ChiComs wanted was Quemoy and Matsu (and implied that he agreed with them that the islands rightly belonged to China). Eisenhower replied that simply was not so, and invited Churchill to examine Chou's statements, which consistently said that his real goal was Formosa. Churchill dismissed Chou's statements as "just talk." Eisenhower strongly disagreed, telling Churchill that after the ChiComs took Formosa, they would go after Japan.[17] Eisenhower also insisted that it was important to keep the ChiNats on China's flank, always threatening to invade, because that tied down ChiCom forces that might otherwise be used in South Korea or against South Vietnam. On February 16, Eisenhower told the Republican leaders that because of what was at stake, he would have to "sort of hold Chiang Kai-shek's hand throughout this difficult time." Then, Hagerty wrote in his diary, "the President smiled wrily and said almost to himself, 'But those damned little offshore islands. Sometimes I wish they'd sink.' "[18]

But they would not, and to get British agreement to their defense, Eisenhower sent Dulles to London to talk to Churchill. He told Dulles to ask Churchill what position the British would want America to take if Chou suddenly announced his intention to capture Hong Kong, and began building the airfields to make it possible.[19] He also sent along yet another letter to Churchill, in which he brought up a theme he had first used in December 1941, when George Marshall had asked him what strategy to pursue in the Pacific in the face of the overwhelming Japanese attack. At that time, Eisenhower had replied that the United States had to do all it could to defend the Philippines, because the people of Asia "will be watching us. They may excuse failure but they will not excuse abandonment."[20] In 1955, Eisenhower thought the same principle applied. "All the non-Communist nations of the Western Pacific," he told Churchill, "are watching nervously to see what we do next. I fear that if we . . . should attempt to compel Chiang to make further retreats, the conclusions of these Asian peoples will be that they had better plan to make the best terms they can with the Communists . . ."[21]

Churchill, and his Foreign Secretary and heir apparent, Eden, remained unconvinced. They wanted negotiations, a cease-fire, a cooling off, anything. Eden suggested that the ChiNats withdraw from Quemoy and Matsu in return for a ChiCom promise to abstain from attacking Formosa. Eisenhower labeled the suggestion "more wishful than realistic."[22]

After Dulles left London, he flew to Asia, making several stops to assess the situation. He returned to the States in time for a March 10 NSC meeting, where he reported that "the situation out there in the Formosa Straits is far more serious than I thought." He believed the

ChiComs were serious about taking Formosa, and he doubted that Chiang's troops would remain loyal in the event of a ChiCom lodgment on Formosa. He said there was a "need better to inform the American people of the hostilities (probably not leading to general war) in defending Formosa."

Then Dulles turned to the point that made defending Quemoy and Matsu such a risky, indeed scary, proposition. "If we defend Quemoy and Matsu," he said bluntly, "we'll have to use atomic weapons. They alone will be effective against the mainland airfields." Because of the New Look, the United States did not have the strength to defend the islands by conventional arms. Dulles acknowledged that using atomic bombs against China would have "a repercussive effect" on Europeans and the Japanese, so "world public opinion must be prepared."[23] Dulles, at least, was ready to face the worst. He concluded, "Before this problem is solved, I believe there is at least an even chance that the United States will have to go to war." Eisenhower did not disagree; he did say that if war broke out, it "would not be of our seeking."[24]

Nevertheless, the President did not want to use atomic weapons. Among other considerations, he was worried about the European reaction. Although France had ratified the agreements bringing sovereignty to West Germany and allowing German rearmament, other continental nations had not yet ratified, and if the United States started using atomic bombs against China they probably would not. In this "especially delicate situation," Eisenhower told the NSC the following day, March 11, he wanted to know "what is the minimum we could do to protect our ally, Free China, and yet not exacerbate the situation in Europe?" He did not want to talk about atomic bombs, and he refused to even consider sending American ground troops to Formosa, but he did want to do something. Surely, he thought, Quemoy and Matsu could be defended without initiating an atomic strike. Could not napalm be used?[25]

What the President needed was more precise information on the situation on Quemoy and Matsu. He was dissatisfied with the intelligence he was getting from the CIA. He therefore decided to send his closest and most trusted adviser, Goodpaster, to the Pacific. Pulling Goodpaster aside after the NSC meeting, Eisenhower told him to find out "how fast ChiCom attacks in various forms might develop," and how long the ChiNats could hold out on their own if they had American logistical support.[26] Goodpaster went, investigated, and returned to report that the ChiNats were rapidly improving their defense on

Quemoy and Matsu, rushing in troops, and would be capable of defending themselves against a ChiCom attack, *unless* the ChiComs threw their Air Force into the battle. In that case, "U.S. support would be required, and would probably have to include special weapons."[27]

The use of "special weapons" had, by the time Goodpaster returned, become a matter of public debate. On March 12, Dulles said in a speech that the United States had "new and powerful weapons of precision which can utterly destroy military targets without endangering unrelated civilian centers." Three days later, he was even more specific, saying that the United States was prepared to use tactical atomic weapons in case of war in the Formosa Straits.[28] This was a clear and unambiguous threat, much clearer than those Dulles and Eisenhower had made against the ChiComs two years earlier with regard to Korea. Dulles cleared his statement with the President before making it.[29] Inevitably, it set off an uproar within the U.S. and throughout the world.

At Eisenhower's March 16 news conference, Charles von Fremd of CBS asked him to comment on Dulles' assertion that in the event of war in the Far East, "we would probably make use of some tactical small atomic weapons." Eisenhower was unusually direct in his answer: "Yes, of course they would be used." He explained, "In any combat where these things can be used on strictly military targets and for strictly military purposes, I see no reason why they shouldn't be used just exactly as you would use a bullet or anything else." But would not the United States itself be destroyed in a nuclear war? Eisenhower replied, "I have one great belief; nobody in war or anywhere else ever made a good decision if he was frightened to death. You have to look facts in the face, but you have to have the stamina to do it without just going hysterical."[30]

Democrats found it difficult to avoid hysteria when the President started comparing atomic weapons to bullets. Lyndon Johnson warned against undertaking "an irresponsible adventure for which we have not calculated the risks," and Adlai Stevenson expressed "the gravest misgivings about risking a third world war in defense of these little islands." On the other side, Radford could barely suppress his excitement; the chairman of the JCS said that "there is a distinct possibility that war can break out at any time." And Senator Wiley pronounced his judgment: "Either we can defend the United States in the Formosa Straits—now, or we can defend it later in San Francisco Bay." General James Van Fleet wanted to send American troops to Quemoy and Matsu; if the Chinese continued shelling the islands, Eisenhower

could "shoot back with atomic weapons and annihilate the Red effort."[31] Knowland added his perspective—there should be no "appeasement," no matter what the risks. Dulles, in a speech on March 20,
managed to raise the tension even higher by referring to the ChiComs
in terms usually reserved for use against nations at war. The Secretary
said the Chinese were "an acute and imminent threat, . . . dizzy with
success," more dangerous than the Russians. He compared their "aggressive fanaticism" with Hitler's.[32]

Three days later, Eisenhower was walking with Hagerty from the
White House to the Executive Office Building for a press conference.
Hagerty said he had just received a frantic plea. "Mr. President, some
of the people in the State Department say that the Formosa Strait situation is so delicate that no matter what question you get on it, you
shouldn't say anything at all." Eisenhower laughed and replied,
"Don't worry, Jim, if that question comes up, I'll just confuse them."[33]

He did. Joseph C. Harsch asked him about using atomic weapons
in the Formosa Straits, and he responded with a long, rambling reply
that was incomprehensible. Years later, Eisenhower still got a chuckle
out of thinking about the difficulties Chinese and Russian intelligence
analysts must have had in trying to put his remarks into their language
and then explain to their bosses what the American President meant.[34]
Eventually, Harsch interjected, "Sir, I am a little stupid about this
thing," and asked for further clarification. Eisenhower explained that
he could not be precise. "The only thing I know about war are two
things: the most changeable factor in war is human nature in its day-
by-day manifestation; but the only unchanging factor in war is human
nature. And the next thing is that every war is going to astonish you
in the way it occurred, and in the way it is carried out. So that for a
man to predict, particularly if he had the responsibility for making the
decision, to predict what he is going to use, how he is going to do it,
would I think exhibit his ignorance of war; that is what I believe. So
I think you just have to wait, and that is the kind of prayerful decision
that may some day face a President."[35]

Two days later, on March 25, Admiral Carney briefed correspondents at a private dinner. He said the President was considering acting
militarily on an all-out basis "to destroy Red China's military potential and thus end its expansionist tendencies." He also said that he expected the war to break out on April 15. Eisenhower called Dulles to
express his concern and anger. As Ann Whitman took down the conversation, "President said he's going to tell Wilson this is intolerable
and that if he does not do something about it, President himself will

take charge of Defense Department. Meanwhile, he will ask Hagerty to tell press people not to be led astray by such news as Carney gave out, to believe that Administration is being vigilant, and certainly trying to get by without a war."[36] When he talked to Hagerty, Eisenhower complained that Carney and the Navy "are anxious to throw a blockade around the China mainland." Becoming agitated, the President began to pace. Hagerty recorded, "As he walked, he talked rapidly and forcefully and said: 'By God, this has got to stop. These fellows like Carney and Ridgway don't yet realize that they . . . have a boss. I'm going to see Radford in half an hour, and I'm going to tell him to tell Carney to stop talking.' "

Then Eisenhower turned to the substance of what Carney had said. He predicted that Carney was "going to look awful silly when April 15th comes along and there is no incident, because honestly our information is that there is no buildup off those islands as yet to sustain any attack, and believe me, they're not going to take those islands just by wishing for them." Quemoy and Matsu were "well equipped and well defended," and they could only be taken by a prolonged campaign. Eisenhower told Hagerty to tell the press corps "that you are not normally a betting man, but if any of them wanted to bet a thousand dollars that we would be in war on . . . the date they wrote about, you would be happy to bet them."[37]

Eisenhower was not entirely sure he could get through the crisis without a war. On March 26, he wrote in his diary that Carney just might be right, "because the Red Chinese appear to be completely reckless, arrogant, possibly overconfident, and completely indifferent as to human losses." Still, he doubted that hostilities would escalate beyond the shelling of the islands. "I have so often been through these periods of strain that I have become accustomed to the fact that most of the calamities that we anticipate really never occur."[38]

On March 30, Dulles and Eisenhower met with the leaders of both parties. Dulles gave a long presentation. When he finished, Rayburn said that as he understood the situation, if the ChiComs should attack Quemoy and Matsu, the United States would intervene. Eisenhower quickly corrected him. The President said he had *not* made that decision and would not make it until he knew the precise circumstances of any attack. If it appeared that the ChiNats could hold out by themselves, fine. If it appeared that the ChiComs were interested only in Quemoy and Matsu, and did not intend to invade Formosa itself, Eisenhower said the United States would stay out of it. But if an attack on Quemoy and Matsu appeared to be but a preliminary to an attack on Formosa, the United States would intervene. "The tricky business," Eisenhower admitted in a grand understatement, "is to determine whether or not an attack on Quemoy and Matsu, if made, is truly a local operation or a preliminary to a major effort against Formosa."[39]

To the press and public, the critical period in the crisis was the first two weeks in April. The Asian and African nations were scheduled to hold a conference at Bandung, in Indonesia, from April 17 to 24. It was generally assumed that the ChiComs would want to enhance their prestige by taking the offshore islands before the conference began—thus Carney's date of April 15. But Eisenhower and Dulles took an opposite view. First, Goodpaster had reported that the true critical period was the last two weeks in March; by April 1, Goodpaster felt, Chiang's defenses on the islands would be sufficient. Second, Dulles felt that the ChiComs would take a different approach to the Bandung conference. They would not seek a military victory, but rather would try to "clean up" their reputation so as to appear to be a peace-loving nation.[40]

Based on his feeling that the danger point had been passed, Eisenhower began his campaign to find a long-range solution. On April 1, he called Dulles, Wilson, Humphrey, Radford, and Goodpaster to the Oval Office. (It is notable that Eisenhower, for all his staff training and consciousness, and for all his insistence on turning the NSC into a policy-making body, held his most critical conferences during the crisis on an informal basis in the Oval Office.) Radford spoke first. The admiral wanted to put some ten thousand U.S. personnel, primarily Air Force, on Formosa. Eisenhower said "he was thinking rather in terms of small sections of technicians and advisers to be attached to ChiNat units." The President then outlined his position. A war with China over Quemoy and Matsu was "undesirable" because none of America's allies would support the United States in such a war, public opinion within the United States would be badly divided, and the effect on the domestic economy would be disastrous.

Eisenhower said a "desirable solution" would be to convince Chiang to voluntarily evacuate Quemoy and Matsu, then entrench himself on Formosa. To induce the ChiNats to retreat, Eisenhower was willing to offer Chiang a division of United States Marines for Formosa and additional Air Force units. If Chiang would not withdraw, Eisenhower's backup position was to convince him to reduce the size of his commitment to Quemoy and Matsu. The ChiNats had fifty-eight thousand troops on Quemoy and fifteen thousand on Matsu. "That's just too many troops for those small islands," the President said, and he did not want the garrisons to become another Dien Bien Phu. He wanted Chiang to turn the islands into outposts instead of fortresses.[41]

Dulles was not fully convinced; he was concerned about the psychological effect of a retreat. On April 5, in a ten-page, single-spaced memorandum, Eisenhower explained to his Secretary why the United States had to avoid committing itself to the defense of Quemoy and Matsu. Because the ChiComs had overwhelming land forces that they could bring to bear against the islands, "any successful defense would necessarily require counteraction against the mainland of China itself." The President continued, "We have ample forewarning of the adverse character of world reaction that would follow any such action on our part, especially if we felt compelled to use atomic weapons— which we probably would in order to insure success. . . . Public opinion in the United States would, to say the least, become further divided. If conflict in that region should spread to global proportions, we would be entering a life-and-death struggle under very great handicaps . . . We would be isolated in world opinion."[42]

Preserving and strengthening peace, the President decided, required some backing down from the belligerent rhetoric and from the Dien Bien Phu atmosphere surrounding Quemoy and Matsu. On April 20, therefore, he sent Radford and Walter Robertson (who had earlier been his envoy to Syngman Rhee at the time of the POW crisis in South Korea) to Formosa to talk to Chiang. His instructions to Radford and Robertson were delicate in the extreme—too delicate, as it turned out. He wanted them to "lead the Generalissimo into making a proposition that will neither commit the United States to war in defense of the offshore islands nor will constitute an implied repudiation of the Generalissimo by this government." The envoys, in other words, should induce Chiang himself to suggest a reduction of the garrisons on the islands; if he did that, the U.S. would send the Marine division and supporting air units to Formosa. But Chiang should not be allowed to think that the United States was committed to the defense of Quemoy and Matsu.[43]

Radford and Robertson sent back long cables on their talks with Chiang. Eisenhower was disappointed with the results. They reported that Chiang did not want Marines on Formosa; what he wanted was an American commitment to defend Quemoy and Matsu. At one point, Chiang walked out of a meeting. The ChiNat Foreign Minister, Yeh, explained to Radford that "Gimo [Chiang] had not anticipated any proposal from us which would involve abandoning Quemoy and

Matsu to Communists inasmuch as Gimo was so firmly convinced that he had been given positive assurance by President Eisenhower that U.S. would participate in their defense."[44]

Eisenhower was dismayed. He had not wanted to suggest complete abandonment of the islands, only the reduction of their garrisons, and he had wanted his envoys to lead Chiang around to himself proposing such action. But they had failed to understand his point, much less get Chiang to understand it. Eisenhower admitted to Dulles that "it is, of course, possible that no presentation could have brought Chiang to recognizing the wisdom of some arrangement as this . . . but it is clear that as long as Radford and Robertson themselves could not grasp the concept, we simply were not going to get anywhere, and there is nothing in the cable to suggest that such a thought was discussed." So, he concluded sadly, "We are still on the horns of the dilemma."[45]

But in fact, the crisis was already over. On April 23, Chou spoke at Bandung about Chinese friendship for the American people and said that the ChiComs "do not want to have a war with the United States." He offered to negotiate. Eisenhower responded positively, saying he was ready to talk "if there seemed to be an opportunity for us to further the easing of tensions." Chou continued his conciliatory line, saying that the ChiComs "are willing to strive for the liberation of Formosa by peaceful means as far as this is possible." The shelling of Quemoy and Matsu eased off; by mid-May, it ceased entirely. At the end of May, the ChiComs released four American fliers they had held as prisoners; that summer, they released all the prisoners they held. On August 1, talks between American and Chinese representatives began.[46]

Throughout the crisis, Eisenhower had been beset by conflicting advice. As he recounted it in his memoirs, "The administration heard the counsel of Attlee (liquidate Chiang), Eden (neutralize Quemoy and Matsu), [Democratic Senators] (abandon Quemoy and Matsu), Lewis Douglas (avoid entry into a civil war, on legal principle), Radford (fight for the Tachens, bomb the mainland), Knowland (blockade the Chinese coast), and Rhee (join him and Chiang in a holy war of liberation)."[47] But the only counsel Eisenhower really took was his own. As a result, he emerged from the crisis with all his objectives secured. Chiang still held the islands, and the American commitment to defend Formosa was stronger than ever. These results satisfied all but the most extreme members of the China Lobby and the Old Guard.

Eisenhower had gotten a blank check from Congress that gave him total freedom of action. As a result, he had managed to so confuse the
ChiComs as to whether or not the United States would use atomic
bombs against them in the defense of Quemoy and Matsu that they decided not to attack. True, his comparison of an atomic bomb to bullets
scared the wits out of people around the world, but through his actions and press-conference ambiguities Eisenhower had managed to
convince the Europeans, and others, that he was neither hysterical nor
cold-blooded. He never had to use the bomb; he did not plunge the
world into war; he kept the peace without losing any territory or
prestige.

Eisenhower's handling of the Quemoy-Matsu crisis was a *tour de
force,* one of the great triumphs of his long career. The key to his success was his deliberate ambiguity and deception. As Robert Divine
writes, "The beauty of Eisenhower's policy is that to this day no one
can be sure whether or not he would have responded militarily to an
invasion of the offshore islands, and whether he would have used nuclear weapons."[48] The full truth is that Eisenhower himself did not
know. In retrospect, what stands out about Eisenhower's crisis management is that at every stage he kept his options open. Flexibility was
one of his chief characteristics as Supreme Commander in World War
II; as President, he insisted on retaining that flexibility. He never
knew himself just how he would respond to an invasion of Quemoy
and Matsu, because he insisted on waiting to see the precise nature of
the attack before deciding how to react. What he did know was that
when the moment of decision came, he would have the maximum
number of options to choose from.

Eisenhower wanted options within his options. If he had to go to
atomic war, he wanted choices as to the weapons he used. At the beginning of the worst weeks of the crisis, on February 13, he gave his
approval to Operation Teacup, a series of atomic blasts in Nevada. As
a part of the process of putting pressure on the ChiComs, Eisenhower
had Strauss make a public announcement about the tests. They were
small weapons, Strauss explained, under fifty kilotons, designed for
battlefield use. (Small is relative—the Hiroshima blast was twenty kilotons.) Eisenhower called Strauss on the day of the first test; Strauss reported it was "very successful." He also said that Goodpaster had told
him the President was thinking of "taking a look" at one of the shots
(twelve were scheduled), which Strauss said would be helpful to morale.[49] The President was indeed interested; ten days later he told

Hagerty that he had never seen one of the things go off and he wanted to do it. Hagerty worried about the public-relations repercussions; it was early March, the Formosa Straits crisis was at its peak and it would appear much too belligerent for the President to be observing an atomic blast. Eisenhower agreed.[50]

He did so reluctantly, because one aim of Teacup was to "prepare the people," as Dulles put it, for nuclear war. But the tests were already stirring too much controversy, because by early March radioactive rain was registering at high levels across a thousand-mile belt from Nebraska to New Jersey. The AEC conducted an intensive public-relations campaign to convince the public that fear of fallout was groundless, but nevertheless people were concerned, and Eisenhower did not want to add to their fears by drawing even more attention to Teacup. But neither did he want to give the ChiComs the idea that he was backing away from the possible use of nuclear weapons, so on March 7 he told Dulles to put into his next speech a line saying "we regard it as tragic that we must continue to enlarge our arsenal of atomic weapons . . ." Such a sentence, Eisenhower explained, "would remind individuals that we are really regarding these weapons as 'conventional' but at the same time maintain a peaceful and conciliatory tone."[51]

An important development in American nuclear policy came that spring as the Eisenhower Administration quietly dropped as its goal the elimination of nuclear weapons from the earth, and instead committed itself to the more modest aim of arms control. Stassen made this official in his first report to the President as the President's Special Assistant on Disarmament, a position Eisenhower had appointed him to on March 19. Stassen's report reflected Eisenhower's feelings. On February 24, talking about disarmament and the stalled talks in London, Eisenhower remarked to Hagerty that "of course the Reds were proposing to eliminate all atomic weapons, which would have the result of going back to ground forces alone, which would leave them with the preponderance of military power in Europe."[52] As Stassen put it in his first report, the United States would seek arms control only under stringent conditions requiring on-site inspection, and would put the highest priority on guarding against a surprise nuclear attack.[53]

It was with some consternation, therefore, that Eisenhower received the news that the Soviet delegation at the London talks, on May 10, announced substantial acceptance of American proposals for nuclear and general disarmament, including on-site inspection. The President had to do a turnaround. After a decade in which it had always been the Russians who rejected on-site inspection, they had managed to force the United States to do the rejecting. When Eisenhower explained the new American position to a press conference, his words sounded strange coming from a man who had complained about the secrecy of the Iron Curtain so many times. "Are we ready to open up every one of our factories, every place where something might be going on that could be inimical to the interests of somebody else?" Eisenhower asked. "This question of inspection, what we will accept and what, therefore, we would expect others to accept, is a very serious one; consequently, there is just nothing today that I could say that is positive beyond this point."[54]

There was no easy way out of the nuclear dilemma. Eisenhower deplored the existence of the bombs, insisted repeatedly that the United States could never win a war using them, not even with a huge lead and a first strike, and yet felt he had to maintain a lead in atomic weapons, else his New Look rationale would fall apart. The "only area" in which the United States was ahead of the Russians, he said (ignoring the Navy), was in nuclear warfare. Yet America could not use the lead. Did this mean that the arms race would go on indefinitely? Eisenhower told a news conference that he was prepared to do just that, saying that America had to have a defense program that it could support and still maintain a healthy economy, "for fifty years, if necessary. I hope and pray that we are not going to carry it fifty years, but that is the way we must design it."[55]

Was there then no hope? Was mankind doomed forever to a nuclear arms race? The only way that Eisenhower could see to avoid that outcome was to lower tensions by improving relations with the Soviets. After the fright the world had just gone through over Quemoy and Matsu, some kind of peaceful coexistence was a situation everyone wanted. Voices were raised around the world for a summit meeting to settle outstanding issues. Dulles was extremely leery of any summit meeting, because he feared Old Guard criticism for sitting down with the Communists, and he also feared that the Soviets would use the occasion to make propaganda (which was, of course, true; it was equally true that Dulles and the Americans used international conferences for the same purpose).

Eisenhower, too, had objections to going to the summit, although his reasons were different from those of Dulles. Eisenhower believed that the major outstanding problems—two Germanys, two Koreas, two Vietnams, two Chinas, and arms control—were intractable. Therefore nothing positive could come from a meeting at the summit. Peoples' hopes would have been raised only to be dashed.

But despite his objections, Eisenhower was willing to try to reach out to the Soviets. In late 1954, he had made a significant reduction in his demands on the Russians for "proof" of their sincere intentions. Earlier, he had said there could be no talks until the Russians had done a series of things to prove their good faith; but on November 23, 1954, the President said that suitable evidence of Russian good faith could be provided by one simple act. Indeed, it was an act so simple, and so relatively painless for the Russians, that if the Russians were as eager for a summit meeting as they said they were, they could not resist Eisenhower's proposal. Eisenhower said, "A very definite agreement as to the Austrian treaty would be taken as a deed that would indicate real sincerity on the part of the Communist world to go into further negotiations."[56]

There was no further move, by either side, toward a summit until the Formosa Straits crisis cooled. Then the pressure built again. On April 5, Churchill finally retired and Anthony Eden took his place. Eden called for general elections in May, and he told Eisenhower he wanted to campaign on the basis of having arranged a summit meeting to ease world tension. Churchill also called for a summit, as did Senator Walter George, chairman of the Senate Foreign Relations Committee, and Premier Edgar Faure of France.

More important, there was a change of leadership in Russia. Nikolai Georgi Malenkov was gone. Bulganin had become chairman of the Council of Ministers; Nikita Khrushchev was First Secretary of the Communist Party; Marshal Zhukov had become Minister of Defense. Together they formed a troika. What the meaning of these changes was for the United States was unclear, but it appeared that the Red Army would have more influence on the government. Hagerty asked Eisenhower if this meant that "Russia was moving toward war." Eisenhower said he doubted it, and explained: "If you're in the military and you know about these terrible destructive weapons, it tends to make you more pacifistic . . ." Besides, he added, "They're not ready for war and they know it. They also know if they go to war, they're going to end up losing everything they have. That also tends to make people conservative."[57]

In May, the new Soviet leadership reached out to accept Eisenhower's offer, when it announced that it was ready to sign the Austrian peace treaty. The details of that treaty had long since been worked out—Austria would regain her independence as the occupying powers left the country; Austria would be neutral, on the Swiss model, with its own defense forces—but the Russians had put off signing the treaty. The announcement that they would now do so, coupled with Eisenhower's declaration that such an act would provide the proof he required of Soviet willingness to negotiate seriously, made a summit meeting both possible and inevitable.

On May 15, the Foreign Ministers of the four occupying powers signed the Austrian treaty. On June 13, they announced the completion of arrangements for a summit meeting. It would be held in Geneva, beginning on July 18, 1955.

On June 22, the Russians shot down an American Navy patrol plane over the Bering Strait. The Soviet government, in an unprecedented act, issued a statement of regret and paid half the damages. Eisenhower did his part to keep the situation calm. At a press conference, he said that the incident was probably due to a trigger-happy Soviet pilot, that weather conditions at the time were not good, and that it must have been a "misunderstanding." In fact, the Navy plane was on a reconnaissance mission over Soviet airspace. To make sure it did not happen again, on June 25 Eisenhower called Radford on the phone and told the admiral "to issue an order that all planes and vessels should stay well outside the fifteen-mile limit during the period between now and the Summit Conference." The meeting at Geneva remained on track.[58]

Anticipation of the first Summit Conference since Yalta and Potsdam, coupled with the end of the Formosa Straits crisis and the general peace that prevailed around the world, added to a feeling of near-euphoria millions of Americans felt in 1955. Everything was going beautifully for the Eisenhower Administration. For the first time in their lives, Eisenhower took pride in declaring, Americans born after 1929 were experiencing peace, progress, and prosperity simultaneously.[59] The short-lived post-Korean War recession was over, thanks in some part to Eisenhower's extension of Social Security benefits, his stepped-up expenditures during the recession, and his ability to convince Congress to extend unemployment compensation to some four million workers not previously covered. In addition, Eisenhower got Congress to raise the minimum wage from seventy-five cents per hour to one dollar per hour. In mid-1955, George Meany, head of the AFL-CIO, told his associates: "American labor has never had it so good."[60] By early 1955, a boom was on, but without inflation—consumer prices went up only 1 percent. The result was a buying spree. The auto industry benefited most dramatically. In 1955, Detroit sold 7.92 million cars, which was up more than 2 million over 1954 and remained the record for one-year sales until 1965. The percentage of families owning automobiles jumped from 60 percent in 1952 to 70 percent in 1955 (and reached 77 percent by 1960). When some five thousand wives of the National Association of Automobile Dealers came to the White House, Mamie—who met them—told her husband "that is one crowd that is prospering! She never saw so many furs and diamonds." [61]

The American people for their part had never seen so many cars; the problem was that the road system was woefully inadequate. Except in New York, Chicago, and Los Angeles, the major urban areas had few or no high-speed expressways. Except for the Pennsylvania Turnpike and a few other toll roads in the East, the country had no four-lane highways connecting the cities. [62] Ever since his cross-country trip by Army convoy in 1919, Eisenhower had been concerned about America's highways. Like almost every other American who fought in Germany in 1945, he had been impressed by Hitler's system of *Autobahnen*. There had been many stops and starts by Congress over the past two decades in an attempt to upgrade and modernize the American road system, but almost no real action, primarily because of federal-state disputes over who would pay for the construction, a problem compounded by the trucking industry, the American Automobile Association, and the many other parts of the "highway lobby," which was composed of so many different interest groups that it could never present a unified position to Congress.

Eisenhower wanted the highways built. To him, it was an ideal program for the federal government to undertake. First, the need was clear and inescapable. Second, a unified system could only be erected by the federal government. Third, it was a public-works program on a massive scale, indeed the largest public-works program in history, which meant that the government could put millions of men to work without subjecting itself to the criticism that this was "make-work" of the WPA or PWA variety. By tailoring expenditures for highways to the state of the economy, Eisenhower could use the program to flatten out the peaks and valleys in unemployment. Eisenhower was often called by his critics a "Whig President," with the implication that he was a "do-nothing" leader. But by advocating a highway program on a gigantic scale, Eisenhower was putting himself and his Administration within the best and strongest tradition of nineteenth-century American Whigs. John Quincy Adams, Henry Clay, and the other great Whigs had all been advocates of internal improvements paid for by the federal government. Eisenhower's highway program brought that tradition up to date.

Finally, Eisenhower wanted the highways as a part of his overall Cold War program. Throughout the Formosa Straits crisis, he had worried about how to evacuate Washington in the event of a nuclear attack on the capital, and on other cities too. Four-lane highways leading out of the cities would make evacuation possible; they would also facilitate the movement of military traffic in the event of war.

In July 1954, Eisenhower had made his first move. At that time, he was trying to "build up" a possible successor for 1956; as a part of that effort, he sent Nixon to speak to a Governors' Conference and gave him a major policy speech to make. Nixon staggered the audience with the scope of the Administration's proposal. Eisenhower's grand plan advocated a comprehensive program, including roads for farm-to-market travel and rapid intercity and interregional travel. He suggested spending $5 billion per year for the next ten years, in addition to the $700 million already being spent annually. Nixon's speech had an "electrifying effect" on the governors, and on the public.[63] In September 1954, Eisenhower put Lucius Clay at the head of a blue-ribbon private citizens' committee to study methods of financing.

In January 1955, Clay submitted his report. He called for a ten-year building program financed by federal gasoline taxes. Eisenhower talked with Clay, expressing his "tremendous enthusiasm" for the project, but asking why Clay had not recommended tolls rather than taxes to finance the system. Eisenhower said he personally favored tolls. Clay said tolls would work in the heavily populated sections of the East and West Coasts, but not in the heart of the country. Eisenhower accepted the explanation.[64] He then gave a series of pep talks to the legislative leaders in Congress, emphasizing in strong words his total commitment to new highways.[65] On February 22, Eisenhower sent to Congress the Clay report, along with his own message urging "comprehensive and quick and forward-looking action." Financing the multibillion-dollar project would be done through bond issues, backed by a federal gasoline and tire tax specially dedicated to retiring the bonds through an Interstate Highway Trust Fund.[66] The Administration bill passed the Senate, but it died in the House, where Democrats objected to the bond issue and wanted to instead increase taxes on the trucking industry.[67]

Eisenhower also failed to get through Congress his school-construction bill. He had asked for an investment of a billion dollars in federal loans and grants to the states for the construction of school-houses, badly needed as a result of the postwar baby boom. The Old Guard was alarmed at the possible intrusion of the federal government into education; the Democrats wanted a much more expansive program that would include not only school construction but also federal assistance for teachers' salaries and other education expenses. Further complicating the proposed bill was the problem of desegregation; liberal Democrats wanted to deny funds to any state that continued to segregate its schools, something southern Democrats would never accept.

Eisenhower nevertheless wanted to push ahead. He agreed heartily with Nixon, at a Cabinet meeting, when Nixon remarked that "Earl Warren got the reputation of being a great liberal because he built schools and roads" and insisted that nothing could be so popular as schools and roads. Eisenhower said the two tied together nicely, because "you have to have roads to get to schools." [68] But before Eisenhower could get either program going, he had to have a majority in Congress behind him, and in 1955 he failed to get it.

Indeed, the combination of a Democratic Congress and a Republican Administration meant that precious little in the way of domestic legislation could be passed. Both parties were jockeying for position for the 1956 presidential election; neither party was willing to give the other credit for major legislation. The Democrats were unwilling to get behind Eisenhower's health reinsurance program, because they wanted a much broader approach to health care; meanwhile the Old Guard remained opposed to any program at all, and nothing happened. Eisenhower did manage, finally, to get a three-year extension on RTAA (and in addition the authority to cut some tariff schedules by 5 percent a year),[69] although it pained him that he got more Democratic than Republican support on the bill.

Eisenhower thought the most blatant attempt to play politics with legislation was Sam Rayburn's proposal to give every taxpayer a $20 cut for each dependent. Eisenhower, who by 1955 was within $2 billion of balancing the budget, was appalled. He told his closest Democratic friend, George Allen, that it was an "astounding proposal," one of "fiscal frivolity," and he wanted Allen to let Rayburn know that if he pushed the proposal, he could not expect any cooperation from the Administration on legislation that Texas wanted, such as a natural-gas bill. Eisenhower also asked the Republican leaders to "pass the word" to Rayburn and "stop this nonsense." To Allen, Eisenhower remarked that "these are the things that make one grow old and look with longing eyes to life on a farm." [70] Nevertheless the bill passed the

House, but in the Senate the southern Democrats joined with the Republicans to defeat it.

In 1955, it was the Democrats who controlled the committees, and who thus were in charge of investigations. They were, naturally, looking for scandals in the Eisenhower Administration, and they felt they had found one down in Tennessee. Hearings examining the Dixon-Yates contract with TVA had revealed that Adolphe H. Wenzell, a vice-president of the First Boston Corporation, had been a consultant to the Bureau of the Budget on the technical arrangements of the contract while he was simultaneously consulting with Messrs. Dixon and Yates on behalf of First Boston. Senator Estes Kefauver charged that the Administration was trying to conceal Wenzell's obvious conflict of interest. Eisenhower initially tried to deny that Wenzell had had anything to do with Dixon-Yates and TVA,[71] which was a violation of a principle he had recommended to Nixon, a lesson "I learned a long time ago." It was, "Don't try to be cute or cover up. If you do, you will get so entangled you won't know what you're doing."[72] Eisenhower was headed for real difficulties on Dixon-Yates, but his luck held. Memphis announced it would build its own steam power plant, which solved the problem of generating more power within the region without expanding TVA, and thus made Dixon-Yates irrelevant. For Memphis to build its own steam plant had always been Eisenhower's solution, and he eagerly grabbed at it. On July 11, Eisenhower announced that the government was canceling its contract with Dixon-Yates (those gentlemen then sued the government for $1,867,545 to recover money already spent; the Court of Claims awarded the money, but six years later the Supreme Court overruled on the grounds that Wenzell's dual status made the negotiations technically illegal).[73]

Dixon-Yates was a minor irritation in that bright, booming beginning of summer of 1955. So were the failures to get domestic legislation through Congress. What mattered was peace and prosperity. Eisenhower had gotten out of Korea, avoided war in Indochina and the Formosa Straits, reduced defense spending, almost balanced the budget, brought inflation down to 1 percent, managed to avoid an Old Guard dismantling of the New Deal reforms, and enjoyed deep and widespread popularity among the public. Everyone outside the ranks of the professional Democrats, it seemed, wanted him to run again. Even Nehru, so often critical of the United States, declared that "Eisenhower is the greatest force for peace in the world today" and expressed the hope that he would stay in the White House until January 1961.[74]

Would he or would he not run again? Eisenhower told conflicting stories to his advisers, and gave only the vaguest kind of hints to the press and public. In late May, when Gabe Hauge came in to tell Eisenhower that he had an offer to become dean of the Business School at Harvard and wanted to accept, Eisenhower told him exactly the opposite of what he had recently told Hagerty; the President said that "frankly . . . he did not intend to seek the nomination again." He explained that he had not sought to complete a program as President, only to point the way toward "a reversal of the trend of the last twenty years" and to strengthen the Republican Party. He felt he had accomplished both tasks and could be permitted to retire. Therefore he asked Hauge to stay on the team until January 1957, when a younger man could take over the Oval Office. "It isn't that I don't like the job," Eisenhower told Hauge. He enjoyed the "challenge of working with people," and appreciated the "great minds" he had around to help him. He also said, "In many ways I think I am pretty well qualified for this thing," although he admitted that the politicians sometimes gave him fits. "I so despise their methods that there is just a resentment in me that finally renders me relatively ineffective." Therefore, "It isn't just that I want to quit, I believe I should quit."

Hauge asked who could possibly succeed him. Eisenhower said that Bob Anderson "would be the finest candidate we could have." Herbert Hoover, Jr., would be a good President, but he "just hasn't quite got the fire" to get elected. Charlie Halleck would be all right, primarily because "he just loves politics." Next came Nixon, who "has made some enemies and is not considered very matured—but he's got a pretty good experience." Henry Cabot Lodge would be excellent, except that he was "a blueblood from Boston, and you could not elect him." Herb Brownell and George Humphrey were other possibilities. Of all the Republicans, Eisenhower concluded, indeed of all the prominent men in the country, the one who would make the best President was Earl Warren, but Eisenhower knew that Warren did not want to leave the Supreme Court.[75]

The 1956 election was a problem for the future. By telling one man one thing, another man another, Eisenhower was keeping his options open. For the present, at the beginning of the summer of 1955, Eisenhower's concern was with the upcoming Geneva Conference. Although he consistently warned the American people not to get their hopes up too high, so many possibilities suddenly seemed open as a consequence of the resolution of the Formosa Straits crisis that Eisenhower himself was letting his own hopes soar. On June 20, he went to

San Francisco to address the Tenth Anniversary Meeting of the United Nations. In his speech, he said that "the summer of 1955, like that one of 1945, is another season of high hope for the world. There again stirs in the hearts of men a renewed devotion to the work for the elimination of war."[76] To that end he was himself devoted, and he prepared to go to Geneva determined to explore and extend the possibilities of genuine peace.

CHAPTER ELEVEN

Open Skies

June–September 1955

EARLY IN THE EVENING of June 15, as Eisenhower was leaving the Oval Office to go upstairs for a cocktail, an aide rushed up to tell him that "fifty-three of the major cities of the United States had either been destroyed or so badly damaged that the populations were fleeing; there were uncounted dead; there was great fallout over the country." Eisenhower decided that he had "no recourse except to take charge instantly." Congress was in disarray. So were the state and city governments. Eisenhower declared martial law all across the nation.[1]

The "disaster" was part of Operation Alert, the most public in a series of exercises Eisenhower had ordered conducted. Eisenhower and his Cabinet made an annual evacuation practice run to a secret site in the Carolina mountains. There were elaborate exercises, and Eisenhower insisted on not being told in advance when they would come or what the scenario would be, so as to make them more realistic. He hoped to uncover problems. In the case of Alert, he did. At his next press conference, on July 6, Anthony Leviero of *The New York Times* asked him, "I wonder if you would discuss the application of [martial law] and where the governors and other civil authorities would fit into the picture?" Eisenhower said there was no precedent, but then the scenario presented an unprecedented problem. He put Brownell to work on solving the legal aspects of declaring national martial law.[2] Casualty estimates ran up to 60 or even 100 million. Eisenhower recalled the "chaos" during the Battle of the Bulge, when for a few hours

Paris went into a panic and citizens tried to flee the city. Studying the results of the exercise, he declared, "I'm not convinced but what it is better to take money now spent on land forces and use it to build roads from the big cities."[3]

As Alert symbolized, it was an age in which Americans, including their President, lived on the high edge of tension. Every decade of the nuclear age has been full of tension, obviously, but the fifties felt it most. America's leaders in that decade, including Eisenhower, had had Pearl Harbor burned into their souls, in a way that younger men, the leaders in the later decades of the Cold War, had not. And the men of the fifties, already superconscious of the danger of surprise attack, were the first to have to live with long-range bombers, and to know that ICBMs were being built, and Polaris submarines. Most frightening of all, the weapons these delivery systems carried were H-bombs, big enough, in Strauss's words, "to take out a city. Any city."

Eisenhower wanted to lessen, if he could not eliminate, the financial cost and the fear that were the price of the Pearl Harbor mentality. But he could not bring himself to respond to Russian, or any other, calls for nuclear disarmament. To him, security for America required building more bombs, because that was the only area in which America had a lead on the Soviet military machine. But building more bombs only increased the cost and raised the tension. Eisenhower searched for a way out of his dilemma.

The Russians, caught in a similar dilemma, helped in the search. In their latest offer, the Russians had said that they would accept on-site inspection teams, based at crossroads and other key control points. Such teams, the Russians said, could adequately monitor the movement of military units and hardware, and thus guarantee a general disarmament. Eisenhower rejected that specific idea, because of the American experience in Korea. Such fixed on-site teams behind the armistice line in Korea found that the Chinese merely diverted their traffic around the control points. But Eisenhower did not reject the spirit of the offer.

At the July 6 news conference, James Reston asked the President whether it was possible to detect the manufacture of nuclear weapons (Reston was voicing a general American suspicion that the Soviets would agree to disarmament, then make new bombs in hidden factories). Eisenhower said that no, there was no way to detect either bombs in storage or the manufacture of new ones. Then he announced a major policy shift: "There are lots of ways in which this thing can be approached . . . For example, let us take the delivery schemes. We know that when you get to long-range bombing you need very large machines and very large fields from which they take off. Now, those can be detected, and there are other ways of approaching it." Martin Agronsky caught some of the significance of what Eisenhower had said, and immediately asked about guided missiles. How could they be spotted, since they "just need a launching platform." Eisenhower replied, "I don't believe that you could take an extensive guided-missile program and conceal it from any decent or effective system of inspection."[4]

None of the reporters asked Eisenhower what kind of an inspection system he had in mind. If one had, Eisenhower would have responded with vague and confusing generalities, but nevertheless he did have a specific idea. It was one of his boldest. Eisenhower had almost decided to propose that the Soviets and the Americans open their airspace to each other, and to provide each other with airfields from which to operate continuous reconnaissance missions. That simple step, Eisenhower was coming to believe, might solve the disarmament dilemma. Eisenhower maintained that the United States could never launch a first strike, both because of American morality and because of the open nature of American society, which precluded secret mobilization. Thus the United States had nothing to lose and much to gain by opening its airspace to the Russians. If American pilots had the same rights over the Soviet Union, it would be impossible for the Russians to launch an undetected nuclear Pearl Harbor, or to otherwise secretly increase their military might.

The origins of Eisenhower's idea is in dispute. Both Stassen and Nelson Rockefeller, who in December 1954 had become a Special Assistant to the President (taking C. D. Jackson's old spot), later claimed that the idea had come to them, independently but almost simultaneously.[5] The latter at least was true, because they got the idea from Eisenhower. In fact, it was not an original idea anyway. Eisenhower had used air reconnaissance extensively during the war, and was well aware of advances in cameras and photo interpretation techniques that had taken place since 1945. He had already tried various ways of flying over the Soviet Union, without success but without abandoning the project. Lockheed's U-2 was coming along nicely, he was told, and would soon—perhaps within a year—be operational. Then would come satellites, which Eisenhower was told were only two or three years away. They too would be able to carry cameras and beam pictures back to earth. Technology was going to open the skies to spy cameras in any case; whether the Russians agreed or not, the United States was soon going to be taking high-altitude photographs of the Soviet Union. By offering unlimited inspection, Eisenhower was trying to use inevitable technological advances to reduce, rather than raise, tensions.

In late May, Eisenhower sent Stassen and Rockefeller to Quantico, Virginia, with instructions to work with a staff on the details of an air inspection system. By June 10, they had the report ready; Eisenhower read it and gave his tentative approval. He said he was not yet sure he was going to propose it at Geneva, that he wanted to wait and see how things went there. But, as noted above, he gave a clear hint at his July 6 news conference that he was going to make the offer at Geneva.[6]

An hour after that news conference, Eisenhower called Dulles on the telephone. He told the Secretary he wanted the State Department to set up two study groups to further refine the plans that Stassen and Rockefeller had developed. "We open up ours," Eisenhower said, "they do likewise for us." Dulles said that was going to be *his* suggestion. Eisenhower told him to get going on it.[7]

Hanging up the phone, Eisenhower turned to Wilson, Strauss, Radford, and Goodpaster, who had gathered for a conference. He had called them in to discuss the other side of the dilemma, keeping ahead of the Russians. They talked about the "dispersal of special weapons overseas." Radford expressed his concern with the program, saying, "We should not tie our hands by dispersing too many weapons in areas from which we could not use them freely in case of attack." Eisenhower replied that he nevertheless wanted it done, because dispersal would "limit the effects of surprise attack."

Then the discussion turned to the ICBM. Wilson showed Eisenhower some charts on DOD programs for building such missiles. Goodpaster noted, "The President indicated he did not see how it would be possible efficiently to expend more funds and effort on the programs." Eisenhower ended the meeting by telling Wilson that he wanted to be kept up to date on the ICBM development.[8]

The following two weeks were taken up with preparations for Geneva. There were many practical arrangements that had to be made for the American delegation. Eisenhower was delighted that Mamie had agreed to fly over with him, only her second flight across the Atlantic; adding to his pleasure was the fact that his son, John, who had just completed the course at the Command and General Staff School and who thus had a one-month furlough, would also be along. Consequently he was more than usually concerned with the details of travel and living arrangements. He was also a bit snappish. When one hassle bothered him, he complained to Ann Whitman, "If I had had a staff like this during the war we would have lost it."[9]

Another irritating part of the preparation was preserving a link with the Old Guard. The Republican senators were opposed to Eisenhower's going to meet with the Russians. Styles Bridges warned that all international conferences contained seeds of "appeasement, compromise, and weakness." On July 12, Eisenhower convened a bipartisan session of congressional leaders. He assured them that Geneva would not be another Yalta. Many of the leaders were still backing the Bricker Amendment; Eisenhower therefore assured them that he would not enter into any binding executive agreements, but would submit any decision to the Senate.[10]

Eisenhower also needed to prepare the Secretary of State. Dulles was not at all convinced that going to the summit was a good idea. He could not see what good could come out of it, but he could foresee one certain danger. Before the meeting, Dulles warned Eisenhower to maintain "an austere countenance" when being photographed with Bulganin. He pointed out that any pictures taken of the two leaders smiling "would be distributed throughout the Soviet satellite countries," signifying "that all hope of liberation was lost and that resistance to Communist rule was henceforth hopeless." In a more general sense, Dulles feared that any summit meeting would give a distorted idea of the possibilities for peaceful coexistence, and therefore the free world would lower its guard.[11] Eisenhower admitted that was a danger, but he was willing to take the risk, because of the high hopes he had for his inspection proposal.

At a formal briefing by the State Department on July 11, four days before Eisenhower would fly to Geneva, the President read over Dulles' draft of an opening statement. Eisenhower began his comments by praising it in general, but then added "he would like to take the words 'Communism' and 'Soviet' out of it . . . to avoid 'polarization of thought' between Washington and the Kremlin." Then Eisenhower commented on a draft Dulles had given him for his eve-of-departure statement on national TV and radio. Eisenhower said he did not want a written speech, that he had a thought he wished to develop and only wanted some key words on cards. Eisenhower explained what he had in mind to say to the American people. It was in large part a propaganda exercise. Eisenhower said that he was "greatly disturbed" by the success Russian propaganda had enjoyed in convincing millions around the world that Americans were "a militaristic and materialistic people." The truth was, Eisenhower asserted, that "there is no more peaceful nation in the world, we are almost pacifistic." He wanted, therefore, to "both dramatize the need for peace and give each American the feeling of participation." He also wanted to prove to the world that Americans were deeply religious. He therefore proposed that he appeal to the American people—all 165 million of them—to go to church on Sunday to pray for peace.

Dulles immediately objected. He thought it would raise hopes too high, and that it would look like an "artificially stimulated demonstration." Eisenhower said he was going to do it anyway.[12]

Meanwhile Stassen and Rockefeller, especially Rockefeller, were becoming pests. They were insisting on joining the delegation. So was Radford. Eisenhower was not sure he wanted them—this was the State Department's show. Dulles was already having trouble with both Stassen and Rockefeller, Stassen because he wanted to be the one in sole charge of disarmament policy, independent of the State Department, and Rockefeller because he was supposed to be a man supplying ideas, not the head of a large, functioning staff. But Rockefeller had been building up just such a staff, to Dulles' great irritation; Dulles showed Eisenhower a Rockefeller memorandum on his staff and the President "expressed his surprise at the size and complexity of the proposed staff." Eisenhower decided to send Stassen, Rockefeller, and Radford to Paris, where they could be available to him if he wanted them, but out of his way in Geneva.[13]

At 8:15 P.M. on July 15, just an hour or less before he was scheduled to fly across the Atlantic, Eisenhower went on national TV and radio. In his speech, delivered without notes, he turned away from propaganda themes or denunciations of the Russians, did not make specific demands, and held forth no specific objectives. Instead he spoke of a purpose so high, so unobjectionable, and so vague that it was almost a sure thing that he would achieve it. Eisenhower said he hoped to "change the spirit" of Russian-American relations. He repeated the word "spirit" three times in his talk, growing quite carried away with himself: "I say to you, if we can change the spirit in which these conferences are conducted we will have taken the greatest step toward peace, toward future prosperity and tranquillity that has ever been taken in the history of mankind." Dulles groaned at such overblown language, and groaned again when Eisenhower devoted the second half of his talk to encouraging every American to go to church Sunday to pray for peace.[14]

Eisenhower flew to Geneva full of curiosity about the new Russian leaders. He had met Foreign Minister V. M. Molotov in Moscow

in the summer of 1945, and he had always felt a special tie with Zhukov, who had fallen into such disfavor with Stalin that Eisenhower
had at one time thought him dead. He was anxious to see Zhukov
again, find out what had happened, explore the possibility of re-
establishing the working partnership the two of them had created in
Germany after the war, and find out if Zhukov, as Defense Minister,
had become a real leader in the post-Stalin government, or was only
window dressing. Eisenhower had not met either Bulganin, chairman
of the Council of Ministers, or Khrushchev, First Secretary of the Communist Party. He had seen CIA studies on them, as well as estimates of
who was really in charge, but none of it was conclusive. Eisenhower
could hardly believe that four strong-willed Russian Communists were
genuinely sharing power, so he set as one of his objectives at Geneva
discovering who the real boss was. To that end, he set John to work.
Eisenhower recalled that John had been a big hit with Zhukov during
the 1945 trip to Moscow, and asked John to stick by Marshal Zhukov's
side throughout the conference. Zhukov just might, Eisenhower said,
drop something around John that he might otherwise withhold.[15]

Eisenhower's natural curiosity was reinforced by his practical
need to know. If Zhukov, for example, was really in charge of defense
policy, Eisenhower felt certain he could get a positive response to his
inspection proposal. During the opening rounds of cocktail parties,
Eisenhower devoted himself exclusively to the Russians, much to the
dismay of Eden and Dulles. At one party, Eisenhower, John, and Zhukov were together in the garden and Zhukov remarked that his daughter was getting married that day but that he had passed up the ceremony to see his "old friend." Eisenhower turned to an aide and had
some presents brought out, including a portable radio. Zhukov, visibly
embarrassed, said softly that "there are things [in Russia] that are not
as they seem." To both Eisenhowers, Zhukov seemed only a shell of
himself, a broken man, almost pathetic. Father and son recalled the
"cocky little rooster" they had known at the end of the war; now
Zhukov spoke "in a low monotone, . . . as if he was repeating a lesson
that had been drilled into him . . . He was devoid of animation, and
he never smiled or joked, as he used to do." The President noted a
feeling of "sadness" and thereafter dismissed Zhukov from his mind.
Whoever was in charge, it certainly was not Zhukov.[16]

At dinner that evening, Eisenhower sat with Khrushchev, Bulganin, and Molotov. He appealed to their reason. "It is essential,"
Eisenhower declared in a loud voice, "that we find some way of controlling the threat of the thermonuclear bomb. You know we both

have enough weapons to wipe out the entire northern hemisphere from fall-out alone. No spot would escape the fall-out from an exchange of nuclear stockpiles." The Russians nodded their vigorous agreement.[17]

Eisenhower did a masterful job of stage-managing his inspection proposal. On July 18, in his opening statement, he took an extremely tough line, one that indeed seemed intransigent and certainly was not a part of the "spirit of Geneva" he had been promoting. Eisenhower said the first issue the conference should discuss was "the problem of unifying Germany and forming an all-German government based on free elections." Beyond that, "We insist a united Germany is entitled at its choice, to exercise its inherent right of collective self-defense." In other words, the reunified Germany would be a full partner in NATO. Next, Eisenhower wanted to discuss East Europe and the failure to implement the Yalta promises. Then there was "the problem of international Communism." Stirring up revolutions around the world was something the United States "cannot ignore." Eisenhower knew that the chances of getting a Soviet response on any of these demands was zero.

Having established his most extreme position, Eisenhower then began listing items for the agenda that held some hope of fruitful discussion. One was the Atoms for Peace proposal, which was still alive (barely) and which Eisenhower still wanted the Russians to join. Another was the need for more cultural exchanges between the U.S.S.R. and the U.S. "Finally," Eisenhower concluded, "there is the overriding problem of armament." He spoke of the fear both sides felt about a surprise attack. "Perhaps, therefore, we should consider whether the problem of limitation of armament may not best be approached by seeking—as a first step—dependable ways to supervise and inspect military establishments, so that there can be no frightful surprises." Eisenhower called on the Russians to join him in exploring ways of achieving "effective mutual inspection," which would be "the foundation for real disarmament."[18]

The Soviets made no response to the inspection suggestions. Over the next two days, the discussions were generally acrimonious and never profitable. The Russians concentrated on denouncing Eisenhower's position on Germany. Eisenhower asked Khrushchev why the Russians feared free elections in Germany. Because, Khrushchev replied, "The German people have not yet had time to be educated in the great advantage of Communism!" Eisenhower smugly noted that the West was willing to abide by the results of an all-German election (he did not note that the United States was unwilling to do so in Vietnam). The Russians pushed for a disarmed and neutral Germany, which Eisenhower flatly rejected. Bulganin told Eisenhower that the rearming of West Germany and her inclusion in NATO had made reunification impossible. He refused to allow Eisenhower to interfere in Soviet "internal affairs," meaning he would not discuss the satellite countries. He did respond favorably to the idea of cultural exchanges and said Russia would later contribute to an Atoms for Peace pool. Bulganin also picked up on a suggestion Eden had made in his opening remarks, a demilitarized area along Central Europe. Bulganin said he was ready to propose that all foreign troops be taken out of Europe.[19] Although Bulganin did most of the talking, he seemed to consult with his partners in a sincere way before speaking, and Eisenhower found it impossible to tell who was really in charge.

Each side did go to great lengths to assure the other that it was aware of how horrible a nuclear war would be. Eisenhower acknowledged that there could be no specific and immediate progress toward settling issues, but just the fact that they were talking together gave hope. After ten years of Cold War rhetoric, much of it greatly overblown, the leaders needed reassurance that they were indeed all reasonable men. In effect, and without ever saying so to each other, much less to the public, they agreed to a stalemate in Germany. By itself, that was a big step toward reducing tensions.

But Eisenhower wanted more than stalemate; he wanted to reduce costs as well as tensions. Serious disarmament was too much to hope for, but a freeze might be possible, and more important, his inspection proposal might extend the spirit of Geneva over to military problems. On the third day of the conference, Eisenhower called Stassen and Rockefeller to Geneva—they had been pleading with him by telegram to be allowed to come—and with them went over the proposal one last time.

On July 21, at the Palais des Nations, speaking from some note cards, Eisenhower finally made explicit what he had been hinting at for a month. After reviewing the difficulties of achieving agreement on disarmament, Eisenhower said, "I have been searching my heart and mind for something that I could say here that could convince everyone of the great sincerity of the United States in approaching this problem of disarmament." Turning to look directly at the Soviet delegation, he said he wanted to speak principally to them. He thereupon proposed "to give to each other a complete blueprint of our military establishments, from beginning to end, from one end of our countries to the other." Next, "to provide within our countries facilities for aerial photography to the other country." The Americans would make airfields and other facilities available to the Russians, and allow them to fly wherever they wished. The Russians would provide identical facilities for the United States.[20]

When Eisenhower finished, there was a tremendous clap of thunder, and all the lights went out. When he recovered from his surprise, Eisenhower laughed and said, "Well, I expected to make a hit but not that much of one." More than twenty years later Vernon Walters, Eisenhower's translator, said that "to this day, I am told, the Russians are still trying to figure out how we did it."[21]

The French and British expressed their hearty approval of the idea. Bulganin spoke last. The proposal, he said, seemed to have real merit. The Soviet delegation would give it complete and sympathetic study at once. But when the session ended, Khrushchev walked beside Eisenhower on the way to cocktails. Although he was smiling, he said, "I don't agree with the chairman." Eisenhower could hear "no smile in his voice." Eisenhower realized immediately that Khrushchev was the man in charge. "From that moment," he recalled, "I wasted no more time probing Mr. Bulganin." Instead, he stayed after Khrushchev, arguing the merits of what was being called Open Skies. Khrushchev said the idea was nothing more than a bald espionage plot against the Soviet Union.[22]

Why Khrushchev reacted so adversely is a puzzle. Eisenhower made the offer sincerely, and he emphasized that it would be "only a beginning." The President could not see what the Russians had to lose. Overflights, the Russians surely knew, were inevitable within two or three years anyway. How Open Skies would have worked out, no one knows, although the difficulties were surely huge; imagine, for example, the problems involved in having a Soviet air base in the middle of the Great Plains, or in New England, not to mention those of the exchange of military blueprints. But no one knows because Open Skies never was tried. Khrushchev had killed it within minutes of its birth.

Disappointed though he was by Khrushchev's quick rejection, which Eisenhower correctly decided was authoritative, Eisenhower nevertheless continued to build the spirit of Geneva. The next day, July 22, he made his presentation on the need for more trade between the U.S.S.R. and the United States, as well as a "free and friendly exchange of ideas and of people." And his parting words, at the last session of July 23, were: "In this final hour of our assembly, it is my judgment that the prospects of a lasting peace with justice, well-being, and

broader freedom, are brighter. The dangers of the overwhelming tragedy of modern war are less." He was specific about what he had
learned and accomplished: "I came to Geneva because I believe mankind longs for freedom from war and rumors of war. I came here because of my lasting faith in the decent instincts and good sense of the
people who populate this world of ours. I shall return home tonight
with these convictions unshaken . . ."[23]

That final statement, coupled with Eisenhower's proposals, was
what made Geneva a dramatic moment in the Cold War. For the five
years before Geneva, there were war scares on an almost monthly basis,
with major wars going on in Korea and Indochina. For the five years
after Geneva, war scares were relatively rare, except at Suez in 1956,
and no major wars were fought. The leaders of the two sides had met
and agreed among themselves that they were indeed two scorpions in
a bottle. Bulganin's parting words to Eisenhower were "Things are
going to be better; they are going to come out right."[24]

After his return to the United States, Eisenhower told congressional leaders about some of the things he had learned. Khrushchev,
he said, was "the boss," but both Khrushchev and Bulganin were
"amateurs in diplomacy. In conference, they wait for some lead from
Molotov, the old hand. Informally, at luncheons or cocktails, they ignore Molotov." Warning the congressmen to "not let this out of this
room," he reported that Khrushchev and Bulganin "want to come visit
America. They would come fast. They want to be more in the public
eye." Zhukov, he said, was just "window dressing. He's in because they
think he constitutes a bridge to us. That's proof to me they want to be
a little closer to the United States."[25]

Eisenhower was surprised to learn that the Soviet leaders, although dictators, had internal problems. Time and again, he said, they
told him, "We can't go home with that statement or agreement." He
was almost done in by their argument that the Cominform was "very
weak," that they were not supporting international Communism, and
that they cited as "proof" the "great weakness of the Communist Party
in the U.S.A." Eisenhower's comment was "Such logic!"

On the positive side, Eisenhower reported that there "was no
question but that they understand the scope of modern war." He told
them, "Let us remember this, the world's winds go east and west, not
north and south. If there is a war, both of us will be destroyed. Only
the southern hemisphere would be left." The Russians said yes, that
was correct. They really did want a new start, he said, and so did he.
Eisenhower reported that his own first reaction to Bulganin's request

for a visit to the United States was to say, "Good, come on over." But Dulles "thought I had been impulsive enough," so he only told Bulganin the United States would study the proposal.[26]

On July 25, a day after returning from Geneva, Eisenhower went on national TV and radio to report to the American people. In Geneva, he had spoken to the world. In Washington, he had to speak to the Old Guard. He declared, "I can assure you of one thing: There were no secret agreements made, either understood agreements or written ones. Everything is put before you on the record." He assured his audience that he had "specifically brought up, more than once, American convictions . . . about the satellites of Eastern Europe and the activities of international Communism." He admitted that there had been no progress on the German question. He briefly explained Open Skies—which had had a tremendous reception in the U.S.—but tended to downplay it, concentrating instead on the real achievements in the field of cultural exchange.

Having reassured his audience that Geneva was no Yalta, Eisenhower then turned to the real result of the conference. "Each side assured the other earnestly and often," he said, "that it intended to pursue a new spirit of conciliation and cooperation in its contacts with the other."[27] As Dulles had warned would be the case, nothing had been settled at Geneva. But as Eisenhower had determined would be the case, Geneva produced an intangible but real spirit that was felt and appreciated around the world. The year following Geneva was the calmest of the first two decades of the Cold War.

But Geneva had failed to slow, much less halt, the arms race. Two weeks after the conference, the Russians began a series of H-bomb tests. None were as large as Bravo, but they were between two and four megatons. What was worrisome to the Americans was the fact that the Russians had dropped their bombs from airplanes, rather than firing them from a tower as the Americans did. Further, the Pentagon feared that the Soviets had perfected nuclear warheads for future ballistic missiles. After completing their tests, the Russians began advocating a test ban, a cry that was taken up around the world as the fallout from the Russian explosions began to be measured. But with the Russians in the lead in H-bomb technology, Eisenhower would never agree to a test ban.[28]

Eisenhower also wanted to improve and expand the American delivery system. "The earliest development of ICBM capability is of vital importance to the security of the United States," he told the chairman of the Joint Congressional Committee on Atomic Energy, Clinton Anderson. "The Soviets may well have begun top-priority work on this weapon shortly after World War II." Eisenhower said that the ICBM had been neglected by the Truman Administration, but asserted that "excellent work has been done during the past two years." He further assured Anderson that "we are moving forward on this project without tolerating any of the delays which may attend normal peacetime development or procurement programs."[29]

And so the arms race went on, despite the spirit of Geneva.

In late August, the Eisenhowers flew to Denver for their summer vacation. The fishing was the best Eisenhower could remember. He enjoyed cooking the trout for his gang and the press corps. The weather for golf at Cherry Hills, Eisenhower's favorite course, was perfect. Lowry Air Force Base in Denver provided him with a complete communications hookup, and an office where he could work a couple of hours a day.

Eisenhower used his vacation to do some thinking and talking about the 1956 presidential election. His friends told him that they would feel he was letting them down if he retired. He resented their pressure, and insisted that he had given them no reason to think he would run again, so he could not be guilty of letting them down. He told Milton that he wanted to "retain as long as possible a position of flexibility," but barring some unforeseen crisis, he would not run again.[30]

He had his health to think about. He was not at all sure he could or should take the mental pounding for another four years. He had another worry. Churchill had not been at Geneva. Eisenhower had found it strange to be at an international meeting without him, but he also knew from his own dealings with Churchill before the old man finally retired that Churchill had held on to power far too long. What worried Eisenhower was, as he told Swede, "Normally the last person to recognize that a man's mental faculties are fading is the victim himself." Eisenhower said, "I have seen many a man 'hang on too long' under the definite impression that he had a great duty to perform and that no one else could adequately fill his particular position." Eisenhower feared that this might happen to him, because "the more important and demanding the position, the greater the danger in this regard."[31]

On September 12, Eisenhower wrote Milton. "It never occurred to me that enthusiasm for the *cause* is necessarily an indication that I am visualizing myself, indefinitely, as the leader of the cause." Then Eisenhower seemed to have a premonition. "I think that if I thought the end of my days would come even before I returned to Washington," he said, "I would probably be even more emphatic and insistent in supporting the things in which I believe than I am under the mere normal uncertainties of life."[32]

CHAPTER TWELVE

Heart Attack

September–December 1955

EISENHOWER SPENT September 19 to 23 at Aksel Nielsen's ranch at Fraser, Colorado. On the morning of the twenty-third, he was up at 5 A.M. to cook breakfast for George Allen, Nielsen, and two guests. He skipped the wheat cakes and made only bacon and eggs. At 6:45 they left Fraser and drove to Denver. Eisenhower went to his office at Lowry; Ann Whitman later wrote in her diary that "I have never seen him look or act better." He was in a good mood, went through his work cheerfully, read a letter from Milton and handed it to Whitman, saying, "See what a wonderful brother I have." About 11 A.M. he and Allen drove out to Cherry Hills and began to play. Twice Eisenhower had to return to the clubhouse for phone calls from Dulles, only to be told that there was difficulty on the lines. He had a hamburger with slices of Bermuda onion for lunch and returned to the course. Again he was called to the clubhouse to talk to Dulles, there to be told that it was a mistake. He was scoring badly, his stomach was upset, his temper flaring. Giving up on golf, he and Allen drove to Mamie's mother's home, where they were spending the evening. Eisenhower and Allen shot some billiards before dinner, declining a cocktail. At 10 P.M., Eisenhower went to bed.[1]

About 1:30 A.M. Eisenhower woke with a severe chest pain. "It hurt like hell," he later confessed, but he did not want to alarm Mamie.[2] Nevertheless his stirring about woke her. She asked if he wanted anything. Thinking of his indigestion the previous afternoon,

270

Eisenhower asked for some milk of magnesia. From the tone of his voice, she knew there was something seriously wrong. Mamie called Dr. Snyder, who arrived at the bedside about 2 A.M. Noting that the patient was suffering with pain in the chest area, Snyder broke a pearl of amyl nitrite and gave it to Eisenhower to sniff while he prepared a hypodermic of one grain of papaverine and immediately thereafter one-fourth grain of morphine sulphate. He then told Mamie to get back into bed with her husband and keep him warm. Forty-five minutes later, Snyder gave Eisenhower another one-fourth grain of morphine to control the symptoms.[3]

Eisenhower slept until noon. When he woke, he was still groggy, had not shaken off the effects of the morphine, did not know what had happened to him. But his first thoughts were of his responsibilities. He told Snyder to tell Whitman to call Brownell "for an opinion as to how he could delegate authority."[4] Snyder insisted on taking an electrocardiogram first; it located the site of the lesion in the anterior wall of the heart. Eisenhower had suffered a coronary thrombosis. Snyder decided to transfer him to a hospital immediately. As the stairs were too narrow for a stretcher, and as Snyder thought it better for both physical and morale factors for the President to walk, Eisenhower walked, heavily supported, to the car for the drive to Fitzsimons Army Hospital in Denver. Before leaving his bedroom, and once again in the car with Snyder, Eisenhower asked about his wallet, about which he was terribly concerned. He asked Mamie several times about it. She assured him she had brought it along.[5]

In the hospital, Eisenhower was put into an oxygen tent. Snyder continued his medication, discontinuing morphine after the second day. John flew down from Fort Belvoir. Arriving at Fitzsimons, he conferred with Mamie, who was being tough, strong, and confident. Then he went to see his father. "You know," Eisenhower said after their greeting, "these are things that always happen to other people; you never think of them happening to you." Then he asked John to hand him his wallet. He explained that he had won a bet from George Allen and wanted to give the money to Barbara. John withdrew to let his father rest; Hagerty told him in the corridor that the heart attack was moderate, "not severe but not slight either."[6]

Whitman, meanwhile, had called all the gang. The members were worried about Snyder, wondered if he was up to the challenge, exchanged among themselves their fears about leaving Eisenhower in the hands of Army doctors. They agreed to force Snyder to accept some outside civilian help. Bill Robinson took the lead, arranging

for the famous heart specialist Dr. Paul Dudley White of Boston to
come to Fitzsimons.[7] Robinson was upset two days later when White
announced that he had examined all the medical evidence and was
satisfied that the treatment had been appropriate and that the patient
was making satisfactory progress, then flew back to Boston.

By the end of the second day, Eisenhower was resting comfortably,
feeling well, beginning to talk about getting back to work. Mamie was
living on the eighth floor of the hospital with him, doing her best to
cope with the shock and find some therapy for herself (she lost ten
pounds during the first two weeks) to keep her busy. She decided to
answer, by hand, each of the thousands of letters and cards that were
coming in from all over the country. John confessed, "I thought she
was out of her mind," but he later saw the wisdom of her finding
something for herself to do. And she actually completed the task.[8]

Eisenhower, meanwhile, was already making decisions. Not until
the second day did Snyder tell him he had had a heart attack. Eisenhower then went into conference with Hagerty and Snyder. Hagerty
wanted to know how much information about the illness the President
wanted given to the public. Eisenhower's mind went back to 1919. In
that year President Wilson had had a stroke. He had been kept in bed
in the White House; the public had not been informed of his condition. Eisenhower thought that the public had a right to know the
status of the President's health, so he told Hagerty, "Tell the truth,
the whole truth; don't try to conceal anything."

Eisenhower also recalled that in 1920 Mrs. Wilson had been
furious when Secretary of State Lansing called Cabinet meetings with-
out President Wilson's knowledge, and persuaded her husband to fire
Lansing. To make certain there was no repetition, Eisenhower had
Hagerty send a message to the effect that all regular meetings of the
NSC and the Cabinet would be held, under the chairmanship of the
Vice-President.[9]

The President's heart attack inevitably put a great strain on the
relations among the members of the Administration. In the first
couple of weeks of Eisenhower's recuperation, no one knew whether
or not he would be able to resume his place as President at any time,
much less in the near future. There was a general and widespread assumption that whatever else it meant, the heart attack precluded a
second term. Thus any jockeying for power in September 1955 was
over not just the next year but the next five years.

Nixon was in the most difficult position. Almost anything he did would be wrong. If he shrank from seizing power, he would look uncertain and unprepared; if he attempted to seize power, he would look ruthless and uncaring. But he managed to find a narrow middle ground, helped in no small part by Eisenhower's early insistence that Cabinet and NSC meetings go forward as scheduled, with Nixon in the chair. On September 29, Nixon met with the NSC, the next day with the Cabinet. He issued a press release which emphasized that "the subjects on the agenda for these meetings were of a normal routine nature." He also called in photographers to observe the harmony among Eisenhower's "family" and to record how the teamwork was so effective that the government was functioning "as usual."[10]

Despite the appearance of unity in the Administration, an intense behind-the-scenes struggle for power was going on. Dulles, not Nixon, was the leading figure at the meetings, and Dulles insisted on sending Sherman Adams to Denver to be at the President's side to handle all liaison activities. Nixon questioned this arrangement, indicating that he thought Adams ought to stay in Washington while he, Nixon, went to Denver. But Dulles prevailed. Dulles also stressed that there would be no further delegation of powers by the President.[11]

The best reporters in Washington, however, could hardly miss the real story. James Reston had already reported, on September 26, that the Eisenhower Republicans were anxious to keep control in the hands of Sherman Adams and away from Nixon, because they were not going to hand over the party to Nixon, and with it the 1956 nomination.[12] Dulles, Humphrey, Adams, Hagerty, and the others felt that Nixon would allow the right wing to dominate the party, and that he would lose to Stevenson (a Gallup Poll in October showed Nixon losing to Stevenson while Warren came out ahead in a race with Stevenson). Richard Rovere observed, in *The New Yorker*, that Adams "regards himself as the President's appointed caretaker and is doing everything he can to cut Mr. Nixon down to size." Nixon, meanwhile, received a telegram from Styles Bridges, which advised, "You are the constitutional second-in-command and you ought to assume the leadership. Don't let the White House clique take command."[13]

As the power struggle progressed, Eisenhower was having a smooth convalescence. His color, his appetite, his energy, and his general demeanor all improved rapidly. He rather enjoyed his enforced rest. His doctors decided to keep the newspapers from him, but after the first few days allowed Whitman and Hagerty to bring him news and an-

swer questions. The timing of the heart attack was fortunate in the
extreme; if it had come at any time during the series of war scares of
1954 and 1955, when Eisenhower's firm hand was crucial to keeping
the peace, there is no way of knowing what might have happened.
(Eisenhower agreed with Hagerty's analysis that if Knowland had
been President, the U.S. would have gone to war many times in the
last two years.[14]) But the world scene was quiet in the fall of 1955,
thanks in large part to the spirit of Geneva, and during the crisis over
the President's illness the Russians stayed discreetly silent and in the
background. Had it come later, when the 1956 campaign was already
under way, Eisenhower would not have had time to recuperate or
think through his options, and Nixon would have had the nomination
by default. Eisenhower was also lucky in that the attack came when
Congress was not in session, so there were no bills for him to sign or
veto. If there ever was a time when the United States in the Cold
War could get by without a functioning President for a few weeks, it
was the fall of 1955.

So Eisenhower was free to rest and recuperate, and—like most pa-
tients—get involved in the daily routine of the hospital. He got to
know the nurses. As they assisted at his electrocardiograms, or administered his medication, or brought in his meals, he would chat with
them. Typically, he wanted to know where they were from, something
about their families, and about their jobs. They were only too anxious
to talk about the jobs. He discovered that they had many legitimate
complaints, so when he was able, he wrote their ultimate boss, Army
Chief of Staff Maxwell Taylor (who had recently replaced Ridgway;
Eisenhower had also gotten rid of Carney in the Navy). Eisenhower
told Taylor that he was shocked by the working conditions of the
Army Nurse Corps. In a four page, single-spaced letter, the President
was quite specific about the nurses' situation. Their quarters were
substandard. Promotions were slow, slower than in any other branch
of the Army. The Army Nurse Corps had only one colonel, when it
deserved at least three. The nurses were moved around every year,
overseas every other year. They were required to retire at fifty-five,
even if they were only a year or two short of their required twenty
years. Eisenhower told Taylor that such a policy "assumes that every
woman of fifty-five is decrepit, something which I don't for a moment
believe." Eisenhower told Taylor to correct all these conditions, and
in general to give the nurses "the feeling that they are needed, respected, and appreciated." Taylor did as told; soon the ANC had a
general and three colonels, and other improvements were made.[15]

Eisenhower's concern for the nurses was a good sign. So was his request for an easel, paint, and canvas. So was his willingness to joke with the doctors. One morning, about five days after the attack, four of them came into his room and earnestly advised him to avoid tobacco. Eisenhower listened "politely and attentively." All of the doctors were smoking. Eisenhower grinned at them and remarked that he had not used tobacco for more than six years, and asked why he should be in bed with a heart attack while they were up and working, apparently suffering no ill effects from their cigarettes.[16]

On September 30, following the Cabinet meeting, Adams flew to Denver. The next day, Eisenhower conferred with him. Eisenhower directed that the normal routine of government should continue, but that when decisions had to be made, the NSC and the Cabinet should make recommendations, then bring the matter to Denver for Eisenhower's personal consideration. Eisenhower also ordered that the "proper channel" for submitting such matters was through Persons in the White House, to Adams in Denver, and then to the President. On October 8, two weeks after the attack, Eisenhower called Nixon to Denver. Eisenhower told Nixon how much he appreciated all that he had done, and asked him to arrange, through Adams, for the members of the Cabinet to fly to Denver, one at a time, for consultation.[17] He also handed Nixon a letter. The Foreign Ministers were about to meet in Geneva to follow up on the summit meeting. Eisenhower wanted to make certain that everyone understood Dulles spoke for him. Therefore, in his letter to Nixon, he told the Vice-President that Dulles had "my complete confidence." He also warned Nixon against making any anti-Communist attacks while the meetings were going on. Returning to Dulles, Eisenhower told Nixon, "He must be the one who both at the conference table and before the world speaks for me with authority for our country."[18] For Nixon, all the pointed references to Dulles' authority must have been painful in the extreme, but he suppressed whatever emotion he felt and did as he was told.

On October 11, Dulles himself flew to Denver. The doctors warned him not to talk to Eisenhower as if he were a helpless invalid; Eisenhower himself cut short expressions of good cheer and told Dulles to get down to work.[19] Dulles nevertheless began by congratulating Eisenhower on his magnificent achievement in building a team that was "so harmonious, so imbued with principles . . . that we were able to carry on the business of government effectively without serious interruption." He cited Wilson as an example of an incapacitated President who had failed to build such a team, so that when Wilson was stricken, "the situation fell into disarray." Eisenhower thanked him for the compliment, saying how pleased he was that matters were going so well, because he had long been an opponent of "one-man" government.

Then they got down to details. Dulles handed Eisenhower a draft of a reply to a recent letter from Bulganin on the subject of Open Skies. After praising the draft, which was general and noncommittal, Eisenhower pointed out that Dulles had failed to repeat something that Eisenhower had told Bulganin in Geneva, namely that the United States would also be willing to accept the Russian proposal for on-site inspection teams within each country. Dulles had the letter rewritten and Eisenhower signed it that afternoon. Next Dulles expressed his alarm over a recent Soviet arms deal with Egypt, and showed Eisenhower another draft of a separate letter to Bulganin, telling Bulganin that the United States was disturbed by the implications of the deal. Eisenhower approved and signed it. (His signature was still shaky, but legible.) Dulles said that at the coming Foreign Ministers' meeting in Geneva, he intended to continue to insist on Germany's right to unity, Germany's right to arm itself, and Germany's right to enter NATO. Eisenhower agreed that that was the right line to take. On disarmament itself, Dulles said the subject was so complex he wanted to take it up later with the President. They then agreed on trying to establish commercial air flights between the U.S.S.R. and the United States. Dulles assured the President that he intended to meet with congressional leaders before departing for Geneva.

After discussing some ambassadorial appointments, the two men talked about the political future within the U.S. Eisenhower said he "had tried very hard to introduce new and solid principles and his great concern was lest his illness should interfere with this effort before there was full understanding and acceptance of these principles by the American people." Descending from the level of principle to practical politics, Eisenhower then expressed the hope that "a successor to him should be found within the inner circle of his Administration," a successor who could hold together the team that he, Eisenhower, had built and of which he was "so very proud." Eisenhower thought that such a man should be relatively young, preferably in his forties. But he was not sure "that he could see around him a person who had the desired youth and vigor, and who at the same time was respected by the country as having maturity of judgment." Like Eisenhower, Dulles never mentioned Nixon directly in his reply. He did say he thought that "maturity of judgment" was "almost too much to expect of any one in his forties." In any event, Dulles said, "it was much too early to be worrying about these matters now."

The conference lasted twenty-five minutes. Throughout, Dulles noted, Eisenhower "seemed cheerful and alert and to be enjoying renewed contact with matters in which he was so interested." On the memorandum he wrote about the conversation, Dulles scribbled by hand, "One copy to Gov. Adams—no other distribution. JFD." In short, no copy to Nixon.[20]

The following day, October 12, Milton Eisenhower paid a visit. Like many heart-attack victims, Eisenhower found that his thoughts were turning from the immediate future, the kind of issues he had discussed with Dulles, to the long-range future. In Eisenhower's case, he was concerned about soil and water conservation, and with his stewardship of the public lands and waterways. There "are things that must be done," he told Milton, such as flood control, drainage, enrichment of the soil, and so on. He knew that programs of this type would cost a great deal of money and take a long time, so he wanted to get started in the summer of 1956 so as to insure "a soil in our country that was permanent and lasting and could be turned over to coming generations as an enriched soil rather than a depleted soil."[21]

Eisenhower did not consider this a subject suited only to idle hospital-room conversation. When Benson came to see him, on October 29, Eisenhower returned again and again to it. He told Benson, "We are as much trustees of the soil and water for future generations as we are trustees of the liberties we are trying to pass on." He said he was thinking of a half-billion-dollar program, which he wanted to call a Soil Bank. The basic idea was an old one that had been a central feature of the New Deal's agricultural policy, to take marginal land out of production by paying the farmers to leave it idle. That would not only save and build the soil, but would also reduce surplus in basic commodities, thereby raising prices and bringing the farmers out of depression. With regard to the current surplus, Eisenhower wanted Benson to do what he could to get congressional legislation that would allow the United States to sell wheat to the Russians. Eisenhower pointed out that "some day the world was going to be out of exhaustible resources." Currently, however, the Russians had metals for sale. Eisenhower said that so far as he was concerned, "there was no indestructible metal in the world he would not trade perishable items for."[22] Later, Eisenhower told Adams that he wanted to have the government begin acquiring the marginal land, especially in the Great Plains, that had been homesteaded in the nineteenth century.

That land should be taken out of wheat, Eisenhower said, and returned to grass or forest. Adams protested that the Old Guard would
be strongly against any such purchases by the government. Eisenhower
said he knew that was so, but pointed out that "when you do buy up
such marginal land, you protect yourself against improper use of such
land." He added that the government had to "protect the soil of
America just as we want to protect our freedom of speech, right to
worship, etc. We must pass on a heritage of rich land for the Americans we hope will be here five hundred years hence."[23]

Having the government buy back land it had given away three-
quarters of a century ago was an idea Eisenhower could not sell, even
to his own Cabinet. Benson was opposed to adding to the public lands.
Humphrey, later, expressed his strong disapproval. The Secretary of
the Treasury thought it was "just giving away money." But Benson
was willing to get behind the Soil Bank, and arranged with Eisenhower to make it one of the Administration's major legislative goals
for 1956.[24]

When Wilson came for his visit, the President was sharp with him.
Wilson reported that the JCS said they were "bleeding," that Eisenhower's demand that the armed services be cut to 2.8 million would
leave America virtually defenseless. Eisenhower said he wanted reductions, that Wilson should get on it, that the President could not be
expected to decide where each little cut could be made. Eisenhower
told Wilson to "get tough."[25]

In his six weeks in the hospital, Eisenhower saw sixty-six official
visitors. The work was clearly good for him, even dealing with Wilson.
He felt fine. He was an obedient patient, never overtaxing himself. He
brought most conferences around to long-range goals, not long range
from a politician's perspective (four years) but long range from the
perspective of a steward. He would not discuss, and his visitors dared
not bring up, his immediate plans about 1956. Eisenhower would not
waste his time thinking about something he could not control. His
fate was controlled by the doctors, and until they told him what his
chances for a full recovery were, he could not make a decision. On
October 26, he told Whitman that in mid-February the doctors would
"take all sorts of tests—and can then predict to a certainty how much
of my previous activity I can renew. For myself," he mused, "I don't
care, I have had a pretty good life."[26]

When he did turn his mind from his stewardship role, he enjoyed
thinking about his own retirement. After his meetings with the various

Cabinet officers, Eisenhower wanted to see some of his own gang. He asked especially for Slater. On November 3, Slater flew to Denver. When he arrived at Fitzsimons the following day, he found Eisenhower in Mamie's room helping her balance her checkbook. The President showed him a portrait he was doing from a photograph of his grandson, David. Eisenhower wanted to talk about his retirement. They conversed at length about Angus cattle, about Eisenhower's plans for the Gettysburg farm. Eisenhower said he wanted to plow as much money as he could into the farm now, while he was in a high tax bracket. He was concerned about improving the soil at Gettysburg, so he was irritated with Art Nevins, who ran the farm for him. Nevins had grown "government subsidized wheat" rather than getting a new pasture started.[27]

On October 25, Eisenhower went for his first walk since entering the hospital. By November 5, the doctors were ready to release him, but said that he would have to be taken to and from the airplane in a wheelchair. When he asked how long it would be before he could walk to and from the plane, they said another week. In that case, Eisenhower said, he would stay in the hospital until he could make his first public appearance on his feet. On November 11, he and Mamie flew to Washington, where a crowd of five thousand greeted him at the airport. Eisenhower walked to the microphone and said a few words ("The doctors have given me at least a parole if not a pardon, and I expect to be back at my accustomed duties, although they say I must ease my way into them and not bulldoze my way into them.").[28] The next day, a Saturday, Eisenhower had a conference with Hagerty and Adams to fix a schedule. On Monday, the Eisenhowers would drive to Gettysburg, where the house was ready for occupancy and where Eisenhower intended to finish his recuperation. The President said that on November 21 he wanted to meet with the NSC, and on November 22 with the Cabinet, in both cases at Camp David. He expected to spend only one hour at each meeting, and said he did not want a briefing beforehand because he already knew the material pretty well, and he felt he could maintain his interest better when he was not completely familiar with the subjects. The doctors had insisted that Eisenhower take a rest each midday; Hagerty said he could move a couch into the Oval Office, but Eisenhower wanted to avoid the appearance of an invalid and told him to use the secretarial office next door for the couch. Eisenhower remembered to tell Hagerty to stay after Taylor about improving conditions in the Army Nurse Corps.[29]

Eisenhower had been offered the use of a vacation home in Florida, and had been sorely tempted to accept. But, as he explained to Cliff Roberts, "the insurmountable difficulty comes from Mamie's aversion to the coastal areas. Since naturally any vacation would be completely unsatisfactory unless she could go along, I simply had to say No." Instead, he decided to stay at Gettysburg until a few days before Christmas, then spend Christmas in the White House.[30]

Gettysburg was the ideal place for his recovery. The house was large and comfortable. The major feature was a glassed-in porch, where the Eisenhowers spent most of their time. It had large sliding glass doors that opened onto a terrace; beyond the terrace there was a putting green, farther out a pasture. The doctors said Eisenhower could practice his putting so long as he did not overdo it. The Slaters came for a visit; Mamie took them for a tour of the house. Slater noted that it was beautifully done, "but what makes it really charming is Mamie's enthusiasm over the whole place and her own pride and delight in having created her first home of their own." Eisenhower had Slater join him in a golf cart for a tour of the farm. When they got to the pasture where the Angus cattle were grazing, the President grinned impishly, pulled out a cattle horn, blew it, and laughed delightedly when—to Slater's surprise—the cattle came running. The men went down to the barn, where they watched the birth of a Brown Swiss calf. The barn was painted a shade of light gray-green. Eisenhower explained to Slater that he had mixed the color himself, because the old red color of the barn stood out too much.[31]

In January 1956, at a news conference, Eisenhower was asked if he missed "the bustle of the Presidency" while he was at Gettysburg. Eisenhower admitted that "anybody who has been busy, when he doesn't have immediately something at hand, has a little bit of a strange feeling." Nevertheless, he was hardly "bored to death," because "there are so many things that I have to do." He said he had "piled up stacks of books I never had a chance to read." He had his painting. "I like the actual roaming around on a farm. I love animals. I like to go out and see them. I have got a thousand things to do in this world, so I don't think I would be bored, no matter what it was."[32]

Like millions of other Americans, Slater was intensely curious about Eisenhower's political plans. He assumed that Mamie wanted no part of a second term, especially so since her home was now complete and after her husband's heart attack. Mamie never said that directly to him, however, and although Slater himself, like the rest of the gang, wanted Eisenhower to retire and thought he deserved it,

Slater also noted that "he's been too active to sit at home on the farm and wait for people to come to him."[33]

Mamie was one of the first to sense this truth. Dr. Snyder had told her, while Eisenhower was still in Fitzsimons, that her husband's life expectancy might be improved if he ran for a second term rather than withdraw to a life of inactivity. She knew Snyder was right, that inactivity would be fatal for Eisenhower. John was with her when Snyder gave her his view; as the three of them talked, Mamie volunteered another reason for a second term. "I just can't believe that Ike's work is finished," she declared.[34]

Neither could he. In mid-December, Eisenhower had a series of talks with Hagerty about politics and 1956. Eisenhower said that he was concerned about the welfare of the country, particularly in the foreign field. Hagerty recorded in his diary, "He was appalled by the lack of qualified candidates on the Democratic side and particularly pointed to Stevenson, Harriman, and Kefauver as men who did not have the competency to run the Office of President." Harriman, currently the governor of New York, was in Eisenhower's view "a complete nincompoop. He's nothing but a Park Avenue Truman."[35]

During his conversations with Hagerty, Eisenhower threw out ideas. At one meeting Adams was also present. "You know, boys," Eisenhower said, "Tom Dewey has matured over the last few years and he might not be a bad presidential candidate. He certainly has the ability and if I'm not going to be in the picture, he also represents my way of thinking." The remark left Adams and Hagerty speechless. The following day, Eisenhower brought up Dewey again. This time Hagerty said that if Eisenhower tried to foist Dewey off on the Republican Party again, the right wing would revolt and nominate Knowland. "I guess you're right," Eisenhower sighed, dismissing Dewey from his mind.[36]

Eisenhower asked about Nixon's chances. Hagerty, who from early October on had insisted that Eisenhower would have to run again, said he thought "Nixon is a very excellent vice-presidential candidate," but not ready for the top spot. On December 14, Hagerty showed Eisenhower a David Lawrence column in the *Herald Tribune*. Lawrence speculated that if the doctors told Eisenhower he was physically capable of continuing in office, Eisenhower would say, "I had no desire to come to public office in the first place . . . But if the people want me to serve, I shall obey their wish and serve if elected." Eisenhower read it through, laughed, and exclaimed, "Well, I'll be goddamned." Turning to Hagerty, Eisenhower said, "Jim, . . . that's almost exactly the words that are forming in my own mind should I make up my mind to run again." Then he speculated on other possible Republican candidates. What about George Humphrey, Eisenhower asked, with Milton on the ticket as Vice-President? "George is one of the ablest men I know," Eisenhower declared, and Milton would add the Eisenhower name to the ticket. Hagerty doubted that Humphrey could get the nomination. Eisenhower groaned and remarked, "You know, I just hate to turn this country back into the hands of people like Stevenson, Harriman, and Kefauver."

Hagerty warned that if Eisenhower did not run, Knowland would get the nomination. "I can't see Knowland from nothing," Eisenhower snapped. "Who else have we got?" Hagerty mentioned Earl Warren. "Not a chance," Eisenhower replied, because Warren was happy where he was, and he was doing a good job. Eisenhower explained that "Earl is one of those fellows who needs time to make decisions and his present spot is the best spot in the world for him. . . . He has a lifelong job and I think he means it when he says he will not enter political life again."

It was Hagerty's turn to ask who else was available. Eisenhower said he thought he knew four Republicans who were "mentally qualified for the Presidency." They were Humphrey, Brownell, Adams, and Bob Anderson. The problem was that none of them could get the nomination. Hagerty asked about finding someone in the Senate. "Actually," Eisenhower replied, "I can't see anyone in the Senate who impresses me at all on both sides of the aisle."

Finding a Republican candidate other than Eisenhower who could win the nomination, get elected, and adequately discharge the duties of the Presidency was proving difficult if not impossible. "Let me try you on something else," Eisenhower said to Hagerty as he began pacing the room. "I think my brother would do anything I wanted him to. I think he would run for President, if I wanted him to." Eisenhower thought he could get the Pennsylvania delegation to go to the convention committed to Milton as a favorite son. Hagerty was as sure as Eisenhower that Milton could do the job, but he warned the President that the American people would resent any attempt to build a family dynasty. Hagerty then repeated that in his opinion the only ticket that could win for the Republicans was Eisenhower-Nixon.[37]

Even as Eisenhower's thoughts were becoming absorbed with his own immediate political future, he continued to worry about long-range problems. On December 5, he wrote a thoughtful letter to Dulles on "the continuing struggle between the Communistic and the free worlds." He said the Soviets had abandoned the Stalinist tactic of using force to achieve their objectives, because the buildup of the U.S. nuclear arsenal had deterred Stalin's successors from continuing that method. Instead, they were turning to economic competition. "Now we have always boasted that the productivity of free men in a free society would overwhelmingly excel the productivity of regimented labor," Eisenhower said. "So at first glance, it would appear that we are being challenged in the area of our greatest strength." But because the Soviets were on the offensive, even in economics, they could be selective in deciding where and when to use their money.

To counter the Soviet economic threat, Eisenhower told Dulles he wanted to start creating "economic associations, somewhat as we have done in the military area. . . . What would be even more effective, however, would be the opportunity to plan together *over the long term.*" Now was the time to move, when America was prosperous, producing two or three times what the Russians could achieve. "If we, at such a time, cannot organize to protect and advance our own interests and those of our friends in the world, then I must say it becomes time to begin thinking of 'despairing of the Republic.'" Eisenhower said that early in the new year he wanted to get together for informal talks with Dulles, Adams, and Humphrey on the subject.[38]

At his Cabinet meeting at Camp David, Eisenhower made the Soil Bank and his idea of buying back the homesteads on the Great Plains and returning them to grass the only topics of discussion. At the NSC meeting, he concentrated on the next generation of weapons, the ICBMs. All three services were working on various ballistic-missile projects; Eisenhower said he approved of this approach, but only "with some qualms" because he feared interservice rivalry would lead to duplication and thus delay development. Eisenhower followed up with a memo for Wilson, in which he told the Secretary of Defense "I want to be amply clear that nothing in the way of rival requirements is to delay the earliest development of an effective ballistic missile with significant range." He said, therefore, that he was making an addition to the NSC's Record of Action of the Camp David meeting. He wanted the record to indicate that the NSC "noted the President's statement that the political and psychological impact upon the world of the early development of an effective ballistic missile with a range in the 1,000–1,700-mile range would be so great that early development of such a missile would be of critical importance to the national-security interests of the United States." Further, Eisenhower ordered that the record indicate that "the President directed that the IRBM and ICBM programs should both be research and development programs of the highest priority above all others." Interservice squabbles should be avoided "so far as practicable," and if a conflict should develop, "then the matter will be promptly referred to the President."[39]

A week before Christmas, the Eisenhowers drove down to the White House. Eisenhower chaired a series of NSC and Cabinet meetings. One of his major concerns was opening trade with the Communist world. He was especially interested in selling surplus agricultural commodities. Radford told him that the JCS were opposed to any relaxation of controls on trade with the ChiComs. Eisenhower replied that "he was not afraid of Communist China—not in this decade, at least." Commerce Secretary Weeks said he agreed with Radford. Eisenhower told Weeks that "the history of the world down to this time proved that if you try to dam up international trade, the dam ultimately bursts and the flood overwhelms you. Our trouble is that our domestic political situation compels us to adopt an absolutely rigid policy respecting our trade with Communist China and the Soviet Union."[40]

After the meeting, Eisenhower talked privately with Dulles. The Secretary of State said he had "come to the conclusion that our whole international security structure was in jeopardy." The basic defense of the West was nuclear deterrence, Dulles said, but "that striking power was apt to be immobilized by moral repugnance. If this happened, the whole structure could readily collapse." Dulles said he had "come to feel that atomic power was too vast a power to be left for military use of any one country, but that its use should be internationalized for security purposes." Dulles was therefore ready to propose that if the Soviet Union would forgo the right to veto, then the United States could transfer responsibility for using the bomb to the U.N. Security Council "so as to universalize the capacity of atomic thermonuclear weapons to deter aggression." Actually, this was no more than a return to the old Baruch proposal of 1946, and Eisenhower knew it was unacceptable to the Russians, who were so badly outvoted in the Security Council. Nevertheless, Eisenhower told Dulles that it was "an interesting idea" and promised that he would study it.[41]

By Christmas 1955, Eisenhower felt fully recovered. He found that he could conduct Cabinet and NSC meetings without undue difficulty, meet with his advisers on a regular basis in the Oval Office, and perform his other duties, all without fatigue or weariness. He was ready to resume a full daily work schedule and was convinced that his recovery from his heart attack would be complete. But that did not mean he would necessarily run again. He was still keeping his options open, although he remained distressed by the failure to locate anyone in the Republican Party who could successfully replace him. John, Barbara, and the grandchildren came to the White House for the holidays; on Christmas Day, as the family was driving to church, Eisenhower turned to John and said, "I *told* the boys four years ago that they ought to get someone who'd want to run again for a second term."[42]

The day after Christmas, Eisenhower called Nixon into his office for a private chat. A number of Eisenhower's aides, led by Adams, had been urging him, if he decided to run again, to dump Nixon. They provided Eisenhower with the results of current polls, which indicated that Nixon would cost Eisenhower three or four points in a race with Stevenson. Eisenhower cited the figures to Nixon, then said that in his opinion Nixon could strengthen himself for 1960 by accepting a Cabinet post, where he could get some experience in administration. Eisenhower offered Nixon any post he wanted, except that of Secretary of State or Attorney General, but urged him to replace Charlie Wilson at Defense. Nixon smelled the very obvious rat. He knew—and he at least suspected that Eisenhower knew—that the press would interpret such a move as a demotion, so serious a demotion as to probably ruin Nixon's chance to ever be President. Nixon told Eisenhower that putting someone else on the ticket in 1956 would "upset the many Republicans who still considered me [your] principal link with party orthodoxy." Nixon then asked Eisenhower, directly, whether the President believed that the Republicans would be better off with someone else as the vice-presidential candidate. Eisenhower did not answer. He would not order Nixon off the ticket. Still, he wished Nixon would leave voluntarily, and suggested again that Nixon could pick up some badly needed experience as Secretary of Defense. The conversation ended on that inconclusive note.[43]

Two days later, on December 28, Eisenhower read through and approved an NSC policy statement on the CIA. He then issued a directive for CIA covert activities. It was a sweeping, tough-minded document. It told the CIA to "create and exploit troublesome problems for International Communism, impair relations between the U.S.S.R. and Communist China and between them and their satellites, complicate control within the U.S.S.R., Communist China, and their satellites, and retard the growth of the military and economic potential of the Soviet bloc." In addition, the CIA should seek to "discredit the prestige and ideology of International Communism, and reduce the strength of its parties." It should also "counter any threat of a party or individuals directly or indirectly responsive to Communist control to achieve dominant power in a free-world country." Finally, "to the extent practicable" in the Soviet Union, China, and their satellites, the CIA should "develop underground resistance and facilitate covert and guerrilla preparations." [44]

The man who issued that directive did not have a weak heart. He was obviously tough enough mentally to stay on the job for four more years, and he felt strong enough physically to do so. That did not necessarily mean that he was going to do it, only that he felt capable. But he insisted on keeping his options open, and certainly was not going to make a final decision until after the doctors had run their series of tests in mid-February.

CHAPTER THIRTEEN

Recovery

January–March 1956

AT THE BEGINNING of the new year, Eisenhower flew to Key West for a week in the sun. Slater, Bill Robinson, George Allen, and Al Gruenther joined him there. Eisenhower's friends agreed that there had been a "great change . . . in his apparent health, his enthusiasm, and completely relaxed attitude . . ." They played bridge almost nonstop, with "a great deal of banter and kidding and laughing." When Eisenhower reneged, he was the butt of the jokes for the remainder of the evening. Slater said he feared they were overdoing the bridge, that they were taxing Eisenhower's strength. Allen replied that he had "never seen the President in such good spirits," and told Slater that their bridge games were as nothing compared to the poker games he used to play with Truman in the White House; Truman's games sometimes began early in the morning and would "go on and on until late at night," often with "dire results" for Truman.[1]

Inevitably in an election year, much of the talk around the bridge table was political. The burning question was, of course, whether or not Eisenhower would run again. The members of the gang agreed among themselves that he would. Allen had it straight from Mamie— who was in Gettysburg—that she wanted him to stay in office. Slater too thought Eisenhower would stand for re-election, because he had done such a good job of organizing his office that "things seem to move with clocklike precision." Slater reasoned that "the team [Eisenhower] has developed is now so well trained and experienced, his work is not

287

at all detailed, in fact it has been reduced pretty much to conference and decision status, which isn't difficult for a man who has been doing that sort of thing for so long." [2]

On January 8, on the eve of flying back to Washington, Eisenhower held a news conference at Key West. He said he was feeling "better—stronger—and much more able to get about." The week in Florida "has been a very splendid period of just sheer recreation for me, and I am going back . . . as ready to go to work as a person could be, after the physical experience I have been through." But he refused to answer questions about his intentions.[3]

When he got back to Washington, Eisenhower had a consultation with his doctors. They told him he would have to stick to a fat-free diet, that he had to lie down for a half hour before lunch, that he should spend the hour after lunch talking with personal friends about noncontroversial subjects, and that he should take a ten-minute rest at the end of each hour during Cabinet and NSC meetings. Dr. Snyder told Eisenhower something he had known all his life—"that it is not the really big problems that upset him, it is the little silly annoyances." Later, talking to Whitman, Eisenhower said that he had been more determined to quit in September, before his heart attack, than he was now.[4]

On January 10, Eisenhower arranged a dinner to discuss the question of a second term. He invited Dulles, Humphrey, Brownell, Summerfield, Hagerty, Adams, Lodge, and Milton Eisenhower. He wanted it to be a "top secret" affair and had Whitman phone the secretary of each of the men invited, issuing the invitations but swearing the secretaries to secrecy. Only Eisenhower and Whitman knew whose names were on the list, or so they thought, but there was a leak and the list was published. Eisenhower decided to postpone the dinner until January 13.[5] Meanwhile, he tried to figure out the source of the leak. Talking to Hagerty about it, Eisenhower remembered that back in late December, when he had conferred with Nixon about Nixon's future, he had mentioned the dinner to the Vice-President. Eisenhower said he had then told Nixon, "Ordinarily you would be the first one I would ask to such a dinner. Since you are going to be so much the object of conversation, it would be embarrassing to you. I have no secrets from you." Then, Eisenhower recalled, he had given Nixon the list. Since he knew that neither he nor Whitman had released it, Nixon had to be the culprit.[6] Evidently Nixon felt that as he had not a single friend among those Eisenhower had decided to consult, his best bet was to try to break up the meeting. But Eisenhower ignored Nixon's leak, and went ahead with the meeting anyway, on a secret basis, three days later.

Before consulting with his advisers, Eisenhower consulted with his family and friends. Milton and John Eisenhower joined George Allen in opposing a second term, primarily on the grounds that Eisenhower would live longer without the aggravations of four more years as President. Mamie, however, insisted that they were wrong. She told her husband that "idleness would be fatal" for a man with his temperament.[7]

On Friday night, January 13, Eisenhower hosted the dinner for his advisers. After the meal, the President asked each man to outline the pros and cons of running again. Without exception, each adviser was for it. Dulles spoke first. He said "there was no one person in the world, and perhaps there never had been any person in the world, who commanded the respect of as many people as did the President."[8] The others insisted that Eisenhower was the "only man" who could rebuild the Republican Party—without him, it would be captured by the right wing (Knowland had already announced that if Eisenhower did not run again, he would enter the race). To Eisenhower, that was the great danger. Before the meeting, he had scribbled down the names of men he could support as his successor. These included Adams, Lodge, Robert Anderson, and Hauge, all of whom got an "A-plus" from Eisenhower, and Nixon and Brownell, each of whom got an "A." The notable thing about his list was the absence of any member of the Old Guard, except Nixon. But his advisers were unanimous in insisting that Eisenhower was the only Republican who could be elected in 1956. On the negative side, the advisers admitted that Eisenhower had "earned the right" to "lay down the burden." Further, "no man is indispensable." Eisenhower's health precluded a vigorous campaign, and all agreed that if Eisenhower had a setback after taking the nomination, "it would be calamitous." If he died in office, after winning re-election, it would be "difficult." There was another consideration; would the people who liked Ike the most vote against him, on the grounds that "the party and the nation are now asking too much of him?"[9] Milton, who was still against his brother's running again, warned him that he might actually lose the election on the issue of his health, which the Democrats would be certain to raise. Milton also pointed out that there were "vast possibilities for good" that Eisenhower could accomplish as a private citizen.

Eisenhower summed up. He said he was surprised at the strength of the sentiment for his being a candidate. He warned the group about the danger of his winning re-election, then suffering another heart attack that might kill him or leave him incapable of performing his duties. He repeated that under no circumstances would he campaign as actively as he had in 1952. He then promised to think it all over, thanked the men for their advice, and at 11:15 P.M. the meeting broke up.[10]

When the others had left, Milton went upstairs with his brother. "If I were in your place," Milton said, "I would [insist] that I had the full right, beyond all possibility of reproach, to decide negatively." Milton thought the President ought to take into account his personal desires, his health, the alternative opportunities for service, and "what duty might require." A couple of days later, Milton summed up in a letter to his brother the arguments presented at the dinner, then added one last point of his own. "If you decline to run," he wrote, "you will clearly go down in history as one of our greatest military and political leaders, with no major domestic or international difficulty to mar your record." If Eisenhower stayed in office, he might enhance his standing and "contribute mightly" to peace, "or you might face serious economic setbacks at home and upheavals abroad." Then his reputation would be ruined. Eisenhower scribbled in the margin of Milton's letter that the question of protecting his reputation was "of no great moment; even though history might condemn a failure it cannot weigh the demand of conscience."[11]

But if Eisenhower was not worried about his reputation, he was deeply worried about his health. Besides his concern about what would happen if he had another attack after being nominated, but before the election, he was not at all sure he could do the job. He told one of the doctors at Fitzsimons, who had given him a "most encouraging prognosis," that it was rather like a quarterback on a football team. "He may have all of the wisdom to be derived from years of experience in the game, but when the need arises, he has to throw himself unreservedly into the play. . . . If we merely needed a brain on the field, a quarterback could play if he had to be in a wheelchair; but that isn't true in his case, nor is it in the Presidency."[12] To his brother Edgar, Eisenhower wrote that "my attempt to do something for my country in the post I now occupy has cost me a lot in health, much in wear and tear on mind and disposition, to say nothing of some hundreds of thousands of dollars."[13]

The wear and tear of being the President told on his sleeping habits. Eisenhower told Swede that although he had no trouble at all going to sleep, after five hours or so in bed, "I find that when I have weighty matters on my mind I wake up extremely early, apparently because a rested mind is anxious to begin grappling with knotty questions." Eisenhower assured Hazlett that while he never fretted over a decision already made, and did not "indulge in useless regrets," he always found that when he came awake "I am pondering some question that is still unanswered." Thus it was "a desire to attack the future" that cost him sleep. Now that he was back in the White House, Eisenhower said his routine included a short swim in the pool each day, a half-hour walk, and climbing one full set of stairs. In addition, he had started swinging his golf clubs again, although he had not yet attempted to actually play a game. The doctors had told him to avoid "all situations that tend to bring about such reactions as irritations, frustration, anxiety, fear, and, above all, anger." In reply, he asked the doctors, "Just what do you think the Presidency is?" He confessed he was also unable to heed their advice to "eat slowly." All this made his decision about how he was going to spend the next five years more difficult.[14]

A number of factors made the decision in 1956 more difficult for Eisenhower than 1952 had been. He was sixty-five years old, had suffered a heart attack, had persistent stomach problems, was not sleeping well, and claimed that he resented the idea that one man was indispensable. He also claimed he had grown immune to the argument that he had a "duty" to serve. Surely neither the nation nor the Republican Party had any right to ask more of him. His supporters could not agree. Virgil Prettyman, a former Columbia University faculty member, quoted to him a statement written by George Washington, which Prettyman wanted Eisenhower to put under his pillow at night. Washington had written, in 1787, that nothing could draw him out of retirement "unless it be a conviction that the partiality of my countrymen had made my services absolutely necessary, joined to a fear that my refusal might induce a belief that I preferred the conservation of my own reputation and private ease to the good of my country."[15] Eisenhower replied that Washington's statement was all very nice, but wondered on what basis Washington had reached the conclusion that "the partiality of my countrymen had made my services absolutely necessary."[16] To another friend, Eisenhower quoted Lincoln's famous remark to the effect that deputations and platoons came to him daily to define for him God's will, which led him to wonder why God never revealed His will directly to the President. "I, too," Eisenhower concluded, "desire to know wherein my duty lies."[17]

As with every recovering heart-attack patient, death was very much on his mind. "As I embark on the last of life's adventures," he wrote by hand on a sheet of White House stationery in early February, "my final thoughts will be for those I've loved, family, friends and country."[18] Under the circumstances, would it be fair and right for him to run again? What if he died or were incapacitated between the convention and the election, or after the election? Such questions added not only to his personal anxiety, but also to his concern about what would happen to his party and his country. His choice of a running mate in 1956 would be far more critical than it had been in 1952, not so much in terms of voter appeal, but in the possibility that the running mate might have to become the candidate, or succeed Eisenhower upon his death. That was why Eisenhower had tried to persuade (and continued to try to persuade) Nixon to take a Cabinet post.

Eisenhower's feelings about Nixon were ambiguous. In their three years together, they had not developed an intimate relationship. Eisenhower appreciated Nixon for his obvious qualities—he was extremely hardworking, highly intelligent, loyal, devoted to Eisenhower and the Republican Party, an effective campaigner who could take the low road, allowing Eisenhower to stay on the high road. On January 25, in a press-conference briefing, Eisenhower told Hagerty that "it would be difficult to find a better Vice-President." As compared to Knowland and most other prominent Republicans, Eisenhower much preferred Nixon, who had, in the President's view, learned a great deal since 1952. But, Eisenhower added, "People think of him [Nixon] as an immature boy." Eisenhower did not say that he agreed with that judgment, but did indicate that he thought Nixon should leave the Vice-Presidency, where he might become "atrophied," to assume a post in the Cabinet.[19]

In a conversation with Dulles, Eisenhower was more direct. He said "he was not sure" it was a good idea for Nixon to stay on the ticket. Using the approach that he had fixed in his mind as the best way to ease Nixon out, he claimed that another term as Vice-President would ruin Nixon politically (a judgment neither Nixon nor anyone else accepted, not only because a "dump Nixon" move would be sure to damage his career, but for the more obvious, if crass, reason that as Vice-President, Nixon had only a recent heart-attack victim between himself and the White House). Eisenhower nevertheless seriously told Dulles that Nixon ought to become Secretary of Commerce. Dulles doubted that Nixon would take it, and suggested that Nixon succeed him as Secretary of State. Eisenhower laughed and said Dulles was not going to get out of his job that easily, then added that "he doubted in any event that Nixon had the qualifications to be Secretary of State." [20]

In a January 25 press conference, Eisenhower was asked if, in the event he decided to seek re-election, he wanted Nixon for a running mate. Eisenhower replied that "my admiration, respect, and deep affection for Mr. Nixon . . . are well known." Then he said, in a statement that was the direct opposite of the truth, that "I have never talked to him under any circumstances as to what his future is to be or what he wants it to be, and until I confer with him I wouldn't have anything to say." [21] That fell far short of an endorsement and left Nixon in agony, but it allowed Eisenhower to keep his options open.

If not Nixon, who? Earl Warren was the most obvious choice. The polls indicated that an Eisenhower-Warren ticket would run as much as five points ahead of an Eisenhower-Nixon ticket. Eisenhower had great admiration for Warren, probably considered him the best man in the Republican Party (aside from himself), but was sure Warren would never resign from the Supreme Court in order to become Vice-President. On the other hand, if after his physical checkup in mid-February Eisenhower decided (or was told by his doctors) not to run again, Warren would make an excellent presidential candidate, one behind whom the whole Eisenhower wing of the party could unite to defeat Knowland, Nixon, or some other representative of the Old Guard. But when Eisenhower was asked at a press conference about the possibility of Warren becoming a candidate, Eisenhower said that "the Supreme Court and politics should not be mixed." Later, on January 30, Hagerty told Eisenhower that Warren had gone out of his way at a private party to express his annoyance at Eisenhower's remark. Did that mean Warren was considering running if Eisenhower withdrew? Eisenhower did not know, but commented in his diary that if it did, "it would be a great relief to me," because he would feel easier about retiring if he knew that Warren would succeed him. But for a Warren candidacy to be "feasible and ethical," Warren would have to wait for a draft. Only then could he submit his resignation and accept the nomination. Eisenhower wrote that "unless I could have personal assurances in advance that [Warren] would respond to a draft, my own problem remains more difficult to solve." [22] At a February 8 press conference, Eisenhower was asked if he would be opposed to a Warren candidacy. "Opposed? For goodness sake, I appointed him as Chief Justice of the United States; and there is no office in all the world that I respect more. Of course I admire and respect and have a very deep affection for Mr. Warren."[23]

But despite the flattering words, Eisenhower had doubts about Warren. He had told Hagerty, "Earl likes to take a long time to make up his mind." That was the perfect temperament for the Chief Justice, but it was a luxury the President could not afford. And if Eisenhower had doubts about Warren, they were dwarfed by the doubts he had about every other potential candidate in the Republican Party. At one point in February, Eisenhower's thoughts turned again to a new party, one encompasing southern Democrats and Republican moderates. He even toyed with the idea of running as a Democrat. He tried out the idea with Len Hall, chairman of the RNC; Hall, nonplussed, managed to reply that he would rather not discuss such a possibility. Well, Eisenhower explained, "All this business of batting your head against the wall" with the Old Guard, "you finally get worn down." Eisenhower said "he thought he could get better discipline on the other crowd." If he ran as a Republican, his coattails might bring back Republican control of Congress, a prospect he dreaded. "Why should I help such people as [Knowland] to get chairmanships—it becomes a terrible thing to do to our country almost."[24]

That was another problem with dumping Nixon; it would rid Eisenhower of the only member of the Old Guard he respected, and leave the rest. Eisenhower tried another idea. He asked Hall about inviting Governor Frank Lausche of Ohio, a Democrat, to jump sides and accept a Republican nomination for the Vice-Presidency. Hall liked the idea. They recalled Lincoln's selection of Andrew Johnson in 1864, when Lincoln had run not as a Republican but as a National Union Party candidate. Lausche was a Catholic, a moderate, friendly to the South, a man Eisenhower admired. The President said he "would love to run with a Catholic." Hall pointed out that if the Republicans did not nominate a Catholic in 1956, the Democrats would do so in 1960, probably "young John Kennedy, an attractive guy." Then Eisenhower indulged in another fantasy; there were any number of southern Democratic senators he could think of who would make good candidates for the Vice-Presidency and possible successors. But he caught himself up; the segregation problem precluded a southerner. Eisenhower returned to the Lausche idea; if the Republicans would accept him as the vice-presidential candidate, Eisenhower said, "It would just knock the props out of the [Democrats]." But in the end, Eisenhower realized it was all pipe dream, and he told Hall to talk to Nixon, "but be very, very gentle."[25]

Eisenhower's sense of himself as the nation's steward, meanwhile, which had come on him so strongly after the heart attack, had grown in the months of recuperation. As will be seen, it was at this time that Eisenhower put his greatest efforts into such programs as the Soil Bank and the Interstate Highway System. As another example, he made more diary entries in January 1956 than in any other month of his Presidency, or indeed during the war. Most of the entries were concerned with long-range problems. One was about a report he had read on the damage that could be anticipated in the United States in the event of an all-out nuclear war. There were a number of scenarios, but even at best, the country would suffer 65 percent casualties. To Eisenhower, this was "appalling." Even if the United States were "victorious," "it would literally be a business of digging ourselves out of ashes, starting again."[26]

Nuclear war had to be avoided at all costs. But so did surrender. Eisenhower looked around him and could see no one whom he could trust to take his place. He could not trust Nixon or Knowland to act deliberately in a crisis; he could not trust Warren to act soon enough. That was one reason why he never told Nixon—as FDR had told two of his Vice-Presidents, Garner and Wallace—that the time had come for them to part. There was no one else around he liked or trusted any more than he did Nixon, except Warren, but Warren could not be asked to leave the Court to be a Vice-President. So Eisenhower was stymied, both by the actual situation and by his own perception of himself and his contemporaries. In finding shortcomings in every possible successor, Eisenhower was coming to see himself as indispensable. He never said so directly, in fact denied it vehemently every time his supporters told him he was the "only man" who could keep the peace. He never said it to himself, never wrote it in his diary. But nevertheless, he had come to think of himself as indispensable.

His associates reinforced the belief. At every opportunity, they told him it was so. Nixon did so, of course, at some length. So did Hagerty and all the aides. So did the Secretary of State, who met with the President over cocktails two days before Eisenhower announced his decision. In his memo on the conversation, Dulles wrote, "I expressed my feeling that the state of the world was such as to require the President to serve." Dulles believed that America's standing in the world had never been higher, that Eisenhower was the most trusted leader around the world and the greatest force for peace. Eisenhower wrote in his diary, "I suspect that Foster's estimate concerning my own position is substantially correct."[27]

There was no escaping. As Eisenhower later told Swede, he had been forced to "bow my neck to what seemed to be the inevitable." What made it inevitable was his own belief that no one else could get the country through the next four years. As he explained to Swede, a major factor in his thinking was "a guilty feeling on my own part that I had failed to bring forward and establish a logical successor for my-self." On the positive side, by running again he could "hope that I may still be able to do something in promoting . . . peace. And that I can help our people understand that they must avoid extremes in reaching solutions to the social, economic, and political problems that are constantly with us. If I could be certain that my efforts would really promote these two things, I shall certainly never have any cause for sympathizing with myself—no matter what happens."[28]

Eisenhower's mind was made up. He would run again if the doctors gave him a go-ahead. On February 12, he went to Walter Reed for a series of tests; two days later the doctors declared, "Medically the chances are that the President should be able to carry on an active life satisfactorily for another five to ten years."[29] After the tests, Eisenhower went down to Humphrey's plantation in Georgia for some quail shooting. On February 25 he returned to Washington. Four days later he announced his decision at a press conference. He would be a candidate for re-election.

Eisenhower's announcement was tantamount to his nomination. Thus he immediately had to face the question every nominee faces: Who would be his running mate? Eisenhower refused to answer, "in spite of my tremendous admiration for Mr. Nixon." The President said "it is traditional . . . to wait and see who the Republican Convention nominates" before announcing the vice-presidential candidate. That was too coy to satisfy the reporters. Charles von Fremd of CBS asked for clarification: "Would you like to have Nixon?" Eisenhower replied, "I will say nothing more about it. I have said that my admiration and my respect for Vice-President Nixon is unbounded. He has been for me a loyal and dedicated associate, and a successful one. I am very fond of him, but I am going to say no more about it."[30]

Eisenhower began his campaign the night he made his announcement. On nationwide TV and radio, he went through his medical record, informed the public of what the doctors had told him, said that he would not be able to travel as extensively or attend as many ceremonial functions as he had in his first term, and admitted that he would need to take regular rest periods, and vacations. "But let me make one thing clear," he added. "As of this moment, there is not the slightest doubt that I can perform as well as I ever have, all of the important duties of the Presidency." He had in fact been doing so for many weeks. But he also wanted delegates to the Republican Convention to know that he would "wage no political campaign in the customary pattern."[31]

The idea of being the candidate but not campaigning bothered him. Nixon, Hagerty, and others had assured him he could be just as effective by making four or five major television addresses, but Eisenhower confessed to Dulles that he "attached importance to the motorcades where he had an opportunity to look in the eyes of hundreds of thousands of people on each occasion." He drew strength from such contact.[32] But he knew he had to avoid the fatigue of a whistle-stop campaign, and in any case he thought it unseemly for a President to go barnstorming. Still, as he told Swede, "I am a competitor, a fighter." When the campaign neared its climax, he knew he would be told that the outcome was in doubt and that he simply had to throw himself into active campaigning. When that time came, Eisenhower feared "my own reluctance ever to accept defeat might tempt me into activity that should be completely eliminated from my life."[33]

But that time would not come until October; meanwhile, in March, Eisenhower's political problem was what to do about Nixon. He continued to urge Nixon to pick a Cabinet post for himself (but not State or Justice), to insist on something that seemed ridiculous to every other observer, that Nixon would thereby strengthen himself for 1960. In Eisenhower's press conferences that spring of 1956, Nixon was the number-one topic. The more Eisenhower tried to praise him, it somehow seemed, the more tongue-tied he got; the more he tried to endorse Nixon's leadership qualities, the more doubtful he sounded. Thus on March 7, in response to a question as to whether he would "dump Nixon" or not, he began indignantly: "If any one ever has the effrontery to come in and urge me to dump somebody that I respect as I do Vice-President Nixon, there will be more commotion around my office than you have noticed yet." Then he said he "had not presumed to tell the Vice-President what he should do with his own future." He added that he had told Nixon that "I believe he *should be* one of the comers in the Republican Party. He is young, vigorous, healthy, and certainly deeply informed on the processes of our government. *And so far as I know*, he is deeply dedicated to the same principles of government that I am." Well, then, if Nixon wanted to stay on the ticket, would Eisenhower be content? Eisenhower snapped back, "I am not going to be

pushed into corners here . . . I do say this: I have no criticism of
Vice-President Nixon to make, either as a man, an associate, or as my
running mate on the ticket."[34] What Eisenhower did not tell the press,
but did say to Nixon, was that Nixon would be better off running one
of the big departments, but "if you calculate that I won't last five years,
of course that is different." It was cruel, really, of Eisenhower to put
it that bluntly—what on earth could Nixon answer? The Vice-President contented himself with mumbling that "anything the President
wanted him to do, he would do."[35]

A week later, at a press-conference briefing, Eisenhower told Hag-
erty, "The idea of trying to promote a fight between me and Dick
Nixon is like trying to promote a fight between me and my brother.
I am happy to have him as a personal friend, I am happy to have him
as an associate, and I am happy to have him in government." That
sounded like an endorsement, but Eisenhower immediately added,
"That still doesn't make him Vice-President. He has serious problems.
He has his own way to make." Eisenhower said he did not know what
Nixon was going to do, "but there is nothing to be gained politically
by ditching him." Ambiguous as always about Nixon, Eisenhower then
said he did not want to give Nixon the inside track to the nomination
in 1960. "I want a bevy of young fellows to be available four years
from now."[36]

Despite the lack of intimacy between the two men, despite Eisenhower's frequently expressed private doubts about Nixon's ability
either to run the government or to win votes, despite Hagerty's warning to Eisenhower that "not one person was for Nixon for Vice-President for a second term," Eisenhower would not act decisively to get
rid of Nixon.[37] Despite Eisenhower's undoubted admiration for many
of Nixon's talents, despite Eisenhower's frequently expressed public
satisfaction with Nixon's actions as Vice-President, despite Nixon's
popularity with the Old Guard, which was insisting that he stay on the
ticket, Eisenhower refused to endorse Nixon. Instead, he remained indecisive.

One aspect of Eisenhower's refusal to act resulted from a personal
trait of Eisenhower's. For all his rough talk about getting rid of the
incompetent, Eisenhower found it extremely difficult to fire anyone
who had been loyal to him. Way back in 1943, at the time of the battle
of Kasserine Pass, Eisenhower had told Patton, "You must not retain
for one instant any man in a responsible position where you have become doubtful of his ability to do the job. . . . This matter frequently
calls for more courage than any other thing you will have to do, but I

expect you to be perfectly cold-blooded about it."[38] But even during the war, except in the most extreme cases, Eisenhower could seldom bring himself to fire a man. So too as President; he never said one good word about Charles Wilson, and often recounted Wilson's shortcomings in detail to his staff, but he never fired Wilson. Nor could he bring himself to fire Nixon.

January was a busy month, not only for presidential but also for congressional politics. Congress was back in session. Eisenhower wanted to establish a record for the upcoming campaign, but so did the Democrats. Eisenhower asked Congress for action on the Soil Bank, the Interstate Highway System, school construction, statehood for Hawaii, and natural-gas regulation. On every item he was frustrated. The only place he was able to enforce his will was on the level of defense spending—and the Democrats quickly made defense spending one of the major issues of the campaign.

The agricultural bill for 1956 embodied some, although not all, of Eisenhower's ideas on striking a balance between conservation and production. It did not incorporate the President's hope that the federal government could buy back some of the submarginal land that had been homesteaded in the late nineteenth century. It did give farmers a choice; they could leave fallow the land that they would otherwise plant to wheat or corn, and the government would pay them in either cash or kind the value of their probable yield, the old New Deal program. What was new in Eisenhower's vision was his proposal to encourage a longer-range program, the Conservation Reserve. In the latter case, a farmer could receive federal payments over a period of years for putting land back into ungrazed grass or forest, or water storage. The purpose was nicely summarized in the words "Soil Bank." Benson's department estimated that the Soil Bank would reduce total cultivated acreage in the United States by 12 percent. This would cut the surplus, which would then lead to an upsurge in commodity prices. It would cost about $350 million annually, but much of that money would come back simply through reduced costs to the government for storing charges on the surplus. Benson, personally, did not think much of the plan. Benson said, "I could not get enthusiastic . . . about the idea of paying farmers for not producing." Indeed, he said, it "outraged my sensibilities." But the President wanted it, and the Soil Bank went to Congress as the Administration's bill to deal with the farm problem.[39]

More congenial to Benson, whose ultimate goal was to free farmers from the government altogether, was the Administration's insistence that the Soil Bank be tied to flexible price supports. This was the point at which the Democrats drew the line. Their best issue for 1956 was the depressed condition of the American farmer. Every other major segment of the economy was booming; inflation was at 1 percent; Eisenhower had made and kept the peace. On the personal side, the Democrats could question Eisenhower's physical ability to carry on, or argue that a vote for Eisenhower was really a vote for Nixon. But on the national level, the Democrats could do nothing with the race issue, because of the South. There were precious few other issues available to them. Eisenhower had so effectively staked out the middle of the road as his territory, Democrats hardly knew whether to attack him from the left or the right. (On many of the crucial votes in that session, Eisenhower got more Democratic than Republican support.) Thus the appeal of the farm-parity issue to the Democrats. It was one on which they could break cleanly with Eisenhower and one that had broad appeal among a major segment of the population. Eisenhower had tied the Soil Bank to flexible and lower parities; the Democrats offered more than one hundred amendments to his farm bill, most of them calling for a rigid 90 percent parity. The Democrats were offering a deal—they would give Eisenhower his Soil Bank if he would let them give the farmers increased price supports.

If the two were joined together in one bill, Eisenhower swore he would veto it. He believed that rigid supports had created the surplus problem in the first instance, and to tie them to a program designed to reduce the surplus was irresponsible and unworkable. "I will not go out of office with rigid supports in being to ruin our agriculture," the President told a meeting of the Republican leaders.[40] But Eisenhower feared that the Democrats had him on this one; he told his aides "the Democrats are going to do a very simple thing, write a bill that has something for everybody and if I then veto it, a lot of people will be mad."[41]

Which is exactly what happened. After months of debate, Congress finally passed a farm bill, one that tied the Soil Bank to 90 percent parity payments. By then, mid-April, it was too late to have any significant impact on the 1956 crop, much of which was already in the ground. On April 16, Eisenhower vetoed the bill. That night, on national TV, he explained his action. "I had no choice," he declared. "I could not sign this bill into law because it was a bad bill." He said he was glad that the Soil Bank was in it, but "other provisions of the bill would have rendered the soil bank almost useless. The fact is that we got a hodge-podge in which the bad provisions more than canceled out the good." He told Congress to try again.[42]

In January, Eisenhower and Humphrey talked on the phone about exercising greater direction over economic movements through a judicious use of government expenditures. One of Eisenhower's favorite programs for reducing the peaks and valleys on the GNP chart was the Interstate System. Back in November 1955, the President had talked to Hauge, then informed Weeks that he wanted Commerce to plan to use the Interstate System for managing the economy. As Hauge put it, "That was the fundamental purpose of the plan in the initial instance." The bill had failed in 1955 due to Democratic objections to the method of financing (bonds). The Democrats wanted to tax the users to pay for the highways. Eisenhower had originally wanted tolls, as had Humphrey, but in January they agreed to cooperate with the Democrats in order to get started on construction. In the House, Hale Boggs of Louisiana and George Fallon of Maryland had introduced a bill providing for users' taxes to pay for the system. Eisenhower gave the word to the Republican leaders—cooperate with Boggs and Fallon and "yield to Democratic insistence on financing," until a bill was passed. Through the late winter and early spring, Boggs and Fallon, with Republican cooperation, worked on their bill.[43]

Oil and taxes make for intense politics. With millions, even billions, of dollars involved, the politics of oil are played with stunning intensity. In 1955, the House passed a bill that deregulated independent producers of natural gas. In early 1956, it came up for debate in the Senate. The oil-producing states favored the bill, the consuming states opposed. It was quite that simple—there were no liberal-conservative, Republican-Democratic divisions over the bill, only a division between the haves and the have-nots. Insofar as either side made a serious argument, the issue was whether or not deregulation would encourage exploration and thus ultimately lower prices by expanding supplies. On balance, Eisenhower thought that the bill would accomplish those goals, and in addition he had a general objection to federal regulation that led him to favor the bill.

On February 7, the bill passed the Senate, but only after a scandal had been revealed. The oil lobby was accused of trying to buy votes, openly and brazenly, and of using strong-arm tactics to get a favorable vote. Eisenhower was distressed. He had many close friends in the oil industry, especially in Texas, and he knew they all wanted the bill.

But he recognized that "there is a great stench around the passing of the bill." It was, he wrote in his diary, "the kind of thing that makes American politics a dreary and frustrating experience for anyone who has any regard for moral and ethical standards."[44] To Gabe Hauge, he broadened his complaint, saying that he "was greatly irritated with business because of the gas bill." Hauge said quietly that business must have an honorable place. Eisenhower replied, "I want to give businessmen an honorable place, but they make crooks out of themselves." Still further broadening his complaint, Eisenhower told Hauge that it was a dangerous fact that the American economy had become so dependent upon the decisions of a handful of men, the directors of the great corporations, who could make decisions (such as a recent U.S. Steel announcement of a price rise) that could bring on great inflation, despite the government's efforts. What bothered Eisenhower most was that the board of directors represented, at most, 2 percent of the stockholders. In his youth, Eisenhower said, a man was risking his own money. "There is something to be said for the tycoon age as against the directorship age."[45]

The next day, February 14, his ire still aroused against big business, Eisenhower informed the Republican leaders that he intended to veto the natural-gas bill. He explained that in addition to the lobbying efforts that had become public knowledge, Brownell had "uncovered other bad stuff." Eisenhower made it clear he did not believe that any vote was bought, "but when things were done like what the oil industry did in this instance . . ." Knowland cut him off. The minority leader said a veto was out of the question, that it would make every man who voted for the bill look like a crook, "and would play into the hands of the left-wingers . . . and encourage similar demagoguery against other bills." Eisenhower rejoined that the Republican Party could not afford to be known as the party of big business, and he would hate to leave the Administration open to the charge "that business could get this bill by throwing sufficient money around." He cursed the "incredible stupidity of the industry."[46]

On February 17, Eisenhower vetoed the bill, citing the "arrogant" lobbying efforts of "a very small segment of a great and vital industry" as his reason.[47] Given the publicity the lobbying effort had already received, and given what Eisenhower knew might soon be revealed (and was; that summer Brownell got a number of indictments), the President had little choice. Still, given that he liked the objectives of the bill, and given that the Republican Party was counting on millions in contributions from the oil industry for the upcoming campaign, the veto was an act of some courage. Eisenhower wrote private letters to a number of his oil-industry friends, including Sid Richardson, explaining his motives and assuring them that he felt the "questionable aura that surrounded its passing" had been created "by an irresponsible and small segment of the industry." (To give some idea of the amounts of money Richardson, at least, controlled, it should be pointed out that about a month earlier, George Allen had told Ellis Slater that Richardson was the richest man in America. Slater had protested that Roy Cullen—another of Eisenhower's oil friends, from Houston—and H. L. Hunt were richer. No, Allen assured him—Richardson was worth "a billion dollars."[48] A billion dollars in 1956 was almost 2 percent of the entire federal budget.)

In January, Eisenhower had sent to Congress a revised and broadened program for school construction. The shortage of classrooms that had existed when Eisenhower took office had become more acute in the past three years, as the baby-boom generation swelled the school-age population. Eisenhower had been trying to get Congress to provide federal aid to the most impacted areas and the poorest states, rather than a program that would provide aid to every state, regardless of need. Between 1953 and 1956 he failed to get action. His latest proposal was to provide more than a billion dollars in federal grants, to be matched by the states, for the neediest school districts over the next five years. Two amendments were attached to the bill in the House. One allocated the money on the basis of a state's school-age population, making the bill much more attractive to congressmen from New York City, Philadelphia, and other wealthy and heavily populated areas, less to those from the poorer states, especially in the South. The second amendment also drew northern votes at the expense of southern support. It was introduced by Adam Clayton Powell, a black congressman from Harlem. It would deny any school-construction funds to any state that refused to comply with the *Brown* decision and integrate its schools.

In public, Eisenhower opposed any linking of school-construction funds with integration. As he explained to the Republican leaders, such an amendment was sure to kill the bill, because the southerners would "filibuster it to death." But he also admitted "that in view of the Supreme Court decision, a vote against Powell would seem to be a vote against the Constitution."[49] Powell got his amendment attached to the bill; Eisenhower failed to support him; the bill was defeated.

• • •

By keeping his distance from the Powell Amendment, Eisenhower was consistent. Ever since the *Brown* decision was announced, and even before, he had gone to great lengths to divorce himself from the problem of race relations, and especially integration of the schools. Integration, he said over and over, was the responsibility of the courts. The judges should exercise the leadership. There was no executive responsibility. He would not involve himself or his Administration.

In early January, in his State of the Union address, Eisenhower called for a bipartisan commission to investigate the racial situation and make recommendations for appropriate legislation. He hoped that such a commission would act as a buffer to keep the race issue out of partisan politics and reduce tension. Brownell, meanwhile, was eager to sponsor a new civil-rights bill (none had been passed since Reconstruction, eighty-five years earlier).[50] Eisenhower told Brownell to get to work on it.

On January 25, at a news conference, Eisenhower was asked how he felt about the Powell Amendment. Eisenhower began his answer by asserting "these things aren't simple." He reiterated, "My devotion to the decisions of the Supreme Court, particularly when they are unanimous, I hope is complete." He said, "I believe in the quality of opportunity for every citizen of the United States," but immediately repeated, "It isn't quite as simple at that." Eisenhower emphasized that "we want the schools now," and reminded the reporters that the Supreme Court itself had said that desegregation should be "implemented gradually." The President said he had to recognize "the deep ruts of prejudice and emotionalism that have been built up over the years in this problem." He wanted a school-construction bill passed, he concluded, and he wanted moderation on the race issue.[51]

Moderation was hard to find. To the black community, words like "moderate" and "gradual" had come to mean "never," which was exactly what the majority of the white South wanted—never. Racial violence, always endemic in the South, increased, almost always by the whites against the blacks. For Frederic Morrow, the "black man in the White House," it was an agonizing time. Morrow was a forty-six-year-old black lawyer, former field secretary for the NAACP, and veteran of World War II, who joined the Administration in July 1955 as a White House staffer. He was the first Negro ever to be named to a presidential staff in an executive capacity. Initially he had numerous personal problems—the other staff aides would not eat with him, none of the secretaries in the White House pool would work for him, and so on—but they paled beside his massive political problem, which was how to get the Administration to act in defense of civil rights. In late 1955, in Mississippi, a fourteen-year-old Negro from Chicago, Emmett Till, was accused of wolf-whistling at a white woman in a store. Shortly thereafter, his trussed and mutilated body was found in a river. Through memoranda and conversations, Morrow tried to persuade the President to speak out on the Till incident, but without success. Morrow warned that such indifference contributed "to the Negro's thinking that the Republican Party deserts him in crisis." No one listened.[52]

Indeed, Eisenhower and his aides felt that the black community was guilty of pushing too hard, too fast, and of ingratitude. In February 1956, Eisenhower expressed his disappointment at the results of a study of black voting in the 1954 congressional elections. Eisenhower felt that after all he and the Republicans had done for Negroes—the desegregation of military base facilities and of Washington, D.C., the appointment of Morrow—the percentage of Negroes voting Republican should have gone up. But it had not. Max Rabb, who was in charge of minority problems for the President, told Morrow that "most of the responsible officials in the White House had become completely disgusted with the whole matter." Rabb said the Administration felt that "Negroes were being too aggressive in their demands; that an ugliness and surliness in manner was beginning to show through." Rabb added that "he could no longer argue that Negroes would be an asset politically or that doing things for them would gain any support for the Administration."[53]

Rabb's tough and ugly-sounding words need to be tempered by an observation Morrow made in his diary at this time. Citing Eisenhower's public commitment to equality of opportunity for all Americans, Morrow wrote: "During my lifetime I have never known of any other President who made such a statement publicly, with such complete conviction, and wholly without reservation."[54]

But, as Morrow well knew, black Americans needed more than moral support and words. The South's counterattack against *Brown* by 1956 was being launched with vigor and imagination. In February, four southern state legislatures passed interposition resolutions that claimed the Supreme Court decision in *Brown* had no force or effect in their states. Eisenhower was asked at a February 29 news conference about his reaction to the doctrine of interposition. Eisenhower ducked: "Now, this is what I say: there are adequate legal means of determining all of these factors." He would leave interposition to the courts. He expected that "we are going to make progress," but emphasized that "the Supreme Court itself said it does not expect revolutionary action

suddenly executed. We will make progress, and I am not going to attempt to tell them how it is going to be done."[55]

On March 1, Eisenhower showed again his capacity for caution on
the race issue. A federal judge ordered the University of Alabama to
enroll Autherine Lucy; university officials then expelled her on the
astonishing grounds that in her suit against the university, she had
lied when she said that her race was the reason she had earlier been
denied admittance. To Morrow, and to millions of others, this seemed
a clear-cut case of defiance of federal court orders, something Eisenhower had sworn many times he was pledged to (and determined to)
enforce. But he remained aloof, strengthening the view in the South
that the Eisenhower Administration would never intervene to enforce
integration.[56]

In early March, the South's counterattack escalated from the state
to the federal level, as 101 southern members of the House and Senate
signed a "manifesto" in which they committed themselves to try to
overturn the *Brown* decision. On March 14, Eisenhower was asked to
comment. He managed to see the thing from the South's point of view.
"Let us remember this one thing," he said, "and it is very important:
the people who have this deep emotional reaction on the other side
were not acting over these past three generations in defiance of law.
They were acting in compliance with the law as interpreted by the
Supreme Court [in the *Plessy* case]." *Brown* had "completely reversed"
Plessy, Eisenhower pointed out, "and it is going to take time for them
to adjust their thinking and their progress to that." How much time?
"I am not even going to talk about that; I don't know anything about
the length of time it will take." Eisenhower criticized "extremists" on
both sides, and offered this advice: "If ever there was a time when we
must be patient without being complacent, when we must be understanding of other people's deep emotions as well as our own, this is it."
As to the manifesto, Eisenhower was quick to point out that the signers
"say they are going to use every legal means," that they did not intend
to act outside the law, that "no one in any responsible position anywhere has talked nullification," which Eisenhower admitted would put
the country in "a very bad spot" if it happened.[57]

Eisenhower hoped that would be the end of his involvement, but
when 101 congressmen formally declare they intend to change a Supreme
Court decision, the President cannot escape that easily. At his next
news conference, Eisenhower was asked how he, the Chief Executive,
felt about defiance of Supreme Court orders. Eisenhower asserted that
no one had used the words "defy the Supreme Court," again spoke of

the difficulty southerners had readjusting from *Plessy* to *Brown,* then said, "These people [white southerners] have, of course, their free choice as to what they want to do." He could hardly have meant it the way it sounded, but he was getting irritated by the whole issue and wanted to be done with it. His conclusion was less than resounding: "As far as I am concerned, I am for moderation, but I am for progress; that is exactly what I am for in this."[58]

Martin Luther King, Jr., was leading a bus boycott in Montgomery, Alabama, protesting segregated seating on the city buses. Black citizens were shot, their homes and churches were bombed, but the city police were arresting the boycotters. Eisenhower told his Cabinet that he was "much impressed with the moderation of the Negroes in Alabama," and that he thought the South had made "two big mistakes," one in not admitting Miss Lucy and the other in opposing the reasonable demands of the Montgomery black community.[59] But when Robert Spivack asked Eisenhower to comment publicly, at a press conference, on King's Montgomery crusade, Eisenhower backed away. "Well, you are asking me, I think, to be more of a lawyer than I certainly am. But, as I understand it, there is a state law about boycotts, and it is under that kind of thing that these people are being brought to trial." He could see no reason for federal involvement.[60]

A common white southern assertation at this time was that integration was a Communist plot. Eisenhower was hardly so naïve as to believe that, but he did fear that the Communists would take advantage of the racial unrest. On March 9, J. Edgar Hoover presented to Eisenhower and his Cabinet a twenty-four-page briefing on the explosive situation in the South. Hoover damned the extremists on both sides, the NAACP and the White Citizens Councils. He said blacks were so terrified that they would refuse to testify as to the violence they had seen or suffered, or even talk to FBI agents. But Hoover emphasized that his greater concern was with the efforts of the Communists to infiltrate the civil-rights movement and use it to add to social unrest. For his part, Eisenhower feared that the Communists were trying to "drive a wedge between the Administration and its friends in the South in that election year. . ."[61]

After Hoover made his presentation, Brownell outlined the civil-rights bill he was proposing. It called for a bipartisan commission, created by Congress, with the power to subpoena and to investigate alleged civil-rights violations; for a new Assistant Attorney General in charge of civil rights in the Justice Department; for new laws enforcing voting rights; and for strengthening existing civil-rights statutes to

protect privileges and immunities of citizens. Eisenhower was enthusiastic about the proposals and told Brownell to go ahead with them. But
Humphrey objected to Brownell's bill, which he charged went too far
and too rapidly toward desegregation. Humphrey insisted that progress
had to be evolutionary. He also gave a warning. "We've talked about
the Deep South," he said, "but your worst problems can come in Detroit, Chicago, *et al*. All they need to run wild is a little expectation of
backing."[62] Wilson agreed that there were real dangers in Detroit. He
pontificated: "A social evolution takes time. You can't speed it up."

     "I'm at sea on all this," Eisenhower confessed. "I want to put some-
thing forward that I can show as an advance." But he too was fearful.
"Not enough people know how deep this emotion is in the South. Unless you've lived there you can't know . . . We could have another
civil war on our hands." More probably, pressure from the North
might lead the South to abandon public education altogether. The
whites would then have their own church-related schools, Eisenhower
said, while the blacks would have no education at all. He used the
word "dilemma." "I must enforce the law," but he did not know how
to do it. "They come in and say I should force the university to accept
Miss Lucy," he complained. He could not do it, because education was
a local matter. His hands were tied.[63]

     Eisenhower's hope was that if the desegregation crisis moved be-
yond the courts, his bipartisan commission would act as a buffer between the contending sides and the Administration, so that he would
not have to use force in a specific case. He had another approach to
noninvolvement—asking the churches to exercise the leadership. In
March, Eisenhower had a long talk with the Reverend Billy Graham;
he followed it up with a letter of March 22 in which he repeated his
main point: "Ministers know that peacemakers are blessed. They should
also know that the most effective peacemaker is one who prevents a
quarrel from developing, not the one who has to pick up the pieces
remaining after an unfortunate fight." Progress achieved "through conciliation will be more lasting and stronger than could be obtained
through force and conflict."[64] Graham heartily agreed and promised to
work with southern ministers to improve race relations. But he also
advised the President to stay away from the race issue during the campaign.[65]

     Eisenhower's moderate, middle-of-the-road stance with regard to
race relations was, of course, consistent with his general approach to all
his problems. He often asserted that a person who stood at either extreme on a political or social question was always wrong. And in his

memoirs, he made the best possible case he could for his position of refusing to act even while violence flared all across the South. He said he was committed to the cause of civil rights, but "I did not agree with those who believed that legislation alone could institute instant morality, [or] who believed that coercion could cure all civil rights problems . . ."[66]

Whenever Eisenhower stated his position on extremists always being wrong, he would add, "except on a moral issue." He did not see the desegregation crisis as a moral issue, but rather as one of practical politics, in which every point of view (meaning that of the white southerners) had to be considered and responded to. His critics charged that he was guilty of moral equivocation; his supporters replied that he was carefully and safely guiding the country through dangerous times.

In the field of civil rights, almost all of what Eisenhower did was in full public view. By refusing to take the initiative or otherwise provide leadership, he had put himself in a position in which he could only react to events, not control them. In the field of defense, where Eisenhower's involvement and commitment were much deeper, the opposite situation prevailed—he had the initiative, he operated secretly, and he controlled events.

On January 24, Dulles came to see Eisenhower, filled with anxiety. Russian Ambassador Zaroubin had asked for an interview with the President. Dulles feared that Zaroubin was going to make a "very strong protest" against the Air Force "weather balloons." These balloons were part of an on-again, off-again project to obtain photographic reconnaissance information from over the Soviet Union. The U-2 was coming along, but was not quite ready; the Air Force had therefore received Eisenhower's permission to try yet another type of balloon. As a cover, the Air Force had released hundreds of the balloons, then announced that they were weather balloons participating in research for the International Geophysical Year. The things were floating over Japan, Oklahoma, the Pacific Ocean, everywhere. But the ones that mattered were over the Soviet Union, and the Russians had managed to shoot some down. Dulles thought Zaroubin would use the incident to denounce Open Skies, and that the Russians might well launch "a worldwide propaganda campaign against the United States, picking up the old charges of warmongering and all the rest." Eisenhower was a bit chagrined. "Foster may be right on his guess" about Zaroubin's mission, the President told Hagerty. "I haven't thought too much of this balloon thing and I don't blame the Russians at all. I've always thought it was sort of a dirty trick. But that was the gamble we took when we made the decision and they ought to have a good answer ready for me if I have to use it when I see the ambassador."[67] But the only answer the State Department could come up with was to stick to the "weather research" story.

The next day, Zaroubin arrived, met with Dulles and Eisenhower, and left. Eisenhower called Hagerty into his office. "Well, Jim," he said, laughing, "it wasn't what we thought. There is no mention of the balloons." Dulles joined the laughter and commented, "Maybe that's what you get for having somewhat of a guilty conscience." What Zaroubin had brought was a proposal for a twenty-year friendship treaty between the United States and the Soviet Union, an idea Dulles thought preposterous.[68]

In early February, the Russians did make a loud and public protest against the balloons, charging that the United States was engaged in military espionage. Dulles conferred with Eisenhower. The President "recalled that he . . . had been rather allergic to this project and doubted whether the results would justify the inconvenience involved." Eisenhower said he thought the operation should be suspended. Dulles cautioned that they should suspend in such a way "so it would not look as though we had been caught with jam on our fingers." But of course they had. The next day, February 7, Dulles informed the Soviets that no more balloons would be released. He did not apologize, nor did he retreat from the weather-research story.[69]

Five weeks later, Air Force Chief of Staff Twining proposed a new balloon project, one that would involve "very high-flying balloons" and that with proper funding could be ready in eighteen months. Goodpaster wrote a memorandum for the record on Eisenhower's response: "Pursuant to the President's direction, I called General Twining and told him that the President is not interested in any more balloons. General Twining said he fully understood and that would be the end of it."[70]

At the beginning of 1956, Eisenhower made an effort to revive his original Atoms for Peace proposal, and simultaneously to stop all production of fissionable material for military purposes. On January 13, acting on Strauss's recommendation, the President allocated twenty thousand kilograms of U-235 for commercial atomic power purposes, the uranium to be distributed over a period of ten years. Eisenhower also directed that if the Russians joined an international atomic pool, the U.S. would be willing to immediately allocate one thousand kilograms to it.[71] At the time, the Americans were demanding an Open Skies inspection system, while the Russians were insisting on stationary posts established within the United States and the U.S.S.R. There were so many nuances involved that Eisenhower expressed his sympathy for Stassen, the American negotiator at the disarmament talks, "because of the inherently almost insoluble character of the project." But Eisenhower told Dulles and Strauss that if the inspection system broke down, "then the international pool theory becomes an alternative that it seems to me the world would seize upon with great relief and enthusiasm." He hoped that with such a pool, both the U.S. and the U.S.S.R. could "suspend the production of fissionable material except for peaceful purposes." The pool, he thought, should be larger than the arsenal of any one nation.[72]

Disarmament was on Eisenhower's mind because he had read, in late January, a new DOD study of the damage the U.S. would suffer in a nuclear exchange with the Russians. The results were so terrifying that Eisenhower felt more strongly than ever the need to do something, anything. Aside from the inspection problem, the disarmament talks were stalled over the question of where and how to undertake reductions. The Russians wanted to reduce and even eliminate nuclear weapons, an area in which America had a clear lead; the Americans wanted to reduce ground forces, an area in which the Russians had a clear lead. Eisenhower told Goodpaster that Stassen was going to have to come up with something new. The specific American offer—to reduce the total U.S. armed forces personnel by a half million to 2.5 million total—was old, stale, and unacceptable to the Russians. And in any case, as Eisenhower told Goodpaster, "There is nothing so illusory as reduction of armament through reduction of men." Eisenhower wanted some different and more hopeful approach, but could not find it. Thus he reiterated the Atoms for Peace idea.[73]

On March 2, Eisenhower sent his formal proposal to Bulganin. If the Russians would accept Open Skies, the Americans would accept on-site inspection teams. He abandoned the previous American demand that the Russians match a 15 percent reduction in American ground forces by a 40 percent reduction of the Red Army. Instead, Eisenhower wanted to attack head on the problem of the nuclear arms race. He proposed that thereafter neither side use fissionable materials to make bombs, but instead put their production into some type of Atoms for Peace program. "My ultimate hope is that all production of fissionable materials anywhere in the world will be devoted exclusively to peaceful purposes."[74]

The JCS were uneasy with such an offer. Eisenhower assured them that he "felt it was very unlikely that the Soviets would accept our proposal, and if they were to accept, it is very unlikely that we would suffer disadvantage."[75] Eisenhower was right. Bulganin spurned the offer. The United States won some propaganda points, but the arms race went on. Its momentum was such that not even Eisenhower could slow it down, much less halt it, not to mention reverse it through actual disarmament.

The Democrats, as noted, were hard pressed to find an issue other than health or farm prices to use against Eisenhower in the presidential campaign. In February, Senator Symington of Missouri tried an issue that did not quite catch on in 1956, but which came to be a major one in 1960. It was the missile gap.

The American ballistic-missile program got started shortly after World War II, but in the cost-cutting days of the Truman Administration only a few millions of dollars had been appropriated for it (less than $7 million for ICBMs, for example). Nor did Eisenhower put any emphasis on it during his first year in office. But in 1954, following the Castle series of tests in the Pacific, the AEC reported to Eisenhower that nuclear weapons could be so drastically reduced in size that a missile could be designed and built powerful enough to carry the bombs. (Previous atomic warheads weighed nine thousand pounds.) Eisenhower then ordered research and development on missiles speeded up; in 1955 he put a half billion dollars into it, and asked for $1.2 billion in 1956. One reason for doubling the budget in 1956 was another recommendation from the scientists, that the U.S. develop an IRBM with a range of fifteen hundred miles. Eisenhower agreed, but he also divided the program and then split them again. The Air Force had two separate projects for ICBMs, Atlas and Titan; the Army (Jupiter) and the Navy (Thor) had IRBM responsibility. Within the Administration, there was some grumbling about this division of responsibility, and Eisenhower worried about the inherent waste involved because of duplication, but the President nevertheless decided that competition and the full use of all existing resources would speed development. In addition, in connection with the International Geophysical Year (which would begin in July 1957), in 1955 Eisenhower had created yet another program, Project Vanguard, designed to put an earth satellite in orbit.[76]

With all the money involved, at a time when Eisenhower was continuing to reduce appropriations for conventional forces, the President told his Cabinet that he expected "to be called on to justify this money." But to his surprise, "I find out that newcomers are saying why aren't you doing more."[77] The newcomer he had in mind was Senator Symington, who at the beginning of February 1956 charged that the United States lagged seriously behind the Soviet Union in the production and development of guided missiles. At a press conference on February 8, Eisenhower was asked to comment. "Well," he began, "I am always astonished at the amount of information that others get that I don't." He protested that he was putting money into the missile program as fast as it could be absorbed. "Now," he admonished, "there are only so many scientists." In any case, the President did not want anyone to get the idea that the Russians were in fact ahead, or that missiles were an ultimate weapon. Because they were so inaccurate, to be effective you needed to have great numbers of them, each loaded with a powerful (and thus heavy) warhead. America already had the assured capability of destroying Russia many times over. "Now, I just want to ask you one thing," Eisenhower said to the reporters, "and if there is anyone here that has got the answer to this one, you will relieve me mightily by communicating it to me here or in private: Can you picture a war that would be waged with atomic missiles . . . ?" It would just be complete, indiscriminate devastation, not "war" in any recognizable sense, "because war is a contest, and you finally get to a point [with missiles] where you are talking merely about race suicide, and nothing else."[78]

Despite Eisenhower's assurances about America's position in the missile race, and despite his warnings about the outcome of such a race, the Democrats continued to go after the President for not spending enough on missiles. At a Republican leaders' meeting on February 14, the congressmen asked Eisenhower how to respond to the attack. He told them to point out that the B-52 was a much better means of delivery of much larger bombs. So was the Russian bomber, the IL-28, which "cannot adequately be defended against. We know that and the Russians know it." But, Eisenhower concluded, he "did not want to belittle the importance of missiles for there was obviously a large psychological factor." Charley Martin said the Democrats were charging that the President did not know what was going on. "When I listen to Symington," Eisenhower said, laughing, "I think I don't!!" Then he added, "I want guided missiles as soon as possible."[79]

The Democrats kept pounding. At the next leaders' meeting, on February 28, Eisenhower assured the anxious Republicans that "the agitation is purely political in my opinion." He said the Administration was spending as much as could be spent. "It is clear that more money cannot be used." He reminded them again of the great destructive power the U.S. already possessed. "After a certain point, there is no use in having more, no matter what quantity. If we have all we need to create the devastation we know we can create, what the hell is the use of more?" Eisenhower also expressed his serious doubts about missiles in general: "I'll wager my life I can sit on any base we've got and in the next ten years the Russians can't hit me with any guided missile."[80]

Symington, along with Senator Henry Jackson of Washington, was saying that the Russians had developed an IRBM with a range of fifteen hundred miles. The AEC told Eisenhower that the Russians "have never got any up to one thousand miles." The various American programs, Eisenhower asserted, were stressing accuracy, not distance. The President told Hagerty, "If we stopped guiding and other things, we could get all sorts of distances that would scare them to death."[81]

Much as Eisenhower yearned to take missiles out of the area of partisan politics, he could not. Reporters continued to ask him about various Democratic charges; he continued to be calming and reassuring in his answers, admitting only that missiles had "a very great psychological value."[82] Eisenhower also had to deal with Bernard Baruch, who wrote the President a series of alarming letters about the need for greater progress in missiles. Baruch's sense of self-importance was unlimited, as was his penchant for being a bore, but as Eisenhower noted, "because of his standing and reputation in the public mind," he had to be treated seriously. Eisenhower spent part of the afternoon of March 28 with Baruch, trying to explain to him the entire strategic situation. Further, Eisenhower recorded in his diary, "I tried to show him that we are already employing so many of the nation's scientists and research facilities that even the expenditure of a vastly greater amount could scarcely produce any additional results." Baruch wanted Eisenhower to appoint a missile czar and put him in charge of a "Manhattan Project." Eisenhower repeated that the scientific community could not absorb any additional funds, and that the military was doing satisfactory work on the missile projects already in place.[83]

In January 1956, Prime Minister Eden flew to Washington for talks with Eisenhower and Dulles. They discussed numerous international problems, such as the admission of Red China to the United Nations (Eisenhower was firmly opposed) and the situation in the Formosa Straits (quiet). Both sides agreed to support Diem of South

Vietnam in his refusal to hold the nationwide elections that had been promised in the Geneva Accords, and to cite as a reason the various violations of the accords by the North Vietnamese.[84] But the real subject that was on Eden's mind was the Middle East.

The situation in the Middle East was the most intractable political problem in the world. In January 1956, Eisenhower came face-to-face with it, and as he said in his memoirs, from that time on "no region of the world received as much of my close attention . . ."[85] Like his predecessor and his successors, Eisenhower found that when he faced the problem, he was beset by a bewildering variety of conflicting desires and demands. Some of these difficulties emerged in the Eden talks. The PM hinted that he thought Nasser would have to be removed. The President expressed surprise at this. He recalled that Nasser had come to power two years earlier, promising reform and modernization for Egypt, and that he had worked out an arrangement with the British whereby the British had withdrawn their eighty thousand troops from Egypt, but retained their share of ownership of the Suez Canal (France was the other principal owner). Eisenhower wondered why Eden had lost confidence in Nasser. The notetaker recorded, "Mr. Eden replied it was difficult to evaluate Nasser who was a man of limitless ambition." Dulles remarked that "he did not mind ambition, which was a healthy thing that could be played upon." Dulles said his own fear about Nasser was that he "might have become a tool of the Russians."[86]

Dulles was referring to another of the dilemmas in the Middle East—namely, how to keep the Russians out of the area. But bumbling by the State Department, and by Eisenhower, had practically invited them in. A few months after taking power, Nasser asked for American arms. He needed them for the border war being waged along the Gaza Strip, and to strengthen his army, which was inferior to the Israeli Army in numbers, equipment, leadership, and morale. The State Department agreed to sell $27 million worth of arms to Egypt, but only for cash. Nasser turned to the Communists. In October 1955, he concluded an arms deal with Czechoslovakia. Egypt got five times more hardware than it would have received from the U.S. and was allowed to pay by barter arrangement, Egyptian cotton for Czech arms.[87]

The shipment of Communist arms to Egypt, Eden said, violated the Tripartite Declaration of 1950 in which the United States, the U.K., and France had pledged to maintain the *status quo* in the Middle East by not selling major quantities of military equipment to either the Jews or the Arabs. Eden proposed that the three Western powers "put teeth" in the declaration by turning it into a military alliance designed to enforce the arms embargo. Neither Eisenhower nor Dulles liked that idea. Then Eden tried to draw them into the Baghdad Pact, which had a long and tortuous history. Dulles had first proposed the pact to seal off Russia from the south. The line ran from Pakistan through Iran, Iraq, and Turkey. In 1955, Eden, enthusiastic about the idea, joined with those four countries in the Baghdad Pact. Then he learned that the United States had decided not to join. Dulles wanted Britain to take the lead in the Middle East, as the U.S. was doing with SEATO. Further, neither Dulles nor Eisenhower could see why the United States should alienate both Egypt and Israel by joining a pact whose avowed goal was to stop Soviet expansion but whose real purpose was, according to Egypt, to preserve British colonial power in the Middle East. For their part, the Israelis feared that the pact was intended by the British to create a unified Arab world to crush the Jewish state. America had nothing to win by joining, Eisenhower told Eden, and would not. So Eden went home with nothing to show for his troubles except a final communiqué grandly titled "The Declaration of Washington." It noted the "unity of purpose of our two countries," and it vowed that "we shall never initiate violence."[88]

For all his professions to Eden about "unity of purpose" and for all his promises about coordinating policies in the Middle East, Eisenhower in fact had set out on a course of his own. Like his predecessor and his successors, he could not resist the temptation to try personal diplomacy. He would send an American envoy who enjoyed the President's absolute confidence to act as a mediator between Egypt and Israel, and to offer financial inducements for them to make peace. The man Eisenhower chose was Robert Anderson. They met on January 11 in the White House to discuss the offer Anderson was going to take on his secret mission. Eisenhower wanted to avert an arms race in the Middle East, with the United States and the U.S.S.R. as suppliers, but he knew to avoid it there had to be peace between Israel and Egypt. Eisenhower gave Anderson a letter to Nasser and to the Israeli Prime Minister, David Ben-Gurion, establishing Anderson's credentials to speak for the President. Eisenhower then authorized Anderson to verbally offer both sides almost whatever they might want in the way of material aid as a reward for making the concessions necessary to achieve peace. "Eisenhower," Anderson later recalled, "just about gave me carte blanche."[89]

Anderson left in the middle of January. He tried everything. He flew back and forth, held secret meetings, promised American money to solve all the problems of both countries. Both sides were willing enough to take American money, but neither would yield on any specific issue. Anderson proposed that the Palestine refugees be resettled throughout the Arab world at American expense. Nasser could not agree to such a callous destruction of a people. Israel was ready to accept an American guarantee of her borders, but not to withdraw to the borders assigned to her by the U.N. in 1948. Nasser agreed that Anderson could serve as an intermediary between him and Ben-Gurion, but said he could not meet with the Israeli leader because he would be assassinated if he did. Ben-Gurion said he would meet with Nasser, but would not agree to use Anderson's services as an intermediary. Then Ben-Gurion asked about arms from the U.S. That Eisenhower had not authorized Anderson to offer, and he did not.[90]

Anderson made one further trip, with equally fruitless results. Eisenhower was distressd, but he could see no alternative to continuing the basic course of attempting to be "friends with both contestants in that region in order that we can bring them closer together. To take sides could do nothing but to destroy our influence in leading toward a peaceful settlement of one of the most explosive situations in the world today." But he was already tilting against Nasser, because he blamed Nasser, not Ben-Gurion, for the failure of the Anderson mission. That was a patently unfair judgment—each side was intransigent—and Eisenhower's deeper motivation was his fear of the Pan-Arab movement Nasser was trying to create. More aware than most observers of the dependence of Europe on Arab oil, Eisenhower's worst-case scenario had Egypt forming a united Arab world that would be allied with the Soviet Union. So in his diary entry of March 8, in which he said he would not take sides, he went on to write, "We have reached the point where it looks as if Egypt, under Nasser, is going to make no move whatsoever" to make peace. Meanwhile "the Arabs . . . are daily growing more arrogant." Therefore "it would begin to appear that our efforts should be directed toward separating the Saudi Arabians from the Egyptians." This was the germ of an idea Eisenhower would soon be pursuing actively, that of making King Saud of Saudi Arabia into Nasser's rival for leadership in the Arab world, then linking Saud firmly to the West.

Eisenhower concluded his diary entry, "I am certain of one thing. If Egypt finds herself thus isolated from the rest of the Arab world, and with no ally in sight except Soviet Russia, she would very quickly get sick of that prospect and would join us in the search for a just and decent peace in that region."[91]

On March 28, Eisenhower met with Dulles, Radford, Wilson, and others to discuss Nasser. At Eisenhower's request, Dulles had a memorandum ready, proposing a new policy, one designed "to let Colonel Nasser realize that he cannot cooperate as he is doing with the Soviet Union and at the same time enjoy most-favored-nation treatment from the United States." Dulles also wished to avoid an open break "which would throw Nasser irrevocably into a Soviet satellite status." To achieve these contradictory goals, Dulles proposed to maintain the Western arms embargo against Egypt, to "continue to delay the conclusion of current negotiations on the High Aswan Dam," to suspend CARE package shipments to Egypt, to "give increased support to the Baghdad Pact without actually adhering to the pact," and to speed negotiations with the Saudis by assuring King Saud "that some of his military needs will immediately be met and others provided for subsequently."[92]

There was no solution, easy or hard. By refusing to support Egypt or to sell arms to Israel, and by insisting on coordinating American policy with Britain's, Eisenhower had lost control of the situation. Or rather failed to gain control, as neither he nor anyone else had ever gotten a grip on the Middle East. Eisenhower and his advisers were reduced to speculation on what they might have to do if the worst happened. Both Dulles and Radford told Eisenhower that if Egypt attacked Israel, using Russian arms, "there is no question that war would be forced upon us." In that event, "We would have to occupy the entire area, protect the pipelines and the Suez Canal, etc."[93]

CHAPTER FOURTEEN

The Tyranny of the Weak

April–September 1956

IT WAS A CURIOUS FACT, but true—the man who made the D-Day decision, and countless others since, the man who insisted upon keeping control of events in his own hands, in 1956 was unable to decide who his own running mate should be and left control of the decision in other people's hands.

Had he wanted Nixon, all he needed to do was say one word at any time in the first half of 1956 and that would have been that. Had he wanted to dump Nixon, all he needed to do was say one word and he would have been rid of the Vice-President. But instead of saying the word on this momentous subject, fraught with significance for the post-Eisenhower Presidency, Eisenhower remained silent, thereby turning the decision over to others. His indecision can only be seen as an indication of his ambiguous and complex attitude toward Nixon.

The adjectives Eisenhower used to describe Nixon in his private diary are generally cold and indifferent; Nixon was "quick," or "loyal," or "dependable." Eisenhower told Arthur Larson (the leading Republican intellectual, a law school dean who had joined the Administration as director of USIA) that Nixon "isn't the sort of person you turn to when you want a new idea, but he has an uncanny ability to draw upon others' ideas and bring out their essence in a cool-headed way."[1]

Eisenhower's most persistent complaints about Nixon were that he was too political and too immature. As to the first charge, it was as much Eisenhower's fault as Nixon's. Although obviously Nixon enjoyed blasting the Democrats, and although Eisenhower frequently told him to tone it down, it was nevertheless the case that Eisenhower used Nixon in both presidential campaigns, as well as in the off-year congressional elections, for the hard-hitting partisan speeches, which allowed the President to stay above the battle. As to the second charge, Eisenhower's comments to Larson were typical of those he made to many others. When Nixon was forty-five years old, in 1958, Eisenhower told Larson, "You know, Dick has matured." Six years later, in 1964, Eisenhower repeated, "You know, Dick has matured." Three years after that, in 1967, Eisenhower reminded Larson, "You know, Dick has really matured."[2] But in the spring of 1956, when Eisenhower had to make the crucial decision about Nixon's career, he told Emmet Hughes (who had taken a leave from Time-Life to write speeches for the campaign), "Well, the fact is, of course, I've watched Dick a long time, and he just hasn't grown. So I just haven't honestly been able to believe that he *is* presidential timber."[3]

Or so at least Hughes claimed Eisenhower said, and perhaps he did, but if so that leaves another problem. In 1956, Eisenhower was a sixty-five-year-old heart-attack victim. There was a good chance he would not live through a second term. Eisenhower loved his country and wanted the best for it. If he thought Nixon was not the best, much less unqualified to be President, Eisenhower was the one man in America who could push Nixon out of the Vice-Presidency, in order to get a man whom he trusted to serve as his potential successor. But he either could not find such a man, or, having found him, could not persuade him to take on the job of ousting Nixon.

Eisenhower's personal choice was Robert Anderson. He said so in his diary frequently, in his private correspondence, and in his conversations with his closest friends. And he said so to Anderson himself. In early April 1956, after Anderson had returned from his abortive mission to the Middle East, Eisenhower invited him to the Oval Office. "I want to talk with you about *your* future," Eisenhower began. "I've observed what you've done. We work well together. As President I have to spend all my time on international affairs; I'd like you, as Vice-President, to spend most of yours with the leaders of the party." Anderson, who had already had a number of feelers from Eisenhower about his interest in the vice-presidential nomination, was hardly surprised, and was firm in his rejection. He pointed out that as a lifelong Democrat he would not be acceptable to the Republican Party, and in any case he had neither the ambition nor the drive to be President.

Eisenhower accepted Anderson's decision, but did not give up; in 1960 he again urged Anderson to try for the nomination, saying that "I'll quit what I'm doing, Bob, I'll raise money, I'll make speeches. I'll do *anything* to help. Just tell me I'm at liberty." Still Anderson said no.[4]

Having failed to persuade Anderson, Eisenhower returned to his passive role in the selection of his running mate. He was detached and seemingly uninterested. When Eisenhower said at a March 7 press conference that he had told Nixon to "chart out his own course," most observers took this to mean (in Nixon's words) "varying degrees of indifference toward me, or even an attempt to put some distance between us." Nixon, perplexed and irritated, drafted an announcement saying he would not be a candidate in 1956. He showed it to an aide, who informed the White House. Within hours Jerry Persons and Len Hall came to Nixon's office to urge him to destroy the draft, because if he withdrew, "the Republican Party would be split in two." Nixon said that it was impossible for the Vice-President to "chart out his own course." If Eisenhower did not want him on the ticket, he was not going to fight for it. "I can only assume that if he puts it this way, this must be his way of saying he'd prefer someone else." Hall said this was not at all the case and reassured Nixon that the ticket would be Ike and Dick.[5]

On April 9 Eisenhower met with Nixon. The President, to Nixon's consternation, continued to urge him to take a Cabinet post, perhaps HEW or Commerce, in order to build his administrative experience. But, Eisenhower added, "I still insist you must make your decision as to what you want to do. If the answer is yes, I will be happy to have you on the ticket." He urged Nixon to take his time. After Nixon left, Eisenhower called Hall into his office to tell him that "in some areas there were still great oppositions to Dick." Hall, one of Nixon's strongest supporters, demurred. Eisenhower said, "I personally like and admire Dick, and he could not have done better, [but] I think he is making a mistake by wanting the [VP] job."[6]

On April 25, at a press conference, Eisenhower was asked if Nixon had yet charted his own course and reported back to the President. "Well," Eisenhower replied, "he hasn't reported back in the terms in which I used the expression . . . no." The following morning, Nixon asked for an appointment with the President. That afternoon, in the Oval Office, Nixon told Eisenhower, "I would be honored to continue as Vice-President under you." Eisenhower said he was pleased with Nixon's decision. The President got Hagerty on the telephone. "Dick has just told me that he'll stay on the ticket," Eisenhower said. "Why don't you take him out right now and let him tell the reporters himself. And," he added, "you can tell them that I'm delighted by the news."[7]

That seemed simple and straightforward enough, but difficulties ensued. On June 7, Eisenhower was stricken with an ileitis attack. He had suffered serious stomach problems for years, but this time the pain was so severe that he was rushed to Walter Reed Hospital. A proper diagnosis was finally made (ileitis is a young man's disease, which was why it had not been suspected previously). Eisenhower was informed that he would have to undergo an immediate, serious operation. He indicated his approval, and between 3 and 5 A.M. on June 8, a successful bypass operation was conducted. There was tremendous concern about subjecting a heart-attack victim to such a long operation, but it could not be avoided, and Eisenhower's quick recovery soon laid to rest the Republican fears that he would not be able to run again. Eisenhower himself, at a press conference, compared the excitement caused by his illness to the Battle of the Bulge. He said that in December 1944, "I didn't get frightened until three weeks after it had begun, when I began to read the American papers and found . . . how near we were to being whipped." So too with the ileitis operation; he claimed he had never been afraid until he began to read the papers.

When William McGaffin of the Chicago *Daily News* suggested that the American people loved Eisenhower so much that they would vote against him because "they are afraid you won't live for another four years," Eisenhower replied: "Well, sir, I would tell you, frankly, I don't think it is too important to the individual how his end comes, and certainly he can't dictate the time." There was never any doubt in his mind; he intended to stay in the race.[8]

To prove his capacity to serve, in July, after recuperating from his operation at Gettysburg, Eisenhower made a trip to Panama for a meeting of the Presidents of the Americas. On July 20, the day before Eisenhower left Washington, Harold Stassen came to see him. Like nearly every other Republican, Stassen was delighted that Eisenhower was staying in the race. Like some other Republicans, Eisenhower's surgery had Stassen worried about the increased importance of the vice-presidential nomination. The possibility of Nixon's succeeding Eisenhower was not, however, what Stassen talked about. Instead, he showed Eisenhower a private poll he had taken which indicated that Nixon's name on the ticket would cost the Republicans 4 to 6 percent of the electorate. Such losses, Stassen asserted, would in turn cost the Republicans control of Congress.

How Eisenhower replied is unknown. He did not turn his recording device on, and when the subject was purely political, Goodpaster
stayed out of the office. Eisenhower had earlier fretted over polls that
roughly paralleled Stassen's, and may have been impressed by Stassen's
figures. But in his memoirs, Eisenhower claimed that "Mr. Stassen's
attitude was astonishing to me . . ."[9] That could hardly have been
so; the fear that Nixon would cost votes in November was a frequent
topic of his conversation. Whatever Eisenhower said to Stassen (according to his memoirs, it was: "You are an American citizen, Harold,
and free to follow your own judgment . . ."), he did not tell Stassen
to stop.[10] That he did not may indicate how tempted he was by the
thought of getting rid of Nixon, an interpretation that gains strength
when one considers Stassen's suggested replacement, Governor Christian Herter of Massachusetts. Herter's name had not appeared on any
of Eisenhower's numerous lists of possible successors. Although Eisenhower had a high opinion of Herter, he could not have expected
Herter to add much to the ticket. Herter was sixty-one years old, suffered badly from arthritis, was identified with Harvard and the East
Coast Republicans, and was not a lively campaigner. Herter was, in
fact, one of the worst possible choices Stassen could have made, which
makes it all the more remarkable that Eisenhower did not put a stop
to the "dump Nixon" move immediately.

July 20 was a hard day for Eisenhower. Before meeting with Stassen, he had dealt with Nasser's vehement protests over the announcement that the United States would not help Egypt finance the Aswan
Dam. When Stassen left the office, Larson went in. "Art," the President asked, "have you ever been Nasserized and Stassenized on the
same day?" Then he referred to Stassen's poll and said that if Nixon
was going to cost him 6 percent, "that's serious."[11]

On July 23, while Eisenhower was in Panama, Stassen called a
press conference. He announced that Eisenhower had approved the
idea of an open convention, and that he personally was supporting
Herter for Vice-President. When Eisenhower was told, he instructed
Hagerty to issue a statement stressing Stassen's right as an American
to campaign for whomever he wished, but that he could not conduct
independent political activity and remain a member of the "official
family." Eisenhower was therefore giving Stassen a leave of absence
without pay until after the convention.[12]

It was all quite unusual, and had most observers confused—but
not Nixon. He reasoned that what Stassen was doing was *not* promoting Herter, but rather using the obviously unsuitable Herter to
throw the vice-presidential nomination open. There were, Nixon

darkly observed, "several potential vice presidential candidates eagerly waiting in the wings for just such a situation."[13] Nixon was quite possibly right in thinking that Eisenhower was trying to use the Stassen/Herter combination to open the nomination, which is to say, to get rid of Nixon. Eisenhower had tried Anderson and failed. He evidently was not averse to trying Stassen/Herter.

But by the time Eisenhower got back to Washington, on July 26, he discovered that Stassen had blundered. The Republican Party was outraged. Among numerous protests Eisenhower received from prominent politicians, the one that stood out was an endorsement of Nixon by 180 of the 203 House Republicans.[14] That was a statement of party preference so direct and clear that Eisenhower could not ignore it. The party as a whole had not previously had an opportunity to speak out on Nixon (although he had done very well with write-in votes in the New Hampshire primary). Eisenhower's offer to Anderson of second spot on the ticket was made in private; Eisenhower's offer to Nixon to chart his own course had been worded in such a way that few dared protest. But the Stassen news conference gave the party regulars the chance to speak out, and they did. When they did, they showed that Nixon had a power base of his own. It was neither as wide nor as deep as Eisenhower's, except within the Republican Party organization, which was where it counted at a convention. Old Guard Republicans still did not regard Eisenhower as a true Republican, they objected strongly to nearly all his domestic programs, and they saw Nixon as the only link between the RNC and the Administration. If Eisenhower tried to dump Nixon, they would rebel, especially over such an inappropriate substitute as Herter. Nixon had built his strength through his Checkers speech, through his exemplary behavior as Vice-President, most of all following Eisenhower's heart attack, and through his unflagging efforts on behalf of the party. There was scarcely a Republican county chairman in the country who did not owe Nixon a favor. If Eisenhower wanted to be rid of Nixon, he was going to have to do it himself, not through the bumbling Stassen.

Eisenhower chose not to do it himself. Instead, he decided to act behind the scenes to put a stop to the Herter nonsense. The President had Sherman Adams tell Herter that there was a job waiting for him in the State Department, but that if he wished to be a candidate for the vice-presidential nomination, that was his choice. However, if Herter did enter the race, the State Department position "would not be possible." Herter said that he was not a candidate, and in fact that he would place Nixon's name in nomination at the San Francisco convention.[15]

Eisenhower still held back from a public endorsement of Nixon. At Eisenhower's August 1 press conference, James Reston asked if it was fair to conclude that Nixon was his preference. Eisenhower said Reston could conclude whatever he pleased, "but I have said that I would not express a preference. I have said he is perfectly acceptable to me, as he was in 1952 [when] I also put down a few others that were equally acceptable to me."[16] Eisenhower insisted that the Republicans were going to have an open convention and nominate the best men for the ticket. Merriman Smith reminded him that he had said some weeks earlier that if anyone came into his office to propose a "dump Nixon" move, he would create quite a commotion in his office. "Have you created such a commotion in the wake of Mr. Stassen's recommendation?" "No," the President replied, because "no one ever proposed to me that I dump Mr. Nixon. No one, I think, would have that effrontery."[17]

That was just an outright denial of the plain truth, and thus an indication of how impossible Eisenhower found his situation to be. No matter how often he insisted that the choice of a vice-presidential candidate was the responsibility of the delegates to the convention, and not his, he knew perfectly well that he could dictate that choice if he wanted to do so. But except for Anderson, he saw no rival to Nixon who did not also have, like Nixon, severe disadvantages. Eisenhower did not decide to dump Nixon, nor did he decide to keep him. He turned the decision over to Len Hall, the RNC, and the delegates, and their overwhelming choice was Nixon.

Eisenhower almost seemed to enjoy keeping Nixon in a state of high tension. When Cliff Roberts called him on July 27, Eisenhower pointed out that "there's one little thing" about the Stassen business: "It did stir up some interest." The Democrats were engaged in a highly publicized contest for the presidential nomination (between Stevenson, Harriman, and Kefauver, among others); the Republicans, by contrast, were dull and stodgy. Eisenhower said he was pleased about Stassen's attempt, because "our program has been so cut and dried, a little interest won't hurt."[18] But he must have known that his failure to issue a clear endorsement of Nixon hurt Nixon personally and politically and added to the coldness between the two men that had started at the time of the Nixon fund crisis of 1952.

Despite Eisenhower's muddled response to the dump Nixon movement of 1956, however, it must be emphasized that it would be incorrect to state that Eisenhower found Nixon unsatisfactory. Given Eisenhower's health and age, the chances of the VP nominee of 1956 becoming President sometime before 1960 were high. Potentially,

Eisenhower's choice of a running mate in 1956 was among the most important decisions of his life. While it was true that he did not choose Nixon, it was also true that he did not reject Nixon. When he said Nixon was acceptable, he meant it. At his August 1 news conference, he pointed out the obvious to the press: "If any man were nominated as Vice-President that the President felt he could not, in good conscience, run with, he would have just one recourse; to submit his own resignation."[19] Eisenhower did not think that there was anyone in the country, other than Anderson and himself, qualified to be President. But he was willing to turn the country over to Nixon. That in itself was the highest possible compliment he could pay to Nixon.

Aside from the excitement over the VP, the Republican preconvention activity was quiet and dignified. In 1952, Eisenhower and the Republicans had won a campaign in which they took the offensive, leveling various accusations against the Democrats. In 1956, Eisenhower intended to run on the defensive, pointing to his record of accomplishments instead of to the shortcomings of the opposition. Given the record levels of employment, the general prosperity, and the achievement of peace in the world, pointing to the record was obviously a wise and prudent decision. In addition, Eisenhower had many specific pieces of legislation he could point to with pride; his own favorite was the National System of Interstate and Defense Highways, which he signed into law on June 29, 1956.

There were, however, three outstanding problems the Republicans had to face in the weeks before the convention. First was civil rights. Second was the Middle East, where the situation threatened to escalate to a war that would damage Eisenhower's reputation as a peacemaker. Third was the festering sore in East Europe, recently made worse by Khrushchev's secret speech denouncing Stalin and hinting at a liberalization of the Soviet control of the area.

On civil rights, Eisenhower's chief initiative in the summer of 1956 was Brownell's civil-rights bill. Republican leaders were cautious about the bill; although they loved putting the Democrats on the defensive by forcing the southern senators to take a stand, they worried about losing their best chance to crack the Solid South. They therefore advised Eisenhower to go slow, and told him Brownell's bill was too stringent. Eisenhower told the leaders that Brownell had been under terrific pressure "from radicals on his staff" to write an even tougher bill, and that the one Brownell had produced could hardly be "more moderate or less provocative." He complained that the southerners, who were already denouncing the bill, had not even bothered to read it. But then he turned his attention to the other side, saying that "these civil-rights people" never consider that although the President could "send in the military," he could not "make them operate the schools." He then repeated a little story he had heard from Bobby Jones down at Augusta; one of the field hands was supposed to have said, "If someone doesn't shut up around here, particularly these Negroes from the North, they're going to get a lot of us niggers killed!"[20]

Brownell sent his civil-rights bill to Congress. After prolonged infighting, in July the House passed the two mildest provisions of the bill, one creating a bipartisan commission to investigate racial difficulties, the other establishing a civil-rights division in the Justice Department. Voting rights and federal responsibility for enforcing civil rights were dropped from the compromise package. Nevertheless, the bill died in the Senate Judiciary Committee, where the chairman was Senator James Eastland of Mississippi.

Despite his formal support for Brownell's civil-rights bill, the President was not badly disappointed. He believed that "civil rights will not be achieved by law alone." He told Jerry Persons that "leaders must be encouraged to appeal to the moral obligation of our people rather than refer only to the law." Eisenhower indicated to Persons that he thought racial progress had been set back, not gone forward, as a result of the *Brown* decision.[21]

Two weeks later, a few days before the convention, Eisenhower told Whitman that he felt civil rights was the most important domestic problem facing the government. He said he wished that the Court had ordered desegregation first in the graduate schools, later in the colleges, then the high schools, and only after that in the grade schools.[22] Meanwhile the Republicans had a platform to write. Eisenhower called Deputy Attorney General William Rogers to tell him that the Justice Department draft of its plank in the platform had to be softened. "What are you going to do," Eisenhower demanded of Rogers, "get an injunction against the governor of Georgia, for instance?" Eisenhower indicated that he deplored the possibility of a federal-state confrontation on desegregation.[23] The next day, August 14, Eisenhower called Brownell, already in San Francisco, to tell Brownell to rewrite the section that said "the Eisenhower Administration . . . and the Republican Party" supported the *Brown* decision. Eisenhower ordered the words "Eisenhower Administration" deleted. Then he told Brownell "that in this business he was between the compulsion of duty on one side, and his firm conviction, on the other, that because of the Supreme Court's ruling, the whole issue had been set back badly." Brownell argued his case, with some success: Eisenhower eventually allowed him to state that "the Republican Party accepts" school desegregation.[24]

A major feature of the 1952 Republican platform had been the call for "liberation" of the East European satellites. Nothing that Eisenhower or his associates had done since had brought liberation any closer; indeed, as noted, Dulles thought that Eisenhower's going to the Geneva summit had signaled an American acquiescence in Soviet domination of East Europe. But in the spring of 1956, as a result of action by the Russians, not the Americans, the prospects for liberation suddenly seemed bright again.

In his famous secret speech to the Twentieth Party Congress, Khrushchev denounced Stalin for his crimes against the Russian people, and seemed to promise that in the future there would be a relaxation of Communist controls both inside Russia and in the satellite countries. The CIA obtained a copy of the speech; with Eisenhower's permission, Allen Dulles gave it to *The New York Times*. On June 5, the paper printed the speech in its entirety. Publication caused great excitement throughout East Europe. Perhaps, just perhaps, the long-awaited breakup of the Soviet empire was at hand. Republicans wanted another strong plank on liberation. Eisenhower insisted that they proceed cautiously. He told Persons "that this particular plank should make it clear that we advocate liberation by all peaceful means, but not to give any indication that we advocate going to the point of war to accomplish this liberation."[25]

Nor was Eisenhower ready to go to war over Suez. Some were, especially the British. Eden was engaging in provocative warmongering against Egypt; Israel was conducting border raids against her neighbors; Nasser was making inflammatory speeches. Eisenhower wanted to be friends with all sides. On April 7, in a telephone conversation with Dulles about the Middle East, Eisenhower said, "We can't do any one of these things in a vacuum—have to look at rounded picture—everybody has got to have something."[26] Since "everybody" included the British, the French, the Egyptians, the Israelis, and the other Arabs, that policy statement contained some major inherent contradictions, but they did not keep Eisenhower from trying. On April 10, Eisenhower again called Dulles, to remind him of the key importance of Saudi Arabia. Eisenhower "wondered if there was any way we could

flatter or compliment King Saud," and later in the conversation returned to the subject, saying, "We must find some way to be friends
with King Saud."[27] On April 30, Eisenhower wrote David Ben-Gurion,
the Israeli Prime Minister, who had asked to buy arms from the
United States. "We are not persuaded that it would serve the cause of
peace and stability in the world for the United States now to accede to
your request for arms sales."[28]

Within the context of those three goals—something for everybody, improvement of American relations with the Saudis, and avoiding an arms race in the Middle East with Russia and America as the
suppliers—Eisenhower wanted his own military option. On May 1, he
talked to Dulles about putting some American arms on a ship in the
eastern Mediterranean "for quick delivery to whichever country was
the victim of aggression." Eisenhower said he liked the idea and
wanted it implemented. Eisenhower also told Dulles to "be prepared
to give some substantial amount of armaments to the Saudis."[29]

Nasser, meanwhile, continued to provoke the Americans. In late
May, he announced that Egypt was withdrawing recognition of
Chiang's government and recognizing that of Red China. He also
seemed to be blackmailing the United States over the most important
immediate question in U.S.-Egyptian relations, the financing of the
Aswan Dam. In December 1955, the United States, in Eisenhower's
words, had "all but committed ourselves" to help in the financing of
the dam. No great sums were involved (a grant of $70 million and a
loan of $200 million, with Britain paying about 20 percent), but op-
position was strong. Pro-Israeli senators, southerners worried about increased Egyptian cotton production, and Old Guard opponents of any
kind of foreign aid banded together to try to block the deal. Humphrey warned that the Egyptians would not be able to pay back. Eisenhower wanted to reduce Nasser's influence. Dulles was furious with
Nasser because of the arms deal with the Czechs and the recognition
of Red China. The Aswan Dam deal, in short, had almost no support
within the United States. Eisenhower could see nothing to be gained
by going through with it. He therefore agreed with Dulles to stall on
the talks to build the dam. That added to American annoyance and
led Eisenhower to mutter about blackmail.[30]

Nevertheless, Eisenhower felt "obligated" to go through with the
offer, and on June 20 sent Eugene Black, president of the World Bank,
to Cairo to brief Nasser on a final offer. Nasser objected to some of the
conditions and made a counterproposal that included conditions "unacceptable" to Eisenhower. This gave Eisenhower the excuse he had

been searching for to back out. On July 19, the Egyptian ambassador called on Dulles. According to Eisenhower's memoirs, he came to "issue a new demand for a huge commitment . . ." According to Eisenhower's contemporary diary, "Nasser sent us a message to the effect that he had withdrawn all of the conditions that he had laid down and was ready to proceed under our original offer."[31] But it was too late for Nasser. Eisenhower had decided that he wanted to "weaken Nasser." The deal was off. Dulles so informed the Egyptian ambassador that afternoon.

Nasser said he was astonished. Dulles replied that he had no reason to be. Eisenhower was nevertheless bothered by the charge of a double cross, and expressed to Dulles his concern with the "abrupt" manner in which the Egyptians had been informed. Dulles explained to the President that "telephone conversations of which we learned indicated that the Egyptian government knew that when they came . . . to get a definitive reply it would be negative."[32] Dulles' interpretation was shaky—the phone-tap information he had was based on Egyptian conversations *before* Nasser withdrew his conditions; surely Nasser expected his act of compromise to elicit a favorable response from the Americans.

Whether Nasser knew in advance or not, his next act was a bold one. On July 26, Nasser nationalized the Suez Canal and took control of its operations. "The fat," as Eisenhower said in his memoirs, "was now really in the fire."[33]

Eden was ready for action. On July 27, he sent a cable to Eisenhower, arguing that the West could not allow Nasser to seize Suez and get away with it. They must act at once, together, or American and British influence throughout the Middle East would be "irretrievably undermined." He said that the interests of all maritime nations were at stake, because the Egyptians did not have the technical competence to run the canal. Eden said he was preparing military plans and said the West must be ready, as a last resort, to "bring Nasser to his senses" by force.[34]

Eisenhower hardly viewed the situation so seriously; he felt "there was no reason to panic." He dispatched Robert Murphy to London, with instructions to "just go over and hold the fort. See what it's all about."[35] More particularly, he wanted Murphy to make certain "that any sweeping action to be taken regarding Nasser and the Canal should not be an act of the 'Big Three Club,' " and he warned Murphy to keep the French from relating the canal seizure to the Egyptian-Israeli hostilities. In order to stall and delay, so that emotions could quiet down, Eisenhower also wanted Murphy to propose a conference of interested nations.[36]

Murphy convinced Eden to agree to a conference. On July 31, with that news in hand, Eisenhower met with the Dulles brothers, Admiral Arleigh Burke, the Chief of Naval Operations, Under Secretary Hoover, Humphrey, and Goodpaster to discuss the situation. But then another message from Eden arrived. According to Goodpaster's notes, "In essence it stated that the British had taken a firm, considered decision to 'break Nasser' and to initiate hostilities at an early date for this purpose (estimating six weeks to be required for setting up the operation)." Eisenhower opened the discussion by saying "he considered this to be a very unwise decision on [Eden's] part." The United States could not support military action without prior congressional approval, which would not be forthcoming in this case, and in any event Eisenhower "felt that the British were out of date in thinking of this as a mode of action." He thought serious and effective counterproposals could be made via the agency of a conference of maritime nations; if the British rejected them, or attacked before they could be made, "the Middle East oil would undoubtedly dry up, and Western hemisphere oil would have to be diverted to Europe, thus requiring controls to be instituted in the United States." Eisenhower said he thought Dulles himself should go to London at once to make the American position clear to Eden.

Humphrey supported Eisenhower. He said the British "were simply trying to reverse the trend away from colonialism, and turn the clock back fifty years," which could not be done. Admiral Burke, however, said "the JCS are of the view that Nasser must be broken." Therefore, if the United Kingdom used force, "we should declare ourselves in support of their action." Eisenhower interjected the view that "it was wrong to give undue stress to Nasser himself. He felt Nasser embodies the emotional demands of the people of the area for independence and for 'slapping the white Man down.'" To join with the British against Nasser, he warned, "might well array the world from Dakar to the Philippine Islands against us." Better to try to split the other Arabs, especially the Saudis, away from Egypt and Nasser than to try to destroy Nasser. Dulles' position was complex. He thought that "Nasser must be made to disgorge his theft," but he also reminded the group that "the British went into World War I and World War II without the United States, on the calculation that we would be bound to come in," and they were thinking they could make it happen again.

Eisenhower too was drawn in different directions by his various desires and needs. He said that the U.S. "must let the British know how gravely we view this matter, what an error we think their decision is, and how this course of action would antagonize the American people . . ." But as to the British claims that Egypt had committed a crime, Eisenhower could only say that "the power of eminent domain within its own territory could scarcely be doubted," and that "Nasser was within his rights." As to the British claim that the Egyptians could not run the canal, Eisenhower scoffed at it. The Panama Canal, he said, was a much more complex operation; he had no doubt the Egyptians could run it. But he also said that "thinking of our situation in Panama, we must not let Nasser get away with this action." He decided to place his hopes on a conference, which would at least slow things down.

Humphrey asked what the repercussions would be if Dulles came back with an obvious split of views between the two countries. "The President said such an event would be extremely serious, but not as serious as letting a war start and not trying to stop it." In conclusion, Eisenhower told the group he wanted "not a whisper about this outside this room."[37]

For Eisenhower to take a stance in such direct opposition to the British, at a time when Eden felt Britain's basic interests were involved, pained him deeply. "I can scarcely describe the depth of the regret I felt . . ." he wrote in his memoirs. Eden, and many members of his Cabinet, had stood beside Eisenhower in World War II. Nevertheless, he "felt it essential" to oppose precipitate action, and told Eden so in a blunt letter of July 31. He said there had to be a conference. If the British acted before negotiating, there would be a wave of anti-British feeling sweeping across America and the world. "I do not want to exaggerate, but I assure you that this could grow to such an intensity as to have the most far-reaching consequences." The President also warned that while "initial military successes might be easy, . . . the eventual price might become far too heavy."[38]

Dulles went to London, conferred with the British and the French, and returned to report that he had persuaded them to postpone military action until after a conference, scheduled to open on August 16 in London, involving twenty-four nations, including Egypt. But Nasser immediately announced that Egypt would not participate, since the conference was called only under a threat of armed force. He began moving reserve units into the Suez Base area. Dulles thought he still might be persuaded to accept a reasonable solution, and the Secretary and the President then worked out the American position.

APRIL–SEPTEMBER 1956   333

Dulles would propose, in London, the creation of an international authority to operate the canal, with Egypt getting the bulk of the revenues from the tolls. Eisenhower accepted that position, even though he had little hope that Nasser would, but he also emphasized to Dulles that if Nasser were to prove he could run the canal and that he intended to maintain it as a world waterway, "then it would be nearly impossible for the United States ever to find real justification, legally or morally, for use of force."[39]

Eisenhower spoke most eloquently on the subject of colonialism in a letter to Swede, written on August 3, at a time when "Nasser and the Suez Canal are foremost in my thoughts." Eisenhower said that "in the kind of world that we are trying to establish, we frequently find ourselves victims of the tyrannies of the weak." American policy, in general, was to support colonial peoples attempting to win national independence. In this situation, Eisenhower said, "we unavoidably give to the little nations opportunities to embarrass us greatly." The great Western nations had no choice but to swallow their pride, accept the insults, and attempt to work to bolster "the underlying concepts of freedom," even though this was "frequently costly. Yet there can be no doubt that in the long run such faithfulness will produce real rewards."[40]

On August 12, before Dulles left for the London Conference, and on the eve of the Democratic National Convention, Eisenhower called together the Democratic and Republican leaders in Congress, to brief them on developments. As they were gathering in the White House, Eisenhower met privately with Dulles, who pointed out that if the British and the French did decide to attack, they would do so knowing that there would be no active American support. But they would expect economic assistance, and especially access to American oil. Most of all, Dulles said—pointing to a central feature of the emerging British-French (and, unknown to the Americans, Israeli) strategy—"they would hope that we would neutralize Soviet Russia by indicating very clearly to Russia that if it should enter the conflict openly, the United States would enter it on the side of Britain and France."[41]

Then, at the meeting with the congressional leaders, Eisenhower outlined the situation. Lyndon Johnson thought the proper response was to "tell them [the British and the French] they have our moral support and go on in." Eisenhower demurred, although he agreed with Johnson's point that the United States could not support Europe's need for oil by itself. Republican Senator H. Alexander Smith complained that "we get a picture that Nasser is the bad man, but Nasser is the end of a long line." Smith thought that Nasser might perhaps "be better than what we might get." Dulles disagreed. "He's the worst," Dulles said of Nasser. "Not in terms of personal morals, but he's a Hitlerite personality." Dulles also reminded the senator that "we've put two world wars and a Marshall Plan into Europe," and it would be foolish "to throw our chips away." Eisenhower then assured the congressmen that he did not "intend to stand impotent and let this one man get away with it. . . . I hope there's no doubt that we will look to our interests." And with that, the meeting broke up, as the politicians went off to their national conventions. Eisenhower had hoped that two senators, one from each party, would join Dulles in London, but none would do so. They were satisfied to leave the crisis in Eisenhower's capable hands.[42]

Dulles flew off to London. Within a few days he had worked out an agreement for an international board to run the canal; it specified that the board would do the "operating, maintaining, and developing of the canal." Eisenhower told Dulles, by cable, that "Nasser may find it impossible to swallow the whole of this as now specified." He suggested that if Dulles changed the key word from "operating" to "supervision," Nasser might find it possible to accept.[43] But although Eisenhower tried to downplay the difference as inconsequential, the French and the British let Dulles know immediately that the difference was everything. "It is felt," Dulles reported, "very strongly here by most of the countries that if all the hiring and firing of pilots, . . . and engineers is made by the Egyptians . . . then in fact Egypt will be able to use the canal as an instrument of its national policy." The reality of control was at stake, and on this point, Dulles said, the British and the French could not be budged. Eisenhower reluctantly told Dulles to go ahead with the initial wording.[44] The majority (18 to 4) of the nations at the London Conference then accepted the American proposal and appointed a committee, headed by Prime Minister Robert Menzies of Australia as chairman, to take the proposal to Nasser.

Eisenhower, meanwhile, flew off to San Francisco on August 21 to attend the Republican National Convention. It was a welcome respite. Throughout the second half of July and the first half of August, as the Suez crisis escalated, he was at his coolest and best. Nevertheless, the long hours and complex problems had taken a toll on a man still recovering from major surgery. Eisenhower had not gained back all the weight he lost after the operation. When he left for Panama on July 21, he told Persons, "If I don't feel better than this pretty soon, I'm going to pull out of this whole thing [the campaign]." Persons related what happened: "So he goes down to Panama, almost gets crushed by the mobs, . . . suffers through all the damn receptions—and . . . three days later, he comes waltzing back looking like a new man."[45] The Suez crisis also had a rejuvenating effect on him, but the real lift he needed he got from the RNC.

It was San Francisco in August, and it could hardly have been better. Everyone had on "I Like Ike" buttons, or "Ike and Dick." Peace and prosperity were the theme. Eisenhower had Mamie, John, Barbara, Milton, and Edgar with him. All the members of his gang came out. The only unpleasant note of the week was one last attempt by Harold Stassen to dump Nixon. Stassen wrote an appeal to every delegate, and tried to persuade Eisenhower to declare for a genuinely open vice-presidential race. But Eisenhower refused to see him unless Stassen promised in advance that he would second Nixon's nomination. Stassen finally agreed, saw Eisenhower, and withdrew. Eisenhower announced to the press that Stassen had become convinced that "the majority of the delegates want Mr. Nixon," so he was ending his effort to nominate someone else.[46] That afternoon, August 22, the convention nominated Eisenhower by acclamation, and Nixon as vice-presidential candidate. Eisenhower made an appropriate acceptance speech, then went off for a few days' vacation on the Monterey Peninsula, at the Casa Munors Hotel. The gang was along and they played golf and bridge for four days. On the plane ride back to Washington, Eisenhower had his friends join him on the *Columbine,* where they played nonstop bridge for eight and one-half hours.[47] Eisenhower returned to the White House sun-tanned, buoyant, eager to go to work on his problems.

Politics had provided an interlude in the Suez crisis, but only a brief one. As soon as Eisenhower returned to Washington, the Middle East—not the upcoming campaign—was his central concern, to which he wanted to give his undivided attention. But of course he could not. The issue of elementary schools, for example, was pressing in on him, because simultaneously with the Suez crisis and the campaign, the 1956–1957 school year began across the nation. At all levels, college, secondary, and elementary, it was the largest opening in the history of the Republic. The classroom and teacher shortage was acute. Eisenhower often said that education was as important, or even more important, than defense, yet the sole significant contact his government had with these millions of children, who everyone agreed were the nation's greatest asset, was a school-lunch program. The two great needs of the education system, teachers and classrooms, were not addressed in any way by the federal government. The baby-boom children were being shortchanged in their education.

By no means was it entirely Eisenhower's fault, but at least some of the responsibility for this situation was his. Although he had no proposal to help the teacher crisis, beyond urging the states to raise salaries, he did propose a federal program of loans and grants to the states for school construction. He put conditions on his program, however, that made it—as he had certainly been told that it would—unacceptable to Congress. His principal condition was that the money go to the poor states; rich states like California or New York could solve their own problems. In practice, that meant most of the money appropriated for schools would go to the Deep South. There it would be used to strengthen a segregated school system existing in open defiance of the Supreme Court. That was what opened the way to the Powell Amendment, which amendment, by denying funds to segregated school systems, gave "rich state" congressmen the perfect reason to vote against the bill. Eisenhower himself said that if he were a congressman, he would have to support Powell, on the merits of the case. But having said that, he refused to widen his proposal to send money to all the states, which would have ensured passage. Instead, he did nothing. He hoped the states would solve the problem, or that it might otherwise somehow go away.

It did not, could not, has not. As schools opened, mob violence broke out in Clinton, Tennessee, and in Mansfield, Texas, as school officials attempted to carry out court-ordered desegregation. On September 5, Eisenhower was asked at a press conference whether he thought "there is anything that can be said or done on the national level to help local communities meet this problem without violence." Eisenhower thought not. It was a local problem. "And let us remember this," he said, "under the law the federal government cannot . . . move into a state until the state is not able to handle the matter."[48] But he could not get off that easily, because the desegregation crisis was getting closer to the basic point every year. That point was the question, Would the federal government use force to insure court-ordered desegregation? If it would, then integration would prevail, and the South (and the nation) thereby changed forever. If it would not, segregation would continue.

Everyone involved in the crisis knew those basic facts. Everyone knew that the ultimate test had to come. Eisenhower admitted to Whitman, "Eventually a district court is going to cite someone for contempt, and then we are going to be up against it," that is, forced to act.[49] As in Suez, Eisenhower wanted to delay as long as possible, to allow people to cool down. But others wanted the test now. Governor Allan Shivers of Texas, who had supported Eisenhower in 1952, sent Texas Rangers to defy a court order, reassigned the Negro pupils, and then said, "I defy the federal government. Tell the federal courts if they want to come after anyone, to come after me and cite me in this matter." Edward Morgan of ABC asked the President, "Would you consider that an incident in which the federal government had a responsibility, and, if not, can you give us an idea of what the formula is that would have to be followed for the government to intervene?"

Eisenhower was clear in answering one part of the question, while managing to ignore the other. If a federal court cited someone for contempt, Eisenhower said, of course U.S. marshals would serve the warrants and take the man to jail or force him to pay a fine. But as to using marshals, or any other form of federal force, to put the Negro children back into the school to which the court had assigned them, Eisenhower said not a word. Instead, he deplored violence, then expressed the hope that the states would meet their responsibilities, both to maintain law and order and to enforce the court orders on desegregation.[50]

Eisenhower was asked if he had any advice for young people in the border states who would be attending desegregated schools that fall. Eisenhower's thoughts immediately turned to the white children, not to the Negro students. He expressed his sympathy for their situation, said he recognized that "it is difficult through law and through force to change a man's heart." The South, he said, was "full of people of good will, but they are not the ones we now hear." Eisenhower then condemned "the people . . . so filled with prejudice that they even resort to violence; and the same way on the other sides of the thing, the people who want to have the whole matter settled today." (Eisenhower's comparison of civil-rights activists to southern mobs infuriated the NAACP.) Eisenhower also said, "We must all . . . help to bring about a change in spirit so that extremists on both sides do not defeat what we know is a reasonable, logical conclusion to this whole affair, which is recognition of the equality of men."

That statement led to the next question: Did Eisenhower endorse the *Brown* decision, or merely accept it, as the Republican platform did? Eisenhower replied, "I think it makes no difference whether or not I endorse it. The Constitution is as the Supreme Court interprets it; and I must conform to that and do my very best to see that it is carried out in this country."[51]

It was an attitude he carried with him through the campaign. He refused to discuss the *Brown* decision or the topic of desegregation, except to point with pride to his ending of Jim Crow in Washington, D.C., and at Army and Navy posts. Since desegregation was not a subject the Democrats could afford to raise, Eisenhower managed to successfully avoid the issue for another year. At what cost to the nation's children, and especially those who were black and lived in the South, no one can say.

On September 2, the Menzies committee arrived in Cairo. Nasser was cordial and willing to make many promises—among them, freedom of passage of the canal; proper maintenance of the canal; equitable tolls. But as Eisenhower had warned, he would never agree to international control. Anticipating this response, on September 2 Eisenhower wrote Eden, to say that the next step had to be to refer the problem to the U.N. and to warn that "there should be no thought of military action before the influences of the U.N. are fully explored." British mobilization and the evacuation of British citizens from Egypt were counterproductive, Eisenhower said, because they were "solidifying support for Nasser, which has been shaky." Turning to the American position, Eisenhower was forceful and could not have been clearer: "I must tell you frankly that American public opinion flatly rejects the thought of using force . . ." Then he explained to Eden why turning to force could not work for Britain: The British economy could not sustain prolonged military operations, nor the loss of Middle East oil. Further, the peoples of the Middle East, and of Asia and all of Africa, "would be consolidated against the West to a degree which, I fear, could not be overcome in a generation . . . particularly having in mind the capacity of the Russians to make mischief." Finally, Eisenhower pointed to an alternative to force. "We have friends in the Middle East," he said, "who tell us they would like to see Nasser's deflation brought about." But these Arabs were unanimous in saying that Suez was not the issue on which to bring that about. Eden should wait before acting.[52]

Eden would not wait. He replied, on September 7, in a letter that warned Eisenhower about appeasement and Munich (only fair; Eisenhower had used the historical example himself against the British when it suited his purposes during the 1954 Indochina crisis). Eden searched for words to express the depth of feeling in Britain. Assuring Eisenhower that he was conscious of the burdens and perils of military action, he then asserted: "But we have many times led Europe in the fight for freedom. It would be an ignoble end to our long history if we tamely accepted to perish by degrees."[53] Eisenhower called Dulles to confer; Dulles told him a story that made it clear he had fools on both sides of the Atlantic to deal with. Dulles said "that he had had a number of senators in yesterday to discuss the situation—and he said that in general they wanted the canal closed so that America could sell oil to the British." Scornfully, Eisenhower asked, "With the British using what for money?"[54]

To Eden, in a reply of September 8, Eisenhower deplored the use of such language as "ignoble end to our long history." He said Eden was "making of Nasser a much more important figure than he is." Eisenhower expressed his alarm at continued British mobilization, and urged Eden to consider how effectively economic pressures against Egypt, and Arab rivalries, could be exploited "if we do not make Nasser an Arab hero." Further, Eden should consider the possibilities of new gigantic tankers that could go around Africa, new pipelines, and oil sales from North America. Then, in a prophetic warning, Eisenhower said, "Nasser thrives on drama." He urged Eden to drain some of the drama out of the situation, to go about deflating Nasser slowly.[55]

That evening, Eisenhower talked with Dulles about their next step, in view of Nasser's rejection of an international control board. What they were looking for was another way to stall; they found it in a "Users' Association." It was an absurd idea; it called for maritime nations to band together, hire pilots, put control ships at each end of the canal (which had no obstacles through its length), use the canal, and put the tolls in escrow. Dulles managed to make the proposal complex enough to force the actors to spend weeks discussing it. Nasser, however, undercut the Users' Association idea before it was hardly born. On September 14, the British pilots walked off their jobs at the canal. The next day, Egyptian pilots brought through a convoy of thirteen ships. By the end of the week, 254 ships had passed through, a record. Nasser was operating the canal more efficiently than the British had. Thus, as Eisenhower wrote in his memoirs, "The assumption upon which the Users' Association was largely based proved groundless." Eisenhower felt that Nasser's action made "any thought of using force . . . almost ridiculous."[56] In his opinion, the British

340

should accept the Egyptian offer for compensation for their 44 percent interest in the Suez Canal Company, and get back to their real problems, such as restoring their economy and making their contribution to meeting the Russian threat.

The split between America and Britain over Egypt was having repercussions in areas of secret military collaboration, specifically on the bases for the U-2. By early 1956, Richard Bissell had twenty-two U-2s, plus trained pilots, ready to go. Bases were necessary to overfly East Europe, the first target. As to what happened from that point on, much of the story must be based on oral history interviews, because most of the documents (and especially those that deal with the British) remain sealed. But the chief informants—Bissell himself, John Eisenhower, who joined the White House staff as Goodpaster's assistant in 1958, and Goodpaster—agree on all the major events, and the few documents that are available substantiate their account.

Bissell flew to London to confer with Eden sometime in the spring of 1956. Eden agreed that the CIA could fly U-2 missions from a SAC base northeast of London. In May, flights over East Europe began. The Russians protested against the violation of airspace. On May 28, Eisenhower met with Allen Dulles, Radford, Twining, and Goodpaster to discuss the subject. Eisenhower expressed his concern over the effects the spy flights might have on the chances for peace, his readiness to see how far the Soviets might go to put relations on a better basis, and his consequent determination to be "wise and careful in what we do."[57] Eden, meanwhile, had grown skittish over the Russian protests, and—more important—could hardly see the point to maintaining American spy-mission airfields within his country at a time when the British were secretly preparing for war. Eden told Eisenhower he did not want any more British-based U-2s flying over Communist territory. Bissell then went to West Germany. Adenauer gave him permission to base the U-2 in Wiesbaden; later the planes were based farther east, near the East German border. Bissell also arranged for bases in Turkey.

On May 31, while these arrangements were being made, Eisenhower approved, in principle, a program for U-2 flights over the Soviet Union itself. By June 21, Bissell was ready and asked for a final approval. Eisenhower quizzed him about the "yield to be expected," operating conditions, control and direction of the missions, and other details, as well as what Bissell proposed to do if a U-2 malfunctioned. Bissell said the CIA would claim it was on a weather reconnaissance flight. Eisenhower told Bissell that he authorized the initial flights for a period of ten days. Bissell said he assumed that meant ten days of good weather, not just ten calendar days. Goodpaster said, "No, you have just ten calendar days and you will have to take your chances with the weather." Eisenhower then told Bissell he wanted to be kept thoroughly informed, and had to be consulted before any "deep operations are initiated."[58]

The first flight went, successfully, five days later. In the following week, there were six additional missions. Then came a great shock— the Russians sent in a private but firm diplomatic protest. The CIA and the Defense Department had assumed the spy planes flew too high (more than eighty thousand feet) to be tracked. American radar could not follow them; its upper limit was sixty thousand feet. But the Russians could. Eisenhower told Bissell to slow down, "and it was quite a few months before he was ready to authorize another flight."

As Bissell explained in a 1979 interview, the entire program "was controlled very tightly by the President personally." Before each flight, Bissell would draw up on a map the proposed flight plan and spread it out on the President's desk. Along with Goodpaster, the Dulles brothers, Wilson, and Radford, Eisenhower would study it. "The President would ask a lot of questions. He would ask me to come around and explain this or that feature of the flight, and there were occasions, more than once, when he would say, 'Well, you can go there, but I want you to leave out that leg and go straight that way. I want you to go from B to D because it looks to me like you might be getting a little exposed over here,' or something of that kind. So we had very, very tight ground rules," Bissell concluded, "very tight control by the President."[59]

As Bissell emphasized, Eisenhower was cautious about overflying the Soviet Union. Overflying France or Britain was out of the question. But still the U-2 could be used to gather intelligence from the Middle East. Sometime in the late summer or early fall of 1956, Eisenhower ordered it done. In mid-October, he noted one discovery in his diary: "Our high-flying reconnaissance planes have shown that Israel has obtained some sixty of the French Mystère pursuit planes, when there had been reported the transfer of only twenty-four."[60] In the three weeks that followed, he found that the U-2 was his best source of information—but only with regard to the British, French, and Israelis, not the Russians, against whom it had been intended to be directed.

Like the U-2, Eisenhower wanted to keep American nuclear testing secret, and if that were not possible, at least relatively quiet. But the fear of fallout was widespread—the President shared it—so interest was high. Further, the tests could not be hidden from the Russians, who were sure to announce them anyway, so some publicity was inevitable. Khrushchev himself had made sure that it would be; in November 1955, he boasted that the Soviet Union had detonated "the most powerful" H-bomb ever. Western observers calculated the blast at between two and four megatons, much smaller than Bravo. What impressed the Americans was the Russian ability to drop a weapon of that size from an airplane, something the Americans could not yet do.[61]

Further American testing was necessary, Strauss and the AEC told Eisenhower, to find a configuration that would fit into a plane, and another, smaller one, to fit into the nose cone of an ICBM. Eisenhower was hesitant, but when in March 1956, the Soviets undertook another series of tests, the President gave his final approval to Operation Redwing, a series of tests of more than a dozen different nuclear explosions at proving grounds in the Pacific. In doing so, Eisenhower "pointed out that without the H-bomb the guided missile amounts to nothing—if they stop tests they would have to stop work on the missiles."[62] Redwing began on May 5; on May 21, an Air Force plane released a hydrogen bomb over Bikini. It exploded with a force of ten megatons.[63]

To Eisenhower's consternation, Stevenson had meanwhile tried to make testing a partisan political issue. In April, running for the Democratic nomination, he called for an end to testing. Stevenson said he found little "sense in multiplying and enlarging weapons of a destructive power already incomprehensible." Then he criticized Eisenhower for being "dangerously dilatory" in the development of missiles.[64] At an April 25 press conference, Eisenhower was asked to comment on both Stevenson's points, and on Khrushchev's latest boast, that the Russians would soon have guided missiles with H-bomb warheads capable of hitting any point in the world.

Eisenhower replied that it was difficult to build missiles, it took a long time, and they were far from dependable. Did he think it important for America to stay ahead of the Russians in missiles? He did, stressing that "you can scarcely overemphasize the psychological value of such a weapon." But he repeated that they were expensive and took a long time to build. Did he then think the United States was spending enough? The reporter added, "There are Democrats who say we are not." "Not only Democrats," the Presidnt said, laughing. "There are lots of people saying we are not." But there were only so many scientists, only so many facilities. They were being used to the maximum.

May Craig brought the wandering discourse back to one of Stevenson's points. She asked Eisenhower to comment on the call for a halt to nuclear testing. He immediately brought in Stevenson's other point—more money for missiles—into his answer. "It is a little bit of a paradox," he pointed out, "to urge that we work just as hard as we know how on the guided missile and that we stop all research on the hydrogen bomb, because one without the other is rather useless." He said he was going to go forward with the Redwing tests, "not to make a bigger bang, not cause more destruction—[but] to find out ways and means in which you can limit it, make it useful in defensive purposes . . . reduce fallout, make it more of a military weapon and less one just of mass destruction. We know we can make them big," he said. "We are not interested in that anymore." The Redwing tests were designed to go along with the missile research, "so if you don't work on one . . . , why work on the other? . . . Research without tests is perfectly useless, a waste of money."[65]

The logic and the authoritative tone in which "General Ike" delivered that statement put Stevenson very much on the defensive on the issue. Eisenhower had made him look like a bumbling amateur trying to interfere in a business that was beyond his competence.

The only way out of testing and missile development was through an acceptable disarmament plan. In the spring of 1956, even while Redwing was going on, Eisenhower remained committed to disarmament. At a meeting with Republican leaders on May 18, however, Knowland spoke up for the Bricker Amendment. Knowland said the nation needed the amendment, because all this disarmament talk could lead to a treaty taking away the people's constitutional right to bear arms. Eisenhower replied that if the people's right to bear arms became an issue in a disarmament treaty, then the Constitution should be amended to remove that right. "If he had to give up the objective of getting a disarmament agreement, the President said, there would be no reason for staying here. A decent disarmament treaty is an absolute must!"[66]

But with Stassen on leave to plot against Nixon, nothing was done on disarmament in mid-1956. Then on August 24, the Russians resumed testing. They also renewed their call for an international test-ban agreement, saying they were ready to stop testing when the United States was also ready.[67] Eisenhower was tempted. On August 30, he wrote Strauss, "I have spoken to you several times about my hope that the need for atomic tests would gradually lift and possibly soon disappear." He said that Isidor Rabi, the Columbia physics professor, had just told him that he thought it was now possible to stop testing. Therefore, Eisenhower concluded, "I should like to talk to you about this when you have an opportunity."[68] Strauss continued to insist on the need for further testing.

By September, however, Stassen had gone back to disarmament concerns, and was pressing for an American initiative on the test-ban issue, and disarmament generally. On September 14, Eisenhower held a major White House conference on the subject. Present were Stassen, Dulles, Strauss, Wilson, Radford, Goodpaster, and the President. Stassen had a series of ideas on arms reduction to present, and he said he proposed to set July 1957 as the date to initiate actual disarmament. All those at the conference, save the President, were taken aback. That was "totally unrealistic," they asserted. Dulles thought "two or three years" was more like it. Eisenhower broke in. He said "we could sit and find obstacles to the plan without end. Something, however, must be done. . . . We must set some date, and work toward it." The conferees then agreed to set December 1, 1957, as the date.

What Goodpaster described as "spirited discussion" ensued over the subject of a test ban. Eventually, "agreement was indicated that any stopping must be predicated upon an inspection plan." Along the way, however, Eisenhower had grown irritated at his people arguing among themselves. He told Stassen to get together with Strauss, Dulles, and Wilson and "work out an agreed staff position. He said he was not accustomed to have his staff come in to him with disorganized point of view so that he would have to argue each aspect with separate individuals." Eisenhower told them to go back to work on the problem, "and not come back until they had a common position to present."[69]

Poor staff work was becoming an increasing problem for Eisenhower. He had hoped, in January 1953, to put together a team that could operate like the one at SHAEF, but he had soon realized how impossible that was in an organization so much larger than even SHAEF had been, and in the past three years had turned increasingly to small, private meetings in the Oval Office when making his decisions. In the public view, and according to the Democrats, Eisenhower's weakness was that he spent too much time with, and paid undue attention to, staffs and committees. The truth was that they were all, from legislative leaders' meetings right through to NSC meetings, *pro forma* gatherings for the President. He used them to explain what he was going to do, and to get support for it, not to discuss what to do.

Whitman made this point clearly in an August 28 letter to Milton, who had asked her to describe for him how the President spent his official time. Whitman replied with a six-page letter, "written with all the frankness I can command," which she asked Milton to keep strictly to himself.

The most time-consuming meetings, Whitman began, were those of the NSC. She thought they could be cut back considerably, because Eisenhower "himself complains that he knows every word of the presentations as they are to be made." But he said that to maintain interest among those present, "he must sit through each meeting—despite the fact that he knows the presentations so well." Next worse were Cabinet meetings. Whitman noted that "little briefing, if any, is required for these meetings." Then there were the press-conference briefings, where for a half hour each week the staff went over possible questions. "Especially in the last year or so," Whitman wrote, "it has seemed to me that the President knows full well how he is going to answer any given question, without assistance from the staff." Eisenhower used the briefings, she continued, "to urge the staff members to be a little more definite and not always to beg the issue (as so many want to)." The meetings with Republican leaders, held weekly when Congress was in session, lasted only half an hour "and only about five minutes' preparation is required."

Eisenhower's important meetings, Whitman said, were those he held weekly with Drs. Burns and Hauge, to discuss the economy, and the more frequent but *ad hoc* discussions he held with Foster Dulles. But the most time-consuming Cabinet officer was Wilson, who turned to Eisenhower to solve the frequently bitter interservice rivalries, and for help on such matters as budget, manpower, etc. In a fascinating juxtaposition, in the next paragraph Whitman wrote that in contrast to Wilson, Strauss and the AEC took hardly any time at all. "As far as I can judge, the President has only to make the top decisions in this field, and they take a minimum amount of time." In other words, Eisenhower was sure of himself in DOD matters and spent hours on details, but was unsure of himself in the nuclear field and thus let Strauss run it.

One-half hour of each day was devoted to Goodpaster's early-morning briefing on intelligence and foreign-affairs reports. Then there were appointments with senators and congressmen, which had been "drastically curtailed" since the heart attack. Additional appointments with visiting groups, heads of organizations, signatures, and a dozen other things also took time. One of the worst was speeches; Whitman wrote, "I guess he spends twenty to thirty hours on each major speech." Often he caught mistakes that had gotten by everyone else. "I shall never forget the time a phrase 'consumer demands have not changed in 2,000 years' got by everybody," Whitman wrote, until it got to the President—"But of course he caught it!" [70]

Whitman was describing only Eisenhower's official meetings, activities, and schedule. He did even more work unofficially. He was, obviously, a very busy man. Not so busy, however, that he could not find time to worry about some details in the upcoming campaign. One of his pet projects was getting out a big vote. On September 6, he wrote Cliff Roberts, suggesting that Roberts get some signs worked up urging people to vote, and told him to quote the President in doing so. Eisenhower told Roberts to distribute the signs through the U.S. Golf Association. He said he wanted to see one of them up in every clubhouse in the country, and warned that he would be looking for such a sign at Burning Tree. [71] The President called Arthur Sulzberger on the phone to ask why the *Times* was hesitating in endorsing the Republican ticket. "It is your running mate that bothers me," Sulzberger replied. Eisenhower asked Sulzberger to come down for lunch sometime soon to talk about it. Sulzberger said he would be there the next day. The *Times* then endorsed the Republican ticket. [72]

Most of all, Eisenhower wanted to get going on the campaign because of the way Stevenson kept opening himself to criticism for not knowing, or thinking through, what he was talking about. On September 5, addressing the American Legion, Stevenson simultaneously called for an end to the military draft and an end to nuclear testing. On issues such as those, Eisenhower was eager to do battle.

CHAPTER FIFTEEN

Election, Suez, Hungary

September 19–December 31, 1956

BEFORE THE CONVENTION, Eisenhower had warned the Republicans that if they nominated him, he would not undertake a strenuous or wide-ranging campaign. Instead, he intended to limit himself to four or five major speeches on national TV. One reason was his health; another was that unlike 1952, he had a record to run on; a third was that, as President, he simply did not have the time to devote to campaigning that he had had when he was only a candidate. One month after the nomination, on September 19, he made his first address. He gave a sober review of the world situation, stressing his Administration's success in maintaining peace. He dismissed Stevenson's call for a nuclear test ban as a "theatrical national gesture."[1]

Eisenhower's private view of the opposition was scathing. He told Gruenther, "Stevenson and Kefauver, as a combination, are the sorriest and weakest pair that ever aspired to the highest office in the land." Eisenhower never had any doubts that he and Nixon would prevail, so he felt comfortable in letting Nixon do the vast majority of the campaigning. But, as in 1952, professional Republicans could imagine all sorts of things going wrong. "I notice that as election day approaches," Eisenhower wrote Gruenther, "everybody gets the jitters. You meet a man and he is practically hysterical with the confidence of overwhelming victory, and sometimes you see that same man that evening and his face is a foot long with fright."[2]

Pressed by the RNC to do more talking, Eisenhower convinced

himself that it was necessary. He explained to Swede that he not only wanted to win, but to win by a substantial margin. Without a mandate, he said, he would "not want to be elected at all." He gave two reasons. First, his work in "reforming and revamping the Republican Party" was far from complete, and his influence over the party would depend, in large measure, on the size of his victory. Second, he expected the Democrats to retain the House and Senate. Working with the Democrats, although it often came easier to Eisenhower than working with the Republicans, would depend on his margin of victory. He therefore decided to "do a bit of traveling in the campaign," and made campaign speeches in half a dozen cities. He went partly for the fun of it—he always enjoyed traveling—and partly "to prove to the American people that I am a rather healthy individual."[3]

Insofar as there was an issue that got him going, it was Stevenson's call for a test ban. Insofar as there was a reason for his increasing contempt for Stevenson, it was the inept and confused way in which Stevenson raised and used the issue. Stevenson's campaign was indeed a mishmash; he wanted to end the draft, end testing, but greatly accelerate spending on missiles. Eisenhower thought that testing was far too complex and dangerous a subject to be discussed in a political campaign, and he would have preferred to leave it alone. Stevenson's advisers also told him that he was foolish to attempt to attack Eisenhower on any question concerning national defense. Stevenson nevertheless insisted on making an end to testing a central theme in his campaign.[4]

Eisenhower would not respond in his prepared speeches, but at a press conference on October 5, he did react to Stevenson's proposal. One problem with a moratorium, Eisenhower said, was that it took "months and months" to prepare for a series of nuclear tests. If the U.S. stopped, the Russians could use the moratorium to make secret preparations for resumption, and thus "make tremendous advances where we would be standing still." So the President concluded, "I think it would be foolish for us to make any such unilateral announcement." The following day, the White House released a statement on a unilateral test ban. In it Eisenhower pointed out how vital nuclear weapons were to offset superior Communist manpower, stressed the need to continue testing to reduce fallout, insisted that inspection was necessary to supervise a moratorium, and concluded, "This specific matter is manifestly not a subject for detailed public discussion—for obvious security reasons."[5]

On October 11, at the next press conference, a reporter asked

Eisenhower to comment on rumors that the NSC had recommended ending the draft and stopping nuclear testing. Growing red in the face, Eisenhower refused to answer questions about national-security issues in a political campaign. "Now, I tell you frankly, I have said my last words on these subjects."[6] Four days after that, Stevenson delivered one of his major campaign speeches, on national TV. He devoted the whole of the speech to the test ban, entitling the talk "The Greatest Menace the World Has Ever Known." He offered four reasons to stop testing. First, the United States already had bombs large enough to destroy any major city—why improve them? Second, a moratorium on testing did not require inspection, because "you can't hide the explosion any more than you can hide an earthquake." Third, a prohibition on testing would halt the spread of nuclear weapons. Fourth, a test ban would eliminate fallout, especially of strontium-90, which Stevenson called "the most dreadful poison in the world."[7]

Eisenhower replied on October 18 in a speech in Portland, Oregon. He said that the people had to choose between "hard sense and experience versus pie-in-the-sky promises and wishful thinking." At Los Angeles the next day, Eisenhower belittled those who "tell us that peace can be guarded—and our nation secure—by a strange new formula. It is this: Simultaneously to stop our military draft and to abandon testing of our most advanced military weapons." There was no cheap or easy way to peace, the President said, before concluding, "I do not believe that any political campaign justifies the declaration of a moratorium on ordinary common sense."[8]

Despite Eisenhower's scorn, Stevenson's appeal was making converts. The White House mail was running heavily in favor of a suspension of testing. Stevenson's advisers were ready to conclude that he had been right, and they wrong, about the wisdom of taking on Ike on national defense. But then Stevenson had the worst possible luck. Bulganin wrote Eisenhower, in a letter made public by the Russians, calling for a test ban. Bulganin said such a moratorium would provide "the first step toward the solution of the problem of atomic weapons." Then Bulganin noted with approval that "certain prominent public figures in the United States" were advocating a test ban.

The press interpreted Bulganin's letter as blatant interference in the American presidential election. So did Eisenhower, who wrote a scathing answer to Bulganin; *The New York Times* called it "one of the most strongly worded diplomatic communications in recent years." Eisenhower rejected the offer to enter into a test-ban agreement. More important, he told Bulganin that his letter "departs from accepted international practice," as it constituted "an interference by a foreign nation in our internal affairs of a kind which, if indulged in by an ambassador, would lead to his being declared *persona non grata* in accordance with long-established custom."[9]

Nixon, meanwhile, went after the hapless Stevenson, already made thoroughly miserable by Bulganin's "endorsement." Nixon described Stevenson as a "clay pigeon" for Soviet sharpshooters, compared him to Neville Chamberlain, said that his test-ban proposal was "the height of irresponsibility and absurdity" and vowed that "the Stevenson leadership would increase the chances of war."[10] But after exploiting the Bulganin letter so brilliantly, Eisenhower wanted to de-emphasize the issue, not highlight it as Nixon was doing. Eisenhower knew he had Stevenson beat anyway. When his son, John, told him, about this time, that "you've got to get moving. You're going to fall behind," Eisenhower, laughing, said, "This fellow's licked and what's more he knows it! Let's go to the ball game." With that, they were off to see the opening game of the World Series.[11]

Under the circumstances, Eisenhower wanted to turn the public mind away from testing and fallout. He told Dulles to issue an Administration statement on testing, and to write a document "so factual as to be uninteresting." He wanted no personal criticism of Stevenson, and he cautioned Dulles against the use of any rigid language that could "publicly tie his [the President's] hands so that in the future [he could] do nothing" about stopping testing.[12] Eisenhower himself, after all, had written Strauss in August asking if testing could not be stopped and indicating that he did want to stop as soon as possible. An overreaction to Stevenson's proposal would therefore reduce the chances for achieving a moratorium.

In the statement as released, Eisenhower was reassuring. Fallout from testing was not dangerous, he said, citing a National Academy of Science report as evidence. Nevertheless, the United States was dedicated to peace, and wanted a ban on testing, and disarmament, as quickly as possible after a satisfactory inspection system had been put in place. In a separate statement the same day, the White House listed the various disarmament proposals made by the United States from the Baruch plan of 1946 to Eisenhower's offer of Open Skies in 1955, and put the blame for failure to achieve disarmament on the Russian refusal to agree to adequate inspection systems.[13]

Through September, the British and the French had continued to mobilize on Cyprus. Nasser rejected the Users' Association proposal and insisted on maintaining Egyptian control of the canal. Eisenhower retained his interest in wanting to promote King Saud as a rival to Nasser while attempting to restrain his NATO allies. On October 8, Herbert Hoover, Jr., the Under Secretary of State, told Eisenhower that "one of our agencies" had devised a plan that was quicker and more direct "on how to topple Nasser." Whether or not that was a euphemism for assassination, Eisenhower rejected the premise. Goodpaster noted, "The President said that an action of this kind could not be taken when there is as much active hostility as at present. For a thing like this to be done without inflaming the Arab world, a time free from heated stress holding the world's attention as at present would have to be chosen." [14]

What then to do about Nasser, indeed about the whole crisis? Eisenhower talked to Hoover later that day on the telephone, then wrote him a letter summarizing his orders. He wanted to issue "a frank warning that the United States will not support a war or warlike moves in the Suez area." He told Hoover to issue another statement announcing that the United States was ready to begin construction of sixty-thousand-ton supertankers. This "might have a calming effect," because the tankers would give Britain access to North and South American oil. Eisenhower said he wanted State to come up with a plan, "any plan," that might have some appeal to Nasser, so that "through some clandestine means we might urge Nasser to make an appropriate public offer." He wanted Hoover to find some role for Nehru and the OAS to play in furthering negotiations, and to think about the idea of Eisenhower's calling for a conference in Washington. Eisenhower concluded, "As you know, I am immersed [in problems] . . ." but said he wanted to give a "clear indication of my readiness to participate in any way in which I can be helpful . . ." to keep the peace. [15]

The British and the French, meanwhile, had gone to the United Nations, whether in a sincere search for a peaceful solution or as a cover to go to war, Eisenhower frankly did not know. He instructed Lodge to support Secretary-General Dag Hammarskjold, who by mid-October had managed to achieve agreement on "Six Principles" as a basis for beginning negotiations. Britain and France approved, because the principles included a Users' Association to insure international control. [16] Hammarskjold prepared to go to Cairo to begin talks with Nasser.

On October 15, Eisenhower received a new piece of information. Dulles reported that U-2 flights had revealed an Israeli mobilization, and the presence in Israel of some sixty French Mystère jets. Eisen-

hower was incensed, because under the terms of the 1950 Tripartite
Declaration, the United States, the United Kingdom, and France were
committed to maintaining a *status quo* in arms and borders in the
Middle East. France had earlier asked for, and received, American
permission to sell Mystères to Israel, but only twenty-four, not sixty.
Thus Eisenhower now knew that the French were arming the Israelis
in contravention of the 1950 agreement, and lying to the Americans
about it. Dulles also reported that Israel was acting aggressively, sending raids into both Gaza and the West Bank of the Jordan. The Secretary said it was being taken "as a foregone conclusion" that Jordan
was breaking up, and Israel was going to be "anxious to get her share
of the wreckage." Complicating this situation was the existence of a
treaty between Jordan, a former British protectorate, and the United
Kingdom. If Israel launched a full-scale invasion of Jordan, Britain
would have to come to Jordan's defense.

"Should this occur," Eisenhower wrote later in a memorandum,
"we would have Britain in the curious position of helping to defend
one of the Arab countries, while at the same time she is engaged in a
quarrel . . . with Egypt." Eisenhower did not suspect an Israeli attack on Egypt; his attention was riveted on Jordan. He told Dulles
to "make it very clear to the Israelis that they must stop these attacks
against the borders of Jordan." If they continued, the Arabs would
turn to the Russians for arms, and "the ultimate effect would be to
Sovietize the whole region, including Israel."

Eisenhower told Dulles he thought "Ben-Gurion's obviously aggressive attitude" was due to his desire to take the West Bank, coupled
with his belief that Western and Egyptian preoccupation with Suez
would "minimize the possibility" of war with Egypt while simultaneously impeding Britain's capability for supporting Jordan, and finally
Ben-Gurion's belief that the political campaign in America would
hamstring the Eisenhower Administration. Eisenhower told Dulles to
set the Israelis straight: "Ben-Gurion should not make any grave mistake based upon his belief that winning a domestic election is as important to us as preserving and protecting the peace." Dulles should
also tell Ben-Gurion that in the long term, aggression by Israel "cannot fail to bring catastrophe and such friends as he would have left
in the world, no matter how powerful, could not do anything about
it." [17]

How powerful Eisenhower thought the Jewish vote was in the
United States he revealed in a conversation with his son. One evening in October in the White House, Eisenhower mused, "Well, it

looks as if we're in for trouble. If the Israelis keep going . . . I may have to use force to stop them . . . Then I'd lose the election. There would go New York, New Jersey, Pennsylvania, and Connecticut at least."[18] Nevertheless, he would do whatever he had to in order to prevent or turn back Israeli aggression. Thus his last words to Dulles were, "I will not under any circumstances permit the fact of the forthcoming elections to influence my judgment. If any votes are lost as a result of this attitude, that is a situation which we will have to confront, but any other attitude will not permit us to live with our conscience."[19]

Over the next two weeks, there was a virtual blackout on communication between the United States on the one side and the French and the British on the other. Simultaneously, American interceptors picked up heavy radio traffic between Britain and France. American code breakers were unsuccessful in unraveling the content of the messages; they could only report that the sheer volume of traffic was ominous. Eisenhower's own expectation was that the Israelis would attack Jordan, supplied by the French and with covert British sanction, and that the British and the French would then take advantage of the confusion to occupy the canal. He was, in other words, badly misinformed, and had reached the wrong conclusions. He was about to be as completely surprised as he had been on December 7, 1941, by Pearl Harbor, or on December 16, 1944, by the Ardennes counteroffensive. The difference was that this time it was his friends who were fooling him.

How could it have happened? The United States maintained a huge, complex, and generally efficient intelligence system, of which the CIA was only one part. There were American reporters in London, Paris, and Tel Aviv, all filing daily dispatches about activities in the capitals. The State Department had flourishing embassies in all three capitals, plus a secret line of communication to send word on developments. The U-2s were overflying the eastern Mediterranean and sending back photographs that revealed major military moves. The CIA had spies at various levels scattered through the area. Most of all, Eisenhower had close personal friends in Eden's Cabinet and in the British military, as well as in the French government and military. But there is no evidence he made any attempt to get in touch, secretly, with his friends (Macmillan, for example, or Mountbatten, both of whom opposed Eden's adventurism) in order to find out what was going on. As a result, he was surprised.

Part of the reason was, obviously, preoccupation with the campaign, precisely the point the British, the French, and the Israelis relied upon as they did their plotting together. The more important reason for the American intelligence failure was the nature of the act itself. As a general rule, the easiest way to achieve complete strategic surprise is to commit an act that makes no sense, or is even self-destructive. In 1941 it made no sense for the Japanese to initiate a war with the United States; thus the surprise at Pearl Harbor. It made no sense for the Germans to invade Russia; thus the surprise of Operation Barbarossa. In 1944 it made no sense for Hitler to use up his armor in a hopeless counterattack, rather than reserve it for the defense of the Rhine; thus the surprise in the Battle of the Bulge. To Eisenhower in 1956, it made no sense—indeed was self-destructive—for the British and the French to attempt to seize and hold the canal, or for the Israelis to act aggressively when they were surrounded by a sea of Arabs, and it especially made no sense to him for Britain and France to attempt to act independently of the United States, much less against the expressed policy of the Eisenhower Administration.

So Eisenhower was badly surprised. He hated to be surprised, but experience had taught him—as he said so many times—that he had to expect to be surprised. The proper response was to remain cool, gather all the information he could, consider the options, and use them to take control of events. That was what he had done in December 1944, in one of his greatest moments as Supreme Commander. It was what he intended to do, and did, in October–November 1956, in one of his greatest moments as President.

While Britain, France, and Israel were completing the preparations for their bizarre plot, great events were occurring in Eastern Europe. Disturbances and riots in Poland, sparked by publication of Khrushchev's secret speech to the Twentieth Party Congress, swept the Soviet-dominated government out of power and brought in Wladyslaw Gomulka, a man earlier dismissed by the Soviets as a Titoist. Gomulka announced that "there is more than one road to Socialism," and warned that the Polish people would "defend themselves with all means; they will not be pushed off the road of democratization." On October 22, the Poles' successful defiance of the Soviets set off demonstrations throughout Hungary, where the demand was that Imre Nagy, who had been deposed by the Soviets in 1955, be returned to power.

Although these were spontaneous events, and quite unpredictable, they nevertheless had long been expected by the Eisenhower Administration, where it was an article of faith that sooner or later the satellites would rise up against Russia. But although the United States had anticipated a revolt, and had indeed encouraged it, both through Voice of America and Radio Free Europe broadcasts and through CIA-created underground resistance cells within Eastern Europe, when the revolt actually came, the government had no plans prepared. There was a good reason for this shortcoming—there was nothing the United States could do anyway. As always in grand strategy, geography dictated the options. Hungary was surrounded by Communist states, plus neutral Austria, and had a common border with the Soviet Union. It had no ports. There was almost no trade going on between the United States and the Russians. There was no pressure, in short, save for the amorphous one of world public opinion, that Eisenhower could bring to bear on the Soviets in Hungary. He knew it, had known it all along, which made all the four years of Republican talk about "liberation" so essentially hypocritical.

On October 23, the Hungarian government installed Nagy as Premier; he promised "democratization and improved living standards." But the riots went on, and the Soviets sent troops to Budapest to restore order. The following day, Hungarian freedom fighters began hurling homemade Molotov cocktails at Russian tanks in Budapest. Eisenhower issued a statement deploring the intervention, but he turned down frantic requests from the CIA that it be allowed to fly over Budapest and air-drop arms and supplies. The Agency was deeply disappointed; as William Colby, at the time a junior CIA officer, later director, wrote: "This [Hungary] was exactly the end for which the Agency's paramilitary capability was designed." But Eisenhower said no. "Whatever doubts may have existed in the Agency about Washington's policy in matters like this vanished," Colby wrote. "It was established, once and for all, that the United States, while firmly committed to the containment of the Soviets . . . was not going to attempt to liberate any of the areas within that sphere . . ." Liberation was a sham. Eisenhower had always known it. The Hungarians had yet to learn it.[20]

On October 26, Eisenhower presided over a meeting of the NSC. Allen Dulles reported on the entry of Soviet troops into Hungary, the desertion of large numbers of Hungarian Army troops, and the fighting in Budapest. Eisenhower said he wanted to proceed cautiously, that he did not want to give the Soviets any reason to think that the United States might support the Hungarian freedom fighters. Point-

ing to the dangers involved, he wondered if the Soviets "might not
. . . be tempted to resort to extreme measures" to maintain their hold
over the satellites, "even to start a world war."

Foster Dulles then reported on the developments in the Middle
East, where Egypt had joined with Jordan and Syria in the Pact of
Amman, which provided for military cooperation among them, and
an Egyptian commander to take charge of their armed forces in the
event of war with Israel. Ben-Gurion said the pact put Israel in "direct and immediate danger," and Dulles said he expected an Israeli
attack on Jordan momentarily.[21]

On October 28, Eisenhower learned that Israel had ordered a
general mobilization of her reserves. In addition, there was heavy
radio traffic between Israel and France. Eisenhower decided to evacuate American dependents from the Middle East. He also sent a stern
warning to Ben-Gurion "to do nothing which would endanger the
peace."[22] U-2 flights revealed heavy military concentrations by the
British and the French on Cyprus. Most disturbing was the increase
in the number of troop transports and air forces. It appeared that
they had concerted a plan to take advantage of the imminent Israeli
attack on Jordan to occupy the canal. Whitman, monitoring a call to
Dulles, recorded, "President said he just cannot believe Britain would
be dragged into this." Dulles said he had just talked to the French
ambassador and the chargé. "They profess to know nothing about
this at all . . . But, he [Dulles] said, their ignorance is almost a sign
of a guilty conscience, in his opinion."[23]

That afternoon, Eisenhower talked with Emmet Hughes, who
was trying to write campaign speeches in the midst of the excitement.
"I just can't figure out what the Israelis think they're up to," Eisenhower confessed to Hughes. "Maybe they're thinking they just *can't*
survive without more land. . . . But *I* don't see how they can survive
without coming to some honorable and peaceful terms with the whole
Arab world that surrounds them." Turning to intelligence reports on
French activities, he said, "Damn it, the French, they're just egging
the Israelis on—hoping somehow to get out of their *own* North African
troubles. Damn it, they sat right there in those chairs three years ago,
and we tried to tell them they would repeat Indochina all over again
in North Africa. And they said, 'Oh, no! [Algeria's] part of metropolitan France!'—and all that damn nonsense."[24]

At 8 A.M. the following morning, October 28, Dulles called Eisenhower. The Israelis had not attacked Jordan, and the Russians appeared to be exercising restraint in Budapest. At least, Dulles said,

"we have gained twenty-four hours." The President wanted more substantial achievements. Whitman summarized his remarks: "The President said that they [the Russians] might be willing to talk sense now more than at any time since Administration has been in power. Said approach might be that things are not going the way any of us want, better have a meeting that recognizes these points." Dulles replied that "undoubtedly there was a battle on in the Presidium . . . some of the people probably would want to go back to the old Stalinistic policies—but Dulles said, that was now too late. He said they [the Russians] were 'up against a tough problem.'" Eisenhower agreed, and said the United States should take advantage of it: "Now is the time to talk more about reducing tensions in the world." Dulles reminded the President, "We would have to be very careful not to do anything that would look to the satellite world as though we were selling them out." [25]

Hanging up the phone, Eisenhower and Mamie left the White House for a political trip to Miami, Jacksonville, and Richmond. About midafternoon, while his plane, the *Columbine*, was en route between Florida and Virginia, the Israelis attacked on a broad front with everything they had. But their target was Egypt, not Jordan. And the Israelis were sweeping the Egyptians before them. Eisenhower got some of the news in Richmond. He went ahead with his speech, then flew up to Washington, arriving at 7 P.M. He met with the Dulles brothers, Hoover, Wilson, Radford, and Goodpaster. Radford thought that it would take the Israeli forces three days to overrun Sinai and get to Suez, which would be the end to the whole affair. Foster Dulles disagreed. "It is far more serious than that," he said. The canal was likely to be closed, the oil pipelines through the Middle East broken. Then the British and the French would intervene. "They appear to be ready for it," Dulles said, "and may even have concerted their action with the Israelis." [26]

Finally, the Americans had caught on. Britain, France, and Israel had entered into a cabal, aimed against Egypt, not Jordan. The details of their plot had yet to be revealed, but that they had plotted together there could be no doubt. Dulles speculated that they must have convinced themselves that in the end the United States would have to give its grudging approval, and support. Three weeks earlier he had warned Eisenhower that the British and the French "keep on assuming that they can count on the United States to pull their chestnuts out of the fire wherever the fire occurred." [27]

•   •

The moment for decision had come. Eisenhower's strategy of delay had to give way to action. His British friends, men who had fought beside him in the war, men he admired and loved without stint, had convinced themselves that they had reached a critical moment in their history, and at such a moment they expected the United States to stand beside them. They could not believe their great friend Ike would desert them. The French counted on Eisenhower's unbreakable commitment to NATO to force Eisenhower to tilt toward them. The Israelis thought that the election, and the importance of the Jewish vote in it, would force Eisenhower to at least stay neutral, if not support them. But good as their reasoning appeared to them to be, the conspirators were as badly wrong about Eisenhower as he had been about their plans.

Eisenhower's immediate decision, from which he never retreated one inch, was that the cabal could not be allowed to succeed. The plot reeked of nineteenth-century colonialism of the worst sort; it reeked of bad planning; it reeked of bad faith and perfidy. It also violated the 1950 Tripartite Declaration. Under the circumstances, Eisenhower said (as summarized by Goodpaster): "We cannot be bound by our traditional alliances, but must instead face the question how to make good on our pledge [in the Tripartite Declaration]." As a first step, he wanted to take a cease-fire resolution to the U.N. in the morning. "The President said, in this matter, he does not care in the slightest whether he is re-elected or not . . . He added that he did not really think the American people would throw him out in the midst of a situation like this, but if they did, so be it." He wanted to tell the British, immediately, that the U.S. would side with Egypt, even though "we recognize that much is on their side in the dispute," because "nothing justified double-crossing us." Eisenhower announced that he intended to support the Tripartite Declaration, one part of which pledged the United States to support the victim of an aggression in the Middle East. The only honorable course, he said, was to carry out that pledge. He issued a White House statement to that effect.

Then Eisenhower, Dulles, and Goodpaster met (8:15 P.M.) with the British chargé, J. E. Coulson (the ambassador had flown back to London). Eisenhower told Coulson "the prestige of the United States is involved," and that it was "incumbent" upon him to redeem America's pledge to support any victim of aggression. He said that he had told both the Egyptians and the Israelis, earlier in the year, when he declined to sell them arms, "our word was enough" to insure their security. "If we do not now fulfill our word Russia is likely to enter the situation." In view of the information he had received in the last few days, Eisenhower said "he could only conclude that he did not understand what the French were doing," but he wanted them to know, too, that the President would call Congress into a special session if he had to do so "in order to redeem our pledge . . . We will stick to our undertaking." Coulson asked if the U.S. would not first go to the Security Council. Eisenhower replied that "we plan to get there the first thing in the morning—when the doors open—before the U.S.S.R. gets there." Then he told Coulson, for the third time, that he "would not betray the good word of the United States," and asked him "to communicate these ideas urgently to London . . ."[28]

Eisenhower began the next day, October 30, by reading a message Goodpaster handed him from Ben-Gurion, saying that Israel had to strike to save herself and rejecting any thought of a cease-fire in Sinai, much less a retreat. Arthur Flemming came in to warn that Western Europe would soon be in critical need of more oil. "The President said he was inclined to think that those who began this operation should be left to work out their own oil problems—to boil in their own oil, so to speak."[29] Cabot Lodge called from New York; he had talked to the British ambassador to the U.N., Pierson Dixon, to ask him to join the Americans in calling for a cease-fire, in accordance with the 1950 Tripartite Declaration. Dixon told Lodge that the declaration "was ancient history and without current validity."

At 10 A.M., Eisenhower went into a meeting with Dulles, Hoover, Sherman Adams, and Goodpaster. There was a wire-service report that British and French landings in Suez were "imminent." Eisenhower said "that in his judgment the French and the British do not have an adequate cause for war . . . He wondered if the hand of Churchill might not be behind this—inasmuch as this action is in the mid-Victorian style." He also wondered what they proposed to do to meet their oil needs; Dulles said they probably figured "we would have no choice but to take extraordinary means to get oil to them." Eisenhower said that "he did not see much value in an unworthy and un-reliable ally and that the necessity to support them might not be as great as they believed." But that was just agitated talk; he knew Dulles was correct in saying that "the U.S. could not sit by and let them go under economically."[30]

At midday, Eisenhower exchanged a series of messages with Eden, arguing about whether the Tripartite Declaration was still valid or not. In New York, the Security Council was considering the U.S. reso-lution asking all members of the U.N. to refrain from using force in the Middle East. When the vote came that afternoon, Britain and France vetoed it. They also used the veto to defeat a Soviet resolution calling on Israel to pull back to the starting line.

At 2:17 P.M., still October 30, Dulles called to tell the President that Britain and France "gave a twelve-hour ultimatum to Egypt that is about as crude and brutal as anything he has ever seen." Dulles saw no point to studying it, because "of course by tomorrow they will be in." But Eisenhower wanted Dulles to read the ultimatum to him, as he had just received a copy and had not had time to read it. The ultimatum revealed, for the first time, the scope of the plot. Britain and France told Egypt and Israel that unless both sides withdrew ten miles from the canal and permitted Anglo-French occupation of the key points along it, Britain and France would take the canal by force to keep the two sides apart. The Israelis, of course, agreed. If the plot worked, Israel would get to keep Sinai, the British and French would have the canal, Nasser would be toppled.[31] To Eisenhower, such pipe dreams bordered on madness. He sent urgent cables to Eden and Mollet, at 3:30 P.M., pleading with them to withdraw the ultimatum.[32]

At 5 P.M., Eisenhower met with Hughes. Hughes found him "more calm (as usual) than either White House staff or State Department—all of whom are whipping themselves into an anti-British frenzy." But calm or not, the President was clearly unhappy. "I've just never seen great powers make such a complete *mess* and *botch* of things . . ." Eisenhower moaned. "Of course, there's just nobody, in a war, I'd rather have fighting alongside me than the British. . . . But—*this* thing! My God!"[33] At 5:24, Eisenhower called Dulles to discuss Eden's latest message, which Eisenhower said had one positive note—Eden was attempting to explain his position, so at least he "wants us to try to understand." They talked about the possibility of issuing a statement, and rejected it. Eisenhower expressed his "concern that if we let this go along until we are completely apart, where do we get against Communism?" After another half-dozen phone calls, the President joined Mamie for dinner, did a bit of painting, went to bed—and got up at 10:30 P.M. for another call from Dulles. Eisenhower mumbled that they could deal with the matter in the morning, and went to sleep.[34]

At dawn, October 31, the news included the results of a vote of confidence on Eden in Commons; he had survived, 270 to 218. Israeli forces were still driving westward across Sinai. But Allen Dulles, who gave the morning briefing, had some good news. The Russians had announced they would withdraw their troops from Hungary, had apologized for past behavior toward the satellites, and had pledged "noninterference in one another's internal affairs." Eisenhower feared it was too good to be true. Allen Dulles said, "This utterance is one of the most significant to come out of the Soviet Union since the end of World War II." Eisenhower replied, "Yes, if it is honest." [35]

At 9:47 A.M., Senator Knowland telephoned from California to ask if Eisenhower intended to call a special session of Congress. Eisenhower said he did not. Knowland expressed his shock at British actions. Eisenhower said what amazed him was that Eden was going ahead with the thing on the basis of a 270 to 218 vote. "I could not dream of committing this nation on such a vote." Eisenhower went on to say, "I am about to lose my British citizenship. I have done my best. I think it is the biggest error of our time, outside of losing China." But, he concluded, "Don't condemn the British too bitterly." [36]

In New York, meanwhile, Lodge had told the General Assembly that the United States intended to introduce a resolution calling upon Israel and Egypt to cease fire, on Israel to withdraw to its original borders, and on all U.N. members to refrain from the use of force, and to participate in an embargo against Israel until it withdrew.

At 11:45 A.M., Lodge phoned Eisenhower to tell him that "never has there been such a tremendous acclaim for the President's policy. Absolutely spectacular." The small nations of the world could hardly believe that the United States would support a Third World country, Egypt, in a struggle with colonial powers that were America's two staunchest allies, or that the United States would support Arabs against Israeli aggression. But it was true, and the small nations were full of admiration and delight. The introduction of the American resolution to the U.N. was, indeed, one of the great moments in U.N. history. Eisenhower's insistence on the primacy of the U.N., of treaty obligations, and of the rights of all nations gave the United States a standing in world opinion it had never before achieved. Lodge quoted some of the remarks he had heard for the President. Hammarskjöld had given him a note: "This is one of the darkest days in postwar times. Thank God you have played the way you have. This will win you many friends." The Colombian ambassador ("A very shrewd fellow," Lodge said.) reported that the Latin-American republics were "behind the President as never have they been before." The Pakistan Under Secretary said that "anybody who is an American citizen can be very proud." A "New Deal Democrat" in the U.N. Secretariat ("who always looks at me with a jaundiced eye"), told Lodge, "You make me proud to be an American." All the Asian and African nations were overjoyed. Even the busboys, typists, elevator operators at the U.N. "have been offering their congratulations." [37]

Despite this overwhelming demonstration of world public opinion (even the small nations of Europe were privately telling Lodge what a great thing this was), despite the narrow vote in the House of Commons, despite Eisenhower's warnings, despite a thoroughly botched preparation for an invasion (the British and the French forces were in disarray even before they went into action), Eden gave the order to strike. By midday, October 31, Eisenhower learned that British planes were bombing Cairo, Port Said, and other targets. Nasser had resisted, ineffectively, but he had managed to block the canal by sinking a 320-foot ship, previously loaded with cement and rocks; in the next few days, he sent thirty-two ships to the floor of the canal, blaming all the sinkings on the British.

Eisenhower spent most of the afternoon with Hughes, preparing for a national TV broadcast at 7 P.M. For Hughes, it was a "fearfully tense" time. He was working on a Dulles' draft which he did not like, but Eisenhower was unhappy with what Hughes was producing. Dulles joined them. Eisenhower told the two men to get it done, then went out on the lawn to hit some golf balls. At 6:15 Hughes took the latest draft to Eisenhower, who was dressing in his bedroom. Eisenhower made some changes, putting more emphasis on the importance of the alliance with Britain, and told Hughes to get a final copy typed. At 6:45 Eisenhower came down to the press room and began to go over it, page by page. At four minutes to seven, Hughes gave him the last page. "Boy," Eisenhower said, grinning, "this is taking it right off the stove, isn't it?" Hughes noted that the "press was edgy with expectancy, since no moment since Korea has seemed so charged with war peril. Even technicians around cameras were hushed and anxious." [38]

Eisenhower began with Poland and Hungary. He said the U.S. was ready to give economic help to new and independent governments in Eastern Europe without demanding any particular form of society, and reassured the Soviets by saying the United States wanted to be friends with these new nations but did not regard them as potential allies. Turning to the Middle East, Eisenhower said the United States wished to be friends with both Arabs and Jews. He pointed out that he had not been consulted in any way about the assault on Egypt. Britain, France, and Israel had the right to make such decisions, just as the U.S. had the right to dissent. American policy was to support the U.N. in seeking peace, and to support the rule of law.[39]

•   •

At 9 A.M. on November 1, Eisenhower presided over an NSC meeting, one of the few formal meetings of the NSC he called during the three-week crisis. Allen Dulles began with an intelligence briefing. Egypt had broken diplomatic ties with Britain and France, and Nasser had pulled most of the Egyptian Army out of Sinai to fight the British and the French in defense of the canal. In Hungary, the new Premier, Imre Nagy, told the Russians that Hungary was withdrawing from the Warsaw Pact (created in 1955 as the Soviet answer to NATO), declaring its neutrality, and appealing to the U.N. for help. The developments in Hungary, Dulles said, "are a miracle. They have disproved that a popular revolt can't occur in the face of modern weapons. Eighty percent of the Hungarian Army has defected. Except in Budapest, even the Soviet troops have shown no stomach for shooting down Hungarians." Eisenhower thanked Dulles for his presentation, then said that "he did not wish the council to take up the situation in the Soviet satellites." Instead, he wanted to concentrate on the Middle East.

Foster Dulles took the floor. His pessimism was as deep as his brother's optimism was high. The Secretary of State declared that "recent events are close to marking the death knell for Great Britain and France." They had acted contrary to the Americans' best advice, contrary to principle, and contrary to their own self-interest. He thought "we had almost reached the point of deciding today whether we think the future lies with a policy of reasserting by force colonial control over the less-developed nations, or whether we will oppose such a course of action by every appropriate means." Like Eisenhower, Dulles was furious with the French, British, and Israelis for plotting behind his back. Adding to the fury was the lost opportunity to exploit Soviet difficulties in Eastern Europe. "It is nothing less than tragic," Dulles said, "that at this very time, when we are on the point of winning an immense and long-hoped-for victory over Soviet colonialism in Eastern Europe," that Western colonialism in Egypt was the center of the world's attention. It was maddening that the British and the French were forcing the U.S. to choose between them ("our oldest and most trusted allies," Dulles called them, "the allies we would most surely depend upon" in the event of war) and Egypt. Dulles concluded, "Yet this decision must be made in a mere matter of hours—before five o'clock this afternoon." At that hour, Dulles was scheduled to address the U.N. General Assembly, at which time he had intended to formally introduce the American cease-fire resolution.

The minutes of the NSC meeting continue: "The President broke the tension which followed Secretary Dulles' statement" by quoting a telegram he had received from Adlai Stevenson, cautioning against the hasty use of American armed forces (Stevenson had earlier urged Eisenhower to send arms to Israel). Laughing and shaking his head at "politics," Eisenhower said, "It would be a complete mistake for this country to continue with any kind of aid to Israel, which was an aggressor." Dulles said he had prepared a statement, announcing that the United States was withholding certain types of government aid to Israel. Eisenhower said he thought "the sanctions outlined seemed a little mild." Dulles agreed that they were, but said more could be added later, after the General Assembly condemned Israel for aggression. Humphrey wanted to stall. He suggested that instead of introducing a resolution calling for a cease-fire, Dulles should call for an investigation by the U.N. to determine who was the aggressor. "The President replied that it seemed to him foolish for people, who know as much as we do about what is going on, to continue to give, as a government assistance to Israel." He therefore ordered Dulles to issue the statement about sanctions against Israel, and to go ahead that afternoon in New York with the original American cease-fire resolution.

After the meeting, Eisenhower sent Dulles a memorandum outlining the policy he wanted Dulles to pursue in New York. The President said the United States must take the lead in presenting a cease-fire resolution, because a resolution from some other country might be "harshly worded" against France and Britain and thus "put us in an acutely embarrassing position." Further, "at all costs the Soviets must be prevented from seizing a mantle of world leadership through a false but convincing exhibition of concern for smaller nations. Since Africa and Asia almost unanimously hate one of the three nations, Britain, France and Israel, the Soviets need only to propose severe and immediate punishment of these three to have the whole of two continents on their side." Eisenhower instructed Dulles, when he made his speech to the U.N., "to avoid condemning any nation, but to put his stress on the need for a quick cease-fire."[40]

Dulles did as he was told. As darkness fell on November 1, the General Assembly began its debate on the American cease-fire resolution. That evening, Eisenhower made his last campaign speech, in Philadelphia. Referring to the Middle East, he declared, "We cannot subscribe to one law for the weak, another law for the strong; one law for those opposing us, another for those allied with us. There can be only one law—or there shall be no peace."[41] Eisenhower then canceled the rallies he had been scheduled to attend in the last week of the campaign.

The next day, November 2, Eisenhower dictated a letter to Gruenther, beginning, "Life gets more difficult by the minute." He confessed that "sleep has been a little slower to come than usual. I seem to go to bed later and wake up earlier—which bores me." But the news that morning was good—the U.N. General Assembly had adopted the U.S. cease-fire resolution by a vote of 64 to 5 (Britain, France, Australia, New Zealand, and Israel opposing). Lester Pearson of Canada then proposed a U.N. police force to interject itself between the warring parties to insure the effectiveness of the cease-fire. By this time, Israeli forces had taken virtually all of Sinai and of the Gaza Strip. The Egyptian Air Force had been destroyed; the Israelis had five thousand Egyptian prisoners and large quantities of Soviet-made arms. British and French planes continued to bomb Egypt, but their troops had not yet landed (poor planning and worse execution of a joint British-French amphibious assault was repeating itself; Suez in 1956 was as badly botched as the Gallipoli landing of 1915).

Eisenhower was appalled by both British tactics and British strategy. "If one has to fight," he told Gruenther, "then that is that. But I don't see the point in getting into a fight to which there can be no satisfactory end, and in which the whole world believes you are playing the part of the bully and you do not even have the firm backing of your entire people." Eisenhower said he had talked to an old British friend who was "truly bitter" about Eden's gunboat diplomacy, and who had declared, "This is nothing except Eden trying to be bigger than he is." Eisenhower said he "did not dismiss it that lightly. I believe that Eden and his associates have become convinced that this is the last straw and Britain simply *had* to react in the manner of the Victorian period."[42] To Swede, Eisenhower wrote that he was astonished Britain could commit such "a terrible mistake." At the time the aggression began, the canal was being run more efficiently than it ever had been. Eisenhower said he had "insisted long and earnestly that you cannot resort to force in international relationships because of your fear of what might happen in the future," but the British had acted on just such fears. The Israelis too had reacted to their fears, and attacked, thinking, no doubt, Eisenhower told Swede, that they could "take advantage" of the United States because of the election. But, the President declared, he had informed Ben-Gurion that "we would handle our affairs exactly as though we didn't have a Jew in America."

Turning to the French, Eisenhower said they had been "perfectly cold-blooded about the matter." Their only concern was the war in Algeria, and they had provided Israel with the arms to "get someone else fighting the Arabs." [43]

At the end of the day on November 2, Eisenhower told Gruenther, "I have heard many people say a fellow would go crazy doing nothing." Then, as he had done so often during critical moments in the war, when he wrote to Mamie about his retirement fantasies, he indulged himself in a bit of wishful thinking about his retirement. At the moment, at least, he thought that a life filled with cattle raising, quail hunting, fishing, and lots of golf and bridge, with perhaps a bit of writing—"maybe such a life wouldn't be so bad." [44]

The next best thing to retirement was a weekend with the gang. Eisenhower had Whitman call the boys, and on Saturday, November 3, they arrived—George Allen, Bill Robinson, Pete Jones, and Ellis Slater. They watched Navy play Notre Dame on the television, then played nonstop bridge until dinner. At dinner, Eisenhower expressed his contempt for Stevenson, who told "outright lies." After dinner, they played more bridge. At breakfast, they talked politics, speculating on the results of the election. Eisenhower got on the subject of the men around him. He praised Bob Anderson and Arthur Larson. Slater noted in his diary, "He rates Nixon high in many respects, particularly when it comes to summing up the various positions taken on any given subject and then arriving at a decision. He may not be the most able at innovation."

After church, Eisenhower tried to take a nap "but got nowhere," so he started thinking about the Gettysburg farm and called Art Nevins on the telephone to talk about his Angus herd. In the afternoon, he played bridge. At six, he watched Sherman Adams on *Meet the Press,* ate dinner, and played more bridge until eleven. Slater was "most impressed" by Eisenhower's "equanimity during periods of stress. Here were so many crises of one kind or another—here were, as the President himself expressed it, the ten most frustrating days of his life, and yet there was no evidence at all of pressure, of indecision or of the frustration he mentioned." Eisenhower took it all "in stride as part of a day's work." [45]

The news over the weekend was quite disheartening. On Saturday, Dulles had entered Walter Reed for an emergency cancer operation, which took place that day. For the immediate future, Herbert Hoover, Jr., would be the Acting Secretary. In the Middle East, the

Syrians blew up oil pipelines running through their country from Iraq to the Mediterranean. In Britain, Eden rejected the U.N. call for a cease-fire, unless Egypt and Israel accepted French-British possession of Suez until a U.N. force could arrive. On Sunday morning, at 3:13 A.M., the Security Council met to consider an American resolution calling upon the Russians to withdraw from Hungary. The Soviet Union vetoed the resolution. That morning the Red Army launched a major assault on Hungary, following an ultimatum that Hungary rejected. Some 200,000 troops accompanied by 4,000 tanks moved on Budapest. Nagy fled to the Yugoslav Embassy, and a new Hungarian government, under Janos Kadar, took office. The Hungarian freedom fighters resisted. Eisenhower sent a message to Bulganin, reminding him of the Soviet declaration of "nonintervention" made only four days earlier, praising him for that statement, and urging him to put it into action. Meanwhile, U-2 flights revealed that the British-French armada from Cyprus was finally approaching the Egyptian coast. Eisenhower again asked Eden to turn back. Eden replied that "if we draw back now everything will go up in flames in the Middle East. . . . We cannot have a military vacuum while a U.N. force is being constituted."[46]

The Hungarians, meanwhile, wanted help. They thought they had been promised it by Radio Free Europe, and by Dulles' many references over the years to liberation. Eisenhower, however, had no intention of challenging the Russians so close to their borders. American intervention, of any type, would have appeared to the Russians as an attempt to break up the Warsaw Pact, and they would fight before they would allow that to happen. Eisenhower again refused the CIA permission to air-drop arms and supplies to the Hungarians, and he would not consider sending U.S. troops to Hungary, which he characterized as being "as inaccessible to us as Tibet." Eisenhower knew that there were limits to his power, and Hungary was outside those limits. "So . . ." he wrote in his memoirs, "the United States did the only thing it could: We readied ourselves . . . to help the refugees fleeing from the criminal action of the Soviets, and did everything possible to condemn the aggression."[47]

On Monday morning, November 5, the day before the election, all hell broke loose. British and French paratroopers landed around Port Said on the Suez Canal. Amphibious landings soon followed. Bulganin sent messages to Eden, Mollet, and Ben-Gurion, telling them that the Soviet Union was ready to use force to crush the aggressors and restore the peace. There was a thinly veiled threat to use nuclear missiles against London and Paris if the Franco-British force was not withdrawn from Suez. Bulganin also wrote Eisenhower, proposing that the U.S. and the Soviet Union join forces, march into Egypt, and put an end to the fighting. "If this war is not stopped, it is fraught with danger and can grow into a Third World War," Bulganin warned.[48]

At 5 P.M., Eisenhower summoned Hoover, Adams, and Hughes to discuss a reply to Bulganin's preposterous proposal that the United States and the Soviet Union join hands against Britain and France. To Hughes, Eisenhower seemed "poised and relaxed," although fatigued. The discussion was somber. The conferees agreed on the word "unthinkable" in dismissing Bulganin's suggestion. They worried about the Russians, whom they recognized were torn by hope and fear—hope that the Suez crisis would lead to a breakup of NATO, and fear that Hungary would lead to a breakup of the Warsaw Pact. Eisenhower described their position: "Those boys are both furious and scared. Just as with Hitler, that makes for the most dangerous possible state of mind. And we better be damn sure that every intelligence point and every outpost of our armed forces is absolutely right on their toes." Under the circumstances, Eisenhower said, "We have to be positive and clear in our every word, every step. And if those fellows start something, we may have to hit 'em—and, if necessary, with *everything* in the bucket."[49] Eisenhower directed Hoover to issue a statement that would include clear warnings—if the Russians tried to put troops into the Middle East, the U.S. would resist with force.

November 6 was election day. At 8:37 A.M., Eisenhower met with Allen Dulles, Hoover, and Goodpaster for the latest intelligence briefing. Dulles reported that the Soviets had told the Egyptians they intended to "do something" in the Middle East. He thought it possible that they would send air forces into Syria. Eisenhower told Dulles to send U-2 flights over Syria and Israel, "avoiding, however, any flights into Russia." If the Soviets attacked the British and the French, Eisenhower said, "we would be in war, and we would be justified in taking military action even if Congress were not in session." If reconnaissance "discloses Soviet air forces on Syrian bases," Eisenhower said, he thought "that there would be reason for the British and French to destroy them." Goodpaster's memo on the conference concluded on a chilling note: "The President asked if our forces in the Mediterranean are equipped with atomic antisubmarine weapons."[50]

At 9 A.M. Eisenhower and Mamie drove to Gettysburg to vote, then took a helicopter back to Washington, arriving around noon. Goodpaster met him at the airport to report that the U-2 flights had discovered no Soviet planes on Syrian airfields, or any moving into Egypt. World War III was not about to begin. In the White House Cabinet Room, Eisenhower met with Radford. The question was, Should the U.S. mobilize? Eisenhower wanted mobilization put into effect by degrees, "in order to avoid creating a stir." As a start, he wanted Radford to recall military personnel on leave, an action that could not be concealed and that would give the Russians pause.[51]

At 12:55 P.M., Eisenhower put through another call to Eden, who had just announced British willingness to accept a cease-fire. (The war had already cost the British nearly $500 million; further, the British and the French now claimed control of the canal.) Eisenhower said, "I can't tell you how pleased we are . . . After the cease-fire it seems like the little technical things would be settled very quickly, and when Hammarskjold comes along with his people you people ought to be able to withdraw very quickly." Eisenhower added that the U.N. peace-keeping force was "getting Canadian troops—lots of troops." Eden wanted American troops. Would they be a part of the U.N. force? Eisenhower said he wanted none of the great nations in it. "I am afraid the Red boy is going to demand the lion's share. I would rather make it no troops from the big five." Eden reluctantly agreed. "If I survive here tonight [he faced a vote of confidence]," Eden concluded, "I will call you tomorrow." Then he asked how the election was going for Eisenhower. "We have given our whole thought to Hungary and the Middle East," Eisenhower responded. "I don't give a damn how the election goes. I guess it will be all right."[52]

Eisenhower spent the afternoon resting, to prepare for the excitement of the long night ahead. He canceled his plans to go to Augusta the next day, because of the Suez situation, a decision that he hated to make. "He's as disappointed as a kid who had counted out all the days to Christmas," Whitman reported. At 10 P.M. he left the White House for the Republican headquarters. As predicted, the early returns showed that he was winning by a landslide, but that the Democrats were going to retain control of Congress.

In the excitement of the contest, Eisenhower shed his supposed indifference to the outcome. He told Hughes, "There's Michigan and Minnesota still to see. You remember that story of Nelson—dying, he looked around and asked, 'Are there any of them still left?' I guess that's *me*. When I get in a battle, I just want to win the whole

thing . . . six or seven states we can't help. But I don't want to lose
any more. Don't want any of them 'left'—like Nelson. That's the way
I feel."

By midnight, he was growing irritated at Stevenson for not con-
ceding. "What in the name of God is the monkey waiting for?" the
President demanded. "Polishing his prose?" Eisenhower loved to win,
but not to gloat. In North Africa in 1943, and in Europe in 1945,
he had refused to be present at the surrender ceremony. On November 6, 1956, when Stevenson finally appeared on the television screen
to concede, Eisenhower stalked out of the room, saying over his shoulder that the others should stay "to receive the surrender."

Eisenhower got the mandate he wanted from the American people, who voted 35,581,003 for him, 25,738,765 for Stevenson. That
10,000,000-vote margin was almost double the margin of 1952. Stevenson carried only seven southern states.⁵³

Eden too survived his vote of confidence. At 8:53 A.M. on November 7, he called Eisenhower to ask for an immediate—that day or the
next—summit conference in Washington between himself, Eisenhower,
and Mollet. Eisenhower feared that Eden was trying to back out of
British acceptance of a cease-fire and a U.N. force taking control in
Suez, but Eden said that what he wanted to discuss was what happened
next. Well, Eisenhower replied, "If we are going to talk about the
future and about the Bear—okay."⁵⁴

Eisenhower next met with Adams and Goodpaster. They both
told him the proposed conference was a terrible idea. Goodpaster
emphasized that such a meeting would give the appearance "that we
were now concerting action in the Middle East independently of the
U.N. action." Hoover joined them. He agreed with Goodpaster and
said he had just talked to Dulles, who also opposed the meeting.
Hoover also said he had a report from Allen Dulles stating that the
Soviets had offered Egypt 250,000 volunteers and that preparations
for their departure were under way. Eisenhower asked Goodpaster to
check on that report. While he did so, Eisenhower called Eden to inform him that the meeting would have to be postponed. Goodpaster
returned to report that there was nothing solid in the intelligence
data, but certainly the Soviets did not have 250,000 troops on the
move.⁵⁵

That morning, Ben-Gurion issued a statement saying Israel rejected the U.N. order to withdraw Israeli forces from Sinai and Gaza
and to permit U.N. forces to enter. Eisenhower sent him a strong pro-

test. Then the President received a message from Bulganin: "I feel urged to state that the problem of withdrawal of Soviet troops from Hungary . . . comes completely and entirely under the competence of the Hungarian and Soviet governments."[56] The fighting in Budapest, meanwhile, had passed its peak. Hungarian refugees were fleeing to Austria at the rate of three to four thousand a day; there were forty thousand dead freedom fighters. As had happened so many times before, and would again, the United States found itself unable to influence in any significant way events in Eastern Europe. The Russians violated their pledge of safe-conduct to Nagy, seized him, held a secret trial, and executed him. All that Eisenhower could do was announce that the U.S. was ready to accept 21,000 of the 150,000 Hungarian refugees, and that he would ask for emergency legislation to let more Hungarians enter the U.S.

On the morning of November 9, Eisenhower met with the NSC to begin planning for picking up the pieces in the Middle East. He wanted American oil companies organized for a major effort in providing France and Britain with oil, saying—with a smile—that "despite my stiff-necked Attorney General" he could give the industry members a certificate that they were acting in the national interest, thus removing the threat of antitrust suits. And if the heads of the oil companies nevertheless landed in jail, he laughed, he would pardon them. Eisenhower said he would not actually send any oil, however, until the British and the French had completely withdrawn and the U.N. force was in place. In the meantime, he did not want to aggravate the situation any further. "The way of the peacemaker is proverbially hard," he sighed.[57]

It was indeed. At 8:45 A.M., the newly appointed British ambassador, Sir Harold Caccia, arrived to present his credentials. After an exchange of pleasantries, Eisenhower told Caccia that it baffled him "that the Russians, as cruel and brutal as they are, can get away with murder . . . However, if we breach the smallest courtesy, the whole world is aflame." In the Far East, he complained, where anti-British sentiment was white-hot, no one paid any attention to the Russian actions in Hungary. To the people of Asia, Eisenhower said, "colonialism is not colonialism unless it is a matter of white domination over colored people." The Asians just shrugged off the murders committed in Hungary—that was a case of whites killing whites, of no concern to them. But anything Britain did in the Middle East was of concern.[58]

At 4:48 P.M., Lodge called from New York. Another resolution condemning the Russians in Hungary was under discussion. Lodge told Eisenhower that "there is the feeling at the U.N. that for ten years we have been exciting the Hungarians through our Radio Free Europe, and now that they are in trouble, we turn our backs on them." Eisenhower protested strongly. He insisted that was wrong—"we have never excited anybody to rebel." [59] The President put through a call to Dulles, still in Walter Reed recovering from his surgery. He repeated Lodge's statement about telling the Hungarians to revolt and then "turning our backs to them when they are in a jam." Dulles assured Eisenhower that "we always said we are against violent rebellion." Eisenhower agreed that that was so, and expressed his "amazement" that Lodge was in ignorance of that fact. In addition, Eisenhower said, the Europeans at the U.N. were "asking why we are so fretful about France and Britain with a few troops in Egypt, while we don't show as much concern about Hungary." Eisenhower was concerned about "putting ourselves in the wrong" by urging the French, British, and Israelis to pull back, while not putting more pressure on the Russians.

But the President could put no meaningful pressure on Bulganin. The Russians did not need Arab oil, or American arms or money, and they had complete military preponderance in Eastern Europe. As Eisenhower later told C. D. Jackson, who was frantic about the lack of action in Hungary by the United States, the only option available to him was to use atomic weapons. "But to annihilate Hungary . . . is in no way to help her." [60] Britain and France, on the other hand, desperately needed American oil and money; Israel needed American money and good will. They could be pressured. Eisenhower applied it.

Eisenhower called his ambassador to the Court of St. James's, Winthrop Aldrich, to tell Aldrich to talk to Rab Butler and Harold Macmillan, the most likely successors to Eden when he resigned (talk of his resignation filled the air), and tell them that "as soon as things happen that we anticipate, we can furnish a lot of fig leaves." He wondered, "Will that be enough to get the boys moving?" Aldrich thought so. [61]

But having invested so much, the British were reluctant to pull out. Eisenhower kept the pressure on by withholding American oil and financial assistance. The British tried a bit of counterpressure. Lord Ismay wrote Eisenhower, accusing him of deserting his friends "in their hour of trial, and now won't even help them out with oil and gas, etc." The accusation pained Eisenhower. He told Dulles, who had gone to Key West to recuperate, that he and Ismay "have been the best of friends over the years." But he would not release the oil until the British were well on their way out.[62] Churchill also wrote the President a long letter suggesting that they leave it to the historians to sort out the arguments and themselves look to the future. The danger was that the Soviets would succeed in their attempt to convince the Arabs that it was their threats, not Eisenhower's actions, that had saved the day for Egypt. Eisenhower replied that he was fully aware that "the Soviets are the real enemy of the Western world, implacably hostile and seeking our destruction." But he could not resist giving Churchill a four-page summary of events of the past few weeks, with the emphasis on how many times he had warned Eden against using force. He also pointed out that "even by the doctrine of expediency the invasion could not be judged as soundly conceived and skillfully executed." Eisenhower did resist any temptation to point out that the last time the British engaged in an amphibious assault, it was in June of 1944; he had been in command and everything had gone successfully. Instead, he concluded with the hope that the Suez crisis would be "washed off the slate as soon as possible," because "nothing saddens me more than the thought that I and my old friends of years have met a problem concerning which we do not see eye to eye. I shall never be happy until our old-time closeness has been restored."[63]

Others among Eisenhower's British wartime friends wrote him letters of protest. To Lord Tedder, Eisenhower replied, "I do not conceive it to be the function of a friend to encourage action that he believes in his heart to be unwise and even inexpedient." He insisted that in trying to prevent Eden from taking action, and now forcing him to withdraw, he was acting "as a *true* friend."[64] He repeated those statements in a letter to Freddie de Guingand.[65]

By the end of November, the U.N. force was moving into place, and the British and the French were almost out. Eisenhower lifted the embargo on oil sales to Britain, and the United States soon was shipping 200,000 barrels a day. The Americans loaned money to the British to tide them over. By Christmastime the French and the British troops were gone and the Egyptians had started to clear the canal.

At a meeting with Republican leaders on New Year's Eve, Eisenhower was asked about British and French attitudes toward the U.S. "Underneath," the President replied, "the governments are thankful we did what we did. But publicly, we have to be the whipping boy." Anyway, "The whole darn thing is straightening out very rapidly." A recent NATO meeting had gone "very well." The alliance had survived the crisis.[66]

• •

After all the nuclear saber rattling that had gone on, relations with the Russians were still tense. Three days after the election, Eisenhower had proposed to Hoover that the United States take advantage of the worldwide fright, a fright that Bulganin presumably shared, to make some progress on disarmament. Eisenhower was willing to make a dramatic offer, such as pulling NATO forces behind the Rhine and withdrawing American ground troops in Germany. Hoover doubted that Dulles would agree. Eisenhower said he just wanted the Secretary to have the thought, because "as long as we are before the world, just calling each other names, being horrified all the time by their brutality, then we get nowhere." But nothing came of the President's idea.[67]

One reason was Soviet reaction to continued U-2 overflights. During the crisis, Eisenhower had to know what military moves the Soviets were making, and after the election he authorized additional flights. The Soviets protested, privately but strongly. On November 15, Eisenhower met with Hoover, Radford, and Allan Dulles to discuss the flights. Eisenhower thought that they were beginning to "cost more than we gain in form of solid information." Hoover pointed out that "if we lost a plane at this stage, it would be almost catastrophic." Eisenhower agreed, and pointed out that "everyone in the world says that in the last six weeks, the U.S. has gained a place it hasn't held since World War II." The country had to "preserve a place that is correct and moral." Still, he worried about those Russians and what they might do with the Red Army, so he approved flights over Eastern Europe, "but not the deep one." The pilot should "stay as close to border as possible."[68]

The Russians continued to protest. One month later, on December 18, Eisenhower talked to Foster Dulles about the overflights of Eastern Europe. Eisenhower said he was "going to order complete stoppage of the entire business." As to the Russian protests, Dulles said, "I think we will have to admit this was done and say we are sorry. We cannot deny it." Eisenhower said he would call Charlie Wilson "and have him stop it." Dulles reminded the President that "our relations with Russia are pretty tense at the moment." Eisenhower agreed that this was no time to be provocative.[69]

The problem of the Hungarian refugees remained. On November 26, Eisenhower gave a warm and heartfelt greeting to the first arrivals, who came to the White House to see the President. He expressed his shock and horror at Russian actions and assured the Hungarians that they were most welcome in the U.S.[70]

On the day after Christmas, Eisenhower held an 11 A.M. meeting with Nixon, who had just returned from a trip to Vienna to get an overview on the refugee situation. Nixon remarked on the high caliber of the refugees. They were mostly young, well-educated, leadership types who had to flee because they had participated in the rebellion. Eisenhower recalled a remark that Zhukov had made to him in the summer of 1945: "If you get rid of the leaders of a country, you can do anything you want to." But the only thing the Americans could do for poor Hungary was accept refugees—yet the law prevented that. Nixon said there were still seventy thousand in Vienna. Eisenhower remarked that the Hungarians were productive people, and that it would be "a tremendous thing" if some of the Middle East countries would take in refugees. The Latin Americans also ought to try to take some—God knew they could "use the skills the Hungarians have." Meanwhile, he wanted the State Department to continue to process applications, even if the quota had been used up, because if the processing stopped, "the pick of the refugees will go to other countries."[71] The best of Hungary's young people but not freedom for Hungary—that was what the United States got for four years of agitation about liberation.

CHAPTER SIXTEEN

The Eisenhower Doctrine

January–July 1957

"NEW FORCES and new nations stir and strive across the earth," Eisenhower declared in his Second Inaugural Address. "From the deserts of North Africa to the islands of the South Pacific one-third of all mankind has entered upon an historic struggle for a new freedom: freedom from grinding poverty." Across this world, he said, "the winds of change" were blowing. The Communists were trying to get those winds blowing their way, in order to exploit the Third World. The great battleground of the Cold War had shifted away from Europe and Korea and Formosa, where the situation was relatively stable, to Africa, the Middle East, and the Indian subcontinent, where the situation was in active ferment. Suez was only the most spectacular event in the process of the breaking up of European colonialism. New nations were emerging, or struggling to emerge, from the wreckage. Most had not been prepared by their rulers for independence. Many had raw materials unavailable elsewhere, particularly oil and minerals that were crucial to the Western industrial system. All of the new nations appeared to be more or less in danger of falling to the Communists.

Suez made Eisenhower almost painfully aware of the importance of the Third World to the United States, which was why he made it not only the theme of his second inaugural but of much of his second term. "No people can live to itself alone," he told the American public. If living conditions were not improved in the Third World, it would go Communist. "Not even America's prosperity could long survive if other nations did not also prosper." [1] Even before the inaugural, Eisenhower had set his Administration to work on what Burt Kaufman has called "the most searching review of the U.S. foreign-aid program since the adoption of the Marshall Plan." When the reports came in, two months later, they concluded—as Eisenhower already had—that economic assistance to the Third World would lead to economic developments which would lead to political stability and the evolution of democratic societies. To get the process started, soft loans on a long-term, continuing basis were necessary. [2]

Convincing the American people was the trick. Over the next four years, Eisenhower would try every form of persuasion at his command to demonstrate to his countrymen the importance of the Third World to the United States. It was one of the most frustrating experiences of his life. He could not convince the people; he could not convince the Republican Party; he could not even convince his own Secretary of the Treasury. Eisenhower recognized that one of the fundamental truths the Suez crisis taught was that the Arabs were more important to the West than the West was to them, but he could not get enough of the American people to see it that way, much less that what happened in Central Africa or Algeria or India made any difference in their lives. Eisenhower tried to explain, on February 5, to a group of Old Guard China Lobby Republicans, that "Formosa, if lost, is a blow, but not a major world defeat." But if the West lost the Middle East, "that would be major." The Republicans did not believe him, and could not see the point to giving away money to Africans and Asians (other than those in South Korea and Formosa). [3]

One of Eisenhower's great concerns was the raw materials that would be lost to the West if the Third World went Communist. Fearful that it might happen, he made stockpiling one of his pet projects, a subject he raised innumerable times in Cabinet meetings. He was particularly eager to trade the grain in storage for minerals or oil that could be stockpiled. At a leaders' meeting, "the President again set forth his belief that the U.S. should miss no opportunity to replace perishables with nonperishable resources which might some day be exhausted." But he could never get his Cabinet or his party to agree. "The President told the leaders how he had shocked Secretary Humphrey when he stated his preference for manganese instead of gold in Fort Knox, on the basis that you can't make bullets out of gold." [4]

Humphrey objected to stockpiling because it was expensive and would disrupt the world market; he objected to loans to developing countries because they would never be paid back and would unbalance the American budget. Eisenhower patiently tried to avoid a split with Humphrey by educating the Secretary to the realities of the modern world. "Few individuals understand the intensity and force of the spirit of nationalism that is gripping all peoples of the world today," Eisenhower said. Humphrey protested that the United States should not encourage the emerging nations, that it should instead support the French in Algeria, the British in Rhodesia, and so on, because the Europeans ran the colonies more efficiently and thus would improve living conditions faster. Eisenhower replied that "it is my personal conviction that almost any one of the newborn states of the world would far rather embrace Communism or any other form of dictatorship than to acknowledge the political domination of another government even though that brought to each citizen a far higher standard of living." Citing his own experiences in the Philippines, Eisenhower explained the obvious to Humphrey, that through national independence people obtained "fierce pride and personal satisfaction."

Eisenhower wanted Humphrey to understand "that the spirit of nationalism, coupled with a deep hunger for some betterment in physical conditions and living standards, creates a critical situation in the underdeveloped areas of the world." He pointed out that "Communism is not going to be whipped merely by pious words, but it can be whipped by . . . a readiness on the part of ourselves . . . to face up to the critical phase through which the world is passing and do our duty like men." [5]

Eisenhower's exhortation to Humphrey to be a man did not succeed. The President himself, indeed, agreed with one part of Humphrey's position. On July 2, at a leaders' meeting, the Republicans told Eisenhower that Senator Kennedy was going to make a long speech on Algeria, and propose a resolution in support of Algerian independence. They wanted to know how to reply. Eisenhower, citing Humphrey, admitted that "the people of Algeria still lacked sufficient education and training to run their own government in the most efficient way." Eisenhower was also concerned about the effects on relations with France if the Senate supported Algerian independence.

But strong as those arguments were, the President continued, they had to give way to even stronger ones. "The United States could not possibly maintain that freedom—independence—liberty—were necessary to us but not to others." Therefore, the Republicans could not argue against the Algerian cause. "Perhaps," the President concluded, "Republicans might best just chide Mr. Kennedy a bit for pretending to have all the answers." [6]

When Eisenhower entered office in 1953, he was in agreement with the moderate Republican notion that aid programs, and preeminently the Marshall Plan, had served their purpose and ought to be abandoned in favor of more trade; thus his attempt to lower tariffs. "Trade, not aid" was the slogan. Humphrey was the strongest advocate of this policy, with its emphasis on private American investment in underdeveloped countries. Eisenhower, however, had learned during his first term that the flow of private capital into the Third World was a mere trickle, and that the money that did go in was invested to provide profits for the West, not improvements in living conditions for the recipient nation. He decided to make a major policy shift.

By 1957, as Kaufman notes, Eisenhower's slogan had become "trade *and* aid," with the emphasis on government to government, soft, long-term loans to Third World countries. He therefore called for a Development Loan Fund of $2 billion, spread over a three-year period.[7] Even as he made his proposal, however, Eisenhower feared that his chances of getting it through Congress "were approximately nil."[8] Nevertheless, he made it a top priority of the Administration for 1957, along with direct-aid packages to such countries as India and military-assistance programs to neutral as well as allied nations.

Eisenhower put his time, prestige, energy, and persuasive powers into the effort to get his foreign-aid package through Congress. He met interminably with the Republican leaders, with the Democratic leaders, with groups and associations interested in the subject. He made speeches. He devoted nearly every one of his stag dinners to convincing his guests to become missionaries for foreign aid.[9]

A conversation Eisenhower had with Senator Styles Bridges on May 21 illustrates the President's methods. Bridges had characterized the foreign-aid program as nothing but "a do-gooder giveaway." Eisenhower called him into the Oval Office. "It is pretty hard," he said, "when I have to bear the burdens not only of the Presidency," but also those of head of a party in which "one of the principal people"—Bridges—could so characterize his program. "I think nothing could be further from the truth" than to call it a "do-gooder" program, Eisenhower said. The program was necessary to meet the Communist menace. "If I knew a cheap way out of this one," he added, "I certainly would take it . . . I think my party ought to trust me a little bit more when I put not only my life's work, but my reputation and everything else, on the line in favor of this."

Bridges protested that what he had in mind was money going to Yugoslavia, India, Indonesia, and other neutrals. Eisenhower said he had been making a study of neutrality, that "I'm reading Horace now for that purpose," and that in the case of India, or Yugoslavia, he highly approved of their neutral stance. Take India, he said; suppose it declared, "We take our stand with the West." India had an eighteen-hundred-mile border with China. "How much have we got to put into India to make it reasonably safe for them even to exist?" Could the United States afford to arm India sufficiently so that it could defend itself? Could the United States afford to send the troops necessary to defend that long border? India was better off neutral.

But India had to develop. It contained 350 million people, many of them practically starving. "You could put all the defense in the world in there, and they will go Communistic." Eisenhower reminded Bridges of his responsibilities: "You are the United States Republican senator who has been in the longest; you are respected; you are intelligent and can look these problems in the face." He admitted that "sometimes I think it would be wonderful if only we could go back to the days of 1896," but insisted that "we cannot . . . Freedom happens to be something that, if it becomes practiced only in one place on earth, then it can no longer be practiced even there." As the President talked, he grew agitated and began pacing. "Look," he told Bridges, "I want to wage the Cold War in a militant, but reasonable, style whereby we appeal to the people of the world as a better group to hang with than the Communists." Bridges managed to put in a protest—he did not like giving money to Yugoslavia. Eisenhower snapped back, "Tito is the only man in Europe who succeeded in breaking away completely from the Soviets." The United States had given him six jet aircraft, obsolete ones "but which are all right for him." Eisenhower said he wanted more aid for Yugoslavia because "I do not by any manner of means want Tito to find that he has no place to go except back to the Soviets." Bridges asked about the danger of Tito using the military equipment against the United States. Eisenhower scoffed at the notion—"I would say that two bombs in Yugoslavia would make the country helpless."[10]

Despite Eisenhower's efforts with Bridges and other senators, the Senate and House continued to cut back on his requested $4 billion appropriation. Eisenhower called in the ten members of the House and Senate most concerned in the appropriation debate to tell them that he felt so strongly about his program that he would sacrifice part of his own salary "to meet the pressing need of adequate funds for foreign aid." He repeated this unique offer the next morning at his regular meeting with Republican leaders. It did not work. In the final bill, Congress cut his request by almost one-third, to $2.7 billion.

This was, according to Republican Senator N. Alexander Smith, "a devastating defeat . . . for the President."[11]

Eisenhower was furious. To Swede, he wrote, "I am repeatedly astonished, even astounded, by the apparent ignorance of members of Congress in the general subject of our foreign affairs." He realized that congressional penny-pinching "reflects abysmal ignorance" among the general public as well. Each congressman, he said, "thinks of himself as intensely patriotic; but it does not take the average member long to conclude that his first duty to his country is to get himself re-elected," a conviction that led to a "capacity for rationalization that is almost unbelievable." "Again and again," he said, he had patiently explained to congressmen that foreign aid represented America's "best investment." It helped keep down the cost of the American military establishment and provided consuming power in recipient nations. Most of the foreign-aid money was spent in the United States to provide goods and services for the Third World countries. It was a program that, to the President, was so obviously good for America that he could not understand how anyone could be opposed.[12] But opposed Congress was, and his virtual one-man attempt to push through an adequate foreign-aid program failed.

What Congress was willing to give the President, although only after intense debate, was the Eisenhower Doctrine. Immediately after the Suez crisis, Eisenhower decided that the President needed, in advance, authorization to intervene in the Middle East before the next crisis got out of hand. He also wanted authorization to send military and economic aid to the Arab nations. At an extraordinary meeting on New Year's Day, 1957, that lasted from 2 to 6 P.M., and that included the top thirty senators and representatives from both parties, plus thirty-two men from the Executive Branch, Eisenhower explained his reasoning. As summarized in the minutes of the meeting, Eisenhower said "that should there be a Soviet attack in that area he could see no alternative but that the United States move in immediately to stop it, other than suffering loss of that area to Russia." Soviet control of the Middle East "would be disastrous to Europe because of its oil requirements." Eisenhower said that in his view "the United States must put the entire world on notice that we are ready to move instantly if necessary." He assured the congressmen that he would always follow constitutional procedures if possible, "but pointed out that modern war might be a matter of hours only." If Congress would give him the authority he sought, Eisenhower added, "it might never have to be used."

382 EISENHOWER

The congressmen voiced several reservations or objections, and protested that the President already had the power to act without a congressional authorization. Eisenhower said that "greater effect could be had from a consensus of executive and legislative opinion," and pointed out that the countries of the Middle East wanted reassurance that the United States was ready to help them. If the Russians started to move whole armies into the Middle East, it would take time, and in that instance, Eisenhower said, he would be able to go to Congress. But if the Communists began fermenting internal coups within the Arab states, he would have to move fast. He would not, however, intervene unless asked to do so by the government that was threatened. The resolution he was offering, he said, would "contain clear indications that the United States would act only where requested, and that the United States was not being truculent."[13]

At noon on January 5, Eisenhower went up to Capitol Hill to deliver in person his special message on the Middle East. After a brief review of the situation there, he asked Congress for authorization to provide economic aid and military assistance to "any nation or group of nations which desires such aid." Further, he wanted authorization to employ American armed forces "to secure and protect the territorial integrity and political independence of such nations, requesting such aid, against overt armed aggression from any nation controlled by International Communism." To implement the economic and military aid portions of his request, the President asked for $200 million beyond the foreign-aid money already appropriated. Eisenhower assured Congress that he would not use the authority for American military intervention "except at the desire of the nation attacked," and expressed his "profound hope that this authority would never have to be exercised at all." In justification for his request, he said the "greatest risk" in the Middle East "is that ambitious despots may miscalculate. If power-hungry Communists should . . . estimate that the Middle East is inadequately defended, they might be tempted to use open measures of armed attack." In that event, the United States could not stand aside. "I am convinced that the best insurance against this dangerous contingency is to make clear" America's readiness and willingness to act.[14]

The problem with going to Congress for prior authorization was that the ensuing debate revealed America was neither ready nor willing to act. Politicians who were unwilling to support Eisenhower's overall economic-aid program for the Third World in general were just as unwilling to authorize money and arms for the Arabs. Speaker Rayburn told Dulles that neither he nor any other Democrat would cosponsor the resolution, nor in any other way identify themselves with the unpopular proposal. But he also promised that the Democrats "were not going to put in a counterresolution." Then Rayburn himself proposed a substitute declaration: "The United States regards as vital to her interest the preservation of the independence and integrity of the states of the Middle East and, if necessary, will use her armed force to that end." Eisenhower refused to accept it because it eliminated economic and military aid. In the Senate, Richard Russell of Georgia made a similar proposal. Like Rayburn, he linked his substitute to the ongoing battle over the budget and the need to eliminate the deficits. Eisenhower thought Russell's argument was a case of penny-wise and pound-foolish. He said his original resolution was directed against two dangers, direct armed aggression and indirect subversion. "To counter one and not the other would destroy both efforts." The Arabs needed arms, and "their peoples need hope for improving economic conditions." Further, Eisenhower feared that the Russell substitution "would suggest that our country wants only to wage peace in terms of war."[15] But Congress was not convinced. Some members, known as prominent friends of Israel, objected to any aid to the Arabs. Others objected to relinquishing, in advance and without knowledge of the particular circumstances, the Constitution's delegation of the authority to declare war to Congress alone. Still others feared it would weaken America's ties to the NATO countries, to the U.N., or both.[16] The debate continued.

While Eisenhower bemoaned what he regarded as the stupid short-sightedness of the Congress toward the Arabs, and regretted its ability to delay and even destroy his foreign policy, there was an area for action available to him that did not require congressional approval. It was personal diplomacy, and he went after it with a vengeance. As soon as the Suez crisis had simmered down, Eisenhower invited a series of Arab and Asian leaders to the White House, where he greeted them with enthusiasm, showered them with honors, and talked to them at length about their problems and what America could do to help. It was, in effect, a blitz of the Third World.

The first to come was the Premier of Tunisia, Habib Bourguiba. His primary concern was the French in Algeria. Then came Nehru, followed by the Lebanese ambassador, who was worried about the effect of Nasser's appeals to pan-Arab nationalism in his country. Eisenhower deplored the intervention and agitation in Lebanon's internal affairs and promised to do all he could to help the Lebanese.[17]

The most important visitor was King Saud, who remained Eisenhower's personal choice as the man who could successfully challenge Nasser for leadership of the Arab world, turning pan-Arab nationalism away from the Soviet Union toward the West. More specifically, the West needed Saudi Arabian oil for Europe, and the Americans needed to extend their lease on Dhahran airfield. For his part, Saud needed American arms. Throughout the Suez crisis, Eisenhower had treated Saud with the most exquisite care, flattering him, making promises, repeating assurances ("Your Majesty's needs have been always in our mind.").[18] When Saud indicated that he wished to visit the United States, Eisenhower was enthusiastic, although he had one worry—"Will he bring his harem?"[19]

It was the wrong worry. On January 9, Dulles called Eisenhower to report that Saud had sent word "that he will not come to the U.S. unless the President would meet him at the airport." Saud's demand posed two major problems for Eisenhower. First, it would shatter precedent. American practice had always been for the President's first greeting of a foreign head of state to take place at the White House. If Eisenhower went to the airport to greet Saud, he would have to do so for every subsequent visitor, a time-draining act that could also jeopardize the President's health (Eisenhower was trying to cut down on, not add to, the physical demands of his job). It was a mark of how important the role was that Eisenhower had projected for Saud that Eisenhower told Dulles, "I don't know how we can get out of it, unless we don't want him to come at all." But Eisenhower definitely did want Saud to come, so he told Dulles, "Of course I will meet him."[20]

The other problem posed by Saud's demand was that it highlighted the king's visit at a time when pro-Israeli forces in the United States vigorously objected to any visit at all by Saud. When Saud arrived, on January 29, Eisenhower had escort ships of the Navy meet him in New York harbor. Cabot Lodge was there, along with other dignitaries, but the mayor of the city, Robert Wagner, refused to grant Saud the customary reception, saying that the king "is not the kind of person we want to officially recognize in New York City." Saud flew to Washington, where Eisenhower met him at the airport. That evening, at a formal dinner at the White House (white ties and tailcoats, or flowing robes), Eisenhower entertained Saud, helped by the chief executives of Aramco, Jersey, Socony, Texaco, and Standard of California, all of whom had had a great year in 1956, thanks to the Suez crisis.[21]

Saud was the first non-European monarch Eisenhower had met, and he was more than a bit astonished. He got Saud to talking about hunting, and asked what kind of rifle and shotgun the king preferred.

Saud said he hunted with falcons and never used a gun. The heavy robes that Saud and his people wore had a musky odor, Eisenhower found, and when he was surrounded by Saudis "I nearly suffocated." The king, he discovered, "is strictly medieval. When he says 'my people,' he means just that." Saud handed out $50 and $100 bills to the waiters as tips; Eisenhower never allowed tipping in the White House, but on this occasion he held his tongue.

Insofar as there were substantial discussions, Saud gave his grudging approval to the Eisenhower Doctrine, assured Eisenhower that he would never allow Saudi Arabia to go Communist, pointed out that he had refused numerous Soviet offers to provide him with arms, and said he had no intention of making any threats about forcing the Americans out of Dhahran. But, Saud added, "My people would revolt if I renew the Dhahran lease without an arms agreement." The chances of a Saudi revolt against the king were about nil, but Eisenhower suppressed his smile and promised to do his best to get arms for Saud. He also promised that no American Jew would serve in the U.S. Air Force in Dhahran (this was long-standing practice; the oil companies too promised the Saudis that no Jew would ever work for them in Saudi Arabia).[22] Overall, Eisenhower thought Saud "introspective and shy," which hardly qualified him to challenge the charismatic Nasser for Arab leadership. But there was no one else in sight, and Eisenhower decided that Saud would be "the person we tie to."[23]

Saud's visit coincided with a crisis in American-Israeli relations, one that also threatened to weaken or defeat the Eisenhower Doctrine. Three months after the crisis, Britain and France had withdrawn from Suez and the Egyptians were clearing the canal. But the Israelis refused to leave Gaza, as they had promised to do and as had been required by the U.N. resolution. By the end of January, the Egyptians were threatening to stop the process of clearing the canal unless and until Israel withdrew from Gaza. On February 3, Eisenhower sent Ben-Gurion a strongly worded three-page telegram, urging him to pull out of Gaza and warning that unless Israel did so, the U.N., already being pressed hard by the Arabs on the subject, would impose sanctions on Israel.[24]

The President then went down to Humphrey's plantation in Thomasville, Georgia, for two weeks of bridge and hunting. The newspapers, at that time, were speculating on a rift between the President and the Secretary of the Treasury over the budget and over the foreign-aid proposals, but as Slater said in his diary, "If there is a rift it is be-

cause of that stupid club lead George made last night." The quail
shooting was superb, and Eisenhower managed to shoot a twenty-two-
pound wild turkey, his first. The hunters rode in wicker buggies drawn
by white mules and driven by "the old colored retainers." Perfect
weather helped make the vacation even more enjoyable.[25]

But Eisenhower had to cut it short because of the Middle East
situation. On February 16, Dulles flew down to Thomasville, along
with Lodge, to talk to the President and Humphrey about Ben-
Gurion's response to Eisenhower's telegram. Unless Israel retained civil
administration and police power in Gaza, Ben-Gurion said, and had a
guaranteed right to use the Gulf of Aqaba, she would not withdraw.
Dulles was angry. He told Eisenhower that the United States "had
gone just as far as was possible to try to make it easy and acceptable
to the Israelis to withdraw." Dulles said that to give any further help
to Israel "would almost surely jeopardize the entire Western influence
in the Middle East and make it almost certain that virtually all of the
Middle East countries would feel that United States policy toward the
area was in the last analysis controlled by the Jewish influence in
the United States and that accordingly the only hope of the Arab countries was in association with the Soviet Union."

Eisenhower thought that was a powerful, indeed overriding, argument. He decided to step up the pressure on Israel. Lodge told him
that he would have to hurry, because the Arabs were pressing for a
General Assembly vote condemning Israel, and Lodge could not delay
the vote much longer. Dulles went over the options. The United States
could support a resolution of condemnation (insufficient, Eisenhower
said); it could support a resolution calling for a suspension of governmental support for Israel (we have already done that, replied the President); support a resolution calling on the members to suspend not
merely governmental assistance but private assistance to Israel (I like
that, said the President, and he told Humphrey to call the tax people
in Washington to find out how much money was involved); a resolution calling for present sanctions against Israel and prospective sanctions against Egypt if she did not open the Gulf of Aqaba to Israel
shipping (good, Eisenhower nodded).

Humphrey returned to report that the rough estimate was about
$40 million a year went to Israel as private gifts (tax deductible), and
about $60 million worth of Israeli bonds were sold each year in the
United States. Eisenhower calculated that the threat to stop the flow
of that money should be sufficient to get the Israelis out of Gaza, and
he told Humphrey to "get in touch with one or two leading Jewish

personalities who might be sympathetic to our position and help to organize some Jewish sentiment."[26]

It is curious but true that Eisenhower himself never attempted to make contact with American Jewish leaders. In nearly every other instance—Soil Bank, foreign aid, NATO relations, oil prices, and so many more—it was his customary practice to call in the spokesmen of the groups involved. He would hear them out, then turn the full power of his personality on them in a summation that exhorted them to see reason and support his position. He would also carry on an extensive correspondence, urging his rich and powerful friends to support his program. But in two areas, Israel and civil rights, he did not follow that pattern. Eisenhower had no close Jewish friends, but he did have many acquaintances who were leaders in the Jewish community, including Baruch, Strauss, and Louis Marx. But he never reached out to them, or to the wider Jewish community. Similarly, Eisenhower had no Negro friends, nor even more than one or two acquaintances. He gave the white South and its leaders the full Eisenhower treatment, but he ignored the Negro community. While he was in Thomasville, Martin Luther King asked for an opportunity to talk to him. Eisenhower refused. He was uncomfortable with Jews and Negroes, so much so that he did not want to hear their side.

He did reach out to Congress. Returning to Washington, on February 20 he called in two dozen of the leading Democrats and Republicans to tell them he intended to support sanctions on private gifts to Israel. He gave them the full treatment—a long, impassioned speech of his own, reviewing the situation and stating the reasons for his decision, followed by a half hour of Dulles giving his supporting arguments. Eisenhower then allowed the congressmen ample time to ask questions, propose their own alternatives, and generally be heard. Knowland said that in view of Israeli intransigence, "voting *against* sanctions did not seem to be feasible," but he also wanted to impose sanctions on the Soviet Union for its failure to comply with the U.N. resolution calling for withdrawal from Hungary. Lodge said that "the U.N. will never vote sanctions against either Russia or the United States." Senator Lyndon Johnson protested that in "cracking down" on Israel, Eisenhower was using a double standard of following one policy with regard to the weak, another toward the strong.

In general, the politicians were somewhat less than enthusiastic about imposing sanctions on Israel, and eager to dissociate themselves from such a policy. When one of them asked whether it was agreed by everyone that Israel had to withdraw, "Senator Fulbright was not so sure all agreed unless it could be certain that Israel would get justice in the future." Senator Russell said there was no possibility of getting unanimous agreement. It was up to the President to "crystallize the thinking of the American people." Speaker Rayburn commented "that America has either one voice or none and the one voice was the voice of the President even though not everyone agreed with him." In short, Congress wanted no part of the responsibility, and was more than glad to leave it to Ike.[27]

Eisenhower moved quickly. He cabled Ben-Gurion, warning him to get out of Gaza before the vote came at the U.N. Then he took his case to the people, on national TV and radio, eloquently and earnestly explaining his policy. The pressure worked. Ben-Gurion pleaded for a bit more time; Lodge managed to stall in the U.N.; on March 1 the Israeli Foreign Minister, Mrs. Golda Meir, went before the General Assembly to announce Israel's plans for a "full and complete withdrawal." A U.N. peace-keeping force moved in, and another Middle East crisis had cooled.[28]

On March 2, the Senate voted 58 to 28 against the Russell proposal to eliminate any funds for economic and military assistance for the Eisenhower Doctrine. On March 5, the Senate passed the original resolution, 72 to 19. On March 9, Eisenhower signed the Eisenhower Doctrine into law. Although he still had to go to Congress for the funds to implement the resolution, he had managed to achieve congressional support, however reluctant, for whatever he might do in the Middle East. It was an impressive achievement.

Not so impressive was his handling of Congress over the issue of the 1958 federal budget. Even before he submitted it, indeed within less than a week after the election, Eisenhower began to build bridges to the majority Democrats, especially the southerners, and seek support from them. On November 13, he told Jerry Persons, himself from Alabama, to talk to Byrd, Thurmond, Stennis, Lyndon Johnson, and other leading southerners. He wanted Persons to tell them to forget "antiquated loyalty to two parties," and to say, "If we do have to stress party differences, let us do it on relatively small matters."[29] At his meeting with thirty congressmen on New Year's Day, Eisenhower remarked at the conclusion of the day that despite the lateness of the hour he wanted to say a few words to the Democrats. He spoke of the need for the executive and legislative branches to get along and work together. He warned of the dangers of inflation, and of the need to keep expenditures down. If they felt it necessary to propose additional spending, he asked them to first talk to him. "You know you are as welcome in this house—in this office—as anyone." He wished them a happy new year "from the bottom of my heart, even though we belong to different clubs. And of course I belong to the better one!!!"[30]

The budget that Eisenhower feared the Democrats would try to increase was already at $73.3 billion for 1958, up $2.8 billion from 1957. Eisenhower had worked hard to keep it down to that figure, his principal difficulty coming with the DOD. The JCS wanted $40 billion; Eisenhower said the highest he would go was $38.5 billion. Wilson was "kicking and storming" about the inadequate funding, while Humphrey was furious at the overspending. At a Cabinet meeting on January 9, Humphrey said he did not "want to give even an appearance of division among us," but he had to point out that "we're throwing away forty billion in capital every year—on the dump heap—serves only our security for that year, then on the dump heap." But Wilson was unconvinced, and more inclined to support the JCS than he was the President on the issue of the budget. (Eisenhower told Humphrey, over the telephone, "I have got a man [Wilson] who is frightened to make decisions. I have to make them for him."[31]) For himself, Eisenhower made a signed pledge: "During my term of office . . . I will not approve any obligational or expenditure authorities for the Defense Department that exceed something on the order of 38.5-billion-dollar mark."[32]

Other than in defense, it was almost impossible to cut the budget. Even at more than $73 billion, Eisenhower's budget was less than 18 percent of the gross national product, the lowest percentage since 1939.[33] Still, Eisenhower tried to persuade his Cabinet to cut deeper. He wanted the members to reduce personnel in their departments. He swore that he would veto any bill raising salaries. "We're going to economize," he said. "This is the time to do it." Hold the line on new construction.[34] But when the figures came back from the departments, the savings were minimal. As Eisenhower presented it to the Congress on January 16, it projected spending $73.3 billion in 1958.

That same afternoon, Humphrey held a press conference. Instead of supporting the Administration's budget, he seemed to attack it. "I would deplore the day that we thought we couldn't even reduce expenditures of this terrific amount," he said. He feared the long-range effect of "the terrific tax we are taking out of this country." He hoped Congress could cut the budget, because "if we don't [reduce expenditures], over a long period of time, I will predict that you will have a depression that will curl your hair."[35] That colorful phrase, not

Eisenhower's budget, was the headline item the next day, and the lead question at Eisenhower's next press conference.

Eisenhower tried to calm everyone down. He emphasized that the Secretary of the Treasury was not predicting an imminent depression. "When he said a hair-curling depression," Eisenhower said, "he is talking about long-term continuation of spending of the order of which we are now doing." Eisenhower said he too was eager to cut the budget, and he encouraged Congress to study it carefully. If it could find places to cut, he would be delighted. But he warned that because of the services the people demanded from government, there was little room to cut. The reporters, eager to find a split between the President and Humphrey, pressed on. Did Eisenhower agree with Humphrey's statement that "deficit spending is never justified even as a tool to ease a recession?" Eisenhower gave a wandering, discursive answer, finally ending up: "If the thing got serious . . . you would go into every single thing, and very quickly, that would . . . correct the situation. And there would be no limit, I think, to what should be attempted as long as it was constitutional."[36]

At the following week's press conference, reporters asked Eisenhower about growing Republican criticism of his budget. Republicans were saying that Eisenhower had gone over to the New Deal, that what the American people wanted was not more services from the government, but a break in inflation and a cut in taxes. Would the President comment? Eisenhower would. "I was talking about the kind of things that have now become accepted in our civilization as normal," he said, "that is the provision of Social Security, unemployment insurance, health research by the government, assistance where states and individuals are unable to do things for themselves." He cited the schoolroom shortage as an example.[37]

Suddenly, inexplicably, the Democrats joined the Republicans in criticizing Eisenhower for spending too much. Gleefully citing his invitation to Congress to find places to save, the Democrats spent the late winter and early spring chipping away (foreign aid was the easiest and favorite target). Knowland, Styles Bridges, and other Republican senators joined them. It was a case of American politics at its worst, as the congressmen tried to outdo each other in irresponsibility.

The hardest part for Eisenhower was increasing Republican criticism that he had deserted his party's principles. One part of the criticism centered around Arthur Larson, who had written a book entitled *A Republican Looks at His Party,* which called for a "Modern Republicanism" that followed the middle of the road. Eisenhower had frequently used the phrase "Modern Republicanism" in the campaign, and it was widely known that he had a high opinion of Larson and the book. At a press-conference briefing on May 15, Adams told him to expect a hostile question on Modern Republicanism from the press corps. Eisenhower mused that he had been "forced down the throats of a lot of people" when he captured the 1952 nomination. "Some will never forget it." Even George Humphrey had been against him, Eisenhower said. "There is so much resentment, and those people will never give up."[38]

At the press conference later that morning, Laurence Burd of the Chicago *Tribune* asked him if it was true that he had moved to the left since 1952. "Far from it," Eisenhower replied. "If anything, I think I have grown more conservative." But, he added, "At the same time I thoroughly believe that any modern political philosophy [has] to study carefully the needs of the people today, not of 1860; of today . . . I believe the federal government cannot shut its eyes to these things." After mentioning specifically the disruptions in industrial employment, old age, disability, and related social problems, Eisenhower said, "I believe that unless a modern political group does look these problems in the face and finds some reasonable solution . . . then in the long run we are sunk."[39]

But Congress cut and cut, eventually approving a budget some $4 billion below Eisenhower's original proposal (much of the cut was later restored in emergency authorizations). "I think it is a mistake to cut as seriously as these people have," said the President. He lost on school-construction costs again. But when he was asked if he intended to tell Senator Knowland, who had fought against many of the Administration's appropriation requests, to resign as minority leader, Eisenhower replied blandly that the organization of the Senate "is a matter for Senate decision."[40] Taken altogether, the Battle of the Budget for 1958 was, in Sherman Adams' words, "a serious and disturbing personal defeat" for the President.[41]

Fortunately for Eisenhower, as he battled with Congress over his budget, foreign aid, and other problems, he was able to get away most weekends to Gettysburg. There he could relax, check on his cattle, oversee the planting of his vegetable garden, play golf and bridge with the gang, and take pleasure in Mamie's happiness as she put the finishing touches on the place. Eisenhower enjoyed everything about the farm, even the drive from Washington to Pennsylvania. In March, he got into a discussion with the Republican leaders about advertising

along the Interstate highways. The President admitted "he rather liked
to read the Burma Shave signs along the way," but did say he was opposed to billboards beside the new highways.[42] Everything about
Gettysburg was not perfect, however. As a farmer, Eisenhower wanted
to operate independently from the federal government, as he was urging other farmers to do. In April he reported to his Cabinet that the
preceding week he had been delighted to find that his tenant had not
planted wheat that spring, so would not be applying for wheat support
payments. But when he "joyfully commented" on this development to
the tenant, he learned that the county agent had sold the tenant on
the merits of the Soil Bank and consequently the farm was now receiving Soil Bank payments. "I'm so mad," said the completely frustrated
President.[43]

Invitations to spend a weekend with the First Family at the farm
were rare and precious. Ordinarily, only Eisenhower's closest personal
friends received one. Field Marshal Montgomery solved that problem
by inviting himself. He arrived in June. Eisenhower took Monty on a
tour of his favorite battlefield. As the two old generals scrambled over
the rocks on Little Round Top, or studied the lay of the land from
Cemetery Ridge, Eisenhower explained the action to Monty, reporters
trailing behind recording every word.

"As you know," Eisenhower later told his old friend "Gee" Gerow,
"Monty can never resist a newspaper reporter nor a camera." Finally,
Eisenhower said, "I got a bit tired of Monty raising his voice, knowing
well that he was doing it for the benefit of eavesdroppers." So Eisenhower walked over to the car, while Montgomery kept talking. "Taking advantage of this golden opportunity to try for something sensational, he called over the heads of the crowd, 'Both Lee and Meade
should have been sacked.' " He added something about incompetence,
then called over to Eisenhower, "Don't you agree, Ike?" Eisenhower,
by now "resentful of Monty's obvious purpose and his lack of good
taste," merely replied, "Listen, Monty, I live here. I have nothing to
say about the matter. You have to make your own comments."[44]

Nevertheless, the story got page-one space on Sunday, the reports
claiming that Eisenhower had agreed with the Field Marshal that Lee
and Meade should have been sacked. At his Tuesday press conference,
Eisenhower was asked about it. He would not comment directly, but
he did point out that he had the portraits of four men on his Oval
Office wall—Franklin, Washington, Lincoln, and Lee—and insisted on
his great admiration for Lee.[45]

Monty gave Eisenhower a set of the galley proofs of his memoirs, indicating passages that discussed Eisenhower. The President read the marked sections, then told Whitman that Montgomery "is pretty clever . . . He says I am so loving and kind . . . that I let him have his own way and he really planned the war." When he read that "Ike reached his greatest heights as President of the United States," Eisenhower grunted and said, "He doesn't want to say I was responsible for winning the war." [46]

Eisenhower could hardly have expected praise from Monty, but he did receive that year some high praise from an unexpected source. Henry Wallace, the Progressive Party candidate for President in 1948 and a leading critic of American policy in the Cold War, sent Eisenhower a copy of a talk he had given in which he said he found certain similarities in the characters of Presidents Washington and Eisenhower. Eisenhower was quite sincerely flattered. He wrote Wallace, "My sense of pride is all the greater because I've never been able to agree with those who so glibly deprecate his [Washington's] intellectual qualities." Subconsciously describing himself as well as Washington, Eisenhower went on: "I think that too many jump at such conclusions merely because they tend to confuse facility of expression with wisdom; a love of the limelight with depth of perception." Speaking directly of himself, Eisenhower concluded, "I've often felt the deep wish that The Good Lord had endowed me with his [Washington's] clarity of vision in big things, his strength of purpose, and his genuine greatness of mind and spirit." [47]

CHAPTER SEVENTEEN

The High Cost of Defense, Nuclear Testing, Civil Rights

January–July 1957

ON EVERY possible occasion, Eisenhower told the press, the politicians, and the public that the only way to reduce the budget, stop inflation, and cut taxes was through disarmament. So long as the arms race went on, the United States would be putting $40 billion or so, nearly 60 percent of the total budget, into what Humphrey had called the "dump heap." Even at those levels, however, the JCS were unhappy and demanding more; indeed they had originally requested $50 billion for 1958. In December of 1956, while the budget was being written, Eisenhower told Dulles he was going to "crack down on defense people," and complained that "I am getting desperate with the inability of the men there to understand what can be spent on military weapons and what must be spent to wage the peace."[1]

With no disarmament treaty in sight, Eisenhower concentrated on making savings where he could. Personnel was a major item; he ordered the armed forces, especially the Army, to make even further cuts in their manpower. Wilson and the JCS protested. Eisenhower told his Cabinet, "I think I know more about this subject than anyone else. What would we do with a large Army if we had it? Where would we put it?"[2] Eisenhower told Wilson to reduce, and where to do it. The President wanted to streamline the forces in Germany, saving thirty-five thousand men there; he ordered a reduction of forty thousand in Japan and another twenty-five thousand elsewhere. Wilson made the point that keeping these troops in place gave the United

States bargaining chips in the disarmament talks. He therefore thought the forces ought to be kept at current strength in order to keep the pressure on the Russians to agree to make reductions in their forces in Eastern Europe. Eisenhower told Wilson to go ahead and make the cuts, just don't advertise them.[3]

Eisenhower was disturbed by the high cost of the CIA, and by the way in which the Agency was spending its money. At a January 17 Oval Office conference (the Dulles brothers, Radford, Wilson, Humphrey, Nixon, Goodpaster, and three deputies), Eisenhower conducted a review of the CIA, which was costing $1 billion per year. Eisenhower thought that "because of our having been caught by surprise in World War II, we are perhaps tending to go overboard in intelligence effort." He also complained about the quality of the intelligence he was getting, and the way in which it was presented to him. Eisenhower did not say so, but everyone in the room knew that with regard to the covert-action side of the CIA, Hungary had shown its extreme limitations, indeed helplessness, in Eastern Europe, which was precisely the area in which the Republicans had hoped that the covert-activity capability of the CIA could be used most effectively. One billion dollars a year was a considerable sum, especially for poorly gathered and prepared intelligence and little effective action on the covert side.

Eisenhower had asked General Lucian Truscott to conduct a thorough review of the CIA's activities in Hungary just before the uprising. Truscott reported that one major problem within the CIA was Allen Dulles, because the head of the Agency was more interested in covert actions than in intelligence gathering. At the January 17 meeting, Dulles told Eisenhower he was thinking of bringing Truscott into the CIA to take over the intelligence side of the operation. Eisenhower said he wanted it done "the other way around." He told Dulles to perform the coordination, and give covert operations to Truscott.[4] Dulles ignored the instructions; when Truscott came to the CIA, he took charge of coordinating intelligence reports, and Dulles kept control of covert operations.

As difficult as the CIA was to control, the DOD was worse. Not only did Eisenhower complain about having to run Wilson's department for him, but he also objected to the way in which DOD kept spinning off new projects. At a March 11 Cabinet meeting, Eisenhower protested against the $200 million bill for development of an atomic plane. The Air Force was simultaneously trying to develop a power plant small enough to be carried on an airplane, and an airplane large enough to carry a nuclear reactor. Eisenhower felt that the

Air Force should concentrate on the reactor, and until a smaller version was developed, to leave off the research on the plane.[5] The Air Force went ahead on both fronts anyway.

On June 26, at an Oval Office meeting with Wilson, his new Deputy Secretary, Donald Quarles, and Goodpaster, Eisenhower brought up the subject again. Quarles reported that great progress was being made, that General Electric was "within gunshot distance of the desired goal." But when Eisenhower pressed him, Quarles admitted that the weight "kept creeping up" and an aircraft of 700,000-pound capacity would be required. Eisenhower said to forget the plane and concentrate on the reactor. Then the President brought up the latest Air Force balloon operation. Although he had ordered the Air Force to get out of the balloon business, it had gone ahead anyway on a new program. Eisenhower told Wilson and Quarles to "step in" and stop it, and added: "If the Air Force continues to take on projects of its own which have not been approved, I think I will send some of these projects to the Comptroller General and make sure that someone besides the Executive Branch pays for them."[6]

Eisenhower also objected to the great cost of ballistic missiles. He "did not think too much of [them] as military weapons"; he was concerned only with their "great psychological importance." Wilson said the Air Force was almost ready to begin testing its first ICBM, and that ninety were programmed for test purposes. Eisenhower wanted to know at what rate the Air Force intended to build operational models. About one every other day, Wilson said. No, General Twining interjected; it was more like one per day. At what cost? asked the President. About $5 million per missile, Wilson replied, not counting the cost of the warhead. Good Lord, said the President, with all the bombers and submarines we already have, we have to be careful that "we do not produce too many." Wilson thought 150 ICBMs would be sufficient; Eisenhower thought that would be too many. The President said he did not want "to put a dollar sign on defense," but he had to point out that "many other programs contribute to making the nation strong, and that I myself am probably the only man in a position to bring all these together." As one evidence, he cited his instructions to the Cabinet to cut costs wherever possible; he had told the Cabinet to "hold down on construction, even the road program in which I am so keenly interested."[7]

But the pressure for ICBMs was too great to resist. The scientists were eager to develop them; the Pentagon wanted them; Democrats continued to criticize the President for not doing more to build them.

At a February 6 press conference, Eisenhower was asked about a recent report by Senator Symington that claimed "the United States has never been more vulnerable to Soviet attack than now." Eisenhower admitted that "the vulnerability of any nation is probably greater today than it ever was, because one bomb today can do the damage of probably all that we dropped on Germany in World War II." But as to America's relative position, "We are in as good a position as we have ever been in time of peace. And I don't believe that that position by any manner of means is deteriorating at the rate that some people would have you think." Well then, did the President think that it was possible that the Soviets might launch a first strike? "Oh, for goodness' sake," Eisenhower responded, "of course anything is possible in this world in which we live. The older you grow the more you will understand that." But he thought the chances of a nuclear war went down, rather than up, as the arsenals increased, and that the Russians were fully aware that a first-strike attempt "is just another way of committing suicide." [8]

Eisenhower also objected to the size of the funding of Project Vanguard, designed to put an earth satellite into orbit. He told the Republican leaders that "in a weak moment" he had approved "half of what the [developers] want," but swore he would go no further. [9]

With the President striving to cut or at least hold down research and development expenditures, and to reduce the size of the armed forces, while he simultaneously asked Congress for the resolution authorizing the Eisenhower Doctrine, reporters wanted to know how he proposed to defend the Middle East. Would he use atomic weapons there? Eisenhower's response was that if necessary, yes he would. He explained that "we do regard these smaller [atomic] weapons as an almost routine part of our equipment nowadays." [10]

Nuclear testing, meanwhile, went on at as fast a pace as the scientific community could make it go. In January and March, the Russians conducted a new series, followed in April by five tests within two weeks, tests which created a heavy fallout that circled the globe. The Kremlin ignored the resulting uproar, indeed fed it when Khrushchev told journalists that the Soviets had perfected an H-bomb too powerful to test, one that "could melt the Arctic icecap and send oceans spilling all over the world." [11] In May, the United States began Operation Plumbob, detonating six atomic weapons (none larger than eighty kilotons) designed to perfect tactical weapons and to produce a relatively clean atomic trigger for the nation's H-bombs. Fallout was minimal.

Nevertheless most people, including the President, worried about fallout. Still, the President was willing to defend the tests. The day before Plumbob began, he wrote Representative Sterling Cole of the congressional oversight committee for the AEC. Eisenhower asserted that "our tests continue to develop very valuable information, not so much in the enhancement of the destructive power of atomic weapons as in civil effects tests to improve our protective measures in event of attack . . . and in the further development of the feature of cleanliness . . ."[12]

On June 3, in the middle of the Plumbob tests, Eisenhower called Strauss into his office to discuss his own worries about fallout. The President said he saw little need for more tests, and certainly no reason to speed up the testing process, much less for building new weapons. "You've been giving us a pretty darn fine arsenal of atomic weapons," he told Strauss, and asked why more tests and bombs were needed. Strauss put his emphasis on the need to develop small warheads that could be used for air defense. The idea was to destroy incoming missiles with small atomic weapons, and for that purpose, Strauss said, the "numbers have to be so much greater." But the estimates on Russian production indicated that the United States had a clear lead; therefore, the President said, "By now reducing our program, we are doing a pretty fine thing." He could see little point to speeding up the tests or adding to the arsenal, and objected strongly to the costs.[13]

Two days later, however, when asked at a press conference about the dangers of fallout, Eisenhower's public position remained that it was necessary to continue testing. American chemist Linus Pauling, among many others, had warned that fallout would lead to genetic damage and result in physical deformities and shortened life-spans for millions of unborn around the world. Eisenhower pointed out in his response that "here is a field where scientists disagree," and charged that "scientists that seem to be out of their own field of competence are getting into this argument, and it looks like almost an organized affair." He said he was ready to stop testing as soon as a general system of disarmament had been agreed upon, but until then "we do have the job of protecting the country." Eisenhower again asserted that the purpose of testing was to find clean bombs, and claimed that the United States had "reduced the fallout from bombs by nine-tenths." James Reston picked up on Eisenhower's charge about "an organized affair." Did the President think that scientists who objected to testing were part of a conspiracy? "Oh, no, I didn't say that at all," Eisenhower responded. "I didn't say a wicked organization." He acknowledged that "many" of the scientists opposed to testing "are just as honest as they can be." It was just that men like Pauling were out of their fields in discussing radiation.[14]

Still the President worried. On June 24, he met with Strauss and three atomic scientists, Ernest Lawrence, Mark Mills, and Edward Teller (the "father of the H-bomb"). Lawrence assured him that "we now believe that we know how to make virtually clean weapons . . . all the way down to small kiloton weapons." But more tests were needed to achieve that goal. Teller concentrated on the need to build tactical atomic weapons, "easily packaged." Within six or seven years, the United States should have bombs "which would have their effect only in the damage sought, i.e., only in the area of initial effects, free of fallout." Teller, who had been briefed by Strauss and who knew that one of Eisenhower's great concerns was the utilization of atomic energy for peaceful purposes, then turned to the advantage of testing in producing bombs that could be used for constructive goals, such as oil exploration, or cutting through mountains to make tunnels or to alter the flow of rivers, "and perhaps even to modify the weather on a broad basis through changing the dust content of the air." As Teller anticipated, Eisenhower liked those arguments, but still he returned to the problem of fallout and the danger of world public opinion turning against the United States. He did not want the nation "crucified on a cross of atoms." Would the scientists accept a test ban if the Russians agreed to one? Both Mills and Teller were quick to say no, because the Russians would then carry on with their tests secretly, and they could not be detected.

In that case, the President wondered, could not the American scientists give the "other fellow" information from Plumbob, so that the Russians could develop their own clean weapons. The scientists were emphatic in saying no. They claimed that "our weapons incorporate other technological advances of great value that we do not wish to give to the Soviets." As a final point, Teller assured Eisenhower that after the clean weapons were developed, "it is possible to put 'additive materials' with them to produce radioactive fallout if desired."[15]

The following day, June 25, Eisenhower talked to Secretary Dulles on the telephone. Dulles was concerned about world reaction to testing. Eisenhower either had not understood what Teller and the others told him, or he believed what he wanted to believe. In any case, he told Dulles that the "real peaceful use of atomic science depends on their developing clean weapons," which Teller had not said, and that clean weapons could be produced in "four to five years." Teller had said it would take six or seven years. Eisenhower was correct in saying that the scientists had warned him the Russians could conduct tests without fear of detection. "They feel we are playing with fire suggesting banning of tests," Eisenhower reported.[16]

The result was that the United States continued testing. As Robert Divine writes, "Ike was the prisoner of his technical consultants on such issues as testing and fallout." It could hardly have been otherwise, especially in view of Strauss's ability to keep the President from consulting with a broad spectrum of the scientific community and limiting him to contact with such convinced atomic scientists as Lawrence and Teller.[17] At a press conference on June 26, Eisenhower repeated all the arguments he had heard from Lawrence and Teller, whom he characterized as "the most eminent scientists in this field." But he again shortened the time from six to seven years down to four or five years. He asserted, without offering proof, that American bombs now had "96 percent less fallout than was the case in our original ones," and that peaceful uses of the atom were just around the corner. Testing had to continue, the President said, so that atomic energy could be used "some day for the building of a civilization instead of tearing it down."[18]

Privately, to the NSC and to the Republican leaders, Eisenhower expressed his reservations about the growing relationship between the scientists and the government. At an NSC meeting, "The President observed with a smile that it seemed to him that every new survey of our problems by a scientific team seemed to result in recommendations that we undertake additional things." He said he "rather wished we could find a team which would recommend programs which we could dispense with."[19] In March, he told the Republican leaders that he was opposed to government sponsorship of basic scientific research. "We've always depended on universities and private concerns" for such work, he declared, and wished the situation had remained that way. But, he admitted, "When I object, I'm just a reactionary old so and so who doesn't understand." He could not slow the momentum of federally sponsored research that put many of the nation's top scientists to work on projects designed to destroy, not improve, the human condition.[20]

On July 17, John Herling asked at a news conference if, "in view of the overwhelming importance of science to modern life," the President had considered adding a scientist to his staff. Eisenhower said he already had the scientists in the AEC and Defense Department reporting to him, and that "it hadn't occurred to me to have one right in my office." But, he added on reflection, "Now that you have mentioned it I will think about it." [21]

The intricate, complex, and almost ritual-like maneuvers in the disarmament dance continued. On January 14, Lodge presented a five-point program to the U.N. General Assembly. It called for an end to the production of nuclear weapons under strict international supervision. Afterward, Lodge continued, the United States would be willing to negotiate a treaty to ban all testing. In addition, the American proposal included reductions in conventional forces, registration of ballistic-missile tests, and a new variation on Open Skies. Although this was the first time the United States had indicated a willingness to include a test ban in its disarmament package, the proposal had no appeal to the Russians—as Lodge knew in advance.[22] (Assured suspension of production, if achievable, would have left the United States far ahead of the Russians in the total nuclear arsenal.)

Meanwhile, there was an intense struggle going on between Harold Stassen, Eisenhower's Special Assistant on Disarmament since 1955, and Secretary Dulles. There was a policy difference between them— Stassen was willing to go much further than Dulles in making disarmament proposals—but the real difficulty was over jurisdiction. Stassen insisted on an independent course and direct access to the President; Dulles wanted all disarmament proposals cleared through the State Department, and he wanted Stassen to report to the President only through the Secretary of State's office. In December 1956, Eisenhower told Dulles that he had been "brutally frank" in telling Stassen that Dulles was his superior, and in February 1957, Eisenhower told Dulles over the phone that he thought "it would be awkward to keep on calling Stassen the Special Assistant to the President, since it might give him the feeling he has a right to continue his attendance at meetings, which is the thing we are trying to avoid." [23] On March 1, Eisenhower announced that henceforth Stassen would report to him through Dulles.

Getting rid of Stassen was not going to be that easy. In May, Stassen attended the London disarmament talks, where he made the same proposal Lodge had put forward to the General Assembly. The Russians rejected the package, but said they were ready for an immediate and unconditional halt to tests, without any inspection. Stassen knew that was unacceptable to Eisenhower, but he suggested that the United States should at least consider a test ban as a possible "first step" in disarmament. When the world press lauded Stassen's suggestion as a possible breakthrough, Admiral Radford responded. "We cannot trust the Russians on this or anything," the chairman of the JCS declared. "The Communists have broken their word with every country with which they ever had an agreement."[24]

Radford had expressed the President's own convictions, but too bluntly. At his next press conference, on May 22, Eisenhower went out of his way to make his standard speech on the crucial importance of disarmament. "It seems to me that the more any intelligent man thinks about the possibilities of war today," Eisenhower said, "the more he should understand you have got to work on this business of disarmament." Eisenhower added, "Our first concern should be making certain we are not ourselves being recalcitrant, we are not being pica-yunish about the thing." He wanted to keep an "open mind" and be prepared to meet the Russians "halfway." But then he repeated Rad-ford's warning that the Soviets could not be trusted, and that an iron-clad inspection system had to be part of any disarmament package.[25]

Three days later, Eisenhower met with Stassen, Dulles, Radford, Strauss, Quarles, and Cutler. For two hours, they debated disarma-ment policy, specifically the wisdom of entering into a temporary test-ban agreement with the Russians as a first step toward arms con-trol. Eisenhower eventually authorized Stassen to return to London with a written "talking paper" that would offer the Soviets a mora-torium on testing in return for future limitations on nuclear weapons production. The President stressed that the new offer was tentative and that Stassen was to show it to the French and the British and get their approval before presenting it to the Russians.[26]

The Russians, meanwhile, had picked up on one part of Lodge's January proposal. Khrushchev announced that he was willing to with-draw his troops from Europe if the United States did the same. Asked at a June 5 press conference how he planned to respond, Eisenhower replied that it was obvious that the Russians were trying to "drive a wedge" between the United States and its NATO allies. As to pulling troops out of Germany, without a comprehensive disarmament agree-ment, Eisenhower said he would not do it until Germany was reuni-fied. Reporters then asked about the rumors that Stassen was about to make a major new proposal in London. Had American policy shifted? Was Eisenhower ready to accept a test ban without inspections and without general disarmament? The President was cautious in his re-sponse; he said he would like to have "a total and complete ban of all testing," but it had to be based "upon total disarmament . . ."[27]

Stassen, meanwhile, was back in London, where he botched everything. Macmillan, who had replaced Eden after Suez, was opposed to any test ban (Britain had just exploded its first hydrogen bomb and wanted to conduct further tests); the French, hoping to develop their own arsenal, were also opposed. Nevertheless, and despite Eisenhower's strict instructions, Stassen gave a copy of his "talking paper" to the Russian negotiator, Valerin Zorin. Zorin then announced that the United States and the Soviet Union were close to agreement. Macmillan was furious; he fired off a cable to Eisenhower. The President answered with a cable of his own, saying that he was "astonished and chagrined" by Stassen's action and assuring Macmillan "that there is no agreed-upon American position which is to be interpreted as a basis of negotiation with the Soviets." Eisenhower concluded, "Everybody here deplores this occurrence as deeply as I do." [28]

A week later, after Stassen had been called to Washington for a reprimand, Eisenhower had Dulles send a message to London. Dulles had proposed that Eisenhower say, "I feel that there is little likelihood that there will be any repetition . . ." Eisenhower changed it to read, "I feel certain that there will be no repetition" and told Dulles to send it off.[29]

On June 14, Zorin announced that the Soviets were giving up their demand for a complete test ban in favor of "a two- or three-year moratorium," and that they were ready to accept a system of international control, with monitoring posts on British, American, and Russian soil. The next day, Robert Clark reminded Eisenhower at a press conference that the American position had been that there would be no halt to testing "until there was a firm agreement that they [the bombs] would never be used in war. Does this apply to the temporary ban proposed by the Soviet Union?" Eisenhower said, "I would be perfectly delighted to make some satisfactory arrangement for temporary suspension of tests," and admitted under further questioning that such a moratorium would mark a major shift in American policy. For the first time since 1945, there suddenly seemed to be some hope for progress in disarmament.[30]

It was not to be. The Pentagon and the AEC scientists were firmly opposed to any moratorium; Strauss brought Teller, Lawrence, and Mills to the Oval Office to express their objections; Teller told the Joint Congressional Committee on Atomic Energy that a moratorium would be "a crime against humanity" because it would keep the United States from developing a clean bomb. Khrushchev scornfully asked, "How can you have a clean bomb to do dirty things?" Nevertheless, Eisenhower bowed to the pressure from the scientists. On June 25, he had Dulles tell a press conference that the United States would accept a moratorium only if the Soviets agreed to a future cutoff in weapons manufacture.[31] And so nothing was done, and the arms race, and testing, went on. The truth was that the United States was no more ready to enter into genuine disarmament than were the Russians. Despite all Eisenhower's eloquence on the subject, despite his firm conviction that an arms race could only lead to disaster, he could not bring himself, or his nation, to trust the Russians. On disarmament, he did exactly the opposite of what he had promised to do—he was picayunish and recalcitrant. Eventually, in August, Stassen was authorized to announce American agreement to a two-year test ban "under certain conditions and safeguards." That came close to Zorin's proposal for a two- to three-year moratorium, and forced the Russians to react. Exactly as Dulles had predicted, Zorin flatly rejected the final American proposal. In August, the Soviets began a new series of tests, and the London talks broke down. Both sides blamed the other for the failure and appealed to world public opinion to note that the fault lay with the other guy.[32]

Actually, everyone was responsible, including America's NATO allies, and most especially France and Britain, two countries that had nuclear pretensions but little or no reality and therefore strenuously objected to both a test ban and a prohibition of nuclear arsenal development. Because of the strength of anti-testing sentiment in Britain and on the Continent, however, London and Paris protested only in private, thus placing the onus on the United States and the Soviet Union. Eisenhower never complained, because he was happy to have the Europeans making their contribution to the Western nuclear deterrent.

Eisenhower was also pleased by two other European developments, the European Economic Community (EEC) and the European Atomic Energy Community (Euratom). Back in October of 1956, on the eve of the Suez crisis, at an NSC meeting, Eisenhower led a discussion on EEC. Eisenhower said he welcomed the talks then going on in Europe to create a Common Market. Stassen did not. He was worried about the "danger of a European Third Force," one that might negotiate separately with the Soviets. Better, Stassen thought, to keep Europe weak and divided. The official notes recorded that "the President, turning to Governor Stassen, stated with emphasis that weakness could not cooperate, weakness could only beg." Therefore, the United States had to help the Europeans "build up self-confidence and strength." Dulles added that "it would actually be a healthy thing for these nations to try to mold themselves into a Third Force," something he and Eisenhower had been advocating for a long time.[33]

In February 1957, Eisenhower met with a group of European leaders who were making plans for the first nuclear electric power stations on their Continent, the Euratom program. Eisenhower told them he thought "Euratom is a great hope for the whole free world." The President "recalled that he has strongly supported a united Europe as a third great force in the world. He had urged Jean Monnet on, as he now urges this group . . . He said that they may be sure of our cooperation, commenting that he hopes he will live long enough to see a United States of Europe come into existence. He has thought the European nations must learn the biblical concept that to save their lives they must lose them." Eisenhower warned that if the Europeans did not get together, "deterioration and ultimate disaster were inevitable." And Eisenhower instructed Strauss to make certain that Euratom got, from the United States, sufficient raw material to build the power plants.[34] Thus encouraged, the Europeans returned home and on March 25, in Rome, the NATO Continental powers signed treaties establishing EEC and Euratom.

Two days earlier, Eisenhower had met with Quarles, Foster Dulles, Strauss, and Goodpaster to discuss a project of giving IRBMs to the British. Macmillan wanted them, and Eisenhower wanted him to have them, although he stated "very emphatically that he did not want to make a commitment to production until we have a successful missile." Quarles assured him that such a missile was coming along nicely, and that it should be possible to deploy a "handful" of missiles in Britain within a year. The first full squadron could be in place by mid-1959, with three more to follow by mid-1960.[35]

In July 1957, Dulles disclosed that the President was considering a plan for establishing nuclear stockpiles of weapons in Europe. (Actually, the decision had already been made and implemented.[36]) Peter Lisagor asked Eisenhower at a July 17 news conference, "If one of our purposes . . . is to prevent the spread of nuclear weapons, . . . can you tell us what the logic is of establishing a stockpile in which fifteen other nations will have nuclear weapons?" Eisenhower replied that the Europeans, if subjected to a nuclear attack, "ought to have the right, the opportunity, and the capability of responding in kind." Further, if the Europeans had nuclear weapons from America already available, they would not have to spend their resources on building their own and "creating a situation [that, with] everybody acting independently, could be very dangerous."[37] In any case, so long as the SACEUR was an American, the United States would make the ultimate decision on the use of nuclear weapons.

Meanwhile, as the President had hoped would happen, and had helped make possible, Euratom got off to a good start, thereby achieving another of Eisenhower's goals—freeing Europe from its total dependence on Arab oil. The man who was most closely identified with the liberation of Europe from the Nazis, and with the creation of SHAPE, thereby continued to play a leading role in the creation of modern Europe.

As difficult as Congress had been for Eisenhower to deal with on such issues as the budget and the Eisenhower Doctrine, it was worse when the subject was civil rights. In his State of the Union address on January 10, Eisenhower had again submitted Brownell's civil-rights bill. It was a multifaceted bill, but Eisenhower put his own emphasis on the right to vote. He was "shocked" to discover that out of 900,000 Negroes in Mississippi, only 7,000 were allowed to vote.[38] He investigated and found that the registrars were asking Negroes attempting to register to vote such questions as "How many bubbles are there in a bar of soap?" In Louisiana, the registrars had closed their doors in the face of five thousand Negroes lined up to register; a local grand jury found "no case" against the state officials. Eisenhower told the Republican leaders a story about a young Mississippi law student who failed the bar exam twice. His father went to the bar and asked to see the questions. "For goodness' sake," the father said, "you have given him the Negro examination!"[39]

Through the late winter and early spring, the House debated the civil-rights bill. Eisenhower gave it public and private support. At press conferences, he emphasized that "I want a civil-rights bill . . . In it is nothing that is inimical to the interests of anyone. It is intended to preserve rights without arousing passions . . . I think it is a very decent and very needful piece of legislation."[40] He pushed the bill in his meetings with Republican leaders. He met with Arthur Hays Sulzberger of The New York Times to urge him to support the bill. (Sulzberger "shamefacedly admitted, for private use only, that even he would not want his granddaughter to go to school with Negro boys."[41]) On June 18, the House passed the bill, which then went to the Senate. Lyndon Johnson warned Eisenhower over the phone that "the Senate is going to fight on the civil-rights issue—he said tempers were flaring already and would be worse . . . Then he said, you can let us fight July and August and if necessary into September." Eisenhower protested that what he was asking for was "the mildest civil-rights bill possible—he stressed that he himself had lived in the South and had no lack of sympathy for the southern position. He said he was a little struck back on his heels when he found this terrific uproar that was created."[42]

But the uproar was there. On July 2, Senator Russell of Georgia described the bill as "a cunning device," designed not to guarantee the right to vote, but to use the power of the Justice Department and "the whole might of the federal government, including the armed forces if necessary, to force a commingling of white and Negro children." At a news conference the following day, James Reston asked Eisenhower to comment. The President was mild and hesitant in his reply. Certainly his own desire was only to protect and extend the right to vote, "simple matters that were more or less brought about by the Supreme Court decision, and were a very moderate move." Now, he said, he discovered that "highly respected men" were making statements to the effect that "this is a very extreme law, leading to disorder." Eisenhower confessed that he found such a reaction "rather incomprehensible, but I am always ready to listen to anyone's presentation to me of his views on such a thing." Reston asked if Eisenhower was willing to rewrite the bill, so that it dealt only with the right to vote. Eisenhower said he did not want to answer, "because I was reading part of that bill this morning, and there were certain phrases I didn't completely understand. So, before I made any more remarks on that, I would want to talk to the Attorney General and see exactly what they do mean."[43]

It was a stunning confession of ignorance. Eisenhower had been pushing the bill for two years, had managed to get it through the House and considered by the Senate, and yet now said he did not know what was in it. Eisenhower's admission was an open invitation to the southern senators to modify, amend, emasculate his bill, and they proceeded to do just that. They offered an amendment that would assure a jury trial to anyone cited for contempt of court in a civil-rights case. Insofar as the jury lists were made up from the voting lists, which were virtually all white, the amendment would have the practical effect of nullifying the bill, since it was unlikely, indeed almost unthinkable, that a southern white jury would convict another white man of violating the rights of a Negro. But the right of an accused to a trial by a jury of his peers was so deeply ingrained in the American tradition, and so sacred, that the amendment attracted support from such northern liberals as Joseph O'Mahoney of Wyoming and Frank Church of Idaho. Eisenhower appealed to Republicans to resist the amendment, and Knowland said on the Senate floor that a vote for jury trial "will be a vote to kill for this session . . . an effective voting-rights bill." Lyndon Johnson replied, "The people will never accept a concept that a man can be publicly branded as a criminal without a jury trial."[44]

On July 10, in the Oval Office, Eisenhower had an hour-long meeting with Russell. Ann Whitman wrote in her diary that Russell, "while emotional about the matter, had conducted himself very well." Then Whitman, always loyal to Eisenhower and nearly always unquestioningly on his side, noted that the President "is not at all unsympathetic to the position people like Senator Russell take." Eisenhower was "far more ready than am I, for instance, to entertain their views." Whitman chided him for supporting segregationists. "I have lived in the South, remember," the President reminded his secretary. She hoped, and believed, that "he is adamant on the fact that the right to vote must be protected." Then, speaking for millions of Americans, Negro and white, Republican and Democrat, North and South, liberal and conservative, Whitman declared, "It seems so ridiculous to me, when it has been in the Constitution for so many years and here at last we get around to believing it might be possible for some of our citizens to really have that right."[45]

On July 22, as the Senate debate continued, Eisenhower wrote Swede, who had lived in North Carolina for two decades. "I think that no other single event has so disturbed the domestic scene in many years," the President said, "as did the Supreme Court's decision of 1954 in the school segregation case." In his view, "Laws are rarely effective unless they represent the will of the majority." Further, "when emotions are deeply stirred," progress must be gradual and take into account "human feelings." Otherwise, "we will have a . . . disaster." The South had lived for three score years under *Plessy* as a law-abiding area; it was therefore "impossible to expect complete and instant reversal of conduct by mere decision of the Supreme Court."

Such views, which Eisenhower had also expressed to Russell (to Whitman's consternation), gave great comfort to the southerners. They did not mean, however, that Eisenhower was going to ignore his duties and responsibilities. Eisenhower told Swede that just the other day "a violent exponent of segregation [Russell] was in my office," where "he delivered an impassioned talk on the sanctity of the 1896 decision [*Plessy*] by the Supreme Court." When Russell finally ran out of words, Eisenhower said, "I merely asked, 'Then why is the 1954 decision not equally sacrosanct?' " Russell "stuttered," then said, "There were then wise men on the Court. Now we have politicians." Eisenhower asked him to name one justice on the 1896 Court. "He just looked at me in consternation and the subject was dropped."

Then, in one paragraph, Eisenhower gave Swede the most eloquent and concise statement on the role of the Supreme Court in American life that he ever delivered. "I hold to the basic purpose," he began. "There must be respect for the Constitution—which means the Supreme Court's interpretation of the Constitution—or we shall have chaos. We cannot possibly imagine a successful form of government in which every individual citizen would have the right to interpret the Constitution according to his own convictions, beliefs, and prejudices. Chaos would develop. This I believe with all my heart—and shall always act accordingly." [46]

That was a private letter to a private citizen. The day he wrote it, the President received a letter (already made public) from Governor Byrnes of South Carolina, supporting the sacred right of trial by jury. In response, Eisenhower said that "as I read your letter, it seems to me that what you are really objecting to is the giving of authority to the Attorney General to institute civil actions." Eisenhower told Byrnes that the right to vote was what was really sacred. Although "the last thing I desire is to persecute anyone," Eisenhower told Byrnes that "the right to vote is more important to our way of life" than anything else. Noting that Byrnes had expressed the hope that the President would show "confidence in the people of the South," Eisenhower wrote: "I am compelled to wonder why you have to express such a thought as nothing more than a hope. Many of my dearest friends are in that region. I spent a not inconsiderable part of my life in the South." Therefore, "I do not feel that I need yield to anyone in my respect for the sentiments, convictions, and character of the average American, no matter where he may happen to dwell." [47]

Taken altogether, the President's various statements on civil rights, whether made in private, or in meetings, or in letters to southern governors, or in news conferences, confused more than they clarified. As southern politicians chose to hear what he was saying, the President had a firm commitment to the Constitution, but it was more ritualistic than active. What came through to them was Eisenhower's sympathy for the white South, and his extreme reluctance to use force to insure compliance with *Brown*. The President's moderation, the southerners felt, gave them license to defy the Court, and to emasculate the civil-rights bill.

At a July 17 news conference, Eisenhower as much as said so directly. Merriman Smith asked the first question. Was the President aware that under laws dating back to Reconstruction, he had the power and authority to use military force to put through integration? Yes, Eisenhower said, he was aware that he had such power. But, he added, "I can't imagine any set of circumstances that would ever induce me to send federal troops into . . . any area to enforce the orders of a federal court, because I believe that [the] common sense of America will never require it." Few paid any attention to his qualification, because after further questioning he said, "I would never believe that it would be a wise thing to do in this country."

The President then reiterated his most basic belief, that the right to attend an integrated school was not so important as the right to vote. "If in every locality every person . . . is permitted to vote, he has got a means of getting what he wants in democratic government, and that is the one on which I place the greatest emphasis." In that case, Rowland Evans wanted to know, would the President veto a civil-rights bill that did not give the Attorney General the power to use the injunction to enforce integration and the right to vote? The President refused to say, but he did declare, "I personally believe if you try to go too far too fast in laws in this delicate field that has involved the emotions of so many millions of Americans, you are making a mistake." [48]

For Eisenhower, the whole experience was one of the most agonizing of his life. He wanted to uphold the Supreme Court, but he did not want to offend his many southern friends. He wanted to enforce the law, but he did not want to use force to do so. He did not want to antagonize anyone, but "anyone" always seemed to turn out to be white southern segregationists. He had waged two successful campaigns to become the nation's leader, but he did not want to lead on the issue of civil rights. The upshot of his conflicting emotions and statements was confusion, which allowed the segregationists to convince themselves that the President would never act.

In his letter to Swede, Eisenhower had concluded, "Possibly I am something like a ship which, buffeted and pounded by wind and wave, is still afloat and manages in spite of frequent tacks and turnings to stay generally along its plotted course and continue to make some, even if slow and painful, headway." [49] But to many observers, it appeared that the ship of state was in fact caught in a storm without a rudder, without power, without a captain; that it was, if the truth be told, drifting aimlessly in unknown and uncharted waters.

CHAPTER EIGHTEEN

Little Rock, Sputnik

August–November 1957

IN AUGUST and September 1957, the efforts by southern segregationists to resist *Brown* and its implications reached a peak. The climax began on August 2, in the wee hours, after an exhausting session of Senate debate over Eisenhower's civil-rights bill, when the Senate voted, 51 to 42, to adopt the jury-trial amendment to the bill. Eisenhower, told of the vote when he woke, was furious. At a 9 A.M. Cabinet meeting, he opened by saying the vote was "one of the most serious political defeats of the past four years, primarily because it was such a denial of a basic principle of the United States," the right to vote. Eisenhower said he could not find much forgiveness in his soul for those Republicans who had voted with the South (twelve had done so, including Barry Goldwater of Arizona). In a statement issued later that morning, the President declared that the jury-trial amendment would make it impossible for the Justice Department to obtain convictions of southern registrars who refused to enroll Negroes. He spoke of how "bitterly disappointing" the result of the Senate vote had been to the millions of "fellow Americans [who] will continue . . . to be disenfranchised."[1]

Despite the President's relatively strong words, the Senate proceeded, on August 7, to pass the emasculated civil-rights bill, 72 to 18. It then went to a Senate-House Conference (the House had earlier passed the bill Eisenhower wanted), where the differences would be worked out. At a news conference on the seventh, May Craig praised

411

Eisenhower for his attempts to wipe out discrimination based on race, creed, religion, and color. Then she asked, "Why have you not been as active in trying to wipe out discrimination based on sex, namely, the equal-rights amendment?" Caught by surprise, Eisenhower's response was "Well, it's hard for a mere man to believe that woman doesn't have equal rights." That standard line brought a standard guffaw from the nearly all-male press corps. Eisenhower added that it was not a question he had thought about, but "I am in favor of it [the perennial equal-rights amendment]. I just probably haven't been active enough in doing something about it." Mrs. Craig persisted. "Will you?" she asked. Eisenhower said he would "take a look at it."[2]

But what he was really looking at and wondering about was what he should do if the House agreed to the crippling jury-trial amendment. He was getting conflicting advice. The White House mail mainly urged him not to sign a "phony" bill. Prominent Negro leaders joined the chorus. Ralph Bunche wrote, "It would be better to have no bill than one as emasculated as that which has come out of the Senate." Jackie Robinson, the baseball player, wired to state his opposition. "Have waited this long for bill with meaning—" Robinson said, "can wait a little longer." Robinson was one of the newest civil-rights leaders; one of the oldest leaders, the grand old man of the movement, A. Philip Randolph, joined him in opposition. "It is worse than no bill at all," Randolph declared.[3] But the NAACP concluded that half a loaf was better than no bread at all, and therefore wanted Eisenhower to sign it. So did Martin Luther King, Jr. Nixon reported at a meeting of Republican leaders on August 13 that he had talked to King, who had said that when the bill was passed, "he will touch off a massive Negro registration drive." King added that although he was not a member of either party, he and his associate, Ralph Abernathy, had both voted for Eisenhower, and indicated that they expected most new Negro voters would be Republican.[4] Eisenhower doubted that there would be many new Negro voters, given the jury-trial provision. He also feared that if he signed this bill, "it will mean that no other legislation can be enacted for at least a decade or two."[5]

But he had not given up on getting a better bill out of the Senate-House Conference. On August 13, he told Republican leaders that he was "in favor of fighting it out to the end to prevent the pseudo liberals from getting away with their sudden alliance with the southerners on a sham bill."[6] He found it difficult, however, to work effectively with the House minority leader, Joe Martin. Eisenhower characterized Martin as "a courageous fighter," but complained that "it was almost impossible to get him to understand any subtle suggestions." [7] Martin was able, however, to get Sam Rayburn and Lyndon Johnson to agree to a minor compromise. It gave a federal judge the right to decide whether a defendant should receive a jury trial in a criminal contempt action concerning the right to vote. If there were no jury trial, the maximum penalty would be a $300 fine and forty-five days in jail; if there were a jury trial, the maximum penalty would be six months and $1,000. On that basis, the House passed the conference bill; on August 29, so did the Senate.

The bill created a Civil Rights Commission with a two-year life; it set up a Civil Rights Division in Justice; and it empowered the Attorney General to seek an injunction when an individual was deprived of the right to vote. [8] But the penalties for violation were so relatively light, and the obstacles in the way of the Attorney General so relatively heavy, that the final bill was a long way away from providing the guarantees of basic civil rights that Eisenhower had insisted were the birthright of all Americans. Some civil-rights leaders blamed the southern senators for this outcome, but others said it was Eisenhower's responsibility, because of his failure to speak forcefully and clearly on the issue. His leadership had been, at best, tepid; Emmet Hughes, disgusted, wrote that "his limp direction of the struggle in Congress for the Civil Rights Act . . . had served almost as a pathetic and inviting prologue to Little Rock." [9]

The battered and bruised bill was hardly Eisenhower's exclusive fault, but the bill's confused and hesitant approach to the problem of civil rights did symbolize the President's own confusion and hesitancy. He still could not make up his mind whether to sign it or not. By the time he did decide, on September 9, to sign, events in Little Rock had overshadowed the bill, and its enactment into law passed virtually unnoticed. Nor can it be said that its enforcement ever attracted much attention, or much action. Essentially, Eisenhower passed on to his successors the problem of guaranteeing constitutional rights to Negro citizens.

On September 4, weary from his battles with Congress, Eisenhower and Mamie flew to Newport, Rhode Island, to spend their summer vacation at the naval base there. Upon their arrival in Newport, Eisenhower said a few words at a reception by the mayor and other local dignitaries. "I assure you no vacation has ever started more auspiciously," he said. He and Mamie were looking "forward to the time of our lives . . ." [10]

Actually, no vacation had ever begun more inauspiciously, because the previous day the governor of Arkansas, Orval Faubus, had presented Eisenhower with exactly the problem he had most wished to avoid, outright defiance of a court order by a governor. Faubus had called out the Arkansas National Guard, placed it around Central High School in Little Rock, and ordered the troops to prevent the entry into the school of about a dozen Negro pupils. Before departing for Newport, Eisenhower had reviewed the situation with his staff. The President made it clear that he had no desire to get the Administration involved in the controversy. He doubted that the Justice Department had a right to intervene and said the real problem was "these people who believe you are going to reform the human heart by law." [11]

That Eisenhower had great sympathy for the white South was, of course, well known, and Faubus counted on it to keep the President inactive while he battled the federal court. On September 4, when Eisenhower arrived in Newport, he was given a telegram from Faubus. The governor asked the President for his understanding and cooperation in his efforts to forestall integration. Faubus complained that federal authorities were threatening to take him into custody and that his telephone had been tapped by the FBI. The following day, before leaving for the golf course, Eisenhower replied in a telegram. He told Faubus, "The only assurance I can give you is that the federal Constitution will be upheld by me by every legal means at my command," and insisted that no one planned to arrest the governor or tap his telephone.[12] Various legal maneuvering ensued, while the National Guard remained around Central High, blocking the entry of nine Negroes who were still trying to get in. The federal judge set September 20 as the date for a hearing on the legality of Faubus' action.

On September 11, Sherman Adams called Eisenhower to report that Arkansas Congressman Brooks Hays had been conducting negotiations with Faubus. Hays told Adams that Faubus "would like to find a way out of the situation in which he has gotten and would be amenable, would like to, ask for a meeting with the President." Hays wanted to arrange a meeting between Eisenhower and the governor. Adams further reported that he had discussed the proposal with Brownell, who was strongly opposed to such a meeting, because Faubus had "soiled" himself badly. For his part, Adams believed that Faubus "realizes he has made a mistake and is looking for a way out." Brownell insisted that there was nothing to discuss with Faubus; the Attorney General thought it was a simple case of "this is the law" and "it must be complied with." Eisenhower said that the situation was not that simple, that the Administration had to "take into consideration the seething in the South." He wanted Brownell to make it "very clear" at the September 20 hearing that the Administration was "appearing in court only as a friend of the court . . . By no means does the federal government want to interfere with the governor's responsibilities." Adams told Eisenhower that Hays said Faubus was not a true segregationist, that his son attended an integrated college, and that his only objection to the court-ordered integration of Little Rock was that it started in the high schools, rather than in first grade. Eisenhower told Adams that if Faubus "honestly wanted to talk with him, he would see him any time any place." [13]

After talking to Adams, Eisenhower called Brownell. He said that the preservation of law and order was the governor's responsibility; "consequently we cannot in any way question the rights of governors to call out National Guard whenever they want." He also said that "the whole U.S. thinks the President has a right to walk in and say 'disperse—we are going to have Negroes in the high schools and so on.' That is not so." Under the circumstances, Eisenhower said he thought he should see Faubus. Brownell thought he should not. The Attorney General pointed out that the Brooks Hays intervention was the fifth attempt to negotiate with Faubus; two senators, a Little Rock newspaper publisher, and Winthrop Rockefeller had all tried, and "all came to the conclusion it was hopeless." Well, Eisenhower replied, "Perhaps the time is now ripe." He told Brownell to get together with Adams and compose a proper telegram for Faubus to send to Newport, requesting a meeting. Then he called Adams again to inform him of his decision. Adams warned that Senator Russell had told Jerry Persons that "Faubus was going to try to force a court decision which would be conciliatory to the problems of the South, which would serve as sort of bellweather in future cases." Eisenhower scoffed at that and ordered Adams to get the telegram to Faubus. [14]

That afternoon, September 11, Faubus' telegram arrived. It was not completely satisfactory. Faubus admitted that "all good citizens" must obey court orders and said "it is certainly my desire to comply . . . consistent with my responsibilities under the Constitution of the United States, and that of Arkansas." The last qualifying phrase was ominous, but Eisenhower chose to ignore it. He replied that he would be happy to see Faubus, and a meeting was arranged on the Newport Naval Base for September 14. [15]

The meeting took place in Eisenhower's tiny office at his vacation headquarters. For twenty minutes, the President and the governor talked, alone. Eisenhower later dictated to Whitman his version of what was said. Faubus began by protesting "again and again [that] he was a law-abiding citizen . . . and that everybody recognizes that the federal law is supreme to state law." He said he had been one of "Ike's boys" in Europe during the war, when he served as a major of infantry and was wounded. Eisenhower said he wanted to give Faubus a way out of the hole he had put himself in. Why not go home, Eisenhower suggested, and instead of withdrawing the Guard, simply change the orders, directing the Guard to maintain the peace while admitting the Negro pupils. If he would do that, Eisenhower promised, the Justice Department would go to court to request that the governor be excused from the hearing. Eisenhower said it was not beneficial to anybody "to have a trial of strength between the President and a governor be-cause . . . there could be only one outcome—that is, the state would lose, and I did not want to see any governor humiliated." Faubus seemed to seize the offer. Satisfied, Eisenhower took Faubus to an outer office, where they were joined by Adams, Hays, and Brownell. To that group, Faubus reiterated his intention to change the Guard's orders.[16]

Ann Whitman had the sinking feeling that her boss, in his eager-ness to find a face-saving compromise for everyone, had allowed him-self to be led down the primrose path. "I got the impression," she wrote in her diary that evening, "that the meeting had not gone as well as had been hoped, that the federal government would have to be as tough as possible in the situation." She thought that Faubus "has seized this opportunity and stirred the whole thing up for his own political advantage . . ." She noted that "there was certainly a great frenzy around here." Then she warned, "The test comes tomorrow morning when we will know whether Governor Faubus will, or will not, withdraw the troops" or change their orders.[17]

Faubus returned to Little Rock. He did not withdraw the troops, or change their orders. Brownell had been right in predicting that nothing would come of a meeting with him other than more publicity for Faubus. The governor continued to use the state's armed forces to defy the orders of a federal court. Eisenhower wanted to issue a state-ment denouncing Faubus for his duplicity, but Brownell and Adams talked him out of it. They wanted to wait until the hearing, where they anticipated the court would issue a directive to Faubus to admit the children forthwith. At that time, as Goodpaster noted in a memo-randum, if Faubus still refused to comply, "then an obligation falls upon the federal government to require Faubus to do so by whatever means may be necessary."[18]

At the hearing, on September 20, Faubus' lawyers—but not the governor himself—made an appearance. They read a statement questioning the federal court's authority, then withdrew. The judge promptly enjoined Faubus and the Guard from interfering with the progress of integration at Central High. That afternoon, Eisenhower called Brownell, who told him of Faubus' action, then said that the governor might withdraw the Guard, turning over the streets around Central High to a racist mob, or he might follow a path of "straight defiance." In either case, Brownell said, the President was going to have to make some difficult decisions, including the possible use of the U.S. Army to enforce the court orders.

Eisenhower said he was "loath to use troops." He feared that the "movement might spread—violence would come." He had no doubt whatever about his authority to call out the troops, but said again that he hated to do it. He wanted Brooks Hays told "just how low the governor has fallen in the President's estimation since he broke his promise." Then Eisenhower expressed his deepest and most persistent fear. He asked Brownell, "Suppose the children are taken to school and then Governor Faubus closes the school? Can he do that legally?" Brownell said he would look it up. Eisenhower feared that the federal government would be helpless in the event the South abolished its public school system, and that the precedent thereby set for defiance of constitutional authority could have devastating results, for Negroes, for poor white southerners, and for the nation.[19]

Eisenhower spent most of the weekend playing bridge and golf with his gang. (At the card game, Slater noted, "The President was the big loser and as usual didn't like it.") During the evening, Hagerty flew up from Washington to report that Faubus had withdrawn the Guard. The governor also said that he intended to appeal the injunction, and he asked the Negro parents to keep their children away from Central High. The President was pleased that an immediate confrontation had been avoided. On September 22, a Sunday, he put on his apron and chef's hat and cooked steaks for the gang. At a marathon bridge session, he said he thought the Little Rock situation would get worse. He had tried "desperately" to keep the integration problem "under control, but the agitators won't let it be that way." No one could win, Eisenhower said, but many would be hurt. He recalled previous crisis situations—the North Africa landings, D-day, the Bulge, NATO, the 1952 campaign, Korea, Suez, and others—and commented that while he made his decisions "without the harassment that most men feel," still it "would be much pleasanter to have a short period where things are running smoothly."[20]

Monday morning, September 23, a howling racist mob gathered around Central High, screaming protests against integration. Variously estimated at from five hundred to "several thousand" strong, the mob rushed two Negro reporters. As the mob knocked down and beat up the newsmen, nine Negro pupils slipped into the school by a side door. The mob, learning of this development, grew even more enraged. It rushed the police barricades and fought to get into the school, vowing to "lynch the niggers." On orders from the mayor of Little Rock, the police then removed the Negro students. Integration at Central High had lasted three hours.[21]

That afternoon, Eisenhower was driving to the Newport Country Club when an urgent call from Brownell caused him to return to his office. Brownell informed him of the events in Little Rock. The Attorney General said the President had to act. Eisenhower agreed. He issued a blunt and vigorous statement: "The federal law . . . cannot be flouted with impunity by any individual or any mob of extremists. I will use the full power of the United States including whatever force may be necessary to prevent any obstruction of the law and to carry out the orders of the Federal Court." He expressed the hope that "the American sense of justice and fair play will prevail . . . It will be a sad day for this country . . . if schoolchildren can safely attend their classes only under the protection of armed guards." He followed the statement with a proclamation setting forth the President's authority and responsibility to use troops to enforce the federal law. The President then did "command all persons engaged in such obstruction to cease and desist therefrom and to disperse forthwith."[22]

Eisenhower was in Newport, Brownell in Washington. They had so many telephone conversations the morning of September 24 that Whitman wrote she could monitor only a few of them. At 8:45, Eisenhower told Brownell that an additional statement Brownell had sent up from Washington for the President's approval was too strong. Instead of starting out with a statement that the "law has been defied," Eisenhower said, he had substituted a phrase expressing his sympathy with the South. Brownell said that Max Taylor, Chief of Staff of the Army, wanted to use the Arkansas National Guard, not regular Army troops, if the President decided to use force. Eisenhower thought that it would be a mistake to use units from Little Rock, as that would set "brother against brother," and suggested instead using Guard units from other parts of the state. Brownell protested that it would take six to nine hours to get units into Little Rock, but the President said "that in this case time was not of the essence."[23]

In his four and one-half years as President, Eisenhower had gotten through many a crisis simply by denying that a crisis existed. His favorite approach was to conduct business as usual, stick as close to a routine as possible, speak and act with moderation, and wait for the inevitable cooling down of passions. On the morning of September 24, between telephone conversations with Brownell, Eisenhower found time to write a long letter to Al Gruenther (who had urged him to return to Washington to manage the crisis), explaining his thinking. He would not return to Washington, because to do so "would be a confession that a change of scenery is truly a 'vacation' for the President and is not merely a change of his working locale." Highly sensitive to the criticism that he was only a part-time President who spent far too much of his time on vacation, Eisenhower insisted that "the White House office is wherever the President may happen to be" and that he could make his decisions in Newport as easily as in Washington. Further, "I do not want to exaggerate the significance of the admittedly serious situation in Arkansas." If he rushed back to Washington, he would give the impression of "fretting and worrying about the actions of a misguided governor." To Eisenhower's mind, "The great need is to act calmly, deliberately, and giving every offender opportunity to cease his defiance . . ."[24]

Moderation and deliberation, however, were hard to find in Little Rock that morning. There the mob, now swollen in size to many thousands, again took control of the streets. The mayor, Woodrow Wilson Mann, sent Eisenhower a frantic telegram: "The immediate need for federal troops is urgent. . . . Situation is out of control and police cannot disperse the mob . . ."[25]

Eisenhower realized immediately that his entire policy had broken down. By allowing events to run their course, by attempting to negotiate with Faubus, by failing to ever speak out forcefully on integration, or to provide real leadership on the moral issue, he found himself in precisely the situation he had most wanted to avoid. His options had run out. Mayor Mann's telegram gave him no choice but to use force.

He did have a choice as to what type of force he would use. At 12:08 P.M., he called Brownell to say that he finally agreed, force would have to be used. And, in a significant switch from his position of only a few hours earlier, he said he wanted to use the U.S. Army. He accepted Brownell's suggestion that he simultaneously call the Arkansas National Guard into federal service and use it side by side with the regulars. At 12:15 he called General Taylor and gave the order. He

wanted Taylor to move quickly in order to demonstrate how rapidly
the Army could respond. Within a few hours, Taylor had five hundred
paratroopers of the 101st Airborne Division in Little Rock; another
five hundred were there by nightfall.[26]

Eisenhower also changed his mind about going to Washington. At
3:30 P.M., he flew to the capital so that he could speak to the nation
that night from the White House. On the plane, he scribbled down
some notes. "Troops—*not* to enforce integration, but to prevent opposition by violence to orders of a court."[27] In his statement to the
nation, the President emphasized that he was not sending U.S. troops
into the South to integrate the schools, but only to maintain the law.
He went out of his way to state that his personal opinion on *Brown*
had no bearing on enforcement. Carefully avoiding any specific reference to Faubus, he blamed the situation in Little Rock on "certain
misguided persons, many of them imported into Little Rock by agitators . . ." In a gesture of conciliation toward the white South, Eisenhower said that the "overwhelming majority of the people of the
South—including those of Arkansas and of Little Rock—are of good
will, united in their efforts to preserve and respect the law even when
they disagree with it." Then he appealed to their sense of patriotism.
He noted with sadness that the United States was taking a terrific beating in the world press—foreigners were aghast that the Army had to
be called out to escort fewer than a dozen youngsters to school. The
Soviets, Eisenhower said, were "gloating over this incident and using
it everywhere to misrepresent our whole nation." Then he returned to
his basic theme, that the troops were there to enforce a court order,
not integration, and that in no way would they be responsible for
running the high school. He concluded by appealing to the people of
Arkansas to return to "normal habits of peace and order," and thus
help to remove "a blot upon the fair name and high honor of our
nation . . ."[28]

Eisenhower's conciliatory words, his call for moderation, his appeal to patriotism, had little effect. Throughout the South, white segregationists were outraged by the "invasion." Marching protestors carried banners that played on the words of the Army's recruiting slogan:
"Join the Army and See the High Schools!" Lyndon Johnson proclaimed: "There should be no troops from either side patrolling our
school campuses." Senator Eastland said that "the President's move
was an attempt to destroy the social order of the South." Senator Olin
Johnston boldly proclaimed, "If I were a governor and he came in,
I'd give him a fight such as he's never been in before." In Louisiana,

a local political boss, Leander Perez, called for secession (calmer heads reminded him that this time around the Feds had atomic weapons).

Few southerners could see the distinction that Eisenhower stressed so carefully, the difference between using troops to enforce integration on one hand, or to uphold the law on the other. The result, after all, was the same. The following morning, the 101st Airborne dispersed the mob, with only minor incidents (one man was pricked by a bayonet), while nine Negro students entered Central High and, under Army guard, sat through a full day of classes. Central High was integrated. That was the result the segregationists had vowed to prevent, and that Eisenhower's orders had made possible. Eisenhower nevertheless continued to insist on his distinction. He told an October 3 news conference, "The troops are not there as a part of the segregation problem." [29] He was careful to tie his actions to such historical precedents as the Whiskey Rebellion, or Grover Cleveland's dispatch of the Army to Chicago during a train strike; his purpose in drawing these historical analogies was to deny that he himself was setting any precedent. But, of course, and inevitably, he was. Faubus had forced Eisenhower to face one ultimate question: Could the southern governors use the state's armed forces to prevent integration? But because Faubus had been forced to pose the question within the context of outright defiance of the orders of the federal court, he gave Eisenhower no choice but to act. He could not have done otherwise and still been President.

Eisenhower had to be pushed to the wall before he would act, but at the critical moment, he lived up to his oath of office. In the process, he convinced most white southerners that they could not use force to prevent integration. Nevertheless, the roar of protest from the segregationists continued, even increased. Senator Russell sent Eisenhower a telegram, protesting the "highhanded and illegal methods being employed by the armed forces of the United States under your command who are carrying out your orders to mix the races in the public schools of Little Rock." He charged that Eisenhower was using Hitler-like storm-trooper tactics on American citizens, and spoke of "bayonet-point rule." [30]

Eisenhower's reply was calm and conciliatory. He began by confessing that "few times in my life have I felt as saddened" as the day he ordered the troops into Little Rock. Without naming him, Eisenhower blamed Faubus for all the trouble. Eisenhower reminded Russell that he had taken an oath of office, an oath that required him to protect American citizens who were peaceably exercising their rights and who were attacked by mobs that the police could not control and the governor would not. Under those circumstances, Eisenhower insisted, "Failure to act . . . would be tantamount to acquiescence in anarchy and the dissolution of the union."

Turning to Russell's analogy, Eisenhower said, "I completely fail to comprehend your comparison of our troops to Hitler's storm troopers. In one case military power was used to further the ambitions and purposes of a ruthless dictator; in the other to preserve the institutions of free government." That was strong, accurate, and a good place to stop, but Eisenhower went on to promise Russell that he would order the Army to investigate Russell's allegations about wrongdoing on the part of individual soldiers (the subsequent investigation revealed none).[31]

The troops were in control, the Negro pupils were at their desks, the mobs had been dispersed. Now Eisenhower's immediate goal was to get the 101st Airborne out of town as quickly as possible. He tried to negotiate with Faubus through a group of four southern governors, but failed; Faubus was up for re-election and his goal was to keep the crisis atmosphere alive. Eisenhower therefore had to abandon his plan to withdraw the regulars and turn command of the Arkansas Guard back to Faubus. Eisenhower's next goal was to dissociate himself with court-ordered integration. He issued a statement which stressed that "the Executive Branch of the federal government does not participate in the formulation of plans effecting desegregation . . ." In an October 3 press-conference briefing, Eisenhower expressed his personal and private view that the courts had gone too far too fast. As Whitman noted, "The President said there was a grave situation raised . . . as to the right of the Supreme Court to go ahead after they find a thing unconstitutional—to work out plans and lay down schemes for implementing plans." Such actions by the courts threatened individual liberties and states' rights. He then announced that he was going to stay as quiet as possible about Little Rock, hoping to play down the situation and allow moderate sentiment in the South to assert itself.[32]

But the news conference was taken up almost entirely with Little Rock. Patiently and clearly, the President restated his reasons for acting. "No one can deplore more than I do the sending of federal troops anywhere," he said. "It is not good for the troops; it is not good for the locality; it is not really American . . ." He did not publicly criticize the federal court for its orders to integrate Central High, but rather praised the plan the court had agreed to (drawn up originally by the Little Rock School Board) as moderate and reasonable (indeed the NAACP had denounced it as much too slow). He preached patience, tolerance, and understanding.[33]

Eisenhower's open appeal to southern moderates to step forward and assume leadership was a dismal failure. It could hardly have been otherwise, given that nearly all the voters in the South were whites committed to segregation. By letters, phone calls, and stag dinners, Eisenhower tried to rally some southern support, but as he told Oveta Culp Hobby, a Texan, the only prominent southerner who had rallied to his side was Ralph McGill, editor of the Atlanta *Constitution*. The President had concluded sadly that southern politicians were not "in a position" to support him.[34]

Slowly, the crisis faded. Faubus continued to shout defiance, but by October 14 the situation was stable enough for Eisenhower to withdraw half the Army troops and to defederalize 80 percent of the Guardsmen. The next week, Brownell carried out his long-standing intention of resigning, to return to private practice, an act that helped cool passions, as many southerners saw Brownell as the villain in the piece. By October 23, Negro students entered Central High without military protection. In November, the last of the 101st left. The Guard remained, under federal control, until the end of the school year, in June 1958. In September of that year, Faubus did what Eisenhower had so feared—he closed Central High altogether (it was reopened on an integrated basis in the fall of 1959).

Little Rock had been, for Eisenhower, "troublesome beyond imagination."[35] By the time the crisis ended, however, it had become little more than an irritant, because by then it had been eclipsed by another crisis in American education, this one brought on by the Russians.

Eisenhower had endured many a discouraging autumn. In 1942, he was stuck in the mud of Tunisia, in 1943 in the mud of Italy, in 1944 along the West Wall. In 1954, he lost control of Congress in the fall elections. In late September 1955, he had suffered his first heart attack. In October 1956, it was Suez, and in September 1957, Little Rock. That should have been enough for any man, but still the dreary list grew. On October 4, 1957, the Soviet Union fired into orbit the world's first man-made satellite, named Sputnik ("traveling companion"). This impressive achievement came as "a distinct surprise" to Eisenhower and his Administration. But as Eisenhower confessed in his memoirs, "Most surprising of all . . . was the intensity of the public concern."[36]

He had no excuse for being surprised by the near-hysterical reaction of the American press, politicians, and public to Sputnik. He himself had said repeatedly, when discussing the American missile program, that the ICBMs were far more important in terms of psychological factors than as military weapons. He had predicted that the achievement of operational ICBMs by the Russians would throw the American people into a fright bordering on panic, because the idea that the enemy could send nuclear warheads across the oceans to obliterate American cities was certain to create uncontrollable anxieties. But predicting and experiencing were two distinct things, and Eisenhower was indeed almost overwhelmed by the intensity of the American response to Sputnik.

Eisenhower had anticipated the fear that Sputnik engendered; what really surprised him was the way in which Sputnik swept away certain basic American assumptions and caused a crisis in self-confidence. For a dozen years, since the victory in the war, Americans had taken for granted that theirs was not only the richest and freest and most powerful nation in the world, but also the best educated and most technologically advanced. As generalizations, those assumptions were more or less appropriate to the mid-1950s. The trouble was that, at the time, few of those who boasted so frequently about American achievements bothered to point out that this was an abnormal and unique situation, brought on by the way in which World War II had been fought. America's allies, and her enemies, had been pulverized while the American industrial system had boomed. It was geography, not inherent American goodness or skill, that had brought about that result, just as it was geography, not American money or scientific knowhow, that brought the atomic project out of Britain and over to America. Americans thought of the Manhattan Project as an achievement of American science, when in fact it had been an international project, with anti-Nazi scientists from all over Europe making crucial contributions.

As almost any general history of the 1950s points out, it was a decade characterized by complacency. In this, it was unique. In the thirties, there was the trauma of the Depression. In the forties, there were the horrors of a world war, followed by Korea. In the sixties, there would be a civil-rights revolution and war in Vietnam; in the seventies, Watergate, an oil embargo, and inflation. But the fifties were unique and blessed, or so people thought. Except for the problem of race relations, which even after Little Rock was minor compared to the events of the sixties, and for minor problems with the economy, and of course, the continuing problems of the Cold War, Americans could find little to worry about, and much to praise, in their assessment of the state of the nation.

Most commentators, then and later, linked this remarkable self-satisfaction to President Eisenhower. "Trust Ike" was the watchword. He was so comforting, so grandfatherly, so calm, so sure of himself, so skillful in managing the economy, so experienced in ensuring America's defenses, so expert in his control of the intelligence community, so knowledgeable about the world's affairs, so nonpartisan and objective in his above-the-battle posture, so insistent on holding to the middle of the road, that he inspired a trust that was as broad and deep as that of any President since George Washington. Even southern Democrats could not bring themselves to dislike Ike, and the Democratic Party as a whole never hated Eisenhower as the Republicans hated FDR and Truman, or as the Democrats later hated Nixon. Thus Eisenhower is praised—or blamed—for the complacency and consensus of the fifties.

Actually, Eisenhower was given far too much credit—or blame—for the character of the fifties. In large part, it was plain good luck. The economic boom would have taken place even if Taft or Stevenson had won in 1952. America's preponderant position in military and financial power was a legacy Eisenhower inherited. Eisenhower had been a participant in the process of changing the isolationist America of 1939 into the world colossus of 1952, but not the maker of that policy. His task as President was one of managing America's rise to globalism, not bringing it about. As Eisenhower himself was always first to point out, it was plain silly to give all the credit, or blame, to one man.

It is also wrong to think of the fifties as a whole as an era of good feelings. The 1952 presidential campaign was one of the most bitter and divisive of the twentieth century. The events in Little Rock signified the breakdown of consensus; Sputnik destroyed the complacency. Modern nostalgia for the fifties is in reality nostalgia for a period of only slightly more than four years, from July 1953 (the end of the Korean War) to September–October 1957.

After Little Rock and Sputnik, the Democrats were after Eisenhower with a vigor and enthusiasm previously unknown. They did not attack the President personally, to be sure, because his popularity was consistently high, but they did lambast his Administration, with great success. The consensus had always been fragile, and it was incapable of dealing with such a basic issue as race relations. Eisenhower always wanted to widen the middle of the road, but Little Rock narrowed it down to little more than a tiny strip. Northern Democrats and liberals

426

generally were critical of Eisenhower's hesitant response to Faubus' challenge; southern Democrats and conservatives generally were even more vocal in their criticism of his decision to use the Army. Eisenhower's policy of delay and obfuscation, which he had used so successfully in various foreign crises, had only made the civil-rights crisis worse.

Similarly, the complacency had always been fragile, as was demonstrated when one Russian satellite, weighing less than two hundred pounds and carrying no scientific or military equipment, broke it down. Democrats cashed in on the shame, shock, and anger Americans felt, as they blamed the Republicans for various "gaps"—in education, in missiles, in satellites, in economic growth, in bombers, in science, and in prestige. Almost all Americans wanted to be "number one" in everything, which helped explain the overreaction to Sputnik and gave the Democrats the rallying cry that would carry them to victory in the 1958 and 1960 elections—Let's get the country moving again. "If we do have to stress party differences," Eisenhower had told the Democratic leaders at the beginning of 1957, "let us do it on relatively small matters." But after Little Rock and Sputnik, the differences were over big matters, civil rights and national defense, as complacency and consensus disappeared.

Three days after Sputnik went up, the AEC finished the Plumbob series of tests. There had been twenty-four bombs set off in all, including an underground test. The Russians had tested fifteen bombs in 1957, the British four. The American lead in nuclear weaponry, both in technology and in size of the arsenal, remained substantial.[37] Still Strauss and the AEC wanted more, specifically twenty-five tests in 1958 in a series code-named Hardtack. Almost all the tests would be of hydrogen bombs. On August 9, Strauss met with Eisenhower to go over Hardtack, with Major John Eisenhower keeping the notes. (John was substituting for Goodpaster, who was on vacation.) The President opened the meeting by expressing his reservations about the scope of Hardtack—twenty-five explosions seemed far too many to him. Strauss said he had pared the number down from the thirty tests requested by the Defense Department. Next Eisenhower objected to the duration of the series, scheduled for May through August. He said he was trying to get disarmament negotiations under way, and publicity from the tests would hamper his efforts. Strauss explained that "perfect meteorological conditions" were necessary for each test, "particularly for the large-yield weapons." Why do we need to test bigger bombs? the President wanted to know. Because, Strauss replied, although neither State nor the AEC could "justify a need for the very large weapons," the DOD wanted to ascertain how big a bomb could be carried by the B-52 (Hardtack included a bomb that weighed twenty-five thousand pounds). John noted that "the President pointed out that the scaling laws apply on a cube route basis, which would give a forty-megaton weapon a radius of damage only about one and one-half the size the radius of damage of the ten megaton." Strauss then said he would not go any higher than the Bravo test of 1954, which was fifteen megatons.

Eisenhower said his dilemma was that in conducting tests of this magnitude the United States "was planning and carrying out extensive tests on the one hand while professing a readiness to suspend testing in a disarmament program on the other." He was concerned that he would be charged with bad faith. However, he said with a sigh, "having gone this far," it was necessary to go through with Hardtack. He did instruct Strauss to explode no bomb bigger than Bravo, and to condense the time span of the series.[38] Eisenhower's reluctance in approving Hardtack only highlighted his determination to stay ahead of the Russians in nuclear weaponry.

Sputnik also highlighted another aspect of the nuclear dilemma— delivery systems. In fact, the American B-52 fleet of 1957 was incomparably the best delivery system in the world of that time, far superior to the Russian bomber fleet, and enjoying the additional advantage of access to airfields around the Soviet Union. Sputnik, however, coupled with Soviet boasting about their progress in ICBMs, suddenly made Americans feel naked and vulnerable, stripped of a retaliatory capacity. American weapons, Khrushchev declared, including the B-52, belonged in museums. Eisenhower knew how ridiculous such an assertion was, but like so many of his countrymen he nevertheless was fearful that the Russians had stolen a march on the United States, that Sputnik proved the enemy had better rockets and missiles than the Americans possessed.

Eisenhower's first response to Sputnik was to call a meeting with the appropriate officials from the Defense Department to review American missile development and find out how the Russians had won the race to space. The backbiting and blame fixing had already begun, the day after Sputnik, when two Army officers said that the Army had a rocket, Redstone, that could have placed a satellite in orbit many months ago, but the Eisenhower Administration had given the satellite program to the Navy (Project Vanguard), and the Navy had failed.

On October 8, at an 8:30 A.M. conference, Eisenhower asked Deputy Secretary Quarles if that was true. Quarles said it was worse than true—he claimed that Redstone could have accomplished the task as much as two years earlier. But DOD had decided that it was "better to have the earth satellite proceed separately from military development," in order to stress the peaceful character of the satellite program. Well, the President commented wryly, when the congressmen find out about this "they are bound to ask why this action [Redstone] was not taken." Quarles said that the Army could still beat the Navy; Vanguard was at least five months away, while Redstone could gear up and send a satellite into space within four months.

Quarles then pointed out that "the Russians have in fact done us a good turn, unintentionally, in establishing the concept of freedom of international space . . ." Eisenhower wanted to know what were the prospects for a reconnaissance vehicle, a satellite that could take pictures and beam them back to earth. Quarles said the Air Force had a research program in that area that was coming along nicely.[39] Later that morning, Eisenhower met with Wilson (who had dismissed Sputnik as "a neat scientific trick"). They discussed the Army and the Air Force programs for missiles. Wilson gave some background on each, then concluded that the choice was to go ahead with both, hoping one would work out, "or to chop off one program now." Eisenhower said "he did not feel in a position to make such a decision, not being a technician." Despite the several millions in cost, he decided to go ahead with both; he also said that what the United States really ought to do was abolish the Army, Navy, Air Force, and Marines "and go to task forces under Defense—but such an idea is probably twenty years away."

Wilson warned that "trouble is rising between the Army and the Air Force over this missile." The Navy, too, was going to make trouble if Vanguard was neglected. "The President interjected, with some vigor, that he thought we are going to have to go to a 'Manhattan Project' type approach in order to get forward in this matter." He then instructed Wilson to remove the restrictions on overtime work at missile research stations, and to get Redstone into the business of putting a satellite into orbit as soon as possible.[40]

Shortly thereafter, Eisenhower met with the Joint Chiefs in the Red Room, for what he described as "a kind of seminar." His subject was rivalry between the services. General Taylor complained that the Air Force was trying to block Redstone. General Nathan Twining, an Air Force officer who had, in August, replaced Radford as chairman of the JCS, immediately "intervened to say that this is one point that is clear—the Army is to have no missiles more than two-hundred mile range." Eisenhower refused to accept such fixed mile limitations. He said there were great advantages to the Army having missiles that could be more centrally located, farther back from the battle area, "which is bound to be a turbulent one, and able to fire on all parts of the sector." He wanted the Army to go ahead with Redstone. Then the President gave a long lecture on teamwork, citing AFHQ, SHAEF, and SHAPE as examples he wanted the Chiefs to emulate. They all nodded their heads.[41]

Sputnik not only set the Chiefs to bickering among themselves; it had a remarkable effect on the White House press corps, usually so friendly to Eisenhower. On October 9, five days after Sputnik, Eisenhower held a news conference that was one of the most hostile of his career. Merriman Smith, ordinarily a great admirer of Eisenhower, set the tone in his opening question. Reading from a note card, Smith began, "Russia has launched an earth satellite. They also claim to have had a successful firing of an intercontinental ballistic missile, none of which this country has done." Raising his eyes, Smith looked directly at the President. "I ask you, sir, what are we going to do about it?"

Eisenhower began by denying that there was a link between a satellite and the ICBM. He gave a brief history of American involvement in a satellite program. He denied that there ever was a race to get into space first. He promised to have an American satellite in orbit before the end of 1958. As to the Russian ICBM, Eisenhower said that Sputnik had certainly proved that "they can hurl an object a considerable distance." It did not prove that the ICBMs could hit a target. American missile research was going forward full speed, and the United States had a lead in the ICBM race.

Eisenhower was asked if the B-52 was "outmoded," as Khrushchev claimed. Absolutely not, the President replied. Robert Clark wanted to know how the Russians had gotten ahead in launching an earth satellite. Eisenhower replied that "from 1945, when the Russians captured all of the German scientists in Peenemunde, . . . they have centered their attention on the ballistic missile." (Don't worry, Mort Sahl was telling his audiences; all Sputnik proves is that the Russians captured better German scientists than we did.) Eisenhower then downplayed the Russian achievement, although he admitted that they had gained a "great psychological advantage."

May Craig wanted to know if the Russians could use satellites as space platforms from which to launch rockets. "Not at this time, no,"

Eisenhower replied. "There is no . . ." he went on, but paused, smiled, and commented, "Suddenly all America seems to become scientist, and I am hearing many, many ideas."

Hazel Markel of NBC then asked the question all of America was asking. "Mr. President," Markel said, "in light of the great faith which the American people have in your military knowledge and leadership, are you saying at this time that with the Russian satellite whirling about the world, you are not more concerned nor overly concerned about our nation's security?" Eisenhower spoke to the whole nation in his reply, in an attempt to calm a jittery public. "As far as the satellite itself is concerned," he said, "that does not raise my apprehensions, not one iota. I see nothing at this moment, at this stage of development, that is significant in that development as far as security is concerned." [42]

Later that day, Eisenhower met with Lyndon Johnson. Senator Symington was beginning an investigation into the American missile program, with the obvious purpose of putting the blame for the loss of the space race on the Republicans. Eisenhower hoped to keep the whole subject out of partisan politics. He told Johnson that Symington and his friends should be aware "that the Democrats could be blamed." Truman had spent literally nothing on missile research before 1950, and only a pittance after that. Eisenhower promised that the Republicans "would not be first to throw the stone." Johnson said he had been urged to call a special session of Congress; Eisenhower said "he saw no need of it now." After Johnson left, Eisenhower told Whitman that he had "said all the right things. I think today he is being honest." [43]

Having faced the Chiefs, the press corps, and the politicians, Eisenhower met next with the scientists. On October 15, he called fourteen of the leading scientists in America to the Oval Office. It was his first meeting with so broad-gauged and representative a group. Strauss had always previously managed to control the access of scientists to the President, and brought him only such men as Drs. Lawrence and Teller. (Teller, incidentally, had called Sputnik a greater defeat for the United States than Pearl Harbor, which was exactly the kind of talk Eisenhower deplored.) Shortly before the Oval Office meeting began, Jerry Persons came in to say he was worried about the guided-missile program, because "it was more than rivalry between services, there was rivalry between German and American scientists, between civilian groups, etc." Eisenhower said he knew that already. [44]

The meeting started at 11 A.M. and it was a long one. Eisenhower began by asking "whether the group really thought that American science is being outdistanced, and asked for an expression of the state of mind of the members." Dr. Isidor Rabi, a Columbia physicist whom Eisenhower knew and admired, spoke first. He said that he, and all the group, wanted federal support for scientific research and training, not because America had fallen behind, but because the Soviets "have picked up tremendous momentum, and unless we take vigorous action they could pass us swiftly just as in a period of twenty to thirty years we caught up with Europe and left Western Europe far behind." Then Dr. Land, who had developed the camera equipment for the U-2, "spoke with great eloquence." He said that science "needs the President acutely." The Russians were in a pioneering stage and frame of mind. They were teaching Russian students basic sciences and beginning to reap the rewards. "Curiously, in the United States we are not now great builders for the future but are rather stressing production in great quantities of things we have already achieved," Land said, while the Russians looked to the future. Land wanted the President to "inspire the country—setting out our youth particularly on a whole variety of scientific adventures." He complained that "at the present time scientists feel themselves isolated and alone."

Eisenhower disagreed with Land's analysis. He said that the Russians had "followed the practice of picking out the best minds and ruthlessly spurning the rest." Nor did he think that he alone could give a new spirit to scientific training and research in America. He did agree that "perhaps now is a good time to try such a thing. People are alarmed and thinking about science, and perhaps this alarm could be turned to a constructive result." Rabi pointed out that Eisenhower lacked a scientific adviser. Eisenhower admitted that such an individual could be "most helpful."[45] Soon thereafter he appointed Dr. James Killian, the president of MIT, to the post, making the widely popular Killian the head of the President's Science Advisory Committee (PSAC).

Two weeks later, on October 29, Rabi and Strauss came to see the President. Rabi said that "we now enjoy certain advantages in the nuclear world over the Russians and that the most important of these gaps can be closed only by continuous testing on the part of the Russians." Rabi and his associates had therefore reached the conclusion that the United States, "as a matter of self-interest," should agree to a suspension of all nuclear testing, if the Russians would allow the United States to place a half-dozen or so listening posts inside Russia. Rabi admitted that there were "certain advantages" to continuing testing and keeping the Hardtack series in place, but "the expected advantage would be as nothing compared with maintaining the particular scientific gap that exists in the design of the Russian H-bomb as compared to ours." He explained that the nature of the gap was that Russian bombs were unshielded against certain types of radioactivity, so that if the United States exploded a small atomic weapon in the path of incoming ICBMs, they would reduce the effect of the Russian weapon by "something like 99 percent."

Eisenhower was more than interested. A freeze on testing would save money, maintain an American lead, quiet the fears about fallout—it had everything going for it. But Strauss intervened to say that neither he nor the AEC scientists, led by Lawrence and Teller, agreed with Rabi. They thought that despite the listening posts inside the Soviet Union, the enemy could set off undetected explosions, and thus successfully cheat on any test ban. Further, they were "keenly afraid" that if America stopped testing, "the Russians would, by stealing all of our secrets, equal and eventually surpass us." They insisted that America had to protect itself through continuous testing. Eisenhower shook his head—in the face of such conflicting advice from the experts, how could he decide? He told Strauss to get together with other scientists and get some agreement on what should be done.[46]

When the meeting ended, Eisenhower asked Strauss to stay for a moment. Goodpaster kept notes of their private talk. Eisenhower said that Rabi "is a brilliant scientist and a friend of long standing to whom he is deeply devoted." He wanted Strauss to make a thorough study of Rabi's proposal. "The President recalled that he had many times thought that if in fact we are ahead in the types of atomic weapons we have, we should stop testing at once in order to 'freeze' our lead." Strauss again insisted that in the event of a test ban, the Russians would steal American secrets. He also told Eisenhower that "the mutual antagonisms among the scientists are so bitter as to make their working together an impossibility . . . Dr. Rabi and some of his group are so antagonistic to Drs. Lawrence and Teller that communication between them is practically nil."[47]

The following day, Eisenhower met with Twining to discuss ways and means of cutting down costs in the nuclear development field. The President wondered why the AEC and JCS wanted so many bombs. He asked, "What is going to be done with this tremendous number of enormous weapons?" With an existing arsenal of thousands of weapons, Eisenhower said, "we are certainly providing for elaborate reserves, and making very pessimistic estimates as to what can get to the target." He thought the B-52 had "great penetrating power."

Twining confirmed that assumption, but then said that "the Air Force will not be happy until they get one [hydrogen bomb] for every aircraft plus a sizable reserve."[48]

Costs were very much on Eisenhower's mind. Sputnik had stimulated almost unmanageable demands for more spending, on space and missile research, for conventional forces, for federal aid to colleges and universities, for fallout shelters, and a myriad of other projects. But the economy was slipping; 1957 was a recession year, federal income was down as a result, and the balanced budget of the previous two years was about to become a deficit budget. George Humphrey had resigned as Secretary of the Treasury (Robert Anderson replaced him), but he continued to have a strong influence on Eisenhower. Humphrey wrote the President an alarmist letter, predicting a major disaster if the expenditures were not reduced sufficiently to balance the budget. Eisenhower responded that if Humphrey was correct, "there better be some looking for storm cellars," because he was going to have a hard enough time holding to current levels of spending, and had no chance to reduce them.[49]

Humphrey had been, by far, the leading watchdog on spending in the Cabinet. With his departure, the remaining members felt freer to propose new projects. At a November 1 meeting, they bombarded Eisenhower with proposals. "Look," the President finally exploded, "I'd like to know what's on the other side of the moon, but I won't pay to find out this year!"[50]

National sentiment was otherwise. Eisenhower was getting advice from individuals, groups, organizations, all centering around the theme that "security is more important than balanced budgets." The President took the time to respond at length to one such communication, from the Committee on International Policy of the National Planning Association. He deplored the Pearl Harbor atmosphere, the readiness to forget economics and spend whatever had to be spent to win the war. "We face," the President said, "not a temporary emergency . . . but a long-term responsibility." The United States effort "to combat and defeat the Soviets must be designed for indefinite use and endurance. Hasty and extraordinary effort under the impetus of sudden fear . . . cannot provide for an adequate answer to the threat." He said he knew he could get whatever he asked for from Congress in the way of defense spending in the next session, but the suggested expenditures were "unjustifiable." (A week later, Eisenhower told Goodpaster that "about two-thirds of the supplementary funds are more to stabilize public opinion than to meet any real need.") Eisenhower ad-

monished the committee that "we must remember that we are defending a way of life, not merely property, wealth, and even our homes
. . . Should we have to resort to anything resembling a garrison state,
then all that we are striving to defend . . . could disappear."[51]

Still the pressure continued. H. Rowan Gaither, Jr., of the Ford
Foundation, headed a committee that had studied "security in the
broadest possible sense of survival in the atomic age." The conclusions
the committee reached—and, after a leak, made public in the Gaither
Report—included, as Eisenhower typically understated it, "some sobering observations." At a November 6 meeting in the Oval Office,
Gaither told Eisenhower that his group had found that "our active defenses are not adequate," and the passive defenses "insignificant."
Within two years, if the Russians launched a surprise ICBM attack,
they would catch up to three-quarters of the B-52s on the ground.
That prospect so frightened the group that three members advocated
an immediate preventive war, while there was still time.

Gaither practically predicted the end of Western civilization. He
said the Soviet GNP was growing at a faster rate than that of the
United States, that the Soviets were spending more on their armed
forces, that they had fifteen hundred nuclear weapons, forty-five hundred bombers, three hundred submarines, an extensive air defense system, an IRBM with a seven-hundred-mile range, a soon-to-be operational ICBM, and so forth. Gaither almost pleaded with Eisenhower
to "do something" about it, something on the order of increasing defense appropriations from $38 billion to $48 billion. Much of that new
money should go into fallout shelters, one for every individual in the
country, at a cost of $100 per person, or a total over five years of $30
billion.

Eisenhower strongly disagreed. There was no defense, he insisted,
except retaliation. Therefore, fallout shelters "rank rather low in the
list of priorities." He thought it would be twenty years or more before
shelters would be built for such places as his Gettysburg farm. He confessed, "I can't understand the United States being quite as panicky
as they are." Even with shelters, Gaither estimated that half the American people would die in a nuclear exchange. Eisenhower said that "we
are getting close to absolutes" at that point. Then he gave his regular
lecture on the need to balance economic and social needs with defense
spending, and his regular warning about the dangers of a "garrison
state." And he reminded Gaither that while it would be easy to get $10
billion more from Congress in this session, "Americans will carry a
challenging load only for a couple of years." In conclusion, Eisen-

hower mentioned "that someone had advised him recently not to say this is a problem that will last forty years, but simply to call for a spurt of activity now. He thought this was inaccurate, and besides we must bring ourselves to carry the load until the Soviets change internally."[52]

With that, Eisenhower rejected the Gaither Report. He refused to bend to the pressure, refused to initiate a fallout shelter program, refused to expand conventional and nuclear forces, refused to panic. It was one of his finest hours. If in September 1957, at Little Rock, he had failed to exercise leadership and consequently suffered through one of the low moments of his Presidency, then in October and November 1957, in his response to Sputnik and the uproar it created, he reached one of the highest points. It is doubtful if any other man could have done what Eisenhower did. The demands for shelters, for more bombers, for more bombs, for more research and development of missiles and satellites, was nearly irresistible. Only Ike could have gotten away with saying no. His unique prestige among his countrymen made him unassailable on the question of national defense. The Ford Foundation, the Rockefeller Brothers, the JCS, Congress, indeed almost all of what would be called in the seventies "the Establishment," clamored for more defense spending. But Eisenhower said no, and he kept saying no to the end of his term. He thereby saved his country untold billions of dollars and no one knows how many war scares. Eisenhower's calm, common-sense, deliberate response to Sputnik may have been his finest gift to the nation, if only because he was the only man who could have given it.

On November 18, Eisenhower wrote Swede. Since July of 1956, when Nasser nationalized the Suez Canal, Eisenhower said he could not "remember a day that has not brought its major or minor crisis . . . But I have the satisfaction of knowing that I do my best . . . and that the Almighty must have in mind some better fate for this poor old world of ours than to see it largely blown up in a holocaust of nuclear bombs." As for himself, "I must tell you that physically I seem to stand up under the burden remarkably well." He had had a physical examination the day before; his blood pressure was 130 over 80 and his pulse was 66.[53] A week later, Whitman told him she thought he was looking "really well." Eisenhower agreed that he felt great.[54] That afternoon, November 25, he had a stroke.

CHAPTER NINETEEN

Problems: Stroke, Dulles, Disarmament, Space Race

December 1957–April 1958

ON NOVEMBER 25, after his lunch, Eisenhower went to his office, sat at his desk, began to sign some correspondence, and suddenly felt dizzy. Shaking off the feeling, he reached for another paper. He had difficulty picking it up, and when he did he discovered that the words seemed to run off the top of the page. Frustrated, bewildered, angry, he dropped his pen. Finding himself unable to pick it up, he got up from the chair, suffered another wave of dizziness, and had to grasp the back of the chair for stability.

He collapsed back into the chair and rang for Ann Whitman. When she came in, he tried to tell her what had happened, only to discover that he could not talk intelligibly. Words came out, but not the ones he wanted to say. Nor were they in any order that made sense. Whitman, of course, was stunned to find the President in the Oval Office talking gibberish. She called for Andy Goodpaster. He came in from his adjacent office, assessed the situation, and took charge. Grasping Eisenhower's arm, he helped him out of the chair and led him toward the door, saying, "Mr. President, I think we should get you to bed." Eisenhower had no difficulty walking with Goodpaster's support, nor did he feel any pain. When they got to his bedroom, Goodpaster helped him undress and lie down. Dr. Snyder was there in a matter of minutes. His patient was comfortable, and turned over to take a nap.[1]

Snyder called in two neurologists, while Goodpaster called John

Eisenhower, and Whitman told Mamie what had happened. The initial medical diagnosis was a minor stroke. Snyder speculated that the President may have had a spasm in one of the small capillaries of his brain. Sherman Adams joined the group in the living room. He said he had called Nixon both to alert him and to ask the Vice-President to replace the President at a state dinner that evening. To their collective horror, the door opened and there stood the President, in bathrobe and slippers, a big grin on his face, expecting to be congratulated on his quick recovery. As he sat down, Mamie gasped, "What are you doing up, Ike?" Softly and slowly, he replied, "Why shouldn't I be up? I have a dinner to go to." Snyder, Mamie, John, and Adams all protested simultaneously that he would do no such thing. "There's nothing the matter with me!" he said. "I am perfectly all right." Mamie explained to him that Nixon would take over at the dinner, and warned that if he went, she would not. Again Eisenhower began to insist that he would go, and to discuss the activities scheduled for the rest of the week that he did not intend to miss. But his words were still jumbled and mispronounced. Aware that he was making no sense, Eisenhower's anger swelled up in him. Mamie turned to Adams in dismay. "We can't let him go down there in this condition," she said. They finally convinced him to go back to bed. As he left the room, he mumbled, "If I cannot attend to my duties, I am simply going to give up this job. Now that is all there is to it." [2]

He slept comfortably, with John and Snyder sharing a night watch at his bedside. In the morning, the doctors found his pulse normal. He continued, however, to have difficulty with words. Pointing toward a watercolor on the wall, he tried to say its name, but could not. The harder he tried, the more frustrated he became. He thrashed about on the big double bed, beating the bedclothes with his fists. John, Snyder, and Mamie shouted any word that came to mind, until Mamie finally remembered the title: *"The Smugglers,"* she blurted out. Eisenhower shook his finger at her, demanding a repeat. But even after hearing it a second time, he could not say it. He sank back into the bed, exhausted. Later that day, he did some painting of his own. Adams and Nixon came to see him. Nixon said that the state dinner had gone well, and that he was planning to substitute for the President at a NATO conference, scheduled for mid-December.

The following day, November 27, a Wednesday, Eisenhower worked in his rooms on various papers; on Thanksgiving, he and Mamie attended church services, then drove on Friday to Gettysburg for the weekend.[3] His speech seemed completely recovered, to everyone but himself. Always very clear and precise in his pronunciation of words, it bothered him thereafter, until the end of his life, that occasionally he would reverse syllables in a long word.[4] But in private conversations or public speeches, few if any listeners ever noticed.

What did bother the American people was the news that the President had suffered his third illness in two years. At sixty-seven years old, the chances of his completing the three remaining years of his second term appeared to be poor. More immediately frightening, especially to insiders who were aware of his dizziness and speech difficulties, and to reporters who heard garbled accounts of what had happened, was the prospect of his becoming incapacitated either physically or, worse, mentally. What would happen if the President was in such bad condition that he was unable to recognize his own incapacity and therefore unable to delegate power to Nixon? What if he went clear out of his mind? What if . . . The list was endless. The Constitution was silent.

That Sunday morning, at Gettysburg, the newspapers the President read were full of suggestions. Walter Lippmann recommended that Eisenhower delegate his powers to Nixon; many other editors and columnists urged him to resign. The effect on the President was to strengthen his determination to take up his full duties on Monday morning, thereby proving that he had enjoyed a complete recovery and could do his job.

Eisenhower's resolve frightened his aides, who wanted him to rest for at least a few more days. Jerry Persons called Dulles at 1:45 P.M. to tell the Secretary about the President's decision to return to work. Dulles said "that itself is a very bad sign, the fact that he does not realize that he needs rest." Then Dulles told Persons, "Someone must get control of the situation."[5]

Dulles was the senior member of the Cabinet, the man closest to Eisenhower. He was also the nephew of Secretary of State Robert Lansing, who had tried to take control of the government when Wilson was incapacitated in 1919, and had been ousted as a result. At 2 P.M., Dulles called the one man in the world more directly and personally affected by the crisis than he was, the Vice-President. Dulles said, "We are liable to run into a situation where the President is incapable of acting and does not realize it." He was "very much disturbed about the situation." Persons had told him that Eisenhower intended to attend a Cabinet meeting on Monday, a Republican leaders' meeting on Tuesday, an NSC meeting, and so on. Nixon said, "It looks like his judgment is not good and the people around him are not able to exercise judgment or control." Inevitably, on both men's minds was the question, Should we declare him incompetent? Dulles told Nixon that "for the first time" he had the "impression the President was sensitive about the Vice-President." He complained again about the "lack of judgment" of Persons and the other aides, but pointed out that if he and Nixon tried to overrule the decision and prevent Eisenhower from returning to work, then "that is a reproduction of the Wilson problem, jealousy and usurpation of power." Dulles concluded by telling Nixon that he had just heard Drew Pearson on the radio appealing to Eisenhower to resign.[6]

Hanging up, Dulles called Gettysburg, this time talking to one of the Army doctors who had accompanied Snyder to Pennsylvania. The doctor told Dulles about Eisenhower's irritation at the newspapers; calls for his resignation "deeply affected him; he is feeling too well." Further, the doctor said, it was not such a bad idea for Eisenhower to return to work, because "continued frustration" would be worse than "active participation." Still, he wished the President would rest a few more days. Dulles said he "detected bad judgment; if the President were thinking right, he would see that he should accept medical advice."[7]

Dulles then got Hagerty, also in Gettysburg, on the phone. The Secretary asked Hagerty whether his presence and appeal might sway the President to rest. Hagerty said "he is beyond any appeal, however we would like to try." Dulles repeated that "this looked like bad judgment, that he understood the President was upset about some newspaper article." Hagerty said it was not the editorial, "it was the President himself, he wanted to come."[8]

Dulles' genuine concern for his friend's health, and his official concern for the continuity of government leadership, lasted less than twenty-four hours. Neither he nor Nixon made any further attempt to keep Eisenhower in Gettysburg, much less an attempt to declare him incompetent, and when they saw him at the Cabinet meeting on Monday, they were satisfied that his health was good. Following the one-and-a-half-hour Cabinet meeting, Dulles met privately with Eisenhower for another hour. They talked about the agenda for the Republican leaders' meeting, about MSA appropriations, about various diplomatic functions, and about the NATO meeting. Eisenhower said he wanted to go. Dulles had earlier protested strongly against this, but now he "urged that the President should take all possible care of himself so as to be able to go." Eisenhower, not Dulles, was the one who brought up a possible resignation. The President said that if, three weeks after his attack, he was not able to go to Europe, "it would in his opinion raise a serious question as to whether he should not then 'abdicate.' "[9]

Like Dulles and Nixon, and indeed almost everyone else, Eisenhower too worried about presidential succession. He talked to Nixon about it, to the Attorney General, to others. He could imagine all sorts of scenarios—"What if I was in an automobile accident and in a coma?"—and cast about for ways in which a committee could be formed that would decide when he was disabled and when he was ready to resume his duties.[10] Eventually he decided that in lieu of a constitutional amendment, his only choice was to make a common-sense agreement with Nixon that would not be binding on his successors. Accordingly, on February 5, 1958, he sent Nixon a letter outlining what they had already agreed to in conversation. If the President were disabled, and aware of it, he would inform Nixon and Nixon would take over. But if the President were so disabled he was incapable of recognizing it, Nixon would be "the individual explicitly and exclusively responsible . . . You will decide." Eisenhower expressed the "hope" that Nixon would consult with Dulles, Adams, and the doctors before acting, but emphasized that "the decision will be yours only." By the same token, "I will be the one to determine if and when it is proper for me to resume . . ."[11]

Nixon never had occasion to test this remarkable grant of power, but there must have been times in the next few weeks and months when he thought he might have to do so. Not that Eisenhower ever again lost control of his speech as he had on November 25 and 26, but the President was, in the winter of 1957–1958, noticeably more irritable and short-tempered, and complained about his job more than he ever had. The Presidency had begun to take its toll. From the time of Suez onward, as Eisenhower had told Swede, his life had been a succession of crises. They did not bother him so much as did the swelling criticism of his Administration. Although few Democrats were ready to go after General Ike personally, many columnists were, especially on such specific issues as the Middle East crisis, Hungary, Little Rock, and, most of all, Sputnik. Critics were questioning his leadership abilities, and pointing to the botched "Battle of the Budget" of 1957, the inept attempt to put through a civil-rights bill with some meaning, and the recession as examples of his failures. The charge that hurt the most was that he had "lost" the space race and had neglected the nation's defenses. Implicit in all the criticism was the idea that he was too old, too tired, too sick, to run the country.

Furthermore, the strong men in his Administration, except for

Dulles, had left the team. Humphrey resigned on July 28, 1957; Wilson on October 8; Brownell on November 8. All three men had told Eisenhower, in early 1956, that he had a duty to serve a second term. And he had told them that if he had to stay four more years, so did they. But within a year of the election, all three had quit. Eisenhower could not prevent their going and did not try to; it is possible that he was glad to see them go. Although his personal friendship with Humphrey was intact, Humphrey's "curl your hair" depression phrase and his single-minded doomsday approach to the budget (balance it or lose everything) made him expendable. Wilson had been a liability since the day he was nominated and said he would not sell his General Motors stock, and he had never taken control of the Pentagon as Eisenhower had hoped he could. His managerial talents were suspect at best; certainly he had never turned out missiles the way he had turned out automobiles. Brownell was a liability in the South, and in any case he had become more insistent on integration than Eisenhower wanted him to be. But whatever their shortcomings, they were the three men—along with Dulles—who did almost all the talking at Cabinet meetings, and who were capable of talking back to the President, telling him he was wrong, or cracking jokes with him, or really touching him with their infrequent, but thus more sincere, praise. He would miss them all.

The effect of the breakup of the team, and of the political criticism, and of the strain of the job in general was clear to the professional observers of the Presidency. At press conferences, reporters asked him on a number of separate occasions about his health, his mood, his temperment, his job. Andrew Tully, among others, commented on his displays of irritation and said that they were signs that the strain of the office was beginning to tell. Eisenhower denied it. He said the job was no more difficult than he thought it would be when he took over, and that he was more than capable of carrying on.[12]

Mamie had her doubts. In February, they went down to George Humphrey's plantation for some quail shooting, but the weather was cold and Eisenhower spent all his time indoors. He took frequent rests, and while he was in bed, Mamie told the gang she was terribly disturbed about his health. Slater mentioned talking to him that morning about a library he wanted to add to the Gettysburg place. Mamie quietly remarked, "I'm not so sure we're ever going to be able to live in Gettysburg." She said the enlarged arteries in his temples frightened her; Slater pointed out that they had always been there and said in his opinion Eisenhower looked a bit better today than he had yesterday.[13]

•   •

One of the things that most bothered Eisenhower during this low point in his Presidency was his relationship with John Foster Dulles. By late 1957, except for the President, the Secretary seemed to have no defenders left anywhere, while he faced a veritable army of critics. He was blamed for the debacle at Suez and in Hungary, for the failure to achieve disarmament or to halt nuclear testing, for all the shortcomings of American foreign policy. In addition, Dulles was widely regarded, in Eisenhower's words, as "legalistic, arrogant, sanctimonious, and arbitrary."[14] But Dulles' personality, objectionable as it was to most people, was not the real issue. His policies, or what people thought of as his policies, were. According to his critics, he was too rigid in his anti-Communism, too simplistic, too moralistic. Actually, he was no more so than Eisenhower himself. The truth was that Eisenhower, not Dulles, made the policy, as anyone who knew anything about the inner workings of the Eisenhower Administration realized. But it was easier, more convenient, more profitable to blame Dulles, rather than Eisenhower, for specific failures. Thus Eden and Mollet blamed him for their failure at Suez; Nasser blamed him for the withdrawal of the Aswan Dam money; Khrushchev blamed him for the inability to achieve disarmament; Hungarians blamed him for the revolt in Budapest; Asia-firsters blamed him for the loss of North Vietnam; and so on. In general, critics regarded him as much more bellicose than Eisenhower. The contrast was too sharply drawn, but it was true that having Dulles available to serve as a lightning rod served Eisenhower's purposes and helped maintain Eisenhower's popularity.

Dulles was not overly sensitive to the criticism. He was concerned about the effect for his country. The day after Christmas, 1956, he had a meeting with James Reston. The Secretary charged that *The New York Times* was not "doing a good job of reporting the foreign policy of the United States," and put part of the blame on antipathy toward himself. He told Reston, "I knew that plenty of people would not like me personally. I did not ask to be liked." But he did object when the top people on the staff of the *Times* were quoted as having "an avowed purpose to get me."[15]

But the *Times* was by no means the only critical voice. In the months after Suez, Democrats contended that Dulles' policies had been disastrous to the British and the French allies. John Scali asked Eisenhower, at a January 30, 1957, news conference, if he agreed that Dulles' actions had "contributed to our present international difficulties." Eisenhower's answer was that Dulles "has never taken any action which I have not in advance approved." (That was a standard reply that Eisenhower perhaps overused; people got the impression that he protested too much, and that the truth must be otherwise, else Eisenhower would not feel it necessary to say it so often.) Eisenhower went on to praise Dulles. The Secretary, he said, had "studied and acquired a wisdom and experience and knowledge that I think is possessed by no other man in the world." (That too was standard, and was too much an exaggeration, and said too often, to be believable.) Eisenhower concluded by admitting that mistakes had been made, but insisted that they were his mistakes, not Dulles'.[16]

The Eisenhower-Dulles team got through 1957 without any crises to compare to Hungary and Suez of 1956, but no progress was made on achieving disarmament. The day after Christmas of 1957, Dulles talked to Eisenhower about this failure. He said "that it was quite obvious that the Soviets from Khrushchev down were trying to make it appear as though I personally was the principal obstacle to a peaceful accommodation and that perhaps quite a few people were coming to believe that." Certainly many Democrats were already making that charge. Dulles therefore offered to resign in February 1958, on the occasion of his seventieth birthday. But Eisenhower was "very emphatic" that Dulles "should stay on." Dulles noted that Eisenhower said "he really could not think of anyone who could adequately take my place." Dulles therefore decided to stay at his post.[17]

A week later, Republican Congressman Walter Judd told Eisenhower that there was an organized attack on Dulles from within the government. Eisenhower said it was the first he had heard of such activity, and asked Judd to name names. Then he expressed his "total confidence" in Dulles, telling Judd: "Dulles' traits of character—as well as his intellectual honesty and diplomatic knowledge—all make him as nearly indispensable as a human ever becomes."[18]

As the barrage against Dulles intensified, Eisenhower had had to respond with more effective support. Cy Sulzberger wrote a piece about the Secretary in *The New York Times* in which he called Dulles a "tragic-comic figure." He said Dulles was too ideological, too inclined to see the world in terms of black and white. Eisenhower wrote a long rebuttal and sent it to Al Gruenther, who was a close friend of Sulzberger's, asking Gruenther to "find the time and the inclination to send Cy a letter to tell him just how stupid he is beginning to appear."[19] The same day, January 15, at a news conference, Michael O'Neill asked Eisenhower about rumors that Dulles would shortly resign. Eisenhower asked him where he got his information. O'Neill said,

"It was in the newspapers." "It was?" Eisenhower responded. "Well, then, I would say, I would class it as trash." Dulles was the last person he would want to resign, the President continued, before going into another of his exaggerated descriptions of the Secretary. Dulles, Eisenhower said, "is the wisest, most dedicated man that I know. I believe he has got greater knowledge in his field than any other man that I know." The President pointed out that he personally knew most of the leading statesmen of the world, and claimed that they all shared his high opinion of Dulles.[20]

Privately, however, Eisenhower was beginning to worry a bit about Dulles. He complained to Slater about Dulles' "excesses" in his frequent denunciations of Communism. It was not that the President disagreed with Dulles' analysis, but that he could not see how denunciation was going to get anyone anywhere.[21] Furthermore, Dulles followed a frantic schedule—Dulles must have logged more flight hours in the fifties than any man living—and tended to get too involved in the details of foreign problems, rather than seeing the bigger picture. In 1957, Eisenhower had explored with Dulles the idea of bringing C. D. Jackson down from New York to take up the slack by becoming Eisenhower's adviser on Cold War matters, with an office in the White House. What the President had in mind was something like the role Henry Kissinger later played as Nixon's National Security Adviser. But Dulles was unalterably opposed—he would brook no rival, especially not one as influential with Eisenhower as Jackson—so Eisenhower had quietly dropped the idea.

Then in January 1958, he revived it, in reverse form. Eisenhower asked Jackson to explore with Dulles the idea that Dulles become Special Assistant and Adviser to the President, while Jackson took over the State Department.[22] Jackson did talk to Dulles, and on January 17 reported to Eisenhower. Jackson claimed that Dulles "is eager for some kind of solution which would give him time to think about the incredible problems which face our foreign policy . . . Furthermore, if he were to step out of his present title it would relieve a certain amount of tension here and abroad."[23] But Jackson either misunderstood Dulles or heard what he wanted to hear. Dulles talked to Eisenhower, who then wrote Jackson to offer him a position, but not that of Secretary of State. Eisenhower said he wanted Jackson to take a position "under Dulles in the State Department as Under Secretary of State." Eisenhower said that his "duties would be to head up the Cold War effort," but Jackson realized that such a grant of power would be impossible so long as Dulles was his boss. He turned it down.[24]

So Dulles stayed on, his powers undiminished, and he continued to resist any changes in the rigid American position on disarmament, and to warn Eisenhower against making any more trips to the summit (Bulganin was calling for a meeting). On January 24, Eisenhower complained to Goodpaster that Dulles had "a lawyer's mind. He consistently adheres to a very logical explanation of these difficulties in which we find ourselves with the Soviets and in doing so—with his lawyer's mind—he shows the steps and actions that are bad on their part; and we seek to show that we are doing the decent and just thing." Eisenhower said Dulles' approach put the President in the position "of becoming a sort of international prosecuting attorney in which I lay out all of the things that I intend to prove before the jury." [25] To Dulles himself, Eisenhower practically pleaded for some "new ideas" to help reduce tensions in the world. He said he knew that Bulganin's letters asking for a meeting were "monotonous" because they always contained the same charges against the Americans, but "I am ready to admit also that our replies are necessarily hammering away on exactly the same keys." He hoped that "possibly we can ignore some of their arguments or do anything else that may have the appearance of something new." [26]

Dulles did not change, however, because he could not believe there was any possibility of a relaxation of tensions between the implacable enemies. At bottom, Eisenhower agreed with that assessment; he often said that there could be no genuine peace until the Soviet system changed internally. But he did want propaganda victories, which was the motive for his search for new ideas. Failing to get any from Dulles, he came up with one of his own. In February 1958, he proposed asking some ten thousand Russian students to come to the United States, at the expense of the U.S. government, to spend a year in American colleges. The idea was not altogether a propaganda stunt—Eisenhower was a great believer in promoting international understanding through exchange of students. In a handwritten draft of a letter to Bulganin proposing the idea, he declared, "For if history teaches us anything, it is this: Nothing but evil has ever come of misunderstanding. And nothing but good has ever come of genuine increased understanding between fellow human beings." [27]

But Eisenhower's main concern was propaganda, and he told Dulles so. Dulles' initial reaction, typically, was negative. He was alarmed at the thought of all those young Communists roaming freely across the United States, and warned Eisenhower that Bulganin would take the opportunity to introduce additional spies into the country.

Eisenhower asked J. Edgar Hoover about the danger; Hoover thought that "the security dangers, which the FBI would have to handle, might be increased somewhat, but that it was well worth it."[28] Eisenhower then told Dulles that although the idea might not be "completely sound, we need some vehicle to ride in order to suggest to the world that we are not stuck in the mud." He explained that "our public-relations problem almost defies a solution. The need always for concerting our views with those of our principal allies, the seductive quality of Soviet promises and pronouncements in spite of their unreliability, the propaganda disadvantage under which we operate because of the monolithic character of Soviet News broadcasts . . . all serve to make us appear before the world as something less than persuasive in proclaiming our peaceful purposes and our effectiveness in pursuing them." But the State Department staff, after studying Eisenhower's proposal, convinced Eisenhower that Bulganin would never let that many young people come to the United States and would therefore denounce the idea. The idea died.[29]

In March, Eisenhower had another sharp disagreement with Dulles, this one over oil import policy. Since 1951, the percentage of imported crude oil as part of the nation's total supplies had climbed from 6 percent to more than 12.6 percent. The cheap foreign oil was a source of profit for the major refiners, but Eisenhower was alarmed at America's growing dependence on the Middle East sources of that oil. In 1957, Eisenhower had tried voluntary quotas, but they were not working, and he was leaning in the direction of making the quotas compulsory. There were serious problems involved in such a move, including the antitrust implications. The Justice Department was attempting to prosecute the major importers of oil for establishing a cartel; to enforce mandatory quotas would force them to share the market between them in outright violation of the antitrust laws. Eisenhower's Texas oil friends told him they wanted no part of cutting back imported oil in any case, as what little profit they made came from it. "Some of these oilmen are coming into my office," Eisenhower told the Republican leaders on March 4, "and saying, 'Gosh, man, my third Cadillac is two years old!!' "[30] But despite Sid Richardson and the others, Eisenhower thought mandatory quotas were necessary. At a March 21 Cabinet meeting, he said he was going to impose them. Dulles objected. He said that he believed voluntary quotas had "worked very well." "I don't," replied Eisenhower. Dulles said that a compulsory system "will end in socializing the whole industry. Besides, it vio-

lates six or eight treaties. There are far-reaching implications." Eisenhower shook his head; he said a voluntary program would not work.
Dulles shot back, "It has worked." "Not as far as I'm concerned,"
Eisenhower replied.[31] The following year, Eisenhower did impose
mandatory quotas.

Eisenhower and Dulles agreed that disarmament was their most
important problem, but they could not find ready agreement on how
to approach it. The American position, that the United States would
cease testing nuclear weapons only when the Soviets simultaneously
accepted a ban on further weapons production, had been consistently
turned down by the Russians. Instead, Bulganin proposed, on December 10, 1957, a two- or three-year moratorium on nuclear tests. When
Eisenhower went to the NATO meetings a week later, he discussed a
test ban with the British and the French. They were unalterably opposed; Britain had tests scheduled, and the French were striving to
perfect their own atomic bomb. The Western nations decided to stall
by proposing disarmament talks on the Foreign Ministers' level. The
British and the French also agreed to accept American IRBMs on
their soil when the missiles were operational.

Not until January 12, 1958, did the President respond to Bulganin's call for a summit meeting and his offer of a moratorium. Eisenhower said he was willing to meet with Bulganin (and Khrushchev,
who was the real power in Russia), but only after meetings at the
Foreign Ministers' level. He could not agree to a moratorium that was
not linked to a cutoff in nuclear weapons' production. Bulganin rejected the proposal.

Harold Stassen was disappointed by Eisenhower's rigidity. As the
President's Special Adviser on Disarmament, he felt a need for more
flexibility, and suggested that Eisenhower test out Soviet sincerity by
meeting with Khrushchev and accepting a moratorium, without insistence on linking it to disarmament. On January 6, at an NSC meeting, Stassen made his presentation, complete with an array of charts
and graphs. Henry Cabot Lodge supported him; from his experiences
in the U.N., Lodge knew what a terrible propaganda beating the
United States was taking on the test-ban issue. Robert Anderson also
supported Stassen; as Secretary of the Treasury, his concern was with
the costs of the arms race. But Secretary of Defense Neil McElroy and
General Twining opposed on military grounds. So did Strauss. After
a lengthy discussion, Eisenhower reluctantly agreed to table Stassen's
proposal.[32] A month later, Eisenhower asked Stassen to resign as disarmament adviser and take another position in the Administration.

Stassen instead left federal service altogether to make an unsuccessful bid in the governor's race in Pennsylvania.

Neither Strauss nor Dulles had ever liked Harold Stassen and they had resented his presence among Eisenhower's advisers, especially so since he was advising the President on matters that Strauss and Dulles thought were their exclusive responsibility. With Stassen out of the way, both men felt freer to come up with their own ideas on disarmament, and both made proposals to the President.

Strauss came first. He advised the President to take the initiative by offering a three-part program, calling for (1) a three-year moratorium, (2) ceasing production of all fissionable material, and (3) cannibalizing existing weapons to provide fissionable material for power and other peaceful needs. Eisenhower was intrigued, but he had some questions. What would happen to the AEC organization? Strauss said he could keep it intact. Could this arrangement be properly supervised? Strauss said it would be more easily inspected than earlier proposals. Eisenhower then pronounced it a "fine idea, of great promise, and worthy of full-scale further study and evaluation."

Strauss's extreme, all-or-nothing approach may have been designed to satisfy the President's oft-expressed desire that something be done about real disarmament, but it had the appearance of just a propaganda stunt that he felt certain the Russians would reject. Strauss wanted to leave his obviously unacceptable proposal as his legacy, as he expected to be leaving the AEC shortly. He reminded Eisenhower that his term as chairman expired on June 30. Eisenhower said he would simply renominate him. Strauss asked the President to "weigh this very carefully, since he had accumulated a number of liabilities, including most of the columnists in the Washington press." Eisenhower joked that he shared the same liabilities, but Strauss insisted that Eisenhower think some more about it (and, in June, Strauss did step down).[33]

While Strauss's proposal was being studied, Eisenhower had to respond to Bulganin's offer of a moratorium, and to the growing worldwide opposition to further testing. As always, Eisenhower was of two minds—he wanted nuclear testing stopped and disarmament begun, but he insisted on staying ahead of the Russians. He tried to brush aside the fears of radioactivity, saying they came from only Senator Hubert Humphrey and a few others. He thought of the British and the French and their desire to test. He could hardly agree to a moratorium.[34]

That was on February 5. Six weeks later, Eisenhower had changed his mind. He called Strauss to his office and handed him a statement: "After reviewing and confirming the plans for nuclear testing in the Pacific next summer [the Hardtack series], President Eisenhower announced that he did not intend to authorize any additional testing of nuclear weapons." Strauss was greatly alarmed. Forgetting all about his own more extreme proposal, he threw questions at Eisenhower. "What becomes of clean-weapon development?" "What about our anti-missile work, which is enormously important?" He said the reports of genetic damage from radiation resulting from the tests were wildly exaggerated, and warned once again of Russian cheating and spying. Eisenhower broke before the onslaught. He never released the statement.[35]

He did not, even though Dulles strongly recommended that he do so. On March 24, the Secretary, his brother, McElroy, Quarles, Strauss, Twining, and Goodpaster met with the President at Dulles' request. Allen Dulles reported that the CIA had learned that Khrushchev was going to announce a unilateral suspension of testing upon the conclusion of the Soviet's current series of tests (the Russians had exploded eleven bombs in the past two weeks). Hardtack was scheduled to start in ten days and run until September. Foster Dulles was visibly upset. He predicted that while Hardtack was going on, "We will be under heavy attack worldwide. The Soviets will cite their test suspension and their call for a summit meeting while we continue to test." The result would be a major propaganda loss for the United States.

Foster Dulles wanted to beat the Russians to a unilateral test-ban announcement. He advised Eisenhower to make "an immediate announcement . . . that following [Hardtack] he would not thereafter order new tests during his term in office." Dulles said he was aware that such a statement would represent a major shift in the American disarmament position, since it would not be linked to inspection systems or a stoppage of weapons' production, and that critics would therefore charge "that we are giving in to the Soviet line." But, he continued, "I feel desperately the need for some important gesture in order to gain an effect on world opinion."

Dulles was proposing almost exactly the announcement Eisenhower had told Strauss he wanted to issue, and he ran into exactly the objections Strauss had made to Eisenhower, plus some new ones. Speaking for DOD, Quarles said the suspension of tests would be disastrous for America. Specifically, he was concerned about defense against nuclear attack. Although Eisenhower had often said that the only defense was retaliation, the Pentagon was still searching for some way to blunt the effect of a Soviet missile attack. The current favorite was an antiballistic missile (later called an ABM). The idea was to develop an extensive radar system to give early warning, then explode a small atomic bomb in the path of the incoming Soviet ICBMs. Quarles said that perfecting the ABM depended on "tests yet to be conducted, even *after* the Hardtack series." (No one present at the meeting pointed to the logical fallacy in the argument—civilian scientists, not connected to the AEC, had pointed out that the vulnerability of Soviet missiles to an ABM was based on the fact that the Soviets had not yet learned how to shield them from such radioactivity, but if testing continued, they would discover how to do it.) Quarles added the other standard arguments against a test ban—America would not be able to build a clean bomb, and progress toward lighter, smaller atomic weapons would end.

Strauss took the floor. "Testing does not result in any significant health hazard," he declared. The "real hazard today is nuclear war, which our weapons' development helps to prevent." Completely contradicting what he had told Eisenhower on February 5, Strauss said that a test suspension would have a "severe" effect on the AEC. The atomic scientists "would lose tone, impetus, and personnel." He urged Eisenhower to stick to the original American position, linking a test ban to a suspension of production. Dulles interrupted to say that "we could not do this without agreement of our allies in advance, whereas we could state unilaterally that we are not intending to test in the next couple of years." He predicted that France and Britain would never agree to a suspension.

Then Dulles undertook a fundamental critique of the DOD-AEC position. According to Goodpaster's notes, "He went on to say that Defense was approaching the problem in terms of winning a war. State must, however, think in terms of all means of conducting the international struggle. He said that we are increasingly being given a militaristic and bellicose aspect toward world opinion, and are losing the struggle for world opinion." Strauss interjected that the tests were "a trivial threat," that the weapons themselves were "the real threat." Dulles told him that "we are open to the charge of not being completely sincere, since we have in fact put impossible conditions on disarmament." He also pointed out that Strauss's proposal to dismantle existing stockpiles as part of a disarmament package was a mere stunt, because "we would not, in fact, agree to give up weapons," and Strauss knew it.

For the first time, Eisenhower entered the debate. He told Dulles that "he thought we would do so [dismantle the arsenal] if we could be sure that all had done so." What worried him was that for the first time in its history, the United States was "scared," and this was "due simply to these tremendous weapons." The argument continued for some two hours. At one point, Eisenhower seemed ready to make a factual statement that after Hardtack "we have no more tests scheduled for the next couple of years," but DOD and the AEC were unwilling to go along, nor would they accept a limitation of tests to underground explosions only. Eisenhower commented that it was "intolerable that the United States . . . seeking peace, is unable to achieve an advantageous impact on world opinion." Strauss said that the search for a clean bomb should satisfy world opinion as to American sincerity; Eisenhower said that was not realistic, as the world had been made to believe that radioactivity was evil, and that therefore any tests were dangerous. On the other hand, however, Eisenhower feared that an American unilateral test suspension would allow the Democrats to charge that "this is our Munich."

Eventually, a weary and disappointed Secretary of State said that he thought, "in light of the discussion, perhaps the best course of action would simply be to pass up his proposal. He said he wished to tell the group, however, that if we cannot act along lines such as this, 'we are going to get licked.' " Allen Dulles then suggested a one-year moratorium. McElroy liked that idea. He said the AEC could not hold the scientists for two years, but they would stay on the job if it was a one-year suspension. "The President said that he thought scientists, like other people, have a strong interest in avoiding nuclear war." But neither DOD nor the AEC would budge.

At the end of the meeting, Eisenhower asked the group, rather wistfully and helplessly, "to think about what could be done to get rid of the terrible impasse in which we now find ourselves with regard to disarmament."[36] Two days later, he sent Dulles a private note, expressing his personal commitment to ending the arms race. "To my mind," he wrote, "this transcends all other objectives we can have. Security through arms is only a means (and sometimes a poor one) to an end." He vowed not to stop "searching for ideas to stem and turn the tide of propaganda success."[37]

While the Eisenhower Administration debated, the Soviets acted. On March 27, Bulganin resigned, making Khrushchev the Russian dictator in name as well as in fact. On March 31, Khrushchev announced that Russia was unilaterally halting all further tests of nuclear weapons. The overwhelmingly positive worldwide response made

Eisenhower and his advisers furious, because they felt it was so transparently insincere. The Russians had only just concluded their most extensive series of tests ever, and they knew that Hardtack was just about to begin. Especially infuriating was the Russian statement that if the United States and the United Kingdom did not stop their tests, "the Soviet Union will, understandably, act freely in the question of testing atomic and hydrogen weapons." It would be some months before the Soviets could prepare for a new series of tests in any case; Khrushchev's shrewd maneuver gave him a built-in excuse to resume testing without disruption in the Russian nuclear program, and to put the blame on Hardtack.[38]

On April 2, at a news conference, Eisenhower responded to Khrushchev's move by dismissing it as "just a side issue." He said, "I think it is a gimmick, and I don't think it is to be taken seriously, and I believe anyone that studies this matter thoroughly will see that."[39] The editors of *The Nation* commented, "If all this is a 'gimmick,' one can only wish to God that our statesmen could concoct such gimmicks once in a while."[40]

In April, a new group entered the debate. In the wake of post-Sputnik demands that the President have a full-time scientific adviser, Eisenhower had created the President's Scientific Advisory Committee (PSAC) and put Dr. Killian at its head. Killian and his people, especially physicists Hans Bethe and Isidor Rabi, undertook a thorough review of American policy. They concluded that an inspection system could be created that, although not absolutely foolproof, could detect any nuclear blast down to as low as two kilotons. Dulles then telephoned Eisenhower to recommend that the President write Khrushchev, accepting an earlier Soviet offer to undertake technical talks on a possible test-ban inspection system. Eisenhower said that was fine, then added, "Our position is that we want to look on testing as a symptom rather than a disease."[41]

The closer the President came to accepting a test ban, the more frantic Strauss became. He repeated endlessly all his arguments against a ban. His position, however, was steadily weakening, partly because in March he had handed in his resignation, effective at the end of June, and was now a lame duck, partly because Eisenhower was getting advice from physicists other than Lawrence and Teller. On April 17, Killian told the President that the PSAC had concluded that "cessation of testing, in the judgment of the group, would leave the United States in a position of technical advantage for a few years, which would otherwise be lost." The PSAC had therefore decided "it would be to our overall advantage" to agree to a test ban. Killian also pointed to a factor previously not discussed—the Soviets were ahead in missile testing, and if there were no ban on testing weapons, there would soon be a worldwide demand that missile as well as weapon testing cease. That would be damaging to the United States. Killian thought that "an early announcement on nuclear testing would reduce the danger of pressures on us for cessation of missile testing." Eisenhower confessed to Killian that "he had never been too much impressed or completely convinced by the views expressed by Drs. Teller and Lawrence that we must continue testing of nuclear weapons." Killian resisted whatever temptation he may have felt to point out that Eisenhower had nevertheless always before given in to their arguments. He merely reported that the AEC and DOD were opposed to a ban, primarily because they wanted to develop the ABM.[42]

With Eisenhower beginning to lean toward a ban, Dulles decided to add a push of his own. On April 26, at his home, he met with Gruenther, Robert Lovett (Truman's Secretary of Defense), Bedell Smith, and John J. McCloy. It was a carefully selected group—Eisenhower had great admiration for each member of it, and would be impressed by a recommendation from such men. Dulles gave them a full briefing, then got their assent to advise Eisenhower to take the initiative in seeking a test-ban agreement. With their backing, Dulles wrote a draft of a letter from Eisenhower to Khrushchev, repeating his earlier proposal for technical talks on an inspection system, and saying, "Studies of this kind are the necessary preliminaries to putting political decisions into effect." In other words, Dulles wanted to take a decisive step and divorce production of future weapons from a nuclear test ban. That marked a fundamental change in the American disarmament position. To Strauss's consternation, and Dulles' delight, Eisenhower accepted the recommendation and on April 28 sent the letter to Khrushchev. Three days later, Eisenhower told Dulles he had made the historic shift in position because "unless we took some positive action we were in the future going to be in a position of 'moral isolation' as far as [the] rest of the world is concerned."[43]

Eisenhower had decided that the political advantages outweighed the military risks. One reason, unmentioned but obvious, was Hardtack's success. Beginning on April 28 and continuing until August, Hardtack was the most extensive series of tests yet held. There were some thirty-four tests of different types of weapons. Strauss wanted still more series scheduled, but on June 30 he left the AEC, and by then Khrushchev had accepted Eisenhower's proposal for technical talks that began, at Geneva, in early July.⁴⁴ For the first time in the nuclear age, the superpowers were engaged in serious disarmament talks that offered some prospect of success. Ironically, the man most responsible for convincing Eisenhower to accept the inherent risk in agreeing to such talks, John Foster Dulles, was the man who got most of the blame for the long delay.

By 1958, Dulles had softened considerably on the question of spending for national defense. During Eisenhower's first term, the Secretary of State had been the leading proponent in the Cabinet for more funds for DOD. He had insisted that America had to maintain a clear lead over the Russians in order to have an effective foreign policy. But in the greatest crises of his career, Suez and Hungary in late 1956, Dulles had learned that American military strength was irrelevant in Eastern Europe, where he had hoped for so much, and equally irrelevant in the Middle East, where American economic pressure, not military force, had compelled the French, British, and Israelis to withdraw. After those experiences, and with George Humphrey out of the Cabinet, Dulles became the leading proponent of less spending by DOD.

Not that Eisenhower had lost his concern over defense spending. In the wake of the post-Sputnik hysteria, the President had stood firm against emergency appropriations and crash programs. When on January 28 the Republican leaders told him that the demands for more B-52s was "irresistible," he complained that "we do things in defense that are just so damn costly," and pointed out that he could not conceive of any Russian attack that was so successful "that there wouldn't be enough bombers escaping to go do their job. If six hundred won't do it," Eisenhower continued, "certainly seven hundred won't."⁴⁵ But on March 20, in a meeting with Killian, Eisenhower authorized the production of more B-52s at the rate of five per month for the next year, plus some millions of dollars for an accelerated missile and ABM program. But he also told Killian, when informed that the Pentagon was asking for $10 billion in new money, that "he found it hard to retain confidence in the heads of the services when they produce such proposals as these." The most he would approve of was $1.5 billion in new money.⁴⁶

At an April 25 NSC meeting, Eisenhower continued to complain about the exorbitant cost of defense. He said that every time there was a test firing of a Titan missile, "we are shooting away $15 million." At that price, "he hoped there would be no misses and no near-misses!"

After the DOD people gave a spirited defense of their program, and justified its costs, Eisenhower commented that "we are now beginning to think of aircraft as becoming obsolescent, and so it is also with first-generation ballistic missiles." He thought it a mistake to "go ahead full steam on production," and predicted that the B-52s would remain usable long after the early missiles were obsolete. To attempt to mass-produce both more bombers and new missiles "will create unheard-of inflation in the United States."

Dulles then entered the discussion. To everyone's surprise, he thought even the President was going too far in defense spending. Dulles raised fundamental points about the arms race. He reminded Eisenhower that the President had often quoted to the NSC George Washington's words on "the desirability that the United States possess a respectable military posture." In his view, Dulles said, "The United States should not attempt to be the greatest military power in the world, although most discussions in the NSC seemed to suggest that we should have the most and the best of everything." He wondered if "there was no group in the government which ever thought of the right kind of ceiling on our military capabilities?" Dulles suggested that a "respectable military posture," not overwhelming superiority, was the proper goal. "In the field of military capabilities," Dulles said, "enough is enough. If we didn't realize this fact, the time would come when all our national production would be centered on our military establishment." He wanted the Russians to "respect" the American military, not be frightened to death by it.

Eisenhower was startled. Since Taft's death, he almost never had to defend his Administration from charges that it was spending too much on defense; it was usually the other way around. And he had not anticipated that Dulles, of all people, would advocate spending less, not more. He therfore replied to Dulles' basic critique that saving money was, of course, "one of the great preoccupations of the JCS." Dulles interrupted to say "that he was not at all sure that this was so." He recognized that it was the business of the JCS "to recommend military capabilities which would provide the utmost national security. He did not blame them for this. It was right and it was their job." But there was another side to the problem, and he complained that it never came out in NSC discussions.[47]

Allen Dulles and the CIA provided some support for the Secretary of State's position. The CIA was, at this time, a source of discomfort to the President. The Russians were protesting vigorously against continuing U-2 flights. On March 7, Eisenhower told Goodpaster that he should inform the CIA that the President had ordered the flights "discontinued, effective at once."[48] A week later, Bobby Cutler brought in the CIA's latest "Estimate of the World Situation," pronouncing it "a very superior piece of work." Eisenhower did not agree. He told Cutler that it "could have been written by a high-school student."[49] But in June, the CIA brought in its latest estimates on Soviet bomber and missile production, and although the report admitted that the Agency had previously grossly exaggerated the scope of the Soviet effort, Eisenhower was pleased with the new conclusions, as the report indicated there was not so much to worry about after all. For example, in August of 1956 the CIA had estimated that by mid-1958 the Russians would have 470 Bison and Bear bombers and 100 ICBMs. But in June of 1958, the estimate was that the Soviets actually had 135 bombers and no operational ICBMs.[50] Eisenhower commented that "the Soviets have done much better than have we in this matter. They stopped their Bison and Bear production, but we have kept on going, on the basis of incorrect estimates and at a tremendous expense in a mistaken effort to be 100 percent secure." Secretary Dulles heartily concurred.[51]

With such strong backing from the CIA and the State Department, Eisenhower was able to hold off the political demands for more military spending. At a Republican leaders' meeting on June 24, he declared flatly that he did not want any nuclear carriers, because "they would be useless in a big war" and were not needed in a little one. As for more missiles and B-52s, the President said he "just didn't know how many times you could kill the same man!" Senator Saltonstall said the country needed more Army reserves, more National Guard, and more Marines. "The President wanted to know why." He said he had "great admiration" for the Marines, but pointed out that "he had made the two largest amphibious landings in history and there hadn't been a Marine in them. To hear people talk about the Marines, you couldn't understand how those two great landings were ever accomplished!"[52]

No matter how often the President assured the country that America was well ahead in nuclear delivery systems, few people would believe him until the nation had put a satellite into orbit. In December 1957, amidst extensive publicity, the United States had tried with a Vanguard rocket, but it had caught fire, fallen back to earth two seconds after takeoff, and was totally destroyed. Such an embarrassment might prove as costly to the budget as to American pride. Knowland, on January 7, warned Eisenhower that if the United States did not get a satellite into orbit soon, the demands on the budget were going to go "hog-wild."[53]

Nelson Rockefeller, running for governor of New York, was one of those who thought there was no limit to the amounts of money available for every conceivable project, including flying to the moon. On January 16, he told the President that if the United States used nuclear explosions for propulsion, it could launch a satellite that could reach the moon and return, and predicted that it would be "the most notable accomplishment of our time."[54] Eisenhower was dubious. On February 4, he told Republican leaders that "in the present situation, he would rather have a good Redstone [IRBM] than be able to hit the moon, for we didn't have any enemies on the moon!"[55] But the idea of flying to the moon was too exciting to pass up. On February 25, at a meeting in the Oval Office, Killian and Quarles proposed a nuclear aircraft, and expenditures of $1.5 billion over the next few years in order to send a nuclear-powered rocket to the moon.[56]

Eisenhower was not convinced. He regarded such talk as Buck Rogers fantasy, unrelated to reality. On March 6, he announced that he was rejecting any proposal to build atomic-powered airplanes, holding that such a prestige effort was a waste of scarce resources and talent. Scientists were critical. Eisenhower ignored them, except to complain to the Republican leaders that when a scientist got before a TV camera, he "got excited" and said the damnedest things. "Last night, for example," Eisenhower said, "I heard one of them talking about a shot to the moon." Yet, "We haven't even put up a full-size satellite." He was aware of the pressures, but thought that space "was certainly an easy subject to make a speech about, but hard to do anything about."[57]

On January 31, the United States had put its first satellite into orbit, but it was almost as much of an embarrassment as Vanguard, because the satellite, named Explorer I, weighed only thirty-one pounds. In March, the Navy finally got a Vanguard rocket to work, but the satellite it put into orbit weighed only three pounds. The embarrassment deepened in May when the Russians put Sputnik III into space—it weighed three thousand pounds.

Eisenhower's basic approach to missiles and satellites had been to let each service develop its own program and hope that one of them would score a breakthrough. The result had been failure. The generals and admirals squabbled with one another, made slighting remarks about their fellow services' efforts, and ignored the Secretary of Defense. In January 1958, Eisenhower proposed a reorganization of the Pentagon, to give more power to the Secretary and to keep the service Chiefs away from congressional committees (where they always said that the Eisenhower Administration was not giving them enough funds to carry out their missions). But Congress was extremely reluctant to give up its power to appropriate separately for the services, and some of Eisenhower's critics charged that he was trying to create a Prussian General Staff. Others pointed out that Eisenhower was asking for centralization at the top, but ignoring the real problem, which was waste and duplication in the space program; they wanted him to put all space activities into one super agency, outside the Department of Defense.

Eisenhower was opposed to the creation of a separate Department of Space. He feared it would put its priority on satellites, while he wanted to keep the priority on missiles. He regretted not putting all space activities into the office of the Secretary of Defense in the first instance, but thought it was too late now. As he told Killian, "Personal feelings are now so intense that changes are extremely difficult." But he wanted nothing to do with any moon shots, or other prestige operations, because he did not want to "put talent etc. into crash programs outside the Defense establishment."[58]

At a February 4 meeting, Nixon warned the President that the pressure to create a civilian space agency was already great, and it was growing. He told Eisenhower that the space program had to have some nonmilitary component, and that the scientists would join the Democrats in demanding that it be done. Eisenhower replied that he would not get into a "pathetic race" and called a lunar probe "useless."[59]

But the President could not hold his ground in opposition to nearly every Democrat, most Republicans, and a majority of columnists, and scientists. On April 2, he retreated. He asked Congress to establish a National Aeronautics and Space Agency (NASA). It was not a surrender; the bill gave NASA control of all space activities "except those that the President determined were primarily associated with national defense."[60] At a press conference two weeks later, James Reston said he had "often wondered why" it had taken the President five years to get around to establishing NASA. "I think the answer to that is I have had plenty of troubles over the five years," Eisenhower snapped back. He then became completely incomprehensible. Even after the editors of his transcripts had smoothed out his reply, it read: ". . . it did not seem that that was a big factor that we should advance in an argument that, to my mind, has become very, very important."[61] But jumbled syntax or not, and Eisenhower's misgivings notwithstanding, the United States had a civilian space agency.

Eisenhower also took a licking on another post-Sputnik demand, that of federal aid to education. Eisenhower's position was that the federal government ought not make direct grants to the states or schools. Nor should it provide help to students in general fields, only to those studying science or math who could not otherwise afford to go to college. The education Establishment, and most Democrats and many Republicans, wanted a much larger program than the one Eisenhower recommended in a January 27 special message—more scholarships more widely spread out, with a means test eliminated, and much larger and more direct grants to the states and schools for education. But Eisenhower was determined to keep the program down to ten thousand scholarships, all based on need and subject, and to relatively small matching grants to the states to help them employ more science and math teachers. At that, he was proposing more than he wanted to; at a long session with Killian and the Republican leaders, in December of 1957, when discussing the education bill, Eisenhower had tried to insist that there be no grants, however small and whether matching or not, to the states. The politicians convinced him that he had to offer something.[62]

Still, some of the ideas being proposed frankly horrified him. One was a tax rebate for parents who were sending their children to college, regardless of their income bracket. Eisenhower mused, "I can't understand the United States being quite as panicky as they really are." When his Secretary of HEW, Marion Folsom, pressed him to be more generous, Eisenhower changed the subject to curriculum. He said he wished the high schools would concentrate on math, foreign languages, and English. Folsom said he wanted $15 million to support medical education; Eisenhower replied that the medical schools ought to lower the number of years of preparation and thus turn out more doctors without raising costs. Folsom spoke up for direct grants, which led Eisenhower off into a discussion of "where socialism will stop."[63]

The House, meanwhile, had eliminated federal scholarships altogether, substituting long-term, low-interest loans instead. The bill did retain graduate fellowships. It also authorized grants to improve instruction in science, math, and—to a much lesser extent—foreign languages. It called for expenditures of about $1 billion over the following seven years. Eisenhower signed the final bill, with some reluctance, on September 2.[64] The National Defense Education Act was law.

Its impact was relatively slight. Indeed, the truth is that NDEA represented a great opportunity wasted. Eisenhower could have used the post-Sputnik hysteria to vastly strengthen the educational system in the United States. It was at this time, in the late fifties, that virtually every Japanese and German student began an intensive study of English, for example. At the same time, the Germans and the Japanese—and the Russians and others—improved their curriculum not only in math and science, but in the liberal arts as well. In the decades that followed, they reaped the benefits, while American education languished, with incalculable results. It is ironic that Eisenhower, who was a fanatic on the subject of international understanding, was the man who spurned the chance to make every educated American speak a foreign language.

Eisenhower's severe limitations on spending for education were part of his overall program of balancing the budget and avoiding inflation. That program, however, had run afoul of a major recession, the first since the Korean War. It began in August 1957, and by April 1958, unemployment was up to 7 percent, while corporate profits were down more than 25 percent. Democrats demanded a tax cut to stimulate the economy, and massive public-works projects to put people back to work. Even Arthur Burns, who had been the chairman of the Council of Economic Advisers to the President during Eisenhower's first term, advised Eisenhower to cut taxes. "I realize that to be conservative in this situation," Eisenhower wrote Burns in reply, "can well get me tagged as an unsympathetic, reactionary fossil." Nevertheless, he was dead set against public-works programs, because they took years to get under way, and against any "slash-bang kinds of tax cutting . . ." He said he did support accelerating those public-works projects already under way, and promised that if the economy got worse he was prepared to pump more money into it, but insisted that the proper response to the recession was to wait for the business cycle to go into an upward phase.[65]

In the face of Eisenhower's unalterable opposition, the Democrats were unable to pass a tax cut. They did, however, pass a public-works project—the Rivers and Harbors Bill, which authorized appropriations for rivers, harbors, and flood-control projects of $310 million. "I cannot overstate my opposition to this kind of waste of public funds," Eisenhower said in his veto message.[66]

Farm state Republicans, meanwhile, had joined with the Democrats to offer a 1958 farm bill that maintained high federal price supports for one year. Delegations of Midwestern Republicans came to the White House to urge the President to support it. One declared passionately, "It's high time the Republicans gave better evidence they're in the farmers' corner." Another delegation, the congressmen from Nebraska, warned Eisenhower that if he did not support the bill (and in the process fire Secretary Benson, who was firmly opposed to it), it would cost the Republicans from twenty to thirty seats in the 1958 elections. Eisenhower told the delegation that "he was in thorough accord with the program Secretary Benson is advocating and he feels that the farmers will be better off if they are freed from government domination and regulation." Eisenhower also insisted that firing Benson would cost seats.[67]

In late March, nevertheless, the bill passed both houses of Congress. On March 28, five Midwestern Republican senators called on Eisenhower to urge him to sign it. They argued that if he did not do so, "the Democrats will pick up fifty or sixty House seats, and we will get radical Democrats who will spend us into bankruptcy." Eisenhower gave them a lecture on the free marketplace. Later that morning, he took up with his aides the bill itself. He said he "hated to veto the bill," because "his action would be taken as 'kicking the farmer in the teeth.'" Eisenhower complained that he was "unhappy and irritated over his position," but in the end his principles overrode his politics, and he reluctantly signed a veto message.[68] There was a predictable storm of protest.

All in all, the first four months of 1958 had been a terrible time for Eisenhower. His problems with the stroke, with Dulles and disarmament, the space race and Congress were well-nigh overwhelming. His only escape came in late February, when he managed to spend ten days at Humphrey's place in Georgia. The shooting was great—Eisenhower and his gang put up thirty-six coveys in one morning—but for the most part it was too cold for hunting or golf, so Eisenhower played bridge endlessly—a total of 140 rubbers.[69]

CHAPTER TWENTY

Lebanon, Sherman Adams, Disarmament, Quemoy and Matsu, Other Woes

May–September 1958

IN JANUARY of 1958, Nasser had announced that Egypt and Syria were uniting into a new nation, the United Arab Republic (UAR). The UAR then began propaganda broadcasts over the radio to appeal to pan-Arab sentiment in Jordan, Iraq, Saudi Arabia, and Lebanon. In response, the feudal monarchies of Jordan and Iraq formed their own federation, the Arab Union. In Saudi Arabia, meanwhile, King Saud—on whom Eisenhower had placed such high hopes—was forced into virtual abdication. Saud granted his pro-Nasser brother, Crown Prince Faisal, full power over the nation's foreign, internal, and financial policies.

There was a great deal of loose talk within the Eisenhower Administration about Nasser. Officials assumed he had a "timetable" for taking over the Middle East, country by country, just as Hitler had taken over Europe. They also assumed that Nasser was a Communist, and argued that his acceptance of arms and money from the Soviets proved it. If Nasser succeeded, it was felt, the Russians would take control of the Middle East and its oil. Before Eisenhower would let that happen, he said on many occasions, he would fight.

True, in public Eisenhower too called Nasser a Communist. And in private, he frequently discussed with the CIA and others possible ways of getting rid of the Egyptian leader. But the President in fact was ambiguous about Nasser. In November 1957, Eisenhower wrote Dulles. His opening sentence was "Do you think there would be any percentage in initiating a drive to attempt to bring back Nasser to our side?" He wanted Dulles to make some discreet inquiries to find out what Nasser "would be prepared to do in the way of easing tensions in the Middle East if we on our part would resume efforts to help him over some of his difficulties." It would have to be "skillfully done—certainly we don't want to be in the position of 'bootlicking a dictator.'" Eisenhower said he did not want a written answer, but did want to talk to Dulles about the subject.[1] But Dulles, burned once by Nasser at Suez in 1956, hesitated to take the plunge, and before he could, Nasser had created the UAR.

By that time, too, a situation had developed that Eisenhower had said he never wanted to see take place—there was an active arms race in the Middle East, with the United States supplying Saudi Arabia, Iraq, Jordan, and (to a slight extent) Lebanon with military equipment, while the Russians supplied Syria and Egypt, and the French sold arms to Israel. As the Middle East became an armed camp, Eisenhower's worries increased. Although for public-relations purposes he said his concern was with internal Communism in the Arab countries, he had no evidence to support such a charge, and solid evidence against it, beginning with the fact that the Communist Party was outlawed in Egypt.

What Eisenhower really feared was radical Arab nationalism. Nasser was almost openly appealing to the Arab people of the feudal states of Jordan, Iraq, and Saudi Arabia to revolt against their monarchs and join the UAR. If he succeeded, and continued to rely on the Soviets for arms and money, Khrushchev might possibly get a stranglehold on the Western world's basic energy source, and Israel could be crushed. Under those circumstances, Eisenhower could only conclude that America's vital interests were at stake. He therefore began searching for a way to demonstrate, unequivocally, America's readiness and capability for action, and its determination to use force to prevent the domination of the area by anti-Western pan-Arab nationalism. He searched, in short, for a place and time to implement the Eisenhower Doctrine.

He found it in Lebanon, a country without oil, almost without an Army (nine thousand men), but with a strong democratic tradition. Indeed, Lebanon was the first country he thought of in relation to the Eisenhower Doctrine, precisely because it was weak but democratic. In April of 1957, only a couple of months after the adoption of the Eisenhower Doctrine, he had almost intervened there. Camille Chamoun, a pro-Western Christian and President of the Republic of

Lebanon, had complained to him that pan-Arab agitators from Jordan were stirring up trouble in Lebanon, and wanted to know if Eisenhower would send troops to help him through the crisis. Eisenhower responded by ordering units of the Sixth Fleet, plus Marines, into the eastern Mediterranean, and offering to send them to Beirut if necessary.[2] But the crisis passed before that could be done.

In late April 1958, another crisis had begun, this one brought on by Chamoun himself. In violation of Lebanese tradition and constitution, he decided to amend the constitution to allow himself to serve an unprecedented second term. Moslems began rioting in protest. In early May, armed bands of Christian and Moslem militia began fighting in Beirut. The Lebanese Army Chief of Staff, General Fuad Chehab, also a Christian but Chamoun's strongest political rival, held his troops out of the struggle.

In his memoirs, Eisenhower wrote that he had a "deep-seated conviction that the Communists were principally responsible for the trouble . . ."[3] He never cited any evidence. He did have Communists very much in his mind, however, because simultaneously with the crisis in Lebanon, he had a crisis in Venezuela to deal with. Vice-President Nixon, on a good-will trip, had been attacked, spat upon, and otherwise insulted and threatened by Communist-inspired mobs. To Eisenhower, and to Foster Dulles, it looked suspiciously like part of a conspiracy. "The Communists," Dulles told Eisenhower, "are stirring up trouble in area after area." He cited Venezuela, Indonesia, and Burma as current examples. The situation in Venezuela was so tense that Eisenhower, on the morning of May 13, ordered a thousand troops flown to Cuba and Puerto Rico to be on hand should the Venezuelan government need help in getting Nixon out of the country.

The President then called a meeting in the Oval Office, with the Dulles brothers, Under Secretary of State Herter, Twining, Gruenther, and Goodpaster. Allen Dulles gave a short briefing, concluding with a summary of a letter from Chamoun asking if the United States would join the British and the French to intervene in Lebanon if he requested such action. Eisenhower's first response was to dismiss any French connection out of hand. Then he ordered the Sixth Fleet, with Marines, to steam toward Lebanon. Foster Dulles was worried about justification. He asked, "On what theory would intervention be based?" The best Dulles could come up with was to protect American life and property, and he warned that "if we should go in, we must expect a wide reaction—the pipelines to be blown up, the canal denied

to us, and a wave of feeling against us throughout the Arab world."
Dulles also said he was opposed to backing Chamoun for a second
term.

Allen Dulles too was opposed to intervention. He said, "We should
not take overt action immediately. The situation might collapse within
twenty-four hours, or General Chehab might move in to bring the
situation under control."

The President interrupted. He pointed out that "while there are
difficulties and dangers in taking action, we must think of the difficulties and dangers of not doing anything." Foster Dulles then changed
his position, saying he thought "we are at a very fateful point in our
affairs in the Middle East . . ." Dulles acknowledged Eisenhower's
point, that usually in cases of Communist agitation, the United States
was powerless, but "here is a case where we can clearly respond on
the basis of a call for help." Eisenhower then told Twining to put
the Sixth Fleet on a full war footing, and to arrange for cooperation
with the British. The President wanted a joint operation, with a
British officer in overall command. Dulles demurred; he cited "resentment toward Britain throughout the Middle East." Eisenhower reluctantly accepted that judgment, but he did tell Twining to cooperate
fully with the British. It was an exciting thought, the first Anglo-
American amphibious operation since June 6, 1944.

It was correspondingly risky. At the conclusion of the meeting,
Foster Dulles brought up the real danger, more important even than
the probable adverse Arab reaction. As Goodpaster recorded the exchange: "Secretary Dulles then said that we must think of the possibility of Soviet reaction. The President said he considered it doubtful
if we stay in Lebanon. If we were to have to hit Syria, however, that
would be something else again."[4]

Eisenhower's prediction was not put to the test, because the next
day Chehab put his troops into action and took control of the city.
Beirut became quiet, although some fighting continued in Tripoli.
The Sixth Fleet stood down. The crisis appeared to be over.

But within a week, new fighting broke out. Chamoun, on May 22,
asked for an urgent meeting of the U.N. Security Council to consider
his charge that Egypt and Syria had been instigating revolt and arming the rebels. On June 10, the Security Council voted to send a military observation team to Lebanon. It began arriving two days later.
Simultaneously, Nasser tried to calm the situation. He contacted
Eisenhower and offered to use his influence to end the trouble; he
would propose that Chamoun give way to Chehab, and that the rebels

EISENHOWER

should be accorded amnesty. Eisenhower was impressed, and thought it sincere. He regretted having backed King Saud, rather than Nasser, in the Middle East struggle. Saud, he told Ann Whitman, "was too weak an individual." He wondered how one could save a country from its own leaders. "Chamoun, for example, has not yet fired Chehab, despite more than ample cause." Then the President mused, "No matter what you think of Nasser, at least he is a leader."[5]

That afternoon, June 15, from 5:10 to 6:45, Eisenhower met with Dulles, Quarles, Twining, and Allen Dulles to discuss Lebanon. The minutes of that meeting, kept by the State Department, remain heavily censored. It was a tense meeting, as the men explored the possibilities and consequences of action. Positions shifted as new points were made. Someone evidently advocated sending in the Marines immediately. Dulles was horrified. The notetaker recorded: "The Secretary felt it would be catastrophic to lay ourselves open" to a charge of acting before the U.N. team had a chance to report. He insisted that "we ought not to make an immediate military response . . ." Eisenhower agreed that "we would be in a bad spot" if the United States intervened before hearing from the U.N. But, expecting the U.N. to fail, he wanted to find a reason for intervening. After all, he pointed out, the Eisenhower Doctrine "had been directed only against external aggression. The President wondered, therefore, what possible future there would be if we intervened except to remain indefinitely." That was an unhappy prospect, as he recalled the warnings he had given the British and the French before Suez. Those warnings were "Where would it lead? Where would it end?" He again bemoaned the lack of leadership in Lebanon. "There seems nobody on whom we can pin our hopes." Chamoun was a virtual prisoner in his hotel room—he had not been out in more than two months—and a victim of a recent heart attack. Under the conditions prevailing on June 15, Eisenhower told the group "he had little, if any, enthusiasm for our intervening at this time."

Foster Dulles then faced the prospect of another letter from Chamoun requesting American intervention. If that happened, Dulles said, "and we do not respond, that will be the end of every pro-Western government in the area. This leaves us with little or no choice, even though every alternative is 'wrong.'" Eisenhower agreed "and noted that in such circumstances we would have to fulfill our commitments."[6] Exactly what those commitments consisted of, no one knew or asked. The United States had no treaties with Lebanon. The Eisenhower Doctrine, as the man who wrote it himself confessed, did not apply, because Lebanon was not being invaded by external armies.

466

On June 18, the U.N.'s Dag Hammarskjold arrived in Lebanon. A few days later, he reported that Chamoun's charges about Syrian and Egyptian infiltration into Lebanon were exaggerated. Fighting in Lebanon became sporadic as a truce settled in. Whatever excuse the United States may have had for an intervention seemed to have gone.

Sherman Adams, meanwhile, was in deep trouble. No one, except Eisenhower himself, had ever liked him very much. Adams' abruptness and absence of emotion were one reason for his vast unpopularity. The man just seemed to have no human feelings at all. Once Eisenhower had painted a portrait of Adams, taken from a color photo. The President worked on it many hours. When he presented it, Adams' only remark was "Mr. President, thank you, but I think you flattered me." He then turned on his heel and walked out.

Foolish stories, wildly exaggerated, about Adams' supposed immense influence with the President were a standard feature of Washington gossip and newspaper columns. The truth was that Adams had almost no influence on the President's policies—he was the gatekeeper, the schedule maker, the man who smoothed things over, but never was he involved in making decisions. Nevertheless, every man who had had a request turned down by the White House blamed Adams; every man whom Eisenhower did not want to see in the Oval Office blamed Adams for his failure to gain admission; every man who objected to a specific Eisenhower decision, whether to veto the farm bill or to resist putting sufficient funds into NDEA, or whatever, blamed Adams. Old Guard Republicans hated the man, whom they blamed for Eisenhower's refusal to adopt their pet projects. The Democrats hated him because he was a Republican, and because in January 1958, he had delivered a blistering attack on the Democratic Party, blaming it for Pearl Harbor and the loss of the space race. (The President was dismayed by Adams' speech; he told Whitman he had consistently refused to blame Pearl Harbor on the Democrats, because he knew that the real blame lay with the military.[7])

The Democrats controlled Congress, and thus the committees and investigations. Like the Republicans from 1953 to 1955, they wanted to use that power to expose their political enemies. In early June 1958, a subcommittee of the House Interstate and Foreign Commerce Committee charged that Adams had allowed a New England industrialist named Bernard Goldfine to pay some of his hotel bills in Boston, and that in return Adams had engaged in influence peddling for Goldfine, who was having tax and regulatory problems with the SEC. Adams might have cited Eisenhower's blanket protection against testifying before committees for White House employees, given in 1954 during the Army-McCarthy hearings, but instead he decided to face his accusors directly. He explained to Eisenhower, "I made a mistake, but I'm no crook." Eisenhower had no doubts about that, but he was distressed by the business of gifts (it turned out that Adams had accepted not only payments on his hotel rooms, but expensive coats and other items from Goldfine). Eisenhower himself, after all, accepted gifts from his gang and other rich friends, gifts worth far more than anything Goldfine had given Adams. The President told Slater that "the gift situation is a very difficult one. It's a custom the world over and where do you stop?" Slater assured him that no one expected him to refuse a personal gift, and that the donors did not expect special favors in return.[8]

On June 17, Adams made his appearance before the committee. He admitted to a lack of prudence in his dealings with Goldfine, but insisted that the only thing he had done for the man was to place one phone call to the SEC, asking it to expedite its hearings in Goldfine's case. The following day, Eisenhower opened a news conference with a prepared statement. He issued a ringing defense of Adams. No one, the President said, could doubt Adams' "personal integrity and honesty." As for himself, Eisenhower said, "I personally like Governor Adams. I admire his abilities. I respect him because of his personal and official integrity. I need him."[9] But the Democrats, smelling blood, were not deterred. The investigation continued, more Goldfine gifts were uncovered, and the Old Guard Republicans, seeing their opportunity, began demanding Adams' resignation (Barry Goldwater and Bill Knowland were the first to do so).

On June 23, Eisenhower expressed his feelings about the uproar to Paul Hoffman. "Nothing that has occurred has had a more depressive effect on my normal buoyancy and optimism than has the virulent, sustained, demogogic attacks made upon Adams," he said. Eisenhower admitted that Adams had been "less than alert" in his dealings with Goldfine, but "the fact remains that he is not only honest, effective, and dedicated, but in most cases, *his attackers know this to be true*." At the least, Eisenhower said, he would have hoped the Republicans would not add to the clamor. "I grow to despise political expediency more every day."[10]

Nevertheless, Eisenhower could not completely ignore what was becoming an almost unanimous Republican demand that Adams resign. In July, the President sent Nixon to talk to Adams about the situation, emphasizing that he felt such deep loyalty to Adams "that he did not want to even discuss the possibility of a resignation." But he did want Nixon to point out to Adams what a liability he had become. In his talk later that morning with Adams, Nixon put the stress on the upcoming congressional elections. He warned Adams that if the Republicans did badly (which was widely anticipated), they would inevitably, if unfairly, blame Adams. But Adams refused to resign. He told Nixon that only Eisenhower could decide what the proper course of action should be.[11] Meanwhile the investigation went on. Goldfine appeared before the committee and made an awful impression. The Republican Party was distraught, Eisenhower hardly less so.

On July 14, the day before Nixon talked to Adams, the President had a great deal more on his mind than Bernard Goldfine. Pro-Nasser forces in Iraq had pulled off a coup in Baghdad that morning, overthrowing the Hashemite monarchy and assassinating the royal family. Although there was no direct evidence linking Nasser to the coup, Radio Cairo was urging regicide throughout the feudal Arab states. Hussein was the target of plots in Jordan; Saud was worried and demanding that the United States send troops to the Middle East, else he would be forced to "go along" with the UAR. In Lebanon, Allen Dulles reported to the President, Chamoun had again requested British and American intervention. The entire Middle East seemed on the verge of falling into the hands of anti-Western pan-Arabs controlled by Nasser.

Since the basic Western policy was to keep the Arab states weak, divided, and dependent on the West, this was a major crisis. To deal with it, Eisenhower did not turn to the NSC, but to an informal group of key advisers, meeting in his office. He told Bobby Cutler the trouble was that the NSC meetings were so large (usually more than twenty people present) that top-secret material could not be discussed anyway, and in addition, the large group provided an audience that was too tempting for the Dulles brothers to resist attempting to impress. Eisenhower told Cutler that he had "real impatience" with Allen Dulles, because his briefings were "too philosophical, laborious, and tedious." Eisenhower admitted that "one must recognize the personality of the individual involved," and confessed that "he really had not sought to do anything about it." The President also told Cutler that Foster Dulles' briefings "were frequently too long and in too much detail in historical account."[12]

So, on July 14, when he had to make a decision, Eisenhower endured an NSC meeting, where he was noncommittal, then called the Dulles brothers, Nixon, Anderson, Quarles, Twining, Cutler, and Goodpaster into the Oval Office. Cutler recalled that the President "sat sprawled back in the chair behind his desk in a comfortable position, the most relaxed man in the room . . ." Cutler had the feeling that Eisenhower "knew exactly what he meant to do."[13] He did indeed; as Eisenhower put it in his memoirs, "This was one meeting in which my mind was practically made up . . . even before we met. The time was rapidly approaching, I believed, when we had to move into the Middle East, and specifically into Lebanon, to stop the trend toward chaos."[14] As the President explained privately to Nixon, just before the meeting (when he had also asked Nixon to talk to Adams about resignation), "We have come to the crossroads. Since 1945 we have been trying to maintain the opportunity to reach vitally needed petroleum supplies peaceably, without hindrance on the part of any one." Eisenhower thought the current unrest came about "by the struggle of Nasser to get control of these supplies—to get the income and the power to destroy the Western world." The President concluded, "Somewhere along the line we have got to face up to the issue."[15]

So, in the Oval Office, Eisenhower listened patiently to yet another of Allen Dulles' briefings, then turned to Twining to discuss the readiness of the Sixth Fleet and the Marines in the eastern Mediterranean. Secretary Dulles asked, almost plaintively, "Would you wish to hear my political appreciation?" Obviously embarrassed, Eisenhower replied: "Go ahead, Foster . . . please." Dulles said the Russians would be content with making noise, but he warned that "if the United States went into Lebanon we could expect a very bad reaction from most Arab countries." He feared for the pipelines and the canal. But he assured Eisenhower that from a legal viewpoint, an American landing in Lebanon was far different from that of the British-French attack on Suez, because Chamoun had invited American troops into his country. He also warned, however, that few people would get the distinction.

Eisenhower knew all that already. Cutler noticed that the President, "calm, easy, and objective . . . was dealing with something which he thoroughly understood. His unruffled confidence was apparent to all." He told Dulles to have Lodge request an emergency meeting of the Security Council for the following morning; he told Jerry Persons to assemble the legislative leaders that afternoon; he told Twining to start the Sixth Fleet and the Marines toward Lebanon.[16]

That afternoon, intervention proved to be a difficult proposition to sell to Congress. The legislative leaders were not at all enthusiastic. Some argued that intervention would undo America's good reputation; Sam Rayburn feared that America was getting into a civil war; Senator Fulbright doubted seriously that this crisis was Communist-inspired. Only three men supported action. But Eisenhower had not called the congressmen together to elicit support, or for consultation—he had called them in to inform them of what he intended to do.[17] At the conclusion of the meeting, he met with the Dulles brothers, Twining, Quarles, Hagerty, and Goodpaster to "fix firmly upon specific action steps." Eisenhower told Twining to send the Marines ashore at 3 P.M. Lebanon time, which was 9 A.M., July 15, Washington time. No one, not even Chamoun, should be given advance notice, because the President did not want to give the rebels in Lebanon an opportunity to prepare resistance. Eisenhower instructed Foster Dulles to have Lodge tell the Security Council that the United States sought only to stabilize the situation until the U.N. could act.[18]

Eisenhower then called Macmillan. The Prime Minister had also received Chamoun's call for help, as well as one from Hussein of Jordan—"the two little chaps," Macmillan called them. Eisenhower informed Macmillan that American Marines were on their way to Lebanon.[19] Macmillan laughed and said, "You are doing a Suez on me." Eisenhower laughed at his end. Macmillan wanted to act jointly; Eisenhower insisted on a unilateral American intervention in Lebanon, and asked Macmillan to be prepared to move into Jordan with British paratroopers. The President did not want to give the impression that the two countries were acting in collusion (although obviously they were), so he promised full logistical support for the British in Jordan, but refused to include American armed forces in that movement. He also assured Macmillan that he would not abandon his ally.

Thus did Eisenhower unleash the American military for the only time in his Presidency. A quarter of a century later, his motives still seemed unclear. Lebanon was under no real threat; Chamoun had already announced that he would not seek a second term; evidence of any Russian, or Egyptian, involvement in either Lebanon or in the coup in Iraq was lacking; there were no vital American interests in Lebanon itself. Eisenhower's decision to intervene, in addition, contrasted sharply with his response to the various crises in the Far East from 1953 through 1955. Then he had been cautious and prudent, far more so than his professional and political advisers. Now he was much more eager to intervene than were the politicians or the State Department people, indeed had been eager to go into Lebanon for more than a year, and was just waiting for a proper excuse. Why was he so much more aggressive in the Middle East than in the Far East?

For one reason, because the chances of a clash between the super-powers was so much less in Lebanon, and the potential for indigenous resistance was far less than in Indochina or on the Chinese coast. Further, by 1958 one of the Democratic charges against Eisenhower had become his defense policy, with its emphasis on big planes and big bombs. Maxwell Taylor, as Army Chief of Staff, had joined the Democrats in this criticism, which had become widespread and claimed that for America it was all or nothing—the country had no capability of making a flexible response appropriate to the occasion. By inter-vening in Lebanon, Eisenhower proved that was not true. Within two weeks, he had the equivalent of a full division in the country, equipped with Honest John rocket batteries that had atomic weapons, with another two divisions alerted to go on a few hours' flight from Ger-many. Lebanon, in short, was a show of force—and a most impressive one.

Against whom was it directed? Not the Soviets, who already knew, roughly, what American capability was. Not the Lebanese, virtually unarmed. The real target was Nasser. As Eisenhower later summed it up, he wanted to bring about a change in Nasser's attitude. Nasser, according to the President, "seemed to believe that the United States government was scarcely able, by reason of the nation's democratic system, to use our recognized strength to protect our vital interests." Eisenhower wanted to impress Nasser, and to show him that he could not count on the Soviets, in order to give him "food for thought."[20] Eisenhower was also anxious to demonstrate to King Saud that the United States could be counted on to support its friends. (The Presi-dent had told the legislative leaders that Saud had made it clear that "if we do not come in we are finished in the Middle East."[21]) Most of all, Eisenhower's gunboat diplomacy in the Middle East was based on his perception of the importance of the area to the United States and its allies. In his judgment, the Middle East was immeasurably more within an area vital to the interests of the United States than the Far East ever would be.

Eisenhower kept the intervention limited in scope and duration. Three hours after the Marines landed, he talked to Macmillan again. The Prime Minister, Eisenhower later told Twining, "wants to get us to commit ourselves now to clearing up the whole Middle East situation" through a massive joint intervention into not only Lebanon, but Syria, Jordan, and Iraq as well. Eisenhower confessed that the proposition "gives me a good deal of concern." He wanted to limit, not escalate, and refused Macmillan's request.[22]

The Marines landed without incident, to find a country going about its business. Having made the commitment, Eisenhower downplayed its significance. In a special message to Congress, in Cabot Lodge's announcement to the Security Council, and in his own nationwide radio and television address that evening of July 15, Eisenhower expressed the hope that the U.N. could quickly come into Lebanon and "permit the early withdrawal of United States forces." He used the words "stationed in" Lebanon rather than "invading." American forces would secure the airfield and the capital, but would otherwise not operate in Lebanon.

In justifying the intervention, however, Eisenhower overstated his reasons. He linked Lebanon in 1958 with Greece in 1947, Czechoslovakia in 1948, the Chinese Communist victory in 1949, and the Korean invasion of 1950. But then he could hardly have said that he was sending in the Marines in order to impress Nasser, Saud, and the others, or to show that the American armed forces were not musclebound, or to protect feudal monarchies.

Two days later, on July 17, the British sent twenty-two hundred paratroopers to Jordan to bolster King Hussein's shaky regime. Macmillan still wanted direct American participation; Eisenhower again refused. The next day, Eisenhower sent Robert Murphy to Beirut to act as his special representative; Murphy talked with Chamoun and persuaded him to hold new elections at the end of July. Chehab won the election, and by early August the United States began to withdraw from Lebanon. The Russians, as Eisenhower had predicted, limited their response to diplomatic maneuvers (Khrushchev was calling frantically for a summit meeting to deal with Lebanon, while denouncing American aggression). In less than four months, the crisis was over; by October 25, the last American troops were withdrawn. Eisenhower had accomplished his basic objectives without risking general war (Nasser had flown to Moscow in July, only to find that the Soviets had no interest in challenging the United States in the Middle East). The whole affair, Eisenhower noted in his memoirs, brought about "a definite change in Nasser's attitude toward the United States."[23]

For Eisenhower it had been an exciting experience, not one to be compared to Overlord, to be sure, but nevertheless hardly something that was all in a day's work. On May 13, the day he sent a thousand

American troops to Puerto Rico and Cuba to rescue Nixon, if necessary, and the day he started units of the Sixth Fleet toward Beirut, he
told Whitman, "I am about ready to go put my uniform on." That
night, he told Mamie he was thinking of "digging out my uniforms
to see whether they still fit." 24 In July, when the intervention took
place, Dr. Snyder worried about the "anxious hours" the President
was putting in on the crisis. Snyder thought Eisenhower was "tense,"
and feared "he might blow a valve again." But Ellis Slater, who spent
the evening of July 16 with Eisenhower, thought he looked great.
Eisenhower told Slater that although things were "a little tough," he
was confident they would come out all right. Slater talked to Whitman
("that most devoted friend and slave," he called her). "She said things
had been hellish but that she never ceased to admire more and more
the attitude of this man under pressure." 25 It almost seemed to rejuve-
nate him.

The aftermath was not so pleasing. Charges of American gunboat
diplomacy, of bullying, of militarism, filled the world's airwaves. Khrushchev blustered and threatened. The Arab world was inflamed.
Eisenhower thought it all terribly unfair. He complained about the
way Nasser was able to "inflame an illiterate populace" and about the
way Khrushchev "can stir all this fuss and the world stands quiet—
only two years after Hungary!" 26

On July 23, Eisenhower conducted a thorough review of world
reaction. Dulles began the discussion, saying that "we must regard
Arab nationalism as a flood which is running strongly. We cannot
successfully oppose it, but we can put up sandbags around positions
we must protect." America's major difficulty, Dulles said, was that
"Israel is a hostage held against us." Eisenhower heartily agreed, pointing out that "except for Israel we could form a viable policy in the
area." In his mind, he said, "the question is how to take a sympathetic
position regarding the Arabs without agreeing to the destruction of
Israel." He feared that "if our policy is solely to maintain the kings
of Jordan and Saudi Arabia in their positions, the prospect is hopeless,
even in the short term."

The President's tone of voice, as well as what he said, worried
Dulles, who now feared an overreaction. Contradicting what he said
at the beginning of the meeting, the Secretary told Eisenhower, "We
must not overestimate . . . Arab nationalism and Arab unity." There
was no real alliance between Egypt and Syria, he said, and Arab unity
"is not a valid, permanent movement." Eisenhower disagreed. He

thought, with regard to Arab unity, that "we must either work with it or change it, or do some of both." The President noted that he had tried to "work out a line of action with Saud, but it availed us very little." Dulles disagreed; he pointed out that "it has gained us at least a couple of years in which the area did not go Communist." Eisenhower had rather hoped that more than a mere couple of years of buying time could result from American policies, but in the end he agreed with Dulles that so long as the United States was forced to support Israel, "we are laboring under an inherent disadvantage in this area." And with that expression of helplessness, the meeting broke up, having decided nothing.[27] The intervention in Lebanon had not solved anything.

On July 22, Eisenhower wrote a seven-page letter to George Humphrey. He described some of his problems with Congress, with the AEC, with DOD, with State, with Sherman Adams, with the CIA, and others. "With this list of things to command my attention," he declared, "you can easily understand that calm, continuous, searching analysis of all factors in the complicated Middle East question is indeed difficult."[28]

The failure of his subordinates to carry out his orders was especially irritating to Eisenhower. Back in 1952, Truman had warned that Eisenhower would find the Presidency much more frustrating than being the Supreme Commander, because as President he would say, "Do this!" or "Do that!" and nothing would happen. The Air Force's addiction to balloon projects showed how right Truman was. Eisenhower had twice, unequivocally, ordered the Air Force to cease sending reconnaissance balloons over the Soviet Union, but in late July, he was chagrined to receive another protest from the Soviets about intrusion of their airspace by Air Force balloons.[29] Eisenhower tried to get Secretary McElroy on the phone, but he had gone home, so the President talked to his deputy, Quarles, instead. As Whitman recorded his end of the conversation, Eisenhower "complained, in salty language, about the laxity in the defense forces—he said he would have, if he had done some of the things that have been done in the last few days—shot himself . . . The President suggested firing a few people—and said that people in the service either ought to obey orders or get the hell out of the service."[30]

Eisenhower followed up with a formal memorandum for the Secretary of Defense, telling him that "there is disturbing evidence of a deterioration in the processes of discipline and responsibility within the armed forces." He cited, in particular, "unauthorized decisions which have apparently resulted in certain balloons falling within the territory of the Communist bloc," and U-2 flights over routes "that contravened my standing orders." He wanted action taken, "at once," to tighten discipline.[31] Five days later, Eisenhower groaned and cursed in helpless anger when Foster Dulles reported to him yet another protest from the Soviets about balloons.[32]

The Air Force motivation was less to get information from inside Russia, more to compete with the CIA's U-2 project, which the Air Force had tried to persuade Eisenhower to give to its care. He had refused. Nevertheless the competition flourished, and not just over intelligence. Each service continued to criticize its rivals and demand more appropriations for itself. Each service had its own champions in Congress, and among the large contributors to campaign funds. John J. McCloy explained to Eisenhower that "the interservice game extends right down through the corporations, depending upon which branch their contracts flow from and it even goes into the academic institutions depending from where their research grants flow." Eisenhower agreed with McCloy, and added that "it is from these vested interests that a great deal of the objection to unification springs."[33]

Eisenhower knew full well that there was an artificial, self-serving quality to many of the demands for more spending on the military, but he hardly knew how to cope with it. Again and again he stressed to his Cabinet, his Republican leaders, his friends, and the public that unless defense spending was cut, there would be annual deficits of $10 billion or more, extending as far as forty years into the future. Under those circumstances, he warned, "we just can't compete" with a closed society.[34]

Part of Eisenhower's difficulty in dealing with DOD resulted from the ingrained habit of disgruntled officers in the Pentagon leaking information to sympathetic congressmen. In August, an Air Force officer told Stuart Symington that the Pentagon was undertaking studies to determine under what conditions the United States might have to negotiate a surrender following a nuclear attack. Symington made this the subject of a major speech that attracted widespread attention. Republican senators asked Eisenhower about it. The President "asserted that he might be the last person alive, but there wouldn't be any surrender in the next two and one-half years, at least." He said he knew of no such study, and commented that Symington's allegations "were about the same as saying 'there is no sun!' "[35]

Two weeks later, on August 29, Symington wrote Eisenhower directly, to say that he had information (from undisclosed sources) "that would appear to show that Allen Dulles heavily underrated Soviet missile development to date, as well as planned capabilities." Symington charged that because of this, and because of Eisenhower's refusal to spend more on defense, "we leave ourselves and our allies subject to overt political, if not actual military aggression . . . with a relatively slight chance of effective retaliation against such aggression between 1960 and 1962."[36]

Eisenhower asked Symington to come to his office, with only Goodpaster present. The President explained that Symington had it backward—what Allen Dulles had really done was overestimate Soviet development and capability. In a grand understatement of his own, "the President said he thought it would be out of character for him to be indifferent to valid assessments of Soviet strength." Symington was not convinced.[37]

Neither were John McCone, Strauss's successor as head of the AEC, Quarles, or McElroy convinced that Eisenhower's desire for a test ban was good for the country. Even after the Hardtack series, they wanted more tests. In late July, they proposed to the President a new series designed to test the ABM. The AEC and DOD proposed conducting the tests from Eglin Airfield, on the Florida Gulf coast, firing out into the Gulf. Secretary Dulles was appalled; he said it would do great damage to relations with both Cuba and Mexico. (No one at the meeting raised the question of what the American residents of the Gulf coast might think.) On the basis of Dulles' advice, Eisenhower ordered the series canceled.[38]

In Geneva, meanwhile, the technical experts from Russia and the United States continued their deliberations in an attempt to agree on an inspection system that would justify a test ban. On August 4, Killian reported that they were making progress. Eisenhower told Killian that "if full technical agreement is reached, the weight of argument for doing so [ceasing the tests] would be very great." Both Twining and McCone strongly protested, but Eisenhower insisted.

On August 21, the Geneva experts adopted their final report. It concluded that "it was technically feasible" to create "a workable and effective control system to detect violations of an agreement on the worldwide suspension of nuclear weapons' tests." There was some disagreement among the experts on the number of control posts needed, and on the ability to detect small underground blasts, but that could not obscure the fact that for the first time in the nuclear age, Soviets and Americans had reached an agreement on atomic matters. Eisenhower told the State Department to begin test-ban negotiations with the Soviet Union.

DOD and the AEC were not the only ones opposed. Macmillan told Eisenhower that a test ban would be a great mistake, and reminded him that Britain had a new series of tests scheduled for the early fall. Eisenhower replied that he had a personal commitment to a ban, and insisted that the moment for action was "psychologically correct."[39]

Eisenhower was greatly concerned by the British military position, which the JCS told him was woefully weak. McElroy reported that the British had gone "very far downhill" since the war. Eisenhower thought the reason was too much emphasis on atomic weapons, not enough on conventional forces. The President wanted to divert the British away from strategic weapons and toward more ships and ground troops; to persuade Macmillan, he offered to send more American nuclear weapons to England and to share more atomic information with the British.[40] But the AEC and DOD were opposed to such sharing, and they cited the McMahon Act, which forbade giving atomic information to foreign countries. Eisenhower insisted that although he did not want to violate the law, he did want to treat the British as "true allies" and "be full and generous" in exchanging information. The President recalled British assistance during the war, mentioning specifically the way they shared Ultra with the United States, and their radar discoveries, not to mention their original contribution to atomic research.[41]

The French, under the leadership of Charles de Gaulle since the spring of 1958, were also adamantly opposed to a ban, as they wished to develop their own bomb. The project was part of de Gaulle's determination to restore the glory and prestige of France, which in turn was part of his program of freeing France from her military dependence on NATO and the United States. De Gaulle's insistence on French independence greatly alarmed many Americans; C. D. Jackson, for example, wrote an editorial for *Life* full of foreboding about de Gaulle and his effect on the alliance. Eisenhower read it, then told Whitman that "sometimes C. D. finds ghosts in the attic where none is there." He thought he could work successfully with de Gaulle, as he had in the past, and that de Gaulle would be good for France.[42] Eisenhower also told congressmen, who feared that the end of NATO was at hand, that "a Frenchman looking for power and one exercising power are two different things." He admitted that de Gaulle was "very vain," but insisted that he was "realistic in the military sense."[43]

Eisenhower did not think, however, that de Gaulle was very realistic about nuclear weapons. He could see no reason for the French to have their own nuclear arsenal, and on August 21 he told the new French Foreign Minister, Maurice Couve de Murville, just that. The President said that he was about to make a public statement calling for negotiations for a ban to begin on October 31, and as a sign of good faith, to suspend all American testing for one year, provided the Russians did not test. Couve de Murville was unimpressed; he said the French would conduct their tests regardless of what the United States and the Soviet Union did. Eisenhower said he wished they would not.[44]

The AEC and DOD had hoped that the British and the French could persuade Eisenhower to oppose a test ban. When that did not work, they made one last attempt of their own. Quarles told Eisenhower that the JCS believed a ban "will be disadvantageous militarily," and McCone told him that every member of the AEC agreed with the JCS. Eisenhower curtly told McCone he was aware of that fact, but pointed out that the AEC was "not concerned with the question of the world political position."[45] The next day, August 19, on the verge of Eisenhower's announcement, McCone made one last, desperate effort. Fully aware of Eisenhower's great interest in using atomic power for peaceful purposes, he told Eisenhower that if only the AEC were allowed to continue underground testing, it would soon be able to use atomic energy to extract oil from deep deposits, blast tunnels through mountains, and achieve other goals. Could not the President at least announce that America intended to continue underground testing? Eisenhower said that if he made such an exception, "we would lose the political gains we are seeking," so "no matter what our military might say" he was going ahead with his announcement.[46]

On August 22, Eisenhower issued his statement, offering to enter into test-ban negotiations with the Russians on October 31. As he explained to McCone, his responsibilities compelled him "to take some risk" in order to "do away with atmospheric testing, thus eliminating the health hazard, and at the same time . . . slow down the arms race."[47]

On August 27, before Khrushchev had replied to Eisenhower's proposal, McCone met with Eisenhower to ask for "one more test." He said he needed a decision "immediately." Eisenhower "expressed some irritation, saying that he had announced the tests' suspension and now 'they' wanted to have another big test." But McCone persisted, and finally got a weary President to agree; Eisenhower said "he supposed that the AEC might as well go ahead."[48] Part of the reason was undoubtedly the roar of protest that had greeted his announcement, from such people as Teller, Strauss, Hanson Baldwin, and Henry Kissinger. Another factor may have been Macmillan's actions; on August 22, the day of the announcement, the British began their latest series of tests with an explosion at Christmas Island. On August 29, Khrushchev indicated his willingness to enter into negotiations at the end of October; that same day, the AEC began a new series, officially named Hardtack II but called Operation Deadline by the press. Hardtack II set off nineteen separate explosions, most of them in the low-kiloton range, and including one of a nuclear bazooka shell designed to be fired by two men at a range of less than two miles. The Soviets also participated in this orgy of last-minute testing, starting their own series on September 30 and setting off fourteen weapons, most in the megaton range, and in the process releasing vast quantities of radioactive material.[49] In all in 1958, the year that saw the first respite in testing since 1945, the three nuclear powers set off more bombs than in any other year (the Soviets set off more in October 1958, alone, than they had in all of 1957). The final total was eighty-one blasts. Radioactivity levels were at their peak. But at least there was, for the first time, some genuine hope that it all might soon end.

Hopelessness, meanwhile, was the dominant mood in the Republican Party as the off-year elections came closer. Eisenhower's veto of the farm bill was one reason, and the relatively lackluster candidates the party was offering was another. Little Rock and Sputnik added to Republican woes. The Democrats, anxious to increase their lead in Congress and thus lay a base for the 1960 presidential election, were conducting a vigorous campaign, one in which they were able to reverse the roles of the 1952 campaign—they were on the offensive, while the Republicans were thrown back on the defensive. Under the circumstances, a Democratic sweep seemed certain.

Almost every Republican wanted a scapegoat. Some settled on Benson, but most put the blame on Sherman Adams. In early September the demands for his resignation became irresistible. Still, Eisenhower hated to let Adams go. Both as general and as President, Eisenhower found it extremely difficult to fire a man who had served him well and loyally, no matter how great a handicap the man had become. So it was with Adams.

Eisenhower was unmoved by demands from Goldwater, Knowland, and other Republican senators that Adams be forced out of the Administration, and by Nixon's warnings that keeping Adams would cost two dozen or more seats in Congress. But when his own gang began to put the pressure on, it was a different matter. Cliff Roberts sent him a handwritten note, saying that the Adams' affair was the cause of "hopelessness" in the party. Eisenhower wrote back on September 4, trying to argue with Roberts. The President said that Adams "admittedly made a mistake, but no one has ever accused him of crookedness. Yet this [Goldfine-Adams business], almost alone, seems to account for the alleged Republican 'hopelessness.' " Eisenhower protested that Adams had worked with "extraordinary dedication," and cited "the round-the-clock days that he has devoted to the service of the country." But all that work was "seemingly forgotten by the public with a consequent readiness to make [Adams] a greater villain than almost anyone in current history." Eisenhower said it all left him "puzzled and resentful."[50]

But no matter how patently unfair it was to blame Adams for Republican difficulties, there was no escaping it. After Eisenhower dictated to Whitman his letter to Roberts, he called Winthrop Aldrich on the phone. Aldrich was a friend of Adams', but he told Eisenhower that "this man has got to go or we are done." Eisenhower then called Meade Alcorn, chairman of the RNC. Alcorn said he was having trouble raising money for the campaign, and he put the blame on Adams. Eisenhower, greatly depressed, finally said "my mind is pretty well cleared up as to what would be the better thing to do. The difficulty is to find a good way to do it." He asked Alcorn to get together with Nixon and talk to Adams. Alcorn said he would.[51]

They did, without results. Adams told them, "I will have to talk to the boss myself."[52] Eisenhower agreed to a meeting, then commented to Whitman, "How dreadful it is that cheap politicians can so pillory an honorable man."[53] At the meeting, on September 17, Adams indicated that he was willing to hand in his resignation, but that he wanted to wait a month or so to get the personnel situation straightened out. Eisenhower told him, "If anything is done and we make any critical decision, as I have always said, you will have to take the initiative yourself." But after the meeting, the President changed his mind and called Adams on the telephone to tell him that he could not drag the thing out for a full month. Then he added that he wanted to protect Adams "from anything that looks cold and indifferent."[54]

Five days later, on September 22, Adams announced his resignation. Eisenhower accepted it with the "deepest regret." The boil had been lanced, but whether the surgery would cure the desperately ill Republican Party remained to be seen.

The ChiNats and the ChiComs were at it again, over Quemoy and Matsu. Eisenhower first learned of the latest crisis on August 25 in appropriate Dr. Strangelove conditions. He was deep in the bowels of the earth, in a bombproof shelter in the North Carolina mountains, surrounded by the most advanced electronic gadgetry, participating in the annual Operation Alert. The crisis brought on a war scare with a potential for a nuclear exchange, thus emphasizing the importance of the government's ability to carry on in the event of an atomic attack.

Allen Dulles gave the briefing. The ChiNats had been steadily increasing their strength on Quemoy and Matsu, to the point that Chiang had 100,000 men, a full third of his total force, on the islands. The ChiComs had protested against this act of provocation, to no avail. On August 24, they began shelling the islands. Dulles said the physical damage from the artillery barrage was slight, although casualties were substantial. He expected the ChiComs to throw a blockade around the islands, in an attempt to starve out the garrisons. He did not, however, think they intended to launch an assault, because they had not brought their mainland forces and amphibious lift to a level that would make it possible for them to do so.

Goodpaster recorded that "the President thought it desirable to make some show of force, with a few calculated leaks regarding our actions to strengthen our forces." Eisenhower ordered two aircraft carriers from the Sixth Fleet to steam through Suez and join the Seventh Fleet in the Formosa Straits. Quarles pointed out that this might have an effect on the ChiComs, "but might also have the effect of Chiang being more provocative." Eisenhower said he would not give Chiang a full commitment. "The Orientals can be very devious," he admonished, and if he told the ChiNats that they had his full support, the ChiNats "would then call the tune." [55]

Still, in Eisenhower's view, what was at stake was much more than Quemoy and Matsu. Using his domino image, he predicted that if Quemoy and Matsu were lost, it would "lead to the loss of Formosa," which would threaten "the future security of Japan, the Philippines, Thailand, Vietnam, and even Okinawa . . . and United States vital interests would suffer severely." [56] By August 29 the President was back in Washington. The artillery barrage continued, the ChiComs had introduced their Air Force into the conflict, and were blockading the islands. If they actually attempted an invasion of Quemoy and Matsu, Eisenhower declared, he was considering authorizing the use of tactical atomic weapons against ChiCom airfields. However, he added, "We cannot be sure this would be necessary, and since we do not want to outrage world opinion, perhaps we had better reserve this."[57] Instead, he authorized the use of the Seventh Fleet to provide convoy protection to ChiNat supply ships attempting to get through to the islands, although he carefully instructed Twining to make certain that no American ships went within the three-mile limit. To his disgust, however, the ChiNat supply ships turned and ran when the Americans left them and the ChiComs began shelling the convoys.

On September 4, Eisenhower met with Goodpaster and Foster Dulles to talk about what to do next. Dulles was all for using tactical atomic bombs. Eisenhower demurred. According to Dulles' memo on the conversation, he then told the President, "I thought we had acknowledged the risk of the political and psychological dangers of the use of these weapons when we decided to include them in our arsenal." According to Goodpaster's notes, "Mr. Dulles directed attention to the point regarding atomic weapons, recalling that we have geared our defense to the use of these in case of hostilities of any size, and stated that, if we will not use them when the chips are down because of adverse world opinion, we must revise our defense setup." Eisenhower pointed out that if the United States used atomic weapons against ChiCom airfields, the Communists might well retaliate with nuclear weapons against Formosa (in his memoirs, Eisenhower said that he was convinced that the Russians were behind this latest ChiCom aggression). Under the circumstances, he was not ready to authorize the use of atomic bombs.[58]

A good thing too, as two days later, on September 6, Chou En-lai made a statement that indicated he was ready to negotiate. Dulles was suspicious. He offered the President a draft of a statement that was full of threats. Eisenhower "suggested modifications," saying "he wanted to add something in the way of a concrete and definite acceptance of Chou En-lai's offer to negotiate." The President thought "that some honorable way out of the Offshore Islands dilemma was desirable," although he recognized that "his views . . . were somewhat at variance with the Secretary of State's."[59]

Chiang, meanwhile, like Dulles, wanted to escalate. So did the JCS. On September 6, Twining gave the President a proposal that gave complete freedom of action to the commander of the Seventh Fleet. If the admiral thought it necessary, he could order atomic air strikes against the ChiCom mainland. Eisenhower refused; the President insisted that any attacks against the mainland "could be ordered only upon his approval."[60] Thus rebuffed, the JCS then completely reversed themselves; on September 11, Twining told Eisenhower that in the view of the JCS, "the islands are not defensible and probably not required for the defense of Formosa."[61]

The problem was to convince Chiang of that fact, and it was insurmountable. Chiang's goal, Eisenhower and his advisers felt, was to embroil the United States in a war with the ChiComs. Gordon Gray, former president of the University of North Carolina, who had in July replaced Cutler as the President's Special Assistant for National Security Affairs, discussed the problem with Eisenhower. Gray wondered "how long we should continue to encourage Chiang in the notion that we would support his return to the mainland by force inasmuch as it seemed to me that this was no longer a reasonable possibility." Eisenhower replied that Chiang hoped "that there would be disintegration from within Communist China and that in the ensuing chaos he would be in a position, with our support, to move in and take over." The President thought that was "a possibility," and that "as long as the possibility existed it was important to maintain the morale of Chiang and his people."[62]

That evening, September 11, Eisenhower went on national television to talk to the public. The bombardment and blockade were still going on, and no negotiations had gotten started. Eisenhower stated that the United States was bound by its treaties, its principles, and its pledge in the Formosa Resolution of 1955. There would be no retreat, he promised. "There is not going to be any appeasement." But he added, "I believe there is not going to be any war."[63]

The reaction to Eisenhower's statement, except from Republicans who automatically gave the President their support, was disastrous. Hardly anyone was willing to risk World War III over Quemoy and Matsu. By September 23, talks had begun between the American and Chinese Communist ambassadors to Poland, but Dulles reported that the initial discussions were not productive, and he still wanted action. Eisenhower told Dulles that "as much as two-thirds of the world, and 50 percent of U.S. opinion, opposes the course which we have been following."[64] None of the NATO allies was willing to support the defense of Quemoy and Matsu, a situation that led Dulles to complain to Eisenhower about "the regrettable failure of any of our allies to stand by us publicly . . ." He feared that NATO, and possibly even SEATO, were "beginning to fall apart."[65]

McElroy suggested one way out of the dilemma. He told Eisenhower he had "been wondering whether, if we cannot persuade Chiang to get off the island . . . there isn't someone else who could step into the position." [66] Eisenhower was not, however, ready to consider assassination. He did say that "something must be done to make Chiang more flexible in his approach." He added that he did not want to wage a fight "on the ground of someone else's choosing, and this is the case in Quemoy and Matsu where we are at a great disadvantage in terms of world opinion." [67] The President's own solution was to give Chiang some American landing craft, so that he would be in a position to return to the mainland if conditions seemed favorable, while he simultaneously "removed all or nearly all his garrison from the offshore islands." [68] He sent Dulles to Formosa to make the proposition to Chiang. The ChiNat leader refused to retreat, but he was willing to issue a statement renouncing the use of force as an acceptable means of regaining the mainland.

The ChiComs responded. After a brief cease-fire, they announced that they would fire on the ChiNat convoys only on odd days of the month, permitting resupply operations on the even days. Eisenhower "wondered if we were in a Gilbert and Sullivan war." [69] Chiang did reduce the garrison, although not to the extent Eisenhower thought he should, and the ChiComs ceased firing. The crisis passed, without war, without retreat, without putting an intolerable strain on NATO, and without a loss of face by the ChiNats or the United States. Eisenhower had used a combination of threats, firmness, and resolve, combined with a willingness to negotiate and be reasonable, to achieve an outcome satisfactory to him.

Early in the Formosa crisis, at a time when the Adams furor was at its height and the test-ban debate was intensifying, and while the Lebanon crisis was still unresolved, Ellis Slater and the rest of the gang spent a weekend at the White House with the First Family. Just before Saturday's dinner, nine-year-old David came in to present his grandfather with a bill for the work he had done on the farm the past two weeks. David had put the bill in an envelope addressed to "President Dwight Eisenhower"; it tabulated his days and hours—twenty-four hours' total at thirty cents per hour. Eisenhower reminded David that he owed forty cents for a previous loan, so David deducted that amount from the bill, which Eisenhower then paid. At the President's suggestion, David marked the bill paid in full and signed it.

Eisenhower cooked Sunday breakfast—cantaloupe from his farm, stacks of wheat cakes, and big link sausages—all served on trays on stands while the guests sat in easy chairs. They talked for three hours, mainly about farming and cattle and fertilizer and fields. Eisenhower said he was desperately looking forward to January 20, 1961, when he could retire and "just sleep and rest and be himself." Mamie commented that she had a lot of work to do before they left the White House, and said "it wasn't going to be fun getting ready to vacate that place." The morning, Slater wrote in his diary, was "refreshing and diverting" for the President.

Toward the end of the breakfast session, however, Eisenhower got to talking about what a terrible year he had had; he called 1958 "the worst of his life." He then commented that years ending in eight always seemed to be bad ones for him. In 1918, he said, he had missed World War I. In 1928, he had been in Paris, writing a guidebook— pleasant enough, but it had given him a feeling of treading water in his career. In 1938, his last year in the Philippines, he had gone through some bitter battles with MacArthur and feared he would never get away from the islands or the man. In 1948, he had retired from the Army and gone to Columbia, where he found much frustration and little satisfaction. In 1958, he had suffered a stroke, found himself in frequent disagreement with his chief foreign-policy adviser and with Congress, lost Sherman Adams and Lewis Strauss, endured a series of international crises and an economic recession, and had to anticipate major Republican defeats in the next election. Small wonder he was looking forward to retirement.[70]

But he was naturally an optimist. In a letter full of grousing to George Humphrey, he concluded, "Actually, of course, the sun is shining . . . the United States is still populated by relatively happy people, and by and large our grandchildren do not seem too much worried." He thought everything would work out all right.[71]

CHAPTER TWENTY-ONE

Elections, Test-Ban Talks, Berlin, Fidel

October 1958–February 1959

EVEN WITH THE DEPARTURE of Sherman Adams, Eisenhower and the Republican Party were gloomy on the eve of the off-year elections. The Democrats were hitting them hard in the campaign, concentrating on Benson's unpopularity in the Midwest, on Taft-Hartley's "right to work" clause in the industrial states, on Republican responsibility for integration in the southern states, on unemployment throughout the nation, and most of all on the charge that "six years of leaderless vacillation have led us to the . . . brink of having to fight a nuclear war inadequately prepared and alone."[1] The charge that Eisenhower had allowed a "missile gap" to develop, which Stevenson had tried without much success in 1956, and which Symington had been using since, began paying off for the Democrats in the 1958 elections.

Eisenhower tried to keep the issue out of politics. His first effort was to attempt to convince the Democratic critics that they were wrong; to do so, he had Allen Dulles give them a briefing. But he would not allow Dulles to reveal any hard information about the U-2 program, so Dulles, unable to cite his sources, was unconvincing. In his press conferences, meanwhile, Eisenhower always managed to say a word or two about how adequate America's defenses were, and to pooh-pooh any missile gap, but he did so in such a vague manner, without citing statistics or sources, that he too was unconvincing.[2]

Another favorite Democratic charge was that the Republican Party was hopelessly split between the Old Guard and the moderate Eisenhower Republicans. Eisenhower tried to turn that one on its head. On October 20, in a major campaign speech in Los Angeles, the President declared that the Democratic Party "is not one—but two— political parties with the same name. They unite only once every two years—to wage political campaigns." One wing consisted of southern conservatives, the other of "political radicals," the wild spenders. A Democratic victory would mean innumerable new social programs, more money for defense, and a tax cut, all of which would lead to uncontrollable inflation and an unstoppable growth of the federal government.[3]

On November 4, 1958, the Republican Party, despite Eisenhower's warnings and efforts, suffered its worst defeat since the advent of the Depression. In the new Congress, Democrats would outnumber Republicans by nearly two to one in both houses. The Democrats had thirty-five governors, the Republicans only fourteen. Rockefeller's victory in New York had been balanced by Knowland's defeat in California, where he had run for governor. It was, all together, a humiliating defeat for the Republican Party, which had been decisively rejected by the people even though its leader was a highly popular President. It left Eisenhower with the "dubious distinction" of being the first President to face three successive Congresses controlled by the opposition party.

One might have thought that would have made him downcast, but it did not. Early in the campaign, when he was making a speech on another subject, he had questioned Arthur Larson on the need for a certain passage. Larson said that it was there for its effect on the elections. "Frankly," Eisenhower said, crossing it out, "I don't care too much about the congressional elections." Senator Bricker was among the defeated, as were a number of Old Guardsmen whose passing hardly displeased Eisenhower. He had told Larson that "I'd just as soon see [Republican Senator Karl] Mundt get beat."[4] Eisenhower had told the party leaders that getting rid of Adams would not do them any good, and now look, Adams was gone, the Republicans were still badly beaten, and all Eisenhower had to show for it was poor staff work. (He complained to Whitman that since Sherman left "the staff seemed to descend upon him in droves and dump everything in his lap."[5])

The reason Eisenhower was so unconcerned by Republican losses was his faith in his informal alliance with the southern Democrats. What Eisenhower wanted from Congress was some common sense on defense spending, a balanced budget, no new social programs, and freedom to conduct foreign affairs and nuclear testing without congressional interference. Since that was precisely what most of the southerners also wanted, Eisenhower knew he could count on Sam Rayburn in the House and Lyndon Johnson in the Senate to support him. He realized that he would have to veto any number of spending bills, but with the help of the southerners he could make the vetoes stick.

So, at a news conference the day after the election, he reached out to the southerners. Merriman Smith began the questioning by asking how Eisenhower proposed to get along with the Democrats after having called them "left-wing extremists . . . apostles of wholesale reckless spending, . . . demagogic excess." Eisenhower replied that Smith had not read his speeches carefully enough. The President insisted that he had talked only about the "spender-wing" of the Democratic Party. "There are a lot of them [Democrats] . . . that want to do what is good for the country. I assure you that I'm talking about a good many people in that party." He said he was counting on the "conservative Democrats . . . and every kind of person that has got brains" to keep the fiscal situation in order.

Still, Democrats were Democrats. Walter Ridder wanted to know how Eisenhower felt about working with all those Democrats when he was prohibited from running again himself. Ridder asked if Eisenhower believed he would have a stronger hand if the possibility existed that he could serve a third term. Eisenhower said that the question did not apply to him, because whatever was in the Constitution, he would never run again in any event. He explained, "Any man . . . more than seventy should not be in this office. Now, that I am certain of." [6]

Speculation on the effect of the losses on the 1960 presidential campaign was inevitable. Nixon, rightly concerned about his own chances when his party was in such disarray, met with Eisenhower in early December to plan a program. They agreed on various projects, such as setting up a committee to analyze the last election, but Eisenhower's interest was less than great, and nothing came of it.[7] As he explained to Harold Macmillan, who had written a letter of condolences on the election, "If I could devote myself exclusively to a political job, I'd like to take on the one of reorganizing and revitalizing the party." But he had more important things to do, he said.[8]

Far more important to Eisenhower than saving the Republican Party from itself, for example, was the test-ban issue. On October 31, in Geneva, the Conference on the Discontinuance of Nuclear Weapons

Tests commenced. One week earlier Gordon Gray met with the President to discuss the line the American negotiating team should follow. Gray was taking his post as National Security Adviser seriously. He was more forward than Cutler had been in raising subjects with Eisenhower, more bellicose and more active. He had even less trust in the Russians than Foster Dulles had, and he warned Eisenhower to be extra cautious in the test-ban talks. Eisenhower, however, thought it was necessary to take some risks. Although he insisted he would never jeopardize the real security interests of the United States, Eisenhower said that because of the numbers of such weapons and the improving means of delivery, "he would wish in any negotiation to err somewhat on the liberal side." To continue testing and the arms race, he said, "frightened him."[9]

Despite the President's attitude, the talks got off to a bad start. On the first day, they deadlocked. The issue was the agenda. The Russians wanted to begin by discussing a comprehensive test ban, while the Americans insisted on starting with discussions of an inspection system. These were becoming classic positions—they dated back to the original U.N. discussions on atomic energy in 1946—that left little room for negotiating anything. But at least there was a voluntary moratorium on testing. Although the Russians had cheated and conducted two tests in the first week of the Geneva talks, Eisenhower had promised if they would stop testing, so would he, and after November 3 the Russians did no more testing. Thus, as *Time* magazine pointed out, Eisenhower had done what he had always claimed he would not do, "stopped [American] tests primarily on good faith, without any provision for inspection."[10]

Having gotten from Eisenhower the unsupervised test ban they had wanted, the Russians finally agreed at Geneva to put the inspection system first on the agenda. The negotiators accepted a 180-post inspection system, but then deadlocked again when the Russians insisted on a veto in the seven-nation control commission. Eisenhower, eager to find a way out of the impasse, was therefore receptive to a mid-November proposal from Senator Albert Gore, a member of the American delegation in Geneva. Gore had concluded that there was no hope for a comprehensive test-ban agreement because of the inspection problem. He therefore urged Eisenhower to announce a three-year unilateral ban on atmospheric tests, the type that spread radioactivity around the world. Gore told Eisenhower that the Russians have been "whaling us over the head" on fallout, but if the United States limited itself to underground tests, "the Soviets would have to do the same or be put on the defensive propaganda-wise."[11]

Eisenhower was perplexed. He wanted a test ban badly; he wanted more than just a ban, in fact—he wanted some real disarmament. But he felt he could not trust the Russians. On December 9, he explained to the visiting Queen Frederika of Greece that "we cannot be naïve and put the whole safety of the free world in their [the Soviets] hands." If America pulled out of NATO and surrendered her lead in nuclear weaponry, "then we have no recourse except to try to accept the Communist doctrine and live with it." Eisenhower said "he would not want to live, nor would he want his children or grandchildren to live, in a world where we were slaves of a Moscow Power," because at that point "you would pay too big a price to be alive." [12]

One part of the talks at Geneva concerned inspection systems designed to insure against surprise attack; it was on the agenda at Eisenhower's insistence. On January 12, Dr. George Kistiakowsky, a Ukrainian-born chemist who was a member of the PSAC, told Eisenhower that he wished the topic had never been brought up. According to Kistiakowsky, if the Russians happened to agree to the American proposals, "such a system would reveal detailed information on our deployments, our readiness, and the protective strengths and arrangements for our striking forces," thus operating to the net benefit of the enemy. Kistiakowsky said that the United States should accept nothing short of an arms-limitation agreement with an adequate inspection system. Eisenhower responded that all or nothing was too nonproductive. The President said "he did not see much hope for a world engaged in all-out effort on military buildup, military technology, and tremendous attempts at secrecy." He was willing to try a step-by-step approach, beginning with a ban on testing; "then we may be able to go on to another." He wanted it tried, if only because, he said, "in the long run, no country can advance intellectually and in terms of its culture and well-being if it has to devote everything to military buildup."

Kistiakowsky then warned the President that in his opinion the Russians had an operational ICBM force. Eisenhower remarked that it might possibly be so, but he still doubted that they had the numbers or the accuracy to do much damage with them. "He then asked the question, if the Soviets should fire these weapons at us, where this action would leave them. They would still be exposed to destruction. In his mind there is the question whether this is a feasible means of making war; he granted that it is a feasible way of destroying much of the nation's strength, but the resulting retaliation would be such that it does not make sense for war." [13]

Back in 1956 most of the scientists who later joined the PSAC were opposed to further testing, Killian most of all. In the spring of 1958, Killian and the others had concluded, again, that a test ban would benefit the United States, and that a relatively small number (180) of inspection sites would discover all but the lowest-yield underground tests. It was on that basis that Eisenhower had agreed to the Geneva talks and the unilateral suspension of testing. But once the scientists became formal advisers to the President, a number of them—led by Killian and Kistiakowsky—began to have doubts about the wisdom of a ban. In late December, the PSAC informed the President that it had decided it could *not* detect underground blasts as large as twenty kilotons, and that therefore thousands of inspection sites would be required to police a comprehensive test ban. Eisenhower was understandably furious with the scientists, because he knew that the demand for a quantum leap in the number of inspection sites would give the Russians an opportunity to charge that they had been double-crossed, and because he hated being given the wrong information, and even worse having acted on it. But he felt he had to stick by his scientists, so on January 5, 1959, the American delegation at Geneva revealed the results of its latest findings and demanded more inspection sites. The Russians refused to even discuss the data, and the talks deadlocked again. Eisenhower instructed Killian to set up a new committee to find ways of making adequate inspection without so many sites.[14]

The DOD and AEC, meanwhile, wanted to set off more bombs, and were using the argument that satisfactory inspection systems were impossible (or unreachable) to force the President to agree to more tests. On January 12, Foster Dulles, McElroy, Twining, McCone, Gordon Gray, and Herter gathered in the President's office to discuss testing. John Eisenhower kept the notes. McCone and McElroy began by making the case for a new test series. "The President," John recorded, "then stated that two years ago he had visualized much propaganda mileage to be gained by a positive stand on this question . . . It had been his belief that the Soviets had no intention of allowing a true agreement on nuclear testing and that we would make many gains by pressing the issue." However, he continued, he had given way on this point to the DOD and AEC, both having insisted on the Hardtack series, so "now we will not get the propaganda benefits which we would have received two years ago." Nevertheless, Eisenhower wanted an agreement on banning tests, because it "would be a great advance toward reducing the danger of war," and because of "the further advantage to the free world of obtaining a set of qualified observers within the U.S.S.R." It would all be so easy, the President concluded sadly, "if we were dealing with sensible people, but not when we are dealing with the U.S.S.R."[15]

Four days later, on January 16, McCone came to the President with a request that the AEC be allowed to build a new reactor, in order to produce more bombs, as required by the DOD. Eisenhower exploded that there were no "requirements" until he had approved them, and stated that he could see no point to building bombs at a faster rate than the current pace of nearly two per day. He said the Defense people were getting "themselves into an incredible position— of having enough to destroy every conceivable target all over the world, plus a threefold reserve." He said "the patterns of target destruction are fantastic." Just a few years ago, he said he had thought Defense agreed that there were only seventy targets inside Russia that they needed to hit in order to destroy the Soviet system, but now Defense came to him and said there were thousands of targets that had to be hit. So many ground bursts, Eisenhower said, would be certain to destroy the United States too from radioactivity. But then, as he almost always did, he reluctantly gave way to the AEC and DOD demands, and with a sigh "said he supposed that we have to go ahead with the construction of the reactor."[16]

The President would not, however, leave the subject alone. On February 12, after an NSC meeting, Eisenhower asked McElroy, Quarles, Twining, and Goodpaster into his office, with John Eisenhower keeping the notes. Eisenhower assured the group that he was "not going to fight" the $145 million for the plutonium reactor, but he did insist that DOD had to start scaling down its "requirements." Eisenhower said he had seen a graph on America's projected atomic weapon's figures by 1968, which called for numbers of bombs that he could only regard as "astronomical." "Some of these days," he continued, "we are going to realize how ridiculous we have been and at that time we will try to retrench." Eisenhower claimed that the Executive Branch "has been fairly sensible, but has been pushed by demagogues and special interests."

Quarles said that DOD needed many more small weapons than had previously been estimated, for air defense and missile defense (the ABM concept). Eisenhower replied that the scientists who had once advocated an ABM, especially Killian, were now backtracking, because they had learned from the last explosions in the Hardtack series that the system would not work. They had set off three nuclear explosions some three hundred miles above the earth's surface only to discover that the band of radioactivity that was created was too weak to prevent missiles from re-entering the earth's atmosphere. They had also discovered that the explosions had not been detected, which added immeasurably to the problem of finding a workable inspection system for a test ban. Eisenhower was also critical of DOD for developing small-yield weapons for battlefield use, for which he could not visualize a need. Eisenhower concluded by saying that "we are taking council of our fears," and by suggesting "that we indoctrinate ourselves that there is such a thing as common sense."[17]

Common sense, however, was hard to find. On February 18, Eisenhower met with Gordon Gray. During the course of a wide-ranging conversation, Eisenhower returned to the subject of numbers of weapons, and to earlier JCS claims that by hitting seventy targets inside Russia, the Soviets would be effectively destroyed. The new plans contemplated targets in the thousands, involving tremendous numbers of weapons of megaton size. The JCS were planning on using thousands of weapons averaging 3.5 megatons in an all-out war; Eisenhower "wondered what would be the cumulative effect of ground bursts of such a magnitude of megatonage on the Northern Hemisphere . . . He expressed his concern that there just might be nothing left of the Northern Hemisphere." The United States already had a stockpile of "five thousand or seven thousand weapons or whatnot." * Eisenhower wondered why more were needed.[18]

Common sense was also difficult to locate on the more general question of defense spending. During the 1958 campaign, as a part of their call for more expenditures, some Democrats had revived the proposal for a nationwide system of fallout shelters. That was far beyond anything Eisenhower was willing to do. He contended that a shelter that was not blastproof as well as falloutproof was useless, and, anyway, building such things would only add to the fright of an American public that was already too scared for its own good. For that reason, Eisenhower said, he had refused to have a fallout shelter built for his farm in Gettysburg. Ignoring the calls for a shelter pro-

---

* As noted earlier, getting accurate figures on the American nuclear arsenal was the most difficult research task in this study. The figures were always given to the President in oral form, by the head of the AEC. As far as the author can tell, Eisenhower inherited an arsenal of about fifteen hundred weapons ranging from the low-kiloton yield to bombs of many megatons. If there were six thousand or so weapons by 1959, the AEC had built about forty-five hundred weapons during the first six years of the Eisenhower Administration, or more than two per day.

gram was relatively easy, however, because the JCS were not interested in such a passive defense system, and therefore did not give the proposal their support.

Symington's call for keeping a third or more of the B-52s in SAC airborne at all times was also fairly easy to turn back, partly because of the enormous expense involved, mainly because the JCS were not behind that demand either. Twining told Eisenhower that he could get most of SAC into the air within fifteen minutes of a warning, which was more than adequate. Complaining that people like Symington discounted everything but relative ICBM capabilities, Twining pointed out that "our Air Force is four times the size of that of the Soviets and ten times as good." Eisenhower heartily agreed. He said he "had spoken before about self-appointed military experts," and that he was "considering making another statement about neurotics— either honest or dishonest neurotics—who are so fearful that they advocate taking the entire SAC into the air and keeping it there. He conceded that these people realized the aircraft must come down occasionally to gas up."

Twining then cut to the heart of the matter. What Symington and his fellow critics were really looking for was a return to the kind of security America had enjoyed before World War II. But that would never come again. Twining said "that the public must realize that the U.S.S.R. has a capability to hit the U.S. and to live with this realization." In short, the Department of Defense could do relatively little, if anything, about actually defending the United States. That, Twining said glumly, "is a hard fact of life." The need was to keep the retaliatory capacity sufficient to deter the Russians. Eisenhower agreed, and SAC's readiness posture was not changed.[19]

The American ability to hit the Russians was already awesome. In late November of 1958, the President undertook a review of the DOD budget request for fiscal 1960. The JCS had asked for $50 billion; DOD had brought that figure down to $43.8 billion; Eisenhower wanted it reduced to $40 billion. In a discussion with McElroy, Twining, Quarles, Gray, Goodpaster, and others, Eisenhower examined the current retaliatory capacity. In addition to SAC (which still carried the most and biggest bombs and was virtually invulnerable), there were the various IRBM and ICBM projects going forward, including the implanting of IRBMs in Europe, and six Polaris submarines were under construction. After looking it all over, Eisenhower asked rhetorically, "How many times do we have to destroy Russia?" Still the JCS and DOD wanted more of everything, including a second nuclear-powered aircraft carrier. Eisenhower objected. He said he did not "visualize a battle for the surface of the sea," and that existing conventional carriers provided sufficient mobility to meet the purposes of any small war, or of an intervention as in Lebanon. The DOD and JCS people kept coming back to the nuclear carrier, however, until the President snapped that "our defense depends on our fiscal system." He insisted that the carrier be put on hold, and that other cuts in defense be made, bringing the total down to $40 billion, because "unless the [federal] budget is balanced sooner or later, procurement of defense systems will avail nothing."[20]

Eisenhower was determined to have a balanced budget in fiscal 1960, despite Democratic control of Congress and despite the demands of defense. On January 13, he gathered together the Republican leaders following the debacle in the 1958 elections (Charles Halleck had taken over from Martin as minority leader in the House, while Dirksen replaced Knowland in the Senate). Eisenhower told the politicians that "every sort of foolish proposal will be advanced in the name of national security and the 'poor' fellow . . . We've got to convince Americans that thrift is not a bad word." One of the biggest difficulties, he said, would come because of the pressure groups, where "one of the strongest these days is in munitions." He complained about the cost-plus contracts the defense industry enjoyed, and about the way industry leaders went around the country "talking poor mouth."[21]

Big farmers also gave Eisenhower fits. He had designed the Soil Bank program with the family farmer in mind, but learned that by far the greatest payments were going to large operations. He therefore told Benson to help him establish limits on such payments, and to withdraw all supports for acreage holdings exceeding a couple of hundred acres, so that no check would be larger than $20,000. Eisenhower admitted that his ideas might be "completely impractical," but it made him furious to discover that "we have been making millionaires with federal subsidies."[22] Benson tried, but Congress would not cooperate.

Neither would Eisenhower's Cabinet. Arthur Flemming, Secretary of HEW, wanted new expenditures for education. Eisenhower said that the mere idea of the federal government giving aid to education "shocks me." He wanted to leave education strictly to the states, but he allowed Flemming to convince him that the states just were not doing the job, that America's greatest national resource, her children, was being wasted, and that the amounts he was requesting were so small that they represented no danger to the budget or to local control of education. Eisenhower still was not convinced, although he admitted that "with the world trend toward socialism, maybe we can't get out of it. Maybe we are just like the old guard at the bridge with rusty armor and a broken sword." Finally, acknowledging that if the Administration did not offer a bill, the Democrats would put through one of their own at a much higher level, Eisenhower told Flemming "to put in some sort of a bill," saying he did it "begrudgingly." "I don't know of anything," he added, "that I hate so much, but I think we have to do it."[23]

Eisenhower took his battle for a balanced budget to the people, through his news conferences, through private meetings with business leaders, and through pressure on Congress (he warned that he would veto all budget-busting bills, that if Congress overrode his veto he would propose new taxes to cover the increase in spending, and that he would call a special session for that purpose). "When I'm in a fight," he told the Republican leaders, "I want every rock, pebble, club, gun, or whatever I can get." He enlisted the Chamber of Commerce, the National Association of Manufacturers, and similar groups in his economy drive, and wrote hundreds of letters to the rich and powerful, urging them to help in the struggle.[24]

Eisenhower's campaign for fiscal integrity, coupled with his use of the veto, worked. When the Democrats proposed spending $450 million per year for four years for urban renewal, Eisenhower objected strongly enough, and got enough support from southern congressmen, to defeat the bill. When Congress finally did pass a housing bill, with lowered expenditures, Eisenhower vetoed it. The Senate failed to override the veto, because of southern votes. That pattern held throughout the year, and to his delight Eisenhower ended up fiscal 1960 with a surplus of a billion dollars.[25]

For their part, one of the gains for the southerners from the informal alliance with Eisenhower was a tepid approach to civil-rights questions by the White House. Five years after *Brown*, the school system in the South remained basically segregated. Two years after passage of the Civil Rights Act of 1957, a large majority of Negro citizens in the South were still unable to register to vote. Eisenhower's Civil Rights Commission conducted investigations and issued statements, but could not force southern officials to register Negroes. In buses, restaurants, hotels, theaters, even at drinking fountains, Jim Crow remained the order of the day. Nor was all southern resistance passive;

in 1958 there were fifty bombings of churches, synagogues, and schools. In Atlanta, "the Confederate underground" bombed the Reform Jewish Temple. Eisenhower spoke out, forcefully, but adroitly, as he managed to use even this occasion to reassure his southern friends. "From babyhood," he told a news conference, "I was raised to respect the word 'Confederate'—very highly, I might add—and for hoodlums such as these to describe themselves as any part or any relation to the Confederacy of the mid-nineteenth century is, to my mind, a complete insult to the word." [26]

Eisenhower's concern with civil-rights violations was real, but not strong enough to lead him to express sympathy with the victims of prejudice. In fact, his concern was primarily with America's image abroad. "It's unfortunate that more people don't realize there are five times as many non-whites in the world as there are whites," he told Ellis Slater, because "these non-white nations control a very high percentage of the world's resources, and someday we will want access to these resources when we have mined most of ours." He complained that "all this anti-Negro agitation here isn't helping to make these non-whites friendly to us." [27]

Eisenhower himself, however, had innumerable opportunities to speak out on racial injustice and to promote racial harmony, but he would not seize them. At a news conference on January 21, 1959, for example, William McGaffin told him that "many persons feel you could exert a strong moral backing for desegregation if you said that you personally favored it [the *Brown* decision]. If you favor it, sir, why have you not said so; if you are opposed to it, could you tell us why?" Eisenhower gave his standard reply: "I do not believe it is the function or indeed it is desirable for a President to express his approval or disapproval of any Supreme Court decision. His job, for which he takes an oath, is to execute the laws." [28] The following week, Merriman Smith said that there was a rumor going around to the effect that Earl Warren, responding privately to Eisenhower's remark, had told friends that Eisenhower's stand on *Brown* was "too indecisive." According to Smith's information, Warren was "pained by what was described as your [Eisenhower's] failure to take forceful action." Eisenhower repeated that he would not comment on a Supreme Court decision, then added that "I have regarded the Chief Justice as my personal friend for years." [29]

The Justice Department, meanwhile, wanted to strengthen legislation to get more Negroes on the voting rolls. This was an area in which the President was unequivocal; he thought it a national disgrace that citizens were denied the right to vote on the basis of their color, and said so privately to his southern friends on many occasions. But he had little faith in new legislation, although he was willing to consider a revision of the 1957 Civil Rights Act. In February 1959, Lyndon Johnson paid a call to offer to submit with Dirksen a bill that would strengthen the voting and registration sections of the act. The staff warned Eisenhower that Johnson was "completely untrustworthy," but the President felt that "he had to live with Johnson," who was less extreme than most southern senators. Russell of Georgia, for example, was going around calling Attorney General William Rogers (who was attempting to enforce the 1957 act) a "hydra-headed monster." When Eisenhower reported that to Rogers, Rogers replied that "that was nothing compared with what Johnson was saying about the President" behind his back.[30] As Rogers had feared, no new legislation was forthcoming, and Jim Crow continued his dominance of the South.

In late 1958, Montgomery's memoirs were published. Eisenhower had had an advance look at some sections, and read other excerpts in the newspapers. He told Harry Butcher that "they convinced me that it was a waste of time to read it if I was looking for anything constructive." Consequently, "I have never even opened Monty's book."[31] But he could not escape it so easily, because of Monty's claims. The field marshal contended that he could have won the war before Christmas of 1944, if only Eisenhower had allowed him to make his single thrust across the Rhine. Eisenhower, who had taken so much from Monty, was absolutely incensed. No one had ever made him so furious—not de Gaulle, not McCarthy, not Khrushchev, not Faubus, no one. So angry was he that on January 1, 1959, he sent an identical letter to the top dozen of his British and American subordinates during the war, proposing that they all get together at Camp David for seven to ten days, without wives, in order to exchange information and to "develop an agreed document concerning incidents which are a part of their individual or collective experiences." He had in mind several of Monty's claims—that he had always intended to break out on the right in Normandy, not at Caen; that he won the Battle of the Bulge for the Americans; that his single thrust would have won the war earlier; that he could have taken Berlin if only Ike had let him.

So incensed was Eisenhower that he seriously proposed to take ten days out of his life to devote to a history of the Second World War at a time when he was President of the United States. The men he wanted to help him were all engaged in their own large affairs and weighed down by heavy responsibilities. In the end, Eisenhower reluctantly dropped the idea of a full-blast rebuttal of Monty.[32]

He did write privately to his British friends at length about his reaction. He told Pug Ismay, for example, that "so far as Monty's book is concerned, my opinion is probably so much lower than yours that I would not like to express it, even in a letter." He then went on to say exactly what he thought in a three-page letter. Monty, he said, "would scarcely stand much chance of going down in history as one of the great British captains. Alexander was much the abler. He was also modest." Then Eisenhower went through his list of charges against Monty: the delay in Sicily; the slow-motion campaign in Italy; the failure to take Caen; the lie about his plans for the Normandy break-out; the "preposterous proposal to drive on a single pencil-line thrust straight on to Berlin"; the failure at Arnhem "even after I had prom-ised and given to him everything he requested." Further, "I cannot forget his readiness to belittle associates in those critical moments when the cooperation of all of us was needed."[33]

Eisenhower feared that the furor about Monty's memoirs might strain relations with the British, so he was delighted when he was asked, on January 14 at the National Press Club, to comment on his associations with Churchill during the war. Eisenhower began posi-tively enough, calling Churchill a great man and praising him to an almost embarrassing degree. But he could not resist the opportunity to refute Montgomery's claim that he could have won the war in December 1944. Eisenhower reminded the reporters that the British had always been hesitant about Overlord, because of their memories of World War I. Indeed, the British "could not stand the idea of starting another operation like [Passchendaele] by invading northern France." The Americans nevertheless insisted on invading. Eisenhower quoted Churchill's forebodings: "The tides will flow red with the blood of American and British youths and the beaches will be choked with their bodies," the Prime Minister had said. Still Eisenhower insisted on going.

On the eve of the invasion, Eisenhower continued, Churchill, Roosevelt, and others were predicting victory within two years. Churchill told Eisenhower that if the allies were able to capture Paris by Christmas 1944, "it would be known in history as the greatest of military operations of all time up to that moment." But in fact, under Eisenhower's command, the allies got up to the German border before Christmas, "and if the Germans had any sense they would [have] surrender[ed] then." But although they fought on, nevertheless the final victory was achieved eleven months after D-Day, not the two years that had been predicted. "From that moment," Eisenhower noted, "there became many, many critics who showed how much more quickly it could have been won, and possibly it could have been." But, he concluded, "The only answer I can give you is we won." The reporters, Americans all, jumped to their feet and gave the President a sustained round of applause.[34]

Shortly thereafter, Churchill paid his last visit to the United States. Eisenhower entertained him at a formal state dinner. Ellis Slater commented on how "very feeble" Churchill was. The former Prime Minister leaned heavily on Eisenhower's arm as they went into dinner. Slater "almost wished he hadn't come and had been remembered as a virile man," and another guest remarked, "You know it's possible to live too long."[35]

Eisenhower himself was sixty-eight years old, and was very conscious of his age and of his health. In January of 1959, when his friend Aksel Nielsen of Colorado had a stroke, Eisenhower wrote a letter of advice that also described his own routine: "I believe that if you will reach home at least forty-five minutes before luncheon, go immediately to bed and refuse to read any letters, memoranda, or books, that you will be astonished how much the practice will finally mean to you. The effort to make your mind a blank—to refuse to think—is not an easy one. But a measure of success can finally be attained. As a consequence you will be astonished to find that in a rest period such as that, you will frequently fall asleep and have a good nap of a quarter or half hour."[36]

Eisenhower could not enjoy such enviable equanimity when he had Monty on his mind. Shortly after Churchill's visit, Monty gave a highly publicized television interview in which he repeated that he could have won the war earlier if only Ike had let him. Then Monty had the gall to ask, through Freddie de Guingand, if Eisenhower would be his host on a visit to the United States. In a carefully worded reply to Freddie, Eisenhower said, "It would likely be bad judgment, at this particular time, for Monty to make any attempt to visit me." He assured de Guingand that "my feeling is merely one of disappointment, not of rancor . . ." Churchill had remarked upon it, Eisenhower said, when he noticed that Monty's picture still occupied the same place in Eisenhower's living quarters of the White House. But despite the portrait and the disclaimer of rancor, Eisenhower told de Guingand that any attempt to open a correspondence between himself and Monty "could not be very helpful . . . I feel that if the matter is to be healed in any way, that time will have to be relied on as the healer."[37]

A second wartime ally who was making it difficult for Eisenhower to take a comfortable nap before lunch was Charles de Gaulle. He was proceeding with French nuclear development, and insisting on an independent role for France, much to Washington's displeasure. In December of 1958, Foster Dulles told Eisenhower that "de Gaulle is becoming increasingly troublesome." Eisenhower offered the warning that "de Gaulle is capable of the most extraordinary actions . . . watch out for him."[38] A few days later Dulles flew to Paris for a NATO meeting where de Gaulle argued that either France participate as an equal partner in America's global decisions or France would cease its military participation in NATO. Eisenhower wired a weary Dulles, expressing his sympathy for the frustration Dulles felt, and adding, "It does seem that our friend should cease insisting upon attempting to control the whole world, of course, with partners, even before he had gotten France itself in good order."[39]

A third wartime ally to cause trouble was Russia. On November 10, 1958, Khrushchev announced his intention of signing at an early date a peace treaty with East Germany. According to Khrushchev, that action would have the effect of terminating Allied rights in West Berlin. According to the Allies, it would do nothing of the sort, as the British-French-American right to be in Berlin rested on the wartime agreements at Yalta and had nothing to do with the East Germans, whose regime the Allies did not recognize. Khrushchev did not threaten drastic action, such as the 1948 blockade of Berlin; instead he called on the Western powers to begin negotiations with the East Germans, looking to a complete withdrawal of all foreign forces from the city. Four days later, Soviet troops began harassing American Army truck convoys on the *Autobahn*. On November 27, Eisenhower was in Augusta when his son brought down to him a summary of State, CIA, and JCS reports. Eisenhower was astonished to read that French Foreign Minister Couve de Murville and Macmillan thought some kind of "low level" recognition of the East German government was preferable to risking war. He called Foster Dulles, who assured him that Macmillan at least was not ready to do so. Dulles also said a wire had come in from Moscow that seemed to portend a willingness to compromise. Khrushchev said that there would be no change in the status of Berlin during the next six months, but during that time, negotiations should take place. The Soviets, for their part, proposed making Berlin a free city under United Nations auspices.

Eisenhower said he would be willing to discuss free-city status for Berlin, *if* it included all of Berlin, East and West, and the access routes were under the jurisdiction of the United Nations. Eisenhower also indicated "that somewhere along the line we have to find a way to say that we are going to do what we want to do," which was to stay in Berlin. Eisenhower told Dulles "that he had been worrying late at night as to what the eventual fate of Berlin would be." He said that when Berlin was divided in 1945, he was against it and "had done his best to make the Americans and British see what a trouble the thing was going to be—but that the political leaders, naming Roosevelt and Churchill, had said, 'Oh, we can get along with Uncle Joe.' He said at the time he knew better and that everything he had feared had come to pass." Finally, the President told Dulles to get together with the Foreign Ministers of France, Britain, and West Germany to compose an answer to Khrushchev. Then he mused, he "wouldn't mind asking Adenauer now exactly what does he see as the way to get along . . . He said he would like to say to Adenauer that he has got to increase his Army and devote more of his revenues to it."[40]

Two weeks later, at a December 12 meeting in the Oval Office, Dulles told Eisenhower that West Germany was making real progress in building its forces. Although it had gotten off to a slow start, it had created eight active divisions and would have four more within a year. Dulles also reminded the President that Germany was restricted, by NATO agreement, to twelve divisions, and that the creation of the twenty divisions Eisenhower wanted would scare the French. "The President retorted that he would be glad to scare them; maybe that would have an effect on French pretentions at being a world power."[41]

As to Berlin itself, Eisenhower was sure Khrushchev was bluffing, that he would back down rather than match Eisenhower's bet. "In this gamble," Eisenhower told his advisers, "we are not going to be betting white chips, building up the pot gradually and fearfully. Khrushchev should know that when we decide to act, our whole stack will be in the pot." In January, the JCS told Eisenhower that if Khrushchev actually tried to close down the *Autobahn,* they wanted to go into action on the first day with an entire division. Eisenhower patiently explained to them just how foolish that would be. A single division was far too weak to fight its way through to Berlin against serious opposition, yet far too strong for a mere show of force. A division would force the Soviets to "put up or shut up" and thus back them into a corner from which the only way out was war. Further, if the NATO powers used force to open a route, could they supply the manpower to keep a 110-mile-long road open? What Eisenhower wanted, in the event of an attempted blockade, was a probe, not a war, and he ordered the JCS to get a much smaller unit ready.[42]

In late January, John Eisenhower gathered together for his father information on the supply situation in Berlin. It was good; Berlin could hold on for at least two months without supplies.[43] That gave Eisenhower some needed room for maneuver. On February 3, he met with Dulles, who was about to depart for London, Paris, and Bonn to attempt to reach an accord with the Allies. What Dulles was most afraid of was that the Allies would want to hold a summit meeting, something Dulles—like Eisenhower—wanted to avoid at almost any cost. But during his trip, Dulles found that the pressure for a summit meeting was irresistible, and he so reported to the President when he returned. In order to put it off for as long as possible, and to prepare for some meaningful discussions, the Americans then proposed a meeting in Geneva of the Foreign Ministers of the U.S.S.R., France, Great Britain, and the United States. It could be followed by a summit meeting. The Russians, meanwhile, were giving hints of a possible postponement of the Berlin deadline, and Khrushchev invited Eisenhower to make a visit to the Soviet Union, saying he would be received with "heartfelt hospitality."[44] With test-ban talks going on in Geneva, Foreign Ministers' meetings and possibly a summit conference coming up, and with Khrushchev suddenly opting to reduce tensions, some early improvement in the atmosphere of the Cold War seemed possible.

Since 1954 and the CIA-supported overthrow of the Arbenz government in Guatemala, the United States had more or less ignored Latin America, as Eisenhower and Dulles concentrated on Europe, the Middle East, and Asia. The Administration, and especially its expert on Latin America, Milton Eisenhower, had called for more economic assistance to the area, but obtaining funds from Congress was difficult at best, and little was accomplished. As always, Latin radicals blamed Uncle Sam for the widespread poverty and discontent; as always, the United States ignored the agitation so long as it did not threaten to actually overthrow a pro-American government.

It was in Cuba, one of the most prosperous of the Spanish-speaking countries, that the policy fell apart. There Fidel Castro was leading a revolt against the corrupt and reactionary dictator, Fulgencio Batista. Batista had an odious record; Castro was young, romantic, dynamic, and full of promises about free elections, social reform, new schools, and economic justice. Popular opinion in the United States could not resist Fidel's appeal. Eisenhower was not so sure, but he did refuse to support Batista—American policy was to deny arms to both sides in the Cuban struggle.

On December 23, 1958, Christian Herter sent Eisenhower a State Department memorandum on the situation in Cuba. Herter said that "the Communists are utilizing the Castro movement to some extent, as would be expected, but there is insufficient evidence on which to base a charge that the rebels are Communist-dominated," as Batista was claiming. Herter noted that Batista had managed to alienate as much as 80 percent of the Cuban people. Widely publicized "elections" in November had been a fraud, Herter continued, and the press, both in the United States and in the Spanish-speaking countries, was overwhelmingly anti-Batista. Herter ended with a policy statement: "The Department has concluded that any solution in Cuba requires that Batista must relinquish power . . . He probably should also leave the country."[45]

On the day Herter wrote his memo, however, Allen Dulles gave a briefing to the NSC that undercut the State Department position. "Communists and other extreme radicals appear to have penetrated the Castro movement," Allen Dulles pronounced. "If Castro takes over, they will probably participate in the government." Eisenhower was much provoked by the discrepancy in the two conclusions. In his memoirs, he claimed that this was the "first time" he had heard of possible Communist penetration of the Castro movement (which could hardly have been the case, as the press was filled with speculation about the subject). At the NSC, Eisenhower commented that although Goodpaster and John Eisenhower kept him "well informed as to intelligence reports, he had not known until [now] that the view of the U.S. government was that of wishing to oppose Fidel Castro in any event. He then said that he felt the situation had been allowed to slip somewhat." Eisenhower refused, however, to accept a recommendation that the United States support Batista as the lesser of two evils. He said that if Castro turned out "to be as bad as our intelligence now suggested, our only hope, if any, lay with some kind of nondictatorial 'third force,' neither Castroite nor Batistiano."[46] Thus began the search that ultimately came a cropper at the Bay of Pigs in 1961.

On New Year's Day of 1959, Batista fled Cuba as Fidel entered Havana in triumph. The United States joined other American countries in recognizing the regime. Castro appointed Cuban liberals to the top posts in his new government, a cause for hope in Washington, but in mid-January he made the Communist Party legal in Cuba, and by the end of the month his first Premier had resigned in protest over the executions of Batista supporters and the increasingly anti-American quality of Castro's speeches. On February 13, Castro himself became Premier, and in the ensuing weeks the executions and the attacks on the United States mounted. On the last day of February, Castro announced that he was postponing, for two years, the promised elections, and Allen Dulles reported to Eisenhower that "the Castro regime is moving toward a complete dictatorship. Communists are now operating openly and legally in Cuba. And though Castro's government is *not* Communist-dominated, Communists have worked their way into the labor unions, the armed forces, and other organizations."[47]

The classic American response to radicalism in Latin America was to send in the Marines, an option that Eisenhower would not even consider, because of Castro's popularity not only in Cuba but throughout Latin America and even within the United States, and because of the probable effect of such action on world public opinion. In any event, the CIA gave him an alternative to the Marines.

Under Allen Dulles' direction, and with Eisenhower's encouragement, the CIA had been conducting covert operations around the world. None were as successful or spectacular as Iran in 1953 and Guatemala in 1954, and some—for example, Hungary in 1956—had been disastrous failures. Nevertheless, covert operations remained one of Eisenhower's chief weapons in the Cold War. His problem was one that confronts every head of government in such situations—how to control the supersecret operations. In 1955, Eisenhower had created a special oversight group called the 5412 Committee, because it was chartered in an NSC Paper, Number 5412. The 5412 group consisted of the Under Secretary of State, the Deputy Secretary of Defense, the National Security Adviser (Gordon Gray), and the Director of Central Intelligence, Allen Dulles. In theory, no covert operation could take place without prior approval from 5412. The major function of the group, according to Gray, was "to protect the President." It would scrutinize proposed CIA actions, policies, and programs to make certain they did not get the President or the country in trouble. It reported directly, and only, to the President, who told Gray flatly "that he did not wish the specifics of covert operations to be presented to the NSC."[48]

The difficulty was that the CIA had become so accustomed to

secrecy, and to having its own way, that it was not even reporting its actions to 5412. On January 19, 1959, Gray wrote a memorandum on the problem. He had just attended a 5412 meeting at which Allen Dulles had given a briefing on covert activities over the past six months. Gray complained that all but a handful had never been cleared by 5412. In other words, Allen Dulles was acting, then informing, rather than seeking prior approval. "We need a better understanding of the mission of the Group (5412)," Gray wrote. "It is also clear to me that the criteria with respect to what matters shall come before the Group are ill-defined and fuzzy." Gray thought that the President wanted 5412 to exercise some initiative, but "as long as I have been a member there has been practically none of this." He suggested, for a start, that 5412 direct the CIA to begin organizing youth and student organizations in Latin America in order to counter Fidel's appeal. This was done, as CIA agent Howard Hunt in Mexico City, and other agents elsewhere, began organizing students along the lines of Gray's suggestion.[49]

On January 29, Eisenhower met with Gray, Goodpaster, Allen Dulles, and John Eisenhower to discuss 5412. He covered most of the points Gray had already touched upon, then ordered that "he wished no records kept of 5412 meetings except in the office of the Director of Central Intelligence." He also declared that "covert activities could be carried on only under his responsibility," and that he therefore "wished to be kept adequately informed." He thought this could be done through oral reports from Gordon Gray. When Allen Dulles asked if he should keep the JCS informed, Eisenhower indicated that such an action was not necessary. Thus, in theory at least, CIA covert actions would be known only to the agents themselves, the 5412 people, and the President.[50] The trick now was to find a way to use the CIA capabilities to get rid of Fidel.

Foster Dulles and his department were getting to be almost as difficult to deal with as Allen Dulles and his people. On November 10, 1958, Whitman complained in her diary that "the State Department regards the President as its chattel." Her specific complaints were minor but irritating. Dulles had talked the President out of going to Seattle on a Sunday night for a Monday speech, "frankly because the Secretary wanted the President's suite at the Olympic Hotel." State would not release a copy of the speech until Dulles had approved it, although Hagerty insisted that the President's approval was sufficient. When the presidential party arrived in Seattle, there "were no seats for the White House staff" although State Department flunkies "sat gaily in the second row." Whitman found it all disagreeable.[51]

Far more serious was the state of Dulles' health. He was seventy years old, had been operated on for cancer, and despite some post-operation improvement, he was exhausted. Just before leaving for Seattle, Dulles had had a checkup at the hospital—Eisenhower was so impatient to have the results that he personally telephoned the hospital—which reported that except for some diverticulitis, Dulles was doing as well as could be expected. Dulles nevertheless again offered to resign. According to his notes on his private meeting with the President, Eisenhower "said he hoped very much that I would be willing to stay on . . . He said he had often thought as to whom he could find to take my place if I were unable to carry on and he could not come up with any satisfactory substitute . . . He hoped that the two of us could stay on working together until the end of his term." Dulles said he would be glad to try.[52]

Three weeks later, Dulles was back in Walter Reed with pains in his colon. The cancer had returned and surgery was indicated. Whitman commented that "my hunch is that this may be finis for Dulles as Secretary of State."[53] Still Dulles carried on, flying to Europe to consult with the Allies in early February. When he returned, on February 9, he could postpone treatment no longer. He requested a leave of absence so that he could have an operation and a period of a few weeks for recuperation, during which time he said he "could concentrate on the complicated and grave problems raised by the Soviet threats regarding Berlin and the Allied response thereto."[54] Eisenhower granted the request, naming Herter as Acting Secretary. At a news conference the following day, Eisenhower spoke with typical praise of Dulles: "I believe he is the most valuable man in foreign affairs that I have ever known . . . His performance over six years has been remarkable, a brilliant one, and I think it's almost a miracle that he hasn't had to go for a longer period of rest and healing than he is now undergoing."[55]

Four days later, on February 14, Eisenhower paid a visit to Dulles in Walter Reed. Whitman recorded his reaction: "Obviously he is hard hit by the business about Dulles. He said that if he accepted his resignation, however, he doubted if Dulles would live for more than a few weeks." Eisenhower cited the instance of "another man in government who knows that he has an incurable disease, but he is going about his job cheerfully and well and it is far better for him and for the government too. Mostly the President does not dwell on death and, indeed, I have seen him rarely shaken by the death, or thought of death, of any of his closest friends." But in Dulles' case, Eisenhower said that "it seems so wrong somehow that a man who has given of himself as has Dulles must die in such a painful fashion, held up every moment to the world's prying eyes. Somehow it makes you wonder why and whether it is all worth it." Sadly, the doctors had given up the thought of yet another operation and were resorting to radiation treatment.[56]

With Dulles in the hospital, Gordon Gray, always an organization man, urged the President to change his habits and begin making his policy decisions in NSC meetings, rather than in private meetings with two or three others, or over late-afternoon cocktails with Dulles alone. Eisenhower demurred. The NSC was too big, too cumbersome. Eisenhower used it to announce his decisions, not to explore possibilities. The same was true of his meetings with the Republican leaders and with his Cabinet. His bright hopes at the beginning of his first term for building a "team" with his Cabinet and party leaders had long since disappeared. With the departure of the Cabinet members he respected most—Humphrey, Brownell, and now Dulles, as well as the outspoken Wilson—Eisenhower's Cabinet meetings became less frequent, more general and vague, and boring. The legislative leaders' meetings were worse. Despite Eisenhower's best efforts, his attempt to build an Administration along the lines of SHAEF and SHAPE had failed. The American government was simply too big and represented too many divergent interests to be made into a team. Eisenhower therefore increasingly made his decisions in the privacy of the Oval Office, ordinarily with only the two or three top officials (usually the Secretary of State, or of Defense, or the chairman of the JCS, and always Goodpaster) present to give him advice. What he primarily wanted from his advisers was information, a succinct expression of what his options were. That was one reason Goodpaster (and after 1958 and to a lesser extent John Eisenhower) was so invaluable to him; Goodpaster had the information and knew how to present it the way the President wanted it. Eisenhower rightly thought of Goodpaster as more intelligent, and better informed, than even Allen Dulles.

Thus when Gray suggested that Eisenhower rely more heavily on NSC deliberations, in view of Foster Dulles' condition, Eisenhower rejected the suggestion out of hand. He said he wanted to discuss issues with Herter, McElroy, Twining, Killian, Goodpaster, and John Eisenhower, then inform the NSC of his decisions. Gray protested that at least Allen Dulles should be brought into the discussions; Eisenhower responded that "Goodpaster's presence would suffice," and as to Allen Dulles, "he saw no necessity for his attendance."[57]

So, contrary to the popular image, so assiduously cultivated by the Democrats, that Ike was a part-time President who played golf while his staff and committees made the decisions, Eisenhower kept all the power in his own hands. Whatever response America made to Khrushchev's threats over Berlin, or to the dangers of Castro in Cuba, would be Eisenhower's response, no one else's.

CHAPTER TWENTY-TWO

A Revival

February–June 1959

FOLLOWING THE DISAPPOINTMENTS and frustrations of 1958—the worst year of his life, Eisenhower called it—he rallied, took command, and led his people with all the instincts of the good steward. Soon columnists were talking about a "new" Eisenhower, a man who asserted himself more powerfully than he had ever done before.[1]

The most dramatic expression of Eisenhower's rally from his 1958 experiences was his handling of the Berlin situation, which was masterful throughout. A major characteristic of his diplomacy was his openness, his willingness to be conciliatory, his refusal to treat the situation as a crisis, and most of all his exercise of command and power. He would not be stampeded, despite—as will be seen—intense pressure. His insistence on a calm, measured, low-key approach was based on a principle that he explained to congressional leaders, who were demanding more action. As John Eisenhower recorded it, "The President pointed out the phrase in the Declaration of Independence which stated as one of the human rights, that of the pursuit of happiness. The President applies this to the present situation by stating that we should not worry the public unnecessarily."[2]

In addition to his Berlin management, the "new" Eisenhower was noticeably friendlier toward the Soviets, more willing to see issues from their point of view, more willing to take some risks to achieve a first step toward a test ban, more willing to consider a summit meeting, than he had ever been before. Some observers attributed this development to the absence of Foster Dulles, but that was only partly true at best. A number of factors had come together by February 1959, when Dulles took his leave of absence, that were pushing Eisenhower toward a summit and some form of accommodation with the Soviets.

First of all, after November 4, 1958, he had his last election behind him. The next one belonged to Nixon. This put Nixon in the awkward position of having to be simultaneously a loyal member of the Administration, a supplicant, and his own man. It put Eisenhower in the worrisome position of realizing that in two years he would have to hand over the Presidency to Nixon—or, worse, the Democrats. Were the opposition to take charge, Eisenhower anticipated an orgy of spending on defense and on social programs combined with a tax cut—a prospect he regarded with horror.

Nor could he regard a Nixon succession with optimism. After six years of a standoffish relationship, Eisenhower remained ambiguous about Nixon. He did not doubt the man's loyalty, or honesty, or even ability, but he did worry about Nixon's ambition. On June 11, Whitman recorded in her diary that Eisenhower had breakfast with Nixon. The Vice-President asked the President if he would take some of Nixon's friends—all rich men, potential contributors—for a weekend on a Navy yacht and play some golf with them at Quantico. Eisenhower, who prided himself on not mixing politics and his social life (although of course he did), flatly refused. Later, the President told Whitman, "It is terrible when people get politically ambitious."[3]

One difficulty for the relationship was the difference in their ages. Eisenhower, born in the nineteenth century, saw things differently from Nixon. Nixon's emphasis was on what had been lost, Eisenhower's on what had been gained. At a Republican leaders' meeting, when the discussion was about a tax exemption for tuition payments to private schools, Nixon declared that "what's involved is the whole erosion of the middle class." He pointed to Britain as an example of the leveling that could take place, and said that in America "the very wealthy do very well, but the middle class is sinking." Eisenhower contradicted him. The President said the middle class had not disappeared, but the proletariat had. The laboring man had become middle class, and was sending his sons to college. Nixon wanted to speak for what he regarded as a dispossessed middle class, for the professional and small-business man who resented the advances of the working class. Eisenhower wanted to deny the existence of any class differences at all.[4] At a news conference, in response to a question on organized labor, Eisenhower said he was "disturbed by what seems to be becoming habit in this country, to adopt certain theories that Marx advanced. One is that there is inevitably a bitter and implacable warfare between the man that works and the man that hires him. To my mind this is absolutely and completely un-American." [5]

Another problem in their relationship was that Nixon wanted to do more, be more visible, shoulder more responsibilities, but Eisenhower would not let him.[6] What really made a close relationship impossible, however, was the nature of their concerns. Nixon's position forced him to concentrate all his attention and energies on the 1960 election; Eisenhower's position forced him to concentrate all his attention and energies on what he could accomplish in the next two years. The irony was that Nixon had to make his decisions on a short-term basis of the election, while Eisenhower's short time remaining led him to make his decisions on the basis of long-term considerations. Nixon's goal was votes. Eisenhower's goals were peace, a test ban, disarmament, reconciliation.

But whatever Eisenhower's reservations about Nixon, he hoped to be turning the government over to him. He doubted that Nixon, as President, could achieve what he might be able to achieve in 1959 and 1960. He therefore set himself to the task of bringing peace to the world as his last act of statesmanship.

In striving for a genuine peace, Eisenhower not only had to reach out to the Russians, but simultaneously to hold back his own JCS. On February 12, after an NSC meeting, Twining, McElroy, and Quarles stayed behind to talk to the President. They wanted to discuss the U-2. The President had been allowing only a small percentage of the flights that the JCS wanted to carry out; now the Defense people had a new argument for a more liberal policy on flights. McElroy pointed out that Symington and the other critical Democratic senators took as their starting point inadequate American intelligence. No matter how often Eisenhower had Allen Dulles give a briefing to one of the Democrats, the critics would never believe Dulles' reassurances about the missile gap unless Dulles produced some hard information. McElroy wanted to show them additional photographs, and he wanted more overflights to get the pictures.

Eisenhower demurred. He thought that reconnaissance satellites were "coming along nicely." He wanted U-2 flights "held to a minimum pending the availability of this new equipment." Quarles said the satellites would not be ready for eighteen months to two years. Eisenhower replied that he was not swayed by that argument, because he doubted Soviet ability to build a first-strike force of ICBMs in the near future. McElroy disagreed, citing latest estimates. Eisenhower reminded him that four years ago the CIA estimate was that by 1959 the Russians would have a huge bomber force, but "as it turned out, the threat has been far less than had been initially estimated."

Then the President handed down his decision. He said that the U-2 flights constituted "undue provocation." He added, "Nothing would make him request authority to declare war more quickly than violation of our airspace by Soviet aircraft." (A remarkable statement by a man who since 1956 had been sending U-2 flights over the Soviet Union.) Twining countered that "the Soviets have never fired a missile at one of our reconnaissance aircraft." McElroy and Quarles insisted that more flights were critically necessary. Eisenhower backed down a bit; he said that "while one or two flights might possibly be permissible he is against an extensive program." As the delegation was leaving, Eisenhower reminded his advisers of "the close relationship between these reconnaissance programs and the crisis which is impending over Berlin," and told them again that he did not want to be provocative.[7]

But he also did not want to make it possible for Symington and the others to continue to cry "missile gap," and the U-2 was his best way to disprove the charge. Symington's friends among lower-level officials in DOD and the CIA were feeding him information based on partial information that did not include the U-2 photographs (which showed that the Soviets were *not* building ICBMs on a crash basis). At a meeting with the PSAC, Eisenhower commented "on the way irresponsible officials and demagogues are leaking security information and presenting a misleading picture of our security situation to our people. Some of our senators in particular seem to be doing this. In turn," Eisenhower complained, "the munitions makers are making tremendous efforts toward getting more contracts and in fact seem to be exerting undue influence over the senators." He specifically noted that Symington was often seen in deep discussion with the vice-president of Convair.[8]

So, in order to disprove the missile gap, the U-2s had to fly; but to fly the U-2 was to be provocative at a time when the President wanted to be conciliatory. In the early spring of 1959, Eisenhower authorized two or three flights, then changed his mind. On April 11, he called in McElroy and Richard Bissell, the CIA official who was in charge of the U-2 program, "to tell them that he had decided not to go ahead with certain reconnaissance flights for which he had given tentative approval the preceding day." He said he wanted to give them his reasoning. His first and fourth reasons were censored out of the Goodpaster memorandum on the meeting when, in 1981, the NSC and the CIA declassified portions of it. His second reason was that "there seems no hope for the future unless we can make some progress in negotiation." His third reason was, "We cannot in the present circumstances afford the revulsion of world opinion against the United States that might occur—the U.S. being the only nation that could conduct this activity." Summing up, the President said "he did not agree that this project would be worth the political costs."

McElroy and Bissell protested. Eisenhower agreed that there was a need for information, especially because of the "distortions several senators are making of our military position relative to that of the Soviets," but returned to his worry over "the terrible propaganda impact that would be occasioned if a reconnaissance plane were to fail." And he repeated his concern about timing, pointing out that it now appeared that Khrushchev was ready to meet at the summit to reduce tensions. McElroy then admitted that "it is far easier for Cabinet officers to recommend this activity than for the President to authorize it, and that he accepted the President's decision very willingly."[9] But of course he did not. Within a few days, DOD, the JCS, and the CIA were back, requesting more flights. In addition, the JCS were proposing to get more funds for themselves by cutting back on Eisenhower's favorite project, mutual security. It made the President angry. At a Republican leaders' meeting, he thundered that "I might have to relieve them all and appoint a new group."[10]

But of course Eisenhower could hardly dismiss all his top military commanders, as each of them had his own constituency and supporters in Congress and among the press and public. Among the JCS, Twining was the strongest Eisenhower supporter. He was less bellicose than Radford had been, less likely to urge the use of atomic weapons, and more inclined to accept Eisenhower's basic proposition, that a proper defense posture included a healthy economy and a balanced budget. In March 1959, the other Chiefs tried to use the Berlin situation to strengthen their forces and their appropriations. Twining came to the Oval Office and, with only John Eisenhower and his father present, warned the President that "some members of the JCS (Twining does not concur) fear that we are not going far enough in responding to the Berlin crisis. Some of the Chiefs have recommended actions which General Twining considers provocative." In addition, the

Chiefs were going to go before Congress and, while defending the over-all Defense budget, claim that they could not meet their own responsibilities without more money, and hint that mutual-security funds could be used to make up the difference.

Eisenhower told Twining to go back to the JCS and tell each man "that the military in this country is a tool and not a policy-making body; the Joint Chiefs are not responsible for high-level political decisions."[11]

By no means was the pressure to increase military spending limited to Symington or the JCS. There was a general impression around the country, one that was assiduously spread by the huge Pentagon propaganda machine, the arms industry, the Democrats, and columnists, that Eisenhower was underreacting to the Berlin crisis. There were serious demands, from serious people, that he order a general mobilization. Nor were the advocates of activism limited to the JCS or the opposition. C. D. Jackson was nearly beside himself with excitement. He bombarded (his own word) Allen Dulles with letters, one a week through the months-long crisis, full of specific suggestions on going over to the offensive. He wanted Dulles to stir up the satellites. "There is one thing that still haunts the Kremlin," he declared, "and that is a general uprising in the Eastern European satellite belt." Jackson wanted to go back to liberation, which he said "is not an ugly word; it is a good word; it is an American word; it is an unambiguous word. It is the one word the Kremlin fears." Stirring words, but not Eisenhower's policy, and he had Dulles send noncommittal replies.[12]

But although Eisenhower ignored him, Jackson nevertheless spoke for millions of Americans. The national mood, at least as it was being expressed in the halls of Congress and in the media, was impatient. People wanted to get moving again, to take the offensive in the Cold War, to stop reacting and start acting. Many were eager to shoot the way through to Berlin and teach the Soviets a lesson.

Eisenhower, however, thought much of this aggressiveness was artificially created, by the same forces that created an artificial demand for more missiles, bombers, and other weapons. "I'm getting awfully sick of the lobbies by the munitions," he told the Republican leaders. After looking at the advertisements Boeing and Douglas had published, Eisenhower said "you begin to see this thing isn't wholly the defense of the country, but only more money for some who are already fat cats." Eisenhower also thought, "This seems to be a hysteria that is largely political."[13] (Then he had to endure one hour of listening to

Congressman Jerry Ford arguing for a contract for a Michigan firm in the missile business.)

But whether artificially created or not, the popular impression that more had to be done ran very deep. As Eisenhower had feared would happen, people had become afraid, and in their fright their instinctive response was to strengthen their military. Although they trusted Ike, they were confused by his policies. He talked about being firm in Berlin, but simultaneously announced a cut of fifty thousand men from the armed services. Senator Fulbright spoke to the point at a March 8 meeting, when he "brought up the problem of his constituents. They asked him why we are cutting the Army. The Senator admits that . . . to him it looks strange." Eisenhower told Fulbright to go explain to his constituents the theory of deterrence and point out to them that the Administration was increasing the budget for ICBMs. "The President expressed wonder why human sense cannot keep up with human inventive ingenuity. Senator Fulbright hastily added that his constituents do not keep up. They do not understand ICBMs, but they do understand fifty thousand soldiers."

Senator Russell was also concerned about the reductions. He told Eisenhower that the mutual-security funds were "a most wasteful expenditure of money" and should be spent instead on keeping up America's defenses. Eisenhower shot back that "the U.S. military services are far more wasteful than our mutual-security program. Therefore, by Senator Russell's criterion, we should do away with our military forces." He said he was saving $250 million by reducing the troop strength, and asked Russell to "consider what that would do if spent on the Turk military." Scornfully, "The President stated that if we desire to abolish mutual security and to provide instead some eighty or ninety divisions, deployed around the Soviet Union, this course of action will solve our unemployment problem, but will ensure that we are a garrison state." [14]

As Khrushchev's May 27 deadline approached, a war-scare fever began to sweep the country, one reminiscent of those over the Far East in 1954 and 1955, only even more serious because this one pitted the United States directly against the Soviet Union, and the arsenals had quadrupled or more since 1954. More than any other individual, the man who held the Berlin crisis in check was Dwight Eisenhower. His was an absolutely bravo performance, a combination of a master diplomat, statesman, and politician at his best. He gave Khrushchev the room to retreat, he mollified his allies, he kept the JCS, C. D. Jackson, and the other hawks in check, he kept the risks at a minimum level, he satisfied the public that his response was appropriate, and he kept the Democrats from throwing billions of dollars to the DOD. His most basic strategy was to simply deny that there was a crisis. His most basic tool was patience, as he carefully explained, over and over, fundamental truths about the nuclear age.

Along the way, he seemed to be almost alone. Treasury Secretary Anderson, who hated spending money, consistently supported him, as did Twining and a few others. But Dulles was in the hospital, Herter was feeling his way into his responsibilities, McElroy was on the side of his JCS, and Eisenhower was generally on his own. Even the White House press corps, normally so friendly, turned on him, asking hostile and even insulting questions. On March 4, Merriman Smith wanted to know why, "against the background of continuing tension," SAC was not on an airborne alert. Eisenhower explained, "An air alert would be really worse than useless as defense against bombers. You would be much better to have your bombers on the ground." Well, then, John Scali wanted to know, what about Dean Acheson's suggestion that NATO go to full mobilization? Eisenhower gave another elementary lesson: "Now, did you ever stop to think what a general mobilization would mean in a time of tension? . . . Now, if you are going to keep a general mobilization for a long time in countries—democracies—such as ours, well, there is just one thing you have and that is a garrison state. General mobilizations . . . would be the most disastrous thing we could do."

Garnett Horner asked about McElroy's testimony that week before a congressional hearing; McElroy had hinted at launching an American first strike. Eisenhower replied with an admonishment: "I don't think we ought to be thinking all the time, every minute, that while we are sitting here, we are very apt to get a bombing attack on Washington." He did not even want to discuss an American first strike, he said, "because I believe we create more misapprehension than we do understanding." [15]

One week later, at his March 11 news conference, the hostile questioning continued. May Craig was the worst. She opened by instructing the President on the Constitution, then asked, "Where technically do you get the right to thwart the will of Congress, for instance in cutting the Army and the Marine Corps . . . or for not spending the money which they give you for missiles, submarine missiles, or whatever they be?" Other reporters also expressed their concern about the reduction in the size of the Army.

"What would you do with more ground forces in Europe?" Eisen-hower replied rhetorically. "Does anyone here have an idea? Would you start a ground war?" Speaking with great emphasis and deep emo-tion, he proclaimed: "We are certainly not going to fight a ground war in Europe. What good would it do to send a few more thousands or even a few divisions of troops to Europe?" Chalmers Roberts wanted to know if Eisenhower thought the American public was "sufficiently aware of the possibility of war in this situation?" Indeed, Eisenhower replied, he thought it was *too* aware. "What I decry is: let's not make everything such an hysterical sort of a proposition that we go a little bit off half-cocked." Then it was back to those fifty thousand troops— what if Congress forced him to take them? "Where will I put them?" Eisenhower asked in his turn. "Well, just some place where it's nice to keep them out of the way, because I don't know what else to do with them." Edward Folliard asked Eisenhower to comment on the wide-spread assumption that the Administration "puts a balanced budget ahead of national security." Suppose, Folliard said, there were more money in the budget—would Eisenhower then spend more on the military? Eisenhower replied, "I would say that I would not spend [such] money on the armed forces of the United States . . ."

Eisenhower's responses left the reporters frustrated. Peter Lisagor asked the last question, and he spoke for the others when he expressed his puzzlement. Lisagor quoted the President's previous remark about "nuclear war doesn't free anyone," noted that he had ruled out the possibility of a ground war in Central Europe, and wondered if there was "an in-between response that we could make." The questions gave Eisenhower an opportunity to use the news conference not only to calm the American people, but to send a message to the Soviets. "I didn't say that nuclear war is a complete impossibility," he replied to Lisagor's question. "I said it couldn't as I see it free anything. Destruc-tion is not a good police force. You don't throw hand grenades around streets to police the streets so that people won't be molested by thugs." But you just might use them if the Soviets blockaded Berlin.[16]

One of Eisenhower's major tasks was to calm people down. In March, on three separate occasions—to the JCS, to the Republican leaders, and to the Democratic leaders—he made the same point. As recorded by John Eisenhower at the JCS meeting, "The President then stressed the necessity to avoid overreacting. In so doing we give the Soviets ammunition. The President stressed the view that Khrushchev desires only to upset the United States. He expressed once again his view that we must address this problem in terms, not of six months, but of forty years." The Soviets would always attempt to keep America off balance, Eisenhower said. First, Berlin. Then Iraq. Next Iran. Wherever they could stir up trouble, they would, and "they would like us to go frantic every time they stir up difficulties in these areas."[17] The reason, as Eisenhower explained to the Republican and Democratic leaders, was that—as he claimed anyone who had ever read Lenin knew—"the Communist objective is to make us spend ourselves into bankruptcy." It was wrong to dramatize Berlin, he declared. "This is a continuous crisis . . . that the United States has to live with certainly as long as we are going to be here."[18] He dismissed liberation of Eastern Europe as an illusion, then explained what America's most realistic hope was: "The President went into our long-term policy of holding the line until the Soviets manage to educate their people. By so doing, they will sow the seeds of destruction of Communism as a virulent power. This will take a long time to settle."[19]

It was one of the oddities of the Cold War that each side expected the other to collapse as a result of its internal contradictions. Eisenhower believed deeply that in the end freedom would prevail, but he also recognized—indeed counted on—Khrushchev's equally firm belief that Communism would win. Thus he told his Cabinet on March 13, "There is good reason to believe that the Russians do not want war," because they felt they were winning already. This gave Eisenhower an opportunity to follow a policy of both conciliation and firmness.

The firmness came first. From the beginning, Eisenhower stressed that the United States was not going to abandon the people of West Berlin. He was ready to face the possible consequences of that stand. As he told the Cabinet, "The United States has to stand firm even should the situation come down to the last and ultimate decision, although neither I nor the State Department believe it will ever be allowed to go to that terrible climax. You should not think of this as the beginning of the end, but don't think it is possible to end tension by walking away from it."[20] In innumerable ways, the President conveyed that message to Khrushchev.

Then came the conciliation. It came hard, because at times even Eisenhower's patience ran out and he allowed himself to fantasize a bit about how he might stick it to those impossible Russians. He had no thought of bombing them into the Stone Age, but he did call Herter to ask for a "little study" of what the effects would be of breaking diplomatic relations with the Russians. Eisenhower enjoyed the thought immensely: "Throw out all the Russians in this country," he exclaimed. "Stop all trade . . . who would be hurt? There may be some other things. If we broke relations we could throw the Russians out of the U.N. and deny them visas." Herter interrupted the President's fantasy before he got too carried away by reminding him that "we have a freedom of access agreement in the U.N."[21]

Conciliation, not confrontation, was what Eisenhower wanted anyway, whatever his dreams. He let Khrushchev know that although he was standing firm, he was willing to negotiate Berlin's status. He made new concessions on a test ban, as will be seen, and tried in other ways to reach out to Khrushchev. But his most important act was the declaration of willingness to negotiate, and the hints that he would be willing to attend a summit. The act of negotiation would, in itself, be an agreement to Khrushchev's position that the situation in Berlin was abnormal. But then of course it was—Eisenhower was only admitting the truth—and Eisenhower was ready to discuss a free-city status, so long as the discussions also included reunification of Germany.

The President's proposed solution for this greatest of the outstanding problems left over from World War II, the division of Germany, was to hold nationwide free elections. The Soviets insisted on reunification through merger at the top. Adenauer's position was that reunification was his principal goal, and that no recognition of any sort of the East German regime was possible, but most observers, on both sides of the Iron Curtain, disbelieved him. Khrushchev once told Eisenhower categorically "that Adenauer's support of unification was nothing but a show . . . merely a ruse on Adenauer's part to stay in power."[22] Christian Herter told Eisenhower exactly the same thing. On April 4, over the telephone, Herter reported that Bonn was opposed to talking about free elections at any Foreign Ministers' or summit meeting, although Adenauer was not saying so publicly. "Herter said it was obvious that what Adenauer and the Christian Democrats were scared of was that in a reunified free election the opposition Socialist Party in West Germany would form a coalition with certain East German parties and throw the Christian Democrats out of office." Eisenhower's reply, at least for all those who believe in democracy, was perfect: "The President said if they get a true free unification, then they have to take their chances on politics."[23]

Conciliation included not only declaring a willingness to talk about Germany, but also some concessions on a test ban. These also came hard to Eisenhower, who in February was on the verge of breaking off the talks (currently in recess) in Geneva on a test ban because of the intransigence of the Russians on a veto that would make any inspection system worthless. At a February 18 meeting with Herter and Goodpaster, "The President said we should not tell anyone we are preparing to pull out. Instead we should say we believe negotiations are about to break down because of Soviet insistence on the veto." Eisenhower added that if no agreement on an inspection system could be reached, "he would rather handle the testing problem simply by making a unilateral statement" that the United States would hereafter refrain from testing in the atmosphere.[24]

But Eisenhower did not want to act unilaterally. He had come to a position of placing his hopes on a step-by-step approach to the disarmament problem rather than the all-or-nothing approach the United States had followed up to this time. He wanted an agreement, almost any kind of an agreement, that could serve to start the process of trust and accommodation. So, through February and March, he backed down from his insistence on a comprehensive, verifiable ban to one that sought to achieve something, anything positive.

On February 25, he told Killian and Goodpaster that he was losing his interest in on-site inspection teams. He thought that if the United States could detect explosions in the atmosphere, and large ones underground, "then the idea of teams . . . seems rather secondary in importance." A ban on only large underground and atmospheric tests could be monitored by a small number of instruments in fixed stations.[25]

The President's movement toward an accord with the Soviets was accelerated by a meeting he held on March 17 with the PSAC, Quarles, and Twining, called to discuss the missile program but quickly broadened into more general considerations. On missiles, it was Killian's sad duty to report that the ABM idea had not worked out. Accordingly, dispersal, hardening of airfields and ICBM sites, improved warning and reaction time "all seem more promising than active defense." Killian thought that "passive tactics were cheaper than active." John Eisenhower was keeping the notes, and did not record his father's reaction, if any. But Eisenhower must have thought to himself about all the arguments he had had over the years with Strauss and the AEC and the DOD about the need for testing. They had always cited the ABM possibilities as a major reason. All that money, wasted. All that fallout, created for nothing.

Killian and the DOD people went on to explain some of the costs involved in building a hardened ICBM force that would match the projected Russian force. Eisenhower protested that they were exaggerating Soviet missile production. "He added that if we ever get to the place where these missiles will rain down out of the skies on the United States, much of what we are planning will be useless anyhow." Undaunted, the advisers went on to talk about hardening B-52 airfields, and other measures, including building more nuclear weapons. Eisenhower interrupted to "comment again that when we begin talking of weapons up to certain very great figures, the discussion loses all meaning . . ."[26]

Eisenhower believed there could be no winner in an arms race. Even if it never came to war, the world would bankrupt itself if it did not first destroy itself through fallout. This last was getting to be a worrisome point with Eisenhower, who told Herter on March 20 that he had been doing some reading on strontium 90 and fallout effects, and was therefore "coming to the conclusion that our position should be that we will not test in the atmosphere." He instructed Herter that he would no longer insist on including underground or outer-space tests in a treaty. He explained, "My thinking is that we should go for a system which both sides agree will work," because if there were too many more atmospheric tests, the Northern Hemisphere might become uninhabitable.[27]

Accordingly, on April 13, the day the Geneva negotiations resumed, Eisenhower wrote Khrushchev, announcing that the United States no longer insisted on a comprehensive test ban, but would be willing to move "in phases, beginning with a prohibition of nuclear weapons' tests in the atmosphere." This would require only a simplified control system.[28] Khrushchev, although he denounced a partial test ban as "misleading," nevertheless indicated a willingness to talk, and the negotiations went on.

On a daily basis, Eisenhower was calling Dulles in the hospital to keep him informed of the test-ban progress, a cause to which Dulles had committed himself so strongly. In one of their last conversations, Eisenhower expressed his desire to halt the "terrific" arms race by at least stopping tests in the atmosphere. "In the long run," Eisenhower concluded, "there is nothing but war—if we give up all hope of a peaceful solution."[29]

Dulles' sinking was extremely painful for Eisenhower, made all the more so by the sniping of some Democrats. In late February, shortly after Dulles took his leave of absence, Democratic senators began attacking his policies and demanding his resignation. Eisenhower told the Republican leaders it just made him sick, that he had "heard nothing quite as cheap as this sudden personal attack." Dulles had once told James Reston that "I did not ask to be liked," but then neither had he asked to be kicked when he was down. Eisenhower reported that "he's very sensitive to some of these bitter attacks. He wonders if he is doing the right thing [by not resigning]. I tell him I'm the one to decide that." Still, even the Republicans wanted to know when he would step down. Eisenhower replied, "When Dulles says he can't do his best, he'll be out. When he feels like working, he'll be there."[30]

On March 20, Macmillan came to town for a visit. Along with Eisenhower, Macmillan made his first call on Dulles in Walter Reed. For an hour they talked. Dulles was his old self, warning against appeasement (which he suspected Macmillan of, as Macmillan had just returned from Moscow where he had joined in the call for a summit and seemed to indicate a readiness to back down on Berlin). Dulles said the United States was spending $40 billion per year on weapons; "if appeasement and partial surrender are to be our attitude," he continued, "we had better save our money."

After the visit, Eisenhower and Macmillan went to Camp David for talks. Macmillan informed him that Khrushchev, despite all his bombast and grandiloquent speeches, was willing to be conciliatory too. He had told Macmillan that the May 27 deadline on Berlin was in no sense an ultimatum. Facing an election, Macmillan was much more willing to commit to a summit than Eisenhower was; the President's position was that there should not be a summit unless and until the Foreign Ministers held a successful meeting. They eventually compromised by agreeing to a Foreign Ministers' meeting, to be followed by a summit if developments justified it.[31] On March 30, Khrushchev accepted that proposal. The Foreign Ministers' meeting would begin in Geneva on May 11.

Dulles, meanwhile, was failing to regain his strength or respond to treatment. On April 13, he talked to Eisenhower on the telephone, saying that he had drafted a letter of resignation. Eisenhower sadly decided that he "could not oppose what seemed inevitable." Dulles recommended Herter as his successor. Eisenhower said he had been thinking of Lodge, Anderson, or Allen Dulles. Foster Dulles held out for a promotion from inside. Eisenhower was worried about Herter's arthritis. Dulles said that if it were an appointment for a long term, he would not recommend Herter on the grounds of his health, but for the short time remaining he was much the best choice. Eisenhower agreed.[32] On April 18, the appointment was made.

Herter's first task was to prepare for the Geneva meeting. The issues were many: Berlin, the test ban, a limitation on the deployment of IRBMs in Germany, assurances against surprise attack, and the principles for a peace treaty with Germany. Given the size of the agenda, and the passion surrounding most of the issues, it was hardly surprising that no progress was made. Gromyko came in saying *"Nyet,"* and he kept saying it for the next three weeks. Eisenhower was close to breaking off the meeting in frustration, but Macmillan insisted on continuing to try.

On May 24, the end came for John Foster Dulles. Eisenhower's sense of loss and grief was personal and painful. Dulles had served him faithfully and tirelessly for six years. He had frequently disagreed with the President, especially in the early years over policy in the Far East, but he had always acceded to the President's judgment and carried out Eisenhower's policies with skill and enthusiasm. They were never personal friends in any social sense; Dulles did not play bridge or golf, or spend weekends with Eisenhower at Gettysburg or Augusta. But they had deep personal respect for each other, and they enjoyed working together, because they shared common assumptions about the nature of the Soviet threat and on the need to stand firm to meet it. In Eisenhower's judgment, Dulles was one of the greatest of Secretaries of State. That he could not convince others of that judgment was not for lack of trying.

One of the qualities of Dulles that Eisenhower appreciated most was his comprehensive knowledge. No matter what subject the President brought up, Dulles knew about it, had information and opinions to offer. This quality was best illustrated, albeit in a negative way, some months after Dulles' death in an incident that also showed how on top of things Eisenhower was. Herter was doing a satisfactory job as Secretary of State, but he just was not Dulles. Eisenhower called Herter on the telephone one afternoon to complain about the leaks from the State Department. As Whitman recorded it, "Herter was ineffectual, said he did not read the *Times* this morning . . . Then the President asked Herter about the Konlon report, and there was a dead silence—then Herter said he did not know what it was." Eisenhower informed him that it was a report from the Foreign Affairs Committee.[33] Dulles would have known, would have read it, just as he never missed reading the *Times*.

Dulles' death brought the Foreign Ministers to Washington for the funeral, which ironically was held on May 27—the original "deadline" date Khrushchev had set for Berlin. Before the funeral, Eisenhower asked the Foreign Ministers to the White House for lunch. The President explained to a protesting State Department aide that "what he had in mind was simply to ask them in and tell them that it is, in his judgment, ridiculous that the world is divided into segments facing each other in unending hostility. He felt that decent men should be able to find some way to make progress toward a better state of things."[34]

Later, Eisenhower made a diary entry on the luncheon. He said that Soviet Foreign Minister Gromyko "was personally agreeable, laughing frequently, and expressing the hope that real progress could be made. I told the group that I was personally anxious that such progress be accomplished, because only in this way could America agree to go to a summit meeting." Gromyko, to Eisenhower's surprise, did not disagree, even though it was well known that Khrushchev wanted a summit, whatever happened between the Foreign Ministers. Eisenhower decided that Gromyko's response was an indication of the "relatively minor position held by Gromyko in the Soviet system. In that system there is only one boss and Gromyko is nothing but an errand boy."[35]

When the talks in Geneva resumed, Gromyko was still saying Nyet, except about a summit, which he wanted. So did Macmillan. Eisenhower still insisted on progress by the Foreign Ministers first. The only concession Khrushchev was willing to make was to set another deadline, one year in the future, for the Allies to get out of Berlin. Later he changed it to a two-and-a-half-year deadline. Herter, on instructions from Eisenhower, refused to discuss any deadlines. Macmillan, ready to give up at Geneva, proposed an "informal" meeting of the heads of government. Eisenhower refused. He felt that if he surrendered to Khrushchev on this point, Khrushchev thereafter would regard him as a "pushover." But, unlike Macmillan, he did not want to break up the Foreign Ministers' meeting. Instead he proposed a recess. On June 20, the Foreign Ministers finally agreed on something—a three-week recess.[36]

Almost unnoticed in the publicity and hoopla surrounding the Foreign Ministers' deadlock was the fundamental outcome of the Berlin crisis of 1958–1959—that Eisenhower had gotten through it without increasing the defense budget, without war, and without backing down. The situation in Berlin was unchanged.

There were, of course, other foreign-policy issues to deal with in the spring of 1959. One was Castro. On the day Eisenhower informed

Herter that he was to become Secretary of State, Herter told Eisenhower that "he was sorry in a way that the President had missed meeting Castro." Fidel had come to the United States on April 17, on the invitation of the American Society of Newspaper Editors. ("I was more than irritated by the news of the invitation," Eisenhower commented.[37]) About a week later, Herter reported that Castro was "a most interesting individual, very much like a child in many ways, quite immature regarding problems of government, and puzzled and confused by some of the practical difficulties now facing him. In English he spoke with restraint and considerable personal appeal. In Spanish, however, he became voluble, excited, and somewhat 'wild.' " Herter said that Castro "made a plea for patience while his government tries to deal with the situation in Cuba."[38]

The day after Herter's report the CIA gave Eisenhower an evaluation of Castro's situation. Castro had said that Cuba would stay in the Western camp in the Cold War, but he was unconvincing. The CIA thought that there was a "probability" that the land reform Castro was insisting upon "may adversely affect certain American-owned properties in Cuba." The CIA charged that Castro "confuses the roar of mass audiences with the rule of the majority in his concept of democracy," and said it "would be a serious mistake to underestimate this man . . . He is clearly a strong personality and a born leader of great personal courage and conviction." The Agency admitted that "Castro remains an enigma," but thought there was still a possibility "of developing a constructive relationship with him and his government." Eisenhower scribbled by hand on the margin of the report, "File. We will check in a year!! D. E."[39]

And, of course, there were the perennial domestic and political problems. Protecting the budget against Democratic assaults took much of Eisenhower's time. He conducted one of his letter-writing blitzes to his friends, asking their support in holding back the big spenders, and he urged Republican leaders to stop any movement toward a tax cut. At one session, he said he wanted to tell a story "to see if I can get a smile here." The other morning, it seemed, a friend had come to the Oval Office to tell Eisenhower how terrible taxes were. He took out a piece of paper and the first thing he wrote down was $913,000, his income for 1958. Eisenhower said, "Stop right there. Anyone feeling sorry for himself who makes that kind of money . . ." The man shamefacedly admitted that Eisenhower was right.[40]

The one place Eisenhower was willing to spend money was on roads. At every Republican leaders' meeting that spring, he brought up the subject, stressing "the great need for catching up on the build-ing of roads." He said he wanted to stick to the original idea of finish-ing the Interstate System within thirteen years, and was appalled at the warnings that the program, which had gotten off to a fast start, would have to be stopped in its tracks because of insufficient financing. But costs were higher than anticipated, primarily because of the mas-sive expenditures required to build superhighways through congested urban areas. Either the gas tax had to be raised, or the pay-as-you-go principle abandoned, or the construction stopped. Eisenhower said he was willing to raise gasoline taxes to keep the program going, but the Republicans warned him that a tax increase was out of the question. To Eisenhower's great displeasure, highway construction slowed down.[41]

In holding down spending, other than on roads, Eisenhower re-lied increasingly on the southerners in the Senate. Ralph McGill, edi-tor of the Atlanta *Constitution* and a man Eisenhower respected, wrote to urge Eisenhower to use the talents of the senators from the South more frequently. Eisenhower replied that he was already doing so, except for Senators Olin Johnston, Thurmond, and Eastland, whom he placed in a "special group." Those three, he said, "reflect a viewpoint that is not only extreme but rigid. They seem so entrenched in their prejudices and racial antagonisms that they never show so much as a glimmer of a readiness to see the other side of the problem." Otherwise, he said, he relied heavily upon the southerners, and hoped to get even more benefits from them, because they had "great opportu-nities . . . to rise to real heights of statesmanship." Since their re-elections were practically guaranteed, they "need not worry too much about their political careers. If they should choose to use that ability with the single thought of promoting the *national* good, . . . they could become outstanding figures on the national scene, and in his-tory." He also wished they would break with the northern Democrats, but knew that they would not "when the prize of committee chairman-ships remains so glittering and tempting."

Turning to immediate problems, Eisenhower told McGill that while he believed wholeheartedly in equality before the law, he also believed just as strongly that "coercive law is powerless to bring about [integration] when in any extensive region the great mass of public opinion is in bitter opposition." He cited the carpet-bag governments of the Reconstruction era and the Volstead Act as proof. Progress would be made, he concluded, only through enlightenment, education, persuasion, and leadership example.[42]

In public, he took the same position. At a May 13 news conference, he was asked to comment on the fifth anniversary of the *Brown* decision. Eisenhower asserted his belief that the United States government, "if it is going to be true to its own founding documents, does have the job of working toward the time when there is no discrimination made on such inconsequential reason as race, color, or religion." But, he added, "Law is not going to do it. We have never stopped sin by passing laws; and in the same way, we are not going to take a great moral ideal and achieve it merely by law."[43]

Many Negro leaders were mumbling that Eisenhower was willing to risk nuclear war over the rights of the people of West Berlin but would do nothing about the rights of Negro American citizens. Their criticism, and the general coolness of the Negro community toward the Republican Administration, genuinely puzzled Eisenhower. He recalled that he had integrated the last of the armed forces' units, had integrated Washington, D.C., and the White House staff, had appointed Earl Warren, and had put through the 1957 Civil Rights Act. What more did the Negroes want? "It's a funny thing," Eisenhower told the Republican leaders. "There is no evidence that we have raised any votes with all we've done for the Negroes. The NAACP still fights us." Charlie Halleck gave his opinion: "I never did think there was any political hay in civil rights." Well, Eisenhower said, he was not really looking for votes anyway. He had helped the Negroes because "it is a matter of decency."[44]

Spring in Washington meant baseball. In May, Eisenhower took an afternoon off and together with Dr. Howard Snyder, George Allen, and his ten-year-old grandson, David, went to see the Senators play the Yankees. David knew every player's batting average and was already an expert on the finer points of the game, but unfortunately he had not inherited his grandfather's athletic ability, and was doomed to be a spectator, not a participant. He complained to Grandpa about how hard he had to work at sports, when the games came so easy to many of his friends.

With only a year and a half to go in office, Eisenhower's mind turned increasingly to retirement and death. He told Slater he could not decide how he wanted to arrange his retirement—whether to take the President's pension of $25,000 per year, with $50,000 in allowances, or go back to the Army as a five-star general, which would entitle him free of charge to the services of Colonel Schulz and Sergeants Dry and Moaney. He said he had gotten so accustomed to having those three around "it will be hard to get along without them." Together with the gang, Eisenhower and Mamie talked about their eventual burial spot. They considered Arlington, West Point, or Abilene. Eisenhower liked the idea of Abilene, where a private foundation had already raised the money to build an Eisenhower Museum and was arranging financing for an Eisenhower Library. The gang urged him to choose Gettysburg, on the grounds that it was closer to the major population centers and was already a major tourist site.[45]

In June 1959, Eisenhower had one of the greatest pleasures any grandfather can have—the grandchildren came to live with him. Not at the White House, but the next best thing, as Barbara and the children moved in at Gettysburg, while John took a room on the third floor of the White House. John went up to Gettysburg on weekends, his parents joining him whenever they could.[46]

Eisenhower needed the support of his family that June, because his southern friends let him down in the Senate and he suffered a blow that he described in his memoirs as "one of the most depressing official disappointments I experienced during eight years in the White House."[47] The issue was the confirmation of Lewis Strauss as Secretary of Commerce. Eisenhower had appointed Strauss to the position in October 1958, but confirmation hearings did not begin until March 1959, and they continued into May. Senator Clinton Anderson of New Mexico, a member of the congressional watchdog committee for the AEC, had frequently clashed with Strauss in the past, and now he led the fight against confirmation. Eisenhower was enraged by the bitter personal attacks made against Strauss (who in truth had few friends, especially in the Senate), and was still angry years later when he wrote his memoirs, where he gave over five full pages to refuting Anderson's charges.

When the vote finally came, on June 18, the Senate refused to confirm Strauss by a vote of 49 to 46. The next morning, Eisenhower told Whitman that "this was the most shameful thing that had happened in the U.S. Senate since the attempt to impeach a President many, many years ago." He put the blame on Lyndon Johnson, who had made it a party matter and instructed the Democrats to vote against confirmation. A number of Democrats, including Senators John Kennedy and Edmund Muskie, had promised to vote for Strauss, but capitulated to Johnson's pressure. Johnson himself, Eisenhower's aides felt, had nothing against Strauss personally, but he owed Anderson a favor, and Anderson had asked to have it paid off by opposing Strauss. Shaking his head, the President repeated, "This is the second most shameful day in Senate history."

Eisenhower was not above a little retaliation. He told Whitman he wanted to start an investigation of the 27.5 percent oil depletion allowance that had made the Texas oilmen, including Johnson and his supporters, so rich.[48] But it was an idle threat. Eisenhower was far too busy dealing with Khrushchev to be able to afford to devote time to Lyndon Johnson and the Texas millionaires.

Besides, he was beginning to lose a bit of enthusiasm and stamina. In April, he told Slater, "You know, one way I realize I'm not as young as I once was, is that I'm perfectly willing to have a big conference at ten in the morning—I even look forward to it—but the same situation faced at four in the afternoon finds me unhappy about the prospect."[49]

His mind stayed young. In late June, dictating a letter to Whitman, he used the sentence, "I doubt whether a man of my age changes his habits of thinking and of speech." Then he told her to cross out that sentence, and explained that "he had conscientiously tried to change his habits of speech. That since a child he had always thought faster than he could talk, which accounted for the fact that his tongue would 'run away with him' and he might not finish sentences, etc. Since his 'difficulty' of the last couple of years, he said he tried very hard to think before he would speak—to outsiders."[50]

CHAPTER TWENTY-THREE

Traveling for Peace

July–December 1959

IN THE SECOND HALF of 1959, with Adams, Foster Dulles, and so many others from the original team gone, and with Eisenhower adopting a more strenuous speaking and traveling schedule, talk of the "new" Eisenhower filled columns and editorials. Whitman noted angrily that in 1958 the reporters had been calling Eisenhower an "old and sick and feeble" man, but she was pleased by all the good publicity the Administration was getting by mid-1959. Then she wondered, since she was part of the "old" team, whether she ought not to leave too. Fortunately for the President, Whitman recorded that "I don't want to leave while I still feel that the President has any shred of affection for me or feels that I can in any way serve him better than someone new." Besides, she did not see any "new" Eisenhower, except for one thing: "I believe that he came to office with a healthy fear of Congress, a carry-over from days when he appeared before committees, kowtowing to Congress." Whitman thought he had learned to stand up to Congress, as evidenced by his recent veto of a Democratic housing bill and his success in getting some labor-reform legislation through Congress. Then Whitman put her finger on what was causing all the "new" talk—"While the decisions were always the President's, I think that Herter and Jerry Persons are more inclined to remain in the background than were Adams and certainly Dulles."[1]

In fact, the theme Eisenhower was stressing in 1959 was an old one that stretched back to Atoms for Peace (1953), Open Skies (1955), and other attempts to find some accommodation with the Soviets. At a mid-June meeting with Under Secretary of State Douglas Dillon and Good-paster, Eisenhower said "we must look for added or new subjects or possibilities on which to negotiate. He said he had racked his head to think of such things—that would not appear to be concessions—and was at his 'wits end.' " But he was not, really, for he immediately added that Khrushchev had raised the question of IRBMs, and Eisenhower felt that if ICBM development continued, "it might be possible to give up these IRBM plans."[2]

Two days later, on June 17, Eisenhower met with Dillon, Gray, McElroy, and Goodpaster. Eisenhower said he could see good reason for the DOD policy of placing IRBMs in Germany, France, and Britain, but going so close to the Soviet borders as Greece "seems very questionable." Eisenhower drew an analogy: "If Cuba or Mexico were to become Communist inclined, and the Soviets were to send arms and equipment, . . . we would feel that we would have to intervene, militarily if necessary." In a more general sense, Eisenhower protested against the mushroom-type growth of American military bases around the world; in places like Morocco or Libya, he pointed out, they "impose a political drain on us—a constant burden and handicap."

McElroy insisted that the President "consider the question against the Soviet threats to obliterate Western Europe. It was a situation resulting from threats such as these that led us to offer these IRBMs to our allies, who were showing signs of being shaken by the threat." Then he made the classic argument for more missiles: The weapons could be used as bargaining chips. McElroy "felt we can push the Soviets toward willingness to consider disarmament seriously if these weapons are in fact deployed near them." That position put McElroy (and all those who used his arguments in the sixties and seventies and eighties) in the strange position of advocating building more bombs and missiles in the present in order to *not* have to build more bombs and missiles in the future. And Eisenhower gave McElroy what has become the classic rejoinder: "The President commented that this [missile] deployment does not seem to serve to reduce tensions between ourselves and the Soviets." In other words, the Russians did not scare easily. Eisenhower then insisted that no pressure be put on the Greeks to accept IRBMs, nor on the Italians or the Turks or anyone else. "Only if the Greeks asked for them should they be provided."[3]

With Europe about to be covered with IRBMs, and with the ICBMs coming into production, and with a crisis over Berlin, everyone was getting a little more frightened. Pressure from the Europeans for a summit, especially from Macmillan, was intense and growing.

Khrushchev said he wanted to meet with Eisenhower. For his part, Eisenhower was willing enough to talk, but only after the Foreign Ministers' meeting (currently in recess in Geneva) had produced some progress. Khrushchev said that by defining the differences, they already had made progress, a proposition Eisenhower refused to accept. There were some informal exchanges taking place—in July, an American Exhibition opened in Moscow, as a counterpart to a Russian Exhibition opening in New York. Eisenhower sent Nixon and his brother Milton to Moscow (where Nixon got into his famous "kitchen debate" with Khrushchev), but as Eisenhower told his aides, making a point "he has made many times, that the Vice-President is not a part of the negotiating mechanism of government."[4]

The President was, of course, the supreme negotiator. But Dulles had always warned him against summit meetings unless and until the Foreign Ministers had made some progress, a position that obviously put great stress on the role of the Secretary of State. Eisenhower agreed with Dulles, but Khrushchev did not. Eisenhower liked to pretend that American diplomatic teams, and especially the Secretary of State, were free to conclude deals with the Soviets on the basis of mutual discussions, but complained that none of Khrushchev's agents, including his Foreign Minister, were allowed to make any decisions on their own. But Eisenhower was caught in a contradiction on this point, because he always insisted that every final decision was his, as in fact it was. With the Foreign Ministers' meeting stalled and in recess, and with the test-ban talks, also based in Geneva, and also stalled and in recess, if Eisenhower wanted to use the last year and a half of his term to advance the cause of peace, he was going to have to talk directly to Khrushchev. That was exactly what Khrushchev wanted; indeed he had dropped any number of hints that he would like to visit the United States and then invite Eisenhower to Moscow.

Eisenhower was intrigued by the idea. American domestic politics were at a virtual standstill, as all the politicians were gearing up for the 1960 election and the only significant issue between Eisenhower and Congress was the budget. Further, technology was making travel so much easier, faster, and more comfortable. In 1959, *Air Force One* replaced the *Columbine* as the President's airplane. The new craft dwarfed the old one, had a much greater range and more room inside, and could fly around the world if the President desired. Travel, just for its own sake, had always been one of Eisenhower's chief delights. There were many places he wanted to see—most especially India—and he had been compiling a mental list of the sites he intended to visit after retirement. But how much nicer to visit them while he was still President, and could use *Air Force One,* and—best of all—could use his prestige and position to further the cause of peace, to which he had committed himself and his Administration.

On July 10, Eisenhower told Herter, Dillon, and Goodpaster that if there was some progress at the Geneva Foreign Ministers' meeting (due to resume in three days), he would ask Khrushchev to visit the United States after he had opened the Russian Exhibition and made an appearance before the U.N. Then in October, he said, he would visit Moscow, afterward flying on to India. He wanted Robert Murphy to deliver the invitation orally to First Deputy Premier Frol Kozlov, who was in New York but scheduled to fly back to Moscow on July 12. Eisenhower explained that he thought talking to Khrushchev might do some good at the Geneva sessions. But, he added, his real reason was that a talk with Khrushchev "would be useful for one thing. If Khrushchev were to threaten war or use of force, he would immediately call his bluff and ask him to agree on a day to start."[5]

By July 22, Khrushchev had responded; he would be delighted to come, for a ten-day visit, and there was much he wanted to see. He made no mention of the Geneva meeting. Eisenhower was terribly agitated by this, and grew even angrier when Murphy confessed that he had issued an unqualified invitation, because he had not understood that the proposed visit was dependent upon progress at Geneva. Eisenhower called in Dillon and Murphy and told them that "someone had failed." He could see the point to a two-day visit to Camp David for private talks, but a ten-day visit was another thing altogether. Goodpaster noted, "The President said he is staggered by the situation now presented to him . . . It was a surprise to him that his concept on safeguarding the invitation had not been observed." But he guessed he "would have to pay the penalty." His mind went back to Dulles; the President found he was missing Foster even more than he had feared he would. Goodpaster noted that the President "recalled that he and Mr. Dulles had always talked from ideas or topics and not from papers. Mr. Dulles would then put on paper the idea upon which they had agreed and send it to the President to correct and confirm."[6]

In accepting the invitation, Khrushchev said he had been warned about hot summer weather in the United States and wanted to make the trip a bit later in September. On August 5, the day the Foreign Ministers' meeting broke up after a stalemate had been reached on the German problem, Eisenhower announced the impending Khrushchev

visit. The announcement brought howls of protest from various Cold
Warriors. William Buckley, for example, wanted to fill the Hudson
River with red dye so that when Khrushchev entered New York har-
bor, it would be on a figurative "river of blood." Reporters too were
hostile. At an August 12 news conference, held in Gettysburg, Eisen-
hower was asked what it was in the United States that he wanted
Khrushchev to see. Whitman called Eisenhower's reply a "love song to
America."

"I would like for him, among other things, to see this," Eisenhower responded. "The evidence that the fine, small or modest homes
that Americans live in are not the exception as he seemed to think the
sample we sent over to Moscow was." He wanted Khrushchev to see
Levittown, a town "universally and exclusively inhabited by its work-
men . . . I would like to see him have to fly along in my chopper and
just make a circuit of the District, to see the uncountable homes that
have been built all around, modest but decent, fine, comfortable
homes." Further, "I would like to see him go in the little town where
I was born and pick up the evidence . . . and let them tell him the
story of how hard I worked until I was twenty-one, when I went to
West Point." Referring to Nixon's debate with Khrushchev, Eisenhower reminded the press that the Russian dictator had said to Nixon,
"What do you know about work? You never worked." Well, said the
President, "*I* can show him the evidence that *I* did, and I would like
him to see it." Most of all, Eisenhower emphasized, "I want him to see
a happy people. I want him to see a free people, doing exactly as they
choose, within the limits that they must not transgress the rights of
others."

There was a steel strike going on, one that had Eisenhower worried, because of its adverse effect on the GNP. He had insisted, however, on the principle of collective bargaining and refused to intervene. Reporters and politicians alike thought something should be
done to bring the strike to an end before Khrushchev came over.
Eisenhower would not agree. "Don't we want Mr. Khrushchev to see
this country as a freedom-loving place?" he asked. "Why should we
worry too much about the fact that people can strike in this country?"[7]

Eisenhower did not tell the reporters, but he did say privately,
that he had something else he wanted Khrushchev to see—his opportunity. As Goodpaster recorded it, "The President thought he personally might make an appeal to Khrushchev in terms of his place in history, point out that if he wants to gain such a place through making a
change to improve the international climate, the President is confident

that something can be worked out." Eisenhower intended to stress that while he had about eighteen months to go, Khrushchev would be in command for many years to come. He felt he had to make such an appeal, he said, if only "to satisfy his own conscience."[8]

De Gaulle and Adenauer were predictably and understandably worried, Macmillan only slightly less so. The thought of Eisenhower and Khrushchev making deals together alarmed them. In order to re-assure them, and to try out *Air Force One* and to indulge in some nostalgia, Eisenhower decided to visit the three Western capitals be-fore Khrushchev's Steptember 15 arrival in America. C. D. Jackson, always on the lookout for a psychological-warfare angle, suggested that Eisenhower go to Paris on August 27, which would be two days after the fifteenth anniversary of the liberation of the city, and thus a not-too-gentle reminder to de Gaulle and the French that they owed their freedom to Eisenhower and American arms. Eisenhower liked the idea and made the proposal; de Gaulle deftly turned it down, saying he preferred a September date. Eisenhower therefore decided to go to Bonn first, then London, then Paris, then a vacation in Scotland.

On August 25, on the eve of his departure, Eisenhower held a news conference. Peter Lisagor said there was criticism of all this traveling around the President was going to be doing. The critics feared that it "will erode the presidential prestige . . . Would you care to comment on that?" Eisenhower got into one of his lecturing moods. "We are putting now, . . . something on the order of $41 bil-lion every year [on defense]. No one seems to stop to think about what that is doing to this country." If Eisenhower did not explore every avenue for peace, and the arms race continued "indefinitely into the future, where is the explosion point?" Prestige? He was not worried about his prestige. "We are talking about the human race and what's going to happen to it."[9]

At 3:20 A.M., August 26, Eisenhower climbed aboard *Air Force One* for the first time. Mamie had gotten up to come see him off (she had been tempted to go along, but there was too much flying involved for her taste), and he showed her the accommodations, which dazzled him but bored her. The flight itself, his first ever in a jet, Eisenhower found an "exhilarating experience." As the big jet went into its "silent, effortless acceleration and its rapid rate of climb," whatever doubts Eisenhower may have had about the wisdom of spending most of the remainder of his term on world travels vanished. He was hooked.[10]

●   ●

In Bonn, the talks with Adenauer were primarily about the French problems in Algeria, on which subject Adenauer "seemed almost obsessed . . ." The German Chancellor told Eisenhower that the Communists were behind the Algerian rebellion, and that if Algeria fell, the North African dominoes would fall with it—Morocco, Tunisia, then the Middle East. Eisenhower said he could not "foresee such a chain of disaster."[11] He turned the subject to German rearmament and possible American withdrawals from Europe. (A subject that was much on his mind of late, partly because of a serious balance-of-payments problem and a consequent drain on America's gold resources; in July, he had told Radford that "we are getting into insoluble problems in connection with our bases abroad. They are terribly expensive . . ." and recalled that when he was SACEUR, he hoped to have all American troops out of Europe by 1955.[12]) Adenauer promised that Germany would do more rearming. Eisenhower said he hoped so, and added that he looked forward to the day that the German contingent in NATO was sufficiently large that the Americans could reduce their ground forces in Europe. Adenauer, much alarmed, asked Eisenhower to not even mention the possibility.[13]

In London, Eisenhower talked with Macmillan. Their only disagreement was over the test-ban negotiations. Macmillan was willing to accept something short of a verifiable inspection system in order to get a comprehensive test ban, while Eisenhower favored a ban on atmospheric testing only.

In Paris, de Gaulle was as difficult as Eisenhower had anticipated he would be. De Gaulle had earlier suggested a tripartite pact, between France, Britain, and the United States, that would act together on a worldwide basis, with a common strategy and foreign policy. As a part of it, France would have a veto on the use of American nuclear weapons stationed in France. The State Department, and Eisenhower, thought the first idea absurd (there was a strong suspicion that what de Gaulle really wanted was American support in Algeria), and the second unacceptable. De Gaulle had therefore ordered American nuclear weapons out of France, a process that was going on during Eisenhower's visit. He had also withdrawn the French fleet from NATO. Nor did de Gaulle hesitate to voice his suspicion that the Americans, along with their British friends, wanted to run NATO and indeed the world.

(De Gaulle's suspicion about collusion between the English-speaking nations was not entirely misplaced. It was an idea that had tempted Churchill, and in March 1959, Eisenhower had told the Republican leaders that "it might be a good idea to begin to try to get Britain and Canada, Australia and New Zealand, all together with us in one great government." Referring to the statehood status achieved by Alaska and Hawaii, he said, "In view of the fact that the United States has now gone beyond its own shores, an idea like this—given time—might not be too difficult to sell."[14])

Eisenhower personally had mixed feelings about de Gaulle. At a briefing with General Lauris Norstad, the new SACEUR, "The President said that de Gaulle merely wants to make France the first nation of the world with himself the first Frenchman." He reviewed all the difficulties he had had with de Gaulle during the war. But Norstad, in a sharp insight, said that de Gaulle "is fond of the President personally. This fondness, far from being a comforting matter, can be extremely troublesome," because de Gaulle counted on Eisenhower's reciprocal feeling to help him achieve his goals. And Eisenhower did have an ability, both in the war and in the late fifties, unusual among Americans, to see things from France's point of view. Thus he told Norstad, "In fairness to de Gaulle, on many of these NATO issues, we would react very much as de Gaulle does if the shoe were on the other foot."[15]

But seeing the French point of view and agreeing with it were two different things. On Algeria, for example, where de Gaulle was attempting to quash the rebellion before holding elections, it looked to Eisenhower as if the French were making the same mistake they had made in Indochina. In any case, he told Herter during the State Department briefing on France, "We cannot abandon our old principles of supporting national freedom and self-determination, and we cannot join the colonialists." Eisenhower thought "we are deep enough in Europe's troubles now, and must be tough in saying that we do not propose to go deeper."[16]

In his talks with de Gaulle, Eisenhower was equally firm. He just could not support the French in Algeria. De Gaulle tried to revive the idea of a tripartite worldwide arrangement, to no avail. Eisenhower tried to revive the idea of the European Defense Community, or all-European army. The President reminded de Gaulle that in early 1952, he "swore, prayed, almost wept for the EDC. It was initialed, but after the French Parliament was through with it, there was nothing left." Would de Gaulle like to examine it again? *Non*, replied de Gaulle, as he loftily declared that "an Army can have no morale unless it is defending its own country." Eisenhower blanched, then reminded de Gaulle that "in the Second World War, when a lot of us were fighting on foreign soil, it seemed we had good morale."[17]

•   •

The war was much on his mind. Nothing new had come out of the discussions, but nevertheless the trip gave Eisenhower a great boost, because it brought back so many good memories and because of the evidence it provided of Eisenhower's extraordinary popularity in Western Europe. On the twenty-mile drive from the airport to the American Embassy in Bonn, the roads were jammed with cheering crowds; it was a moving experience for Eisenhower, to be cheered by the people he had only so recently conquered. Eisenhower told Adenauer it was "astonishing"; the Chancellor agreed.

In Paris, the people quite outdid themselves. De Gaulle may not have wanted them to remember Eisenhower's role in their liberation, but they remembered anyway. From the airport to the city, the crowds were huge. De Gaulle and Eisenhower rode in a convertible, waving to the wildly enthusiastic throngs. "How many?" Eisenhower asked de Gaulle. "At least a million," de Gaulle told him. "I did not expect half as many," said Eisenhower, deeply moved.

London was the best, although Eisenhower had feared the worst. He had been warned to expect a cool reception, as the British had by no means forgiven him for Suez, and the Montgomery memoirs controversy was still warm. In addition, Macmillan had given the trip minimum publicity, as the talks were informal and because Eisenhower had given tentative agreement to making another, formal visit at Christmastime. But as the motorcade drove from the airport to the city, through a gathering dusk, the people of Britain turned out to honor the man who had such a special place in their hearts. They turned out by the thousands, by the tens of thousands, by the hundreds of thousands. As the crowds grew denser, Macmillan kept repeating, "I never would have believed it, I never would have believed it." As they got to Grosvenor Square, Eisenhower's wartime headquarters, Macmillan told him, "The state visit in December is off. Anything after this would be anticlimax."[18]

Eisenhower hosted a dinner for his wartime comrades. He paid a visit to the royal family. He spent a weekend at Chequers (ah, the memories). He took a few days' vacation at Culzean Castle, given to him for his lifetime by the people of Scotland. The gang flew over to play bridge.

Not everything was perfect. At his dinner, Eisenhower returned to his idea of getting the top people together at Camp David to write an authoritative history of World War II, as a rebuttal to Monty.[19] (When Eisenhower returned to the States, he gave a television talk about his trip. Working on the script, he noticed the date—September 10, 1959.

Slamming down his blue pencil, he told Whitman that it was the fifteenth anniversary of the day he met Monty at the Brussels airfield, and Monty "made his preposterous proposal to go to Berlin."[20])

London provided the appropriate setting for the climax of the trip. Eisenhower appeared with Macmillan on television, talking extemporaneously. Eisenhower, discussing the need for greater cultural exchange, showed again that the British always brought out the best in him. Turning to Macmillan, he said with great earnestness, "I like to believe that people, in the long run, are going to do more to promote peace than our governments. Indeed, I think that people want peace so much that one of these days governments had better get out of the way and let them have it."[21]

That was the spirit of his trip, the spirit in which he had, however grudgingly, agreed to a Khrushchev visit, the spirit in which he intended to work in the time remaining to him.

On September 7, Eisenhower returned to the States. Khrushchev was due to arrive in a week. Eisenhower made last-minute preparations (there was a major flap over dress at the formal White House dinner, and over Khrushchev's schedule for his tour of the country). Even before leaving for Europe, Eisenhower had tried to give the talks some chance of success by making concessions on testing. McCone and McElroy and the JCS all wanted to resume testing, but after a July NSC meeting "the President grew heated about atmospheric tests," indicating that "he would not approve them."[22] In that case, the AEC and DOD wanted underground testing. But Eisenhower would not approve that either. Instead, he met with George Kistiakowsky, who in July had replaced Killian as the President's science adviser. Kistiakowsky gave him the bad news that the latest scientific information was that underground tests, at least below twenty kilotons, could not be accurately detected. Eisenhower therefore decided, as he had been inclined to do anyway, to accept a State Department proposal that the United States drop its attempts to achieve a comprehensive test-ban treaty and instead try to secure Khrushchev's agreement to an atmospheric test ban. In addition, Eisenhower decided to extend his unilateral test moratorium from its October 31 expiration date to January 1, 1960. There was a "wild reaction" from McCone and McElroy, but on August 26, the President announced it anyway.[23]

Khrushchev arrived for two days of talks, formal dinners, and a helicopter ride over Washington. Khrushchev gave Eisenhower a gift, a model of a projectile called Lunik II, which had just made a trip to the moon. Eisenhower thought it a bit on the blatant side, but then thought to himself "quite possibly the man [is] completely sincere." In his opening statement at the talks, Khrushchev made the most basic point, one that everyone said they recognized but that no one was willing to act on as a basis of policy. We do not want war, said Khrushchev, and we believe that you know that. Eisenhower said he did, that there was no future in mutual suicide. After that, they really had nothing more to discuss, as on all the outstanding issues—the status of Berlin, of Formosa, Soviet (and American) meddling in the Middle East, disarmament—each man had taken a position from which he would not back down.[24]

Primarily, Eisenhower wanted to appeal to Khrushchev's sense of history, in order to get some progress somewhere, most likely on testing. As he told the Republican leaders, he wanted to make "one great personal effort, before leaving office, to soften up the Soviet leader even a little bit. Except for the Austrian peace treaty, we haven't made a chip in the granite in seven years."[25] He did get a chance to make the point to Khrushchev privately; Khrushchev took it graciously, but said that there would have to be movement toward compromise by both sides.

On the helicopter ride, to Eisenhower's disappointment, Khrushchev remained silent. Eisenhower had wanted Khrushchev to see all those middle-class homes, and all those automobiles rushing out of Washington in the late afternoon to get to them. Khrushchev did, but he would not say anything, or even change expression. The following morning, he took off for a tour of the country. Eisenhower assigned Cabot Lodge to accompany him, slighting Nixon in the process. Khrushchev's tour was a media event of the first magnitude. He made great copy and the world press was there to take down his rages, his delights, his off-the-cuff comments, his threats, his blandishments, and to satisfy his desire for headlines.

A highlight came on September 18, when Khrushchev spoke to the U.N. He was proud of his speech—back in Washington, he had tapped his pocket and told Eisenhower, "Here is my speech and no one is going to see it."[26] Thus Eisenhower was completely unprepared for Khrushchev's bombshell, which was nothing less than a call for a total abolition of all weapons, nuclear and conventional, over the next four years, without any provision for inspection or supervision. If the West was not ready for so radical a cure, he was willing to pursue the stalled test-ban issue, which he said was "acute and eminently ripe for solution."[27]

On September 25, Khrushchev returned to Washington. He and Eisenhower took a helicopter to Camp David for two days of talks.

Now it was Khrushchev's turn to try to impress Eisenhower. He grew quite expansive in discussing the military and security posture of the Soviet Union (all through the trip, he had been kidding Lodge about how easily the KGB broke the most secret American communications, and hinted that the KGB had a mole highly placed in the CIA). He said the Russians were building more powerful nuclear submarines than the Americans. Khrushchev claimed that the U.S.S.R. had all the bombs it wanted and would soon have all the missiles it needed, and bragged that the number was a "lot." He said he had decided that small tactical atomic weapons were too expensive. So was atomic power for civilian purposes; Khrushchev said the Russians had stopped work on their nuclear power plants and were relying instead on gas, oil, and coal. But, as Eisenhower later told Twining, "Khrushchev gave great emphasis to the tremendous costs of defense, returning to this subject time after time. He repeatedly emphasized the importance of disarmament."[28]

They had a long talk about World War II. Khrushchev assured Eisenhower, "Your old friend Zhukov is all right. Don't worry about him. He's down in the Ukraine fishing—and like all generals he is probably writing his memoirs." They drove over to Gettysburg, where Khrushchev met Eisenhower's grandchildren. Khrushchev bantered with them, and on the spot asked them to accompany Eisenhower to Moscow. The children were delighted, their parents somewhat less so. Eisenhower showed Khrushchev his Black Angus herd. Khrushchev admired the animals and said he was trying to improve the cattle-breeding industry in Russia. Eisenhower arranged for Lewis Strauss to send Khrushchev a prize-winning bull and two heifers. Then Khrushchev began talking about the subject Eisenhower had hoped he would, American homes and automobiles, and Eisenhower was more disappointed than ever, because Khrushchev said he was not impressed. In fact, he was shocked at all the waste. Those vast numbers of cars, he said, represented only a waste of time, money, and effort. Well, said Eisenhower, he must find the road system impressive. No, replied Khrushchev, because in his country there was little need for such roads because the Soviet people lived close together, did not care for automobiles, and seldom moved. The American people, he observed, "do not seem to like the place where they live and always want to be on the move going someplace else." And all those houses, Khrushchev continued, cost more to build, more to heat, more for upkeep and surrounding grounds than the multiple-family housing in the Soviet Union.

The only positive note to emerge was Khrushchev's willingness to remove any hint of a deadline or an ultimatum from the Berlin question.[29] On that basis, the two leaders made a tentative agreement to meet at the summit, in Paris, in May. After the summit, Eisenhower—and his wife, son, daughter-in-law, and grandchildren—would pay a visit to Russia. Before that, Eisenhower would make another trip, in December, to Europe, the Middle East, and the Italian subcontinent.

In preparation for that trip, which would include a meeting of the heads of government of the United States, Britain, France, and West Germany, and to review his discussions with Khrushchev, Eisenhower called ambassador to the Soviet Union Llewellyn Thompson to Washington for talks. Thompson told Eisenhower that he thought Khrushchev's motive in the Berlin situation was to get a peace treaty with East Germany (the NATO powers had already made peace with West Germany), not so much to make trouble in Berlin as to "nail down the eastern frontiers of Germany and of Poland, and thus remove these sources of future trouble" (and not incidentally to nail down the Russian-Polish frontier, moved far to the west by Stalin in 1945). Thompson also said that Adenauer "does not really want to try to get the eastern provinces back for Germany," and that the last thing de Gaulle wanted was a reunified Germany. Eisenhower said that Khrushchev had made the point to him, and that he thought "there was much in what Khrushchev had said . . . The President said that more and more he is coming to the view that complete reunification of the two parts of Germany is not going to be achieved early."

On testing, Thompson said he thought Khrushchev would continue to hold out for a comprehensive ban, because "his main objective is to keep China and Germany from getting these weapons . . . Resumption of underground tests would permit the Chinese and Germans to develop these weapons ultimately." But, Thompson added, Khrushchev "is far out in advance of many of his people on this issue," even though he frequently put on a show for the benefit of his associates. Eisenhower commented "that Khrushchev cannot be as confident of his position as Stalin was."

Then Eisenhower began to muse on Khrushchev's U.N. call for total disarmament. The President was hardly likely to go that far, but he told Thompson, "Suppose that we disarmed in everything but missiles and bombs. It is hard to see how any serious war could be initiated under those circumstances." It was also difficult to see how Eisenhower could have expected Khrushchev to take such a proposal seriously, as it would have meant disarming Russian strength, the Red

Army, while retaining those weapons, atomic and nuclear, in which America was superior.

Back in Russia, meanwhile, Khrushchev was talking about the "spirit of Camp David," and generally being noticeably more friendly to Thompson. Eisenhower urged the ambassador to see more of Khrushchev informally in the future, because he thought that "someone as voluble as Khrushchev would be bound to disclose useful information in such talks."[30]

Another voluble leader, Fidel Castro, was causing confusion and alarm in Washington, where the great question was, Is Fidel a Communist or not? No one seemed to be certain. What Eisenhower was certain about was Batista's politics, and he found them unacceptable. In July, Batista applied for admission to the United States; Mrs. Batista wrote directly to Mamie asking her to intervene. But Eisenhower would not be moved. "There is one thing we cannot afford," he told his staff, "that is, to be known as a haven for displaced dictators who have robbed their countries." Eisenhower said he had met Batista and thought him a "nice guy," but he still insisted that Batista should not be allowed into the country. It had nothing to do with Castro, he said: "You just can't make a policy of bringing dictators into this country."[31]

By the fall of 1959, Cuban refugees were streaming into Miami. In southern Florida, they were organizing themselves into counterrevolutionary groups, with the avowed purpose of driving Castro from power. On October 27, Herter reported to Eisenhower that the State, Justice, and Defense departments were working together to stop the refugees' activities. But, he said, they were handicapped by the fact that private planes flew out of some two hundred airfields in Florida; in addition, American laws on the subject were weak and it was difficult to obtain a conviction. Eisenhower admitted that it was "impossible to police them all," but he did think that Herter could station inspectors at the major airfields. Then he asked, "Why doesn't Castro just shoot the airplanes down?" Herter did not know, but he did say that "the Cubans have been behaving very badly."[32]

"Every place I go," Whitman told Eisenhower on July 20, "people seem to be choosing up sides on the Nixon-Rockefeller matter." Eisenhower replied that what he wanted for 1960 was a combination ticket of the two, although even better would be a Nixon-Al Gruenther team.[33] Even at that, his first choice for the presidential candidate was not Nixon, but Robert Anderson. But he could not persuade Anderson to consider the idea, and he was fully aware of Nixon's great strength with the party regulars. It was just that he had doubts about Nixon's maturity, doubts that were strengthened by Khrushchev's visit, because Nixon got into a couple of shouting arguments with Khrushchev. But he did not like Rockefeller at all. As governor of New York, Rockefeller had turned out to be a spender and a budget buster. Eisenhower exchanged anxious letters with Bill Robinson and other New York friends about Rockefeller's activities, although of course he could not make his criticism of a Republican governor public.[34]

Above all, Eisenhower wanted party unity going into the presidential election, but it was difficult to maintain. As in 1952, the Republicans were splitting between the moderate, internationalist wing, which was more or less supporting Rockefeller, and the Old Guard, which was enthusiastically supporting Nixon. The two candidates, meanwhile, were sniping at each other. In August, Rockefeller was quoted as expressing disapproval of the invitation to Khrushchev for a visit, and putting the blame for it on Nixon. Eisenhower talked to Rockefeller about it; Rockefeller vehemently denied having made such a statement, which he called a "complete lie."

Eisenhower then wrote Nixon, explaining Rockefeller's position. Eisenhower said that "my concern about the matter is that two people—even should both become candidates for the same nomination—who have supported me so long and faithfully through the years I have been in this office should find themselves publicly at odds about an issue that in fact does not exist." In conclusion, Eisenhower expressed a forlorn hope: "My opinion is that people can be politically ambitious if they so desire without necessarily becoming personal antagonists."[35]

Another man with a monumental ego who wanted badly to be President was Lyndon Johnson. His sensitivity to supposed slights was striking. In August, Eisenhower gave a stag dinner for some correspondents. He was asked, informally, about the Democratic candidates. He decided not to mention anyone who was a serious candidate, and instead commented on Senators Holland and Stennis, who had no chance. A reporter asked him if there was anyone from Texas who could handle the job. Eisenhower mentioned Sam Rayburn.

First thing the following morning, Johnson was on the telephone to Eisenhower. The senator said he was "hurt" by the President's refusal to mention his name, adding "that the thing that distressed him so much was that one whom he has admired so much would be represented to feel bitter toward him." Johnson cited an off-the-record remark by one senator to the effect that the President was "burning mad" at him. But what really hurt was Eisenhower's comment that Mr. Sam would make a fine candidate, while leaving out Johnson's name (although Johnson hastened to add that he had the greatest admiration for Mr. Sam). Then Johnson concluded by stating, with great sincerity and emphasis, that it did not matter to him, because "I have no ambitions politically." The things politicians say to each other![36]

Of all his domestic programs, Eisenhower's favorite by far was the Interstate System. By 1959, it was in bad trouble. Construction costs were far higher than had been anticipated, primarily because of the expense of building urban freeways directly through the inner cities, where land acquisition prices and the problems of building the roads were so much greater than in the countryside. In Eisenhower's vision, the superhighways were not supposed to have gone into the cities, but only around them, as in Europe. His objections were not sociological—few if any of those associated with the building of the Interstates anticipated the tremendous effect the urban freeways would have on housing patterns, schools, inner-city conditions, the spread of the suburbs, or the other nearly limitless ways in which the four- and six- and eight-lane highways changed the face of urban America. Eisenhower's objections were to the cost, not the result. He evidently was unaware that in rounding up the votes in 1956 for the Interstate bill, Jerry Persons and the staff had made a deal with urban representatives, who as a group tended to oppose the whole program. The deal was that in exchange for big-city votes, the cities would get their share and more of the construction expenditures.

The evidence that Eisenhower was unaware of this deal comes from his reaction to seeing, in July of 1959, while driving from the White House toward Camp David, a deep freeway construction gash in the outskirts of metropolitan Washington. Surprised and appalled by what he saw, when he got to Camp David he called the director of the Bureau of the Budget, Maurice Stans, to ask for an explanation. Unsatisfied with the result, he ordered a formal White House study of the urban Interstates.[37] On July 9, he called in the members of the Mass Transportation Survey of the Washington Metropolitan Area and asked them what they were doing about a rapid-transit subway system. The reply was that some $1 billion would be spent over the next twenty years. The President then "stated his concern that too much of the interstate highway money might be going into connections in the cities." Next, the President asked whether the committee had considered placing a special tax on automobiles coming into the central cities, "it being his observation that it was very wasteful to have an average of just over one man per $3,000 car driving into the central area and taking all the space required to park the car."[38]

Clearly, Eisenhower by that time was thinking his way through the thing and anticipating the future better than his planners could do, but neither that fact nor his position made it possible for him to stop the onrushing program. At a special meeting with the highway people in early 1960, Eisenhower indicated that "the matter of running Interstate routes through the congested parts of the cities was entirely against his original concept and wishes, that he never anticipated that the program would turn out this way," but he noted that he had been told, finally, that what "sold the program to the Congress" was the urban feature. Therefore, it was too late to turn it around; Eisenhower said that he "had reached the point where his hands were virtually tied."[39] Nor did he again bring up the idea of taxing suburban cars coming into the cities.

The President was frustrated in other areas too. As the end of his term approached, he increasingly thought in long-range terms—witness such suggestions as a political union of all the English-speaking nations—and by September of 1959 he had some constitutional amendments he wanted to propose. The first would give the President an item veto on appropriation bills, a hardy old perennial that every President wants and no Congress will give. The second would make the term of House members four years instead of two, an idea Eisenhower liked because it would make it possible for congressmen to campaign less and work at their jobs more. The third would require a two-thirds vote of the Senate to turn down a presidential appointee to the Executive Branch, a proposal that only showed how angry he was over the rejection by the Senate of the Strauss nomination.[40] To the end of his life, he tried to talk up these proposed amendments, but without encouragement and without success.

The constitutional amendment that he was stuck with was the one that forbade his running again. At a Republican leaders' meeting early in 1959, Halleck and Dirksen cursed themselves and the Republican Party for passing the Twenty-Second Amendment, just to spite Roosevelt; then they began thinking that what had been done could be undone. Stating the obvious, Halleck said it "would be a major operation for us to switch around." Eisenhower said that he could take either side of the argument. "Had I been voting, I never would have voted for Mr. R *except* the fourth time, in the middle of the war." He insisted that repealing the amendment would have no effect on him, because no one over seventy years of age should ever be President. But, he told Halleck and Dirksen, "You won't hurt my feelings if you speak to repeal—and maybe if I read some of your eloquent speeches I'd be convinced!" From the congressmen's point of view, however, there was no point to repeal if Ike would not run again, and nothing was done.

Perhaps they should not have given up so easily—Eisenhower left them with a broad hint they might have followed up. In explaining why he would have voted for Roosevelt in 1944, Eisenhower said that "in a real emergency, it would be tough to turn over the government. Suppose McClellan had beaten Lincoln in 1864?"[41] Eisenhower did *not* say that he thought the situation in 1960 was in any way to be compared to the crisis of 1944, but the thought persists that he had twice before allowed himself to be persuaded that he was the "only man" who could save the country. Given his doubts about Nixon and his certainty that the Democrats would be a disaster, given his good health, given his intense desire to achieve peace, and given his conviction that he was indeed the best man in the country for the job, he might have allowed himself to be persuaded one more time. But the effort was not made. It is virtually certain that had he been able to and agreed to run in 1960, he could have been overwhelmingly reelected.

Eisenhower devoted most of the Republican leaders' meetings to giving pep talks on holding down spending. In the recession year of 1958 the government had run a $12 billion deficit, but in 1959, revenues were up by nearly $10 billion, and as the economy recovered, spending for antirecession measures was curtailed. In fiscal 1959, Eisenhower cut federal spending by almost $4 billion. The result was a $1 billion surplus, and a projected $4 billion surplus in 1960.[42]

As always, defense was the most difficult place to hold down spending. The generals and the admirals were determined to stick to the cutting edge of the technological revolution, while they simultaneously wanted the largest nuclear arsenal, the best delivery system, the world's most powerful Navy and conventional Air Force, and a large, mobile standing Army. They, and their many supporters, could be most eloquent in stating their position. At a June 23 meeting with the top officials in DOD and the PSAC, for example, Eisenhower was told that there was unanimous agreement on the pressing need to go forward with the project for a nuclear-powered aircraft. But Eisenhower could not be bamboozled. He asked some probing questions, which revealed that the major reason his military advisers wanted to do it was because they thought it was possible to do it. "The President commented that the next thing he knows someone would be proposing to take the liner *Queen Elizabeth* and put wings a mile wide on it and install enough power plant to make it fly. Dr. York begged him not to let the idea get around, or someone would want to try."[43]

It was not that the President was opposed to new ideas, or that he was incapable of changing his mind. Two years earlier, at the time of Sputnik, he had insisted that the bomber was still much the best delivery system; since then, advances in rocketry had been such as to convince him otherwise. What bothered him most, however, was that the Air Force insisted on having both, indeed wanted to fund a new bomber, the B-70, while increasing ICBM construction. Eisenhower said he was "very skeptical" about the need for any new bombers. "If the missiles are effective, there will be no need for these bombers." He said he wished the Air Force officers would make up their minds, and added (he must have had a grin on his face), "I am beginning to think that the Air Force is not concerned over true economy in defense."

McElroy said that DOD wanted to put money into the B-70 because it represented the state of the art, and would provide spin-off benefits in civilian air transport. Eisenhower said "sharply that he cannot see us putting military money into a project to develop a civilian transport. He is 'allergic' to such an idea." But all the PSAC members jumped in to urge funding for the B-70. And Twining said the Air Force planned to send the B-70 over Russia "to search out and knock out mobile ICBMs on railroads." Eisenhower snorted. "If they think that," he said, "they are crazy!" He explained, "We are not going to be searching out mobile bases for ICBMs, we are going to be hitting the big industrial and control complexes."[44]

When Eisenhower met with the JCS, they too pressed him for the B-70. The Air Force Chief of Staff, General Thomas D. White, argued that all the Air Force wanted was research and development money, and reminded Eisenhower of the "premium we gain from having different systems for attack." Eisenhower replied that in "ten years the missile capacity of both countries will be such as to be able to destroy each other many times over." He thought that "we are going overboard in different ways to do the same thing." White replied that "this is the last aircraft under development in the world" and almost begged Eisenhower to leave it in the program. But Eisenhower "reviewed past examples of weapons that had outlived their era and said he thought we were talking about bows and arrows at the time of gunpowder when we spoke of bombers in the missile age."[45] He refused to support the B-70.

Another military expense Eisenhower wanted to reduce was in the American contribution to NATO. In mid-November, he told the people in DOD that he wanted to pull back some air and ground units from Europe. Eisenhower said that the United States had six divisions in Europe, "which we never intended to keep there permanently." The only reason he could see to maintaining them was that "the NATO allies are almost psychopathic whenever anyone suggests removing them." He also wondered why the United States should maintain the Sixth Fleet in the Mediterranean, which was a British and French responsibility and where the U.S. Navy would only be bottled up in time of war. Eisenhower said this was an area in which he had always been in sharp disagreement with Dulles, who "had practically a phobia against raising the question of reduction of these forces." Eisenhower's response, he related, was that by pulling out Americans, the United States could force the Europeans to do more in their own defense.[46]

Eisenhower's consultations with the JCS, DOD, and PSAC took place in Augusta, where he and Mamie spent most of November, surrounded by the gang. John and his family were there much of the time too. On the plane ride down, on October 21, Eisenhower told Slater, "fifteen months from that date" and he would "be a *free man*." The children put on a show for their grandparents; eleven-year-old David topped it off by reciting the Gettysburg Address. Eisenhower did much of the cooking. For one lunch, he sent out for a long list of groceries. First he stewed some chickens, then used the broth to boil the quail. He removed the quail meat from the bones, browned it, put it over hominy grits, and smothered the whole with a sauce from the chicken broth. Mainly, however, he rested himself mentally and physically, in preparation for his journey.[47]

Planning for the trip was in itself a major undertaking. Eisenhower proposed to visit Rome, Ankara, Karachi, Kabul, New Delhi, Teheran, Athens, Tunis, Paris, Madrid, and Casablanca. His purpose in going, he told a December 2 news conference, was that "I have relatively few months left and . . . I do feel a compulsion to visit a number of countries . . . I want to prove that we are not aggressive, that we seek nobody else's territories or possessions; we do not seek to vio-

EISENHOWER

late anybody else's rights." Further, "such prestige and standing as I have on the earth, I want to use it."[48]

He also wanted to get something straight with de Gaulle. In November, de Gaulle had written him about NATO and nuclear matters. Eisenhower said he was "astonished" by some of de Gaulle's points. For example, de Gaulle raised the question as to what would happen in the future to France if the two powers sharing the nuclear monopoly decided to divide the world. Or what would happen to France if the two superpowers decided to limit their battle to Europe. "It is possible to imagine," de Gaulle said, "that on some awful day Western Europe will be wiped out from Moscow and Central Europe from Washington." Finally, de Gaulle had written, "and who can even say that the two rivals, after I know not what political and social upheaval, will not unite?"

Eisenhower's reply was restrained but firm. He said he was "disturbed" that de Gaulle should believe the United States could fall to "such a low moral plane" as to run out on its commitments to its allies. He was "astonished" that de Gaulle could even suggest that the United States might divide the world with the Soviets. He objected strenuously to having his country put into "the same category of nations with the Soviet Union," calling it "unjustified."[49]

When he saw de Gaulle later in Paris, de Gaulle apologized and then some, as he again asked Eisenhower to consider a British, French, American triumvirate that would act together around the world. Eisenhower still had no interest in such a project. At the heads-of-government meeting, the only act of any consequence was an agreement to have a summit meeting in Paris in the spring of 1960.

The trip as a whole was triumph after triumph. In India, Greece, Spain, Afghanistan, Pakistan, Turkey, Italy, Iran, and at other stops the crowds turned out by the millions to see Eisenhower. He in turn did a great deal of sightseeing of his own, and was especially delighted to fulfill a boyhood dream and visit the Taj Mahal (he was appropriately impressed). Mamie had wanted to come along, but there was too much flying involved. John accompanied his father as a staff aide, and Barbara came with him. It was, taken all together, the perfect trip—exhausting but fascinating and satisfying. No real business had been done—none had been intended—but the enthusiastic reception Eisenhower received wherever he went showed that he was the world's most respected and beloved leader. Even in India, people lined up by the millions and stood for hours just to catch a glimpse of Ike. Nehru said they were the largest crowds he had seen since

552

Independence Day, bigger even than the ones Mahatma Gandhi used to draw.[50] Eisenhower had caught the world's imagination, reminiscent of the way Woodrow Wilson had done in 1919, as *the* peacemaker.

For his part, Eisenhower had seen such poverty as he had never before experienced. Upon his return, on December 22, he and Mamie went down to Augusta for the holidays. On New Year's Eve, he met with State, Defense, and PSAC leaders. He told them that as a result of his trip, he had decided that "the most critical question before us is what the rich countries are going to do with their wealth. The underdeveloped countries need the help we can give, and I am convinced we will go down within a short span of time if we do not give them this help. I'm frightened over the likelihood that we will be unable to get our people to support this kind of operation in time . . . If we cannot get a great number of the new countries committed to our side, the U.N. may soon be stacked against us."

Eisenhower also wanted progress on disarmament. He said the United States should agree to any kind of an inspection system the Russians would accept, because "our real aim is to open that country to some degree." He was tempted to take Khrushchev up on his offer of total disarmament, but he thought "it will be necessary to leave atomic weapons to the last." In Eisenhower's view, "If we cut back our armaments to where only a retaliatory force is left, war becomes completely futile." He therefore thought that the United States should strive for an agreement of reducing conventional arms and nuclear delivery systems. Herter reminded him that some years ago Strauss had thought it would be to America's advantage to agree to a total stop on the production of all nuclear material, but that it now appeared that DOD requirements were such that more bombs had to be built. "The President said he is completely unconvinced as to the validity of these so-called requirements."[51]

Nevertheless, production continued. But with a summit coming up, and with Khrushchev in an apparently conciliatory mood, and with all the recent evidence of how beloved he was around the world, with a budget surplus, and with the Berlin crisis surmounted, Eisenhower on New Year's Eve could look back on 1959 with satisfaction. It had been a much better year than 1958, and gave him confidence as he looked forward to 1960.

CHAPTER TWENTY-FOUR

High Hopes and Unhappy Realities

January–June 1960

FOR EISENHOWER, 1960 turned out to be a bad year, almost the worst of his Presidency. He made a series of mistakes, particularly in his dealings with Khrushchev and Castro, mistakes brought on by his own fetish for secrecy and his misplaced trust in the CIA. He had hoped to leave office in an atmosphere of budding trust between the super-powers, with the Communist threat turned back in Latin America, Berlin secure, and disarmament under way. These were, however, in-herently contradictory aims, which was one overriding reason for the lack of success. On the one hand, Eisenhower was trying to inspire Khrushchev, and the American people, with his vision of peaceful co-existence; on the other hand, he was willing to do almost anything to get rid of Castro. His readiness to take major risks in pursuit of dis-armament were counterbalanced by his unwillingness to risk working toward a new relationship with Castro and Cuba specifically or Latin-American radicalism generally.

Forces beyond Eisenhower's control were a factor in the failures of 1960. While he tried to concentrate on peace, his fellow politicians concentrated on the presidential election. It was characteristic of such elections, in the era of the Cold War, for each side to try to outdo the other in promising to get tough with the Communists (Eisenhower himself had used that theme against the Democrats in 1952). Getting tough meant, primarily, spending more money on arms; to Eisen-hower's disgust, both candidates promised to do just that. The press was far more ready to see dangers in peaceful coexistence than it was to envision hope. Powerful men, in such bureaucracies as the CIA, the AEC, the JCS, and the DOD, and their suppliers in the defense industry, were firmly opposed to any outbreak of peace, and together they helped to sabotage Eisenhower's vision. Despite Eisenhower's efforts, the Cold War by the end of 1960 was more dangerous, more tension-packed, than it had been at the beginning of the year.

By January of 1960, Eisenhower and his advisers were determined to do something about Cuba. Castro's verbal abuse against the United States was reaching new levels, as was his confiscation of American-owned property. There were, however, many problems in dealing with Castro. He was far more politically astute and adroit than Arbenz in Guatemala had been. His anti-American diatribes were based on a Latin, not a Communist, critique of Uncle Sam, and he had managed to convince millions of Latins that any attempt by Washington to link him with the Communists was simply the old Yankee trick of accusing all Latin-American reformers of being Communists. He was widely popular among the Latin masses, and retained a certain popularity even among liberals in the United States, who were arguing that the United States ought to try cooperation instead of confrontation with the new Cuban government. Privately, the rulers of Latin America were telling Eisenhower that they hoped the United States could get rid of Castro, one way or another, but neither individually nor collectively, through the OAS, would they speak out against Castro.

The OAS had long since committed itself (in the Caracas Declaration of 1954) to opposition to Communist intrusion in the New World. The problem was proving that Castro was a Communist. As Secretary of State Herter put it in one of his numerous memoranda to Eisenhower outlining his attempts to get an OAS condemnation of Castro, "Successful presentation of the problem of Cuba to the OAS calls for the careful documentation of a 'case' on the Communist issue." The disgusted President wrote by hand in the margin, "This has been almost a zero!"[1]

The reason the Administration could not prove to the OAS that Castro was a Communist was that it could not prove it to itself. The ambassador to Cuba told Eisenhower that he personally did not think Cuba was a Communist dictatorship, and he expected that Castro's foreign policy would be to seek neutrality in the Cold War.[2] Herter reported in March 1960 that "our own latest National Intelligence Estimate [prepared by the CIA] does not find Cuba to be under Com-

munist control or domination . . ." Herter added that because of un-
certainty about the direction in which Castro was moving, the anti-
Castro refugees in Florida were unable to unite in their opposition.
Some wanted to bring back Batista, others only wanted to be rid of
Fidel, none were willing to cooperate to create a government-in-exile.
Herter warned against any action to drive Castro from Cuba until a
responsible Cuban opposition leadership was ready to take over, be-
cause otherwise Cuba might end up with someone worse than Castro.

A further problem was that although Cuba and Latin America
were important to American foreign policy, they were not *that* important. Thus Herter told Eisenhower that in attempting to enlist the
OAS in an anti-Castro move, he should first of all make certain that
"our efforts to enlist Latin-American support will not generate exces-
sive pressures on us to undertake a significantly expanded and more
dramatic economic assistance program for Latin America . . ." In
short, while the Eisenhower Administration wanted to drive Castro
from office, it was not ready to spend money to do it.[3]

In addition to all those difficulties, Herter continually warned
Eisenhower that the OAS would support no move against Castro until
and unless the United States also moved against Rafael Trujillo, the
right-wing dictator of the Dominican Republic. Eisenhower held a
number of conferences with Herter to discuss ways of persuading Trujillo to resign, suggesting at one point setting up a trust fund for Trujillo (although Eisenhower refused to offer Trujillo asylum in the
United States). But Trujillo refused to step down voluntarily. Herter
said that it would not do to push him out, because in that event the
Communists might take over the Dominican Republic in the ensuing
chaos. He promised to keep working on the diplomatic front against
Trujillo.[4]

At a January 25 meeting, a frustrated and angry President said
that "Castro begins to look like a madman." He indicated that if the
OAS would not help remove him, then the United States should go it
alone, for example, by imposing a blockade on Cuba. "If the Cuban
people are hungry," Eisenhower declared, "they will throw Castro
out." Calmer heads prevailed, pointing out that the United States
should not punish the whole Cuban people for the acts of one madman. Eisenhower admitted that that was true.[5]

Eisenhower turned to the CIA for help in solving the Castro problem. The Agency had managed to drive Arbenz from office in Guatemala in 1954; perhaps it could accomplish the same thing in Cuba. In
February, Eisenhower called Allen Dulles to the Oval Office to discuss

Castro. Dulles brought along some U-2 photographs of a Cuban sugar refinery, along with CIA plans to put it out of action by sabotage. Eisenhower scoffed at this puny effort, noting that such damage could be easily repaired and telling Dulles that the CIA had to come up with something better. He told Dulles to go back to his people and return when they had a "program" worked out.

The CIA then began a series of assassination attempts against Castro. There were some harebrained schemes, including using the Mafia to gun Castro down, poisoning Castro's cigars or his coffee, and rigging an exotic seashell with an explosive device to be placed in Castro's favorite skin-diving area. None worked. Whether Eisenhower knew about these attempted assassinations or not, or whether he ordered them or not, cannot be said. There is no documentary evidence that this author has seen that would directly link Eisenhower with the attempts. He could have given such orders verbally and privately to Dulles, but if he did he acted out of character. Further, Eisenhower himself indicated to the CIA that he did not want Castro removed until a government-in-exile had been formed, because he feared that the probable successor to Castro in the event of a premature assassination would be Raúl Castro or Che Guevara, either of whom would be worse than Fidel.[6]

The record is clear on what Eisenhower did approve. On March 17, he met with Dulles and Richard Bissell, the CIA agent Dulles had put in charge of preparing a "program" for Cuba. Eisenhower gave the go-ahead to the program Bissell presented to him. It had four parts: (1) creation of a "responsible and unified" Cuban government-in-exile; (2) "a powerful propaganda offensive"; (3) "a covert intelligence and action organization in Cuba" that would be "responsive" to the government-in-exile; and (4) "a paramilitary force outside of Cuba for future guerrilla action." Eisenhower indicated that he liked all four parts, but put his emphasis on Bissell's first step, finding a Cuban leader living in exile who would form a government that the United States could recognize and that could direct the activities of the covert and paramilitary forces.[7]

Exactly as Herter had warned, meanwhile, the Latin-American governments were using the American obsession with Castro as arguments for increasing the flow of money and military aid to them. They argued that Castroism was spreading to their countries, and that they could stop it only with American help, which they said had to come in much larger quantities than in the past. Eisenhower decided to make a personal good-will trip to the South American continent, with three mutually contradictory aims. First, he wanted to counter Castro's appeal to the masses of Latins. Second, he wanted to convince their governments that they did not need more planes and tanks, although they did need to undertake social and economic reforms. Third, he wanted the Latins to stay firm in their anti-Communism.

The trip, which took place in February, included stops in Puerto Rico, Brazil, Argentina, Chile, and Uruguay. Huge crowds greeted him, and they were friendly enough, but their mood was best summed up by a sign in Rio de Janeiro proclaiming, "We like Ike; We like Fidel too." In thirty-seven speeches and talks, Eisenhower's theme was that the United States did not support right-wing dictators and was not opposed to needed reforms in Latin America. Again and again, he cited the goodness of American intentions, without much effect. Nor could the President convince the Latin leaders to get tough with Castro or to lower their demands for arms. And his attempts to persuade them to institute social reforms themselves were also ignored. About the best that could be said for the journey as a whole was that it got him out of Washington at a miserable time of the year and allowed him to enjoy the South American summer while seeing places he had always wanted to see.[8]

On January 20, 1960, Eisenhower had one year to go in office. That morning, he talked to Ann Whitman about the future. He planned to do some writing, he said, and he wondered if Whitman would come to Gettysburg to set up an office there for him. Whitman recorded in her diary, "I said I would do anything he wanted me to do. He said that he had thought that while I was willing to sacrifice my life for the country for eight years, he didn't think I would want to when he was a private citizen. I said that was the silliest thing he had ever said, that my dedication to him was ten times my dedication to my country. He admitted that might be so."[9]

Eisenhower had already given his papers to the government, eventually to be processed, housed, and made available to scholars at the Eisenhower Library, built with private funds by the Eisenhower Foundation in Abilene, Kansas. First, however, Whitman's extensive file, containing most of the private correspondence, summaries of telephone calls, minutes of Cabinet meetings, and so forth, would go to Gettysburg, where Eisenhower would use the documents in writing his memoirs. An old friend, General Willard S. Paul, currently the president of Gettysburg College, offered Eisenhower the use of the president's house on the campus as an office (Paul said he preferred to live elsewhere). The highly classified material, primarily Goodpaster's files, would be stored in safes at Fort Ritchie, an Army base one-half hour's drive from Gettysburg, so that the files would be available to Eisenhower for the writing of his memoirs. John Eisenhower, who planned to resign his commission effective January 20, 1961, agreed to be the custodian of the papers, and to assist his father in the writing of the memoirs.[10]

In early 1960, Eisenhower's thoughts were primarily on his retirement, and on the upcoming summit conference, where he had high hopes on getting started on some genuine disarmament. Nearly every other politician in America, however, had his thoughts on the upcoming presidential election. Eisenhower stayed aloof from the Democratic struggle for the nomination, although in private he expressed his anger and disgust at Kennedy's constant harping on a "missile gap" and other exaggerated remarks. At a Republican meeting on April 26, for example, Styles Bridges informed the President that Kennedy had said the day before that seventeen million Americans went to bed hungry every night. Eisenhower snorted, then commented, "They must all be dieting!!!"[11]

Similarly, Eisenhower remained aloof from the Republican's pre-convention activities. Early in 1960, Rockefeller was still a candidate, which gave a bit of drama to the Republicans but no satisfaction to Eisenhower, who had long ago decided that Rockefeller did not have either the brains or the character to be President. He did write Rockefeller a long letter of advice, of which the principal point was to stick to the middle of the road, but he so deplored Rockefeller's deficit financing in New York State, and Rockefeller's calls for more defense spending, that he could never support the man for the Presidency.[12] That left him with Nixon, the only viable Republican candidate, but he was not happy with Nixon either. Still, he had no one else to support, and as between Nixon and any of the Democratic candidates, he much preferred Nixon.

He would not, however, give Nixon his support until the Republicans, meeting in convention, actually nominated him. After Rockefeller withdrew from the race, Marvin Arrowsmith asked Eisenhower at a press conference if he would not now endorse Nixon. Eisenhower refused to do so, maintaining "that there are a number of Republicans, eminent men, big men, that could fulfill the requirements of the position . . ." Then he added lamely that Nixon "is not unaware of my sentiments" toward him. Later in the same conference, William Knighton asked if the President did not think that the country ought to have the benefit of his advice as to which Republicans he regarded as qualified. Well, Eisenhower replied, "There's a number of them." Then, from Nixon's point of view, he made things worse by saying, "I am not dissatisfied with the individual that looks like he will get it," but still he would not endorse Nixon by name.[13]

Nevertheless, he was not completely resigned to Nixon's nomination. He tried to persuade Robert Anderson to become a candidate; when that failed, he asked Oveta Culp Hobby to get the Texas Republicans to organize behind Anderson as a "favorite son." If that was not possible, he suggested that she might become a candidate herself. He also tried to get Al Gruenther to run. Nothing worked, as no one was ready to take on Nixon, because his strength with the party organization was too great.[14]

One of Eisenhower's major objections to Rockefeller was that the New York governor was sounding like an echo of Kennedy in his positions on defense spending. That Rockefeller would adopt the Democratic position on defense (spend more, now, on every conceivable weapon) irritated Eisenhower no end. So did the partisan use of the issue by the Democrats. "I don't take it very kindly," Eisenhower told a January 13 press conference, "the implied accusation that I am dealing with the whole matter of defense on a partisan basis." Hauling out his heaviest artillery, he pointed out that with regard to national defense, "I've spent my life in this, and I know more about it than almost anybody." In short, he wanted the people to "trust Ike" and turn away from the Democratic critics.[15]

At his private meetings with Republican leaders, Eisenhower was blunt and direct in castigating the Democratic candidates. "By getting into this numbers racket," he said of Kennedy, Symington, and the others, "and by scaring people, they are getting away with murder." The President wondered "how much deterrent could possibly be wanted by the critics. Did they just want to build more and more Atlases for storage in warehouses? It was unconscionable."[16]

The Air Force was the darling of congressional Democrats, and the Air Force's pet project was the B-70 bomber. Eisenhower did not like the project at all. In February, he received a long memorandum on the B-70 from Kistiakowsky that concluded, "Putting it crudely, it is not clear what the B-70 can do that ballistic missiles can't—and cheaper and sooner at that." The President decided to cancel the B-70.[17] General White, Air Force Chief of Staff, testified before Congress that the B-70 was "vital" to the nation's defense. A furious Eisenhower called Secretary Gates on the telephone. According to Whit-man's notes, "The President said that ever since the days of the Fair Deal and the New Deal, discipline had been lost in the high-ranking officers of the services. Nothing does he deplore more. Everyone seems to think he has a compulsion to tell in public his personal views." Once a decision was made by the Commander in Chief, he insisted, every officer in the armed services was duty-bound to support it.[18] To the Republican leaders, Eisenhower complained that "all these fellows in the Pentagon think they have some responsibility I can't see." He continued, "I hate to use the word, but this business is damn near treason."[19]

Eisenhower was fighting virtually a one-man battle on holding down the costs of defense. The JCS would not support him; neither would his new Secretary of Defense, Tom Gates; nor would McCone, the head of the AEC; nor would the Republican leaders, who tried to convince him that the JCS were not out of line in expressing their own views. Further, not a single member of the White House press corps was on his side; the questions he received at his press conferences were uniformly hostile. Why wasn't the United States doing more? When would we catch up with the Russians? Did not the President fear a Soviet first strike? Was not the President's insistence on fiscal soundness imperiling the nation's security?

With a great effort of will, Eisenhower calmly and patiently an-swered all the questions. He insisted that there was no missile gap, that American prestige was not at stake in the space race, that there was no need to be afraid. He cited history to prove his point: "Only three or four years ago," he said, "there was a great outcry about the alleged bomber gap." Congress appropriated nearly a billion dollars more than Eisenhower had asked for to build new American bombers. "Subsequent intelligence investigation," however, "showed that that estimate was wrong and that, far from stepping up their production of bombers, the Soviets were diminishing it or even eliminating that production."[20] Eisenhower also tried logic. On February 3, Merriman Smith wanted to know, "Do you feel any sense of urgency in catching up with the Russians?" Eisenhower replied, "I am always a little bit amazed about this business of catching up. What you want is enough, a thing that is adequate. A deterrent has no added power, once it has become completely adequate, for compelling the respect for your de-terrent." But, Rowland Evans protested, the Air Force was insisting that unless the B-52s were put on a full air alert, "our deterrent of heavy bombers cannot be properly safeguarded." Eisenhower's reply was short and scathing: "Too many of these generals have all sorts of ideas."[21]

But neither historical truth nor logic was Eisenhower's best weapon. It was his personal prestige that counted most. When Charles Shutt asked him to comment on Democratic charges that he was "complacent in advising the people of the danger we face in world affairs," and that Eisenhower was allowing his commitment to fiscal soundness to "stand in the way of developing some weapons we may need," Eisenhower stiffened, reddened, glared at Shutt, then replied: "If anybody— anybody—believes that I have deliberately misled the American people, I'd like to tell him to his face what I think about him. This is a charge that I think is despicable; I have never made it against anyone in the world." Then he insisted, "I don't believe we should pay one cent for defense more than we have to," and concluded with a personal assurance: "Our defense is not only strong, it is awesome, and it is respected elsewhere."[22]

But wherever he turned, Eisenhower was confronted with the charge that he, the man most responsible for it, had neglected the nation's security. In March 1960, he attended the annual Gridiron dinner in Washington. Senator Symington was the principal speaker, and his theme was the need for more and better weapons. When he finished, Eisenhower took the mike. The President described the day he moved into the Oval Office, and how the JCS started coming in even before he had hung his pictures on the wall or had the carpet put down. The Chiefs insisted that they had to have more of this and more of that. After he had gotten rid of them, Eisenhower related, he paced the bare floor, looked out the window and said to himself, "My God, how did I get into this?" Then he went into what one observer called a "magnificent explanation of the responsibilities of the Presidency and how they far exceed the importance of weapons . . . He went into the responsibilities to the whole nation and to the family and the whole man. He talked about the spiritual things as well as material things. He built an awesome and inspiring and yet heartwarming image of the broad scope and high responsibilities that are a President's. And then he said goodnight."[23]

But no matter how effective the President was in making his case before small groups, or at his press conferences, the critics kept pounding at him. At a February 4 NSC meeting, Kistiakowsky noted in his diary, "McCone gave a rather emotional speech, saying he received many telephone calls from all over the country, complaining about the inadequacy of our deterrent forces." The chairman of the AEC demanded a much larger missile program, and a full B-52 air alert.

"He also wanted vigorous work to increase the explosive yield in Minuteman warheads," which would have required new tests. "The President spoke firmly," Kistiakowsky recorded, "that he would not accept McCone's point of view because: firstly, he was deeply convinced that we have adequate deterrents, and secondly, an increase in military effort would so disrupt the national economy that only a highly regimented society of an armed camp could result, and he was not willing to work for that."[24]

Eisenhower's basic position was that there was no missile gap. The proposition could not be proved, however, without revealing the U-2 flights and showing the photographic evidence demonstrating that the Russians were not building ICBMs on a crash basis. But Eisenhower was extremely sensitive about the flights, and about the resulting Russian protests, and he insisted that the U-2 be kept top secret (within the White House, only he, Gordon Gray, Goodpaster, and John Eisenhower knew about the project). He "exploded," therefore, when *The New York Times* ran a story, based on a leak from unnamed sources, hinting at American knowledge of Russian missile developments at Tura Tam in Central Asia. Kistiakowsky noted that "the President is exceedingly angry and has talked at length about lack of loyalty to the U.S. of these people. In his estimation Joseph Alsop is about the lowest form of animal life on earth . . ."[25]

Eisenhower wanted to not only hold down the costs of defense, but to actually reduce them through a general disarmament program. He recognized that "an effective ban on nuclear testing had become an essential preliminary to . . . attaining any worthwhile disarmament agreement."[26] As with levels of defense spending, however, he found that he stood virtually alone within his Administration. Gates, McCone, the JCS, Teller, and many others insisted on the need to resume testing. So did Nelson Rockefeller, who publicly advocated resumption of testing, because the United States "cannot afford to fall behind in the advanced techniques of the use of nuclear materials." But on the specific issue of testing, Eisenhower had strong support from outside the Administration. Fear of fallout was so great that both Kennedy and Hubert Humphrey, the leading Democratic contenders, said that they wanted to continue the testing moratorium "indefinitely," provided that the Russians did not resume their tests. Nixon also spoke out, saying that men like Rockefeller who called for test resumption were "ignorant of the facts."[27] Eisenhower also had strong support from his science adviser, George Kistiakowsky.

By early 1960, Eisenhower had made a test-ban treaty, to be followed by some actual disarmament, the major goal of his Presidency, indeed of his entire career. It would be the capstone to his half century of public service, his greatest memorial, his final and most lasting gift to his country. To that end, he wanted to make an offer to the Russians that he felt had a good chance of being accepted by Khrushchev at the summit. On February 11, he announced at his press conference that he was willing to accept a test-ban treaty that would end all tests in the atmosphere, in the oceans, and in outer space, as well as underground tests "which can be monitored."[28]

While Eisenhower waited for a Russian response, he had to fend off the Pentagon and its supporters, who were terribly unhappy with the whole prospect of a test ban. The day after he made his announcement, the JCS presented to him a plan for strategic war that indicated the United States could "prevail" in a nuclear exchange, and stating that the radiation problem would not be unmanageable. Kistiakowsky noted that "the President spoke with some feeling about the proposed overkill" (the JCS plan would leave 200 million Chinese and Russians dead), and "cited his disbelief . . . that a complete destruction of the U.S.S.R. would not contaminate the air over America."[29]

A week later, Eisenhower met with Herter, Gates, McCone, and Kistiakowsky to discuss a State Department proposal to call a ten-nation conference to cut off fissionable materials' production for weapons' purposes. Gates protested: the Secretary of Defense said that the armed services needed more, not less weapons, and added that further tests were necessary to improve the bombs. McCone protested: the chairman of the AEC warned Eisenhower that whatever the Russians agreed to in public, they would cheat. According to Kistiakowsky (who favored the proposal, as well as a test-ban treaty), "The President then delivered a strong statement, virtually condemning Gates and the Chiefs . . . for their utter inability to see the positive side. He suggested that the Soviets would also stop production and that he saw no alternative but somehow to stop this mad race . . ."[30]

On March 19, the Russians did indeed respond positively to Eisenhower's proposal of February 11. The Soviets would agree to all of it, provided that the United States agreed to a moratorium on low-kiloton tests underground. By so doing, the Russians were making considerable concessions—accepting a supervised test ban for all atmospheric, underwater, and large underground tests, which meant opening their borders to American inspection teams. All they asked in return was a voluntary cessation of small underground tests based solely on good faith.[31]

Good faith the Americans could not muster. Eisenhower was bombarded with advice to reject any unsupervised ban out of hand—he got it from the Defense Department, the JCS, the AEC, newspaper editorials, and politicians. It was taken for granted that the Russians would cheat; as *The New York Times* put it, an unsupervised ban, even if only for small bombs, "would leave the Soviets free to continue experiments behind the Iron Curtain to develop Premier Khrushchev's fantastic weapons."[32] Macmillan was disturbed by the American hostility—he wanted to accept the offer—and eagerly accepted Eisenhower's invitation to fly to Washington for consultation. But he was not optimistic. "The Americans are divided, and with an Administration on the way out," he commented, "the Pentagon and the Atomic groups are gaining strength."[33]

Macmillan need not have worried. Eisenhower had already decided to make some concessions of his own in an attempt to meet the Russians halfway. He accepted Herter's recommendation that he agree to a two- or three-year unsupervised moratorium on underground tests, which went against his previous policy of never signing a treaty that did not contain proper inspection systems, but which could not fail to impress the Russians. In any case, he had already won the main points—no more tests in the atmosphere, space, or the oceans, and the right, in principle, to send American inspection teams inside the Soviet Union. He announced his decision at a March 24 NSC meeting; after it ended, he called seven men into his office for discussion. McCone spoke first. He stated his objections to any such agreement. Kistiakowsky noted, "The President in a sharp voice rejected McCone's point of view and got obviously angry when McCone suggested that [the agreement] was a surrender of our basic policy. The President said . . . [he] felt that this was in the interests of the country, as otherwise all hope of relaxing the cold war would be gone."[34]

After McCone, the Deputy Secretaries of Defense spoke. They insisted that the Soviets would cheat. Eisenhower calmly reminded them that the United States was preparing a program, code named Plowshare, for exploding nuclear weapons for peaceful purposes, such as building tunnels. He did not need to remind every man in the room that the United States expected to get new military information from the blasts, although publicly insisting that they were for peaceful uses only. In short, the United States was already cheating. Goodpaster noted that "the President commented that the only real hazard is that the Soviets test and we do not. But the fact is that we have been doing some experimenting . . ."[35]

This meeting was, potentially, one of the most important Eisenhower ever presided over. What was at stake was the nuclear-arms race. Never before had the Russians and the Americans been so close to agreement. The details could be finished in time for the summit in Paris in mid-May. It was a dizzying prospect. James Reston wrote in *The New York Times* that the President was "confronted with the most serious decision he has had to make since he ordered the Allied troops to cross the English Channel for the invasion of Europe . . ." Appropriately enough, three of the eight men in the room kept notes—of them, Gordon Gray caught best the President's sentiments. Eisenhower, Gray wrote, made the following points: (1) There must be an agreement. (2) We cannot continue to refuse to go a part of the way. (3) It is in our vital interest to get an agreement. (4) He would prefer a one-year moratorium (the Soviets were asking for an unlimited one) but would accept two years. (5) "If we do not make some progress in one line such as this then there is no hope whatsoever for disarmament." (6) "The President wants to give Khrushchev every chance to prove that he will do what he says . . ."[36]

On March 28, Eisenhower and Macmillan went to Camp David, along with Herter and Kistiakowsky. The Prime Minister was delighted by Eisenhower's decision. When Eisenhower said he would offer a one-year moratorium, while he would be prepared to accept a two-year ban, Macmillan suggested that three years might be a reasonable time. When Kistiakowsky mentioned that the number of on-site inspections would surely be a negotiable point, Macmillan said, "You know, it might happen that you would suggest a hundred, and we ten, and the Soviets might suggest five." Herter said it would probably be necessary to leave the number of on-site inspections blank in the treaty, to be filled in at the summit. Eisenhower agreed that such was the case. Then, as Kistiakowsky noted, "In a simple quick way, [the President] conceded to the Soviets one of their main contentions, namely, that the number of on-site inspections is a political rather than a technical issue."[37]

On March 29, Eisenhower issued a statement outlining his decision. At a press conference the following day, he reassured doubtful reporters at some length. Nothing was being risked or sacrificed, he said. What was really behind it, he added, was his personal belief "that we should try to stop the spreading of this, what you might say, the size of the [nuclear] club. There are already four nations into it [France in February had exploded its first bomb], and it's an expensive business. And it could be finally more dangerous than ever . . ."

Eisenhower also insisted that "all the signs are that the Soviets do want a degree of disarmament, and they want to stop testing. That looks to me to be more or less proved."[38]

At another press conference, a month later, after Eisenhower had announced that he, de Gaulle, and Macmillan agreed that disarmament, not Berlin or Germany, should be the number-one topic at the Paris summit, Laurence Burd wanted to know if disarmament would not mean economic depression for the United States. Eisenhower explained why it would not: "We are now scratching around to get money for such things as school construction . . . , road building. There are all sorts of things to be done in this country . . . I see no reason why the sums which now are going into these sterile, negative mechanisms that we call war munitions shouldn't go into something positive."[39]

Eisenhower was prepared to go to Paris to seek a genuine accord. Never in the Cold War did one seem closer. A President of the United States was on the verge of trusting the Russians in the most critical and dangerous field, nuclear testing. He had de Gaulle and Macmillan with him, and Khrushchev seemed by every indication to be sincere in his own desire for disarmament. There were, however, powerful men determined to stop the progress.

First, the politicians. The Democrats, controlling the Joint Congressional Committee on Atomic Energy, held hearings on the proposal. Dr. Teller, and many others, testified that the Russians would cheat, that the proposed inspection systems were woefully inadequate, that the whole thing was a disaster for American security interests. McCone, purportedly the prime mover behind the hearings, told Kistiakowsky that the proposed ban was "a national peril" that might force him "to resign his job." Arthur Krock believed that the Democrats were holding the much-publicized hearings in order to cast doubts in advance on any treaty Eisenhower managed to obtain, so as to deprive the Republicans of the peace issue in the November election. Eisenhower himself thought "that goddamned joint committee will certainly do anything in its power to embarrass me."[40]

Second, the military. The Pentagon wanted no part of a ban, wanted to resume testing, and wanted a major buildup in ICBMs. At an April 1 NSC meeting, Eisenhower "sharply questioned" the Defense people about the rate of proposed buildup. The reply was that they were seeking a production capacity of four hundred missiles per year. Eisenhower, according to Kistiakowsky, "remarked in obvious disgust, 'Why don't we go completely crazy and plan on a force of 10,000?' "[41]

Third, the scientists. Teller and the AEC scientists, and their friends, were determined to continue testing. Their device was through "peaceful" explosions. They appealed to Eisenhower's great desire to use nuclear energy for the good of mankind to make all sorts of proposals for Operation Plowshare. Teller told an April 26 Cabinet meeting that he wanted to dig a tunnel through Mexico and another parallel to the Panama Canal; he wanted to blast a harbor in northern Alaska, with a short channel and a turnaround basin; he wanted to deposit heat in underground caverns by setting off a bomb, then draw on the energy later; he saw splendid opportunities for strip mining through atomic blasts. Given the opportunity, he said, he could squeeze oil out of the sands. All these glittering prospects could become reality only if he were allowed to test. When Defense Secretary Gates asked him how much these experiments would add to weapons' developments, Teller assured him a great deal would be learned. He also added that the proposed moratorium "can be evaded with complete safety by us . . . it can easily be evaded." Eisenhower gave permission to go ahead with preparations for Plowshare, but insisted that the record show that "final authorization for the actual detonation would be reserved for action by the President." He was not going to have the AEC setting off any bombs, no matter how peaceful the purpose, before the summit meeting.[42]

Fourth, the intelligence community. The CIA and other intelligence gatherers were strongly opposed to any unsupervised ban, and were especially insistent that U-2 flights over the Soviet Union be continued and even expanded. They were concerned about "gaps" in the coverage. In a meeting with the Board of Consultants on Foreign Intelligence Activities, on February 2, General Doolittle urged Eisenhower to use the overflights to the maximum degree possible. Eisenhower, according to Goodpaster's notes, "pointed out that such a decision is one of the most soul-searching questions to come before a President." He added that at Camp David Khrushchev had outlined for him Soviet missile capability, and "every bit of information I have seen [from the overflights] corroborates what Khrushchev told me."

Goodpaster's notes continue: "The President said that he has one tremendous asset in a summit meeting, as regards effect in the free world. That is his reputation for honesty. If one of these aircraft were lost when we are engaged in apparently sincere deliberations, it could be put on display in Moscow and ruin the President's effectiveness."[43]

Despite this basic recognition, Eisenhower approved additional flights, but only at the rate of one per month. One reason was the standard assumption by the intelligence community that even if the Soviets ever shot down a U-2, they never would admit it, because they would then also have to admit that the flights had been going on for years and they had been unable to do anything about them. The logic was questionable, but the eagerness to get more photographs was real enough. In late March, Richard Bissell explained to Eisenhower why the CIA thought the Russians might be building new missile sites, while John Eisenhower and Goodpaster traced out for him on a huge map of Russia the proposed flight route. Eisenhower set aside his personal objections and authorized one flight. It went on April 9. The Russians tracked the U-2 with their radar and made a number of attempts to knock it down with their surface-to-air missiles (SAMs), but the flight was a success.[44] The photographs revealed no new missile construction. In early April, Bissell asked for another flight. Eisenhower authorized him to fly any day in the next two weeks. Every day for the next fourteen days, however, Russia was covered by clouds. The U-2 needed near-perfect weather to get its photographs. When the weather did not improve, Bissell applied for an extension. Eisenhower told Goodpaster to call Bissell and tell him the flight was authorized for one more week. Goodpaster made it formal with a memorandum for the record: "After checking with the President, I informed Mr. Bissell that one additional operation may be undertaken, provided it is carried out prior to May 1. No operation is to be carried out after May 1." Eisenhower had insisted on that date because he did not want to be provocative on the eve of the summit meeting.[45]

On May 1, the weather cleared. That morning, in Adana, Turkey, Francis Gary Powers, a young pilot employed by the CIA, took off for Bodo, Norway, his flight route taking him directly over the Soviet Union.

Meanwhile, Eisenhower prepared for the summit. In March and April, he met with de Gaulle and Adenauer in the White House, getting their agreement to make disarmament the main topic in Paris. He indicated that he intended to follow the test-ban treaty with a new variation on Open Skies, an offer for continuous aerial inspection, divorced from any disarmament aspects, and operating in selected regions, for example Siberia and Alaska. He wrote Macmillan, saying, "I would derive tremendous satisfaction out of seeing some specific practical step agreed upon at the summit, and initiated as soon as possible . . . It would be a ray of light in a world that is bound to be weary of the tensions brought about by mutual suspicion, distrust, and arms races."[46]

With Soviet Ambassador Menshikov, Eisenhower made up an itinerary for his trip to Russia following the summit. He told Menshikov that he hated to say it, but he would not be able to bring the grandchildren along. He truthfully admitted that the reason was that their father and mother, John and Barbara, wished to give them as normal an upbringing as possible, and had therefore insisted they refuse the invitation.[47] (Later, when Khrushchev withdrew the invitation, Mamie blamed it on John; Khrushchev had reneged, Mamie said, because of his hurt feelings about John's unreasonable attitude.)

By late April, Eisenhower was ready for the summit. He expected tough bargaining and intended to do more than a bit of it himself. As he told de Gaulle and Macmillan, just before the end of April, the Soviets wanted to reduce their military burdens, and were particularly anxious to ban nuclear tests because of their fear that the Chinese would get their own bomb. Eisenhower said he planned to "capitalize on these apparent Soviet desires," first of all by making Berlin a *quid pro quo*. He wanted de Gaulle and Macmillan to join him in emphasizing to Khrushchev, privately, "that Communist action against our rights in Berlin would bring a rapid end to the détente, in general, and to any prospect for early disarmament, in particular." Eisenhower also indicated that although he was in favor of a "thaw," he did not want it misunderstood; "we do *not* want to gloss over the difference between freedom and totalitarianism with vague references to 'peaceful coexistence' and 'improved atmosphere.' "[48]

Despite that final statement, Eisenhower's hopes were far higher than his fears. His own desire to make a breakthrough in the arms race, as his final act as a world leader, was greater than ever. His Secretary of State, Herter, was distinctly milder toward the Soviets than Foster Dulles had ever been. Eisenhower had a science adviser who assured him that a test ban would strengthen not only America's moral position but her strategic situation as well. The JCS were no longer his contemporaries, as Bradley and Radford had been in the early years, but relatively junior officers from World War II, men who could not impress him. Macmillan wanted a test ban, de Gaulle wanted peace, Khrushchev wanted an agreement, Eisenhower was ready to take some risks and make some concessions. The atmosphere, on the eve of the summit, could not have been better.

•   •

On the afternoon of May 1, two weeks before Eisenhower was scheduled to fly to Paris, Goodpaster called him on the telephone: "One of our reconnaissance planes," he said, "on a scheduled flight from its base in Adana, Turkey, is overdue and possibly lost." The information was disturbing but not alarming. If the plane had crashed, or been shot down, there was no possibility of the pilot, Francis Powers, escaping alive. Further, the CIA had assured the President "that if a plane were to go down it would be destroyed either in the air or on impact, so that proof of espionage would be lacking. Self-destroying mechanisms were built in." The CIA had *not* told Eisenhower that the "self-destruct mechanism" had to be activated by the pilot, or that it was only a two-and-one-half-pound charge, hardly sufficient to "destroy" a craft as big as the U-2, or that the hundreds of feet of tightly rolled film would survive a crash and/or fire, thus by itself providing the Soviets with all the evidence they would need. Eisenhower assumed that Powers was dead, his U-2 burned to cinders. He thanked Goodpaster for the information and went on to other business.[49]

The next morning, May 2, Goodpaster came into the Oval Office. "Mr. President," he said, "I have received word from the CIA that the U-2 reconnaissance plane I mentioned yesterday is still missing. The pilot reported an engine flameout at a position about thirteen hundred miles inside Russia and has not been heard from since. With the amount of fuel he had on board, there is not a chance of his still being aloft."[50] If Powers was not aloft, he was dead, and his craft destroyed. Eisenhower therefore decided to do nothing, leaving the next move to Khrushchev, who it was assumed (or hoped) would also do nothing. Having shot down a U-2, the Russians had made their point. If Khrushchev was sincere about the summit, he would either downplay the event or ignore it altogether, contenting himself with a private remark or two to Eisenhower in Paris.

Over the next few days, Eisenhower continued his preparations for the summit. On May 5, he awoke to discover that at 7:15 A.M. he had to fly to High Point, North Carolina, for an emergency meeting of the NSC in the Relocation Center there (code named Crystal), a mammoth underground structure containing all the latest electronic and communication equipment. The meeting was part of a continuing civil-defense exercise, designed to test the ability of the members of the NSC to get to High Point, with no previous knowledge of the date or time, as soon as possible. The exercise did not go well—Allen Dulles' Cadillac broke down and he almost did not make it; General

Twining, chairman of the JCS, did not make it at all; Secretary Gates had to be driven to the airport by his wife in her nightgown, had no pass when he arrived at the entrance, and almost did not persuade the guards to let him through. The meeting itself was routine—the major item was a history of U.S. and U.S.S.R. long-range missile development. Kistiakowsky found it boring.[51]

While the meeting was going on, Jim Hagerty learned from the wire services that Khrushchev had that morning made a speech to the Supreme Soviet in which he claimed that the Soviet Union had shot down an American spy plane that had intruded Soviet airspace. Khrushchev angrily denounced the United States for its "aggressive provocation" in sending a "bandit flight" over his country. In the course of a long harangue, Khrushchev said the Americans had picked May Day, "the most festive day for our people and the workers of the world," hoping to catch the Soviets with their guard down, but to no avail. Khrushchev provided his own interpretation of the provocative flight: "Aggressive imperialist forces in the United States in recent times have been taking the most active measures to undermine the summit or at least to hinder any agreement that might be reached." He did not blame Eisenhower, however; instead, he suggested that the militarists were acting without the President's knowledge. "Was this aggressive act carried out by Pentagon militarists?" he asked. "If such actions are taken by American military men on their own account, it must be of special concern to world opinion."[52]

Khrushchev's charge that Eisenhower did not know what was going on in his own Administration, which dovetailed so nicely with the ongoing Democratic campaign, angered the President. Still, he decided to make no rejoinder, nor any explanation. He could have refuted the charges immediately. He might have issued a statement taking full responsibility, pointing out that no U-2 flight ever left the ground without his personal approval, insisting that because of the closed nature of the Soviet Union and because of fears of a nuclear Pearl Harbor, the overflights were necessary to the security of his country. In the process, he could have reminded the world that, as everyone knew, the KGB was far more active in spying on the West than the CIA was in spying on Russia. He might have given a brief outline of the history of the U-2, then made the most fundamental point of all—that the evidence gathered by the overflights provided convincing proof that there was no missile gap, despite Khrushchev's boasting about Soviet rockets, and that as a result of the photographs, the United States had been able to keep some kind of control on its own defense spending.

But he did none of these things, because he had a fetish about keeping the U-2 a secret. The odd thing about this fetish was that the U-2 was no secret to the Soviets, and had not been since the very first flight, back in 1956. Indeed, all the governments involved—British, French, Turkish, Norwegian, Formosan, and others—knew about the U-2. The people who did not know were the Americans and their elected representatives.[53]

Another option available to Eisenhower would have been to state that since the Soviets had turned down Open Skies, he had decided to unilaterally put it into effect anyway, and then invite Khrushchev to fly all he wanted to across the United States. To do that, however, Eisenhower would have had to make public the U-2 flights. Although it is difficult to see, a quarter of a century later, when Russian and American spy satellites are constantly in orbit around the world, what damage could have resulted, Eisenhower decided to make a desperate effort to keep the overflights a secret, or at least to deny their existence. Instead of confessing, he launched a cover-up.

He did so because he thought a cover-up would work. Acting on the assumption that Powers was dead and his plane in ruins, Eisenhower believed that Khrushchev could prove nothing. The irony—or perhaps the tragedy, considering what was at stake at the summit— was that Eisenhower himself had pointed out that his greatest single asset was his "reputation for honesty," and that if a U-2 were lost "when we are engaged in apparently sincere deliberations, it could be put on display in Moscow and ruin the President's effectiveness." But he clung to the hope that Khrushchev, without any physical evidence, would be unconvincing.

On the afternoon of May 5, after returning to Washington, Eisenhower approved a statement that was then issued by the National Aeronautics and Space Administration. It began, "One of N.A.S.A.'s U-2 research airplanes, in use since 1956 in a continuing program to study meteorological conditions found at high altitude, has been miss-ing since May 1, when its pilot reported he was having oxygen diffi-culties over the Lake Van, Turkey, area." Presumably, the U-2 had strayed off course, perhaps crossing the border into Russia. The un-stated assumption was that Powers' weather plane was the one the Russians had shot down.[54]

The following day, Khrushchev released a photograph of a wrecked airplane, describing it as the U-2 Powers had flown. It was not, however, a U-2, but another airplane. The Premier was setting a trap. He wanted Eisenhower to continue to believe that Powers was dead, the U-2 destroyed, so that the United States would stick to its "weather research" story, as it did. Then, on May 7, Khrushchev sprang his great surprise. He jubilantly reported to a "wildly cheering" Supreme Soviet that "we have parts of the plane and we also have the pilot, who is quite alive and kicking. The pilot is in Moscow and so are the parts of the plane." Khrushchev made his account a story of high drama and low skulduggery interspersed with bitingly sarcastic remarks about Eisenhower's cover story. Cries of "Shame, Shame!" rose from the deputies as Khrushchev heaped scorn on the CIA, mixed with cries of "Bandits, Bandits!" [55]

Upon receiving the news of Powers' capture by the Russians alive, news that he found "unbelievable," Eisenhower knew that since Khrushchev had both the plane and the pilot (and the film), there was little point in denying any further the real purpose of the overflights. He was not ready, however, to tell the American people, and the world, that he personally was involved in the distasteful business of spying. Dulles, Herter, and other top officials were frantically trying to find ways to protect the President. (During a 4:30 P.M. phone call, Dulles referred to a statement Herter wanted to release, saying, "There is an inconsistency." Herter replied that "this was to get the President off the hook. Mr. Dulles said he would do anything he could." [56]) On Herter's recommendation, Eisenhower then authorized the State Department to issue a statement denying that Powers had any authorization to fly over the Soviet Union.

That statement was so ill conceived and so poorly timed that it made a bad situation much worse. As James Reston reported in *The New York Times*, "The United States admitted tonight that one of this country's planes equipped for intelligence purposes had 'probably' flown over Soviet territory.

"An official statement stressed, however, that 'there was no authorization for any such flight' from authorities in Washington.

"As to who might have authorized the flight, officials refused to comment. If this particular flight of the U-2 was not authorized here, it could only be assumed that someone in the chain of command in the Middle East or Europe had given the order." [57]

The following morning, May 9, an agitated Secretary of Defense called a disturbed Secretary of State on the telephone. Gates did not like at all the implication that his officers in the field were authorizing unapproved flights over Soviet territory. According to the summary of the conversation, "Gates said we should say that it is a matter of national policy and we have been doing it because everything else has failed. Gates said somebody has to take responsibility for the policy and while the President can say he didn't know about this one flight, he did approve the policy." Herter replied that "the President didn't argue with this but for the moment doesn't want to say anything and we have been trying to keep the President clear on this."

Twenty-five minutes later, Eisenhower himself called Herter. The President wanted Herter to issue a statement admitting that the overflights had been going on for years, under orders from the President, to "get adequate knowledge of the composition of the Russian military and industrial complex." Eisenhower said the statement should also point out that while he, the President, "realizes at times that unusual and unorthodox things are needed to do this," he did not get the details of spying or reconnaissance trips.[58]

The attempt to cover up continued that afternoon, when Goodpaster called Herter to say that Eisenhower wanted a statement from State that would indicate that the U-2 flights were carried out under "a very broad directive from the President given at the earliest point of his Administration to protect us from surprise attack." But, Goodpaster added, "The President wants no specific tie to him of this particular event."[59]

The resulting statements added to a national sense of humiliation, shame, and confusion. Reston reported, "This was a sad and perplexed capital tonight, caught in a swirl of charges of clumsy administration, bad judgment and bad faith.

"It was depressed and humiliated by the United States having been caught spying over the Soviet Union and trying to cover up its activities in a series of misleading official announcements."[60]

Eisenhower personally remained calm. He told Whitman, "I would like to resign," and he seemed to her to be depressed in the morning, "but by afternoon had bounced back with his characteristic ability to accept the bad news, not dwell on it, and so go ahead."[61] That afternoon, Eisenhower gave a briefing to the congressional leaders. He explained the U-2, gave a bit of its history, praised the overflights for the information they had gathered, admitted that he had fallen into Khrushchev's trap, and concluded, "We will now just have to endure the storm."[62]

Over the next two days, humiliation gave way to fright as the headlines became increasingly alarmist. "Khrushchev Warns of Rocket Attack on Bases Used by U.S. Spying Planes," the *Times* announced on May 10. The following morning, the headline read, "U.S. Vows to Defend Allies if Russians Attack Bases." Khrushchev, at an impromptu news conference in Moscow, announced that he was putting Powers on trial and added, "You understand that if such aggressive actions continue this might lead to war."[63] Eisenhower held his own news conference, where he read a prepared statement. In firm, measured tones, without a hint of regret or apology, Eisenhower said Khrushchev's antics over the "flight of an unarmed nonmilitary plane can only reflect a fetish of secrecy." Because of the nature of the Soviet system, spying "is a distasteful but vital necessity." When asked whether his trip to Russia had been canceled, he replied, "I expect to go." When asked if the outlook for the summit had changed, he replied, "Not decisively at all, no."[64]

But of course it had. No one in Washington could have supposed for a minute that Khrushchev would not exploit the fact that he had caught the Americans red-handed, and that they had lied about it. Some of Eisenhower's advisers urged him to take the way out Khrushchev had offered—deny that he knew anything about the flights and punish someone, presumably Allen Dulles, for them. Such action, the advisers argued, might still save the summit. Eisenhower rejected the advice, first of all because it was not true, secondly because it would be manifestly unfair to Dulles, thirdly because if he did such a thing, Khrushchev could refuse to deal with him at the summit on the grounds that Eisenhower obviously could not control his own Administration.[65]

With only a few days to go before the summit, Khrushchev continued to make belligerent statements, but also continued to express his doubts that Eisenhower personally knew about the flights; at one point, he even said that the KGB often carried on activities that he did not know about. Sorting out Khrushchev's motives is a hopeless task. He seemed determined to destroy the summit before it got started—but he was the one who had been most insistent about a summit meeting. He must have known he could never get Eisenhower to say that such a major operation as a U-2 flight could take place without his knowledge, just as he must have realized that Eisenhower would not make a personal apology—yet he insisted on both.[66] His histrionics, wild charges, and pretended outrage sat ill with a man who had satellites flying over the United States daily—indeed Russian newspapers had even published photographs of the United States taken by cameras aboard such satellites. Reston guessed in the *Times* that Khrushchev was pretending shock and outrage because he realized that Eisenhower was not going to pull out of Berlin, so he was using the U-2 "to blame the United States for the breakdown of the Paris meeting."[67]

De Gaulle thought that Khrushchev had had second thoughts about allowing Eisenhower to make a trip through the Soviet Union, because he feared the results if Eisenhower spoke directly to the Soviet people over television. He therefore used the U-2 to cancel the visit. Another possibility is that Khrushchev's scientists had told him what Kistiakowsky had told Eisenhower—namely, that a test ban would favor the Americans. Breaking up the summit over the U-2 would effectively put an end to test-ban talks. Some thought Khrushchev needed to impress the Chinese with his toughness. Eisenhower's own interpretation was that Khrushchev was hoping to break up NATO by using the U-2 incident to split France and Britain away from the United States.

If Eisenhower was correct, Khrushchev was in for a major disappointment, because in fact the crisis brought the Western allies closer. Eisenhower, Macmillan, and de Gaulle had first come together in Algeria in 1943, seventeen years earlier. Their common foe then had been the Nazi dictatorship. Now their common foe was a Communist dictatorship. Their determination to oppose totalitarianism and their resolution to maintain democracy and the Western alliance were as great as ever. They knew each other intimately, these three who had been through so much together. "I don't know about anybody else," Eisenhower said at their first meeting in Paris, "but I myself am getting older." De Gaulle smiled. "You don't look it," he replied. "I hope," said Eisenhower, "that no one is under the illusion that I'm going to crawl on my knees to Khrushchev." De Gaulle smiled again. "No one is under that illusion," he said. De Gaulle mentioned Khrushchev's threat to attack U-2 bases in Turkey, Japan, and elsewhere. "Rockets," Eisenhower replied without smiling, "can travel in two directions." Macmillan nodded his agreement and pledged his full support. "With us it is easy," de Gaulle said to Eisenhower, because "you and I are tied together by history."[68] In the crisis, NATO had held firm, which for Eisenhower was a heartwarming experience that justified all the effort and hope he had put into the Western alliance since December 1950. It was unfortunate that strengthening NATO required deepening the split between East and West, but then it was Khrushchev, not Eisenhower or Macmillan or de Gaulle, who made the decision to ruin the summit conference.

On May 14, Eisenhower and his party flew to Paris. The next afternoon, he met with Herter, ambassador to the Soviet Union Chip Bohlen, and Goodpaster. They informed him that Khrushchev, already in Paris, had told de Gaulle that he was prepared to go ahead with the summit, but that the Russian leader had given de Gaulle a six-page statement asserting that if Eisenhower did not condemn such actions as the U-2 flight, renounce such acts in the future, and punish those responsible, the Soviets would not take part in the summit. Eisenhower wanted to know why Khrushchev had not made such specific demands five days earlier—it would have saved him a trip to Paris. Bohlen remarked that the content of the statement, coupled with the fact that it was in written form, indicated that Khrushchev had already decided to break up the conference.[69]

Eisenhower called on de Gaulle. The French leader reported that along with the written statement, Khrushchev had told him verbally that he could not understand why Eisenhower had admitted publicly that he knew about the overflights. By Khrushchev's standards this indicated not American truthfulness, but rather contempt for the Soviets. De Gaulle said he had told Khrushchev that the Russians could not seriously expect Eisenhower to apologize. Indeed, de Gaulle discussed these matters, according to Eisenhower's interpreter, General Vernon Walters, "with a sort of Olympian detachment. . . . he did not think that the peccadilloes of intelligence services were appropriate matters to be discussed at meetings of chiefs of government."[70]

The following morning, May 16, Eisenhower had breakfast with Macmillan. Eisenhower said that "one thing was very clear in his mind and that is until we get to satellites, we will not do this kind of overflying anymore." Macmillan, who had talked privately with Khrushchev the previous day, was much encouraged by this. Khrushchev, he said, was agitated by American statements that indicated the U-2 flights would continue. "He thought clarification of this point might be of great value in the discussion with Mr. K."[71]

But at the initial meeting, Eisenhower never got a chance to make the point. He had intended to speak first, in answer to Khrushchev's written statement, but de Gaulle, the host, had hardly finished calling the meeting to order when Khrushchev was on his feet, red-faced, demanding the right to speak. De Gaulle looked quizzically at Eisenhower, who nodded his agreement, then indicated that Khrushchev had the floor. Khrushchev launched into a tirade against Eisenhower and the United States. Soon he was shouting. De Gaulle interrupted, turned to the Soviet interpreter, and said, "The acoustics in this room are excellent. We can all hear the chairman. There is no need for him to raise his voice." The interpreter blanched, turned to Khrushchev, and began to translate. De Gaulle cut him off and motioned to his own interpreter, who unfalteringly translated into Russian. Khrushchev cast a furious glance at de Gaulle, then continued to read in a lower voice.

He soon lashed himself into an even greater frenzy. He pointed overhead and shouted, "I have been overflown!" De Gaulle interrupted again. He said that he too had been overflown. "By your American allies?" asked Khrushchev, incredulous. "No," de Gaulle replied, "by you. Yesterday that satellite you launched just before you left Moscow to impress us overflew the sky of France eighteen times without my permission. How do I know you do not have cameras aboard which are taking pictures of my country?" Eisenhower caught de Gaulle's eye and gave him a big grin. Khrushchev raised both hands above his head and said, "As God is my witness, my hands are clean. You don't think I would do a thing like that?"

After Khrushchev finished his diatribe, which concluded with a statement that Eisenhower would no longer be welcome in the Soviet Union, Eisenhower spoke. He said that Khrushchev hardly needed to go to such lengths to withdraw his invitation, that he had come to Paris hoping to engage in serious discussion, and that it was his wish that the conference could now proceed to matters of substance. Khrushchev and the Russian delegation stalked out of the room. As Eisenhower rose to follow them, de Gaulle caught him by the elbow and drew him aside, with Walters to interpret. De Gaulle said to the President, "I do not know what Khrushchev is going to do nor what is going to happen, but whatever he does, or whatever happens, I want you to know that I am with you to the end." [72]

The summit was over before it started, all the hopes for détente and disarmament gone with it. Eisenhower, with only eight months to serve, would not have another chance to force progress toward genuine peace. He returned home, where he had to endure making a series of reports to various groups, including the public. He issued a formal statement, made a radio and television report, met with the congressional leaders and his Cabinet, and with the NSC. At the latter meeting, Herter said something about the need to "regain our leadership." Kistiakowsky recorded, "This made the President angry. He lost his temper and said we did not lose the leadership and therefore we didn't have to regain it, and he would appreciate it if that expression were never used again, especially before congressional committees." [73]

On May 23, Herter reported to him that the CIA and the Defense Department wanted to continue the U-2 flights. Eisenhower replied that "he had no thought whatsoever of permitting more of these . . . that they may as well realize that these flights cannot be resumed in the next eight months."[74] By August 1960, the United States had reconnaissance satellites in operation, although the U-2 continues to this day to provide photographic reconnaissance of outstanding quality. Powers was eventually exchanged for a Soviet spy, Colonel Rudolf Abel (what happened to Powers' U-2 remains a mystery).

In late May, Eisenhower had a private talk with Kistiakowsky. The President said that the scientists had failed him. Kistiakowsky protested that the scientists had consistently warned that eventually a U-2 was going to get shot down. "It was the management of the project that failed. The President flared up, evidently thinking I accused him, and used some strong uncomplimentary language." After Kistiakowsky explained that he meant the bureaucrats, not the President, were responsible, Eisenhower cooled off. He "began to talk with much feeling about how he had concentrated his efforts the last few years on ending the cold war, how he felt that he was making big progress, and how the stupid U-2 mess had ruined all his efforts. He ended very sadly that he saw nothing worthwhile left for him to do now until the end of his presidency."[75]

Eisenhower's depression was deep, genuine, and appropriate. Of all the events in Eisenhower's long lifetime, this one stands out. If only Eisenhower had not given permission for that last flight. If only Khrushchev had not made such a big deal out of such a small thing. If only the two leaders could have trusted their own instincts just once, rather than their technicians and generals. Eisenhower was on the verge of agreeing to an unsupervised test ban; Khrushchev was on the verge of agreeing to inspection teams within the Soviet Union. No one knows where the momentum thus generated might have taken the Cold War and the nuclear arms race. But both the old men allowed their fears to override their hopes, and the summit was gone, and with it the best chance to slow the arms race of the sixties and seventies and eighties.

CHAPTER TWENTY-FIVE

A Bad Summer and
a Terrible Fall

July 1–November 9, 1960

THE DISASTROUS OUTCOME of the Paris summit, combined with Eisenhower's lame-duck status, took much of the energy and vitality out of the President and his Administration. During his last half year in office, Eisenhower had nothing new to propose. He made his criteria for disarmament proposals their propaganda and political value, rather than seeking real accord with Khrushchev. He could not decide even how to define Castro, much less what to do about him. His relations with Khrushchev were characterized by snarling defiance. He grew so frustrated in attempting to deal with the problems of the Congo that he became almost irrational in his response. His control of his own party weakened badly, he could not generate much enthusiasm for his party's candidate as his successor, he was late and ineffective in his campaigning. Even an extensive foreign trip, that proved device for getting headlines, spreading good will, and allowing Eisenhower to indulge in his passion for travel, failed of its purpose, indeed left the President embarrassed.

Eisenhower had expected to go to Russia after the summit, then on to Japan. When the Russian trip was canceled, he decided to visit the Philippines, Korea, and Formosa during the time he would have been in the Soviet Union, then go to Japan. He left on June 12, going first to Manila, where he had a nostalgic visit, which was interrupted by bad news from Japan. The Japanese government had been forced to ask him to "postpone" his visit, because street rioting in protest against it had gotten out of hand and the government could not be responsible for his safety. The riots, organized by the Japanese Communists around the issue of opposition to the mutual-defense treaty the Japanese were on the verge of signing with the United States, had reached a fever pitch. Although the treaty was ratified a few days later, as Eisenhower put it in his memoirs, "viewed from any angle, this [the withdrawal of the invitation] was a Communist victory."[1] The remainder of the Far Eastern trip was routine—huge and friendly crowds greeted Eisenhower in the Philippines, Formosa, Korea, and Okinawa. (The Chinese Communists welcomed Eisenhower to Formosa by giving Quemoy and Matsu a good pasting that day.) Eisenhower talked with the various leaders, reassuring them that America was still their good friend, but offering nothing new.

Not even at home did Eisenhower have the kind of support he had come to count on when he traveled abroad. Lyndon Johnson, and other Democrats, cited "seasoned diplomats of the State Department" as being opposed to "personal diplomacy" and questioning the value of "good-will trips." Eisenhower, when told during a rest stop at Honolulu of the criticism, snapped, "Lyndon Johnson is getting to be one of those smart alecks." Eisenhower wanted to know what else Johnson was saying. Herter mentioned the broken Paris summit, Japan, and Cuba, then assured the President that "it was mostly Lyndon Johnson ranting."[2]

Eisenhower returned to Washington and more problems. Cuba, for one. Although neither Eisenhower nor his advisers could even yet decide if Castro was a Communist or not, they nevertheless wanted to be rid of him and the dangers he represented. That Trujillo could be attacked simultaneously was a bonus, rather than a problem, because it freed the United States from the charge of opposing only left-wing dictators. At every meeting that summer with Herter or the NSC, when Cuba came up, Eisenhower insisted on linking Castro and Trujillo. When, in late June, the CIA got its propaganda radio station on Swan Island into operation, it attacked first Trujillo, then Castro.

There were major differences between the two dictators, however; the one that concerned Eisenhower most was the possibility of Cuba entering into a mutual-security arrangement with the Russians, something Trujillo would never do. In Eisenhower's view, the worst possibility was Castro allowing Khrushchev to use Cuba as a base for Soviet strategic forces. He did not, however, think that was likely to happen. At a June 29 meeting with Gordon Gray, Eisenhower "observed that he did not believe that Khrushchev would enter into a mutual-security treaty with Castro," and added that Chip Bohlen shared that opinion. Khrushchev must know, Eisenhower said, that the United States "could not tolerate" a military alliance between Cuba and Russia.[3]

On July 6, Eisenhower signed legislation authorizing a major reduction in the Cuban sugar quota, and eliminating it altogether for 1961. As he admitted, "This action amounts to economic sanctions against Cuba."[4] By that time, Khrushchev had threatened to use his rockets to protect Cuba against a military attack, and was apparently attempting to incite the Cubans to take control of the American naval base at Guantánamo Bay. He was also insisting that the Soviets were not interested in putting missiles into Cuba, because his ICBMs made them unnecessary. Herter assured the President that Khrushchev's bluster was actually helpful, because as a result "the Latin-American countries have come around very well in the last few days."[5]

Taking advantage of this development, the United States called for a meeting of the American Foreign Ministers, which took place in Costa Rica in August and which condemned "intervention or the threat of intervention by the Sino-Soviet powers" in American affairs. The same conference also condemned the Dominican Republic and called on all members of the OAS to break diplomatic relations with Trujillo (which the United States did shortly thereafter).[6]

Along with his diplomatic and economic moves against Castro, Eisenhower considered a full range of military or paramilitary options. At a July 7 NSC meeting, Gates briefed him on possible moves, ranging from evacuating American citizens from Cuba to a full-scale invasion and occupation. Treasury Secretary Anderson "gave a fairly bloodthirsty long speech about the need to declare a national emergency, . . . [and] argued that what is happening in Cuba represents an aggressive action by the U.S.S.R."[7]

Eisenhower was not ready to sound the bugles and direct a charge up San Juan Hill. As he explained to Republican leaders—who, like Nixon, were desperate for some definitive action against Castro before the November elections—"If we were to try to accomplish our aims by force, we would see all of [the Latin countries] tending to fall away and some would be Communist within two years. . . . If the United States does not conduct itself in precisely the right way vis-à-vis Cuba, we could lose all of South America."[8]

Nixon wanted public action but Eisenhower continued to refuse.

The President was, however, ready to move covertly against Castro. On August 18, he met with Gates, Dulles, and Bissell to discuss implementation of the four-point plan he had approved in March. Bissell reported that point two, a powerful propaganda offensive, was under way; point three, the creation of a resistance organization within Cuba, had been a miserable failure, primarily because of Castro's police-state control. Bissell was making progress on point four, the creation of a paramilitary force from among Cuban exiles. He had moved the original training camp, outside Miami, to the Panama Canal Zone, then to Guatemala, where the CIA had excellent ties with President Miguel Ydígoras Fuentes.

Bissell wanted to expand the training program. Eisenhower agreed. The CIA had shown him photographs of Czech arms in Cuba, which helped convince him. He approved a $13 million budget for Bissell, and authorized the use of DOD personnel and equipment in the operation, although he insisted that "no United States military personnel were to be used in a combat status." Later, he also approved the mounting of a U.S. Navy patrol off the coast of Guatemala, supposedly to block a Cuban invasion, actually to keep the Guatemalan training base a secret.[9]

After giving his approval to Bissell's expanded plans, Eisenhower asked about the original point one—"Where's our government-in-exile?" Bissell and Allen Dulles explained that it was difficult to get the Cubans to work together, because some were pro-Batista, most were anti-Batista, all were hot-tempered and hardheaded, few were willing to compromise. Thus no genuine leader had emerged. Eisenhower, impatient, remarked, "Boys, if you don't intend to go through with this, let's stop talking about it." He would not approve any action, he insisted, without a popular, genuine government-in-exile.[10]

Khrushchev was making trouble not only with his remarks about Cuba, and not only with his continuing belligerent statements about American militarism, but also with his acts. On July 1, when Eisenhower and Mamie were at Gettysburg celebrating their forty-fourth wedding anniversary, the President was informed that a U.S. patrol plane, an RB-47, had disappeared over the Barents Sea, north of Russia. No one knew where the plane was—its mission was to fly along the Soviet border (under orders not to go closer than fifty miles), collecting electromagnetic, radio, and radar information—but Eisenhower had a sense of déjà vu. That sense was increased when Khrushchev, after waiting ten days in the hope that the Americans would issue another contradictory cover story, finally revealed that the Soviets had shot down the plane and picked up two survivors.

Eisenhower, in a telephone conversation with Herter after the announcement, said that he had been told the plane was thirty miles off the coast when last heard from. "This may be true," the President continued, "but he said he has gotten to the point where he doesn't trust them [the Russians] to the slightest degree. The President said they have two of our people and if these two people say maybe they were lost then we are in for it again. The President said if we can prove it was not over [Russian] territory when it was shot down, we will break relations . . ."[11]

The problem was proof. The best information on the location of the spy plane available to the Americans came from radar tracking stations that DOD and the CIA insisted the Russians knew nothing about, and they did not want to reveal their sources. Thus any flat assertion by the Americans that the plane never got within thirty miles of the coast would be met by Soviet demands for proof, which for security reasons Eisenhower would not be able to supply.[12]

A further problem was that Khrushchev was warning Eisenhower of the "seriousness" of the situation, and of the "dangerous conse- quences to which continuation of provocative actions by American aircraft will lead . . ." Khrushchev was also threatening the British (the RB-47 had taken off from a British airfield), telling them that allowing the Americans to use their airfields for "aggressive actions," would "bring great danger" to the British people.

Eisenhower's advisers, nevertheless, wanted to continue the RB-47 missions, and even revive the U-2 flights. The President wished they would pay more attention to world opinion, and proceeded to give them a lecture. As summarized by Goodpaster, Eisenhower said "that all his advisers . . . had missed badly in their estimate regarding the U-2. They had never had an idea of what the reaction . . . would be. He did not wish to say 'I told you so' but recalled that he was the one and only one who had put much weight on this factor, and that he had given it great emphasis." He then ordered all U-2s withdrawn from Japan. Goodpaster brought up a CIA and DOD request to use RB-47s in the Far East. Eisenhower said that "he thought it is essential to allow time for the political picture to develop more stability. He added that another failure would in all likelihood be bound to have a determining, adverse effect upon the election."[13]

On July 19, Eisenhower told Herter "we should not let ourselves be caught out in any story, as in the U-2 case, where we have to change

our story subsequently or acknowledge an untruth." But despite Eisenhower's association of the two spy flights, there was one outstanding
difference. In the RB-47 case, the United States was clearly within its
rights, because in fact the plane had been shot down well off the
Russian coast. Without revealing his sources, Cabot Lodge was able
to make a convincing case in the U.N. Security Council. The Russian
resolution calling for a condemnation of the "provocative action" by
the United States was rejected, 7 to 2. Then the Soviets had to veto
an American resolution calling for an investigation by the International Court of Justice. "Khrushchev's effort to make the RB-47 a
little brother to the U-2," Eisenhower later wrote, "had turned out a
miserable failure." [14] Actually, Eisenhower had enjoyed just a bit of
"Ike's luck" in that miserable summer, because while the U.N. debate
was going on, an American C-47 had, through navigation error, flown
directly over the Kuriles. The Soviets tried to shoot it down but were
unable to hit it because of fog and clouds.

Khrushchev was also making trouble in the Congo. In May, national elections were held in the Belgian colony. Three national
leaders emerged—Joseph Kasavubu, Patrice Lumumba, and in the
mineral-rich province of Katanga, Moise Tshombe. June 30 was
Independence Day. Shortly thereafter, the army, called the Force Pub-
lique, mutinied against its Belgian officers. Belgian paratroopers re-
entered the country. Meanwhile Katanga, the province that held the
mines Belgium was determined to possess, seceded from the Congo,
and Tshombe made his own deal with the Belgians. Lumumba, who
was Prime Minister of the Congo, asked for U.N. troops to restore
order. A peace-keeping force was sent. In late July, Lumumba himself
flew to the United States to ask for arms and other support, so that he
could re-establish control over Katanga. He made a bad impression
on Under Secretary of State C. Douglas Dillon, who reported, "You
had a feeling that he was a person that was gripped by this fervor
that I can only characterize as messianic. . . . He was just not a ra-
tional being." Thus, Dillon concluded, "This was an individual whom
it was impossible to deal with." [15]

Thus began the process of inducing Eisenhower to think of Lumumba as an even greater menace than Castro. The image that Dillon
and others created of the young African leader was irrational, but
Eisenhower found it convincing. What Lumumba was after was arms
with which to crush Tshombe and build a nation; what Eisenhower
saw was a Communist take-over. The image became established after

the United States rebuffed Lumumba's call for help, and he responded by going to Moscow. A Soviet airlift then began. Eisenhower feared that Soviet troops would soon follow. Herter warned him against overreacting, reminding the President that the U.N. position was to support the Congo as an entity, and pointing out that if the United States became identified with any effort to support Tshombe and an independent Katanga, it would be regarded by the other African nations as equivalent to returning Katanga to the Belgians.[16]

On August 18, Dillon reported on developments in the Congo to the NSC. Lumumba and Khrushchev were both demanding that the U.N. peace-keeping force get out of the country. Dillon said that "the elimination of the U.N. would be a disaster which . . . we should do everything we could to prevent." If the U.N. were forced out, he warned, the Soviets would come in. The minutes of the meeting continued: "Secretary Dillon said that Lumumba was working to serve the purposes of the Soviets and Mr. Dulles pointed out that Lumumba was in Soviet pay." Eisenhower commented that it was "simply inconceivable" that the United States could allow the U.N. to be forced out of the Congo. "We should keep the U.N. in the Congo," the President said, "even if such action was used by the Soviets as the basis for starting a fight." Cabot Lodge doubted that the U.N. force could stay in the Congo if the government of the Congo demanded that it leave. Eisenhower responded by stating "that Mr. Lodge was wrong to this extent—we were talking of one man forcing us out of the Congo; of Lumumba supported by the Soviets."[17]

When Eisenhower took office, back in 1953, he had been eloquent in telling Churchill that old-style European colonialism, especially in Africa, could not and should not last. Over the following seven years, he had held consistently to that position—with the French in Vietnam, with the French and British at Suez, in urging de Gaulle to recognize realities and grant a full independence to Algeria. Repeatedly, he had said that because of the intense feelings of nationalism of the colonialized peoples, no vestige of European control or domination could be allowed to continue. Yet here, in a case where the Belgians had simply abandoned their responsibilities in the poorer provinces of the Congo, while blatantly attempting to hold on to Kantanga, Eisenhower sided with the European colonialists and was completely unable to see Lumumba's point of view. His reason was not, incidentally, to keep for the West access to the uranium in Katanga; the United States at this time had an embarrassing excess of enriched uranium and was trying to sell some of the surplus to the French. Eisenhower's concern was that Lumumba would allow the Soviets to turn the Congo into their own military base, which they would then use to expand their influence and power in Africa. Rather than try to prevent that by cooperating with Lumumba, Eisenhower decided to get rid of the man.

On August 25, Dulles, Gray, and Gates met in their capacity as the CIA's watchdog committee (5412) to discuss CIA plans for action against Lumumba. Gray reported that "his associates had expressed extremely strong feelings on the necessity for very straightforward action in this situation, and he wondered whether the plans as outlined were sufficient to accomplish this." The minutes state that the committee "finally agreed that planning for the Congo would not necessarily rule out 'consideration' of any particular kind of activity which might contribute to getting rid of Lumumba." The following morning, Dulles sent a cable to a CIA agent in Leopoldville, telling him that the "removal" of Lumumba was an "urgent" objective.[18]

Before the CIA could act, the swirling events inside the Congo intervened. General Joseph Mobutu seized power via a military coup; Lumumba placed himself in the custody of the U.N. peace-keeping force. He was eventually kidnapped by Mobutu and executed. Thus the CIA was not directly involved in Lumumba's murder (although it had been in on his capture). That begs the question, however, as to whether Eisenhower ordered the man assassinated or not.

In November 1975, the U.S. Senate's Select Committee to Study Governmental Operations with Respect to Intelligence Activities, popularly known as the Church Committee, conducted widely publicized hearings into the CIA's activities, including assassination plots. One of the committee's conclusions was that "the chain of events revealed by the documents and testimony is strong enough to permit a reasonable inference that the plot to assassinate Lumumba was authorized by President Eisenhower."[19] Almost immediately, John Eisenhower, Goodpaster, Gray, and Dillon challenged this finding. In a statement to the Senate, they requested that the committee "disavow" its conclusion. Frank Church, the chairman, and John Tower, vice-chairman, refused to do so. Goodpaster testified unequivocally to the Church Committee, "At no time and in no way did I ever know of or hear about any . . . such an activity. It is my belief that had such a thing been raised with the President other than in my presence, I would have known about it." And in a 1979 interview in the superintendent's office at West Point, Goodpaster said he recalled some assistant once making a joking reference to bumping off Lumumba.

Eisenhower reddened, as Goodpaster recalled the scene, and said sternly, "That is beyond the pale. We will not discuss such things. Once you start that kind of business, there is no telling where it will end."[20]

Yet Gordon Gray admitted that when he told the 5412 committee that "his associate" wanted "very straightforward action," his reference to "associate" was a euphemism for Eisenhower, employed to preserve "plausible deniability" by the President. And Richard Bissell testified that "there isn't any doubt in my mind [that] the President did want a man whom he regarded . . . as a very dangerous one, got rid of. He would have preferred if it could be done in the nicest possible way, but he wanted it done and wasn't prepared to be too fussy about how it was done."[21] The record, in short, is deliberately obscure.* It is impossible to say conclusively whether or not Eisenhower ordered an assassination. Eisenhower's closest associates insist that he never could have ordered a cold-blooded assassination; his critics insist that Dulles never would have sent out such orders on his own responsibility.

That summer of 1960, Khrushchev was making trouble for Eisenhower not only in the Congo, Cuba, and the Barents Sea, but even within the United States itself, or at least that part of it that contained the U.N. headquarters. Khrushchev indicated that he intended to exercise his rights and come to the U.N. as head of the Russian delegation. Eisenhower and his advisers had no doubt that he would indulge in more saber rattling. Eisenhower decided to try to blunt the effects of Khrushchev's speech by exercising *his* rights as host and insisting on speaking at the opening session, on September 22.[22] He did so, calling for support for the U.N. peace-keeping force in the Congo and proposing a Food for Peace plan. Khrushchev followed on the next day with a blistering attack on Western colonialism in the Congo, charging both the U.N. and the United States were trying to maintain

---

* For his part, the author can testify that he has never seen any documentary evidence linking Eisenhower with an assassination plot, much less giving orders to have Lumumba murdered. Like most of the other evidence in this case, however, that testimony is negative and is not based on the total record, as some items remain classified. And of course, Eisenhower would never have put on paper orders to commit murder; he would have given such instructions in the vaguest possible way, using all sorts of euphemisms. But it is difficult for me to believe that he would not have informed Goodpaster of any secret orders to Dulles, although it is true that in his last year as President, Eisenhower did sometimes ask Goodpaster to step out of the room while he talked privately with Allen Dulles.

Belgian control of Katanga. Later in this same session, Khrushchev insulted Macmillan by interrupting him while he was speaking, then really outdid himself by taking off his shoe and pounding it on the table. Castro, who also attended the session, made few friends for himself when he subjected the delegates to a four-hour monologue on the evils of American imperialism.

Overall, the atmosphere could hardly have been much worse, or in sharper contrast to the one that prevailed before the Paris summit. Eisenhower told Herter over the telephone that "he was a rather long sufferer, but one day he was going to call Khrushchev the 'Murderer of Hungary.'" Eisenhower said that in his opinion, "Khrushchev is trying to promote chaos and bewilderment in the world to find out which nations are weakening under this attack and to pick what he can by fishing in troubled waters." The President showed the full depth of his anger when he commented that if he were a dictator, he would right now "launch an attack on Russia while Khrushchev is in New York."[23]

In such an atmosphere, disarmament talks were obviously dead, at least until Eisenhower's successor took office. Eisenhower made a halfhearted effort to keep the Geneva disarmament talks going even after Paris, but on June 27 those meetings came to an end when the Soviet delegation walked out. Their collapse, although hardly unexpected, was a blow to Eisenhower, who had in 1953 set disarmament as one of his major goals, but who by 1960 had to recognize that the arms race was out of control. By 1960, the American nuclear arsenal had grown to proportions that by 1953 and 1954 standards Eisenhower had called "fantastic," "crazy," and "unconscionable." Just how big it was becoming, Eisenhower was reminded on August 15, when McCone informed him that the United States was now producing, each year, more bombs than the estimated total requirement had been back in the mid-fifties.[24] Partly this was a result of Eisenhower's own inability to stand up to the AEC and the DOD over the years and say no to the expansion, but as he said, "being only one person, he had not felt he could oppose the combined opinion of all his associates."[25] America had gone far beyond what it needed for deterrence, at least in Eisenhower's view, without getting anywhere close to a first-strike capability. After paying the cost in money and tension for the arsenal, which now contained more than six thousand weapons of all sizes, the United States was less secure than it had been in 1953. Eisenhower hated that result, but could not do anything about it.

In his last half year in office, Eisenhower's conversations about disarmament proposals were exclusively concerned with propaganda advantage, or the effect of this or that proposal on the election, never with seeking a compromise that could lead to a breakthrough in the talks. Indeed, he agreed, albeit reluctantly and for the first time, to an increase in DOD appropriations, primarily because Bohlen advised him that such action would give Khrushchev some pause, but also because the Democrats were making such an issue out of national security. In so doing (the amount was one-half a billion dollars), Eisenhower admitted that the additional arms were not necessary for military purposes, but perhaps they "would carry sufficient credibility to create the psychological effect desired." [26]

All hint of cooperative activity with the Russians was now gone. In July, Eisenhower met with his closest advisers to discuss Operation Plowshare. One part of that operation was to investigate the detectability of underground nuclear shots, and to do so in cooperation with Soviet scientists. All this had been set up before Paris; at that time, neither DOD nor AEC had protested, because the bombs being used were obsolete and thus would not give the Russians any new information. But after Paris, none of the politicians wanted anything to do with it, for purely political reasons. As John Eisenhower put it in his notes on the conversation in July, no one would support the project, because the voters "would interpret this procedure as giving the Russians something for nothing." [27]

Despite his increasingly belligerent attitude toward the Russians, the President refused to be swept away on the national-security issue. The NSC, DOD, AEC, and Henry Luce all urged him to institute a nationwide civil-defense program. Nelson Rockefeller joined the chorus. Eisenhower responded that such a program would cost the federal government more than $10 billion (Rockefeller argued that it could be done for $3 billion), and that in any case, building fallout shelters was a responsibility that "rests upon the locality and the private citizen." Eisenhower would not put any federal money into shelters. [28]

Eisenhower also resisted entreaties that he spend more on the space race. Nixon, Republican leaders, and the Defense Establishment were all urging him to go all out on Project Mercury, designed to put a man in orbit around the earth, and on a man-on-the-moon project. Eisenhower called the latter "a multibillion-dollar project of no immediate value . . . He said he felt the project is useless at this moment and he would not think it really worth the money . . . The

President said he likes to see us go ahead on useful things but he is
not much of a man on spectaculars. He realizes that some stunts, such
as the Lindbergh trip across the Atlantic, have some virtue, [but] he
emphasized that he would not be willing to spend tax money to send
a man around the moon . . . He said there is such a thing as common
sense, even in research." [29]

Eisenhower was growing weary of holding the same conversations
with the same men on the same subjects. After Paris, he had resolved
to do his duty to the end of his term, but he was finding his job increasingly distasteful, as it seemed all he was doing was saying no to
everyone on everything. He had the sinking feeling that after he was
out of the White House, even if Nixon replaced him, there was going
to be an orgy of spending, as the heads of all the projects he had
turned down over the years would clamor for funds. Small wonder his
thoughts turned more often toward his retirement.

Mamie was busy packing things up and making the other preparations for the move to Gettysburg. John was preparing to resign from
the Army. Eisenhower, meanwhile, made an informal agreement about
his presidential memoirs. He was determined to write them, not only
because of the money involved (he was offered a flat payment of
$1 million from at least one publisher), but because he wanted to de-
fend himself and his Administration while setting the record straight.
He made an informal agreement with his old publisher, Douglas
Black of Doubleday, and set John to work getting the necessary documents up to Gettysburg or nearby Fort Ritchie. [30]

Eisenhower was now almost seventy years old. Like many old
men, his thoughts turned increasingly back toward his youth. On
June 30, 1960, he had a meeting with General William Westmoreland,
a most pleasant affair, as Westmoreland, former chief of staff of the
82d Airborne and commander of the 101st Airborne, was on his way
to West Point to assume the duties of superintendent. Eisenhower
had a long talk with "Westy" about the Academy, a talk full of nostalgia and reminiscence. The only unhappy note came when Eisenhower remarked that the JCS nowadays "tend to kowtow to the Congress and to make speeches inconsistent with the decisions of their
superiors." He wanted Westmoreland to recall to the cadets "the old
simple rule that after a decision is made, officers must be loyal to their
commander." [31] Westmoreland said he would see to it, then rose to go,
already embarrassed by the amount of the President's time he had
taken. But Eisenhower rose from his chair too, came around his desk,

grasped Westmoreland by the arm, and said, "Now, Westy, one more thing. See what you can do about improving that football team!"[32]

What was most on his mind, however, was not his retirement, nor nostalgia, nor the outcome of the next Army-Navy football game, but the election. For Eisenhower, the 1960 presidential election campaign was dominated by three thoughts. First, his intense concern about the future of his country, a concern that expressed itself in a partisan manner, as he convinced himself that victory by the Democrats would mean disaster for the country. Second, his feeling that the election was a vote of confidence and approval of his policies over the past seven and a half years. He knew this was silly, even irrational, that if he himself were the candidate there could be no question of the outcome, but he could not escape the feeling. Nor could he escape a third feeling, one of ambiguity about Nixon.

Since the time of the Checkers speech in the 1952 campaign, Nixon had served Eisenhower loyally and effectively, especially at the time of Eisenhower's 1955 heart attack. For Eisenhower, the problem was that he never seemed to grow, never seemed to consider a problem from any point of view other than the partisan political considerations, never seemed quite ready to take over. In 1956, Eisenhower had agreed to run for a second term primarily because he could not think of anyone qualified to succeed him. In 1960, he had no choice but to turn over the government, but he still could not think of anyone qualified to succeed him. Repeatedly, in the summer of 1960, he told friends that his greatest failure was the failure to develop more Republican "comers." He regretted that Nixon did not have more competition for the nomination. But—and there was always a "but" in the Eisenhower-Nixon relationship—he thought Nixon a far better man than his only serious competitor, Nelson Rockefeller. And as between Nixon and any of the Democratic hopefuls, Eisenhower never hesitated. Although Eisenhower could not believe that Nixon was even yet ready, Nixon was so superior to any alternative that Eisenhower gave him his full backing.

The nature of the campaign put an additional strain on the already difficult Eisenhower-Nixon relationship. It was inevitable that Nixon would stress his experience in government, and in the process claim for himself a leading role in the decision-making process of the Administration. But this was precisely the area in which Eisenhower was most sensitive. The Nixon claim reinforced the standard Democratic criticism of Eisenhower, that he reigned rather than ruled, that he did not make the decisions himself. Eisenhower could not escape thinking of the election as a referendum on his Presidency, and he could not and would not allow it to be said that he delegated his decision-making powers. Nixon, of course, could hardly see the election as a referendum on Eisenhower; it was Nixon versus Kennedy, and he needed all the support from Eisenhower that he could get. He did not want Eisenhower to campaign on the basis of the record of his Administration, but to cite Nixon's great contributions and describe Nixon as "indispensable," "statesmanlike," "judicious," and so forth. But Eisenhower nevertheless spent the campaign defending his own record.

A second major problem revolved around differences in perceptions. When he was a candidate, Eisenhower had instinctively gone into the middle of the road, with the explicit goal of winning the independent vote. He had won the 1952 nomination despite the intense opposition of the Old Guard; he was not a professional politician; he did not draw his strength or his power from the Republican Party; he simply was not a party man. Nixon, by contrast, was the quintessential party man. He drew his strength and his power from the Republican Party. Thus Nixon was more partisan in his approach, especially during the 1960 campaign, than Eisenhower would have wished.

Nixon's felt need to unite the Republican Party, added to his perception of what the voters wanted to hear on the issue of national defense, led to the deepest wound of all. Nixon deserted Eisenhower on defense. Rationally, Eisenhower knew it had to be done, that the clamor for more defense spending had become irresistible. He also knew that Nixon had to be his own man, had to establish himself as something more than "Ike's boy," had to show that the Republican Party was not a standpat party. But emotionally, it felt to Eisenhower like cold rejection of everything he had stood for and fought for over the past seven and a half years.

The result of all these structural difficulties, and of Eisenhower's ambiguity toward Nixon, was that Eisenhower's contribution to Nixon's campaign was worse than unhelpful—it actually cost Nixon votes, and probably the election.

Defense spending was a central issue in the campaign. The Democratic candidates were stumping the country with it, charging that Eisenhower had allowed a "missile gap" and a "rocket gap" to occur, and that as a result America was in retreat around the globe. Nelson

Rockefeller joined the chorus. On June 8, he called for a $3.5 billion increase (about 9 percent) in the defense budget. "I suspect that Nelson has been listening too closely to half-baked advisers," Eisenhower commented at a Republican leaders' meeting. Then he specifically named Emmet Hughes, his former speech writer with whom he had by then completely broken and who was now working for Rockefeller.[33]

That evening, Rockefeller called Eisenhower on the telephone. He wanted to know Eisenhower's thinking on whether or not he, Rockefeller, should once again become an avowed candidate. Eisenhower took the occasion to first of all give Rockefeller a short lecture on defense spending. Whitman recorded that "the President said he did not believe it was right to alarm people unnecessarily—he thought a fair question was whether we were doing these things fast enough." As to Rockefeller re-entering the race, "The President said he was afraid he would be called 'off again, on again, gone again, Finnegan.' . . . The President said he thought Nelson's chances were very remote." Eisenhower told Rockefeller that anyone who wanted a Republican nomination in the next four or five years "would have to get some kind of blessing from the President. He said therefore he hoped that the reasoned and positive approach he had advocated would be adopted by Nelson (instead of jumping on everybody)." He advised Rockefeller to avoid becoming a "lone wolfer—a La Follette." He also advised him, "Don't let anyone else write your speeches."[34]

The following day, Rockefeller announced that although his previous withdrawal from the race still stood, he would accept a draft. That same day, June 11, Eisenhower talked to Mrs. Hobby on the telephone. She had called him to deplore Rockefeller's defense-spending statement, but she also remarked that "the other one [Nixon] is not easy." Eisenhower assured her that "Dick is growing in stature daily." Hobby complained that Nixon's partisanship was driving away independents and Texas Democrats who had voted for Eisenhower. She asked the President to urge Nixon to be constructive and nonpartisan in his approach. Eisenhower did as requested, dictating a letter to Nixon repeating Hobby's advice and noting, "personally I concur."[35]

Eisenhower had never developed any great love for the Republican Party, especially not for that part of it filled by Republican congressmen. In June, the President vetoed a bill raising the pay of Civil Service employees. On July 1, he called in the Republican leaders in the Senate to try to "light a fire" under them to support the veto (he knew he was going to be overridden in the House, but had hopes for the Senate sustaining his veto). But Dirksen argued that in an election year the President could not expect any politician to vote to deny a pay raise to all those constituents. The most Eisenhower could hope for was fifteen Republican and five Democratic votes, all from senators not up for re-election. Bryce Harlow, a presidential assistant who worked for Jerry Persons on relations with Congress, kept the notes. Harlow recorded, "The President expressed deep concern over the news presented by Senator Dirksen—commenting that he is at a loss, assuming Senator Dirksen to be correct, as to what Republicans really stand for. Fiscal integrity is the keystone to which all Republicans have adhered, he said, and he could hardly see how he could contend vigorously . . . that the Republican Party is the party of responsibility when the majority of the Republicans vote exactly the opposite."

Shaking his head, Eisenhower said "he had the feeling that he was being 'read out of the party.' " When the meeting ended, Eisenhower commented to Senators Dirksen and Morton that "maybe it would be better for the boys on the Hill to impeach him and he would be happy to support them in this effort." [36]

Afterward, Harlow told Whitman that "Dirksen is so tired he is lethargic. It even affects his speech to the point where you practically cannot understand him." Eisenhower told her that he personally was "disgusted with the Republican leadership; I don't know why anyone should be a member of the Republican Party." [37]

The Democrats, meanwhile, met in Los Angeles and nominated Senator Kennedy as their candidate. He chose Lyndon Johnson as his running mate. Eisenhower was appalled, even though he had predicted the outcome. He was vacationing at Newport at the time. Bill Robinson was with him. Robinson had breakfast with Eisenhower the morning Kennedy was to announce his choice. Eisenhower asked Robinson who he thought it would be. Symington, Robinson replied, then asked Eisenhower who he thought it would be. "He said, without hesitation, Lyndon Johnson." Robinson remonstrated: "How could Lyndon Johnson—having said all the things he did about Kennedy, having said over and over again he wouldn't be a vice-presidential candidate—even consider it?"

Eisenhower replied, according to Robinson's diary, "Of course, that's very sound thinking and fairly good deduction, unless you know Johnson. He is not a big man. He is a small man. He hasn't got the depth of mind nor the breadth of vision to carry great responsibility. Any floor leader of a Senate majority party looks good, no matter how incompetent he may be. Johnson is superficial and opportunistic."[38]

Eisenhower disliked Kennedy even more. He told Ellis Slater, who was a friend of Joe Kennedy's, that he feared if the Kennedys ever got in "we will never get them out—that there will be a machine bigger than Tammany Hall ever was . . ."[39] Eisenhower told one of his big-business friends, "I will do almost anything to avoid turning my chair and the country over to Kennedy."[40] And he gave Kistia-kowsky "a long discourse on how incompetent Kennedy is compared to Nixon, that even the more thoughtful Democrats are horrified by his selection, and that Johnson is the most tricky and unreliable politician in Congress."[41] In 1956, Eisenhower had pronounced the Stevenson-Kefauver ticket "the sorriest" in the history of the Democratic Party. In 1960, he decided that Kennedy-Johnson was even worse.

In 1956, he could confront Stevenson-Kefauver directly; in 1960, he had to confront Kennedy-Johnson through Nixon. He could and did, however, see to it that Nixon made the confrontation on a platform acceptable to him. The convention was to open on July 25. The week before, Eisenhower talked twice daily at least with Nixon on the telephone; the President told Bill Robinson that he was "quite content with the Nixon position." Then, on July 22, Nixon unexpectedly flew to New York for a meeting with Rockefeller. They hammered out a joint statement, one that reporters immediately called appeasement on Nixon's part, because on most issues (civil rights, housing, schools, and jobs) the statement reflected Rockefeller's more liberal views. But what really upset Eisenhower was the statement on defense: "The United States can afford and must provide the increased expenditures to implement fully this necessary program for strengthening our defense posture. There must be no price ceiling on America's security."

Eisenhower confessed that he found the statement, which echoed Kennedy's charges, "somewhat astonishing," especially as it came from two men "who had long been in Administration councils and who had never voiced any doubt—at least in my presence—of the adequacy of America's defenses." Gabe Hauge called Robinson "in somewhat of a panic." He blamed Emmet Hughes for the offensive passage, then told Robinson that the statement "really involved a repudiation of the President's position on defense." Worse, Rockefeller was insisting on putting the pledge to increase defense spending into the platform. Robinson talked to Eisenhower, who commented that "it would be difficult for Nixon to run on the Administration record if the platform contained a repudiation of it." Eisenhower said he would still be President for six more months "and he intended to stick to his policies. Any position by Nixon or the platform in repudiation of these policies would bring discord and disunity in the Republican Party efforts."[42]

The following day, Eisenhower talked to Nixon on the telephone. Nixon claimed that Rockefeller had put out the statement unilaterally. "What I'm trying to do," he said, "is to find some ground on which Nelson can be with us and not against us." Eisenhower told Nixon that he would find it "difficult . . . to be enthusiastic about a platform which did not reflect a respect for the record of the Republican Administration . . ." Nixon then instructed his lieutenants to eliminate the offensive passage, substituting for it a compromise: "The United States can and must provide whatever is necessary to insure its own security . . . and to provide any necessary increased expenditures to meet new situations. . . . To provide more would be wasteful. To provide less would be catastrophic." That was acceptable to Eisenhower.

On July 26, Eisenhower addressed the convention. He spoke not of Nixon's qualifications to take over the Oval Office, but rather about the accomplishments of his own Administration.[43] Nixon won the nomination easily, then selected Henry Cabot Lodge, Jr., as his running mate. Eisenhower was disappointed—up to the end he had hoped it would be Al Gruenther or Bob Anderson, and he doubted that Lodge would be an effective campaigner—but he accepted Nixon's decision.

Immediately after the Republican Convention, Eisenhower tried to convince Kennedy to tone down his criticism of defense policy. He instructed Allen Dulles to give a briefing to both Kennedy and Johnson. Eisenhower wanted Dulles to put his emphasis on how strong the American defense posture was. But in the briefing, Dulles only wanted to talk about developments in Berlin, Cuba, Iran, the Middle East, Formosa, NATO, and the Congo. The Democratic senators, for their part, were only interested in developments that might arise during the campaign. Kennedy did ask Dulles directly, "How do we stand in the missile race?" Dulles recorded, in a memorandum for the President on the briefing, that "I replied that the Defense Department was the competent authority on this question . . ."[44] That was hardly a satisfactory answer, and Kennedy felt free to continue to speak of a "missile gap."

Kennedy's campaign made Eisenhower more determined than ever to stop him. He met with Nixon and they agreed that the President would save his effort until the last days of the campaign, when he would barnstorm for Nixon. Behind the scenes, however, Eisenhower began the process of persuading his millionaire friends to put some of their money and energy into the election. On August 8, for example, he called Pete Jones on the telephone. Jones was one of his gang, as well as head of Cities Service Oil Company. Eisenhower told Jones to use his influence to see to it that "industry do something to talk a little optimistically, not pessimistically, these next three months." He wanted Jones to get active in fund raising. "The President also said that the government was accelerating some of its spending; that certain companies might do the same."[45]

Besides stimulating the economy and raising campaign funds, Eisenhower could most help Nixon through his press conferences. He tried to do so, but the results were bad. No matter what he was asked about Nixon, it seemed, or what he intended to say, his answers could always be read two or more ways, and never constituted that clear-cut, total endorsement that Nixon so desperately needed. The total effect was almost devastating.

On August 10, a reporter asked if Eisenhower was going to give Nixon "a greater voice . . . than you have in the past, in view of his responsibility as the candidate." Eisenhower replied that he alone could make the decisions. He would continue, as always, to consult with Nixon, but if a decision had to be made, "*I'm* going to decide it according to *my* judgment." Did he think that Nixon had gone too far in trying to appease Rockefeller? "Well," Eisenhower replied, "I don't think he *feels* that he was appeasing." Peter Lisagor asked if Eisenhower had any objections to Nixon holding his own press conference, so that he could speak for himself on the defense issue. Eisenhower said he had no objections: "As a matter of fact I am quite sure that while, with the exception of minute detail, he would be saying exactly the same thing I would be, I have no objection to his going and making any kind of public talk . . ." Sarah McClendon wanted to know if Eisenhower's recent request for a larger military appropriation "is a change that you took in light of the world situation or were you influenced to do this by Mr. Nixon or Mr. Rockefeller." Eisenhower snapped back, "I wasn't influenced by anybody except my own military and State Department advisers and my own judgment." Charles Bartlett asked if there were any differences between Nixon and the President on the question of nuclear testing. "Well," Eisenhower responded, "I can't recall what he has ever said specifically about nuclear underground testing."[46]

Nixon's major claim in his confrontation with Kennedy was that he was experienced in making the tough decisions. But at one half-hour press conference, Eisenhower had denied that Nixon, or anyone else, really participated in the decision making. He specifically denied that Nixon had been consulted on increasing the military budget. And he admitted that he could not even remember what Nixon's advice might have been on the testing issue.

Two weeks later, at the next press conference, things got worse. Sarah McClendon asked Eisenhower to "tell us of some of the big decisions that Mr. Nixon has participated in . . ." Eisenhower replied, "I don't see why people can't understand this: No one can make a decision except me . . . I have all sorts of advisers, and one of the principal ones is Mr. Nixon . . . Now, if you talk about other people sharing a decision, how can they? No one can because then who is going to be responsible?" Later in the same conference, Charles Mohr of *Time* brought the subject up again, justifying it on the grounds that Nixon "almost wants to claim that he has had a great deal of practice at being President." Could not the President give an example of how Nixon fit into the decision-making process? Eisenhower said that Nixon attended the meetings and gave his opinion. "And he has never hesitated . . . to express his opinion, and when he has been asked for it, expressed his opinion in terms of recommendations as to decision. But no one [at the meetings] . . . has the decisive power. There is no voting . . . Mr. Nixon has taken a full part in every principal discussion."

By this point, Eisenhower was obviously becoming irritated at answering the same simple question over and over. But Mohr persisted. "We understand that the power of decision is entirely yours, Mr. President," he said. "I just wondered if you could give us an example of a major idea of his that you had adopted in that role, as the decider and final—" Eisenhower cut him off. "If you give me a week," he said, "I might think of one. I don't remember." And with that, the conference ended.[47]

Eisenhower realized immediately how terrible that remark sounded. When he returned to the Oval Office, he called Nixon to apologize and express his regret. The Democrats, of course, and the press, made the most of it. Shortly thereafter, Nixon made a plaintive appeal to Eisenhower "to be tied into the President's action in Cuba in some way." (Nixon was urging decisive action against Castro and wanted Eisenhower to give him the credit for it.) Eisenhower refused, saying, "This would be very difficult to do in any acceptable way."[48] To Whitman, Eisenhower complained that Nixon had made a big mistake in 1956, when Eisenhower offered him the job as Secretary of Defense. Had Nixon taken that post, Eisenhower argued, he could have gained all the decision-making experience he wanted, and "he would be in a lot better position today in his bid for the Presidency."[49]

On August 30, Eisenhower went to see Nixon in the hospital— the Vice-President was in Walter Reed with an infected knee. When he returned from the visit, Eisenhower told Whitman that "there was some lack of warmth." Whitman's diary continues: "He mentioned again, as he has several times, the fact that the Vice-President has very few personal friends." Eisenhower confessed that he could not understand how a man could live without friends. Whitman wrote that the difference between Eisenhower and Nixon "is obvious. The President is a man of integrity and sincere in his every action . . . He radiates this, everybody knows it, everybody trusts and loves him. But the Vice-President sometimes seems like a man who is acting like a nice man rather than being one."[50]

The highlight of the campaign was the Nixon-Kennedy debates. Eisenhower advised Nixon against agreeing to debate, on the grounds that Nixon was much better known than Kennedy and therefore should not give Kennedy so much free exposure. Nixon rejected the advice, on the grounds that debate was one of his strongest points. Eisenhower then advised him "to talk on the positive side . . . and not try to be too slick." Nixon replied that "he was going to be gentle- manly, let Kennedy be the aggressor." After the first debate, Nixon called Eisenhower on the telephone. Nixon must have been crushed when Eisenhower explained "that he had not been able to hear the debate . . ." And he must have been hurt as Eisenhower nevertheless proceeded to advise him to "once in a while . . . not appear to be quite so glib, to ponder and appear to think about something before answering a question."[51]

In late October, Eisenhower finally began active campaigning for Nixon. What he talked about, however, was not Nixon's superb prepa- ration for the Presidency, but the record of his own Administration. He told a Philadelphia audience, for example, that in the past eight years personal income was up by 48 percent, individual savings were

up by 37 percent, school construction up by 46 percent, college enroll-
ments up by 75 percent, that 9 million new homes had been built,
the most ever in one decade, that the GNP was up by 45 percent, that
inflation had been controlled, that the Interstate Highway System had
become a reality, as had the St. Lawrence Seaway, that in short the
past eight years had been wonderful.[52] Few disagreed, although Nixon
might have said that the point was that the election was about who
was going to lead America forward into the 1960s, not back into the
fifties.

Nevertheless, the Eisenhower speeches were eliciting a response.
The polls had Kennedy ahead. Both Eisenhower and Nixon were
worried. Eisenhower decided he wanted to do more campaigning and
indicated that he wished to have an expanded schedule of speeches.
Nixon was all for it. But on October 30, eight days before the election,
Mamie called Pat Nixon to say that she was distraught at the thought
of her man taking on additional burdens, and told Mrs. Nixon she
feared that Eisenhower "was not up to the strain campaigning might
put on his heart." She had tried to dissuade him, but could not, and
therefore "begged" Pat Nixon to have her husband convince Eisenhower to change his mind, without letting Ike know that she had
intervened. The following morning, Dr. Snyder added his opinion,
telling Nixon to "either talk him out of it or just don't let him do it—
for the sake of his health."

In his memoirs, Nixon related that "I had rarely seen Eisenhower
more animated than he was when I arrived at the White House that
afternoon." He showed Nixon an expanded itinerary. Nixon began
giving reasons why the President should not take on the extra burden.
According to Nixon, "He was hurt and then he was angry." But Nixon
insisted and Eisenhower "finally acquiesced. His pride prevented him
from saying anything, but I knew that he was puzzled and frustrated
by my conduct."[53]

If Nixon was not ready to risk Eisenhower's health in his cause,
he was ready to call into question Senator Kennedy's physical condition. On November 4, Whitman noted that an "air of desperation"
had taken over the Nixon camp. She cited as an example a statement
Nixon said he wanted the White House to put out. Rumors were flying around the country to the effect that Kennedy had Addison's
disease. The proposed statement referred to Eisenhower's position in
1956, when he had made public the results of a complete physical
examination, and called on the 1960 candidates to do the same. Nixon
indicated that after the President signed and issued the statement, he
would immediately make his own physical records public.

Jim Hagerty was furious. He called it a "cheap, lousy, stinking political trick." Eisenhower felt the same way. When an aide tried to explain to the President about the rumors of Addison's disease, Eisenhower cut him off and said, "I am not making myself a party to anything that has to do with the health of the candidates." The idea died.[54]

That same day, November 4, the Nixon people called Whitman with another proposal. Nixon wanted to say in a speech that night that if elected, he would send Eisenhower on a good-will tour to the Communist-bloc countries. Eisenhower was "astonished, did not like the idea of 'auctioning off the Presidency' in this manner, spoke of the difficulty of his traveling once he is not President, and felt it was a last-ditch, hysterical action." He told Hagerty to call Nixon's people and tell them no. Two days later, Nixon's secretary, Rose Wood, called Whitman to ask her to make sure the President listened to Nixon's taped speech at 9 P.M. that night. Eisenhower did, and was again astonished as he heard Nixon make the promise to send Eisenhower on a tour. Eisenhower was so angry he told Hagerty to call Nixon and force him to retract the promise. Hagerty got the President calmed down. Then, Whitman reported, "The President dictated . . . a congratulatory telegram on the speech . . . to send to Nixon." Speaking for everyone who has attempted to plumb the depths of the Eisenhower-Nixon relationship, as well as for that larger group that tries to make sense of American politics, Whitman confessed, "I do not understand."[55]

November 8 was election day. Eisenhower joined John and Barbara to watch the returns. The early reports were discouraging, as Kennedy was sweeping the East. At 11 P.M., Eisenhower went to bed, thinking the worst. When he woke the next morning, Nixon had closed the gap in the popular vote, which stood almost dead equal, but still looked to be hopeless in the electoral vote. Shortly after noon, Nixon called from his California headquarters. He thought he would take California, Illinois, and Minnesota, but it would not be enough. Nixon pointed out that he had run some 7 percent ahead of the Republican Party, and that he lost because of the "weakness of the Republican Party." Eisenhower urged Nixon to take a good rest. Eisenhower then made a remark that summarized nicely his perspective on the campaign and election: "We can be proud of these last eight years." Nixon replied, "You did a grand job."[56]

Nixon later told Eisenhower that he had never heard the President sound so depressed. Eisenhower agreed that it was so. What he did not tell Nixon, but did tell Whitman, was the reason. It was not so much Nixon's defeat as it was his own sense of rejection. All morning, Whitman recorded, "The President kept saying this was a 're-pudiation' of everything he had done for eight years."[57]

At 11 A.M. on the morning after the election, the gang all gathered in the White House to fly down to Augusta with Eisenhower for a vacation. The President muttered that he thought he would cancel the trip; his son practically shoved him out the door, with Mamie telling him to "come on down and knock hell out of the golf ball and forget it." On the plane ride, Eisenhower played bridge. His first comment was "Well, this is the biggest defeat of my life." The postmortem began immediately, Eisenhower saying to Slater, "Dick never asked me how I thought the campaign should be run. I offered him [Robert] Montgomery, who would never have let him look as he did in that first television debate. Cabot Lodge should never have stuck his nose into the makeup of the cabinet—promising a Negro cost us thousands of votes in the South, maybe South Carolina and Texas." After lunch, he mused that if he had written an article for Reader's Digest, that might have turned the trick.[58]

As in any unsuccessful campaign, the losers could not resist torturing themselves by thinking about the might-have-beens. In the case of the 1960 losers, their most frequent thoughts were: if only Eisenhower had hit the campaign trail sooner and harder; if only Nixon had not agreed to the debates; if only Eisenhower had not made that devastating statement about "give me a week I might think of one"; if only Rockefeller had agreed to take second place on the ticket; if only a bit more money had been raised. And the biggest "if only" of all—if only there had been a fair and honest count. The 1960 election brought forth widespread allegations of fraud in the vote count. Some of Nixon's supporters urged him to go to court and demand a recount. Nixon rejected the advice, because he thought it useless and disruptive. Eisenhower rather wanted a recount; more realistically, he wanted the Justice Department to make an investigation. In a November 30 phone call to the Attorney General, Eisenhower "admitted that the election was a closed issue, but he felt we owed it to the people to assure them . . . that the federal government did not shirk its duty." But the Attorney General said he had talked to Nixon about an investigation, and Nixon was against it. Eisenhower let it drop.[59]

CHAPTER TWENTY-SIX

Transition

November 9, 1960–January 20, 1961

THE LAST TEN WEEKS of the Eisenhower Administration were a period of marking time. Because Eisenhower's role was that of caretaker, he undertook no new initiatives. Instead, he worked to keep the options open, so that on such issues as nuclear testing, balance-of-payments problems, Indochina, Berlin, and Cuba the incoming President could make his own decisions. One place where Eisenhower did try to tie Kennedy's hands, however, was the budget. Starting with his vacation at Augusta, he labored over the budget. He told Slater, "You know, I'm going to insist on a balanced budget no matter what Kennedy says he wants. And if he feels otherwise he'll have to declare himself. There just won't be enough money to pay for the already committed things and his new ideas too."[1]

While working on that final budget, Eisenhower was told that such-and-such a program could not be cut. Goodpaster noted, "The President commented that if he were a dictator he thought he could cut the budget before him 20 percent without damage to the country— by knocking out many sacred cows and completely useless but well-established activities."[2] At another budget meeting, this one with Gates and the Defense people, Eisenhower bemoaned the emphasis Kennedy and his advisers were putting on Maxwell Taylor's idea of "flexible response."

Eisenhower's concern was the same in 1961 as it had been in 1953—keeping the economy sound. Goodpaster recorded that Eisenhower said, "We have constantly got to ask ourselves whether we are cutting out everything that can be cut out. For example, he is clear in his mind that the only way we are going to win in the present struggle is by our deterrent. There may be some use in having a few mobile elements but he cannot see any 'little wars.' More and more the matter is a question of big war and the deterrent."[3]

Eisenhower knew, however, that his views had already been examined and rejected by the Kennedy team, which certainly did intend to spend more than it took in, to cut taxes, and to dramatically increase defense spending, both in nuclear arms and delivery systems and in conventional arms, so as to create a "flexible response" capacity. Eisenhower therefore wanted no hint of approval by his team toward the incoming Administration. Thus when Kennedy approached Under Secretary of State Douglas Dillon to inquire as to Dillon's availability for the post of Secretary of the Treasury in the new Administration, Eisenhower strongly urged Dillon not to take the job. The President warned that if he joined Kennedy, Dillon would be classed among the radicals, as he would not be free to pursue sound money policies.[4]

By early January, Eisenhower was getting thoroughly fed up with the press, which was treating Kennedy almost like a savior, as reporters and writers tried to outdo one another in extolling the virtues of the President-elect. In a January 3 letter, Eisenhower said he was amazed at the "constant deterioration in the tone of Ralph McGill's writings." He had always entertained a high opinion of McGill's work, but "now it seems to me that he has sold himself on a naïve belief that we have a new genius in our midst who is incapable of making any mistakes and therefore deserving of no criticism whatsoever. It appears as if he has almost adopted a cult, surrendering completely his own critical ability and his power of analysis."[5]

Despite Eisenhower's resentment at Kennedy's favorable press treatment, and the absence of any critical comment, he had no personal rancor toward his successor, as he had had toward Truman. It helped that Kennedy had carefully, and wisely, refrained from any direct attacks on Eisenhower personally during the campaign. It also helped that when Kennedy came to the White House on December 6, at Eisenhower's invitation, for a briefing from the President, he arrived sitting alone in the back seat of his limousine. Eisenhower and his staff had feared he would show up with a group of assistants preparing to celebrate their victory. The President was also pleased by Kennedy's manner. As John Eisenhower recalled, Kennedy's "warmth and modesty were impressive." At the meeting in the Oval Office, Kennedy listened carefully and intelligently as Eisenhower explained the way the White House functioned.

Turning to the biggest of all the government's operations, the Department of Defense, Kennedy said he had a report from Eisenhower's old nemesis, Stu Symington, that was shocking in its assertions. Eisenhower had seen the report and thought it was "so useless as to be ridiculous," but he did not say so to Kennedy. He did urge Kennedy not to make any changes in a hurry, indeed not to act "until he himself could become well acquainted with the problem." And he warned Kennedy that without a well-organized personal staff, detailed problems would march up to the President for decision in an endless row.

Eisenhower stressed to Kennedy the seriousness of the balance-of-payments problem (and later subjected Kennedy to a forty-five-minute lecture from Robert Anderson on the subject). "I pray that he understands it," Eisenhower wrote in his diary. He was pleased that Kennedy's attitude "was that of a serious, earnest seeker for information." Eisenhower told him that because of the gold outflow, and because of his own conviction that America was carrying far more than her share of the free-world defenses, he intended to let the NATO community know that the United States planned to redeploy some troops out of Europe, unless the Europeans pitched in to stop the outflow of gold. Eisenhower assured Kennedy that he would make the announcement of his intention in such a way as to leave Kennedy a free hand in reversing the policy (which Kennedy did a week after taking office). Kennedy then asked about Eisenhower's personal thinking about Macmillan, de Gaulle, and Adenauer. Eisenhower replied that Kennedy ought to go out of his way to meet them and talk with them individually and as a group; if he did "he would be impressed by their ability and their integrity."

Toward the end of the meeting, Kennedy asked Eisenhower whether he would be prepared to serve the country "in such areas and in such manner as may seem appropriate." Eisenhower replied that of course, "the answer was obvious," but he added that he hoped it would be in the area of serious conferences and consultations on subjects that Eisenhower knew something about, "rather than errands which might necessitate frequent and lengthy travel." Kennedy understood. Finally, Kennedy asked if he could hold Goodpaster for two months or more into the new Administration. Eisenhower was opposed. He said Goodpaster wanted to return to active duty with troops, that a spot was being held for him, and that he wished Kennedy would appoint someone right now who could sit at Goodpaster's side for the final month. But Kennedy replied that "he would be handicapped" without Goodpaster. Eisenhower reminded Kennedy that he would soon be the Commander in Chief and he could then order Goodpaster to do any duty he wished. Kennedy indicated that he would hold the active-duty spot open for Goodpaster. The meeting ended on that pleasant note of agreement. It had been much smoother than the preinaugural meeting Eisenhower had had with Truman back in 1952.[6]

One of the subjects Kennedy had wanted to discuss was Cuba. Eisenhower had responded with a brief summary of a meeting he had held a week earlier. At that meeting, attended by Anderson, Gates, Dillon, Dulles, Bissell, Persons, Goodpaster, Gray, and General Lyman Lemnitzer, chairman of the JCS, the Administration had considered the options with regard to the CIA's program for Cuba. Gray kept the notes. He recorded: "The President said he wished to ask two questions: (1) Are we being sufficiently imaginative and bold, subject to not letting our hand appear; and (2) are we doing the things we are doing, effectively." Without waiting for a response, Eisenhower "adverted to the impending transfer of government responsibilities and said that we would not want to be in the position of turning over the government in the midst of a developing emergency."

Dulles reported that there were some 184 different groups among the refugees, each demanding to become the recognized government-in-exile. "The President asked how might we proceed to bring them all together and Mr. Dulles responded that this was impossible." Eisenhower remarked that the CIA should not "be financing those we cannot get to work in harness. Mr. Dulles said we would find it necessary to continue to finance some . . . notwithstanding."

Dillon spoke up for the State Department, saying that "the State concern was the operation was no longer secret but is known all over Latin America and has been discussed in U.N. circles." Eisenhower responded "that even if the operation were known, the main thing was not to let the U.S. hand show. As long as we pursued that course he was not too concerned." He added that he did not share the State Department concern about "shooting from the hip as he thinks that we should be prepared to take more chances and be more aggressive."[7]

In late December, Dulles and Bissell reported to Eisenhower on their progress. The brigade was up to six hundred men, which stretched the capacity of the training camp in Guatemala. The refugees were highly trained and motivated. Eisenhower asked about political progress: Did the Cubans have a recognized and popular leader yet? No, Bissell replied, not yet. Eisenhower said that he would not approve of any military plans for the utilization of the paramilitary force until there was a genuine government-in-exile. He hoped he would be able to recognize one before he left office.[8]

Castro, however, moved before Eisenhower could do so. On January 2, 1961, Castro ordered most of the State Department personnel in the embassy in Havana to leave the country within twenty-four hours, charging that they were a den of spies. The next day, Eisenhower met with his top advisers. He announced that "the U.S. should not tolerate being kicked around," and indicated that he was inclined to bring every member of the embassy home and withdraw diplomatic recognition of the Cuban government. Herter mentioned the various problems that such a course of action would create. Treasury Secretary Anderson said that rather than break relations, he favored vigorous action, now, "to get rid of Castro." He wanted the CIA to get going. Dulles remarked that Bissell's paramilitary force would not be ready to move until early March. The problem of finding a legitimate government-in-exile remained acute, meanwhile, and there was another difficulty—finding an excuse for an American-sponsored intervention in Cuba. Herter suggested that "we should stage an 'attack' on Guantánamo," copying the technique Hitler had used in 1939 on the German-Polish border before he invaded Poland. Bissell warned that whatever was decided, it had to be done soon, because he did not think he could hold his paramilitary force in Guatemala together beyond March 1. He explained that the CIA agents who were supervising the training "think morale will suffer dangerously if action is not taken by early March."

Eisenhower said that it was his opinion that "we had only two reasonable alternative courses of action: (1) Supporting Cubans to go in March or (2) to abandon the operation." He strongly favored the first course. "When we turn over responsibility on the twentieth," he declared, "our successors should continue to improve and intensify the training and undertake planning when the Cubans are themselves properly organized." Meanwhile, he wanted Bissell to increase the size of the force of refugees. "We should permit the Cubans to expand the forces already planned and then find ways to give arms to broader groups." As to the immediate future, he had decided to withdraw recognition from the Cuban government that day, even though no government-in-exile had emerged. Eisenhower said he was ready to "recognize in a great hurry the leader whenever we do find him." Goodpaster warned that a relatively large military force was being created by the CIA that was not responsible to nor connected with any government, and that the operation was building a momentum of its own which would be difficult to stop. Eisenhower replied that the CIA was only creating an asset, not committing the United States to an invasion of Cuba or anything like that. Whether the refugees would be used or not depended entirely on political developments. There was no need to worry.[9]

For themselves, the Eisenhowers had many chores to do, but they were such old hands at moving that this would be a relatively easy move, physically if not emotionally, because everything was already set up at Gettysburg. Slater spent the first weekend in January at the White House. As he was walking down the hall on Sunday morning, Mamie called him into her bedroom. She was still in bed, but told him she had been up since 5:30 A.M. trying to balance her checkbook. She had already packed the paintings and knickknacks in their bedroom; looking around, she commented to Slater, "Don't things look bare."[10]

Probably no family has ever moved out of the White House gladly, but there were compensations to becoming private citizens. The day after Christmas, 1960, Eisenhower wrote to the members of his gang, and a few other close friends, an identical letter. "During my entire life," he began, "until I came back from World War II as something of a VIP, I was known by my contemporaries as 'Ike.'" He continued, "I now demand, *as my right,* that you, starting January 21, 1961, address me by that nickname. No longer do I propose to be excluded from the privileges that other friends enjoy."[11]

But of course no former President is simply a private citizen. Already Eisenhower was being bombarded with requests that he speak to this club or that charity, to this organization or that university. Honorariums of $1,000 and more were being offered. One such request came from Edgar out in Tacoma, who was rather pleased with himself at being able to extend to his brother a fee of $1,000 for a twenty-minute speech at the University of Puget Sound. Eisenhower replied that Edgar's letter "shows how little you know your younger brother. I have made it a practice for years never to accept an honorarium for any talk; this policy I adopted right after World War II."[12]

He had no financial worries in any case. Pete Jones and other friends had done a good job of investing his *Crusade* money for him; Gettysburg was paid for; he had his full pension; there was plenty of money. Besides, he still had a high income potential, even without speaker's fees. Given Eisenhower's continuing popularity, given the turbulent years he had just presided over, and given the great success of *Crusade,* every publisher in the country wanted to produce his White House memoirs. Eisenhower decided to stay with Doubleday, primarily because of his friendship for the president, Doug Black. He did not sign a contract, but did make an informal arrangement with Black, trusting that Black would treat him fairly, even generously. There was no package deal involved, as there had been with *Crusade;* this time, Eisenhower would receive royalties and pay taxes on a regular basis.

One additional reason Eisenhower made his arrangement with Black was that Black said he could arrange first serial publications in *The Saturday Evening Post.* Eisenhower had been addicted to that magazine when he was a boy—he claimed he read every issue—and he got a great kick out of the idea of appearing in the magazine. C. D. Jackson was miffed. He wrote Eisenhower a long, hurt letter—after all that Time-Life had done for Eisenhower, after all that Henry Luce had done for him, after all that C. D. had done for the President, how could he turn to the *Post?* Eisenhower replied with a long, defensive letter, saying he had accepted Black's proposal because of "my boyhood devotion" to the *Post,* and that he had not intended to slight C. D. or Luce.[13]

In January, by special act of Congress, Eisenhower regained the five-star rank he had resigned in 1952. Sam Rayburn and Lyndon Johnson took the lead in getting the legislation into law. As a former President, Eisenhower was entitled to a $25,000 per year pension, plus $50,000 for office expenses, which was much more than he would receive as a five-star general. The special act gave him the best of both worlds—he got his rank back, and Congress stipulated that he should receive the full presidential pension and allowance. Further, he got to retain the services of Sergeants Dry and Moaney and Colonel Schulz, as aides, their costs to be deducted from the $50,000 allowance.[14]

On December 14, Whitman typed up a note and sent it into the Oval Office. "Norman Cousins called," she told the President. "His suggestions: that you give a 'farewell' address to the country . . . reviewing your Administration, telling of your hopes for the future. A great, sweeping document."[15] Eisenhower liked the idea. He also liked the work of a young political scientist from Johns Hopkins, Malcolm Moos, who had joined the staff in late 1958 as a speech writer. Eisenhower talked to Moos, set him to work on a speech, and over the following weeks consulted closely with him to make the text exactly right.

On January 17, 1961, at 8:30 P.M., Eisenhower went on national radio and television to deliver his Farewell Address. His theme was the Cold War. He spoke of war and peace, of police states and of freedom. "We face a hostile ideology," he declared, "global in scope, atheistic in character, ruthless in purpose, and insidious in method." The danger it posed was of "indefinite duration." There would be many crises, and correspondingly many calls to find a "miraculous solution" by spending ever-increasing sums on research and development of new weapons. Eisenhower warned that every such proposal "must be weighed in the light of . . . the need to maintain balance . . . between cost and hoped-for advantage."

The irony of the Cold War was that to maintain the peace and retain its freedom, the United States had to build a huge military establishment, but the cost of building it threatened to create a garrison state in which there would be no freedom. "Our military organization today bears little relation to that known by any of my predecessors . . ." Eisenhower said. In addition, until after World War II, the United States had "no armaments industry." In earlier days, "American makers of plowshares could . . . make swords as well." But because of the Cold War and the technological revolution, "we have been compelled to create a permanent armaments industry of vast proportions."

Then, in ringing phrases, Eisenhower spoke the sentences that would be the most quoted and remembered of his Farewell Address, indeed of his entire Presidency. The sentences summed up his deepest feelings, gave voice to his greatest fears. They were the words of a soldier-prophet, a general who had given his life to the defense of freedom and the achievement of peace. "This conjunction of an immense military establishment and a large arms industry is new in the American experience," he said. "The total influence—economic, political, even spiritual—is felt in every city, every statehouse, every office of the federal government." Then, the direct warning: "In the councils of government, we must guard against the acquisition of unwarranted influence, whether sought or unsought, by the military-industrial complex. The potential for the disastrous rise of misplaced power exists and will persist." The MIC should never be allowed to "endanger our liberties or democratic processes. We should take nothing for granted."

Eisenhower next spoke of another great change that had occurred in America in his lifetime, and the dangers that change brought. The solitary inventor, working on his own, had been replaced "by task forces of scientists in laboratories and testing fields." Further, in the old days, universities were "the fountainhead of free ideas and scientific discovery." But today, "partly because of the huge costs involved, a government contract becomes virtually a substitute for intellectual curiosity." Therefore, Eisenhower issued a second warning, not so well remembered later as was the military-industrial complex phrase, but equally prophetic. "The prospect of domination of the nation's scholars by federal employment, project allocations, and the power of money is ever present," he said, "and is gravely to be regarded."

Another warning: "We—you and I, and our government—must avoid . . . plundering, for our own ease and convenience, the precious resources of tomorrow. We cannot mortgage the material assets of our grandchildren without risking the loss also of their political and spiritual heritage. We want democracy to survive for all generations to come . . ."

An apology: "Disarmament . . . is a continuing imperative . . . Because this need is so sharp and apparent I confess that I lay down my official responsibilities in this field with a definite sense of disappointment. As one who has witnessed the horror and the lingering sadness of war—as one who knows that another war could utterly destroy this civilization which has been so slowly and painfully built over thousands of years—I wish I could say tonight that a lasting peace is in sight." But the most that he could say was that "war has been avoided." He concluded by praying that "all peoples will come to live together in a peace guaranteed by the binding force of mutual respect and love."[16]

The speech got a highly favorable reception, which put Eisenhower in a good mood the next morning, when he held his 193rd, and last, press conference as President. He thought the transition was going "splendidly," he praised Congress for its cooperation [sic!], he wished Kennedy "Godspeed in his work," he said his greatest disappointment was the failure to achieve peace, he explained his retirement status, and he answered a question about what specific steps he would recommend in dealing with the military-industrial complex. Eisenhower said every citizen should keep well informed, because "it is only a citizenry, an alert and informed citizenry which can keep these abuses from coming about." He added that the potential abuses of power and influence by the arms makers could come about "unwittingly, but just by the very nature of the thing." Every magazine you picked up had an advertisement of a Titan missile or an Atlas or what have you, which represented "almost an insidious penetration of our own minds that the only thing this country is engaged in is weaponry and missiles. And, I'll tell you we just can't afford to do that."

Robert Spivack asked if, over the years, Eisenhower felt the reporters had been fair to him. Eisenhower grinned and shot back, "Well, when you come down to it, I don't see what a reporter could do much to a President, do you?"

William Knighton wanted the President's opinion on the two-term amendment. "A funny thing," Eisenhower replied, grinning again, "ever since this election the Republicans have been asking me this." After the laughter died down, he said he had come to believe that the two-term amendment "was probably a pretty good thing."[17]

The following day, January 19, Eisenhower invited Kennedy to the White House for a final briefing. Eisenhower told Kennedy about the man with the satchel, a satchel that contained the communications equipment that connected the President with SAC and the missile forces. He was, Eisenhower said, "an unobtrusive man who would shadow the President for all of his days in office." To give Kennedy an example of the services available to him, Eisenhower pressed a button and said, "Send a chopper." In six minutes, a helicopter settled down on the lawn outside the Oval Office.[18]

Then they turned to subjects Kennedy wanted to discuss. First on his list was Laos. He wanted Eisenhower's advice. Jerry Persons kept the notes; he recorded that "the President stated that unilateral action on the part of the United States would be very bad for our relations in that part of the world and would cause us to be 'tagged' as interventionists." Herter then informed Kennedy that neither the British nor the French were willing to join in an intervention in Laos, and that if the United States tried to invoke the SEATO obligation, the only result would be that Britain and France would walk out of SEATO. Kennedy asked Eisenhower which he would prefer—a coalition government in Laos that would include the Communists, or an intervention through SEATO. Eisenhower was opposed to any attempt to settle the crisis in Laos through a coalition government, reminding Kennedy of what happened in China when General Marshall tried to form a coalition back in 1948. Intervention, however, would represent "a last desperate effort to save Laos." Changing his domino image, Eisenhower added that "the loss of Laos would be the loss of the 'cork in the bottle' and the beginning of the loss of most of the Far East."

Kennedy was confused. If Eisenhower opposed both a coalition government and intervention, except as a last desperate resort, how did he propose to keep the Chinese out of Laos? Eisenhower said the Chinese did not want a major war. "The President further stated that it is like playing poker with tough stakes and there is no easy solution." He wished that the United States could persuade SEATO to act, but among other problems, there was de Gaulle. Eisenhower told Kennedy that de Gaulle's "thinking on every matter is dominated by an obsession that a triumvirate of the United States, France, and Great Britain should decide on all these matters—that this triumvirate should be organized on a joint staff concept." Eisenhower warned Kennedy against such an organization, because "any action of this type would break up NATO immediately."

Next, Kennedy wanted Eisenhower's judgment "as to the United States supporting the guerrilla operations in Cuba, even if this support involves the United States publicly." Eisenhower replied "Yes," it should be done, because "we cannot let the present government there go on." He told Kennedy that the members of the OAS, who in public consistently spoke against any action designed to eliminate Castro, in private were urging the Administration to "do something." Eisenhower discussed Bissell's operation in Guatemala. He said that this would be a good time to miss "no opportunity to keep our mouths shut." (*The New York Times,* a few days earlier, had carried a story describing the organization and training of the Cuban refugees.) Then Eisenhower outlined his attempts to "find a man who was both anti-Batista and anti-Castro" to head a government-in-exile. It was "very tough," he said, to find a man of standing that satisfied all the refugees. Eisenhower said that Kennedy's "first job would be to find who that man could be." Then, when the paramilitary force of refugees went into Cuba, "it would have the appearance of a more legitimate operation." No specific plans for an invasion had yet been made, Eisenhower added, and that should be done as soon as a government-in-exile was formed.

Kennedy asked about America's limited-war capability. Eisenhower assured him that the armed services were more than strong enough to cope with any situation, then urged Kennedy to hold down the costs of defense, and to strive for a balanced budget (afterward, Eisenhower commented that "I must say that the President-elect did not seem to be impressed."). Eisenhower returned to the subject of Cuba, telling Kennedy that it was his "responsibility to do whatever is necessary." Clark Clifford, who took notes for Kennedy, saw no "reluctance or hesitation" on Eisenhower's part. Indeed, five days later Clifford sent a memorandum to President Kennedy reminding him that Eisenhower had said "it was the policy of this government" to help the Cubans "to the utmost" and that this effort should be "continued and accelerated."[19]

Inevitably, Inauguration Day came. Inevitably, Eisenhower was leaving the Presidency with some reluctance. A few days before January 20, Henry Wriston came to the Oval Office to deliver the report of the Commission on National Goals, which Eisenhower had appointed a year earlier. With the New Frontier about to take over, the report was already a dead letter, of no interest to anyone. But it had to be received, and photographs taken. While that was going on, Eisenhower heard the clatter of hammers across Pennsylvania Avenue, where a reviewing stand was being constructed for the inaugural. "Look, Henry," Eisenhower said, "it's like being in the death cell and watching them put up the scaffold."[20]

The morning of January 20, John Eisenhower remembered an "eerie" atmosphere in the White House. It had snowed heavily the night before, forcing many of the staff to spend the night in the basement. Secretary Gates assured Eisenhower that he would have every soldier in the Army shoveling snow to make sure the inaugural went ahead without a hitch. Eisenhower spent most of the morning leaning on his empty safe, reminiscing with Ann Whitman. The servants lined up, and Eisenhower and Mamie went down the line, saying goodbye to each of them. Many had tears streaming down their faces. The Kennedys, the Johnsons, and "a small entourage" of Democrats arrived for a short visit and a cup of coffee.[21]

At noon, before Chief Justice Earl Warren, the oldest man ever to serve as President to that date gave way to the youngest man elected to the office. After the ceremonies, when all the attention was centered on the Kennedys, the Eisenhowers sneaked away through a side exit. In so doing, Eisenhower later wrote, they made "a fantastic discovery. We were free—as only private citizens in a democratic nation can be free." They drove to the F Street Club, where Lewis Strauss was the host for a luncheon for the Cabinet and Eisenhower's close friends. Then it was off for Gettysburg, along the route they knew so well, and home to the farm.[22]

By special, unprecedented action on Kennedy's part, Eisenhower was retaining the services of his personal Secret Service bodyguard, Special Agent Richard Flohr, for two weeks. Otherwise, he was as free as he felt. When they got to the farm, Eisenhower hopped out the car door to open the gate. For twenty years, he had had every physical need taken care of by others. He never wore his shoes while they were being shined, he had never been in a laundromat, or a barbershop, or a clothing store, or indeed a retail store of any kind. (Exception: Once, in Gettysburg, in 1958, he had taken David into a sporting goods store, where he picked out an assortment of rods and reels, hip boots, and so forth, for his grandson. He had them all bundled up and then just walked out, a Secret Service agent carrying the packages. The store owner was delighted to have the President for a customer, but he could not just let him walk out the store with hundreds of dollars' worth of goods. Merriman Smith hurried forward from the press corps to assure the owner that although the President never carried any money, and had no charge cards, if the bill was sent to the White House, it would be paid.)

There were all sorts of things Eisenhower did not know how to do. Paying tolls at the automatic lanes on the turnpikes, for example. He had forgotten how to type, and had never learned how to mix frozen orange juice or adjust a television picture. He had no idea in the world about how to make practical travel arrangements, how to buy tickets or even where to buy them. He had told Slater, on January 7, that after a few days in Gettysburg following the inaugural, he wanted to go quail shooting down in Georgia at George Humphrey's place. But, he said, "I can't drive all that way and I'm just wondering how I'll get there." Slater assured him that he could "snitch a ride" on Pete Jones's airplane.

Eisenhower did not even know how to place a telephone call. For the past twenty years, whenever he wanted to make a call, he told a secretary to put it through for him. The last time he had placed a call himself, in late 1941, he did so by telling the operator the number he wanted. So, the evening of January 20, he picked up the phone to call his son, tried to give the number, heard only a buzzing at the other end, shouted for the operator, clicked the receiver button a dozen times, tried dialing it like a safe, shouted again, and slammed the phone down. Frustrated, red-faced, he bellowed for Agent Flohr. "Come show me how you work this goddamned thing." Flohr did. "Oh! So that's how you do it!" exclaimed a delighted Eisenhower, fascinated by the way the ring clicked around the dial. He rather thought he might enjoy this business of learning to cope with the modern world.[23]

He would especially enjoy it because, even if he had to place his own phone calls, or get out and open a gate, or wonder how to get from one place to another on his own, he would do so as a private citizen. After a full one-half century in its service, the nation had finally allowed Dwight Eisenhower to retire. He was free.

CHAPTER TWENTY-SEVEN

The Eisenhower Presidency: An Assessment

1953–1961

ANY ATTEMPT to assess Eisenhower's eight years as President inevitably reveals more about the person doing the assessing than it does about Eisenhower. Assessment requires passing a judgment on the decisions Eisenhower made on the issues of his time, and every issue was political and controversial. Further, all the major and most of the minor issues of the 1950s continued to divide the nation's political parties and people in the decades that followed. To declare, therefore, that Eisenhower was right or wrong on this or that issue tends to be little more than a declaration of the current politics and prejudices of the author. The temptation to judge, however, is well-nigh irresistible, and most of the authors who write about the 1950s give in to it.

Thus William Ewald, in *Eisenhower the President,* concludes "that many terrible things that could have happened, didn't. Dwight Eisenhower's presidency gave America eight good years—I believe the best in memory." There were no wars, no riots, no inflation—just peace and prosperity. Most white middle-class and middle-aged Republicans would heartily agree with Ewald. But a black American could point out that among the things that did not happen were progress in civil rights or school desegregation. People concerned about the Cold War and the nuclear arms race could point out that no progress was made in reducing tensions or achieving disarmament. People concerned about the Communist menace could point out that no Communist regimes were eliminated, and that in fact Communism

618

expanded into Vietnam and Cuba. On these and every issue, in short, there are at least two legitimate points of view. What did not happen brought joy to one man, gloom to another.

One of the first serious attempts at assessment was by Murray Kempton in a famous article in *Esquire* magazine in September 1967. Kempton called the piece "The Underestimation of Dwight D. Eisenhower," and in it he admitted that Eisenhower was much shrewder and more in control of events than he, or other reporters, had ever imagined during the fifties. Eisenhower was "the great tortoise upon whose back the world sat for eight years," never recognizing "the cunning beneath the shell." Garry Wills took up the same theme in his 1970 book *Nixon Agonistes*. Such judgments were little more than confessions on the part of the reporters, and they shed little light on the Eisenhower Presidency.

Members of the academic community also confessed. Thus Arthur Schlesinger, Jr., who wrote speeches for Stevenson during the presidential campaigns of 1952 and 1956, was—at that time—critical of Eisenhower for failing to exercise vigorous executive leadership, as Schlesinger's heroes, Andrew Jackson, Franklin Roosevelt, and Harry Truman, had done. Later, after Watergate, Schlesinger wrote *The Imperial Presidency*. In that book, Schlesinger's major criticism of Eisenhower was that Eisenhower went too far in his use of executive powers, especially in his proclamation of the principle of executive privilege when he refused to turn over documents or personnel to McCarthy's investigating committee, and in his insistence on exclusive executive responsibility during foreign-policy crises.

To repeat, then: To say that Eisenhower was right about this or wrong about that is to do little more than announce one's own political position. A more fruitful approach is to examine his years in the White House in his own terms, to make an assessment on the basis of how well he did in achieving the tasks and goals he set for himself at the time he took office.

By that standard, there were many disappointments, domestic and foreign. Eisenhower had wanted to achieve unity within the Republican Party, on the basis of bringing the Old Guard into the modern world and the mainstream of American politics. In addition, he wanted to develop within the Republican Party some young, dynamic, trustworthy, and popular leaders. He never achieved either goal, as evidenced by the 1964 Republican Convention, where the Old Guard took control of the party, nominating a candidate and writing a platform that would have delighted Warren Harding, or even William

McKinley. Franklin Roosevelt did a much better job of curbing the left wing of the Democratic Party than Eisenhower did of curbing the right wing of the Republican Party.

Eisenhower wanted to see Senator McCarthy eliminated from national public life, and he wanted it done without making America's record and image on civil-liberties issues worse than it already was. But because Eisenhower would not denounce McCarthy by name, or otherwise stand up to the senator from Wisconsin, McCarthy was able to do much damage to civil liberties, the Republican Party, numerous individuals, the U.S. Army, and the Executive Branch before he finally destroyed himself. Eisenhower's only significant contribution to McCarthy's downfall was the purely negative act of denying him access to executive records and personnel. Eisenhower's cautious, hesitant approach—or nonapproach—to the McCarthy issue did the President's reputation no good, and much harm.

Eisenhower had wanted, in January of 1953, to provide a moral leadership that would both draw on and illuminate America's spiritual superiority to the Soviet Union, indeed to all the world. But on one of the great moral issues of the day, the struggle to eliminate racial segregation from American life, he provided almost no leadership at all. His failure to speak out, to indicate personal approval of *Brown* v. *Topeka,* did incalculable harm to the civil-rights crusade and to America's image.

Eisenhower had hoped to find a long-term solution for American agriculture that would get the government out of the farming business while strengthening the family farm. In this area, he and Secretary Benson suffered abject failure. The rich grew richer thanks to huge government payments for the Soil Bank, the government in 1961 was more closely and decisively involved in agriculture than it had been in 1953, and the number of family farms had dropped precipitously.

In 1953 Eisenhower had entertained wildly optimistic hopes for the peaceful uses of nuclear power. Electricity too cheap to meter, he believed, was just around the corner, as soon as nuclear power plants went into operation. New transocean canals would be blasted open, artificial harbors created, enormous strides in medicine taken, the world's fertilizer problems solved, the energy for the industrialization of the Third World created. But as he left office in 1961, there had not been any such significant application of nuclear power to civilian purposes.

In foreign affairs, Eisenhower's greatest failure, in his own judgment, which he expressed on innumerable occasions, was the failure to achieve peace. When he left office, the tensions and dangers and costs of the Cold War were higher than they had ever been. In large part, this was no fault of his. He had tried to reach out to the Russians, with Atoms for Peace, Open Skies, and other proposals, only to be rebuffed by Khrushchev. But his own deeply rooted anti-Communism was certainly a contributing factor to the failure. Eisenhower refused to trust the Russians to even the slightest degree. He continued and expanded the economic, political, diplomatic, and covert-operations pressure on the Kremlin for his entire two terms. This was good policy for winning votes, and may even have been good for achieving limited victories in the Cold War, but it was damaging to the cause of world peace.

Allied with the failure to achieve peace was the failure to set a limit on the arms race (never mind actual disarmament, another of his goals). Better than any other world leader, Eisenhower spoke of the cost of the arms race, and its dangers, and its madness. But he could not even slow it down, much less stop it. The great tragedy here is opportunity lost. Eisenhower not only recognized better than anyone else the futility of an arms race; he was in a better position than anyone else to end it. His prestige, especially as a military man, was so overwhelming that he could have made a test ban with the Russians merely on his own assurance that the agreement was good for the United States. But until his last months in office, he accepted the risk of an expanding arms race over the risk of trusting the Russians.

When finally he was ready to make an attempt to control the arms race by accepting an unsupervised comprehensive test ban, the U-2 incident intervened. Fittingly, the flight that Powers made was one Eisenhower instinctively wanted to call off, but one that his technologists insisted was necessary. In this case, as in the case of building more nuclear weapons, holding more tests, or building more rockets, he allowed the advice of his technical people to override his own common sense. That this could happen to Eisenhower illustrates vividly the tyranny of technology in the nuclear/missile age.

Another area of failure came in the Third World, which Eisenhower had hoped to line up with the Western democracies in the struggle against Russia. In large part, this failure was caused by Eisenhower's anti-Communism coupled with his penchant for seeing Communists wherever a social reform movement or a struggle for national liberation was under way. His overthrow of popularly elected governments in Iran and Guatemala, his hostility toward Nasser, his

refusal to seek any form of accommodation with Castro, his extreme
overreaction to events in the Congo, were one result. Another was a
profound mistrust of the United States by millions of residents of the
Third World. A third result of his oversimplifications was an over-
commitment in Indochina, based on an obsession with falling dominoes.

In Central and Eastern Europe, Eisenhower had hoped to take
the offensive against Communism. But his unrealistic and ineffective
belligerency, combined with his party's irresponsible advocacy of up-
risings and liberation within a police state, produced the tragedy of
Hungary in 1956, which will stand forever as a blot on Eisenhower's
record. In his Administration, "roll back" never got started, as "stand
pat" became the watchword. But the free world was not even able to
stand pat, as Eisenhower accepted an armistice in Korea that left the
Communists in control in the north, another in Vietnam that did the
same, and the presence of Castro in Cuba.

These failures, taken together, make at first glance a damning
indictment. According to Eisenhower's critics, they came about because of the greatest shortcoming of all, the failure to exert leadership.
In contrast to FDR and Truman, Eisenhower seemed to be no leader
at all, but only a chairman of the board, or even a figurehead, a Whig
President in a time that demanded dramatic exercise of executive
power. Eisenhower was sensitive about this charge, which he had heard
so many times. When Henry Luce made it, in an August 1960 *Life*
editorial, Eisenhower took time to provide Luce with a private explanation of his methods—"not to defend," Eisenhower insisted,
"merely to explain."

He realized, he told Luce, that many people thought "I have
been too easy a boss." What such people did not realize, he pointed
out, was that except for his "skimpy majority" in his first two years,
"I have had to deal with a Congress controlled by the opposition and
whose partisan antagonism to the Executive Branch has often been
blatantly displayed." To make any progress at all, he had to use
methods "calculated to attract cooperation," and could not afford "to
lash out at partisan charges and publicity-seeking demagogues." In
addition, the government of the United States had become "too big,
too complex, and too pervasive in its influence for one individual to
pretend to direct the details of its important and critical program-
ming." Nothing could be accomplished without competent assistants;
to command their loyalty, the President had to be willing to show

patience, understanding, a readiness to delegate authority, and an acceptance of responsibility for honest errors.

Finally, Eisenhower concluded, "In war and in peace I've had no respect for the desk-pounder, and have despised the loud and slick talker. If my own ideas and practices in this matter have sprung from weakness, I do not know. But they were and are deliberate or, rather, natural to me. They are not accidental."[1]

Shortly after Eisenhower left office, his successor suffered an embarrassing defeat at the Bay of Pigs. In passing his own judgment on the event, Eisenhower concentrated his criticism on Kennedy's failure to consult with the NSC before deciding to act. He chided Kennedy for not gathering together in one room representatives of every point of view, so that he could hear both the pros and cons. Since Eisenhower made such a major point of this failure to consult, it is only fair to apply the same standard to Eisenhower's own Administration. How well did he listen to every point of view before acting?

In some cases, fully. In other cases, hardly at all. In the various Far East crises that began with Korea in 1952 and continued through Dien Bien Phu, the Geneva Conference of 1954, and Formosa, he consulted with every appropriate department and agency, listened carefully to every point of view, and acted only after he was satisfied he had taken everything into consideration and was prepared for all possible consequences. But in other areas, he was surprisingly remiss. He did not give the anti-McCarthy people a full hearing, for example, and only once met with Negro leaders on civil-rights issues. Until 1958, he allowed himself to be isolated from the nuclear scientists opposed to testing. On national defense, he gave the proponents of more spending every opportunity to express their views, but except for one meeting with Senator Taft in 1953 he never listened to those who urged dramatic cuts. Advocates of more spending for domestic social programs or for tax cuts seldom got near Eisenhower. He kept the U-2 such a closely guarded secret that only insiders who were proponents of the program ever gave him advice on how to utilize the spy plane.

But on major questions involving the European allies, he consulted with the heads of government in Paris, Bonn, and London before acting (except at Suez, and the failure to consult there was no fault of his). His record, in short, was mixed, and hardly pure enough to justify his extreme indignation at Kennedy for Kennedy's failure to consult the NSC before acting at the Bay of Pigs.

•   •

How effective, if not dramatic, Eisenhower's leadership techniques were can be seen in a brief assessment of his accomplishments as President, an assessment once again based on his own goals and aspirations. First and foremost, he presided over eight years of prosperity, marred only by two minor recessions. By later standards, it was a decade of nearly full employment and no inflation.

Indeed by almost every standard—GNP, personal income and savings, home buying, auto purchases, capital investment, highway construction, and so forth—it was the best decade of the century. Surely Eisenhower's fiscal policies, his refusal to cut taxes or increase defense spending, his insistence on a balanced budget, played some role in creating this happy situation.

Under Eisenhower, the nation enjoyed domestic peace and tranquillity—at least as measured against the sixties. One of Eisenhower's major goals in 1953 was to lower the excesses of political rhetoric and partisanship. He managed to achieve that goal, in a negative way, by not dismantling the New Deal, as the Old Guard wanted to do. Under Eisenhower, the number of people covered by Social Security doubled as benefits went up. The New Deal's regulatory commissions stayed in place. Expenditures for public works were actually greater under Eisenhower than they had been under FDR or Truman. Nor were Eisenhower's public works of the boondoggle variety—the St. Lawrence Seaway and the Interstate Highway System made an enormous contribution to the economy. Eisenhower, in effect, put a Republican stamp of approval on twenty years of Democratic legislation, by itself a major step toward bringing the two parties closer together.

Eisenhower's positive contribution to domestic peace and tranquillity was to avoid partisanship himself. His close alliance with the southern Democrats, his refusal to ever denounce the Democratic Party as a whole (he attacked only the "spender" wing), his insistence on a bipartisan foreign policy, his careful cultivation of the Democratic leaders in Congress, all helped tone down the level of partisan excess. When Eisenhower came into the White House, his party was accusing the other party of "twenty years of treason." The Democrats in turn were charging that the Republicans were the party of Depression. When Eisenhower left office, such ridiculous charges were seldom heard.

In 1953, Eisenhower had also set as a major goal the restoration of dignity to the office of the President. He felt, strongly, that Truman had demeaned the office. Whether Truman was guilty of so doing depended on one's perception, of course, but few would argue against the claim that in his bearing, his actions, his private and social life, and his official duties as head of state, Eisenhower maintained his dignity. He looked, acted, and sounded like a President.

He was a good steward. He did not sell off the public lands, or open the National Wilderness Areas or National Parks to commercial or mineral exploitation. He retained and expanded TVA. He stopped nuclear testing in the atmosphere, the first world statesman to do so, because of the dangers of radiation to the people who had chosen him as their leader.

In the field of civil rights, he felt he had done as well as could be done. His greatest contribution (albeit one that he had grown increasingly unhappy about) was the appointment of Earl Warren as Chief Justice. In addition, he had completed the desegregation of the armed forces, and of the city of Washington, D.C., as well as all federal property. He had sponsored and signed the first civil-rights legislation since Reconstruction. When he had to, he acted decisively, in Little Rock in 1957. These were all positive, if limited, gains. Eisenhower's boast was that they were made without riots, and without driving the white South to acts of total desperation. Progress in desegregation, especially in the schools, was painfully slow during the Eisenhower years, but he was convinced that anything faster would have produced a much greater and more violent white southern resistance.

In 1952, when he accepted the Republican nomination for the Presidency, Eisenhower called the party to join him in a "crusade." Its purpose was to clean the crooks and the Commies (really, the Democrats) out of Washington. Once those tasks had been accomplished, Eisenhower's critics found it difficult to discover what his crusade was aiming at. There was no stirring call to arms, no great moral cause, no idealistic pursuit of some overriding national goal. Eisenhower, seemingly, was quite content to preside over a fat, happy, satisfied nation that devoted itself to enjoying life, and especially the material benefits available in the greatest industrial power in the world. There was truth in the charge. Eisenhower's rebuttal also contained an elementary truth. The Declaration of Independence stated that one of man's inalienable rights was the pursuit of happiness. Eisenhower tried, with much success, to create a climate in the 1950s in which American citizens could fully exercise that right.

His greatest successes came in foreign policy, and the related area of national defense spending. By making peace in Korea, and avoiding war thereafter for the next seven and one-half years, and by holding down, almost single-handedly, the pace of the arms race, he achieved his major accomplishments. No one knows how much money he saved the United States, as he rebuffed Symington and the Pentagon and the JCS and the AEC and the military-industrial complex. And no one knows how many lives he saved by ending the war in Korea and refusing to enter any others, despite a half-dozen and more virtually unanimous recommendations that he go to war. He made peace, and he kept the peace. Whether any other man could have led the country through that decade without going to war cannot be known. What we do know is that Eisenhower did it. Eisenhower boasted that "the United States never lost a soldier or a foot of ground in my administration. We kept the peace. People asked how it happened—by God, it didn't just happen, I'll tell you that."[2]

Beyond keeping the peace, Eisenhower could claim that at the end of his eight years, the NATO alliance, that bedrock of American foreign policy, was stronger than ever. Relations with the Arab states, considering the American moral commitment to Israel, were as good as could be expected. Except for Cuba, the Latin-American republics remained friendly to the United States. In the Far East, relations with America's partners, South Korea, Japan, and Formosa, were excellent (they were still nonexistent with the Chinese). South Vietnam seemed well on the road to becoming a viable nation. Laos was admittedly in trouble, but it appeared to be the only immediate danger spot.

What Eisenhower had done best was managing crises. The crisis with Syngman Rhee in early 1953, and the simultaneous crisis with the Chinese Communists over the POW issue and the armistice; the crisis over Dien Bien Phu in 1954, and over Quemoy and Matsu in 1955; the Hungarian and Suez crises of 1956; the Sputnik and Little Rock crises of 1957; the Formosa Resolution crisis of 1958; the Berlin crisis of 1959; the U-2 crisis of 1960—Eisenhower managed each one without overreacting, without going to war, without increasing defense spending, without frightening people half out of their wits. He downplayed each one, insisted that a solution could be found, and then found one. It was a magnificent performance.

His place in history is, of course, a relative matter. He has to be judged against other Presidents, which means that no judgment can be fair, because he did not have the opportunities, nor face the dangers, that other Presidents did. We cannot know how great a leader he might have been, because he ruled in a time that required him, at least in his own view, to adopt a moderate course, to stay in the middle of the road, to avoid calling on his fellow citizens for some great national effort. He did not face the challenges that Washington did, or Lincoln, or Franklin Roosevelt. How he would have responded to setting precedents, rather than following them, or to a Civil War, or to a Depression, or to a world war, we cannot know. What we do know is that he guided his country safely and securely through a dangerous decade.

Shortly after Eisenhower left office, a national poll of American historians placed him nearly at the bottom of the list of Presidents. By the early 1980s, a new poll placed him ninth. His reputation is likely to continue to rise, perhaps even to the point that he will be ranked just below Washington, Jefferson, Jackson, Lincoln, Wilson, and Franklin Roosevelt.

In attempting to assess the Eisenhower Presidency, certain comparisons must be made. Since Andrew Jackson's time, only four men have served eight consecutive years or more in the White House—Grant, Wilson, Franklin D. Roosevelt, and Eisenhower. Of these four, only two—Grant and Eisenhower—were world figures before they became President. Of the four, only two—Eisenhower and Roosevelt—were more popular when they left office than when they entered. In contrast to his Democratic predecessors and successors, Eisenhower kept the peace; in contrast to his Republican successors, Eisenhower both balanced the budget and stopped inflation.

Eisenhower gave the nation eight years of peace and prosperity. No other President in the twentieth century could make that claim. No wonder that millions of Americans felt that the country was damned lucky to have him.

CHAPTER TWENTY-EIGHT

Elder Statesman

January 1961–November 1963

THROUGH THE WAR YEARS, through the time of his service in Washington as Chief of Staff, in New York at Columbia, in Paris with SHAPE, and through the eight years of his Presidency, Eisenhower had fantasized about his retirement. The fantasies had taken different forms—a ranch in Texas, a summer place in Wisconsin, a bit of travel, telling stories to Mamie, fishing with a cane pole and a bobber on a small stream. He thought that perhaps he would write an occasional article on some national issue, play a lot of golf and bridge, but mainly concentrate on taking it easy. After a half century of service to the nation, he was, he insisted, bone tired, and had to have some rest. No more meetings, no more speeches, no more conferences, no more decisions to make. George Washington at Mount Vernon was his model.

Eisenhower's Mount Vernon was his farm at Gettysburg. Both he and Mamie loved the farm and the area. The climate, except in winter, was temperate. The location was ideal. They lived in a rural setting, but close enough to Washington and New York for occasional trips to those cities, and convenient for their friends to come to them for weekend visits. The farm was on the edge of the battlefield, which enhanced the sense of being a part of the continuity of American history and allowed Eisenhower to indulge himself in the never-ending game of "what if" about the way in which the Battle of Gettysburg had been fought. Because of its location, there were tourists to put up with—every visitor to the battlefield, it seemed, wanted to see the

628

Eisenhower farm too, and most of them hoped to catch a glimpse and take a picture of the former President walking on his land. Eisenhower enjoyed this visible proof that he had not been forgotten. When he went into town, people would take his picture, or ask for an autograph, or assure him that they had voted for him. He complained about it, but immediately added, "Suppose people didn't like us. That would be terrible, wouldn't it?"

The farm contained 246 acres; in addition, Eisenhower leased another 305 acres. Eisenhower had purchased it, in part, because he liked the idea of living near the place his ancestors had settled in the eighteenth century, and because he relished the opportunity to restore the soil to the fertility it had possessed in those days. He rotated his crops and pastures, raising hay, corn, oats, barley, soybeans, and sorghum. Hay was the main crop; he used it for winter feed for the hundred or so prize Angus cattle that constituted his principal cash crop. He also had horses for the grandchildren to ride, and dogs for them to play with, and fourteen Holsteins to serve as nurse cows for the Angus calves. He butchered most of the mature Angus, rather than selling them for breeding purposes. He knew that any bull or heifer that he put on the market for breeding would fetch a wildly inflated price, but he could not bear the thought of inferior offspring that would be called "Eisenhower Angus." So only the best were sold for breeding; most were sold for slaughter.

The home had a colonial appearance on the outside, but all the modern conveniences inside. The glass-enclosed sun porch was perfect for reading or painting. The furnishings were elegant, the pick of the hundreds of gifts Eisenhower had received over the years from heads of state and American millionaires. Mamie had a priceless collection of Boehm porcelain birds in one room, of which she was very proud but about which Eisenhower would only comment, "God, wouldn't you hate to have to dust them." Through the presidential years, Eisenhower had hardly seen Mamie during daylight; at Gettysburg, he made up for it by spending long hours with her on the sun porch, overlooking the green fields, reading, watching television, or painting. Eisenhower threw away most of his painting efforts. Soon he discovered that Moaney was retrieving the discarded canvases from the wastebasket, so he began painting a big X over the ones that he decided to reject. But Moaney collected them too, so that his private collection of Eisenhower paintings continued to expand.

When the gang or other guests came for a visit, Eisenhower did the cooking, because the only thing Mamie knew how to make, aside from broiling a steak or baking a potato, was fudge. "I was never permitted in the kitchen when I was a young girl," she explained. Otherwise, she was a devoted wife, who appreciated Eisenhower's protective attitude toward her. "For any marriage to be successful," she told one reporter, "you must work at it. Young women today want to prove something, but all they have to prove is that they can be a good wife, housekeeper, and mother. There should be only one head of the family—the man." "As for spats," she told the same reporter, "if a quarrel develops, one should leave the room. It takes two to quarrel."

John, Barbara, and the grandchildren lived on the farm in a small home of their own about a mile away. Eisenhower was extremely proud of his only son. For all of his adult life, John had carried the handicap of being the child of a world-famous father. There was never the slightest chance that John could live out the dream of most American boys and do better in life than the old man had done. Nevertheless, he had been a success in the Army, in war and in peace, and had made himself into an invaluable aide to his father (and to Goodpaster) during the second term. He handled with aplomb the reporters, the sycophants, the supplicants, the publicity seekers, and the merely curious hero-worshipers who had surrounded him. Tall, strong, good-looking, he had his father's facial expressions and grin. He was, by nature, a shy man, reserved, unhappy in large groups when he was the center of attention. Eisenhower knew about these characteristics, just as he knew that John had a much more difficult task in finding his own place in life than he himself had experienced, all of which made Eisenhower even more appreciative and proud of how well John had done. There was more than pride—Eisenhower loved his son as he did no one else, save only Mamie. He also enjoyed working with him, as they had done during the second term and planned to do at Gettysburg. John had left the Army and was preparing to help his father write his memoirs of the White House years.

Having John around carried with it the bonus of having Barbara and the grandchildren there. Mamie and Barbara were very close and happy in their relationship; the Eisenhowers related to Barbara as a daughter, rather than a daughter-in-law. But it was David, Barbara Anne, Susan, and Mary Jean who gave them their greatest joy. "I just love having them around," Mamie declared. "The girls try on my clothes and watch TV with me. We do a lot of talking and laughing." Inevitably, David was his grandfather's favorite. "When he was smaller we spent more time together," Eisenhower told one reporter. "Today, he likes baseball, football, and soccer, like other boys his age, but these are things I can no longer do with him. I do go fishing, skeet shooting, and play golf with him. And often we just sit around and talk seriously." He was aware of the potential for problems arising from the close proximity of the two families. "Grandparents should be helpful," he admonished a reporter (and himself and Mamie), "but not busybodies. They should help out with their grandchildren's education if they can, but under no circumstances should they get in the way and become prime ministers for them. That's the one way to ruin your children's marriage."[1]

The Eisenhower's were, probably, the best-known family in the world. As one result, they were besieged with requests that they allow their names to be used for this or that cause or purpose. Eisenhower indignantly turned down every offer that had the slightest commercial hint to it, saying that he would never sell his name for his own financial benefit. He felt that any such use of his name would demean the office of the Presidency, and his personal reputation. Besides, he did not need the money.

Mamie too had a strong sense of what was fitting, and what was not. In March 1962, the Kennedy Administration asked her to serve as cochairman with Jacqueline Kennedy of a fund drive for a National Cultural Center. Mamie agreed to do it, but only on condition that Bess Truman and Eleanor Roosevelt be added to the group. She also insisted that it be limited to First Ladies, and specifically said she would not serve if any sister of President Kennedy, or of Mrs. Kennedy, was on the list. She added that "she would not care to serve in a capacity subordinate to Mrs. Kennedy."[2]

Eisenhower, for his part, lent his name to various fellowships, scholarships, and similar educational projects, especially if they were designed to provide funds for study abroad for young people. But his favorite project, by far, was Eisenhower College, a small liberal arts, Presbyterian college in Seneca Falls, New York. The project, sponsored by residents of Seneca Falls, began in 1962. Eisenhower agreed to—indeed was flattered by—the use of his name, but insisted that he would take no part in the fund raising. In the event, although he never solicited funds directly, he did write a personal letter of thanks to every contributor, and in countless other ways let his rich friends know that he would be pleased if they could help out.[3]

They almost never traveled at their own expense; usually a friend, the Republican Party, or a corporation would pick up the tab. Eisenhower did some television commentary for Walter Cronkite of CBS, a man he found he liked as much as he admired. A high point in their relationship came in August of 1963, when the Eisenhowers crossed the Atlantic with Cronkite on the *Queen Elizabeth* to film a documentary entitled *D-Day Plus 20*. Eisenhower and Cronkite drove across the Normandy beaches in a jeep (with Eisenhower driving), while Eisenhower explained this or that feature of D-Day. The climax came at the beautiful cemetery overlooking Omaha Beach, where Cronkite asked Eisenhower what he thought of when he revisited the place. In a most revealing remark, the old soldier spoke not of the battle, but of his sorrow whenever he looked at all those graves and thought of the parents of the boys who were buried there, parents who did not have the great blessing he and Mamie enjoyed from their grandchildren.

There were many other trips, beginning immediately after January 20, 1961. In February of that year, the Eisenhowers took a train to Palm Desert, California, where they stayed on the ranch of Floyd Odlum and his wife, Jacqueline Cochran, the famous aviator who had played a key role in persuading Eisenhower in 1952 to run for the Presidency. Eisenhower intended to just play some golf and bridge and generally relax, but he discovered that he could not put national affairs out of his mind. Riding his electric cart around the golf course at Eldorado, he turned on the radio and listened to an account of Colonel John Glenn's around-the-world astronaut flight. Slater felt that Eisenhower was "a little disappointed that the trip hadn't been made during his administration." He also confessed that he was terribly unhappy about the "careless spending" of the Kennedy Administration, and its "complete lack of interest in the soundness of the dollar and the disregard of what inflation will do to the savers." He was also concerned about Kennedy's "build up of the military, the space scientists and armament industries." Eisenhower warned that "this combination can be so powerful and the military machine so big it just has to be used."[4]

As the quotations indicate, after all those years at the center of power, making the decisions, Eisenhower was finding it difficult to relegate himself to an observer's role. His major concern, however, was less with shaping the future, more with justifying the past, and specifically his own Administration. Despite the closeness of the 1960 election, and despite the fact that his name was not on the ballot that year, he continued to think that the American people had, by electing Kennedy, repudiated him. He wanted to prove that Kennedy, and the people who voted for him, were wrong in charging him with having allowed a missile gap to develop, wrong in saying that American prestige had suffered under his leadership, wrong in ignoring his insistence on balancing the budget, and most of all wrong in charging that he had been a lazy, part-time President who delegated his decision-making powers to committees and staffs.

"One thing this book is going to demonstrate," his son declared as the work began, "is that Dad knew what was going on" and was the man in charge.[5] John and his secretary, Rusty Brown, started collecting documents and organizing an office in the president's house on the Gettysburg College campus. They were soon joined by William B. Ewald, Jr., a former English professor at Harvard who had served as a speech writer for Eisenhower and later as an assistant to the Secretary of the Interior. Samuel S. Vaughan, a Penn State graduate and already a senior editor at Doubleday although only thirty-two years old, also became a *de facto* member of the team. Eisenhower had written *Crusade in Europe* in a one-hundred-day blitz, dictating every word of it. This time around, he worked from rough drafts produced by his son or Ewald. Eisenhower ordinarily cut these drafts in half, then rearranged paragraphs, sentences, and phrases, often adding long passages of his own.

Despite all the help, writing the presidential memoirs proved to be a much more difficult task than writing *Crusade* had been. *Crusade* had been the story of an unqualified success with a definitive and happy ending, but the White House memoirs covered issues that were still ongoing, the outcome of which no one knew—Cuba, Laos, Vietnam, disarmament, nuclear testing, and so forth. The cast of characters in *Crusade* was relatively limited; in the presidential memoirs, it was endless. Eisenhower found something good to say about almost everyone who appeared in *Crusade,* even Montgomery, and found little cause for the slightest disparagement of his associates, which was not at all the case in his White House memoirs, but he hated to be critical. *Crusade* covered three and a half tightly compressed years, as compared to the eight years in the White House. Further, in *Crusade* he could tell the story of making a decision, then show how it worked in action, but the situation for the presidential memoirs was more a case of describing a decision made, followed by inaction. That is, he decided *not* to expand the war in Korea, *not* to enter the war in Vietnam at the time of Dien Bien Phu, *not* to accelerate the arms race, *not* to attack McCarthy directly, or support *Brown* v. *Topeka,* or dismantle the New Deal, or lower taxes, or support the British and the French at Suez, or intervene in Hungary. The White House memoirs, in short, necessarily had to be negative and inconclusive, while *Crusade* had been positive and conclusive.

In addition, Eisenhower was more sensitive to criticism as a politician than he had been as a general. In *Crusade,* he admitted mistakes; for example, taking personal responsibility for the German surprise at the Ardennes counteroffensive. In his White House memoirs, he refused to admit any mistakes, which gave the work a defensive and self-serving style that was not at all like *Crusade.* For example, Eisenhower did not want to mention McCarthy at all, but Vaughan, representing the publisher, insisted that he had to recount the story of his relationship with the Wisconsin senator. Eisenhower agreed, but then refused to say anything about the Milwaukee incident, when he had excised the paragraph praising Marshall. Again Vaughan, this time joined by Ewald, insisted that the incident had to be covered. Generally, Vaughan wanted Eisenhower, in John's words, to "bare his soul and admit to more mistakes," but Eisenhower just would not do it.

Eisenhower insisted that, regardless of who wrote the first drafts, it was going to be his book. When they came to the U-2 incident, for example, John wanted him to put the blame on Allen Dulles. (John, who was intimately involved in that operation, once complained that "the CIA promised us that the Russians would never get a U-2 pilot alive. And then they gave the SOB a parachute!") But Eisenhower would not put the blame on Dulles, partly because he did not feel a mistake had been made, mainly because he was so sensitive to the criticism that he did not know what was going on in his own Administration, and blaming Dulles for the U-2 would have reinforced that criticism. Still John insisted. Voices were raised. Finally Eisenhower slapped his hand down on the desk and said, "Damn it, John, I'm writing this book." John replied, "You sure are. Do it your way."

It was a two-volume work that took almost four years to complete. The overall title was *The White House Years.* Volume One, which was published on November 9, 1963, was subtitled *Mandate for Change,* while Volume Two, which came out in 1965, was called *Waging Peace.* In contrast to *Crusade,* which had enjoyed rave reviews, *Mandate for Change* got a mixed reception at best. Many reviewers hinted that they could hardly keep their eyes open, while others pointed to the self-serving and defensive tone of the memoirs. But James Reston gave *Mandate* a strong, positive review in *The New York Times.* Doubleday printed a first run of 125,000 copies, and the book started off with strong sales, quickly reaching the second spot on the best-seller list. But two weeks after *Mandate* appeared, Kennedy was assassinated, and the ensuing national obsession with Kennedy overrode the public's interest in the Eisenhower Presidency, and sales faltered. *Waging Peace* never achieved the kind of sales that *Crusade* had achieved.[6]

Despite their shortcomings, *Mandate for Change* and *Waging Peace* represented a major effort, and they made a major contribution. Neither as salty nor as personal as Truman's memoirs, they nevertheless did cover all the major and most of the minor issues of the Eisenhower Administration. Despite Vaughan's and John's efforts, there were omissions in the treatment of McCarthy and the U-2. Primarily because of security classifications, the memoirs were woefully incomplete on such matters as nuclear testing, covert CIA operations, disarmament policy, and other national-security-related matters. But there were few if any errors of fact, a remarkable achievement in a manuscript of nearly three thousand pages, and a tribute to the thoroughness and accuracy of the research effort. The memoirs did achieve what Eisenhower most wanted them to achieve—he got to explain his side of the story and present his motivation in making this or that decision. They therefore immediately became, as they remain, one of the starting points for any serious study of the politics of the 1950s.

Following the publication of the White House memoirs, Vaughan and others at Doubleday persuaded Eisenhower to write a more informal autobiography, covering those parts of his life not touched upon in *Crusade* or *The White House Years*. In preparing the book, Eisenhower reverted to his old practice of dictating personally. He thoroughly enjoyed going back in his mind to his boyhood days in Abilene, his years as a cadet at West Point, and his experiences as a young officer. He paid handsome tributes to Fox Conner, Douglas MacArthur, George Marshall, to his parents and his brothers, his high-school teachers, and his fellow junior officers. He told some funny stories, and some sad ones, and some revealing ones. He called the book *At Ease: Stories I Tell to Friends,* and it received a much warmer reception, and enjoyed far higher sales and more translations, than *The White House Years. The New York Times* commented that *At Ease* "serves admirably to flesh out and give life to the image of one of the most durable popular heroes of our time."[7]

At Ease contained a chapter entitled "Footnotes for Biographers." The whole book might have been called by that title. Eisenhower had no false modesty. He was well aware that he was one of the most important men of the twentieth century, and that therefore scores of books would be written about him. Naturally enough, he wanted to guide the authors to conclusions and interpretations that were favorable to him. That was why he was willing to devote so much time to writing about himself and his Administration.

But Eisenhower was far too intelligent, and had far too much respect for the documentary record and the truth, and had so much respect for the craft of writing honest history, to ever suppose that historians would be content to, or should, rely on his memory for their interpretations, narratives, and conclusions. After World War II, as Chief of Staff, he had insisted that the American public had the right to know the full story of the Army's efforts in the war, the mistakes and errors as well as the successes. In the same way, after his Presidency, he wanted the full record of his Administration made available. When he left the White House, he sent the bulk of his staff files to the library in Abilene; as he completed sections of his White House memoirs, he sent on his personal papers, memoranda, and correspondence. On May 1, 1962, he and Mamie went to Abilene to dedicate the library (he had earlier, in November 1961, paid a visit to the Truman Library in Independence, Missouri, to see how it was set up and administered).[8]

Located across the lawn from the Eisenhower Museum, kitty-corner from his childhood home (already a shrine open to the public) overlooking the Great Plains of North America, the three-story native sandstone and granite building was suitably magnificent. Eisenhower, much impressed, told Nixon that "the Library itself is one of the most beautiful buildings I have ever seen."[9] It was immediately opened to researchers, and immediately set a standard of excellence in archival management and service to scholars that has continued and, indeed, even improved. Appropriately, it is just two miles off Interstate 70, one of the major east-west links in the national road system Eisenhower did so much to bring about. Together with the Truman Library, which by the mileage standards of the Great Plains is just down the road a piece, it has become an obligatory research stop for every person doing serious study of or writing about the Second World War and the 1950s.

When Eisenhower visited the Truman Library, he did not see Truman personally. The old rancor and bitterness from the 1952 campaign were still there; the two ex-Presidents who had worked so closely together from 1945 to 1952 did not see each other at all from the time of Eisenhower's inauguration to the time of the Kennedy funeral. But if Eisenhower ignored his predecessor, he could hardly escape paying a great deal of attention to his successor. So much so, in fact, both in support and in opposition to Kennedy's policies, that Eisenhower was very nearly as active in politics during his retirement as he had been in the fifties. So much so that he wrote Churchill, in April of 1961, "I don't know whether I am relieved to some extent or dismayed to a large extent to discover that there seems to be little cessation from the constant stream of demands upon my time and energy."[10] His dreams of a quiet, Mount Vernon-style retirement were shattered. As he told a reporter who asked him about retirement, "My wife thinks it's nothing but a word in the dictionary. I think I've more demands made upon me than I've ever had in my life."[11]

Kennedy, of course, had good reasons to court Eisenhower assiduously. Eisenhower's public support for a Kennedy position or policy might well be decisive, and would certainly always be helpful. Further, for all his self-confidence, the young President was aware that there was much he could learn from the oldest President ever. On the day after the 1960 election, Kennedy responded warmly to Eisenhower's grudging telegram of congratulations. During the transition, he had nothing but nice things to say about, and to, Eisenhower. And on January 21, his first day in office, Kennedy dictated his first letter from the White House to Eisenhower, thanking him for his help during the preceding weeks of transition.[12] On every appropriate occasion, Kennedy made military transport available to Eisenhower, and when Eisenhower asked him privately to promote Colonel Schulz (who had spent the past decade in Eisenhower's service, and continued to do so at Gettysburg, handling Eisenhower's appointments and personal affairs), Kennedy did so immediately.

When Eisenhower wrote to thank Kennedy for making Schulz a general officer, he added a personal note. "While it is of course well known that in the domestic field there are governmental proposals and programs concerning which you and I do not agree," Eisenhower stated, "I assure you that my political views, though strongly held and sometimes vigorously expressed, contain nothing of personal animus on my part." He assured Kennedy that "any allegation to the contrary that may come to your ears—and I have heard that such a one has—is either untrue or highly exaggerated and would, I hope, be wholly ignored. I am confident that anyone in your position finds—certainly this was my own experience—that some individuals will never hesitate to distort or even falsify in striving for a feeling of self-importance in the limelight that plays about the Presidency."[13]

April was planting time, and in 1961 by the beginning of the month the Eisenhowers were back at Gettysburg, preparing for the new season. On the seventeenth, Bissell's paramilitary force of Cuban refugees, now grown to some two thousand strong, landed at the Bay of Pigs in Cuba. Deprived of air cover or reinforcements, operating with inadequate communications equipment, the men were quickly killed or captured by Castro's armed forces. It was a debacle.

Kennedy called Eisenhower. Could Eisenhower come to Camp David for consultation? Of course, Eisenhower replied, and on April 22 he flew by helicopter from Gettysburg to Camp David. Kennedy met him when he landed, and the two men went to the terrace at Aspen Cottage to talk. Kennedy described the planning, objectives, and anticipated results of the landing, confessed that it had been a total failure, and said the causes of the failure were gaps in intelligence plus some errors in ship loading, timing, and tactics. Kennedy promised a complete investigation, not—Eisenhower was happy to note—"to find any scapegoat, because the President does seem to take full responsibility for his own decision, but rather to find and apply lessons for possible future action."[14]

The two men began strolling around the grounds, heads bent, deep in conversation. Eisenhower had the impression that Kennedy "looked upon the Presidency as not only a very personal thing, but as an institution that one man could handle with an assistant here and another there. He had no idea of the complexity of the job." Eisenhower asked Kennedy, "Mr. President, before you approved this plan did you have everybody in front of you debating the thing so you got pros and cons yourself and then made your decision, or did you see these people one at a time?" Kennedy confessed that he had not had a full meeting of the NSC to discuss and criticize the plans. He seemed to Eisenhower to be "very frank but also very subdued and more than a little bewildered." He said to Eisenhower, ruefully, "No one knows how tough this job is until after he has been in it a few months." Eisenhower looked at Kennedy, then said softly, "Mr. President, if you will forgive me, I think I mentioned that to you three months ago." Kennedy replied, "I certainly have learned a lot since."

Eisenhower asked Kennedy why on earth he had not provided air cover for the invasion. Kennedy replied that "we thought that if it was learned that we were really doing this rather than these rebels themselves, the Soviets would be very apt to cause trouble in Berlin." Eisenhower gave him another long look, then said, "Mr. President, that is exactly the opposite of what would really happen. The Soviets follow their own plans, and if they see us show any weakness then is when they press us the hardest. The second they see us show strength and do something on our own, then is when they are very cagey. The failure of the Bay of Pigs will embolden the Soviets to do something that they would not otherwise do."

"Well," Kennedy responded, "my advice was that we must try to keep our hands from showing in the affair." Eisenhower, astounded, snapped back, "Mr. President, how could you expect the world to believe that we had nothing to do with it? Where did these people get the ships to go from Central America to Cuba? Where did they get the weapons? Where did they get all the communications and all the other things that they would need? How could you possibly have kept from the world any knowledge that the United States had been assisting the invasion? I believe there is only one thing to do when you go into this kind of thing. It must be a success."

Kennedy seized on the last sentence. "Well," he said, "I assure you that hereafter, if we get in anything like this, it is going to be a success." Eisenhower, pleased, replied, "Well, I am glad to hear that." The former President then told Kennedy, "I will support anything that has as its objective the prevention of Communist entry and solidification of bases in the Western Hemisphere," but also gave him a warning: "I believe the American people will never approve direct military intervention, by their own forces, except under provocations against us so clear and so serious that everybody will understand the need for the move." [15]

In the weeks that followed, Kennedy's people—although not Kennedy himself—tried to spread the responsibility for the debacle to include the Eisenhower Administration, charging that the plans for the Bay of Pigs operation had been completed and approved before January 20, 1961. Eisenhower would have none of that. In early May, he flew to Augusta to host a dinner for the men who had put up the money for Mamie's cottage on the golf course (he had not known who they were, and was only given their names after he left the White House). While there, he indignantly told Slater and the others that the Bay of Pigs "could not have happened in my Administration." That theme was taken up by his associates, who insisted that if Ike had been President, either the operation would not have gone forward with such inadequate and sloppy planning, or if it had, Ike would have provided U.S. air cover for the invaders.

Eisenhower felt so strongly about the controversy that he did something he had never done before, or would again—he ordered the documentary record changed. He wanted to prove that he had never approved any plans, much less a specific one for the Bay of Pigs, and insisted that the distinction between creating an asset and approving a plan remained sharp and clear. He wrote to Gordon Gray, Goodpaster, and others in his inner circle, asking for their impressions and memories of what had been approved and what had not. He believed that there was no record of his discussions on the subject with them, because he had specifically ordered that no notes be kept.

Gray, however, had kept notes. In June of 1961, as the controversy about responsibility for the Bay of Pigs continued and increased, Gray called Eisenhower at Gettysburg. "Would you like to see a record of all your conversations about Cuba?" he asked. "I think I'd give my right arm to have such," Eisenhower replied, "but of course there isn't anything." Gray told him, "There is." Eisenhower asked, "Where is it?" Gray said that it was at Fort Ritchie, where the classified material from the White House years was kept while Eisenhower worked on his memoirs. Eisenhower sent John Eisenhower to Ritchie to fetch the papers, then called Gray to Gettysburg to go over them with him.

The two men sat down with Gray's various memoranda. Eisenhower read them word for word, making such comments as "By golly, that's right" or "Remember this?" Then he came to one that covered the March 17, 1960, meeting in which he had approved Bissell's four-point plan for Cuba (see page 557). Eisenhower looked at it, looked at Gray, looked back at the paper, and declared, "This is wrong." "Well," Gray replied, "all right, sir, what is it?" Eisenhower indicated that Gray had used the word "planning," and insisted that he had *not* given any approval for planning. "We did no military planning," Eisenhower flatly declared, and insisted again that so long as he was President, there had been no military planning as to where, when, or how to use the paramilitary force. "With your permission," Eisenhower said to Gray, "I'm going to have this page rewritten to reflect the facts." Gray said, "That's fine with me," and they then agreed to take the word "planning" out of the memorandum.[16]

Thirteen years later, after the documents had been deposited in the Eisenhower Library, Gray wrote Dr. Don Wilson, the assistant director, to explain the situation. After outlining the story, he wrote: "I agreed with the General that the memorandum [of the March 17 meeting] was misleading and was quite content with the revision made and, of course, signed it. In any event, the memoranda which you now have had his specific approval as to content, and, I might say, that I had his cheerful forgiveness for having violated his instructions [about keeping no notes of discussions about Cuba]."[17]

Eisenhower's unhappiness with Kennedy was increased by one of Kennedy's responses to the Bay of Pigs. Kennedy challenged the Russians to a race to the moon. Eisenhower thought that a terrible mistake, and said so, although only in private. Nevertheless his criticisms got through to the NASA astronauts, and one of them, Major Frank Borman, wrote Eisenhower about it in June of 1965. Eisenhower sent Borman a long, careful reply. "What I have criticized about the current space program," he said, "is the concept under which it was drastically revised and expanded just after the Bay of Pigs fiasco." Eisenhower gave it as his judgment that the challenge to the Russians to race to the moon was "unwise." American prestige should not have been put on the line in that fashion, because "it immediately took one single project or experiment out of a thoughtfully planned and continuing program involving communication, meteorology, reconnaissance, and future military and scientific benefits and gave the highest priority—unfortunate in my opinion—to a race, in other words, a stunt." As a result, Eisenhower said, "costs went up drastically," while the benefits of the space program were lost.[18]

However unhappy with Kennedy the former President was, Kennedy nevertheless was the country's leader, and Eisenhower gave him his support whenever he could. Eisenhower was enthusiastic about Kennedy's program for trade expansion, and wrote letters to all the Republican leaders asking them to get behind Kennedy on it.[19] When Kennedy asked him to use his influence to secure Republican votes for new civil-rights legislation, Eisenhower replied that although he would not presume to tell Republicans how to vote, he was willing to let them know "my personal convictions" favoring new legislation, as well as "the seriousness with which I view the entire problem."[20] After Kennedy fired Dulles and replaced him with John McCone, as head of the CIA, he sent McCone up to Gettysburg on a number of occasions to give private briefings to Eisenhower. In addition, Macmillan, Adenauer, and de Gaulle sometimes asked Eisenhower to pass on to Kennedy their worries and opinions.[21] And Eisenhower gave Kennedy his full support in terminating the nuclear test moratorium.[22]

On October 20, McCone called Eisenhower to ask him to come down to Washington the following morning. Eisenhower agreed to make the trip. When he arrived, McCone gave him a briefing on Soviet missile development in Cuba, then said the government was considering three plans: (1) destruction of the missile sites by bombing; (2) bombing conducted simultaneously with amphibious invasion of the island with overwhelming force; (3) a blockade of the island. Eisenhower listened, asked some questions, discovered that he would not be meeting with Kennedy (McCone had hinted in his phone call that he would), and went back to Gettysburg. The next morning, Sunday,

October 22, Eisenhower, Mamie, and George Allen were sitting on the porch at the farm when Kennedy telephoned. He wanted Eisenhower's views. Eisenhower told Kennedy that he had come to the conclusion that a bombing mission was inappropriate "and would not be useful and would indeed be detrimental to our cause." He added that he could not choose between plans 2 and 3, because "I am not in possession of all the background . . . that would give me the basis for making any selection." Eisenhower did say, however, that whatever Kennedy decided to do, he would have Eisenhower's support. Kennedy said he had decided to put the third plan, a blockade, into effect, and that he was going on national television that evening to announce this action.[23]

A week later, again on Sunday morning, Kennedy called Eisenhower to inform him about the messages he had received from Khrushchev on the Cuban missile crisis. Khrushchev's basic proposal, Kennedy said, was that he would remove the missiles from Cuba in return for an American promise not to invade the island. Kennedy indicated that he was inclined to accept. Eisenhower concurred, but warned him to be "very careful about defining exactly what was meant by the promise." In a memorandum he made on the conversation that afternoon, Eisenhower wrote that "I observed, since we make a point of keeping our promises, that the agreement should not imply anything more than we actually meant. It would be a mistake, I said, to give the Russians an unconditional pledge that we would, forever and under all conditions, not invade regardless of changing circumstances." Kennedy said he understood that point and agreed. Eisenhower then warned him not to allow Khrushchev to drag out the negotiations, but to "hold the initiative that the government had finally seized when it established the quarantine."[24]

Some years later, in 1966, in an oral history interview, Eisenhower recalled telling Kennedy "there is one thing you must do." It was to get Khrushchev's agreement to allow land inspections of the missile sites. As Eisenhower remembered it, Kennedy replied that Khrushchev had so agreed. Eisenhower then told the interviewer, "Of course, it was never done. And I think that Communists probably concluded he wouldn't do anything; but I insisted on this land inspection. . . . It was an opportunity we missed not to go in." Perhaps Eisenhower was as insistent in 1962 as he claimed to be in 1966, but even if true, he did not think the point about land inspection important enough at the time of the event to mention it in his long memorandum written immediately after he finished his conversation with Kennedy.[25]

By November 5, 1962, Castro had told Kennedy that he did not care what agreements Khrushchev had made, that Cuba was his country and he would not allow American inspection teams on his island. When Eisenhower heard that, he called McCone to tell the head of the CIA that "we owe it to ourselves to (a) First, *make certain* all missiles are gone, and (b) To assert our right to take such action, at any time, against Castro as would assure Latin America and ourselves protection against subversion, sabotage, etc." But to the former President's disgust, Kennedy did nothing.[26]

When Khrushchev put up the Berlin Wall, Kennedy did not come to Eisenhower for advice. Eisenhower nevertheless called McCone and said, "John, isn't there going to be any reaction to this, because I read in the papers that they are starting to build a wall." McCone replied, "I haven't heard a word about any thought of resistance." Eisenhower said that in his view the written agreements the Russians had signed on the status of Berlin guaranteed communication between all parts of the city, and that "we had the absolute right to use whatever force was needed to eliminate walls." But again, to Eisenhower's expressed disgust, Kennedy did nothing.[27]

One noteworthy aspect to these Eisenhower-Kennedy exchanges was how belligerent Eisenhower had become. When he was in office, Eisenhower had received a constant stream of advice, whenever there was a crisis with the Communists, whether it was in Korea or Vietnam or Formosa or Hungary or Berlin, to get tough, to stand up to Khrushchev, to use whatever force was necessary. He had consistently rejected such advice. But out of office, as an outsider and a critic, he was much tougher, much more willing to go the whole route, than he had been when the decision was his responsibility.

Eisenhower was not only a former President, but also the former head of the Republican Party. In addition, he was still—according to every poll taken—the most admired, respected, and popular man in the country. Nixon had carried the banner for the Republicans in the 1960 election, but in the months and years that followed, it was to Eisenhower that Republican candidates and officeholders turned for endorsements, help in fund raising, and general publicity. Initially, he was flattered to be remembered, honored to be invited to dinners, eager to help the cause wherever he could. In June 1961, he and Mamie went to New York for a series of $100-a-plate Republican dinners. While in the city, the Eisenhowers went to the 21 Club for dinner on their own, their first night out as private citizens. The next day they went to Belmont racetrack, where Mamie presented a trophy, and the following evening they went to the theater. After a whirlwind few days, Eisenhower had a box of sandwiches packed up and drove back to Gettysburg.[28]

The pressure on Eisenhower to participate in more fund raisers was intense and never ending. It was irritating, and it bothered him to have to say no so often, but as he told Slater, "I don't mind as long as I can be helpful because I figure that when the time comes that a person can't do some good he might as well die."[29] In the course of the 1962 congressional elections, he visited twenty-one states and made twenty-eight speeches supporting Republican candidates, in addition to attending more than two dozen fund-raising dinners. But he was bothered by the way so many Republicans were drifting farther to the right, and he was distinctly unhappy with the way in which party leaders felt free to call on him for speeches and dinners, but equally free to reject his advice to move toward the middle of the road. In July 1962, he complained to George Humphrey that "all that the Leaders want to use me for is to use whatever value I may have to bring more people to the dinners with their hundred dollars in their hands."[30]

In that summer of 1962, Eisenhower tried to take the party leadership away from the Old Guard and the RNC. He helped organize and agreed to serve as honorary chairman of a new group, the Republican Citizens. Back in 1952, and again in 1956, Eisenhower had turned to such a "Citizens" organization to manage his campaign, much to the displeasure of the regulars in the RNC. During his eight years in the White House, he had often entertained the notion of forming a third party, and had tried unsuccessfully to put an adjective such as "Modern" or "Moderate" in front of the word "Republican." The Republican Citizens idea of 1962 was yet another attempt to broaden and liberalize the party (or, in the view of the RNC, to steal it from its rightful owners). Eisenhower wrote dozens, if not hundreds, of letters asking his business and military friends to support the Citizens group, and from them he got a handsome response. Notably absent was the name of Richard Nixon. Notable in their indifference, if not outright hostility, were Dirksen, Halleck, and the other Republican leaders in Congress. Eisenhower had liked the idea so much that he agreed to give up the services of Ann Whitman, who left Gettysburg in 1962 to take a position with the Republican Citizens. He soon heard a "very distressing report" from her; she said the work was dismal, the response to the Citizens almost nonexistent among professional politicians, and that her morale was shot. Eisenhower wrote to the RNC about Whitman's report. He admitted that "she is quite a temperamental lady and sometimes gets very easily discouraged and depressed," but reminded the committee that "her value in the political field and especially her wide acquaintanceship with so many Republican leaders are not to be discounted." He urged the committee to make full use of her services, and those of the Citizens. Still the regulars in the party remained indifferent.[31]

In one of his letters, to a businessman in Cleveland, Eisenhower said he was "completely nonplussed" by the way in which Dirksen, Halleck, and the other leaders were reacting to the Citizens. He explained that "what we're trying to do is build a bridge between the Republican Party on the one hand and the Independents and the dissatisfied Democrats on the other so that these latter people may eventually find themselves more comfortable living with Republican policies and personalities." But as far as he could tell, the Old Guard would rather have control of a minority party than share power in a majority party.[32] If his analysis was correct, the Old Guard got what it wanted out of the 1962 elections—the Republicans remained a distinctly minority party, while the Republican Citizens died.

Following the Republican defeat in 1962, Eisenhower's attention, like that of every other Republican, turned to the 1964 presidential election. Who would lead the Republican Party? Eisenhower was not enthusiastic about either of the front-runners, Senator Barry Goldwater of Arizona (who had been one of the leading critics of the Republican Citizens idea) and Governor Rockefeller of New York. Nixon, who had lost a bid to become governor of California and then made things worse with a disastrous postelection press conference ("You won't have Dick Nixon to kick around any longer."), was out of the running. Eisenhower, for his part, clung to the absurd hope that Robert Anderson would be the candidate; if not Anderson, he liked Lodge; if not Lodge, he was impressed by Governor William Scranton of Pennsylvania. In meetings with Clay, Brownell, and others, Eisenhower mentioned these names as the kind of men he could get enthusiastic about. He did not mention Goldwater, or Rockefeller—or Nixon.

When Nixon was told about Eisenhower's conversations, he commented—at a private party—that he thought it "strange" Eisenhower had left his name off the list. Little in politics is really private; a reporter heard about Nixon's remark and the next day it appeared in the Washington newspapers. Eisenhower saw the story and immediately wrote Nixon. He said he could scarcely believe Nixon could have made such a remark, because "you have frankly told me that you were not available even for consideration," and because "I have always been careful to point out that in naming any possibilities, I do not mean to limit." In conclusion, Eisenhower wrote, "It appears that the newspaper people are never going to cease their attempts to make it appear that you and I have been sworn enemies from the very beginning of our acquaintanceship." That was it—there was no reassurance on Eisenhower's part that he still loved and supported Nixon, or that he always had.[33]

On October 14, 1963, Eisenhower celebrated his seventy-third birthday. He had been in and out of Walter Reed a half-dozen times since he left the White House, but never stayed more than a few days, as all the ailments were minor ones. His general physical condition, for a man his age who had suffered a major heart attack, a stroke, and undergone major surgery for ileitis, was excellent. He was playing golf regularly, walking about his farm, puttering in his garden, keeping active. Shortly after Eisenhower moved permanently to Gettysburg, John wrote that he was "shocked and worried at the Old Man's demeanor." To John, his father's "movements were slower, his tone less sharp, and he had time even during the work day to stop and indulge in what would formerly be considered casual conversation. I feared for his health." But, John soon realized, he was wrong—it was simply that his father was relaxed, more so than he had ever been.[34] Ellis Slater thought that Eisenhower "has seldom looked better—[he] seems quite relaxed."[35] He got tired sooner and more often than in the past, but he still had that remarkable ability to bounce back after a good night's sleep. His mind was as sharp as ever, as was his interest in and concern about public affairs.

His friends were passing from the scene. In March 1962, Pete Jones died. After the funeral, the Eisenhowers flew to Baja, California, with what remained of the gang for some fishing, shooting, and bridge. Eisenhower got up at 5 A.M. each morning in order to be in the ravines when the white-wing doves started flying shortly after sunrise. One day he shot a dozen, the next sixteen, and on the following morning he killed thirty birds, tops in the group. After the shoot, he went marlin fishing, where he was again successful, then spent the afternoons swimming in the pool and the evenings playing bridge. Eisenhower and his gang were well looked after; in addition to Moaney, there was a Mexican manager, a cook, three maids, four workers to handle luggage and other chores, three planes and pilots, two boats with crews, and a platoon from the Mexican Army to arrange for the jeeps to drive to the ravines for the shooting. The pilots flew low over the Gulf of California, at Eisenhower's request, so that he could observe the whales nursing their calves. Eisenhower stayed in Baja for two weeks; when he was not otherwise occupied, he wrote articles for *Reader's Digest* and *The Saturday Evening Post* on the futility of summit meetings and the importance of fiscal responsibility. Taken all together, it was exactly the way he had envisioned his retirement ought to be.[36] And, it might be said, exactly the kind of a retirement most Americans thought he deserved and ought to have.

Certainly Eisenhower's rich friends thought so. Beginning in the winter of 1961–1962, the Eisenhowers took a train each year to Palm Desert, where a home was provided for them by one friend, while Jackie Cochran and Floyd Odlum provided the general with an office and made their ranch available to him for entertaining his friends (at their expense). Another friend provided him with a car. The office was appallingly busy. In his retirement, Eisenhower received an average of seventy-five hundred letters a month; he claimed to answer two-thirds of the mail. It proved to be too much for Ann Whitman. He insisted on dictating to her alone—during the White House years, she was the only human being he ever dictated to. Whitman was accustomed to handling the load, but when her boss was the President, she had twelve typists she could call on. At Palm Desert, and in Gettysburg, she had only two, and unlike the secretaries in the White House, they refused to work more than eight hours a day, five days a week, which meant Whitman had to carry an enormous typing load. Cochran commented that "Ann didn't even take time to eat. I never saw anybody put in the hours that she did in my life." Eisenhower hardly noticed. He was so accustomed to people knocking themselves out for him that he took it for granted.

There was another problem. During the White House years, Mamie seldom saw Whitman, but at Palm Desert and Gettysburg, they were often together. The two women shared a single obsession, Dwight Eisenhower. He took both of them for granted, but they were competitors for his attention, or so it seemed to Mamie, who resented the way in which her husband relied on Whitman. "There was," Cochran remembered, "a lot of dissension between Ann and Mamie." At the end of that first winter in Palm Desert, Whitman went to work for the Republican Citizens, and after that idea died, she joined Rockefeller in New York, which made the general distinctly unhappy. Thereafter, he had little contact with the woman who had given so much of her life to serving him, a woman who had been indispensable when he was President. In 1968 he did write her a short, disapproving note: "I see that your Governor has added Emmet Hughes to his staff of advisers. I can scarcely think of anything that could be less helpful to the Governor, either in the campaign or if and when he became President." [37]

By the fall of 1963, conditions in South Vietnam, which had seemed so stable when Eisenhower left office, had deteriorated badly. A major insurgency was under way. Kennedy had committed nearly sixteen thousand American troops to the country, but political intrigue in Saigon continued and intensified. There was a military coup; one result was the assassination of Diem, the man who had generated such enthusiasm in Eisenhower back in 1954 and in the following years. There was speculation that the CIA was involved in the assassination. Eisenhower commented on the subject in a letter to Nixon. "I rather suspect the Diem affair will be shrouded in mystery for a long time to come," he began. "No matter how much the Administration may have differed with him, I cannot believe any American would have approved the cold-blooded killing of a man who had, after all, shown great courage when he undertook the task some years ago of defeating Communist's attempts to take over his country." [38]

Within the month, there was another assassination, equally mysterious and far more shocking. On November 22, 1963, Eisenhower was in New York for a luncheon at the U.N. when he received the news of Kennedy's death. (Back in April 1954, when Eisenhower was going to Lexington, Kentucky, for a speech, the Secret Service had asked him to change the route of his motorcade, because several Puerto Rican nationalists demanding independence had been seen in the city the previous day. Jim Hagerty wrote in his diary that Eisenhower took "a completely fatalistic viewpoint—'If they're going to shoot me, they're going to shoot me—so what! There's nothing you can do about it.' " [39])

The following day, November 23, 1963, Eisenhower went to Washington to view Kennedy's casket and to pay his respects to the widow. Then, at the request of the new President, he crossed the street and went to the Executive Office Building for a conference with Lyndon Johnson. Eisenhower promised Johnson his full support during the national emergency, urged Johnson to balance the budget, suggested that he speak to a joint session of Congress, and told him "to be his own man." [40] It was the beginning of an association between the new President and the former President that was to dominate much of the remainder of Eisenhower's public life.

CHAPTER TWENTY-NINE

Johnson, Goldwater, Vietnam

November 23, 1963–February 1968

As RICHARD NIXON noted, Dwight Eisenhower "was not the kind of man who appreciated undue familiarity." He would give chilling looks to anyone who tugged at his arm or tried to slap him on the back. Lyndon Johnson was not the kind of man who could resist pulling, tugging, slapping, or punching the people he was talking to. Jerry Persons remembered the time, in 1959, when Eisenhower had an appointment with Johnson. "I want you to stand between Lyndon and me," Eisenhower told Persons. "My bursitis is kicking up, and I don't want him to grab me by the arm."[1]

But grab Johnson did, figuratively if not literally. At their meeting the day after Kennedy's assassination, Johnson indicated to Eisenhower that he intended to call on him regularly for advice and support. As a beginning, he asked for a memorandum containing specific suggestions. Eisenhower responded that night with a dictated message. He urged Johnson to consult with Robert Anderson on general subjects, and particularly fiscal and financial matters. In addition, he advised Johnson to meet regularly with Gordon Gray and Andy Goodpaster. "For the abilities and patriotism of these two men," Eisenhower said, "I personally vouch." He suggested that Johnson call a joint session of Congress to make a speech of not more than ten minutes. "Point out first that you have come to this office unexpectedly and you accept the decision of the Almighty," Eisenhower advised, then promise that "no revolution in purpose or policy is intended or will occur." Further, promise a balanced budget.[2]

649

During his first year as President, Johnson concentrated on domestic affairs. In that area, his policies and programs were far too liberal for Eisenhower. Knowing this, Johnson did not ask Eisenhower's advice or opinions, although he did send birthday and anniversary presents, Christmas greetings, and the like, always writing in a humble and subservient manner. His attempts to ingratiate himself included innumerable invitations to come to the White House for lunch or for dinner parties, sending Mamie flowers on any excuse, and promoting Goodpaster to three-star rank (not that Goodpaster did not deserve it, but Johnson was careful to let Eisenhower know that he had done it as a favor).[3] In February 1964, Johnson went hundreds of miles out of his way to pay his respects at Palm Desert.

In June 1964, Johnson made his first call on Eisenhower for political help. He wanted Eisenhower to urge the Republican leadership to get behind the Mutual Security appropriation. Eisenhower was both amused and irritated. He called Michigan Congressman Jerry Ford on the telephone and said, "I can remember LBJ whimpering and crying that Senator George was defeated because of his support for Mutual Security and he was afraid he would be too when I asked his support." Nevertheless, Eisenhower's commitment to Mutual Security was so strong that he did as Johnson wished, sending a strong telegram on the need for the program to Halleck and Dirksen.[4] But as Johnson began putting his Great Society legislation through Congress, in the summer of 1964, Eisenhower was most unhappy, and scathing in his judgments. He told one caller that "Johnson is unreliable and has no moral courage whatsoever." In large part, Eisenhower's hostility toward Johnson in that first year was pure and simple partisanship. The presidential election of 1964 forced the two men to stay at arm's length. When George Humphrey expressed the fear that Johnson would win by a landslide, and that the size of his vote would "reduce his backbone to stand up to Walter Reuther," Eisenhower said, "He never had any."[5]

Reporters and commentators were saying that Eisenhower was the one without a backbone, because of his refusal to endorse a Republican candidate, and even more because of his refusal to lead the fight against Senator Barry Goldwater, who was in the process of capturing the Republican Party and the nomination. To many members of the press, and to many East Coast Republicans, it was inconceivable that Eisenhower would stand aside while Goldwater returned the Republican Party to the principles of Herbert Hoover, thereby repudiating Eisenhower's middle-of-the-road, moderate policies. But stand aside he did, at least in public.

In August 1963, Henry Cabot Lodge accepted the post of ambassador to South Vietnam. In November, after Kennedy's death, Eisenhower urged Lodge to come home to run for President as the "common sense" candidate. The two men talked; *The New York Times* reported their conversation on the front page; the assumption was that Eisenhower would back Lodge. But a few days later, on his way to Palm Desert, Eisenhower had his private car shunted to a siding in the railroad yards at Harrisburg, where he had dinner with the Republican governor of Pennsylvania, William Scranton. The general pressed Scranton to enter the race. He explained that what he wanted was an open convention, with a number of contestants for the party to choose from for its candidate. Meanwhile, Goldwater continued to pile up delegates.[6]

By early May 1964, the moderate Republicans were growing desperate. A number of them urged Eisenhower to ask Lodge to return from Saigon to stop Goldwater. Eisenhower refused. He would not endorse Lodge, he said, although he would welcome him home if Lodge would resign and become an active candidate. Until then, Eisenhower declared, his position was that "if you want to canter you have to have a horse." He told Walter Cronkite, who had become one of his confidants, that "if Lodge decides to come back fine, the more the merrier."[7]

With Lodge in Saigon, and Scranton in Harrisburg refusing to campaign, the only horse available—other than Goldwater—was Rockefeller, who was even more objectionable to Eisenhower than Goldwater. Nevertheless, in late May, when the *Herald Tribune* asked Eisenhower to describe the ideal Republican candidate, Eisenhower devised a formula that seemed to fit Rockefeller. The *Tribune* published it on the eve of the last primary, in California. Reporters guessed that Eisenhower's strategy was to give Rockefeller a boost in the primary. A defeat for Goldwater in California would, presumably, block his nomination; meanwhile, Goldwater's pledged delegates would never accept Rockefeller. The result would be a stalemated convention, out of which a moderate, middle-of-the-road candidate, either Lodge or Scranton, would emerge. But Goldwater won a narrow victory in California, which gave him a commanding delegate lead going into the San Francisco convention.[8]

Moderate Republicans were distraught and desperate. Goldwater's extremism seemed certain to result in a devastating Republican defeat. For his part, Eisenhower was most concerned about Goldwater's stance on civil rights. The senator had voted against the Civil Rights Act of 1964 and appeared to be actively courting the "white backlash" vote. Eisenhower told Jim Hagerty over the telephone that "if the Republicans begin to count on white backlash, we will have a big civil war." He also talked to the head of CBS, Bill Paley, on the subject. "I have no sympathy with the 'white backlash.' I will not encourage it and if it is encouraged I will vote for the other side." Paley asked him if he would go on national television to express his views. "Not right now," Eisenhower replied. "Let things simmer for a week or two. Maybe later."[9]

On June 6, Scranton drove to Gettysburg to spend the afternoon in conference with the general. They agreed that a Goldwater nomination would have a disastrous effect on all Republican candidates, as well as assuring Johnson a landslide. Scranton got the impression that Eisenhower wanted him to declare his candidacy and would endorse him. Newspapers the following day reported that Eisenhower had finally chosen his candidate. George Humphrey, who was supporting Goldwater, called Eisenhower on the telephone to apply pressure on Eisenhower to remain neutral. Eisenhower then called Scranton. He was concerned, he said, that there had been a misunderstanding. Eisenhower said he would not participate in a stop-Goldwater "cabal." He would not endorse Scranton. Later, Eisenhower said, "I was never trained in politics; I came in laterally, at the top. In the service, when a man gives you his word, his word is binding. In politics, you never know." As Peter Lyon comments, on this occasion "it was Scranton who was bewildered."[10]

Scranton did announce that he was a candidate. Eisenhower talked with reporters. He said he felt strongly that the GOP wanted a candidate who favored civil rights for Negroes, and that he had serious reservations about Goldwater's ability to conduct foreign policy. He also issued a statement: "A free, fair, and active competition among party personalities . . . is good for the health and vigor of the party . . . I welcome the entry of Governor Scranton, whom I have long admired, into the contest." But he stayed neutral.

At the convention, Milton Eisenhower made the nominating speech for Scranton. It was a stirring speech, Milton at his best, and received a highly favorable response—except among the delegates, who were bored. Eisenhower, meanwhile, carefully retained his neutrality by appearing on ABC television on a regular basis. Although he was handsomely paid for the interviews, his gang was opposed to the whole idea, because, as Slater said, the members feared "he would demean himself" by appearing as a commentator. But they thought he did well.

On July 16, Goldwater won the nomination. In his acceptance speech, he proclaimed: "Extremism in the defense of liberty is no vice! . . . Moderation in the pursuit of justice is no virtue!" Eisenhower protested that Goldwater's vice and virtue statement "would seem to say that the end always justifies the means. The whole American system refutes that idea." But he pledged to "do my best to support" Goldwater.[11]

Never had Eisenhower appeared so bumbling or ineffective. Never had he gone so far in appeasing the Old Guard of the Republican Party. Never was he so roundly criticized. He was, however, in an awkward position. With Nixon resolutely on the sidelines, the only man who had a reasonable chance of stopping Goldwater was Rockefeller, who was anathema to Eisenhower and who in any case had lost all hope with the California primary. What the 1964 convention revealed, above all else, was how completely Eisenhower had failed in his eight-year effort to modernize the Republican Party and broaden its base. The result left him with no choice. Having failed as President to form a third party, he could hardly do so now, and he could never bring himself to support the Democrats, especially Democrats led by Lyndon Johnson. So he endorsed Goldwater, and during the campaign he made a television special at his Gettysburg farm. Goldwater was with him; sitting on chairs on the lawn, they discussed the "silly notion" that Goldwater was a right-wing extremist. It was a dismal performance, about which the less said the better. In November, Goldwater and the Republican Party suffered a humiliating defeat.

A much happier experience for Eisenhower in 1964 was the establishment of a project at Johns Hopkins University to publish his papers in a scholarly multivolume set. The original idea came from historian David Donald at Hopkins. Donald approached the head of the university, Milton Eisenhower, to point out that there was a pattern to the treatment of former Presidents by American historians. When a President left office, Donald said, his reputation was usually at its lowest point. It stayed there for two decades or more. Then his personal and official papers were opened to scholars, who began to see the President's problems, options, and choices from the President's point of view. At that time, his reputation began to rise. Donald suggested that in the case of Milton's older brother, whose reputation was shockingly low among intellectuals, the process of raising it could be speeded up through an early publication of his papers.

Milton liked the idea and arranged for a meeting between himself, Donald, and Eisenhower. The former President was enthusiastic and gave his consent. Hopkins raised the money for the project and Milton hired Dr. Alfred D. Chandler, Jr., as the editor. Chandler gathered a staff and began work immediately. In 1970 the first five volumes of *The Papers of Dwight David Eisenhower* were published by the Johns Hopkins Press. They covered the war years, and exactly as Donald had predicted, they added immeasurably to Eisenhower's reputation. By the end of that decade, when four additional volumes covering Eisenhower's career to 1948 had appeared, and the documents from the Eisenhower Administration began to become available, there was a flourishing "Eisenhower revisionism" under way, as American historians began to discover that Eisenhower was not the lazy, ineffective, simpleminded "chairman of the board," a nice guy with a big grin and an empty head, that they had thought he was.

For Eisenhower, one of the nicest things about the Hopkins' project was that it gave him an opportunity, and an excuse, to spend more time thinking about the war years. He enjoyed going over his wartime papers with Chandler and the other editors, answering questions, recalling this or that incident, reliving Overlord and the other great events. In general, in the mid-sixties, historians were relatively uninterested in his Presidency, partly because they wrote it off as a time when nothing happened, mainly because the great bulk of the documents remained classified and unavailable. But, except for the Ultra secret, the correspondence, memoranda, orders, and reports from World War II were available, and there was a flourishing industry around the writing of the history of the war. Nearly all of those doing the writing wanted an opportunity to interview General Eisenhower, and he was generous with his time. He tried to grant interviews to every serious scholar who asked for one.

Milton was in Gettysburg one afternoon in 1965. Eisenhower had spent most of the day doing interviews with historians. After they had all left, as Milton was pouring cocktails, Eisenhower let out a big sigh. Milton remarked on how tired he looked, and Eisenhower admitted that he was exhausted. Milton said it must be a burden on him, answering all those questions, searching his mind, recalling incidents long since forgotten. "Well, that's right," Eisenhower replied. Then he took a drink, grinned, and said, "But it would be worse to be forgotten." [12]

He was finding the life of a gentleman farmer to be all that he had hoped it would be. If he had a complaint, it was that he did not have enough time to oversee the operation. His cattle herd was prospering. He entered his best Angus bulls and cows in various livestock shows in Maryland and Pennsylvania, where they won numerous grand championships, which gave him bragging rights that he fully exercised. The winters in California were a joy to him too, especially because his gang and other friends would fly out and spend a week or two. Golf and bridge remained his great passions. In 1967, he shot his first hole in one. "The thrill of a lifetime," he gloated, thereby putting Overlord and the Presidency in their proper perspective.[13]

After the 1964 election, public life in the United States was dominated by Lyndon Johnson and the war in Vietnam. The man, and the event, became the national obsession. Eisenhower got caught up in it too, because once the election was passed, Johnson increasingly turned to him for advice and support. In December, Johnson called Eisenhower in Palm Desert to invite him to the inaugural. Eisenhower explained that because Mamie refused to fly, they could not make it. Johnson said he understood, then went on to say that he hoped Eisenhower would give him the benefit of his advice and counsel. He "did not want to make a nuisance of himself," Johnson said ("DDE thanked him for that," Eisenhower's new secretary, Rusty Brown, wrote in her summary of the conversation). But, Johnson added, "If he got his 'tail in a crack' he would come running to DDE on foreign affairs."[14]

Johnson meant what he said. As he began to escalate the American effort in Vietnam, he started a practice of writing or calling Eisenhower on the telephone before every significant act, both to report on what he intended to do and to seek Eisenhower's support and to ask his advice. Although Johnson's letters to Eisenhower were so full of overblown praise and gratitude as to be obsequious and phony, Johnson was quite sincere in his requests for Eisenhower's counsel, to which he gave great weight. Johnson had, after all, come to the White House almost completely innocent of any experience in foreign affairs. All through the fifties he had deferred to Eisenhower's judgment on virtually every foreign-policy crisis. Like almost everyone else in politics, he regarded General Eisenhower as the nation's greatest and wisest soldier. He was obviously aware of how valuable Eisenhower's public support of his Vietnam policy could be to him, and he was not above using Eisenhower for his own purposes in this regard, but the record makes it absolutely clear that as Johnson made his crucial decisions on the conduct of the war in Vietnam, he both sought and was influenced by Ike's advice—except on the basic question of the wisdom of fighting in Vietnam.

It is equally true that Eisenhower's advice was consistently hawk-ish, and that the main thrust of Eisenhower's criticism of Johnson on Vietnam—insofar as he was critical rather than supportive—was that Johnson was not doing enough. That had also been true of Eisen-hower's criticism of Kennedy's foreign policy; in both instances, Eisen-hower was far more belligerent, more ready to take extreme action, as an outsider than he had been when he was the man on the spot.

Johnson had *not* consulted Eisenhower before sending the Gulf of Tonkin Resolution to Congress, in August of 1964, or on the other early commitments to Vietnam. Before the next significant escalation, however, early in 1965, he asked Eisenhower to come to Washington for a thorough discussion and consultation. By then the U.S. was at war, so the only concern was how to wage it. Johnson wanted General Ike's advice, not President Eisenhower's. On February 17, 1965, in the Cabinet Room, Eisenhower met for two and one-half hours with Johnson, Robert McNamara, McGeorge Bundy, and Generals Earle G. Wheeler and Goodpaster. The notes of the meeting remained top secret until August of 1982, when they were declassified.

Johnson opened the meeting by asking for Eisenhower's thinking about the situation in South Vietnam. Eisenhower said the first thing that should be done was to get the support of the NATO allies for the American effort in Indochina. His second point was that South Vietnam's security could not be brought about by creating a "Roman wall" composed of American forces. The Vietnamese themselves had to stop the infiltration of supplies to the Viet Cong; the proper role for American forces was to "destroy the will of the enemy to continue the war." Morale was the key, not only in the negative sense of strik-ing at the enemy's morale, but in the positive sense of doing "every-thing possible to raise the morale of our own side." Eisenhower said he did not believe that air strikes against the North, such as the JCS were proposing and Johnson was considering, would be effective against infiltration. "The strikes can, however, discourage the North, and can make them pay a cost for continuing their aggression." He warned Johnson against a start-stop approach, pointing out that the air strikes following the Tonkin Gulf incident in August had raised morale, "which then suffered when there was no follow-up."

Again and again during the meeting, Eisenhower reverted to the question of air strikes. "He said that in his opinion these retaliation actions have helped the situation a great deal. However, he felt it is now important to shift to a campaign of pressure. Targets should be struck north of the border . . . He thought such strikes could be well justified before the world."

Switching to the political situation in South Vietnam, Eisenhower said the many changes in the government there "have been bewildering . . . From his experience in the Orient, however, he thought it was important to find someone who is promising and try to bolster him." He regretted Diem's assassination, because Diem "was a capable man . . . The removal of Diem resulted in a great setback for our cause."

Taking up the possibility of Chinese or Soviet intervention, Eisenhower said "that if they threaten to intervene we should pass the word back to them to take care lest dire results occur to them. . . . He thought we should let them know now what we are seeking to do in South Vietnam, and that we would act against them if necessary. This should not be done publicly, but rather very quietly." As to the possibility of negotiations with North Vietnam, "General Eisenhower felt that negotiation from weakness is likely to lead only into deceit and vulnerability, which could be disastrous to us. On the other hand, if we can show a fine record of successes, or real and dramatic accomplishment, we would be in good position to negotiate. He advised not to negotiate from a position of weakness." Prime Minister Harold Wilson of Great Britain had been urging Johnson to negotiate; Eisenhower commented that Wilson "has not had experience with this kind of problem. We, however, have learned that Munichs win nothing; therefore, his answer to the British would be 'Not now boys.' "

When Eisenhower finished, Johnson began asking questions. He asked Eisenhower whether he thought the Gulf of Tonkin Resolution "was strong enough, and ample to fill the need." Eisenhower said it struck him as being very much like his own Formosa Resolution of 1958, "which had left a large area of discretion and flexibility to the President, and that he thought that this is the way it should be." Johnson assured him that the Formosa Resolution had been his model for the Gulf of Tonkin Resolution.

McNamara asked Eisenhower for further comments on escalation of the military effort, on the ground as well as in the air. Eisenhower replied that "we should be sure that the enemy does not lack an appreciation of our stamina and determination to keep nations free by whatever means required. He thought that if they find we are ready, they will not come in in great strength." He pointed out that America had put her prestige "onto the proposition of keeping Southeast Asia free. We cannot let the Indochinese peninsula go. He hoped it would not be necessary to use the six to eight divisions mentioned, but if it should be necessary, so be it."

Johnson asked how Eisenhower had managed to get the Chinese to stop their aggression in Korea and agree to an armistice. Eisenhower replied that it was simple. "There was a gentlemen's agreement between us and our allies after the very early days of the war—well known to the Chinese—that we would not cross the Yalu or even strike the bridges on the Yalu, nor would we use nuclear weapons." Eisenhower said he had let the Chinese know, by various means, that the "gentlemen's agreement" was off after he became President, and that if the war continued, "he would not feel constrained about crossing the Yalu, or using nuclear weapons." He said that in the present situation in Vietnam, the "greatest danger is that the Chinese get the idea that we will go just so far and no further in terms of the level of war we would conduct. That would be the beginning of the end, since they would know all they had to do was go further than we do."

As they prepared to adjourn for lunch, Eisenhower made his final comment. "We must look at the effect of our actions on the whole world," he said. "When we say we will help other countries we must then be staunch. It is, of course, necessary to work out our tactics, and we should not be unnecessarily provocative." [15]

Shortly thereafter, Johnson began Operation Rolling Thunder, the bombing of North Vietnam. He also began sending in American combat units, as opposed to advisers. On March 12, Eisenhower wrote him to pledge his full support and to assure him that he was doing the right thing. Johnson replied that "you are in my thoughts always and it is so valuable to me to have your thoughts, interest, and friendship." [16]

Beginning in April of 1965, Johnson sent Goodpaster to Palm Desert or Gettysburg on a biweekly basis to give Eisenhower a detailed briefing on what was happening, and to seek his advice. These meetings usually lasted two to three hours. At the first such meeting, Eisenhower told Goodpaster that "he strongly recommended getting rid of restrictions and delaying procedures. These result in many cases from attempts to control matters in too much detail from Washington. Such practices normally result from inexperience on the part of governmental officials." Eisenhower urged Goodpaster to tell Johnson to "untie Westmoreland's hands." The President should give Westmoreland, who had recently become the commander in Vietnam, whatever he requested, then leave him to fight the war. He thought this was "absolutely essential."[17]

On May 13, 1965, at Gettysburg, Goodpaster told Eisenhower that Johnson had "asked me to tell him that many of the views he has given have been among the best received and are now being carried out." Johnson had just instituted the first of his many bombing pauses, with the hope that the North Vietnamese would take the opportunity to begin negotiations. The President wanted to know what Eisenhower thought about the pause. Eisenhower replied that "he just did not feel in a position to judge . . . He was clear, however, that if the Communists fail to respond, and we do resume our attacks, we should hit them heavily from the outset, using 'everything that can fly.'" Goodpaster also told Eisenhower that Johnson wanted him to come down to Washington, or phone him, whenever he had a comment to make. The President was making a helicopter available for Eisenhower for that purpose. Eisenhower was "very appreciative." As a final point, Goodpaster noted, "He asked me to convey a comment to the President that he should not be too surprised or disturbed at the 'chatter' from certain quarters over the firm course the President is pursuing . . . A certain amount of this has to be expected . . . So long as the policies are right, as he believes they are, too much attention need not be given to these people."[18]

At a June 16 briefing in Gettysburg, Goodpaster said that the President wanted Eisenhower's views on the proper use and size of reinforcements being sent to Vietnam. The JCS wanted to send only one brigade of the air mobile division, and use it to defend coastal base areas. Westmoreland wanted the entire division, and he wanted to use it to operate offensively within South Vietnam. Eisenhower "considered the matter at some length." He then commented that "we have now appealed to force in South Vietnam, and therefore we have got to win. For this purpose, simply holding on or sitting passively in static areas will not suffice. He added that there is no use building bases if they are not put to full use. The only reason for creating them is to make it possible to take the offensive and clear the area. He thought . . . we should undertake offensive operations ourselves," and he therefore concluded "General Westmoreland's recommendation should be supported." He added that "he was strongly impressed by General Westmoreland," and that "he very definitely supported operations of the kind he proposed, and thought the first one should be carried out as soon as practicable."[19]

On July 2, 1965, Eisenhower called Johnson on the telephone. Senators Robert Kennedy and Mike Mansfield were becoming increasingly critical of the escalation. Eisenhower urged Johnson to ignore them. "When you once appeal to force in an international situation involving military help for a nation," he said, "you have to go all out! This is war, and as long as the enemy are putting men down there, my advice is do what you have to do!" He advised Johnson to tell the Russians that if they did "not bring about some understanding we will have to go all out."

At this point Johnson asked Eisenhower, in a plaintive voice, "Do you really think we can beat the Viet Cong?" It was his first confession of uncertainty, at least to Eisenhower. Eisenhower was cautious in his reply. He said it was hard to tell, that it depended on how far the North Vietnamese and Chinese were willing to go, and what Johnson was willing to do. As far as Eisenhower was concerned, "We are not going to be run out of a free country that we helped to establish." Johnson, still gloomy, said that if he escalated further, "we will lose the British and Canadians and will be alone in the world." Eisenhower snapped back, "We would still have the Australians and the Koreans—and our own convictions."

Then, as Rusty Brown recorded the conversation, "President Johnson said he wanted General Eisenhower to think about this as he wanted the best advice possible and General Eisenhower is the best Chief of Staff he has." Eisenhower's advice was to go for victory.[20]

Through August of 1965, Eisenhower remained extremely hawkish. On the third, he told Goodpaster, "We should not base our action on minimum needs, but should swamp the enemy with overwhelming force." He wanted to "mine the harbors without delay, telling the world to keep shipping out of Haiphong and making clear that there is to be no sanctuary." He complained that "there seems to him to be too much of a brake on everything we do." Goodpaster said the JCS were worried about getting overextended in Vietnam, which might tempt the Russians to attack in Europe. "General Eisenhower said he was not concerned over this point. If we were to become involved in war in Europe, he would not be for sending large forces into the area, but would be for using every bomb we have."[21] On August 20, after Goodpaster reported on a "search and destroy" mission in Chulai, Eisenhower said that that was "the way to do it. It was highly professional, overwhelming and quick." He told Goodpaster to tell Johnson "that there is no question about his support for what the President is doing. He supports it strongly."[22]

All of this was highly appreciated by Johnson, who increasingly felt like a man under siege. He wrote Eisenhower, "No one knows better than you the accumulated demands of the Presidency. No one gives more attention than you to the best interests of our country. Whatever course of action you believe to be right is the course to which you give your approval and the massive weight of your prestige and wisdom . . . History will surely record that President Dwight D. Eisenhower, both in and out of office, never swerved from what he believed to be the truth nor from giving his courage and his energy to the people he serves as patriot, soldier, President, and now as wise counselor to the nation." [23]

By October 1965, Johnson's major ground reinforcements were beginning to move into Vietnam. Eisenhower was enthusiastic. He told Goodpaster, "We must now be sure to put in enough to win. He would err on the side of putting in too much rather than too little. He thought that overwhelming strength on our side would discourage the enemy, as well as keep down casualties." [24] Eisenhower did warn that sending conscripted troops to Vietnam would cause a major public-relations problem, and he thought Johnson should try to avoid it by sending only regulars or volunteers. Goodpaster responded that there just were not enough of either category. [25]

In January 1966, Johnson wanted Eisenhower's advice on a suggestion that some of the "old heads," retired general officers from World War II, be consulted about operations in Vietnam. Eisenhower was opposed. "He stated that there is no better man than Westmoreland. The thing to do is give him the means and let him alone to the maximum possible extent." [26] Two weeks later, Johnson asked, through Goodpaster, what Eisenhower thought about the idea of adopting an "enclave" strategy, i.e., digging in around the bases and cities while abandoning offensive operations in the hinterland. "General Eisenhower indicated he would have nothing to do with such proposals. They would put us in a situation where hope of a successful outcome would be lost. They in fact could only result in complete failure on our side." [27]

In March 1966, Johnson wrote Eisenhower to say that he was the only other man in the world "who fully understands the problems that come to this desk . . . I cannot tell you adequately my gratitude for your wisdom and your counsel. And, for the fact no one has found it possible to divide you and me.

"I choose to believe that every decision I have taken in Vietnam has met your approval. It is important to me, for both guidance and inspiration."[28] Two weeks later, he wrote again: "I need your wisdom and judgment in these decisions which the President must make and whose depth and solemn agony only you really understand."[29]

By September of 1966, however, Eisenhower was finding it more difficult to approve of "every decision" Johnson had made in Vietnam. His impatience over Johnson's gradual application of pressure on the Communists, and his concern over the way in which the Johnson Administration centralized the decision-making power, not allowing Westmoreland the free hand Eisenhower thought he had to have, were growing daily. Further, Eisenhower was beginning to worry that as the war dragged on, popular support for it would wane. On September 19, Goodpaster recorded that "General Eisenhower said he had been seeing various statements implying that 'small wars,' or hostilities such as those in Vietnam, could go on almost indefinitely. Some comments in fact suggest that such a condition must be regarded as normal, and that our society must be geared to support this as well as other ongoing problems." Eisenhower would not accept such a view. "He felt this is not something that can go on and on, but is something that should rather be brought to an end as soon as possible. He commented that our people inevitably get tired of supporting involvements of this kind which go on for a long time, with no end in sight."[30]

But although he predicted and anticipated antiwar protests, as they increased in volume so did Eisenhower's anger. "Frankly," he wrote Nixon in October 1966, "it seems that the Vietnam War is creating more whimperings and whinings from some frustrated partisans than it's inspiring a unification of all America in the solution of a national problem."[31] And he complained about "the selfish and cowardly whimperings of some of these 'students' who—uninformed and brash though they are—arrogate to themselves the right to criticize, irresponsibly, our highest officials, and to condemn America's deepest commitments to her international friends."[32] No matter how strident the antiwar protests, however, Eisenhower could not believe that America would cut and run. In February 1967, he wrote George Humphrey (who had told him that his fear was that Johnson would negotiate an agreement and "bring the boys home," thereby winning re-election), "America has invested a lot of lives in Vietnam. I cannot believe the nation will be satisfied with any agreement that our people would recognize as 'phony,' or which the Communists would soon, and with impunity, violate."[33]

Eisenhower wanted victory, not negotiations. And he wanted it soon. In April 1967, he told Goodpaster to tell Johnson that "a course of 'gradualism' . . . is bound to be ineffective." To make his point, he used one of his favorite examples: If a general sent a battalion to take a hill, he might get the hill, but would suffer heavy casualties in the process, whereas if he sent a division, the casualties would be minimal.[34] But even if Johnson was sending battalions rather than divisions, at least he was proclaiming his resolution to stay the course, and on that basis Eisenhower was willing to give him his support. Indeed, in July he told Jim Hagerty over the telephone that "he wouldn't mind if the man were elected if he won the war, except for his fiscal policies." But he also responded to Hagerty's remark that "orders come from Washington for every battle" with the comment that "I have pleaded for decentralization."[35]

Also in July, Eisenhower's frustrations were such that he told reporters how opposed he was to a "war of gradualism," and urged Congress to declare war against North Vietnam. That war, he said, "should be given first priority. Other goals, however attractive, should take second place."[36] In October, he said the country should "take any action to win." Asked if he would draw the line at the use of nuclear weapons, he replied, "I would not automatically preclude anything. When you appeal to force to carry out the policies of America abroad there is no court above you."[37] The comment caused great excitement, and required clarification. Tom Dewey, who was present when Eisenhower made it, explained that Eisenhower simply meant "you don't inform the enemy on what you intend to do." Two weeks later, at his seventy-seventh birthday party at Gettysburg, Eisenhower himself told reporters that the idea of using nuclear weapons in Vietnam was "silly." He pointed out that they would destroy friend as well as foe. But he also told Arthur Larson privately that if the Chinese came into the war "we would have to use at least tactical atomic weapons."[38]

For that seventy-seventh birthday, Johnson sent Eisenhower a watch with an alarm clock in it and a tie clasp, each bearing the Presidential Seal. In a covering letter, Johnson commented: "Each passing day, we are stronger in purpose and firmer of faith for the unity we continue to find in your example and voice. You offer us the courage of the soldier and the counsel of the statesman. Each is priceless to our search for peace. But what we treasure most is your wise advice . . . Your friendship will always be cherished."[39]

And, of course, Johnson cherished Eisenhower's support on Vietnam. He got it in the most public way possible on November 28, 1967, when Eisenhower and Bradley made a television broadcast from Gettysburg over NBC. Together with Truman, the two old generals had joined a short-lived group called the Citizens Committee for Peace with Freedom in Vietnam. Bradley defined the object of the committee as to help the American people understand the war, because "when they understand it, they will be for it, we think." Eisenhower argued that a military victory was possible if certain changes in strategy and tactics were made. "This respecting of boundary lines on the map," he said; "I think you can overdo it." He suggested a foray into North Vietnam "either from the sea or from the hills . . . I would be for what we call 'hot pursuit' " into Cambodia or Laos. He ended with a curt dismissal of the " 'kooks' and 'hippies' and all the rest that are talking about surrendering."[40]

But it was not just kooks and hippies who wanted out, as Eisenhower well knew. He told Goodpaster privately that "many of the people who see him—neither 'hawks' nor 'doves'—are talking in terms of discouragement about the course of the war in Vietnam. They say that nothing seems to be going well and that, perhaps, it would be better to get out of it than to continue." Goodpaster responded with a pep talk—things were going well, he insisted, and there was an end in sight. Eisenhower was encouraged. "He said he is optimistic that we can win this war."[41]

Another presidential election was coming up. The agony of Vietnam was obviously going to be a major issue. In October 1967, Eisenhower spoke in general terms about the kind of candidates he wanted to see nominated. "I don't regard myself as a missionary, and I don't want to convert anybody," he said. "But if any Republican or Democrat suggests that we pull out of Vietnam and turn our backs on the more than thirteen thousand Americans who died in the cause of freedom there, they will have me to contend with. That's one of the few things that would start me off on a series of stump speeches across the nation."[42]

In the early spring of 1968, Eisenhower wrote an article on the war for *Reader's Digest.* "The current raucous confrontation," he wrote of the antiwar movement, "goes far beyond honorable dissent. . . . it is rebellion, and it verges on treason. . . . I will not personally support any peace-at-any-price candidate who advocates capitulation and the abandonment of South Vietnam."[43]

About that time, Johnson came to visit at Palm Desert. Afterward, he wrote Eisenhower, "I could not resist dropping in to draw on the strength of your wisdom and friendship again. . . . I will persevere, sustained by your support."[44] Simultaneously, the Communists launched their Tet offensive. They suffered extraordinarily heavy casualties, but the reaction in the United States verged on panic. No one had anticipated the offensive, or so it appeared, nor had they suspected that the Viet Cong were so numerous and well coordinated. It all reminded Eisenhower of the reaction to the Battle of the Bulge. He recalled that in December 1944, when he asked for reinforcements to follow up the victory in the Ardennes, the Allied governments had provided the men he needed to finish the job. But in 1968, rather than send Westmoreland the reinforcements he wanted to follow up his victory, the Johnson Administration put a ceiling on manpower commitments to Vietnam. In New Hampshire, meanwhile, Senator Eugene McCarthy, running on an antiwar platform, did surprisingly well in the Democratic primary against Johnson, and Senator Robert Kennedy entered the race against the President.

Johnson had promised Eisenhower that he would persevere, but he went on national television to announce that he was halting the bombing of most of North Vietnam, and that he was personally withdrawing from the presidential race. Eisenhower was livid with anger, his remarks about Johnson's cutting and running unprintable.[45] Goodpaster went on to a new assignment, and Eisenhower's connection with the Johnson Administration came to an end.

Vietnam was the main, but not the only, cause of unhappiness for Eisenhower in the mid-sixties. Longhairs, hippies, rock music, extensive drug use by teen-agers, and riots in the ghettos were, to Eisenhower, deplorable. He wrote a British friend in 1965, "Lack of respect for law, laxness in dress, appearance, and thinking, in conduct and in manner, as well as student and other riots with civil disobedience all spring from a common source; a lack of concern for the ancient virtues of decency, respect for law and elders, and old-fashioned patriotism."[46]

Eisenhower was also disturbed by the problem of overpopulation. In 1965 Senator Ernest Gruening held hearings on the subject and asked for Eisenhower's comments. Eisenhower called it "one of the most, if not the most, critical problem facing mankind today." He admitted that when he was President, he had resisted attempts to get the federal government involved in programs of population control, either within the United States or in relation to the nations of the Third World. But, he said, he had "abandoned" that position, and had become convinced that without a program of population stabilization, no amount of economic aid would improve the lot of the poor at home and abroad.

In this regard, Eisenhower was ready to take an extreme position.

He suggested to Gruening that the Senate consider "the desirability, in certain cases, of sterilization." Eisenhower explained that there were many cases of illegitimate children born to the same mother, "who has no source of income except the relief checks paid her from public funds." He would not "want to condemn out of hand any woman who might have, because of any emotional reason, given birth to a child out of wedlock or deny to her needed support for its raising." But, he added, "If the mistake should be repeated then I think the public should be guaranteed against the need of supporting more than two illegitimate children. I see no way this can be done except through compulsory sterilization."[47]

Like most older Americans, Eisenhower was appalled by many of the trends of the 1960s. Why could not the youth of the sixties be more like the youth of his day? Why were not draft dodgers an object of scorn, as they had been during World War II? Why could not the kids get their kicks out of the fox-trot and beer and cigarettes rather than rock and roll, marijuana, and LSD? Why was not Norman Rockwell, rather than Andy Warhol, the most popular artist of the day? Eisenhower expressed his concern over the decline in "our concept of beauty and decency and morality," over the use by Hollywood and book and magazine publishers of "vulgarity, sensuality, indeed downright filth, to sell their wares," over the sort of painting "that looks like a broken-down tin lizzie loaded with paint has been driven over it."[48]

A major reason for the decline in morality and good taste, he felt, was the decline in the quality of the nation's leadership. That at least could be set right in the 1968 presidential election. He could not escape a sense of personal responsibility for the Republican debacle in 1964, because of his failure to denounce Goldwater or endorse a candidate of his own choosing, and he was determined not to make the same mistake again.

His candidate was Nixon, and in 1968, unlike 1960, he had no hesitancy about him. It was not so much that Nixon had gone up in his estimation—although he had—as it was a case of having no choice. The other contenders, Nelson Rockefeller, George Romney, and Barry Goldwater, were all for various reasons unacceptable, and in comparison to any Democratic candidate, Nixon was in Eisenhower's view light-years ahead.

As early as 1966, Eisenhower made his opinion public. In November of that year, just prior to the congressional elections, Johnson had issued a blast against Nixon, who was speaking around the country for Republican candidates. Johnson called Nixon a "chronic campaigner" who "never did really recognize and realize what was going on." As proof, Johnson had cited Eisenhower's 1960 press-conference statement, "If you give me a week I might think of one." Eisenhower called Nixon from Gettysburg and said, "Dick, I could kick myself every time some jackass brings up that goddamn 'give me a week' business. Johnson has gone too far . . . I just wanted you to know that I'm issuing a statement down here."[49]

In the statement, which was widely reported, Eisenhower said he had "always had the highest personal and official regard" for Nixon, who was "one of the best-informed, most capable, and most industrious Vice-Presidents in the history of the United States and in that position contributed greatly to the sound functioning of our government. He was constantly informed of the major problems of the United States during my Administration. Any suggestion to the contrary or any inference that I at anytime held Dick Nixon in anything less than the highest regard and esteem is erroneous." (It must be pointed out that somehow, whenever he talked about Nixon, Eisenhower could not get it to come out right. Thus in this case, in the key sentence, he did not say Nixon was "consulted" about the "major problems"; instead, the verb he used was "informed."[50])

On March 14, 1967, Eisenhower held an impromptu press conference at the Eldorado Country Club. The governor of California, Ronald Reagan, was with him. Reporters were clamoring for Eisenhower's attention. From one side, a reporter asked his opinion of Reagan; another newsman, on his other side, simultaneously asked his opinion of Nixon. Eisenhower turned to the man who had asked about Nixon and remarked that "he is one of the ablest men I know and a man I admire deeply and for whom I have great affection." Most of the other reporters, however, had heard only the question about Reagan, and assumed that Eisenhower was talking about the governor. Headlines the next day proclaimed that Eisenhower had said, "Governor Reagan is one of the men I admire most in the world." Walter Cronkite reported it that way on the evening television news. Eisenhower called to straighten him out; Cronkite, according to Eisenhower, "was chagrined to admit that his information came from a newspaper and he hoped sometime to change it." Eisenhower, however, was stuck; he could hardly issue a clarification saying that "Reagan is *not* one of the men I admire most in the world." In any case, he *did* admire Reagan; he told Arthur Larson he did not believe Reagan to be as much of a right-winger as he was portrayed to be. Still, Nixon was his man.[51]

He made that clear to Republican politicians in private meetings and in his correspondence with them. His standard line (in this case to Fred Seaton of Nebraska) was, "I cannot think of anyone better prepared than Dick Nixon is to undertake the responsibilities of the Presidency."[52]

That was a bit short of an unqualified endorsement. Eisenhower did not say that Nixon was "well prepared," or "completely capable," or anything like that, only that he was "better prepared" than anyone else. In March, when the gang came to Palm Desert for the annual visit with the Eisenhowers, the members got to talking politics. Slater recorded that "many of us are still resentful that Nixon did not run a better campaign in 1960 and all had one or more instances to report where things would have been better had he taken advice. The President [meaning Eisenhower] still doesn't understand why Nixon and Lodge didn't call on him for help and why they didn't take the position of wanting to continue the Eisenhower philosophy of how the country should be run." Still, considering the competition, Eisenhower and his friends concluded that "Nixon would probably make the best president."[53] Eisenhower indicated that he intended to do all he could to bring about a Nixon victory.

CHAPTER THIRTY

Taps

March 1968–March 28, 1969

AFTER PRESIDENT EISENHOWER recovered from his September 1955 heart attack, the doctors had told him that there was no medical reason for him not to run for a second term, and they predicted that he could lead an active life for a period of as long as ten years.[1] In November 1965, when he and Mamie were at Augusta for a week, he remarked one night that the ten years were up. The next day, in Mamie's cabin, he suffered a second heart attack. He was rushed to a nearby Army hospital, and two weeks later was transferred to Walter Reed. Recovery was slow, but for a seventy-five-year-old man who had been struck by two major heart attacks, surprisingly good. Soon the doctors were allowing him to play golf again, although they restricted him to a cart and to a par-three course.

Still, his heart was failing, and he knew it. He was a man who had spent his lifetime facing facts, making his decisions on the basis of reality rather than wishful thinking. The end was approaching, and he began to prepare for it. He dispersed his herd of Angus cattle and otherwise put his affairs in order. He had already decided he wanted to be buried in Abilene, where he had had a small Meditation Chapel built, just across the street from his childhood home and just west of the Eisenhower Library and Museum. It was a small, simple, dignified chapel constructed with native sandstone, quite in keeping with the quiet little town on the Plains. In 1967 he had Icky's body moved there from Fairmont Cemetery in Denver, and had it placed at the foot of the places reserved for his body and Mamie's.

That winter, on his way to Palm Desert, Eisenhower stopped off in Abilene to visit the chapel. When he arrived in California, he was still upset and depressed, not at the thought of his own death, but by the tiny plaque on the floor over Icky's body, the physical reminder of what he and Mamie had lost in 1921 when four-year-old Icky died. He soon recovered his natural good spirits, helped by his friends, some good cards at bridge, and the opportunity to play golf in the lovely desert climate. Rather than grouse at being restricted to a par-three course, he made jokes about it, telling an old Abilene friend that "I suppose in another year I will be having to play the ladies' tees even on that course."[2] That was the winter he scored his hole in one, about which he bragged incessantly.

On the golf course one day that winter, he scared the wits out of his friends when he suffered a temporary loss of memory and some confusion. Rusty Brown, his secretary, called Goodpaster, who flew out to California with some Army doctors. By the time they arrived, the next morning, Eisenhower had recovered and wanted to stick to his schedule, which included a talk to a high-school history class from Los Angeles, a lunch with Sam Goldwyn, and a dinner with the President of Turkey. The doctors were able to persuade him to cancel the talk to the history class, but he kept his other appointments.[3]

His thoughts were turning back toward his youth. Visitors noted that he was much more inclined to reminisce about his days as a cadet, or his childhood in Abilene, or his experiences as a junior officer, than he was about SHAEF or the White House. In April 1968, he heard that a proposed governmental reorganization plan included transferring all of the affairs of the American Battle Monuments Commission to the Veterans Administration. He immediately wrote President Johnson: "From my viewpoint, both as a junior officer who once served with the Battle Monuments Commission and as one who has followed its affairs over these many years, I hope that you will decline to approve this particular move." His reason went beyond nostalgia. The commission was in charge of what surely must be some of the most beautiful cemeteries in the world. No American can visit them, especially the one at Omaha Beach, without feeling a surge of pride, so magnificently are they maintained. Eisenhower explained to Johnson that the cemeteries were closed to future burials, and that they were monuments rather than mere cemeteries. "Nearly all of them are in foreign countries and every one of them is precious to the families and relatives of those who died during those two world conflicts. The American Battle Monuments Commission has always maintained the highest possible standards in the care of these cemeteries."⁴ Johnson granted the request.

Eisenhower wrote that letter from the hospital at March Air Force Base, because in April of 1968 he had suffered his third major heart attack. A month later, he had recovered enough strength to be moved to Ward Eight at Walter Reed. Despite his invalid status, he had not lost his flair for giving commands. He ordered the commanding officer at March to give the nurses accompanying him on the flight east a few days' leave in Washington before returning to their duties.

At Walter Reed, Eisenhower had the finest care the Army and modern medicine could provide. Mamie moved into a tiny room next to his suite. Dominated by a high hospital bed, it was cramped and uncomfortable, but it was where she wanted to be. (She would not consider living at Gettysburg alone; she once commented, "Whenever Ike went away, the house sagged. When he came home, the house was alive again.") For a woman who loved to surround herself with knick-knacks and family photographs, it was surprisingly bare. She passed the time by sewing facecloths together and stuffing them with foam to make pillows for her friends.⁵ There was a constant stream of visitors, who were not allowed more than a few minutes with the general, and who therefore spent hours chatting with Mamie. One of her favorites was another patient in the hospital, Mrs. William ("Kitsy") Westmoreland, a bright, cheerful woman who was a favorite of everyone who knew her. Kitsy had contracted a stomach ailment in Vietnam, where she had made herself a hero with the troops by working regular eight-hour shifts in the hospitals there. An Army brat herself, Kitsy was full of jokes about life in the service, and she managed to keep Mamie laughing, despite the surroundings.

By July, Eisenhower had recovered enough strength to take an active interest in the presidential campaign. He remained committed to Nixon, a commitment that was solidified by the courtship then going on between his grandson, David, and Nixon's daughter Julie. He decided to make a preconvention endorsement of Nixon. On July 15, when Nixon stopped in for a short visit, Eisenhower informed him of his decision. Nixon was naturally delighted, but worried about the timing. After he left, Nixon wrote a letter to Eisenhower on the subject. Eisenhower had told him he would make the endorsement public on the day the convention opened. Nixon said that by that time a number of favorite sons planned to release their delegates so that they could cast their ballots for Nixon. Thus, Nixon told Eisenhower, "we face the distinct possibility that in the public mind the decision would have been made before your endorsement was announced . . . I hesitate to bring these additional facts up for consideration because I shall indeed be most grateful for your announcement of support whenever it comes. In view of our discussion, however, I felt that you should know of these possibilities since they bear on the critical question of the timing of your announcement and the relationship of that timing to the effect your announcement will have on the voters in November." In other words, he wanted Eisenhower to make the endorsement immediately.[6]

Two days later, Eisenhower released his statement. He said he supported Nixon for the nomination "because of my admiration of his personal qualities: his intellect, acuity, decisiveness, warmth, and above all, his integrity." He sent Nixon a copy of the press release, with a handwritten note across the top: "Dear Dick—This was something I truly enjoyed doing—DE."[7]

The convention opened in Miami on August 5. That evening, Eisenhower put on a business suit, and television cameras were brought into Walter Reed. He gave a speech to the delegates, who stopped their usual frenetic activity for a few minutes and listened in respectful silence as he gave them some words of encouragement. The next morning, Eisenhower suffered yet another heart attack.

This attack took a new form. It did not cause additional muscle damage, but it did upset the rhythm of the heart, causing it to periodically go out of control and fibrillate. Instead of beating, it merely vibrated, pumping no blood. Whenever a fibrillation began, the doctors were able to restore rhythmic beating through electrical impulses. Everyone feared that this was the end. John and Barbara moved into the guesthouse at Walter Reed while their children stayed with friends around Washington. John bgean the detailed planning for the funeral. But, after a week, the fibrillations stopped, and soon Eisenhower was out of danger. He was even able to receive visitors again.

On Eisenhower's seventy-eighth birthday, General Westmoreland, recently promoted to Chief of Staff of the Army, called, accompanied by Kitsy. Eisenhower congratulated Westy on his appointment and urged him to take good care of the Army. That afternoon, the Army Band gathered outside Eisenhower's room to play a serenade for him. Eisenhower was wheeled to his bedroom window, where he acknowledged the tribute with a smile and a wave of a small five-star flag. His extreme weakness was obvious, and brought tears to everyone's eyes.

He was, however, calm and cheerful. He told John that his mind was eased because a law had been passed that provided widows of former Presidents lifetime Secret Service coverage. "This last August," he said, "when it looked like I might cash in my chips, my only worry was about Mamie. This puts my mind at rest on that count at least."

On October 24, he dictated a letter to Nixon. He said he hoped for, and expected, a big victory, big enough to give Nixon "a strong, clear mandate" and a Republican Congress. Such an outcome would, Eisenhower said, put Nixon in a position to unite the country, deal with dissension and lawlessness, cope with Vietnam, and "change the ingrained power structure of the federal government (the heritage of years of Democratic rule), placing more responsibility at state and local levels." He congratulated Nixon on his treatment of Vietnam during the campaign: "You have stood steady and talked straight, despite what must have been heavy pressures and temptations to reach for popular support through irresponsibility."[8]

Nixon's victory in November was not by the margin Eisenhower had hoped for, but he was delighted that at least Nixon had won. In December, as Nixon began naming his Cabinet, he asked Eisenhower if he would receive each appointee. Eisenhower agreed, indeed told Nixon "I am quite anxious to meet the ones I do not know." He also sent Nixon some advice on replacing Earl Warren, who had resigned, asking Nixon to destroy the memo after he read it (Nixon did not; it is now in the Eisenhower Library). Eisenhower suggested Herb Brownell, or elevating Potter Stewart up to Chief Justice and appointing William Rogers to the vacancy on the Court.[9]

Eisenhower summoned the strength to write by hand on November 29, 1968, the day of the Army-Navy game, a telegram to be sent to the Army football coach. "For 364 days out of the year it is Army, Navy, Air Force, forever," he scribbled. "Today it is Army, Army, Army. My heart, though somewhat damaged, will be riding with you and the team. Good Luck!!"[10]

As the end approached, his thoughts were increasingly with his family. For Thanksgiving, 1968, Mamie arranged for each member of the family to share the turkey feast with him. "With the precision of an Army drill instructor," Julie Nixon recalled, "Mamie arranged for members of each family [the Nixons as well as the Eisenhowers] to share a course of the meal with Ike in his bedroom." Susie Eisenhower and Tricia Nixon had juice with him, David and Julie (both of whom had campaigned for Nixon) shared the fruit cup, and so on, until Barbara Eisenhower and Pat Nixon joined him for the pumpkin pie.

Julie was depressed by his appearance: "He was so thin and wasted under the Army-issue sheet. The blueness of his eyes was startling in his dead-white face." [11]

In December, Eisenhower watched on closed-circuit television the wedding of David Eisenhower and Julie Nixon. David's haircut by the standards of his contemporaries in the late sixties was extremely short and made him something of an object of ridicule, but his grandfather thought it much too long. Eisenhower offered his grandson $100 if he would get it cut before the wedding. David had it trimmed, but not short enough to satisfy his grandfather, who did not pay up. [12]

Christmas and New Year's passed without any celebration by the Eisenhowers, because Mamie had come down with a severe respiratory ailment, which confined her to bed for more than a month. By February, Eisenhower was taking a terrific beating. The doctors informed him that he would have to undergo a major abdominal operation. Complications had arisen from his ileitis operation of twelve years earlier; scar tissue had wrapped itself around his intestine, causing a blockage. The doctors were worried that his heart could not survive the ordeal, but it did. John visited him shortly after the operation. "It's an eerie feeling," Eisenhower told his son, "to have them hit you with one thing and then another." "Well," John replied, "now that you've had that intestinal blockage taken out, you ought to start feeling better. Maybe now you can gain some weight."

"God, I hope so," Eisenhower sighed.

On Monday, March 24, 1969, Eisenhower suffered a severe setback. His heart was failing. The doctors began giving him oxygen through tubes stuffed into his nose. He was aware that he was dying, and he wanted the end to come soon. He asked Billy Graham to come by; together they talked about spiritual matters. He still had the old impulse to give something to those who served him. John had just published a book on the Battle of the Bulge entitled *The Bitter Woods*, which had made the best-seller list. Eisenhower ordered a dozen copies and had John autograph them, so that he could give them to the doctors and nurses who had taken care of him. He gave John last-minute instructions: "Be good to Mamie."

The evening of March 27, the electrocardiogram machine above his bed, which monitored his heartbeat, showed a slight improvement. When John came in to say good night, he told his father that the pattern of the cardiogram was a bit better. Eisenhower winced—he wanted his final release. John, in his turn, winced at the sight of his father;

he wrote later that it "made me resolve to avoid ever being placed in a hospital where my life would be artificially prolonged."

All his life, Eisenhower had been a man of the most extraordinary energy. He had carried a burden of high command and decision making that was heavier, and lasted longer, than any other leader of the free world. Not even Roosevelt, not even Churchill, not even de Gaulle, had met the demands that Eisenhower had. For twenty years, on a daily basis, he had had to render judgments, make decisions, give orders at the highest level. The process had often left him exhausted. He had always bounced back after that miracle that is a soldier's night's sleep.

But he was tired now, more tired than he had ever been. No amount of sleep would help him bounce back. The ultimate weariness had descended.

He was a man born to command. On his deathbed, he was still in charge. On Friday morning, March 28, 1969, John, David, Mamie, the doctors, and a nurse gathered in his bedroom. Eisenhower looked at them. He barked out a command: "Lower the shades!" The light was hurting his eyes. The venetian blinds were pulled; the room became nearly dark.

"Pull me up," Eisenhower told John and one of the doctors. They propped up the pillows behind him and, one on each arm, raised him until they thought he was high enough. Eisenhower looked from side to side. "Two big men," he growled. "Higher." They pulled him higher.

Mamie grasped his hand. David and John stood stiffly at each corner of his bed. The electrocardiogram was fluttering.

Eisenhower looked at John. He said softly, "I want to go; God take me." He was ready to go home, back to Abilene, back to the heart of America, from whence he came. His great heart stopped beating.

ACKNOWLEDGMENTS

I began work on Eisenhower in 1964. In the ensuing two decades, I have piled up debts of such size that I despair of ever discharging them. Still, the attempt must be made.

The list begins with those who made the record, and first of all with General Andrew Goodpaster. A majority of the citations in this volume are to his memoranda. There is a military precision, thoroughness, and accuracy to his reports that make them the single most reliable source for what happened in the Eisenhower Presidency. He was unflagging; he never editorialized; he was always objective. The fruits of his labor are the *sine qua non* of this book. Next comes Ann Whitman, whose devotion to Eisenhower was matched only by her devotion to compiling an accurate record. As a bonus, there is a warmth and humanness to her diary that gives invaluable insights into Eisenhower the man. That Eisenhower could not have gotten through his task without her goes without saying; for my part, I do need to say that neither could I.

Others close to Eisenhower kept diaries that I relied upon heavily. Ellis Slater was not only one of Eisenhower's best friends, but a man who found the time and energy to write full accounts of his intimate gatherings with Eisenhower at Augusta, in the White House, at Gettysburg, and at Palm Desert. In the early years of the Administration, Jim Hagerty kept a copious diary (he gave it up because of lack of time after 1955, a great loss to the historian) that contained much revealing information. In the last years of the Administration, John

Eisenhower often took the notes of meetings in the Oval Office, and he got to be almost as good at it as Goodpaster.

Dr. L. Arthur Minnich, a trained historian (he received his Ph.D. from Cornell in 1948), served Eisenhower from January 21, 1953, to August 6, 1960, as an Assistant Staff Secretary and unofficial historian. He attended the Cabinet and legislative leaders' meetings. He had a keen ear for the good quote and a sophisticated understanding of what was important and what was froth. I read his handwritten notes with excitement and profit, and have quoted from him extensively.

I could not possibly find the words to adequately express my thanks to the individuals listed above. There are dozens of others, members of Eisenhower's staff or his friends, who have placed their diaries and papers in the Eisenhower Library, and on whose labors this book is based. My sincere thanks to all of them.

Those who made the record made my research possible; those who keep the record made my research far more profitable—and fun to do—than it otherwise would have been. Dr. John Wickman and his staff at the Eisenhower Library have created and maintain a world-class archival facility. They are professionals of the highest qualities. I am especially indebted to Mack Teasley, Rod Soubers, Jim Leyerzapf, David Haight, and Hazel Stroda. It is not simply that they provide an attractive, comfortable place to study the documents, or that they cheerfully bring out from the stacks cart after cart filled with box after box of documents, or that they create such a pleasant sense of camaraderie between themselves and the researchers who come to Abilene. In addition, they know the collection better than anyone else, and are eager to pass on what they know. Their finding aids are superb; their verbal advice to look at this or that file about this or that event saves countless hours of time. Best of all, they love Ike as I do, and love to talk about him, so that at coffee breaks and lunch conversations, they provide insights into his personality and policies.

My research at the library was facilitated by the help of Mrs. Elizabeth Smith, a former associate editor on the Eisenhower Project at Johns Hopkins and one of my dearest friends. She worked with me, and independently, at Abilene for many months during 1982 and 1983. She has a keen eye for the good document; without her, I would still be sitting in the research room, going through the boxes. In addition, she was my typist (this is the fifth book she has typed for me) and did her usual excellent job.

This book was written on a solid foundation, and I know, because I helped build it. Most of the writing was done in my office in New Orleans, which I had built in the back of my house for the specific purpose of writing this book. The contractors, Robert Stalder and Chris Clark, designed the office especially for writing, and did a super job. I helped pour the foundation, a tricky business when you are sitting four feet below sea level. The name I gave the office, Eisenhowerplatz, is a bit corny, but I like it.

Dr. Joseph Logsdon, my department chairman at the University of New Orleans, and one of my closest friends for more years than either of us likes to count, read the first draft of each chapter. He has a critical eye that, in my experience, is unmatched. He has an equally unmatched ability to put friendship aside and say what he thinks, no matter how critical. I cannot recall a suggestion that he made that I did not incorporate, much to the advantage of the book.

John Ware, my agent, was a constant source of encouragement. My editor, Alice Mayhew, was a constant source of strength. The copy editor, Patricia Miller, did a superb job.

It is customary for an author at this point to state that all the errors are his own, and I hereby do so. But in so doing, I do not wish to imply that whatever is good about the book is my own doing; rather, I am compelled to say that whatever might be good about it is due in greatest part to the people listed above.

I come to the point of thanking my wife, Moira, for her part in the creation of the manuscript, and I cannot hold back the tears. For hundreds of hours, she sat at my side in Abilene, helping me go through the documents. She was willing to talk to me for seemingly endless periods about Eisenhower, giving me the benefit of her point of view on the man and his policies. She helped me to see things I otherwise never would have noticed. She listened as I read each day's outpouring aloud to her. Every author needs encouragement at the end of the day, and she always told me how wonderful the writing was (before then pointing out gently where this or that change would have to be made). For the past year, I have spent ten hours a day, six days a week, at the typewriter. To say that this created certain difficulties for Moira in arranging our home and social life is to state the obvious. I can't say that she never complained, but I can say that she always made me feel that the effort was worthwhile. Without her help and support, there would be no book.

STEPHEN E. AMBROSE
Sunflower Hotel, Abilene, Kansas
Eisenhowerplatz, New Orleans, Louisiana
The Cabin, Dunbar, Wisconsin
June 1982–August 1983

NOTES

The Key to abbreviations in these citations will be found on page 718.

CHAPTER ONE

1. DDE to Lovett, 11/8/52, AWAS.
2. Acheson, *Present at the Creation*, 706.
3. Ferrell, *Off the Record*, 274–75.
4. DDE, *Mandate*, 85.
5. DDE Diary, 1/21/53.
6. Truman, *Year of Decisions*, 19.
7. Milton Eisenhower interview; Merriman Smith interview, EL.
8. Cabinet meeting, 1/12/53, CMS.
9. Montgomery, *Memoirs*, 484.
10. Neustadt, *Presidential Power*, 9.
11. Quoted in Richardson, *Presidency of Eisenhower*, 25.
12. DDE Diary, 1/6/53.
13. Milton Eisenhower, *The President Is Calling*, 273.
14. DDE Diary, 1/5/53.
15. *Ibid.*
16. *Ibid.*, 2/7/53.
17. Adams, *Firsthand Report*, 89.
18. Hughes, *Ordeal*, 251.
19. Eden, *Full Circle*, 64.
20. Winthrop Aldrich interview, COHP.
21. Immerman, "Eisenhower and Dulles."
22. Adams, *Firsthand Report*, 89.
23. DDE, *Mandate*, 84.

24. Smith, *Dewey*, 604–5.
25. Warren, *Memoirs*, 260.
26. Lyon, *Eisenhower*, 466–67; Geelhoed, *Charles E. Wilson*, 19.
27. DDE Diary, 2/7/53.
28. DDE, *Mandate*, 91–92.
29. *Ibid.*, 92.
30. Parmet, *Eisenhower*, 168.
31. *New York Times*, 12/31/52.
32. *New Republic*, 12/15/52.
33. DDE interview.
34. DDE, *Mandate*, 87.
35. Hatch, *Red Carpet for Mamie*, 255–59; Brandon, *Mamie Doud Eisenhower*, 304.
36. John Eisenhower, *Strictly Personal*, 153.
37. Merriman Smith interview, EL.
38. Slater, *The Ike I Knew*, 39.
39. Minnich notes, Cabinet meeting, 5/17/54, CMS.
40. West, *Upstairs at the White House*, 130
41. Morgan, *Past Forgetting*, 100–125.
42. Parmet, *Eisenhower*, 154; Clark, *From the Danube to the Yalu*, 233; John Eisenhower, *Strictly Personal*, 149–50.
43. DDE, *Mandate*, 95.
44. *New York Times*, 12/6/52; Donovan, *Eisenhower*, 19.
45. *Ibid.*, 12/10/52; *ibid.*, 20.
46. *Ibid.*, 12/11 and 12/12/52.
47. *Ibid.*
48. DDE to Weeks, 12/9/52, WHCF; Donovan, *Eisenhower*, 18–19; Parmet, *Eisenhower*, 156–57.
49. *New York Times*, 12/15/52.
50. MacArthur's memo, dated 12/14/52, is in JFD Papers, '51–'59 subseries.
51. DDE interview.
52. DDE interview, Dulles Oral History Project, Princeton.
53. Lyon, *Eisenhower*, 472.

Chapter Two

1. Hughes, *Ordeal*, 53; DDE Diary, 1/16/53.
2. Minutes, Cabinet meeting, 1/12/53, CMS.
3. *Ibid.*, 1/13/53; Parmet, *Eisenhower*, 159; Donovan, *Eisenhower*, 11.
4. *New York Times*, 1/17/53.
5. Robinson memo, 1/24/53, WRP.
6. *Ibid.*, 1/5/55, WRP.
7. DDE to HST, 1/15/53, AWNS.
8. Ferrell, *Off the Record*, 287.
9. DDE, *Mandate*, 101; Truman, *Mr. Citizen*, 15.
10. DDE to HST, 1/23/53, AWNS.
11. Murphy to DDE, 12/30/52, Preinaugural Papers.
12. PP (1953), 1–8.
13. Parmet, *Eisenhower*, 166.
14. DDE, *Mandate*, 102.
15. Robinson memo, 1/24/53, WRP.

CHAPTER THREE

1. PP (1953), 67.
2. DDE, *Mandate,* 267.
3. Minnich notes, Cabinet meeting, 1/23/53.
4. *Ibid.,* 1/30/53; for Eisenhower's State of the Union message as delivered, see PP (1953), 12–34.
5. DDE Diary, 2/2/53.
6. Parmet, *Eisenhower,* 195.
7. DDE Diary, 2/2/53.
8. PP (1953), 15.
9. DDE, *Mandate,* 141.
10. DDE to Gruenther, 2/10/53, AWAS.
11. DDE Diary, 2/13/53.
12. Lyman Lemnitzer interview.
13. DDE to Draper, 3/16/53, DDE:DS.
14. NSC meeting notes, 2/11/53, NSC series.
15. Minnich notes, Cabinet, 2/12/53.
16. DDE, *Mandate,* 181.
17. PP (1953), 42–55.
18. Ken Crawford interview, EL.
19. DDE Diary, 2/7/53.
20. Bischof, "Before the Break," 85.
21. Griffith, *Politics of Fear,* 198.
22. Milton Eisenhower interview.
23. Bischof, "Before the Break," 87.
24. DDE to Robinson, 3/12/54, WRP.
25. DDE Diary, 4/1/53.
26. Griffith, *Politics of Fear,* 200.
27. *Ibid.*
28. PP (1953), 63.
29. See Greenstein, *Hidden-Hand Presidency.*
30. DDE interview.
31. Minnich notes, Cabinet, 2/6/53.
32. Hughes, *Ordeal,* 94.
33. Shanley Diary, 3/20/53.
34. PP (1953), 130.
35. Bischof, "Before the Break," 111.
36. *Ibid.,* 120.
37. *New York Times,* 3/28/53; White, *Taft,* 240.
38. DDE Diary, 4/1/53.
39. Griffith, *Politics of Fear,* 209.
40. Bischof, "Before the Break," 84.
41. Griffith, *Politics of Fear,* 213; Reeves, *McCarthy,* 477; Bischof, "Before the Break," 102–5.
42. Bischof, "Before the Break," 103.
43. Reeves, *McCarthy,* 480.
44. PP (1953), 62.
45. *Ibid.,* 88.
46. *Ibid.,* 64.
47. Bischof, "Before the Break," 129.
48. *New York Times,* 3/31/53.

49. PP (1953), 155.
50. Bischof, "Before the Break," 100.
51. *Ibid.,* 101.
52. Reeves, *McCarthy,* 461–69.
53. Bischof, "Before the Break," 100–101.
54. DDE to Dulles, 3/18/53, JFD Papers, WH memo series.
55. PP (1953), 81–83; Minnich notes, LLM, 3/9/53.
56. PP (1953), 56–57.
57. *Ibid.,* 81–83; Minnich, LLM, 3/9/53.
58. Minnich, Cabinet, 3/6/53.
59. DDE Diary, 4/1/53.
60. DDE interview.
61. Minnich, Cabinet, 4/3/53.
62. *Ibid.,* 3/20/53.
63. Minnich, Cabinet, 4/3 and 7/17/53.
64. PP (1953), 116–17.
65. Minnich, Cabinet, 3/20/53; Hughes, *Ordeal,* 101.
66. DDE, *Mandate,* 113.
67. West, *Upstairs at the White House,* 155.
68. Slater, *The Ike I Knew,* 32.
69. West, *Upstairs at the White House,* 175.
70. Ellis Slater interview.
71. Slater, *The Ike I Knew,* 33.
72. Lyon, *Eisenhower,* 512.
73. DDE, *Mandate,* 271–72.
74. Slater, *The Ike I Knew,* 37–38.
75. Robinson Diary, 2/15/53, WRP.
76. *Ibid.*
77. Slater, *The Ike I Knew,* 19.
78. DDE, *Mandate,* 271.
79. Whitman Diary, 2/7/53.
80. West, *Upstairs at the White House,* 157–58.
81. Slater, *The Ike I Knew,* 18.
82. DDE Diary, 2/7/53.
83. PP (1953), 94–95.
84. DDE to Hauge, 2/4/53, AWNS.
85. DDE Diary, 4/1/53.

CHAPTER FOUR

1. Jackson memo, 8/7/54, C. D. Jackson Papers.
2. Eli Ginzburg interview, EL.
3. Minnich, Cabinet, 3/6/53.
4. *Ibid.,* 4/3/53.
5. *Ibid.,* 4/10/53.
6. DDE to Sloan, 5/6/53, AWNS.
7. Minnich, Cabinet, 5/22 and 12/9/53.
8. Hughes, *Ordeal,* 140–42.
9. Minnich, LLM, 5/25/53.
10. Minnich, Cabinet, 5/29/53.
11. DDE to Milton, 4/29/53, AWNS.
12. DDE, *Mandate,* 301.

13. Parmet, *Eisenhower,* 254–55.
14. Bischof, "Before the Break," 141–48; Parmet, *Eisenhower,* 260–61.
15. DDE to Wm. Phillips, 6/5/53, AWNS.
16. Bullis to DDE, 5/9/53, and DDE to Bullis, 5/18/53, DDE:DS.
17. Bischof, "Before the Break," 144.
18. PP (1953), 413–15.
19. Dulles memo, 6/15/53, JFD Papers, WH memo series.
20. PP (1953), 427–37.
21. *Ibid.,* 467.
22. Minnich, Cabinet, 6/26/53.
23. Cook, *Declassified Eisenhower,* 242.
24. Dillon to Dulles, 5/15/53 (passed on to DDE by Beetle Smith), WFIS.
25. Jackson memo, 5/27/53, CDJ Records '53–'54.
26. DDE to Miller, 6/10/53, DDE:DS.
27. DDE to John Eisenhower, 6/16/53, DDE:DS.
28. Hughes, *Ordeal,* 80; Minnich, Cabinet, 6/19/53.
29. PP (1953), 446.
30. DDE interview.
31. DDE, *Mandate,* 202.
32. DDE Diary, 5/1/53.
33. Minnich, LLM, 4/30/53.
34. DDE Diary, 5/1/53.
35. Minnich, LLM, 4/30/53.
36. *Ibid.,* 5/12/53.
37. *Ibid.,* 5/19/53.
38. *Ibid.*
39. PP (1953), 209–10.
40. *Ibid.,* 337.
41. Hughes, *Ordeal,* 73.
42. Minnich, Cabinet, 5/22/53; Hughes, *Ordeal,* 138–39.
43. DDE to Spaatz, 5/19/53, SWAS.
44. DDE to Radford, 5/18/53, DDE:DS.
45. Minnich, LLM, 5/25/53.
46. *Ibid.*
46. Minnich, Cabinet, 5/22/53.
47. DDE to Dulles, 4/1/53, DDE:DS.
48. Hughes, *Ordeal,* 103–5.
49. Brookings Institution, *Force Without War,* 128; for Eisenhower's personal authorization on the production of atomic weapons, see Strauss to DE, 5/14/53, AWAS. In that message, Strauss gave Eisenhower a rundown on his powers with regard to the Atomic Energy Commission.
50. Slater, *The Ike I Knew,* 42–44.
51. PP (1953), 179–88; DDE, *Mandate,* 147.
52. Parmet, *Eisenhower,* 279.
53. Slater, *The Ike I Knew,* 45–46.
54. Minutes, NSC, 4/8/53, NSC series.
55. DDE to Dulles, 4/2/53, JFD Papers, '51–'59 subseries.
56. DDE to Rhee, 4/23/53, WFIS.
57. Divine, *Eisenhower and the Cold War,* 30.
58. Dulles to DDE, 5/22/53, AWF Dulles-Herter.
59. Minutes, NSC, 4/28/53, NSC series.
60. DDE, *Mandate,* 183.
61. DDE to Rhee, 6/6/53, WFIS.

62. DDE interview.
63. DDE to Nixon, 6/1/53, WFIS.
64. Minnich, LLM, 6/2/53; Eisenhower, *Mandate*, 215.
65. Minutes, NSC, 4/28/53, NSC series.
66. DDE to Dillon, 5/6/53, WFIS.
67. Parmet, *Eisenhower*, 300–301.
68. DDE, *Mandate*, 185.
69. Minnich, Cabinet, 6/19/53.
70. DDE to Rhee, 6/18/53, WFIS.
71. Minnich, Cabinet, 6/26/53.
72. PP (1953), 463.

CHAPTER FIVE

1. PP (1953), 464.
2. Parmet, *Eisenhower*, 314.
3. DDE to Wilson, 7/17/53, WFIS.
4. NSC minutes, 7/23/53, NSC series.
5. Memo of conversation, 7/24/53, JFD Papers, '51–'59 subseries.
6. PP (1953), 520–22; *New York Times*, 7/28/53.
7. DDE, *Mandate*, 190.
8. DDE Diary, 1/18/54.
9. PP (1953), 522–24.
10. Memo, 7/31/53, AWNS.
11. *Ibid.*, 9/30/53.
12. DDE, *Mandate*, 160–61.
13. Loy Henderson interview, COHP.
14. Eden, *Full Circle*, 211–26, 256.
15. Ambrose, *Ike's Spies*, 197.
16. DDE to Mossadegh, 6/30/53, WFIS.
17. Roosevelt, *Countercoup*, 1–8.
18. Goodpaster interview; on the general subject, see Cook, *Declassified Eisenhower*.
19. DDE, *Mandate*, 163; Ambrose, *Ike's Spies*, 199–200.
20. See DDE to W. B. Smith, 9/21/53, DDE:DS.
21. Smith to DDE, 9/23/53, D/H.
22. See Jackson to Carroll, 9/30/53, CDJ Records '53–'54.
23. Dinner list, 9/23/53, DDE:DS.
24. DDE to Whitney, 6/24/53, SWNS.
25. DDE Diary, 7/24/53.
26. Goodpaster interview, EL.
27. DDE Diary, 7/2/53.
28. *Ibid.*, 7/31/53; PP (1953), 544–46.
29. PP (1953), 534–35.
30. Minnich, Cabinet, 7/3/53.
31. Minnich, LLM, 7/20/53; DDE, *Mandate*, 216–18.
32. Minnich, LLM, 7/20/53; Cabinet, 5/29/53.
33. DDE to Hazlett, 7/21/53, AWNS.
34. Parmet, *Eisenhower*, 326–27.
35. *Ibid.*, 327–29; DDE, *Mandate*, 197–99.
36. DDE to Shanley, 9/26/53, AWAS.
37. PP (1953), 624.

38. *New York Times,* 8/1/53.
39. Parmet, *Eisenhower,* 315.
40. DDE Diary, 1/10/55.
41. Minnich, LLM, 7/7/53; DDE interview.
42. DDE to Montgomery, 7/14/53, DDE:DS.
43. DDE to Adenauer, 7/23/53, DDE Con. SS.
44. DDE to Laniel, 9/21/53, DDE Con. SS.
45. DDE memo for Wilson, 7/1/53, AWAS.
46. *New York Times,* 7/11/53.
47. Bischof, "Before the Break," 155–57.
48. Robinson to DDE, 7/22/53, WRP.
49. DDE to Swede Hazlett, 7/21/53, AWNS.
50. Shanley Diary, 7/9/53.
51. DDE to Wm. Pawley, 8/3/53, AWNS.
52. DDE to Richardson, 8/8/53, AWNS.
53. DDE to Wilson, 8/15/53, DDE:DS.
54. Shanley Diary, 7/9/53.
55. DDE to Dulles, 9/8/53, DDE:DS.
56. JFD to DDE, 9/10/53, JFD Papers, WH memo series.
57. DDE Diary, 5/14/53.
58. Duram, *Moderate Among Extremists,* 63.
59. Memo, 8/19/53, DDE:DS.
60. John Eisenhower interview.
61. PP (1953), 30.
62. *Ibid.,* 108.
63. DDE, *Mandate,* 235.
64. DDE Diary, 7/24/53.
65. DDE to Byrnes, 8/14/53, AWNS.
66. DDE to Nixon, 9/4/53, DDE:DS.
67. DDE, *Mandate,* 227.
68. Brownell interview, COHP; DDE to Edgar, 10/1/53, AWNS.
69. DDE to Dean Smith, 9/14/53, DDE:DS.
70. DDE to MSE, 10/9/53, AWNS.
71. Quoted in Ewald, *Eisenhower,* 81.
72. DDE, *Mandate,* 164.
73. DDE Diary, 10/8/53.
74. Ambrose, *Ike's Spies,* 213–14; DDE Diary, 10/8/53.

CHAPTER SIX

1. PP (1953), 645–46.
2. Oppenheimer, "Atomic Weapons and American Policy," 528–31.
3. Strauss, *Men and Decisions,* 356; Divine, *Blowing on the Wind,* 11.
4. Lear, "Ike and the Peaceful Atom," 11–12.
5. See Jackson to Strauss, 9/25/53, CDJ Papers.
6. See Dulles memo for Bowie, 9/8/53, and Dulles memo of 9/23/53, JFD Papers, WH memo series.
7. Jackson to DDE, 10/2/53, CDJ Papers.
8. DDE Diary, 10/10/53.
9. DDE, *Mandate,* 252; Strauss, *Men and Decisions,* 357.
10. Robinson Diary, 11/6/53, WRP Papers.
11. Stuyvesant Wainwright interview.

12. Minnich, Cabinet, 10/2/53.
13. DDE to Brownell, 11/4/53, DDE:DS.
14. Lyon, *Eisenhower*, 565–66.
15. Ferrell, *Off the Record*, 300–301.
16. Adams, *Firsthand Report*, 137.
17. *New York Times*, 11/7/53.
18. Memo of call, DDE to Brownell, 11/11/53, DDE:DS.
19. Minnich, Cabinet, 11/11/53.
20. PP (1953), 758–65.
21. Minnich, Cabinet, 11/12/53.
22. *New York Times*, 11/17 and 11/18/53; Ferrell, *Off the Record*, 301.
23. Slater, *The Ike I Knew*, 57–58; Roberts, *Augusta National*, 165.
24. Telephone calls, 11/16/53, DDE:DS.
25. Ann Whitman Diary, 11/27/53, ACWD; *New York Times*, 11/26/53.
26. Quoted in Ewald, *Eisenhower*, 123–26.
27. PP (1953), 802.
28. DDE Diary, 12/2/53 and 12/3/53.
29. Ewald, *Eisenhower*, 82–83; telephone calls, 11/16/53, DDE:DS.
30. DDE to Byrnes, 12/1/53, AWNS.
31. Telephone calls, 12/2/53, DDE:DS.
32. DDE to Gruenther, 10/27/53, DDE:DS.
33. *Ibid.*, 11/23/53.
34. Memo, 11/11/53, AWAS.
35. DDE Diary, 11/11/53.
36. DDE to Dodge, 12/1/53, DDE:DS.
37. Minnich, LLM, 12/17/53.
38. PP (1953), 860.
39. Conference, 12/2/53, ACWD.
40. NSC 151/1, 12/4/53, WH Pres. SS.
41. Minnich, Cabinet, 10/23/53.
42. Memo of conference, 12/4/53, JFD Papers, '51–'59 subseries.
43. PP (1953), 813–22.
44. DDE to Dodge, 11/5/53, AWAS.
45. DDE to Hughes, 12/10/53, AWAS.
46. Minnich, Cabinet, 12/11 and 12/12/53.
47. *Ibid.*, 12/15/53.
48. Minnich, LLM, 12/18 and 12/19/53; DDE Diary, 12/19/53.
49. Robinson Diary, 11/7/53, WRP.
50. DDE to MSE, 12/11/53, AWNS.
51. DDE to Hazlett, 12/24/53, AWNS.
52. DDE to Jackson, 12/31/53, DDE:DS.

CHAPTER SEVEN

1. Jackson, "Notes on Ike," 1/4/54, CDJ Papers.
2. Minnich, LLM, 1/11/54.
3. HD, 1/14/54.
4. DDE to Edgar, 1/27/54, AWNS.
5. Telephone calls, 3/19/54, DDE:DS.
6. HD, 1/25/54.
7. *Ibid.*, 2/2/54.
8. DDE to Edgar, 1/12/54, AWNS.

9. Minnich, LLM, 3/29/54; HD, 3/29/54.
10. HD, 1/20 and 3/2/54; for a full discussion, see Kaufman, *Trade and Aid,* Chap. 2.
11. PP (1954), 6–23.
12. *Ibid.;* DDE, *Mandate,* 294. For a detailed discussion, see Adams and Gray, *Monopoly in America,* 142–63.
13. PP (1954), 69–76.
14. DDE, *Mandate,* 303.
15. PP (1954), 193–200.
16. *Ibid.,* 62–68.
17. DDE, *Mandate,* 303.
18. *Ibid.*
19. DDE to Burns, 2/2/54, DDE:DS.
20. Minnich, Cabinet, 4/2/54.
21. DDE, *Mandate,* 287–89.
22. *Ibid.,* 306.
23. See Reichard, *Reaffirmation of Republicanism,* for a detailed discussion.
24. DDE to Robinson, 3/23/54, AWNS.
25. DDE Diary, 1/18/54.
26. Slater, *The Ike I Knew,* 69.
27. Greenstein, *Hidden-Hand Presidency,* 184–85.
28. *New York Times,* 2/24/54.
29. HD, 2/25/54.
30. Telephone calls, 2/25/54, DDE:DS.
31. *Ibid.,* 3/2/54.
32. PP (1954), 288–91.
33. Greenstein, *Hidden-Hand Presidency,* 191–92.
34. DDE memo, 3/5/54, DDE:DS.
35. DDE to Robinson, 3/12/54, WRP; DDE to Helms, 3/9/54, AWNS.
36. PP (1954), 300.
37. DDE to Robinson, 3/12/54, WRP.
38. DDE to Helms, 3/9/54, AWNS.
39. DDE Diary, 1/18/54.
40. HD, 3/24/54.
41. PP (1954), 339.
42. DDE to Brownell, 3/29/54, along with Hoffman to DDE, 3/25/54, AWAS.
43. HD, 4/7/54.
44. *Ibid.,* 4/9/54.
45. *Ibid.,* 4/10/54.
46. *Ibid.,* 4/9/54.
47. PP (1954), 382.
48. DDE, *Mandate,* 312.
49. DDE to Conant, 4/26/54, DDE:DS.
50. DDE to Hazlett, 4/27/54, AWAS.
51. PP (1954), 346.
52. Divine, *Blowing on the Wind,* 13.
53. HD, 3/31/54.
54. PP (1954), 381–82.
55. Divine, *Blowing on the Wind,* 25.
56. Memo of conversation, 4/19/54, JFD Papers, WH memo series.
57. Divine, *Blowing on the Wind,* 25.
58. Ambrose, *Ike's Spies,* 186.
59. DDE to Strauss, 6/14/54, AWAS.

60. PP (1954), 435.
61. *Ibid.*, 329–31.
62. *Ibid.*, 58.
63. *Ibid.*, 324–25.
64. Notes, *Helena* meeting, 12/10/52, Preinaugural Papers.
65. Minnich, Cabinet, 4/26/54.
66. Smith to DDE, 1/18/54, HD.
67. DDE to Churchill, 2/9/54, WFIS.
68. Dulles memo, 4/12/54, D/H.
69. Quoted in Immerman, "Anatomy of the Decision Not to Fight."
70. HD, 2/8/54.
71. NSC minutes, 1/8/54, NSC series.
72. Ewald, *Eisenhower*, 119.
73. Memo for Smith, 3/15/54, WFDS.
74. Dulles memo for DDE, 3/23/54, D/H; various Dulles telephone conversations, 3/24 and 3/25/54, JFDP.
75. Ewald, *Eisenhower*, 119–20.
76. Minnich, Cabinet, 3/26/54.
77. Dulles memo, 3/24/54, JFDP.
78. See Dulles to DDE, 4/2/54, JFDP.
79. Memo, Dulles to DDE, 4/24/54, JFDP.
80. DDE to Churchill, 4/4/54, WFIS.
81. Telephone conversation, 4/5/54, AWDS.
82. PP (1954), 382–83.
83. Nixon, *Memoirs*, 152–53.
84. HD, 4/16/54.
85. Minnich, LLM, 4/26/54.
86. Dulles to DDE, 4/23/54, D/H.
87. *Ibid.*
88. DDE to Dulles, 4/23/54, D/H.
89. Dulles to DDE, 4/25/54, D/H.
90. HD, 4/26/54; Minnich, LLM, 4/26/54.
91. DDE to Gruenther, 4/26/54, DDE:DS.
92. PP (1954), 428.
93. Nixon, *Memoirs*, 153–54.
94. NSC minutes, 4/29/54, NSC series.
95. DDE interview.
96. NSC notes, 5/6/54, NSC series.

CHAPTER EIGHT

1. DDE, *Mandate*, 357.
2. Telephone call, 3/2/54, WF-DDE.
3. DDE Diary, 5/11/54.
4. HD, 5/13/54.
5. *Ibid.*, 5/14/54.
6. *Ibid.*, 5/17/54.
7. PP (1954), 483–84. (Italics added.)
8. Schlesinger, *Imperial Presidency*, 156.
9. PP (1954), 489–90.
10. HD, 3/28/54.
11. *Ibid.*, 4/11 and 5/1/54.

12. PP (1954), 526.
13. HD, 6/8/54.
14. See DDE to Doolittle, 7/26/54, AWAS.
15. HD, 6/18/54.
16. Ibid., 1/25/54.
17. Warren, *Memoirs,* 291.
18. HD, 5/18/54.
19. Warren, *Memoirs,* 291–92.
20. DDE interview.
21. Warren, *Memoirs,* 5–6.
22. PP (1954), 491.
23. DDE to Hazlett, 10/23/54, AWAS.
24. Quoted in Ewald, *Eisenhower,* 84.
25. Brownell interview.
26. Ewald, *Eisenhower,* 85.
27. I am indebted to former Congressman Frank E. Smith of Mississippi for pointing this out to me in a private letter.
28. DDE to Hazlett, 7/22/57, DDE:DS.
29. Immerman, *CIA in Guatemala,* 133; Smith to DDE, 1/15/54, WFIS.
30. Ambrose, *Ike's Spies,* 223.
31. Immerman, *CIA in Guatemala,* 133–34.
32. *Ibid.,* 162.
33. *New York Times,* 5/19/54; Eisenhower, *Mandate,* 424.
34. Ambrose, *Ike's Spies,* 216.
35. Richard Bissell interview; PP (1954), 573.
36. *New York Times,* 6/15 and 6/19/54.
37. Ambrose, *Ike's Spies,* 229–30.
38. PP (1954), 573.
39. HD, 6/18/54.
40. Immerman, *CIA in Guatemala,* 168; Eisenhower, *Mandate,* 425–26.
41. HD, 6/24/54.
42. Immerman, *CIA in Guatemala,* 170–72.
43. See Immerman, *CIA in Guatemala,* and Cook, *Declassified Eisenhower.*
44. Andrew Goodpaster interview.
45. PP (1954), 605.
46. DDE, *Mandate,* 426–27.
47. Minnich, Cabinet, 3/27/54.
48. HD, 6/26/54; Immerman, *CIA in Guatemala,* 172.
49. HD, 6/26/54.
50. *Ibid.,* 6/25/54.
51. Slater, *The Ike I Knew,* 76–79.
52. DDE to Dulles, 8/9/54, DDE:DS.
53. HD, 7/14 and 7/19/54.
54. DDE to Chynoweth, 7/13 and 7/30/54, AWNS.
55. HD, 7/19/54.
56. *Ibid.,* 5/24/54.
57. Minnich, Cabinet, 7/23/54.
58. HD, 5/24/54.
59. *Ibid.*
60. DDE to Adams, 5/11/54, DDE:DS.
61. Minnich, Cabinet, 7/9/54.
62. DDE to Brownell, 8/17/54, AWAS.
63. Benedict memo, 6/8/54, ACWD.

64. HD, 8/6/54.
65. DDE to Gruenther, 7/2/54, DDE:DS.
66. HD, 6/23 and 8/6/54.
67. Ann Whitman Diary, 6/29/54.
68. PP (1954), 680.
69. Ann Whitman Diary, 6/29/54.
70. HD, 7/16/54.
71. *Ibid.*, 7/27/54.
72. DDE to Robinson, 8/4/54, AWNS.
73. Ann Whitman Diary, 8/11/54.
74. DDE memo for Scott, 5/1/54, DDE:DS.
75. DDE to Dulles, 5/7/54, JFD Papers, '51–'59 subseries.
76. Dulles memo, 5/19/54, JFD Papers, '51–'59 subseries.
77. Dulles memo, 5/25/54, JFD Papers, '51–'59 subseries.
78. Dulles memo, 7/7/54, JFD Papers, WH memo series.
79. Cutler notes, 6/2/54, AWAS.
80. HD, 6/19/54.
81. PP (1954), 698, 701.
82. American-Korean talks, 7/27/54, DDE:DS.
83. DDE to Gruenther, 6/8/54, DDE:DS.
84. DDE, *Mandate*, 366.
85. HD, 6/23/54.
86. *Ibid.*, 6/24/54.
87. DDE, *Mandate*, 401.
88. *Ibid.*, 368.
89. PP (1954), 605.
90. Minnich, Cabinet, 7/9/54; HD, 7/9/54.
91. PP (1954), 642.
92. *Ibid.*, 647.
93. Ambrose, *Ike's Spies*, 260.
94. PP (1954), 948–49; the draft of 9/25/54 is in D/H.
95. DDE, *Mandate*, 372.
96. PP (1954), 661.
97. DDE, *Mandate*, 404.

CHAPTER NINE

1. DDE, *Mandate*, 461–63.
2. *Ibid.*, 464.
3. Memo of conversation, 10/30/54, JFD Papers, WH memo series.
4. PP (1954), 1076–77.
5. Memo of conference, 12/20/54, ACWD.
6. Ambrose, *Ike's Spies*, 245–46.
7. Memo of conversation, 10/30/54, JFD Papers, WH memo series.
8. DDE to Collins, 11/3/54, DDE:D.
9. Memo of conference, 11/3/54, ACWD.
10. HD, 11/29/54.
11. Telephone calls, 10/4/54, DDE:D.
12. PP (1954), 889.
13. DDE to Hazlett, 10/23/54, AWNS.
14. Memo of conversation, 10/30/54, JFD Papers, WH memo series.
15. HD, 12/23/54.

16. DDE to Adams, 9/25/54, DDE:D.
17. Telephone calls, 10/7/54, DDE:D.
18. DDE to Dewey, 10/8/54, AWAS.
19. DDE to Hauge, 9/30/54, DDE:D.
20. DDE, *Mandate*, 436–38.
21. DDE to Edgar, 11/8/54, AWNS.
22. Smith interview, 11/23/54, DDE:D.
23. ACWD, 12/4/54.
24. DDE to Roberts, 12/7/54, AWNS.
25. HD, 12/7/54.
26. Conversation with Roy Roberts, 12/54, and with Clay, 11/18/54, ACWD.
27. DDE Diary, 11/20/54.
28. DDE to Hazlett, 12/8/54, AWNS.
29. Memo of conference, 12/22/54, ACWD.
30. Minnich, Cabinet, 11/5 and 12/13/54.
31. PP (1954), 1110.
32. Notes on meeting, 12/1/54, AWAS, and attachments.
33. DDE to Hazlett, 8/20/56, AWNS.
34. Conference with Knowland, 11/23/54, AWAS.
35. Conference, 10/19/54, AWAS.
36. Ambrose, *Ike's Spies,* 188.
37. Memo, 11/24/54, ACWD.
38. Memo, 10/30/54, JFD Papers, WH memo series.
39. Slater, *The Ike I Knew,* 82–83.
40. ACWD, 11/24/54.
41. Slater, *The Ike I Knew,* 90.
42. PP (1954), 1074–77.

Chapter Ten

1. *New York Times,* 1/2/55.
2. DDE, *Mandate,* 466.
3. *Ibid.,* 467; Divine, *Eisenhower and the Cold War,* 57.
4. Telephone calls, 1/20/55, DDE:DS.
5. JCS meeting, 1/21/55, WFIS.
6. HD, 1/22/55.
7. PP (1955), 207–11.
8. DDE to Luce, 1/24/55, JFD Papers, WHMS.
9. HD, 1/25/55.
10. Telephone calls, 1/25/55, DDE:DS.
11. Divine, *Eisenhower and the Cold War,* 59–60.
12. Memo of conference, 1/31/55, WFIS.
13. Memo for record, 1/29/55, DDE:D.
14. DDE, *Mandate,* 472.
15. DDE to Gruenther, 2/1/55, SWAS.
16. DDE to Churchill, 1/19/55, D/H.
17. DDE, *Mandate,* 473.
18. HD, 2/16/55.
19. Telephone calls, 2/16/55, DDE:DS.
20. Ambrose, *Supreme Commander,* 6.
21. DDE to Churchill, 2/19/55, D/H.
22. DDE, *Mandate,* 475.

23. Memo on NSC meeting, 3/10/55 (dated 3/11), WFIS.
24. DDE, *Mandate*, 477.
25. Notes, NSC meeting, 3/11/55, WFIS.
26. Goodpaster memo, 3/16/55, WFIS.
27. Goodpaster memo to DDE, 3/15/55, WFIS.
28. Divine, *Eisenhower and the Cold War*, 62.
29. HD, 3/16/55.
30. PP (1955), 332–33.
31. *Ibid.*, 338; Divine, *Eisenhower and the Cold War*, 62–63.
32. Ambrose, *Rise to Globalism*, 239.
33. DDE, *Mandate*, 477–78.
34. DDE interview.
35. PP (1955), 358.
36. Telephone calls, 3/28/55, DDE:DS.
37. HD, 3/28/55.
38. DDE Diary, 3/26/55.
39. Minnich, LLM, 3/30/55; DDE, *Mandate*, 480.
40. Goodpaster memo, 3/18/55, WFIS.
41. Goodpaster memo of meeting of 4/1/55 (dated 4/4), WFIS; memo for Dulles, 4/1/55, JFD Papers, Meetings w/President.
42. DDE to Dulles, 4/5/55, D/H.
43. DDE conversation with Under Sec. of State, 4/21/55, WFIS.
44. The Radford/Robertson reports are in WFIS.
45. DDE to Dulles, 4/26/55, WFIS.
46. Divine, *Eisenhower and the Cold War*, 64; DDE, *Mandate*, 482–83.
47. DDE, *Mandate*, 483.
48. Divine, *Eisenhower and the Cold War*, 65–66.
49. Telephone calls, 2/23/55, DDE:DS.
50. HD, 3/4/55.
51. DDE to Dulles, 3/7/55, DDE:DS.
52. HD, 2/24/55.
53. Divine, *Blowing on the Wind*, 60–61.
54. PP (1955), 676–77.
55. PP (1954), 1110.
56. *Ibid.*, 1061–62.
57. HD, 2/8/55.
58. DDE, *Mandate*, 508; PP (1955), 661; phone calls, 5/25/55, ACWD.
59. DDE, *Mandate*, 484.
60. *Ibid.*, 491.
61. Telephone calls, 1/31/56, DDE:D.
62. Schwartz, "Urban Freeways," 419.
63. *Ibid.*, 428; Davies, *Age of Asphalt*, 17–18.
64. Memo of conference, 1/11/55, ACWD; HD, 2/16/55.
65. HD, 2/21/55.
66. PP (1955), 275–80.
67. Davies, *Age of Asphalt*, 22; Rose, *Interstate*, 69–84.
68. HD, 1/14/55.
69. DDE, *Mandate*, 498.
70. DDE to Allen, 2/22/55, DDE:DS; HD, 2/22/55.
71. PP (1955), 653.
72. HD, 1/18/55.
73. DDE, *Mandate*, 384; Wildavsky, *Dixon-Yates*.
74. ACWD, 5/19/55.

75. *Ibid.,* 5/25/55.
76. PP (1955), 606.

CHAPTER ELEVEN

1. PP (1955), 672.
2. *Ibid.,* 671–72.
3. Minnich, LLM, 5/25/55.
4. PP (1955), 678–79.
5. John Eisenhower, *Strictly Personal,* 178.
6. Donovan, *Eisenhower,* 345–46.
7. Telephone calls, 7/6/55, DDE:D.
8. Memo of conference, 7/7/55, ACWD.
9. ACWD, 7/10/55.
10. Parmet, *Eisenhower,* 404; Minnich, LLM, 7/12/55.
11. Ambrose, *Rise to Globalism,* 243.
12. State Department briefing, 7/11/55, DDE:DS.
13. Memo of conference, 8/5/55, JFD Papers, WHMS.
14. PP (1955), 702–5.
15. John Eisenhower, *Strictly Personal,* 175.
16. DDE, *Mandate,* 525; John Eisenhower, *Strictly Personal,* 175–76.
17. John Eisenhower, *Strictly Personal,* 176.
18. PP (1955), 707–12.
19. DDE, *Mandate,* 517, 523.
20. PP (1955), 713–16.
21. Walters, *Silent Missions,* 289; John Eisenhower, *Strictly Personal,* 178.
22. DDE, *Mandate,* 521.
23. PP (1955), 718, 722–23.
24. See DDE to Bulganin, 7/27/55, DE:DS.
25. Minnich, LLM, 7/25/55.
26. *Ibid.*
27. PP (1955), 728–30.
28. Divine, *Blowing on the Wind,* 65–67.
29. DDE to Anderson, 9/13/55, AWAS.
30. DDE to MSE, 9/12/55, AWNS.
31. DDE to Hazlett, 8/15/55, AWNS.
32. DDE to MSE, 9/12/55, AWNS.

CHAPTER TWELVE

1. ACWD, 9/29/55; DDE, *Mandate,* 535–36.
2. Nixon, *Memoirs,* 166.
3. See Snyder to Robinson, 10/5/55, WRP.
4. ACWD, 9/29/55.
5. Snyder to Robinson, 10/5/55, WRP; ACWD, 9/29/55.
6. John Eisenhower, *Strictly Personal,* 181.
7. ACWD, 9/29/55; Slater, *The Ike I Knew,* 106–8.
8. John Eisenhower, *Strictly Personal,* 182.
9. DDE, *Mandate,* 538.
10. *New York Times,* 9/29 and 9/30/55.
11. Minnich, Cabinet, 9/30/55; Parmet, *Eisenhower,* 416.

12. *New York Times,* 9/26/55.
13. Rovere, "Letter from Washington"; Parmet, *Eisenhower,* 417.
14. HD, 12/12/55.
15. DDE to Taylor, 11/5/55, AWAS.
16. DDE, *Mandate,* 539.
17. *Ibid.,* 539–41.
18. Quoted in Parmet, *Eisenhower,* 417–18.
19. Adams, *Firsthand Report,* 189.
20. Dulles memo, 10/11/55, JFD Papers, WHMS.
21. Notes on conversation, 10/12/55, ACWD.
22. Memo, 10/29/55, DDE:D.
23. Whitman notes, conference, 12/5/55, DDE:DS.
24. Adams, *Firsthand Report,* 213.
25. ACWD, 10/18/55.
26. *Ibid.,* 10/26/55.
27. Slater, *The Ike I Knew,* 110.
28. PP (1955), 841.
29. ACWD, 11/12/55.
30. DDE to Roberts, 11/28/55, AWNS.
31. Slater, *The Ike I Knew,* 113–14.
32. PP (1956), 191.
33. Slater, *The Ike I Knew,* 115.
34. John Eisenhower, *Strictly Personal,* 183–84.
35. HD, 12/10 and 12/12/55.
36. *Ibid.,* 12/11 and 12/13/55.
37. *Ibid.,* 12/14/55.
38. DDE to Dulles, 12/5/55, D/H.
39. DDE to Wilson, 12/21/55, AWNS.
40. Minutes, NSC, 12/23/55, NSC series.
41. Memo of conversation, 12/26/55, JFD Papers, WHMS.
42. John Eisenhower, *Strictly Personal,* 184.
43. Nixon, *Memoirs,* 167–68; Parmet, *Eisenhower,* 424.
44. Note to NSC, 12/28/55, WH Pres. SS.

CHAPTER THIRTEEN

1. Slater, *The Ike I Knew,* 121–24.
2. *Ibid.,* 123.
3. PP (1956), 32–33.
4. ACWD, 1/11/56.
5. *Ibid.,* 1/10/56.
6. *Ibid.,* 1/11/56.
7. DDE, *Mandate,* 571.
8. Dulles memo, 1/15/56, JFD Papers, WHMS.
9. See MSE to DDE, 1/16/55, AWNS, summing up the arguments.
10. Dulles memo, 1/15/56, JFD Papers, WHMS.
11. MSE to DDE, 1/16/56, AWNS.
12. DDE to Pollock, 1/20/56, DDE:D.
13. DDE to Edgar Eisenhower, 1/18/56, AWNS.
14. DDE to Hazlett, 1/23/56, AWNS.
15. Prettyman to DDE, 1/26/56, WFPCS.
16. DDE to Prettyman, 2/1/56, WFPCS.
17. DDE to Emanuel, 2/7/56, WFPCS.

18. Undated DDE note, AWNS (February '56 folder).
19. HD, 1/25/56.
20. Dulles memo, 2/9/56, JFD Papers, WHMS.
21. PP (1956), 182.
22. DDE Diary, 1/30/56; HD, 1/23/56.
23. PP (1956), 231.
24. Telephone calls, 2/10/56, DDE:D.
25. ACWD, 2/9/56.
26. DDE Diary, 1/23/56.
27. Dulles memo, 2/29/56, JFD Papers, WHMS; DDE Diary, 1/10/56.
28. DDE to Hazlett, 3/2/56, AWNS.
29. DDE, *Mandate*, 572.
30. PP (1956), 266–67.
31. DDE, *Waging Peace*, 4.
32. Dulles memo, 2/29/56, JFD Papers, WHMS.
33. DDE to Hazlett, 3/2/56, AWNS.
34. PP (1956), 287, 295. (Italics added.)
35. ACWD, 2/9/56.
36. *Ibid.*, 3/13/56.
37. *Ibid.*, 3/19/56.
38. Ambrose, *Supreme Commander*, 175.
39. Benson, *Cross Fire*, 294.
40. ACWD, 2/7/56; Minnich, LLM, 1/10/56.
41. ACWD, 3/20/56.
42. DDE, *Mandate*, 560–61.
43. Rose, *Interstate*, 87–89.
44. DDE Diary, 2/11/56.
45. ACWD, 2/13/56.
46. Minnich, LLM, 2/14/56.
47. DDE, *Mandate*, 555.
48. Slater, *The Ike I Knew*, 121.
49. Minnich, LLM, 1/10/56.
50. Duram, *Moderate Among Extremists*, 131.
51. PP (1956), 186–87.
52. Morrow, *Black Man in the White House*, 28–29.
53. *Ibid.*, 47–48.
54. *Ibid.*, 37.
55. PP (1956), 269–70.
56. Duram, *Moderate Among Extremists*, 123.
57. PP (1956), 304–5.
58. *Ibid.*, 340.
59. Minnich, Cabinet, 3/9 and 3/23/56.
60. PP (1956), 335.
61. DDE, *Waging Peace*, 152; Duram, *Moderate Among Extremists*, 124.
62. Minnich, Cabinet, 3/9/56.
63. *Ibid.*, 3/23/56.
64. DDE to Graham, 3/22/56, AWNS.
65. Graham to DDE, 3/29/56, AWNS.
66. DDE, *Waging Peace*, 149.
67. HD, 1/24/56.
68. *Ibid.*, 1/25/56.
69. Dulles memo, 2/6/56, JFD Papers, WHMS: Dulles to ambassador, Moscow, 2/7/56, WHO SS.
70. Goodpaster memo, 3/13/56, WHO SS Alpha.

71. Memo of conference, 1/13/56, DDE:D.
72. DDE to Dulles, 1/23/56, DDE:D; Dulles memo, 2/6/56, JFD Papers, WHMS.
73. ACWD, 2/6/56.
74. DDE to Bulganin, 3/2/56, WFIS.
75. Memo of conference, 3/1/56, DDE:D.
76. DDE, *Waging Peace,* 207–9; Minnich, Cabinet, 2/14/56.
77. Minnich, Cabinet, 2/14/56.
78. PP (1956), 235–36.
79. Minnich, LLM, 2/14/56.
80. *Ibid.,* 2/28/56.
81. Briefing, 2/29/56, DDE:D.
82. PP (1956), 298.
83. DDE Diary, 3/30/56.
84. Eden talks, memo of conversation, 2/7/56, WFIS.
85. DDE, *Waging Peace,* 20.
86. Eden talks, memo of conversation, 2/7/56, WFIS.
87. DDE, *Waging Peace,* 24–25.
88. Eden talks, note, WFIS; Neff, *Warriors at Suez,* 149–55.
89. Ewald, *Eisenhower,* 194.
90. *Ibid.,* 196; Neff, *Warriors at Suez,* 134–36.
91. DDE Diary, 3/8/56.
92. Dulles memo, 3/28/56, D/H.
93. Memo of conference, 3/28/56, DDE:D.

CHAPTER FOURTEEN

1. Larson, *Eisenhower,* 10.
2. *Ibid.,* 10.
3. Hughes, *Ordeal,* 173.
4. Ewald, *Eisenhower,* 197–99.
5. Nixon, *Memoirs,* 170–71.
6. ACWD, 4/9/56.
7. Nixon, *Memoirs,* 172–73.
8. PP (1956), 360–61.
9. DDE, *Waging Peace,* 10.
10. *Ibid.*
11. Larson, *Eisenhower,* 9.
12. DDE, *Waging Peace,* 10.
13. Nixon, *Memoirs,* 174.
14. Parmet, *Eisenhower,* 452.
15. Nixon, *Memoirs,* 174–75; Adams, *Firsthand Report,* 240–41.
16. PP (1956), 633.
17. *Ibid.,* 625.
18. Telephone calls, 7/27/56, DDE:D.
19. PP (1956), 624.
20. Minnich, LLM, 4/17/56.
21. Persons memo, 8/1/56, DDE:D.
22. ACWD, 8/14/56.
23. *Ibid.*
24. *Ibid.,* 8/19/56.
25. Persons memo, 8/1/56, DDE:D.
26. Telephone calls, 4/7/56, DDE:D.

27. ACWD, 4/10/56.
28. DDE to Ben-Gurion, 4/30/56, WFIS.
29. Dulles memo, 5/1/56, JFD Papers, WHMF; Dulles memo, 5/9/56, WHMF.
30. DDE, *Waging Peace*, 30–32.
31. DDE Diary, 8/8/56; DDE, *Waging Peace*, 32.
32. Dulles to DDE, 9/15/56, JFD Papers, WHMS.
33. DDE, *Waging Peace*, 34.
34. *Ibid.*, 36–37.
35. Neff, *Warriors at Suez*, 280.
36. DDE, *Waging Peace*, 37–38; memo of conference, 7/28/56, DDE:D.
37. Memo of conference, 7/31/56, DDE:D.
38. DDE, *Waging Peace*, 41, 664–65.
39. *Ibid.*, 42–44.
40. DDE to Hazlett, 8/3/56, AWNS.
41. Memo for record, 8/12/56, DDE:D.
42. Minnich, LLM, 8/12/56.
43. DDE to Dulles, 8/19/56, DDE:D.
44. DDE, *Waging Peace*, 46–47.
45. Hughes, *Ordeal*, 176.
46. Parmet, *Eisenhower*, 457.
47. Slater, *The Ike I Knew*, 135–38.
48. PP (1956), 735.
49. ACWD, 11/14/56.
50. PP (1956), 758–59.
51. *Ibid.*, 736–37.
52. DDE, *Waging Peace*, 666–67.
53. Neff, *Warriors at Suez*, 301.
54. Telephone calls, 9/7/56, DDE:D.
55. DDE, *Waging Peace*, 669–70.
56. *Ibid.*, 50–51.
57. Memo of conference, 5/28/56, DDE:D.
58. Goodpaster interview; Goodpaster memo, 6/21/56, WHO SS Alpha.
59. Goodpaster, Bissell, and John Eisenhower interviews; Ambrose, *Ike's Spies*, 271–73; memo of conference, 5/18/56, DDE:D.
60. DDE Diary, 10/15/56.
61. Divine, *Blowing on the Wind*, 65.
62. Press-conference briefing, 4/25/56, ACWD.
63. Divine, *Blowing on the Wind*, 77.
64. *Ibid.*, 72–73.
65. PP (1956), 434–35.
66. Minnich, LLM, 5/18/56.
67. Divine, *Blowing on the Wind*, 85.
68. DDE to Strauss, 8/30/56, DDE:D.
69. Memo of conference, 9/14/56, DDE:D.
70. Whitman to MSE, 8/28/56, AWNS.
71. DDE to Roberts, 9/6/56, AWNS.
72. Telephone calls, 9/25/56, DDE:D.

CHAPTER FIFTEEN

1. Divine, *Blowing on the Wind*, 88.
2. DDE to Gruenther, 11/2/56, DDE:D.
3. DDE to Hazlett, 11/2/56, AWNS.

4. Divine, *Blowing on the Wind*, 88.
5. PP (1956), 858, 863–66.
6. *Ibid.*, 82–88.
7. Divine, *Blowing on the Wind*, 93–95.
8. PP (1956), 938–39, 944, 959.
9. DDE to Bulganin, 10/21/56, D/H.
10. Divine, *Blowing on the Wind*, 100.
11. John Eisenhower, *Strictly Personal*, 189.
12. Telephone calls, 10/23/56, DDE:D.
13. Divine, *Blowing on the Wind*, 101.
14. Memo of conference, 10/8/56, DDE:D.
15. DDE to Hoover, 10/8/56, D/H.
16. DDE, *Waging Peace*, 51–54.
17. DDE memo, 10/15/56, DDE:D.
18. John Eisenhower, *Strictly Personal*, 189.
19. Dulles memo on conversation, 10/15/56, JFD Papers, WHMS.
20. Colby, *Honorable Men*, 134–35.
21. DDE, *Waging Peace*, 67–68.
22. *Ibid.*, 70.
23. Telephone calls, 10/28/56, DDE:D.
24. Hughes, *Ordeal*, 212.
25. Telephone calls, 10/28/56, D/H.
26. DDE, *Waging Peace*, 71–73.
27. NSC minutes, 10/4/56, NSC series.
28. Memo of conversation, 10/29/56, DDE:D.
29. Memo of conference, 10/30/56, DDE:D.
30. *Ibid.*
31. Telephone calls, 10/30/56, DDE:D.
32. DDE to Mollet and Eden, 10/30/56, WFIS.
33. Hughes, *Ordeal*, 216–17.
34. Telephone calls, 10/30/56, DDE:D.
35. DDE, *Waging Peace*, 78–79.
36. Telephone calls, 10/31/56, DDE:D.
37. *Ibid.*
38. Hughes, *Ordeal*, 219–21; DDE, *Waging Peace*, 80.
39. DDE, *Waging Peace*, 80–81.
40. Memo, NSC meeting, 11/1/56, NSC series; DDE to Dulles, 11/1/56, D/H.
41. Hughes, *Ordeal*, 41.
42. DDE to Gruenther, 11/2/56, DDE:D.
43. DDE to Hazlett, 11/2/56, AWNS.
44. DDE to Gruenther, 11/2/56, DDE:D.
45. Slater, *The Ike I Knew*, 140–43.
46. DDE, *Waging Peace*, 86–88.
47. *Ibid.*, 89, 95.
48. *Ibid.*, 89.
49. Hughes, *Ordeal*, 222–23.
50. Memo of conference, 11/6/56, DDE:D.
51. DDE, *Waging Peace*, 91.
52. Telephone calls, 11/6/56, WFIS.
53. Hughes, *Ordeal*, 228.
54. Telephone calls, 11/7/56, WFIS.
55. Memo for record, 11/7/56, DDE:D.
56. DDE, *Waging Peace*, 94–95.

57. Minutes, NSC, 11/9/56, NSC series.
58. Memo of conference, 11/9/56, DDE:D.
59. Telephone calls, 11/9/56, DDE:D.
60. Telephone calls, 11/9/56, D/H; DDE to Jackson, 11/19/56, DDE:D.
61. Telephone calls, 11/20/56, WFIS.
62. Telephone calls, 11/27/56, DDE:D.
63. DDE to Churchill, 11/27/56, WFIS.
64. DDE to Tedder, 12/5/56, AWNS.
65. DDE to de Guingand, 12/23/56, AWNS.
66. Minnich, LLM, 12/31/56.
67. Telephone calls, 11/9/56, DDE:D.
68. Handwritten notes on meeting, 11/15/56, WHO SS Alpha.
69. Telephone calls, 12/18/56, DDE:D.
70. Notes, 11/26/56, WFIS.
71. Notes on meeting, 12/26/56, ACWD.

CHAPTER SIXTEEN

1. PP (1957), 60–65.
2. Kaufman, *Trade and Aid,* 99.
3. Minnich, LLM, 2/5/57.
4. *Ibid.,* 7/2/57.
5. DDE to Humphrey, 3/27/57, AWNS.
6. Minnich, LLM, 7/2/57.
7. DDE to Humphrey, 5/7/57, AWAS.
8. Kaufman, *Trade and Aid,* 103.
9. See, for example, Minnich, LLM, 5/9/57, and Slater, *The Ike I Knew,* 121.
10. Conversation, 5/21/57, DDE:D; Minnich, Cabinet, 4/1/55.
11. Kaufman, *Trade and Aid,* 109–10; Minnich, Cabinet, 4/1/55.
12. DDE to Hazlett, 7/22/57, AWNS.
13. Minnich, LLM, 1/1/57.
14. PP (1957), 6–16.
15. DDE to Knowland, 2/28/57, AWAS; telephone calls, 1/9/57, DDE:DS.
16. DDE, *Waging Peace,* 180.
17. Memo of conversation, 2/6/57, WFIS.
18. See, for example, DDE to Saud, 12/24/56, WFIS.
19. Telephone calls, 12/18/56, DDE:D.
20. Telephone calls, 1/9/57, DDE:DS.
21. Lyon, *Eisenhower,* 730–31.
22. Minnich, LLM, 2/5/57.
23. *Ibid.;* DDE, *Waging Peace,* 116.
24. DDE to Ben-Gurion, 2/3/57, WFIS.
25. Slater, *The Ike I Knew,* 148–50.
26. Dulles memo of conversation, 2/16/57, JFD Papers, WHMS.
27. Minnich, LLM, 2/20/57.
28. DDE, *Waging Peace,* 187–89.
29. ACWD, 11/13/56.
30. Minnich, LLM, 1/1/57.
31. Telephone calls, 12/7/56, DDE:D; Minnich, Cabinet, 1/9/57.
32. Undated entry in Jan. '57 folder, ACWD.
33. PP (1957), 273.
34. Minnich, Cabinet, 12/14/56.

35. *New York Times,* 1/17/57; Lyon, *Eisenhower,* 735.
36. PP (1957), 73, 85.
37. *Ibid.,* 99.
38. Press-conference briefing, 5/15/57, DDE:DS.
39. PP (1957), 354–55.
40. *Ibid.,* 400; Lyon, *Eisenhower,* 738.
41. Adams, *Firsthand Report,* 380.
42. Minnich, LLM, 3/12/57.
43. Minnich, Cabinet, 4/12/57.
44. DDE to Gerow, 11/15/58, AWNS.
45. PP (1957), 356.
46. ACWD, 7/15/57.
47. DDE to Henry Wallace, 2/22/57, DDE:DS.

CHAPTER SEVENTEEN

1. Telephone calls, 12/18/56, DDE:D.
2. Minnich, LLM, 3/29/55.
3. Memo of conference, 6/28/57, DDE:DS.
4. Ambrose, *Ike's Spies,* 239, 243; memo of conference, 1/17/57, DDE:DS.
5. Minnich, Cabinet, 3/11/57.
6. Meeting, 6/26/57, DDE:DS.
7. Memo of conference, 12/20/56, DDE:D.
8. PP (1957), 125–26, 130.
9. Minnich, LLM, 3/26/57.
10. PP (1957), 82–83.
11. Divine, *Blowing on the Wind,* 119–20.
12. DDE to Cole, 5/27/57, DDE:DS.
13. Minnich, Cabinet, 6/3/57.
14. PP (1957), 429, 434.
15. Memo of conference, 6/24/57, DDE:DS.
16. Telephone calls, 6/25/57, DDE:DS.
17. Divine, *Blowing on the Wind,* 152.
18. PP (1957), 498–99, 505.
19. NSC, 10/4/56, NSC series.
20. Minnich, LLM, 3/26/57.
21. PP (1957), 551.
22. Divine, *Blowing on the Wind,* 113.
23. *Ibid.,* 115; telephone calls, 2/4/57, DDE:DS.
24. Divine, *Blowing on the Wind,* 143–44.
25. PP (1957), 405.
26. Divine, *Blowing on the Wind,* 144–45.
27. PP (1957), 431, 435.
28. DDE to Macmillan, 6/4/57, D/H.
29. Dulles memo, 6/12/57, D/H.
30. PP (1957), 476–79.
31. Divine, *Blowing on the Wind,* 146–53.
32. *Ibid.,* 155–57.
33. NSC, 10/4/56, NSC series.
34. Memo of conference, 2/6/57, DDE:DS.
35. *Ibid.,* 3/23/57.
36. DDE Diary, 11/21/56.

37. PP (1957), 550.
38. Telephone calls, 7/3/57, DDE:DS.
39. Minnich, LLM, 7/30/57.
40. PP (1957), 127–28.
41. ACWD, 1/3/57.
42. Telephone calls, 6/15/57, DDE:DS.
43. PP (1957), 520–21.
44. DDE, *Waging Peace,* 157–58.
45. ACWD, 7/10/57.
46. DDE to Hazlett, 7/22/57, AWNS.
47. DDE to Byrnes, 7/23/57, DDE:DS.
48. PP (1957), 546–47, 555.
49. DDE to Hazlett, 7/22/57, AWNS.

CHAPTER EIGHTEEN

1. Minnich, Cabinet, 8/2/57; PP (1957), 587.
2. PP (1957), 594.
3. DDE, *Waging Peace,* 160.
4. Minnich, LLM, 8/13/57.
5. Press-conference briefing, 8/7/57, DDE:DS.
6. Minnich, LLM, 8/13/57.
7. ACWD, 8/17/57.
8. DDE, *Waging Peace,* 160–61.
9. Hughes, *Ordeal,* 242.
10. Duram, *Moderate Among Extremists,* 145; press-conference briefing, 9/3/57, ACWD.
11. Press-conference briefing, 9/3/57, ACWD.
12. PP (1957), 659.
13. Telephone calls, 9/11/57, DDE:DS.
14. *Ibid.*
15. PP (1957), 673–74.
16. ACWD, 10/8/57; DDE, *Waging Peace,* 166.
17. ACWD, 9/14/57.
18. Goodpaster memo for Hagerty, 9/19/57, ACWD.
19. Telephone calls, 9/20/57, DDE:DS.
20. Slater, *The Ike I Knew,* 160–62.
21. Adams, *Firsthand Report,* 353.
22. *Ibid.,* 354; DDE, *Waging Peace,* 169.
23. Telephone calls, 9/24/57, DDE:DS.
24. DDE to Gruenther, 9/24/57, DDE:DS.
25. DDE, *Waging Peace,* 170.
26. Telephone calls, 9/24/57, DDE:DS.
27. Undated note, AWAS.
28. Duram, *Moderate Among Extremists,* 157–58; DDE, *Waging Peace,* 172.
29. PP (1957), 704.
30. Duram, *Moderate Among Extremists,* 159–60.
31. DDE to Russell, 9/27/57, AWAS.
32. Duram, *Moderate Among Extremists,* 164–65; ACWD, 10/3/57.
33. PP (1957), 708–11.
34. Duram, *Moderate Among Extremists,* 167.
35. DDE to Reid, 9/28/57, AWNS.

36. DDE, *Waging Peace*, 205–6.
37. Divine, *Blowing on the Wind*, 159.
38. Memo of conference, 8/9/57, DDE:DS.
39. *Ibid.*, 10/8/57.
40. *Ibid.*
41. Memo for record, 11/6/57, DDE:DS.
42. PP (1957), 719–30.
43. ACWD, 11/6/57.
44. Divine, *Blowing on the Wind*, 170; ACWD, 10/10/57.
45. Memo of conference, 10/15/57, DDE:DS.
46. DDE Diary, 10/29/57.
47. Memo of conference, 10/29/57, DDE:DS.
48. *Ibid.*, 10/31/57.
49. DDE to Humphrey, 11/22/57, AWAS.
50. Minnich, Cabinet, 11/1/57.
51. DDE to Altschul, 10/25/57, DDE:DS; memo, 12/5/57, DDE:DS.
52. Memo of conference, 11/4 and 11/7/57, DDE:DS; ACWD, 11/9/57; DDE Diary, 12/30/57.
53. DDE to Hazlett, 11/18/57, AWNS.
54. ACWD, 11/25/57.

Chapter Nineteen

1. DDE, *Waging Peace*, 227–28; John Eisenhower, *Strictly Personal*, 195–96.
2. John Eisenhower, *Strictly Personal*, 196; Adams, *Firsthand Report*, 196–97.
3. Adams, *Firsthand Report*, 197–98; John Eisenhower, *Strictly Personal*, 196–97.
4. DDE, *Waging Peace*, 229.
5. Telephone calls, 12/1/57, JFD Papers, WHMS.
6. *Ibid.*
7. *Ibid.*
8. *Ibid.*
9. Dulles memo, 12/2/57, JFD Papers, WHMS.
10. ACWD, 1/3/58.
11. DDE to Nixon, 2/5/58, AWNS.
12. PP (1958), 93, 355.
13. Slater, *The Ike I Knew*, 171.
14. DDE, *Waging Peace*, 365.
15. Dulles memo, 12/26/56, JFD Papers, '52–'59 subseries.
16. PP (1958), 100–101.
17. Dulles memo, 12/26/56, JFD Papers, '52–'59 subseries.
18. DDE to Judd, 1/4/58, D/H.
19. DDE to Gruenther, 1/15/58, DDE:D.
20. PP (1958), 97.
21. Slater, *The Ike I Knew*, 171.
22. ACWD, 1/14/58.
23. Jackson to DDE, 1/17/58, C. D. Jackson Papers.
24. DDE to Jackson, 1/28/58, C. D. Jackson Papers.
25. ACWD, 1/24/58.
26. DDE to Dulles, 3/7/58, D/H.
27. Draft, 2/24/58, AWNS.
28. Telephone calls, 3/4/58, DDE:D.

29. DDE to Dulles, 3/21/58, D/H.
30. Minnich, LLM, 3/4/58; Kaufman, *Trade and Aid*, 88–91.
31. Minnich, Cabinet, 3/21/58.
32. Divine, *Blowing on the Wind*, 174–77.
33. Memo of conversation, 1/22/58, DDE:D.
34. Telephone calls, 2/5/58, DDE:D.
35. "Draft #1," 3/23/58, JFD Papers, WHMS.
36. Memo of conference, 3/24/58, DDE:D.
37. DDE to Dulles, 3/26/58, DDE:DS.
38. Divine, *Blowing on the Wind*, 200.
39. PP (1958), 262.
40. Quoted in Divine, *Blowing on the Wind*, 202.
41. *Ibid.*, 206–7.
42. Memo of conversation, 4/17/58, DDE:DS.
43. Divine, *Blowing on the Wind*, 210–12.
44. *Ibid.*, 215–17, 221
45. Minnich, LLM, 1/28/58.
46. Memo of conference, 3/20/58, DDE:D.
47. NSC, 4/25/58, NSC series.
48. Memo for record, 3/7/58, WHO SS Alpha.
49. ACWD, 3/13/58.
50. The CIA report is summarized in "Staff Notes," 6/9/58, DDE:DS.
51. Memo of conference, 6/18/58, DDE:DS.
52. Minnich, LLM, 6/24/58.
53. *Ibid.*, 1/7/58.
54. ACWD, 1/16/58.
55. Minnich, LLM, 2/4/58.
56. Memo of conference, 2/25/58, DDE:D.
57. Minnich, LLM, 3/18/58.
58. Memo of conference, 2/6/58, DDE:D.
59. Minnich, LLM, 2/4/58.
60. DDE, *Waging Peace*, 257.
61. PP (1958), 311.
62. Minnich, LLM, 12/4/57.
63. ACWD, 12/30/57.
64. DDE, *Waging Peace*, 243.
65. DDE to Burns, 3/12/58, DDE:D.
66. DDE: *Waging Peace*, 306.
67. Memo for Whitman, 2/27/58, DDE:D.
68. *Ibid.*, 3/28/58.
69. Slater, *The Ike I Knew*, 174–75.

CHAPTER TWENTY

1. DDE to Dulles, 11/13/57, D/H.
2. DDE to Chamoun, 4/25/57, WFIS.
3. DDE, *Waging Peace*, 266.
4. Memo for record, 5/13/58, DDE:DS; ACWD, 5/8/58.
5. ACWD, 6/15/58.
6. Memo of conference, 6/15/58, DDE:DS.
7. ACWD, 1/22/58; Slater, *The Ike I Knew*, 187.
8. Slater, *The Ike I Knew*, 178.

9. PP (1958), 479.
10. DDE to Hoffman, 6/23/58, AWAS.
11. Notes by RMN, 7/15/58, ACWD.
12. Cutler memo, 8/26/58, WH Pres SS.
13. Cutler, *No Time for Rest,* 363.
14. DDE, *Waging Peace,* 270.
15. Staff notes, 7/15/58, WFIS.
16. Cutler, *No Time for Rest,* 363–64.
17. Minnich, LLM, 7/14/58.
18. Memo of conference, 7/14/58, DDE:DS.
19. DDE, *Waging Peace,* 273.
20. *Ibid.,* 290–91.
21. Minnich, LLM, 7/14/58.
22. Memo of conference, 7/15/58, DDE:DS.
23. DDE, *Waging Peace,* 290.
24. *Ibid.,* 519; ACWD, 5/13/58.
25. Slater, *The Ike I Knew,* 177–78.
26. Minnich, LLM, 7/18 and 7/22/58.
27. Memo of conference, 7/24/58, DDE:DS.
28. DDE to Humphrey, 7/22/58, DDE:DS.
29. Goodpaster notes, 7/29/58, Christian Herter Papers.
30. Telephone calls, 7/31/58, DDE:DS.
31. Memo for Secretary of Defense, 7/31/58, DDE:DS.
32. Memo of conference, 8/4/58, WFIS.
33. DDE to McCloy, 5/10/58, DDE:DS.
34. Minnich, Cabinet, 6/27/58.
35. Minnich, LLM, 8/12/58.
36. Symington to DDE, 8/29/58, AWAS.
37. Memo of conference, 8/30/58, DDE:DS.
38. *Ibid.,* 7/24/58.
39. Divine, *Blowing on the Wind,* 226–28.
40. Memo of conference, 9/11/58, and DDE to Macmillan, 7/30/58, DDE:DS.
41. Memo of conferences, 8/20 and 8/23/58, DDE:DS.
42. Whitman to Jackson, 6/5/58, DDE:DS.
43. Minnich, LLM, 5/19/58.
44. Memo of conversation, 8/21/58, DDE:DS.
45. Memo of conference, 8/18/58, DDE:DS.
46. *Ibid.,* 8/19/58.
47. Divine, *Blowing on the Wind,* 228, 231.
48. Gray memo for record, 8/27/58, WH Pres SS.
49. Divine, *Blowing on the Wind,* 229–33.
50. DDE to Roberts, 9/4/58, AWNS.
51. Telephone calls, 9/4/58, ACWD.
52. Nixon, *Memoirs,* 196.
53. ACWD, 9/16/58.
54. Ibid., 9/17/58.
55. Memo of conference, 8/25/58, DDE:DS.
56. DDE, *Waging Peace,* 294.
57. Memo of conference, 8/29/58, DDE:DS.
58. Memo of conversation, 9/4/58, JFD Papers, WHMS; memo of conference, 9/4/58, WFIS; DDE, *Waging Peace,* 293.
59. Memo of conference, 9/8/58, WFIS; Gray memo, 9/12/58, WH Pres SS.
60. Memo of conference, 9/6/58, WFIS.

61. Memo of conversation, 9/11/58, JFD Papers, WHMS.
62. Gray memo, 9/12/58, WH Pres SS.
63. DDE, *Waging Peace*, 301.
64. Memo of conversation, 9/23/58, JFD Papers, WHMS.
65. *Ibid.,* 9/11/58.
66. Memo of conference, 9/15/58, DDE:DS.
67. *Ibid.,* 9/30/58.
68. DDE to Dulles, 10/7/58, DDE:DS.
69. DDE, *Waging Peace*, 304.
70. Slater, *The Ike I Knew*, 179–80.
71. DDE to Humphrey, 7/22/58, DDE:DS.

<h2 style="text-align:center">Chapter Twenty-one</h2>

1. DDE, *Waging Peace*, 377.
2. DDE to McElroy, 10/7/58, AWAS.
3. DDE, *Waging Peace*, 380–81.
4. Larson, *Eisenhower*, 35.
5. ACWD, 2/2/59.
6. PP (1958), 827–29, 836.
7. Memo for record by DDE, 12/6/58, AWNS.
8. DDE to Macmillan, 11/11/58, WFIS.
9. Memo of conference, 10/25/58, WP Pres SS.
10. *Time,* 11/10/58, 30.
11. Memo for record, 11/18/58, DDE:DS.
12. Conversation with Frederika of Greece, 12/9/58, DDE:DS.
13. Memo of conference, 1/12/59, DDE:DS.
14. *Ibid.*
15. Memo of conversation, 1/12/59, DDE:DS.
16. Memo of conference, 1/16/59, DDE:DS.
17. *Ibid.,* 2/12/59.
18. Memo of meeting, 2/18/59, WH Pres SS.
19. Minnich, Cabinet, 10/9/58; memo of conference, 2/9/59, DDE:DS.
20. Memo of conference, 11/28/58, DDE:DS.
21. Minnich, LLM, 1/13/59.
22. DDE to Benson, 11/15/58, DDE:DS.
23. Minnich, Cabinet, 1/16/59.
24. Minnich, LLM, 1/30/59; memo of conference, 1/15/59, DDE:DS.
25. DDE, *Waging Peace*, 387–88.
26. PP (1958), 742.
27. Slater, *The Ike I Knew*, 183.
28. PP (1959), 123.
29. *Ibid.,* 133–34.
30. ACWD, 2/3/59.
31. DDE to Butcher, 3/14/59, AWNS.
32. DDE to Clay (and others), 1/1/59, AWNS.
33. DDE to Ismay, 1/14/59, DDE:DS.
34. PP (1959), 29–31.
35. Slater, *The Ike I Knew*, 195–96.
36. DDE to Nielsen, 1/8/59, AWNS.
37. DDE to de Guingand, 6/29/59, AWNS.
38. Memo of conference, 12/15/58, DDE:DS.

39. DDE to Dulles, 12/16/58, D/H.
40. Telephone calls, 11/27/58, DDE:DS.
41. Memo of conference, 12/15/58, DDE:DS.
42. DDE, *Waging Peace,* 340–41.
43. Status of supplies memo, 2/3/59, DDE:DS.
44. Memo of conference, 2/3/59, DDE:DS.
45. Memo, Herter to DDE, 12/23/58, AWAS.
46. Gray memo, 12/24/58, WH Press SS.
47. DDE, *Waging Peace,* 522–23.
48. Memo of conference, 12/30/58, WH Pres SS.
49. Gray memo for 5412, 1/19/59, WHO SS Alpha; Howard Hunt interview.
50. Memo of meeting, 1/29/59, WHO Alpha SS.
51. ACWD, 11/10/58.
52. Memo of conversation, 11/10/58, WFIS.
53. ACWD, 12/6/58.
54. Dulles to DDE, 2/9/59, D/H.
55. PP (1959), 168–69.
56. ACWD, 2/14/59.
57. Memo of meeting, 2/18/59, WH Pres SS.

CHAPTER TWENTY-TWO

1. PP (1959), 218.
2. Memo of conference, 3/6/59, DDE:DS.
3. ACWD, 6/11/59.
4. Minnich, LLM, 3/3/59.
5. PP (1959), 428.
6. Telephone calls, 3/4/59, CAHP.
7. Memo for record, 2/12/59, WHO SS Alpha.
8. Memo of conference, 2/13/59, WHO SS Intelligence Briefing Notes.
9. Memo of conference, 4/11/59, WHO SS Alpha.
10. Minnich, LLM, 6/30/59.
11. Memo of conference, 3/9/59, DDE:DS.
12. Jackson to Dulles, 2/24/59, CDJ Papers (see entire file for the period).
13. Minnich, LLM, 6/2/59.
14. Memo of conference, 3/8/59, DDE:DS.
15. PP (1959), 226–28.
16. *Ibid.,* 242–52.
17. Memo of conference, 3/9/59, DDE:DS.
18. Minnich, LLM, 3/10/59.
19. Memo of conference, 3/8/59, DDE:DS.
20. Minnich, Cabinet, 3/13/59.
21. Memo of telephone conversation, 3/5/59, CAHP.
22. DDE, *Waging Peace,* 351.
23. Memo of telephone conversation, 4/4/59, CAHP.
24. Memo of conference, 2/18/59, DDE:DS.
25. *Ibid.,* 2/28/59.
26. *Ibid.,* 3/17/59.
27. *Ibid.,* 3/20/59.
28. DDE to Khrushchev, 4/13/59, WFIS.
29. Telephone calls, 4/7/59, DDE:DS.
30. Minnich, LLM, 2/24/59.

31. DDE, *Waging Peace,* 352–55.
32. Memo of conversation, 4/13/59, JFD: WHMS.
33. Telephone calls, 11/4/59, DDE:DS.
34. Memo of conference, 5/28/59, DDE:DS.
35. DDE Diary, 5/28/59.
36. DDE, *Waging Peace,* 402–3.
37. *Ibid.,* 523.
38. Memo of conference, 4/22/59, DDE:DS.
39. Report, 4/23/59, WFIS.
40. Minnich, LLM, 3/3/59.
41. *Ibid.,* 4/28 and 5/26/59, and others.
42. DDE to McGill, 2/26/59, AWNS.
43. PP (1959), 388.
44. Minnich, LLM, 2/17/59.
45. Slater, *The Ike I Knew,* 197–99.
46. John Eisenhower, *Strictly Personal,* 209.
47. DDE, *Waging Peace,* 396.
48. ACWD, 6/19/59.
49. Slater, *The Ike I Knew,* 193.
50. ACWD, 6/27/59.

CHAPTER TWENTY-THREE

1. ACWD, week of August 7–15, 1959.
2. Memo of conference, 6/15/59, DDE:DS.
3. *Ibid.,* 6/17/59.
4. Press-conference briefing, 7/22/59, DDE:DS.
5. Memo of conference, 7/10/59, DDE:DS.
6. *Ibid.,* 7/22/59.
7. PP (1959), 576, 582. (Italics added.)
8. Memo of conference, 8/25/59, DDE:DS.
9. PP (1959), 593.
10. DDE, *Waging Peace,* 415.
11. *Ibid.,* 417.
12. Memo of conference, 7/15/59, DDE:DS.
13. DDE, *Waging Peace,* 418.
14. Minnich, LLM, 3/24/59.
15. Memo of conference, 6/9/59, DDE:DS.
16. *Ibid.,* 8/24/59.
17. Memo of conversation with Spaak, 11/24/59, DDE:DS.
18. DE, *Waging Peace,* 419; Lyon, *Eisenhower,* 798.
19. DDE to Gault, 8/9/59, DDE Confidential SS.
20. ACWD, 9/10/59.
21. PP (1959), 625.
22. Kistiakowsky, *Scientist at the White House,* 17.
23. Divine, *Blowing on the Wind,* 284–86.
24. DDE, *Waging Peace,* 435.
25. *Ibid.,* 432.
26. Minnich, Cabinet, 11/6/59.
27. *New York Times,* 9/20/59.
28. Memo of conferences, 9/28 and 9/29/59, DDE:DS.

29. DDE, *Waging Peace,* 442–44, 446–47.
30. Memo of conference, 10/21/59, DDE:DS.
31. Press-conference briefing, 7/22/59, DDE:DS.
32. Memo of conference, 10/27/59, DDE:DS.
33. ACWD, 7/20/59.
34. See Wm. Robinson papers for 1959.
35. DDE to Nixon, 8/18/59, DDE:DS.
36. Telephone calls, 8/4/59, DDE:DS.
37. Schwartz, "Urban Freeways," 444–45. I am indebted to this careful study for my understanding of the politics of the Interstate program.
38. Memo for record, 7/13/59, DDE:DS.
39. Schwartz, "Urban Freeways," 446–47; memo for record, 4/8/60, DDE:DS.
40. Memo for record, 9/15/59, DDE:DS.
41. Minnich, LLM, 2/24/59.
42. DDE, *Waging Peace,* 459–60.
43. Memo of conference, 6/24/59, DDE:DS.
44. *Ibid.,* 11/16/59.
45. *Ibid.,* 11/18/59.
46. *Ibid.,* 11/16/59.
47. Slater, *The Ike I Knew,* 203–4, 209.
48. PP (1959), 786–87.
49. DDE to de Gaulle, 11/17/59, WFIS.
50. DDE, *Waging Peace,* 485–513 describes the trip in some detail.
51. Memo of conference, 12/31/59, DDE:DS.

CHAPTER TWENTY-FOUR

1. Memo for President, 4/23/60, D/H; see also memo of conference, 4/26 and 5/16/60, DDE:DS.
2. Memo of conference, 1/25/60, DDE:DS.
3. Memo for President, 3/17/60, D/H.
4. *Ibid.,* 4/14/60.
5. Memo of conference, 1/25/60, DDE:DS.
6. Ambrose, *Ike's Spies,* 309.
7. *Ibid.,* 309–10.
8. DDE, *Waging Peace,* 525–33.
9. ACWD, 1/20/60.
10. John Eisenhower, *Strictly Personal,* 281–84.
11. Minnich, LLM, 4/26/60.
12. DDE to Rockefeller, 5/5/60, AWAS.
13. PP (1960), 144, 147.
14. DDE to Hobby, 5/9/60, AWNS.
15. PP (1960), 26.
16. Minnich, LLM, 2/9/60.
17. Memo for President, 2/12/60, DDE:DS.
18. Telephone calls, 1/12/60, DDE:DS.
19. Minnich, LLM, 2/9/60.
20. PP (1960), 126.
21. *Ibid.,* 145.
22. *Ibid.,* 198–99.
23. White to Stepherson, 3/18/60, AWAS.
24. Kistiakowsky, *Scientist at the White House,* 243.

25. *Ibid.,* 250, 252.
26. DDE, *Waging Peace,* 480.
27. Divine, *Blowing on the Wind,* 289.
28. PP (1960), 166.
29. Kistiakowsky, *Scientist at the White House,* 253; memo of conference, 4/27/60, DDE:DS.
30. Kistiakowsky, *Scientist at the White House,* 257–58.
31. Divine, *Blowing on the Wind,* 299.
32. *New York Times,* 3/23/60.
33. Quoted in Divine, *Blowing on the Wind,* 300.
34. Kistiakowsky, *Scientist at the White House,* 282.
35. Memo of conference, 3/24/60, DDE: DS.
36. Memo of meeting, 3/25/60, WH: Pres SS.
37. Kistiakowsky, *Scientist at the White House,* 286, 288.
38. PP (1960), 323–29.
39. *Ibid.,* 362–63.
40. Kistiakowsky, *Scientist at the White House,* 290–91; Divine, *Blowing on the Wind,* 310.
41. Kistiakowsky, *Scientist at the White House,* 293.
42. Minnich, Cabinet, 4/26/60; memo of conference, 3/10/60, DDE:DS; Teller to DDE, 5/11/60, DDE Confi. SS.
43. Memo for record, 2/8/60, and memo of conference, 2/5/60, WHO SS Alpha.
44. Kistiakowsky, *Scientist at the White House,* 328; interviews with Bissell and Goodpaster.
45. Goodpaster memo, 4/25/60, WHO SS Alpha; Ambrose, *Ike's Spies,* 283.
46. Memo of conversation, 1/14/60, WFIS; DDE to Macmillan, 3/18/60, WFIS.
47. Memo of conversation, 1/14/60, WFIS; John Eisenhower, *Strictly Personal,* 262.
48. DDE to de Gaulle and Macmillan (draft, undated), May 1960 file, WFIS.
49. Ambrose, *Ike's Spies,* 283–84.
50. DDE, *Waging Peace,* 543.
51. Kistiakowsky, *Scientist at the White House,* 317; ACWD, 5/5/60.
52. *New York Times,* 5/6/60.
53. See Dulles to Goodpaster, 12/23/60, WHO SS Alpha.
54. Ambrose, *Ike's Spies,* 285.
55. *New York Times,* 5/8/60.
56. Telephone calls, 5/7/60, CAHP.
57. *New York Times,* 5/8/60.
58. Telephone calls, 5/9/60, CAHP.
59. *Ibid.*
60. *New York Times,* 5/9/60.
61. ACWD, 5/9/60.
62. DDE, *Waging Peace,* 552.
63. *New York Times,* 5/13/60.
64. PP (1960), 403–7.
65. DDE, *Waging Peace,* 552–53.
66. Walters, *Silent Missions,* 341.
67. *New York Times,* 5/8/60.
68. DDE, *Waging Peace,* 558–59; Lyon, *Eisenhower,* 811–14.
69. Memo of conference, 5/15/60, WFIS.
70. Walters, *Silent Missions,* 341.
71. Memo of conference, 5/16/60, WFIS.

72. This account is based on Walters, *Silent Missions,* 343–47; DDE, *Waging Peace,* 555–56; memo of conference, 5/16/60, WFIS.
73. Kistiakowsky, *Scientist at the White House,* 335–36.
74. Memo of conference, 5/23/60, DDE:DS.
75. Kistiakowsky, *Scientist at the White House,* 375.

CHAPTER TWENTY-FIVE

1. DDE, *Waging Peace,* 563.
2. Telephone calls, 6/21/60, CAHP.
3. Memo of meeting, 6/29/60, WH: Pres SS.
4. DDE, *Waging Peace,* 535.
5. Memo of conference, 7/21/60, DDE:DS.
6. DDE, *Waging Peace,* 538.
7. Kistiakowsky, *Scientist at the White House,* 363.
8. Minnich, LLM, 8/16/60.
9. Memo of meeting (Gray), 8/22/60, WH: Pres SS; Bissell interview; Ambrose, *Ike's Spies,* 309–11.
10. Bissell interview.
11. Telephone calls, 7/11/60, CAHP.
12. DDE, *Waging Peace,* 570; telephone calls, 7/12/60, CAHP.
13. Memo of conference, 7/13/60, DDE:DS.
14. DDE, *Waging Peace,* 570; memo of conference, 7/19/60, DDE:DS.
15. Church Committee, 53.
16. Memo of conference, 7/19/60, DDE:DS.
17. Church Committee, 58.
18. *Ibid.,* 15.
19. *Ibid.,* 51.
20. *Ibid.,* 64; Goodpaster interview.
21. Bissell interview.
22. See telephone calls, 8/8 and 9/8/60, CAHP.
23. Telephone calls, 10/4/60, CAHP; memo of conference, 10/1/60, DDE:DS.
24. Memo of conference, 8/15/60, DDE:DS.
25. *Ibid.,* 7/11/60.
26. *Ibid.,* 7/19/60.
27. Memo of conference, 7/7/60, WH: Pres SS.
28. DDE to Luce, 7/6/60, AWNS; memo of meeting, 9/14/60, WH: Pres SS.
29. Memo of conference, 10/13/60, DDE:DS.
30. See DDE to Black, 8/22/60, AWNS.
31. Memo of conference, 6/30/60, DDE:DS.
32. Westmoreland interview.
33. Minnich, LLM, 6/9/60.
34. Telephone calls, 6/11/60, DDE:DS.
35. *Ibid.,* 6/11/60, and DDE to Nixon, 6/11/60, DDE:DS.
36. Memo for Record, 7/1/60, DDE:DS.
37. ACWD, 7/1/60.
38. Wm. Robinson Diary, 7/18–25/60, WRP Papers.
39. Slater, *The Ike I Knew,* 229.
40. Telephone calls (Ben Fairless), 8/19/60, DDE:DS.
41. Kistiakowsky, *Scientist at the White House,* 402.
42. DDE, *Waging Peace,* 595; Wm. Robinson Diary, 7/18–25/60, WRP Papers.

43. DDE, *Waging Peace,* 596–97.
44. Memo for the President, 8/3/60, AWAS.
45. Telephone calls, 8/8/60, DDE:DS.
46. PP (1960), 622–27. (Italics added.)
47. *Ibid.,* 651, 653, 657–58.
48. Nixon, *Memoirs,* 219; memo of conference, 10/18/60, DDE:DS.
49. ACWD, 10/4/60.
50. *Ibid.,* 8/30/60.
51. Telephone calls, 9/25/60, DDE:DS; ACWD, 10/14/60.
52. PP (1960), 815–16.
53. Nixon, *Memoirs,* 222.
54. ACWD, 11/5/60.
55. *Ibid.,* 11/8/60.
56. *Ibid.,* 11/9/60.
57. *Ibid.*
58. Slater, *The Ike I Knew,* 230–31.
59. Telephone calls, 11/30/60, DDE:DS.

CHAPTER TWENTY-SIX

1. Slater, *The Ike I Knew,* 231.
2. Memo of conference, 12/30/60, DDE:DS.
3. *Ibid.,* 12/5/60.
4. DDE to Dillon, 12/15/60, AWAS; telephone calls, 12/31/60, DDE:DS.
5. DDE to "Bob," 1/3/61, DDE:DS.
6. DDE Diary, 12/6/60.
7. Memo of meeting, 11/29/60, DDE:DS.
8. DDE, *Waging Peace,* 613–14.
9. Memo of meeting, 1/3/61, DDE:DS; Goodpaster interview.
10. Slater, *The Ike I Knew,* 239.
11. DDE to Slater, Robinson, Jones, and others, 12/26/60, WRP Papers.
12. DDE to Edgar Eisenhower, 1/7/61, AWNS.
13. DDE to C. D. Jackson, 12/31/60, DDE:DS.
14. John Eisenhower, *Strictly Personal,* 280–81.
15. Whitman to DDE, 12/14/60, ACWD.
16. PP (1960), 1035–40.
17. *Ibid.,* 1040–45.
18. DDE, *Waging Peace,* 617.
19. Wyden, *Bay of Pigs,* 88; Persons memorandum, 1/19/61, DDE:DS; Malcolm Moos interview with DDE, 11/8/66, Eisenhower Library.
20. Lyon, *Eisenhower,* 825.
21. John Eisenhower, *Strictly Personal,* 287.
22. DDE, *Waging Peace,* 618.
23. Merriman Smith interview; Slater, *The Ike I Knew,* 241.

CHAPTER TWENTY-SEVEN

1. DDE to Luce, 8/8/60, AWNS.
2. Quoted in Lyon, *Eisenhower,* 851.

CHAPTER TWENTY-EIGHT

1. Ewald, *Eisenhower*, 6–10; *Parade Magazine*, 6/26/66.
2. John Eisenhower, memo for record, 3/7/62, DDE '61–'69.
3. See McGrath to DDE, 1/8/63, and DDE to McGrath, 1/17/63, DDE '61–'69.
4. Slater, *The Ike I Knew*, 243.
5. Ewald, *Eisenhower*, 310.
6. This account of the writing of the memoirs is based on John Eisenhower, *Strictly Personal*, 302–12; Ewald, *Eisenhower*, 1–9; and interview with John Eisenhower.
7. *New York Times Book Review*, 6/17/67.
8. DDE to Truman, 11/13/61, DDE '61–'69.
9. DDE to Nixon, 5/2/62, DDE '61–'69.
10. DDE to Churchill, 4/22/61, DDE '61–'69.
11. Lyon, *Eisenhower*, 833.
12. JFK to DDE, 1/21/61, DDE '61–'69.
13. See DDE to JFK, 5/8/62, DDE '61–'69.
14. Notes by DDE, 4/22/61, DDE '61–'69.
15. Moos interview with DDE, EL.
16. Burg interview with Gray, EL.
17. Gray to Don Wilson, 12/3/74, GGP.
18. DDE to Borman, 6/18/65, DDE '61–'69.
19. DDE to JFK, 1/15/62, DDE '61–'69.
20. *Ibid.*, 6/14/63.
21. See, for example, *ibid.*, 8/31/62.
22. See DDE to Gray, 6/14/61, DDE '61–'69.
23. DDE memo of conversation, 10/22/62, DDE '61–'69.
24. *Ibid.*, 10/29/62.
25. Moos interview with DDE, EL.
26. DDE memo, 11/5/62, DDE '61–'69.
27. Moos interview with DDE, EL.
28. Slater, *The Ike I Knew*, 246–47.
29. *Ibid.*, 248.
30. DDE to Humphrey, 7/5/62, DDE '61–'69.
31. DDE to Gruenther, 7/5/62, and to Sheffield, 8/31/62, DDE '61–'69.
32. DDE to White, 7/11/62, DDE '61–'69.
33. DDE to Nixon, 9/25/63, DDE '61–'69.
34. John Eisenhower, *Strictly Personal*, 293.
35. Slater, *The Ike I Knew*, 246.
36. *Ibid.*, 251–53.
37. Jackie Cochran interview, EL; Slater, *The Ike I Knew*, 259.
38. DDE to Nixon, 11/11/63, DDE '61–'69.
39. Hagerty Diary, 4/23/54.
40. Daily Log, 11/23/63, DDE '61–'69.

CHAPTER TWENTY-NINE

1. Nixon, *Memoirs*, 377–78.
2. Notes for the President, 11/23/63, DDE '61–'69.
3. See DDE to LBJ, 12/20/63, DDE '61–'69.
4. Daily Log, 6/24/64, and DDE to Halleck and Dirksen, same date, DDE '61–'69.
5. Daily Log, 9/4 and 9/10/64, DDE '61–'69.

6. Lyon, *Eisenhower*, 839.
7. Daily Log, 5/15 and 5/19/64, DDE '61–'69.
8. Lyon, *Eisenhower*, 839.
9. Daily Log, 8/3/64, DDE '61–'69.
10. Lyon, *Eisenhower*, 840.
11. *Ibid.*, 841.
12. Milton Eisenhower interview.
13. Slater, *The Ike I Knew*, 258; John Eisenhower, *Strictly Personal*, 329.
14. Daily Log, 12/14/64, DDE '61–'69.
15. Memo of meeting, 2/17/65, DDE '61–'69.
16. DDE to LBJ, 3/12/65, and LBJ to DDE, 3/16/65, DDE '61–'69.
17. Memo for Record, 4/9/65, DDE '61–'69.
18. *Ibid.*, 5/13/65.
19. *Ibid.*, 6/16/65.
20. Telephone calls, 7/2/65, DDE '61–'69.
21. Memo for record, 8/3/65, DDE '61–'69.
22. *Ibid.*, 8/20/65.
23. LBJ to DDE, 8/19/65, DDE '61–'69.
24. Memo for record, 10/11/65, DDE '61–'69.
25. *Ibid.*, 10/25/65.
26. *Ibid.*, 1/4/66.
27. *Ibid.*, 1/25/66.
28. LBJ to DDE, 3/10/66, DDE '61–'69.
29. *Ibid.*, 3/25/66.
30. Memo for record, 9/19/66, DDE '61–'69.
31. DDE to Nixon, 10/7/66, DDE '61–'69.
32. DDE to Anderson, 10/23/66, DDE '61–'69.
33. DDE to Humphrey, 2/14/67, DDE '61–'69.
34. Memo for record, 4/7/67, DDE '61–'69.
35. Daily Log, 7/14/67, DDE '61–'69.
36. *New York Times*, 7/12/67.
37. *Ibid.*, 10/4/67.
38. Lyon, *Eisenhower*, 846; Larson, *Eisenhower*, 191.
39. LBJ to DDE, 10/14/67, DDE '61–'69.
40. *CBS News Special*, 11/28/67.
41. Memo for record, 10/18 and 11/9/67, DDE '61–'69.
42. Lyon, *Eisenhower*, 847–48.
43. *Ibid.*, 848; *Reader's Digest*, April 1968, 49–53.
44. LBJ to DDE, 2/22/68, DDE '61–'69.
45. DDE interview.
46. DDE to Ormerod, 10/25/65, DDE '61–'69.
47. DDE to Gruening, 6/18/65, DDE '61–'69.
48. Lyon, *Eisenhower*, 836.
49. Nixon, *Memoirs*, 275–76.
50. Statement, 11/5/66, DDE '61–'69.
51. Memo for record, 3/14/67, DDE '61–'69; Larson, *Eisenhower*, 191–92.
52. DDE to Seaton, 1/31/67, DDE '61–'69.
53. Slater, *The Ike I Knew*, 269.

CHAPTER THIRTY

1. John Eisenhower, *Strictly Personal*, 328. Except where otherwise noted, this chapter is based on *Strictly Personal*, pages 328–337. I have also stolen the chapter title from John Eisenhower's work.

2. DDE to Pat, 2/14/68, DDE '61–'69.
3. Daily Log, 4/1/67, DDE '61–'69.
4. DDE to LBJ, 4/3/68, DDE '61–'69.
5. Julie Nixon Eisenhower, *Special People*, 192.
6. Nixon to DDE, 7/15/68, DDE '61–'69.
7. Nixon, *Memoirs*, 307.
8. DDE to Nixon, 10/24/68, DDE '61–'69.
9. *Ibid.*, 12/13/68.
10. DDE to Kahill, 11/29/68, DDE '61–'69.
11. Julie Eisenhower, *Special People*, 193.
12. Nixon, *Memoirs*, 361.

BIBLIOGRAPHY

List of Published Works Cited

Acheson, Dean. *Present at the Creation.* New York: W. W. Norton & Co., 1969.

Adams, Sherman. *Firsthand Report: The Story of the Eisenhower Administration.* New York: Harper & Bros., 1961.

Adams, Walter, and Horace Gray. *Monopoly in America: The Government as Promoter.* New York: Macmillan Co., 1955.

Ambrose, Stephen E. *Ike's Spies: Eisenhower and the Espionage Establishment.* Garden City, N.Y.: Doubleday & Co., 1981.

————. *Rise to Globalism: American Foreign Policy Since 1938.* New York: Penguin, 1972.

————. *The Supreme Commander: The War Years of General Dwight D. Eisenhower.* Garden City, N.Y.: Doubleday & Co., 1970.

Benson, Ezra Taft. *Cross Fire: The Eight Years with Eisenhower.* Garden City, N.Y.: Doubleday & Co., 1962.

Bischof, Guenter. "Before the Break: The Eisenhower-McCarthy Relationship." Master's thesis, University of New Orleans, 1981.

Brandon, Dorothy. *Mamie Doud Eisenhower.* New York: Charles Scribner's Sons, 1954.

Brookings Institution. *Force Without War: U.S. Armed Forces as a Political Instrument.* Washington, D.C., 1978.

Clark, Mark W. *From the Danube to the Yalu.* New York: Harper & Bros., 1954.

Colby, William. *Honorable Men: My Life in the CIA.* New York: Simon and Schuster, 1978.

Cook, Blanche. *The Declassified Eisenhower.* Garden City, N.Y.: Doubleday & Co., 1981.

Cutler, Robert. *No Time for Rest.* Boston: Little, Brown and Co., 1966.

Davies, Richard O. *The Age of Asphalt: The Automobile, the Freeway, and the Condition of Metropolitan America.* Philadelphia: J. B. Lippincott Co., 1975.

Divine, Robert A. *Blowing on the Wind: The Nuclear Test Ban Debate.* New York: Oxford University Press, 1978.

———. *Eisenhower and the Cold War.* New York: Oxford University Press, 1981.

Donovan, Robert J. *Eisenhower: The Inside Story.* New York: Harper & Bros., 1956.

Duram, James. *A Moderate Among Extremists: Dwight D. Eisenhower and the School Desegregation Crisis.* Chicago: Nelson-Hall, 1981.

Eden, Anthony. *Full Circle.* Boston: Houghton Mifflin, 1960.

Eisenhower, Dwight D. *Mandate for Change.* Garden City, N.Y.: Doubleday & Co., 1963.

———. *Public Papers of the Presidents, 1953–1961.* Washington, D.C.: Government Printing Office 1954–1962. Cited throughout as PP with the appropriate year in parentheses.

———. *Waging Peace.* Garden City, N.Y.: Doubleday & Co., 1965.

Eisenhower, John S. D. *Strictly Personal.* Garden City, N.Y.: Doubleday & Co., 1974.

Eisenhower, Julie Nixon. *Special People.* New York: Simon and Schuster, 1977.

Eisenhower, Milton S. *The President Is Calling.* Garden City, N.Y.: Doubleday & Co., 1974.

———. *The Wine Is Bitter.* Garden City, N.Y.: Doubleday & Co., 1963.

Ewald, William Bragg, Jr. *Eisenhower the President: Crucial Days: 1951–1960.* Englewood Cliffs, N.J.: Prentice-Hall, 1981.

Ferrell, Robert, ed. *Off the Record: The Private Papers of Harry S Truman.* New York: Harper and Row, 1980.

Geelhoed, E. Bruce. *Charles E. Wilson and Controversy at the Pentagon, 1953 to 1957.* Detroit: Wayne State University Press, 1979.

Greenstein, Fred I. *The Hidden-Hand Presidency: Eisenhower as Leader.* New York: Basic Books, 1982.

Griffith, Robert. "Eisenhower and the Corporate Commonwealth." *American Historical Review,* February 1982.

———. *The Politics of Fear: Joseph R. McCarthy and the Senate.* Published for the Organization of American Historians by the University Press of Kentucky, Lexington, 1970.

Hatch, Alden. *Red Carpet for Mamie.* New York: Henry Holt and Co., 1954.

Hughes, Emmet John. *The Ordeal of Power: A Political Memoir of the Eisenhower Years.* New York: Atheneum, 1963.

Immerman, Richard. *The CIA in Guatemala: The Foreign Policy of Intervention.* Austin: University of Texas Press, 1982.

———. "Eisenhower and Dulles: Who Made the Decisions?" *Political Psychology,* 1979.

Kaufman, Burton I. *Trade and Aid: Eisenhower's Foreign Economic Policy.* Baltimore: Johns Hopkins University Press, 1982.

Kistiakowsky, George B. *A Scientist at the White House.* Cambridge: Harvard University Press, 1976.

Larson, Arthur. *Eisenhower: The President Nobody Knew.* New York: Charles Scribner's Sons, 1968.

Lear, John. "Ike and the Peaceful Atom." *The Reporter,* January 12, 1956.

Lyon, Peter. *Eisenhower: Portrait of the Hero.* Boston: Little, Brown and Co., 1974.

Montgomery, Bernard Law. *Memoirs*. Cleveland: World Publishing Co., 1958.

Morgan, Kay Summersby. *Past Forgetting: My Love Affair with Dwight D. Eisenhower*. New York: Simon and Schuster, 1976.

Morrow, E. Frederic. *Black Man in the White House*. New York: Coward-McCann, 1963.

Neff, Donald. *Warriors at Suez: Eisenhower Takes America into the Middle East*. New York: Simon and Schuster, 1981.

Neustadt, Richard E. *Presidential Power: The Politics of Leadership*. New York: John Wiley, 1960.

Nixon, Richard. *The Memoirs of Richard Nixon*. New York: Grosset & Dunlap, 1978.

Oppenheimer, J. Robert. "Atomic Weapons and American Policy," *Foreign Affairs*, July 1953.

Parmet, Herbert S. *Eisenhower and the American Crusades*. New York: Macmillan Co., 1972.

Reeves, Thomas C. *The Life and Times of Joe McCarthy*. New York: Stein and Day, 1982.

Reichard, Gary W. *The Reaffirmation of Republicanism*. Knoxville: University of Tennessee, 1975.

Richardson, Elmo. *The Presidency of Dwight D. Eisenhower*. Lawrence, Kans.: The Regents Press of Kansas, 1979.

Roberts, Clifford. *The Story of the Augusta National Golf Club*. Garden City, N.Y.: Doubleday & Co., 1976.

Roosevelt, Kermit. *Countercoup: The Struggle for the Control of Iran*. New York: McGraw-Hill, 1979.

Rose, Mark H. *Interstate: Express Highway Politics*. Lawrence, Kans.: The Regents Press of Kansas, 1979.

Rovere, Richard. "Letter from Washington." *The New Yorker*, September 29, 1955.

Schlesinger, Arthur M., Jr. *The Imperial Presidency*. Boston: Houghton Mifflin, 1973.

Schwartz, Gary T. "Urban Freeways and the Interstate System," *Southern California Law Review*, Vol. 49 (March 1976).

Slater, Ellis. *The Ike I Knew*. Privately printed, 1980.

Smith, Richard Norton. *Thomas E. Dewey and His Times*. New York: Simon and Schuster, 1982.

Strauss, Lewis. *Men and Decisions*. Garden City, N.Y.: Doubleday & Co., 1962.

Truman, Harry S., *Mr. Citizen*. New York: Bernard Geis Associates, 1960.

———. *Years of Trial and Hope*. Garden City, N.Y.: Doubleday & Co., 1956.

———. *Year of Decisions*. Garden City, N.Y.: Doubleday & Co., 1955.

United States Senate. *Final Report of the Select Committee to Study Governmental Operations with Respect to Intelligence Activities*. Senate Report 94–755, 94th Congress, 2nd Session. Washington, D.C.: Government Printing Office, 1974. Cited as Church Committee.

Walters, Vernon. *Silent Missions*. Garden City, N.Y.: Doubleday & Co., 1978.

Warren, Earl. *The Memoirs of Earl Warren*. Garden City, N.Y.: Doubleday & Co., 1977.

West, J. B. *Upstairs at the White House: My Life with the First Ladies*. New York: Coward, McCann & Geoghegan, 1973.

White, William S. *The Taft Story*. New York: Harper & Bros., 1954.

Wildavsky, Aaron. *Dixon-Yates: A Study in Power Politics*. New Haven: Yale University Press, 1962.

Wyden, Peter. *Bay of Pigs: The Untold Story*. London: Jonathan Cape, 1979.

MANUSCRIPTS

All the manuscripts used in this work are housed at the Eisenhower Library in Abilene, Kansas. There is a printed guide to the holdings of the library—Historical Materials in the Dwight D. Eisenhower Library.

ACWD (Ann C. Whitman Diary)
AWAS (Ann Whitman Administration Series)
AWDS (Ann Whitman Diary Series)
AWF (Ann Whitman File), Dulles-Herter
AWNS (Ann Whitman Name Series)
C. D. Jackson Papers
C. D. Jackson Records '53–'54
Christian Herter Papers
Daily Log, DDE '61–'69
DDE Confidential SS (Staff Series)
DDE:D (DDE Diary)
DDE:DS (DDE Diary Series)
Dulles/Herter Papers
Hagerty Diary (HD)
JFD Papers, '51–'59 subseries
JFD Papers, Meetings with President
JFD Papers, White House memo series
Minnich, Cabinet (hand-written notes)
Minnich, LLM (Legislative Leaders Meeting)
NSC Series
Preinaugural Papers
William Robinson Diary
Bernard Shanley Diary
WF — DDE (Whitman File, DDE)
WFDS (Whitman File Diary Series)
WFIS (Whitman File International Series)
WHPCS (Whitman File Press Conference Series)
WHCF (White House Central File)
WHMF (White House Memo File)
WHO Alpha SS (White House Office of Staff Secretary, Alpha)
WH Pres. SS (White House, Presidential Staff Secretary)
WHO SS Intelligence Briefing Notes

INTERVIEWS

By author

Richard Bissell	Howard Hunt
Dwight D. Eisenhower	Lyman Lemnitzer
John Eisenhower	Ellis Slater
Milton S. Eisenhower	Stuyvesant Wainwright
Andrew Goodpaster	William Westmoreland

By Columbia Oral History Project (COHP)

Winthrop Aldrich	Loy Henderson
Herbert Brownell	

By Dulles Oral History Project, Princeton

Dwight D. Eisenhower

By Eisenhower Library

Jacqueline Cochran	Andrew Goodpaster
Kenneth Crawford	Gordon Gray
John Eisenhower	Malcolm Moos
Milton Eisenhower	Merriman Smith
Eli Ginzburg	

INDEX

Nixon, Richard M., *continued*
  on school construction, 252
  second term dinner and, 288–90
  on Stassen's opposition, 323–24
  on Stevenson, 350
  on Taft-Hartley revision, 117
  tape-recorded conversations with,
    202–3
  on "undesirables" in government,
    136
  in Venezuela, 464
  as Vice President, 292
  Vietnam War and, 662
  see also election of 1960
Nixon, Thelma Catherine (Pat), 602,
  673
Nixon, Tricia, 673
Nixon Agonistes (Wills), 619
Norstad, Lauris, 539
North Atlantic Treaty Organization
  (NATO), 14, 33, 143–44, 373,
  447, 502
  Berlin crisis and, 503–4
  Eisenhower on U.S.-British col-
    lusion in, 538–39
  Formosa Straits crisis and, 484
  France and, 100, 538–39
  German rearmament and, 119–20,
    215–17, 503, 538
  Germany in, 215–17, 263–64, 276,
    538
  Powers' U-2 flight and, 577
  SEATO and, 183
  U.S. contribution to, 551
nuclear war:
  de Gaulle on, 552
  Eisenhower on, 295, 313, 491
  fallout shelters and, 434–35
  Geneva summit discussions of, 262–
    266
  JCS plan for, 564
nuclear weapons, 658, 660, 663
  delivery systems for, 427, 429, 550–
    551
  in Europe, 405–6
  Gaither Report on, 434–35
  international control of, 284
  quantities of, 405–6, 432–33, 493–
    494, 590
  test ban proposed for, 342–44,
    347–50
  testing of, 341–44, 397–400
  see also atomic weapons; fallout;

hydrogen bombs; test ban;
  specific tests

O'Daniel, John, 175
Odlum, Floyd, 647
oil import policy, 446–47
oil industry:
  natural-gas deregulation bill and,
    301–3
  Suez crisis and, 371–73
Old Guard (Republicans), 60, 76,
  619–20
  Adams and, 467–69, 481
  Asia-first attitude in, 144
  Cold War and, 226
  Communist embargo pushed by,
    62–63, 202
  Eisenhower on, 219–21, 294
  foreign aid and, 118–19
  on French Vietnam War agreement,
    209
  Geneva summit and, 260
  health care and, 199
  immigration and, 116
  Korean settlement and, 99–100
  land purchases and, 278
  1953 State of the Union speech and,
    47–48
  1954 elections and, 218–19
  Nixon supported by, 324
  RTAA and, 156
  Third World and, 377
  Yalta rejected by, 65–67
O'Mahoney, Joseph, 408
Open Skies proposal, 257–59, 267, 311
  at Geneva summit, 264–65
  origins of, 258
Oppenheimer, J. Robert, 131–32, 141–
  142, 166–67
  accusations of Communism against,
    141–42, 166–67, 170, 187–89
Organization of American States
  (OAS), 193, 555–56, 583, 615
overpopulation, 665–66

Pakistan, 209–10
Paley, Bill, 652
Palm Desert, Calif., 632, 639, 644, 653
Panama, Eisenhower's trip to, 322–23,
  334–35
Panama Canal, 332
Papers of Dwight David Eisenhower,
  The, 653–54

STEPHEN E. AMBROSE is currently a professor of history at the University of New Orleans. He was awarded a Ph.D. from the University of Wisconsin and has taught at L.S.U., Johns Hopkins University, and the Naval War College, and was the Dwight D. Eisenhower Professor of War and Peace, Kansas State University. Ambrose was the associate editor of the Eisenhower Papers and has written articles for numerous scholarly journals as well as a biweekly column on foreign and military affairs for the *Baltimore Evening Sun*.